CRM at the Speed of Light, Third Edition:
Essential Customer Strategies
for the 21st Century

Paul Greenberg

McGraw-Hill/Osborne

New York Chicago San Francisco Lisbon London Madrid Mexico City
Milan New Delhi San Juan Seoul Singapore Sydney Toronto

McGraw-Hill/Osborne

2100 Powell Street, 10th Floor
Emeryville, California 94608
U.S.A.

To arrange bulk purchase discounts for sales promotions, premiums, or fund-raisers,
please contact **McGraw-Hill**/Osborne at the above address.

*CRM at the Speed of Light, Third Edition: Essential Customer Strategies for the
21st Century*

1234567890 DOC DOC 01987654

ISBN 0-07-223173-4

Publisher
Brandon A. Nordin

Vice President & Associate Publisher
Scott Rogers

Editorial Director
Roger Stewart

Project Editors
Betsy Manini
Patty Mon

Acquisitions Coordinator
Jessica Wilson

Copy Editor
Lunaea Hougland

Proofreader
Marian Selig

Indexer
Valerie Perry

Computer Designer
Maureen Forys,
Happenstance Type-O-Rama

Illustrator
Jeffrey Wilson,
Happenstance Type-O-Rama

Series Design
Maureen Forys
Happenstance Type-O-Rama

Cover Design
Simone Villas-Boas/
Editora Campus—Brasil

This book was composed with QuarkXPress 4.11 on a Macintosh G4.

I love my family without reservation. My mom, Helen, 87 years old, and my dad, Abraham, 89 years old, who have always been there for me and love me unconditionally as I do them; my brother Bob, a brilliant and wonderful brother, guru in his own right and a personal and business inspiration to me all the time; my sister-in-law Freyda, who astounds me daily—even qualifying and running very well in the 2004 Boston Marathon; and my niece Sara who is all that a young woman should be as she moves through her teen years. I love my mother-in-law, Martha Reid, a source of wisdom and unreserved warmth for so many years.

But this edition of this book is especially for Yvonne, my wife of more than 20 years. Not only has she had to put up with me, but this year, has put up with cancer—and with a never-flagging spirit, indomitable courage, remarkable intellect, emotional power, and fabulous determination, is on her way to beating it. I love her endlessly for all that she is, all that she inspires, and all that she means—not just to me but to everyone around her. I can only dedicate something earthly and bound, but what I feel is celestial and unbound.

TO YVONNE, MY TRUEST LOVE

Contents

Foreword

It's no secret that I've always been a big believer in CRM. It was on a recent trip to Japan, however, that I was totally blown away by just how powerful it can be. As I left the plane, I switched on my handheld. A few years ago, I would have been to check out what appointments I had lined up, or what e-mails I had received, but now—with the advances made in CRM technology and delivery—it meant finding out *every-thing* going on in my organization. I was informed about what had happened while I had been incommunicado: I accessed information about new deals with ADP and SunTrust Bank—all before I made a phone call, before I checked e-mail, and before I got through Customs!

With developments like these, it's an exciting time in the world of CRM. As a former salesperson at Oracle, where I spent 13 years, I've long been fascinated with what CRM provides: a 360-degree view into an organization that can be leveraged at every level to drive the return on investment of marketing programs and to increase efficiency of customer service.

More and more customers are realizing those benefits. Much as Paul Greenberg discusses in this book, the market has exploded. It's rewarding for me to see the marketplace recognize and validate the benefits of CRM—enhanced productivity, competitive edge, and business success.

The increased popularity in CRM solutions makes sense: the products now offered are so vastly improved and the ROI is better than ever before. One key essential in the development of these offerings has been the power of the Internet. As we all know, the rapid evolution of the Internet has profoundly impacted every industry. In our business, it's forever changed the way we deliver and the way we use software applications. The new so-called on-demand or "no software" CRM solutions eliminate the need for traditional software. That means no installation and no upkeep for the user. Not only is it simpler, it's also less expensive. And since the solutions are scalable, users don't have to sacrifice the advanced benefits they demand from their CRM programs. We've come a long way, baby!

I view the newer on-demand model as CRM for the 21st century. The market, which was once skeptical of the idea, has begun to embrace this software-as-service solution as a legitimate and improved way. As I like to say (especially to those who were critical!), "shift happens."

With unmatched understanding, Greenberg captures the spirit of the revolution underway in the latest edition of *CRM at the Speed of Light*.

In a style that's easy to digest (and dare I say, even humorous at times), Greenberg explains why the newer "no software" models have emerged as a viable means to deliver CRM. His chronicle of the industry comes just in time as even the most traditional software companies are starting to view the Internet as the next platform. Microsoft now offers an online version of its CRM product, PeopleSoft features eCenter hosting, and mySAP offers an online solution. There's also Oracle Business Online and e-business On Demand from IBM. Last year, Siebel Systems bought Upshot, a provider of on-demand enterprise software.

This on-demand transformation is just one of the intriguing developments Greenberg covers here. He also covers the transformation of CRM from data-centered to process-driven and the evolution of business from a corporate to a customer ecosystem, in a style that is humor laced but based on powerful content.

With an unbiased view, he explores the entire industry and carefully explains the options available so that executives can make the most informed CRM decisions. There are an overwhelming number of solutions in this space. (Trust me, I have to compete against them every day!) It would take countless hours to investigate them all. Luckily, industry-appointed "CRM Guru" Greenberg has researched the solutions, tested the products, and interviewed users so that you can gain the knowledge he's cultivated over ten years.

Always on top of the latest advancements in CRM, *CRM at the Speed of Light* has been the industry bible since its first edition in 2001. This version—complete with the newest, most original thinking—is the best one yet. As Greenberg discusses here, we are in a new age—it's fast and it's furious, and it's easy to fall behind. With the insights in this book, you'll be up to speed.

In the technology business, we're always talking about change. That's a good thing. At the same time, it's nice to know that some things will always remain the same. Paul Greenberg will always be a Yankees fan, he'll always include a personal mobile phone number in the introduction, and his research in *CRM at the Speed of Light* will always be accessible, up-to-the-minute, and the only place to go to get the tools you need to make the most successful CRM decisions. But don't take my word for it, read on.

—Marc Benioff, chairman and CEO of salesforce.com
Co-chairman, President's Information
Technology Advisory Committee (PITAC)

Acknowledgments

This is always a lot of fun. Once again, I get to award my own Oscars, Emmys, Grammys, and Tonys: the Greenies, my personal acknowledgments of those who helped me with the book. Now, with a few bows to Billy Crystal and Steve Martin after their hilarious opening monologues, on to the Greenie awards. I'll be your host and presenter tonight and I promise we'll all be done by 11:00 P.M., just like the Oscars.

And the winners for:

Best Wife in the Known Universe and Beyond: Mine, Yvonne Greenberg.

Best Family in a Dedicated Environment: My mom, Helen; dad, Chet; brother, Bob; sister-in-law, Freyda; and niece, Sara Rose.

Best Friends in a Supporting Role: Wayne and Dorothy Hintz. I introduced them to each other well over 20 years ago and they remain cornerstones in our life. Also, Liz Giese—living in Chicago, infrequent visits, but while living there, always here (points to heart with grand gesture).

Best Editorial Director Who Doubles as Wonderful Friend (Lifetime Achievement): Roger Stewart, for not only his continual support for all my editions of the book, but his friendship, which means far more than anything in publishing could.

Best Editors Who Kept Me on the Straight and Narrow and Put Up with Bad Jokes (though they edited them out): Project editors Patty Mon and Betsy Manini, and especially, for the third consecutive edition, my copyeditor and guidepost, Lunaea Hougland.

Best Salesperson and Dear Compadre: Karen Schopp for her work on *CRM at the Speed of Light* and for our always delightful conversations and her thinking.

Best Suggestion for a Chapter that I Had Ignored Completely in the Second Edition: Basak Yildirim, who was a student at the time she suggested including what became Chapter 14. She also wins the **Best Future CRM Specialist** award, now that she's starting her career. This is someone with real potential.

Best Marketing People in the CRM Industry Who Also Contributed Significantly Above and Beyond to this Book: John Gill,

ChannelWave (even if he is a Red Sox fan, he's awesome as marketer and as a bud); Jane Hynes, salesforce.com (thoughtful, diligent, and kind); Mei Li, NetSuite (not only one of the best I've ever seen, but a dear, dear, incredibly considerate and bold friend); Donna Parent, Salesnet (knows her profession inside and out and, I think, is an angel disguised as a human); Angela Lipscomb, SAS (a champion and a lovely person, who would be a friend in the industry or out, indeed); and finally, Rose Lee, Unisys (for knowing how to get the word out on budget on time and remain a warm, wonderful person and (d)ear for me while doing so).

Most Influential in My Life: Stan Isaacs, not only as the spark for the "chipmunk" revolution in sports reporting that eventually gave us ESPN, but as prominent columnist for *Newsday* who gave a gawky, shy 13-year-old a real boost in writing confidence by publishing my first awkward attempts at sports poems in "Out of Left Field" (Stan's column) and giving the bar mitzvah boy good advice that was remembered as a kindness and inspiration to write "just like Stan Isaacs" the rest of his life. Thank you.

Best Contributions to *CRM at the Speed of Light* by a CRM Guru: Bob Thompson, founder of CRMGuru, for his continuous mentoring and personal support and for making CRM a business household word; David Mangen, Mangen Associates, for his humor and intelligence in making a difficult subject easier to understand; Dick Lee, Hi-Yield Methods, for his iconoclasm—always speaking his mind and keeping CRM on its toes; Denis Pombriant, Beagle Research Group, for being willing to be a thought leader rather than just run of the mill; Paul Ward, a clarion in CRM who is just getting heard and really should be heard more; and Michael Maoz, Gartner Group, for being both the most trustworthy analyst's voice in CRM—a world that often lacks that voice—and a good friend.

Best Contributions to CRM at the Speed of Light by Vendor and Integrator Heavyweights: Bruce Culbert, senior vice president and general manager of global services, salesforce.com, for not only his innovations and contributions to the entire industry as a Top 20 leader, but for his extraordinary friendship and support, which has been one of the truly important things I've gotten from my association with this industry; Steve Olyha, senior vice president and general manager of global CRM practice, Unisys, for his continuous efforts to be a creative and focused force in CRM, a man I've gotten to know as a great Yankees fan, great cook, and great bud; Marc Benioff, CEO, salesforce.com for bringing some sparkle back into the CRM world, being a good disruption to the industry, and being someone willing to butt heads with me; and Mike Doyle, CEO, Salesnet, for being one of the best human beings in the industry, always timely when it came to this book and someone who cares more than enough for all of us—and whom I can count on.

Best Creative in an Arts Role: Scott Johnson and Colby Waller, both of Rock Creek Creative Service—these guys are not only a graphic arts business, they are artists.

Best Sports Guys Who Understand CRM: Mario Zambas, CIO Norwich City Canaries; Mike Pagliarulo, president of iScout and former third baseman, New York Yankees (1984–89).

Best Special Others in a Supportive Role: Robb Eklund, VP of product marketing, Oracle; Jeff Pulver, VP of marketing, Siebel; Dan Starr, chief marketing officer, Salesnet; Zach Nelson, CEO, NetSuite; Mike Shubra, manager, SAP Global Marketing; George Ahn, group VP and general manager of CRM, PeopleSoft; Beth Miller-Thiel and Kim Stocks, product marketing managers, PeopleSoft. All are outstanding credits to their professions and great supporters of the book. Get to know these people if you can. They are really worth it.

And of course,

Best Actress in a Featured Role: Ashley Judd for her extraordinary performance in "Is CRM Ashley Judd?"

Introduction

I can't keep up with this world. I swear it's getting impossible to track and monitor the monumental changes that have been and are going on in just the few months since I started writing this edition of *CRM at the Speed of Light*. I mean, A-Rod to the Yankees? Awesome.

This is going to be the final edition of *CRM at the Speed of Light*. And, please, I'm not coming out of *CRM at the Speed of Light* retirement to write it after the public clamor for the fourth edition gets so great that I can't ignore it. First, I can ignore it. Second, it's easy to ignore when there is neither hue nor cry.

Why no fourth edition, you ask? Oh, you didn't ask. Well, so what! I'm answering.

Aside from the fact that I have other projects in mind, such as a book on the Negro Leagues, CRM isn't just maturing to a stable state, it's evolving beyond its traditional self, as you're going to see throughout this whole book. CRM, as we know it today, isn't the CRM of three years ago. It isn't the CRM we'll see in five years, if there is a CRM to see (hint). It has become something that I had actually forecast it would in the second edition, an overarching business strategy that reaches every part of your business, and even beyond that into your partners', suppliers', and employees' business and lives. It is not just a system, it is not just software, it's a change to your culture, it's an increased knowledge of the behavior of your customer, it's...wait. I'll tell you all of this in the book so I won't waste the small space where I can talk about stuff only vaguely related to the book, reiterating the book content.

What is relevant is that CRM is now in another dimension and thus, while this is *CRM at the Speed of Light, Third Edition*, you'll note two things. The subtitle has been changed to a relatively bland "Essential Customer Strategies for the 21st Century." The prior subtitle, "Capturing and Keeping Customers in Internet Real Time," is still sort of relevant but not sufficient to cover the scope of CRM as we now know it. Second, if you've read the second edition (or the first), you'll note that this book is brand new. It is not an update of either of the first two editions whatsoever.

Why do that? Isn't that a lot of work? Damn skippy it is. But it's necessary work. It's taken me ten months to write this one—four more months than I expected. Aside from the usual author excuses—the cat shredded the PDF files or my carpal tunnel syndrome had to be cured by a long rest and a series of trips to major league baseball parks—in fact, the amount of research became copious because of major events and sea changes going on in CRM.

What changes were they? Read the book, you'll see them throughout. Except for one, which you will also see, but I'm going to it address here as well.

No, mergers and acquisitions weren't the biggest changes in the landscape. The big one is: I was wrong! Well, sort of wrong. Maybe, in my own defense, I was convinced of something I hadn't been convinced of before.

What I had been "wrongly convinced" about is important to the current state of CRM—the strength, endurance, and scalability of the ASP market. I have to say the good burghers of salesforce.com and Salesnet are the reasons I'm going to publicly admit my mistakes. Man, am I ever a believer.

In my own defense, I've always been a fan of Salesnet, because of my regard for their functionality and product, and equally as important for their leadership who I find to be really good people. But I figured if the ASP market—the enterprise hosted solutions—had a chance, it was by focusing on sales and in the smaller and midsized companies as at best a niche alternative.

But then, in 2003, I got a call from Marc Benioff, the CEO of salesforce.com, saying he had read an article on my skepticism about the market and his company and he loved convincing skeptics. Would I give him a shot at it? I did. Bingo. Right on target. Between my observations of Salesnet's GPS sales system and salesforce.com's dynamic sforce development services, I came to the conclusion that I was an idiot. Totally off. But I'm now right in the head again, because I believe that this is a model that is here to stay. I do. I will prove that to you, if you'll give me a shot, in Chapter 16.

The other sea changes are awash throughout the book and you'll be agog as to what a profound effect they've had on what CRM is.

The Book: The Third Time's the Charm

This edition is organized a lot differently than the first and second editions. That's because the book is far more strategic. For those of you who have faithfully (or faithlessly) read the first two editions or at least one of them, you'll note one definitive change right away. The subtitle of the book is different. The title remains *CRM at the Speed of Light*.

The edition says third edition. But the subtitle is "Essential Customer Strategies for the 21st Century." Why in the world did I do that?

I have no idea.

Just kidding. CRM moved from just a system and technology over the past several years to a centerpiece for all corporate strategies. That means that customer strategy as sculpted by the customer-dominated marketplace is the cornerstone of overall corporate strategy. If you're not forward thinking enough to figure this one out by either inference or observation, woe to you and your company. It is the way the business world has to work to continue on motoring. Customer strategies arc at the core of business, and they are at the core of this book.

That means that you will see a different sort of animal here. This time around, while the systems, technologies, and players are all covered, there is a considerably stronger emphasis on strategy, culture and processes, and the human factors than in the last two editions. More content, but it's funnier too.

I Like the Way This Moves

I've been doing a lot of speaking on CRM around the world the last two years. Each time I speak, I get an introduction that includes a short biography and often even mentions that I'm a huge Yankees fan, a well-known CRM trivia question. The intros are pretty much the same except for one—my all-time favorite, at the SmartCRM East Conference sponsored by SearchCRM and its parent company TechTarget in February 2004. As I was introduced by Jon Panker, the best CRM reporter in the entire business, the song "Hey Ya!" began to blare over the audio system in the room, making me feel like I was going up to get a Grammy, rather than speaking on CRM and the ASP market. It was awesome.

For those of you who haven't hung out in the 21st century, "Hey Ya!" is a gender and age crossing hip hop/rap song sung by the notably named group Outkast. They are a creative, innovative bunch called by one music pundit "the Frank Zappas of Hip-hop." I love them. They are self-parodying, iconoclastic, and immensely talented—all things I aspire to be at the age of, uh, more than 40. Okay, okay, 54. Their name is doubly iconoclastic if you think about it. Not only outcasts, but outcasts with a "k"! Very cool.

I hope that this book is that for you—not just a standard dry volume on CRM, but a relaxed, easy going, content filled encyclopedia of instruction and ideas. Several of them are iconoclastic and, thus, I hope, refreshing. It is not meant to be a typical CRM book, many of which are technically dusty and impossibly standard. Some are marketing trips. Some are just trying to change names and acronyms to protect the oh-too-clever. Some are very, very good. I want this one to be useful, enjoyable, and atypical of the genre, though provocative. You judge whether it is good. In fact, let me know too. Not only am I willing to listen to you sing my praises, but also am willing to listen to you kick me around. Let me know what's right about this book and wrong. I'm not writing another edition, but I will continue to write and speak in all the other CRM venues I am already in and in others that I'm not yet in. So suggestions for improvement or what to do with my book (so to speak) are welcome.

My e-mail is paul-greenberg3@comcast.net. My cell phone number is (571) 213-6988. You can call or write anytime. I will respond. I swear.

PART I
The Overview

1

Is CRM Ashley Judd?

My wife and I went to the IHOP in Manassas, Virginia where we live, one Sunday for no particular reason. It's not a place that we frequent. In fact, she had never been there. For those of you who didn't live in the 20th or 21st century, IHOP is International House of Pancakes. Needless to say, it was mobbed. I'm one of those people who have a cheery outward demeanor and seem even-tempered, but *hate* waiting at restaurants to be seated. So I was about to settle in for a long grumpy sojourn, when I noticed that my wife had a sheet of paper in her hand. "What's that say?" She turned it toward me. It said, "Ashley Judd." Simultaneously I heard from the host, "Tom Cruise, table for four!" Rather than having them sign up to a list, the host gave each customer the name of a famous celebrity. The mere assignation of this star-studded name, and then hearing it called out, had everyone giggling and chattering. "Who do you have? Nicole Kidman? That's so cool!" What could have been an annoying wait turned into a pleasant 20 minutes of smiling and laughing. It made breakfast at this particular IHOP really enjoyable—not usually something that I would associate with a meal there. Edible, yes. Enjoyable…?

Is this Customer Relationship Management (CRM)? Be patient. In the meantime, think about Ashley Judd or Tom Cruise.

Defining CRM: Salute to the General

To get you an answer on whether my restaurant experience was CRM, I'm going to take the long approach to a definition. The entire first part of this book, "The General," is devoted to defining CRM. Why spend so much time on a definition? For a few reasons, all pretty important. Even in these economically challenged times, CRM is considered the second most important initiative after security for businesses, according to a 2002 Goldman Sachs study. With that level of importance attached, defining CRM is not just an exercise in knuckle cracking, but something that can mean success or failure for any CRM proposal you undertake.

We all strive for definition. Definitions provide clarity. Some people want definition of their contract terms so that there are no misunderstandings. Some want clear delineation of their job responsibilities, perhaps worried about the consequences of acting outside the classification. Frankly, I'd like definition of my abs.

Think about it. Do you really want to be in the midst of what is likely to be a substantial CRM initiative and say, "Oops. I didn't know that CRM meant *that!*"

CRM's evolving definition is now significantly more complex and more enigmatic than it was at any time in the last few years. There are countless attempts to come up with a definition, as widely disparate as the agendas of those presenting them. However, there are some universally recognized practices, concepts, and features that can be described by the CRM industry influentials whose takes on Customer Relationship Management grace these pages.

Entering the Mainstream

As of 2004, CRM has a history, an extensive body of experiences, and a significant corpus of literature on its failures, successes and, yes, even its definition. Perception has shifted—traditionally, CRM had been seen as a technology initiative, though there has always been a politically correct insistence that it isn't a technology. That is characterized by the CRM software vendor–created mantra, "It isn't a technology, it's a system." Said, of course, while they were selling you software with oodles of exciting bells and whistles. The CRM-as-technology world view flourished mostly during the heady days of the dot.com boom. The general business world was focused on technology as the driver of the "New Economy" that we giddily thought would make us wealthy. CRM's apparent benefit was that it seemed to be able to automate much of the "customer-facing" activity of a company. It was seen as a system providing a competitive edge, not a mainstream business activity. CRM customers tended to ignore or barely perceive the actual premises that defined CRM.

Now, as this third edition of *CRM at the Speed of Light* is published, CRM is a mainstream initiative, a technology-driven competitive edge no longer. It is recognized as the way that business should be conducted rather than an option in a menu of multiple options to differentiate you from your competitor. The logic here is simple yet compelling. If everyone is "doing" CRM or planning on it, how can it differentiate you from your competitor? And everybody is—47 percent of businesses surveyed by Forrester Research are considering a CRM initiative; another 37 percent were already implementing it in 2003.

What were historically separate business disciplines like Supply Chain Management (SCM) are also becoming part of CRM initiatives, rather than just remaining relatively static production management processes. As you will see throughout this book, the progressive transformation of the business environment created a dramatic, rapid evolutionary change in CRM, how it is perceived and, ultimately, how it is implemented and used.

Much of CRM's transformation stemmed from learning the lessons of its failures. There have been dozens of surveys, reports, and studies done on the reasons for CRM failure, some scientifically valid, some more impressionistic. For example:

- A 2002 Butler Group report found that 70 percent of CRM implementations fail.

- A 2001 Gartner study found that approximately 55 percent of all CRM projects failed to meet software customers' expectations.

- In a 2001 Bain & Company survey of 451 senior executives, CRM ranked in the bottom three categories among 25 popular tools evaluated for customer satisfaction.

- A 2002 Selling Power, CSO Forum study found that 69.3 percent of CRM implementations failed to meet all goals.

Not exactly a ringing endorsement for what had been a techno-functional fair-haired boy not long before that.

But regardless of what color CRM's hair was dyed, as 2002 ended, CRM had obvious problems and not all of them were related to software bugs, over-budgeting, and late delivery. Nor were the problems front-office knockoffs of the same problems that beset that other big technology system, Enterprise Resource Planning (ERP).

One of CRM's persisting problems is that it is still often sold as a technology initiative. There are numerous contemporary examples of companies that buy CRM software *admittedly* without any planning, despite the countless pages on the folly of ignoring just that. That seemed to be the result of two basic meltdowns:

- ▶ No programmatic strategy, even though the software has been purchased. I received a call from a good friend of mine who had a client that bought every module of one CRM suite and had called him to find out what to do with it!

- ▶ No way to measure the return on investment (ROI). In February 2003, *CRM Magazine* in conjunction with CAP Ventures did a survey of 800 end-user executives (and 400 vendors and integrators) who were in the midst of CRM initiatives. About one third of these respondents hadn't planned to measure ROI in any way!

What happens when you don't plan appropriately? CRM applications sit under flowerpots at a 42 percent rate according to a study by Gartner Dataquest in early 2003. Without strategy, without benchmarks and measures, without cultural and process transformation, the software is rendered useless.

However, the potential value of CRM remains clear, despite problems. The lessons learned from CRM's notable failures, in combination with the change in the business climate, plus the continued desire for CRM, leads us to what is a pretty dramatic redefinition of Customer Relationship Management.

The Meta-factors

Several other good and bad events and perceptions impact the change in definition.

Good news on CRM's satisfaction rate Studies began to appear in 2003 that showed CRM wasn't so bad after all. CRMGuru did a landmark study entitled "CRM Blueprint for Success" that identified those factors that led to a satisfaction rate of near 52 percent and a failure rate that reached only 35 percent.

The recognition of human performance factors as a critical part of CRM programs CRM writing became blatant in late 2002 on findings that human performance issues, not technology, were the culprit that led to the biggest failures. Pinpointing problems such as lack of user adoption and where the problem occurred became a refreshing clarifying agent. Finally, it wasn't just murky CRM that caused the problem, but it was, as IDC pointed out (2003), the lack of user input from the beginning of the planning process that was a major contributing factor to failure over 47 percent of the time.

The economic downturn and the uncertainty around recovery The miserable state of the economy and the mixed signals on recovery made positive spending decisions on such high ticket initiatives with long-term ROI a lot less likely, despite the declaration by the Fed that the recession was retroactively over in November 2001. In fact, according to a Gartner Dataquest study released in June 2003, CRM spending declined for the first time ever in 2002. However, its prospects for growth were still excellent through 2006. But CRM spending became a practical decision, based on solving actual business problems rather than a big ticket impulse buy. Numbers like 42 percent shelfware tell you about the sordid past.

Confusion over what was the right way to perceive CRM Was it CRM sales, marketing, and support? Was it field service? How about analytics? Was it data driven, process driven? How had it changed in the last few years? What did the supply chain have to do with the demand chain? How about the argument that it was services, not software? What about partners? Which architecture was the most appropriate? Should it be hosted or not? What did culture have to do with it? Loyalty or satisfaction? Project or program? Carrot or stick? Mantle or Mays? (I'm a Yankees fan, so tread lightly here.) Actually, I wrote the previous two editions to help answer these questions. Most of the existing CRM books had been aimed at a technology audience. I aimed squarely at people like me—business people who are not members of Alpha Geek Omega.

Recognition of these issues and uncertainties provided a new kind of clarity about pinpointing the causes of CRM difficulty, in stark contrast to the many success stories that also came out about CRM. But it also made the business community more cautious when it came to spending money on it. In response to this caution, the vendors began to throw out a multitude of pricing strategies for the software, in a misguided effort to "make the decision easier." This served to confuse the issue even further. All of a sudden potential customers were hit with price choices such as buying both licenses and services, getting the licenses cheaply or free, and paying for just services. Pricing licenses by user, by seat, by module, by server. Paying for services using models for time and materials (for example, hourly plus expenses), or monthly subscriptions, or fixed price, fixed time (accelerated implementation) were proposed, dropped, reinvented, and respun.

Of course, rather than solve the already extensive series of confusing choices and questions raised by the contrasts between CRM successes and failures, these pricing options made the decisions even more confusing.

To make this even more difficult, there had been a number of respectable definitions of "traditional" CRM that stuck in the corporate consciousness, the most celebrated one penned by the admired analyst firm, the META Group, in its "Customer Relationship Management Ecosystem" report in 2000. META Group defined CRM as consisting of operational, analytic, and collaborative subsets (see Chapter 2 for details). This became the industry standard definition that shaped CRM's voluptuous form in its earlier incarnations and still holds to some extent to this day. But both the overall business landscape and the CRM contours had changed too dramatically to not cast the validity of these venerable definitions into doubt.

The questions are extensive, the issues confusing, the models in transition as we head through 2004. That's why this is going to take three-chapters to define CRM appropriately, rather than a single shot across the bow. But it is a great ride—*Pirates of the Caribbean* is nowhere near as adventurous, swashbuckling, fraught with peril, and potentially laden with gold at the end of the day.

CRM Definition: The View from Above Still Needs Binoculars

CRM appeared on the heels of big ticket Enterprise Resource Planning (ERP) initiatives as a big ticket item itself. But by the late 1990s, ERP was notable for problems that befit its size and its lack of identifiable ROI. ERP press was atrocious as large deal after large deal was either scrapped or never made it off the drawing boards, because the ROI seemed to be unknowable and the implementation woes, both technical and functional, were extensive. Bad ERP press or not, CRM was still seen in the late 1990s as, in effect, "customer-facing ERP," a moniker that was to haunt it in 2001–2002.

In fact, my initial awareness of CRM came with the development of what was then called "xRP" or "extended ERP," a gross misnomer, but what was, for a short while, the reference point for CRM's emergence.

To get a look at the birth of CRM's new definition via confusion over its actual nature, take a look at this comment from a panel discussion with several British finance managers excerpted by *CRM Magazine* in November 2000 from *Computers & Finance* magazine:

> For many companies, ERP did not deliver all they expected in the first place, but this doesn't stop them accepting that they need more IT to become more efficient or stop vendors piling on so-called extended ERP offerings.

> However, it does seem that companies are weighing up their options more carefully the second time around and questioning whether e-business or Customer Relationship Management (CRM) may or may not be the way forward for them in their attempts to extend their ERP systems.

> CRM was already being tarred with the extended ERP "big, expensive system" brush. The "big ticket item" tag mars business impressions of CRM to this day.

Early Perceptions

With the META Group definition in 2000, CRM finally was able to begin to break out of the ERP prison it had been placed in. But perception remained ambiguous about what CRM was.

Look at this survey done in 2000 on the definition of CRM by META Group and IMT (apparently multiple answers were okay since the totals add up to 118 percent):

- ▶ 29 percent of respondents saw CRM as a 360-degree view of the customer, which includes a better understanding of customer lifecycles and profitability.

- ▶ 27 percent of respondents defined CRM as "the quality of company/customer interaction." These respondents saw CRM as providing seamless service to customers across all points of interaction.

- ▶ 22 percent saw CRM simply as the tools and technologies used to achieve incremental operational improvements.

- ▶ 20 percent defined CRM as an organizational shift from a product focus to a customer focus.

> ▸ 14 percent of those surveyed saw CRM as a way of delivering customer data to customer-facing employees.

> ▸ 6 percent saw CRM as nothing more than "a new name for an old business practice."

Several observations:

> ▸ The percentages' evenhandedness shows that there was no clear consensus on what CRM was. The only significantly aberrant percentage was from the "same old, same old" group, most of whom, I presume, are not currently employed at the places they made this comment.

> ▸ CRM is seen by the subjects as a result, not an ongoing program. This was typical of early perceptions.

> ▸ Human performance factors are barely recognized and then by implication only.

Fast Forward to Now

In the years between 2000 and 2004, CRM was a constant topic of corporate discussion. The economy was shaky and CRM was seen either as a solution by those who understood it, or a panacea, by those who didn't. But the definition gained some precision. We were that much closer to a truer working definition as the discussions continued.

In January 2003 in an Aberdeen Group interview, Ad Nederlof, CEO of Genesys Telecommunications Laboratories, said, "CRM is a term that can refer to a range of things from the 'management of the relationship with customers' all the way to 'the software and hardware that allow one to manage [his or her] relationship with a customer.' It has become a catchall term. CRM generally is an enterprise-focused endeavor encompassing all departments in a business. For example, in addition to customer service, CRM would also include operations—manufacturing, assembly, product testing—as well as other areas like purchasing, billing, HR, engineering, marketing and sales. When the full company spectrum of departments is focused on building, maintaining, and constantly improving not only the product but also the relationship with the customer, this is what is meant by CRM. This requires a deep look at the goals and objects of the entire business and how those goals at the executive level are carried out in the sublevels of management and employees. In order to understand how goals get accomplished, it is necessary to revisit the way [companies] get [their] business done. Once a baseline is determined, they must determine if the way they do [their processes] makes sense in the current business climate. If not, then they need to be redesigned to be more customer-centric. It is a step most businesses do not do before buying CRM software and are then surprised that they did not get the ROI they wanted after they implemented it."

This was representative of some of the smarter contemporary CRM thinking in the business community. Nederhof, like much of the CRM vendor community, recognizes where CRM has been and is. We are living in a cross-functional, process-driven CRM world. His thinking reflects the changes that have occurred within this morphed business milieu, such as the commingling of the back and front office and the redesign of business processes around customer-focused activities. Perception of the need for the transformation of the business culture and the continuous nature of the ongoing improvements that CRM demands is still more implicit than explicit.

So What Is CRM, Again?

The answer's on the way. In the meantime, keep thinking about Ashley or Tom. By book's end, we will have an intelligible definition, knowledge, and working strategy for CRM, but we've got another roadblock to deal with. Clouding CRM's definition even more, there has been a surfeit of attempts to "move *beyond* CRM" that make things even more opaque. There is a school that would like to throw CRM out altogether rather than learning from the well-documented mistakes of the past. Since CRM is wounded, let's put it out of its misery and do something CRMish, but not CRM. This thinking has the same value as "Since capitalism has problems, let's do something different, like, say, communism." That worked about as well as I think this approach does, though feel free to draw your own conclusions on its value.

Getting beyond CRM seems to be reflected in the call for new acronyms and the failure of the original acronym. For example:

Customer **Relationship Management** Lack of attention to the customer is highlighted the most frequently as the cause for CRM failure. The usual phrase, said by too many naysayers to count, is "We need to put the 'C' back in CRM." But then they add new descriptors like, weirdly, "customer-centric CRM." Is there a non-customer-centric CRM?

Customer *Relationship* Management Kenneth Carleton Cooper, in his book *The Relational Enterprise: Moving Beyond CRM to Maximize All Your Business Relationships*, says, "This requires a redefinition of CRM to include the old front-office CRM, back-office ERP, legacy back-office systems, collaborative channels and analytics. META Group says this is the new definition of CRM. We've been calling it simply, 'RM.'" (This is actually a very useful book that I would recommend.)

Customer Relationship *Management* Frederick Newell, in his book *Why CRM Doesn't Work*, says, "The very phrase explained in [books about CRM]—CRM, or 'Customer Relationship Management'—implies that companies can manage the customer relationship by targeting specific customers for specific product offerings. How audacious, how impudent, how wrong!" Newell proposes CMR—customer managed relationships—that empower customers to determine their own fate. I certainly agree with that. He even quotes me saying I agree with that. You can't make a customer do what he doesn't want to.

These books are far superior to the typical "moving beyond CRM to a place that pushes my agenda" genre out there (see most of the CRM books by big consulting firms). Unfortunately, agendas, not customers, are most frequently satisfied by the majority of these approaches. We're better served by providing:

- ► An agenda-free crystalline definition of CRM

- ► A body of best practices

- ► Refinements to CRM's science and art

This is far more beneficial to business than a new name based on picking at CRM scabs. Better to solve its admittedly numerous problems than create another magic elixir with a bouquet of berries and a finish like cod liver oil.

In the Beginning: CRM's Place in the Business Universe

Trying to understand the physical universe, its evolution over time, and its relationship to the atomic and subatomic particles that comprise it can make one feel small.

Trying to understand the place and importance of the individual in the metaphysical universe can make one (well, me) existential.

Trying to understand the place of CRM in a business universe dominated by a single customer may be difficult, but it is neither existential nor diminishing. Now we can begin to look at that ecosystem and identify who that individual customer is.

We'll all feel better.

Transformation of the Business Ecosystem

What has characterized CRM's move into the mainstream business thinking (see the CRM definition below by Gartner Group guru Michael Maoz) is the integration of its principles into the business ecosystem as it transformed. There is a history to this, as we can see from Figure 1-1. Business has evolved in its structures and its thinking over the past twenty years far more quickly than it had the previous hundred years. It has gone from a reactive product-driven corporate ecosystem to a real-time proactive customer ecosystem, though it is not fully transformed to this state yet.

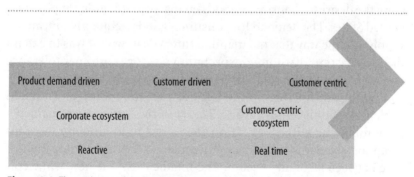

Figure 1-1: The evolution of the business ecosystem

The Product-Driven Corporate Ecosystem

In 1978, the manufacturing world dominated the economy. Processes were based on division of labor; planning consistency triumphed over responsive agility. JIT was the first three letters of a type of taxi, not "just in time." These practices had been around at varying levels for a hundred years.

Materials planning practices were used to improve efficiencies of the manufacturing process at the plant and manufactured goods levels. The facilities used during President Franklin Delano Roosevelt's World War II manufacturing mobilization had been converted to peacetime production. Jobs were plentiful. The workforce skill level was unprecedented. From the late 1950s on, in order to handle the increasing demand for consumer goods from an increasingly affluent United States middle class, there had to be a more scientific scheme of determining what it took to get those desired goods to market. Material requirements planning also called "little mrp," was one technique. It used a bill of materials (BOM), a list of what materials were available to the production process, in combination with a production forecast. This was done one specific product at a time. The result was forecasts for future material needs and materials purchase timing. The capacity to handle those materials was disregarded to a large extent. It was a plodding, monotonous, and steady way to plan. The planning done by the manufacturers did not involve the consumers they served. The processes were aimed internally at the enterprise. But the planning and the processes were able to at least reduce the costs of production.

During this time, Madison Avenue was taking responsibility for creating the desire for consumer goods en masse in this affluent post-war United States. The demand for consumer goods frequently outran the supply, but the way that the manufacturers dealt with it was to extend the delivery time. Customer expectation was low, customer tolerance was high, and so the volatility level was also quite low. People were willing to wait for the branded goods that they wanted. Thorsten Veblen's late 19th century work, *Theory of the Leisure Class*, gained a fresh following with its position that a desire to emulate the consumption standards of the rich influences individuals' allocation of time between labor and leisure. The middle class, the new white collar workers, were willing to work longer hours or have two-income families to get the stuff they wanted. We were flying high. Global competition wasn't a big issue.

It was during the latter part of this period, in the late 1960s and early 1970s, that the American Production and Inventory Control Society (APICS) not only began to grow, but began to develop the concepts to professionalize and organize inventory control and production. They recognized that they had to control the costs of manufacturing and increase the efficiency of the production process.

But another element injected itself into the plan in the late 1970s: Wal-Mart. The demand for consumer goods reached unprecedented heights as the post-war economy continued its long boom and a healthy middle class—with two-income families—continued its buying habits. Large retailers like Wal-Mart became powerhouses and developed the need for a managed supply chain so they could tell manufacturers like Proctor & Gamble what products were needed on the shelves and when. This made planning and collaboration (with the retailers primarily calling the shots) a necessity for successful competition.

By 1984, Manufacturing Resource Planning (MRP) and later its sibling, MRPII, made its appearance. To meet the needs of this product-driven corporate ecosystem, MRP added sales forecasts to do things like calculate the timing of materials flows into the production process, based on the expected numbers of product sales at specific times. Capacity planning and determining on-hand inventory, especially given retailer needs, made the ability to plan the use of materials, given this consumer demand, all that much better. It was a new way to create more efficient production and reduce costs of production and to improve the timeliness of the goods' creation. As that became a commonly used methodology, and production continued to expand, along came Enterprise Resource Planning (ERP) to meet the needs of the expanding corporation and the increasingly complex interdepartmental relationships.

ENTERPRISE RESOURCE PLANNING

ERP was the methodological omega point for the product-driven corporate ecosystem. It took the MRP systems and expanded them to include other critical business departments such as human resources (labor) and finance (capital). ERP added procurement planning and budgeting to its vast libraries of business processes that impacted the overall production process. It took advantage of technologies like relational databases (such as Oracle or IBM's DB2) and graphical user interfaces (GUIs) to make the systems more accessible and acceptable. It was able to adapt to the new paradigm of distributed computing through the use of client/server technologies. What this allowed the enterprises to do is to plan, report, and analyze the processes and methods that were aimed at continually tweaking manufacturing and related practices. But it was still based in the world that was driven by product creation and consumer demand, though a computerized, much more flexible version of that world.

Empowered by the Internet:
The Customer-Focused Corporate Ecosystem

In the mid-1990s, two profound events occurred. First, the buying power of the baby boomers. While there has been a lot made of the Gen Y and Z buyers, in dollar terms, 45- to 55-year-olds spend three times more than the younger generation. Because baby boomers are now "older shoppers," this first Internet-literate generation knows how to get what they want and their expectations are high.

This brings us to the second event: the Internet revolution. Not the dot.com fantasy that was characterized by lots of twentysomething entrepreneurs partying and programming their way (and their companies' way) into oblivion. But instead the growth and rapid acceleration of the newest communications medium: the World Wide Web and email. Customers who had been limited by their geographies, by the limited availability of outlets and options when it came to choosing products, had their reach expanded globally as a cornucopia of choices fell to those who took the online plunge into e-commerce. All of a sudden, they could order from anywhere in the world, and, if they were not satisfied with the service they were getting, with the click of a mouse, they could move to another company. Product research was no longer a matter of receiving a direct mail piece and hoping to read something in the paper about the product, or buying *Consumer Reports*, or waiting for an increasingly creaky Madison Avenue to hype the products they were interested in. With the new-found freedom of billions of web pages of available information, customers began to send information on their experiences with the products to sites like Epinions.com where these real-life experiences became valuable assets. Knowledge became power and value. The ability to know about and to easily purchase a product or to change companies with that mouse click, transformed the customer from a receptacle to a powerhouse. With the development of incredibly fast search engines like Google, consumers had information at their fingertips instantly and had the means to proactively transmit information equally as quickly. This led to a substantial increase in customer expectations; customer reach increased, customer volatility increased.

Roger Blackwell, a marketing professor at Ohio State University, and author of the book *Consumers Rule!*, puts it well, "The 21st century should really be called the century of the consumer. Today Wal-Mart asks the consumer what should be out on the shelves. It's no longer enough to satisfy consumers. Today consumers must be delighted." Jeff Rusinow, former president of Kohl's department store, says, "The consumer has been enormously empowered."

Interestingly, the ERP vendors and other technology purveyors recognized that the consumer of the 1990s was not the consumer of the 1960s, '70s, or '80s. Perhaps the most elegant expression of that was from PeopleSoft, oddly enough, in 1995 with the acquisition of a supply chain management (SCM) solution called Red Pepper (see Chapter 15 for more on SCM). PeopleSoft developed a concept called Enterprise Resource Optimization (ERO). ERO said the marketplace had changed. Demand was no longer pushed to the market, but customers drove demand, and they rapidly changed their desires and criteria for demand. The successful enterprise would adjust to that by having available real-time or near real-time data so that they could change their production accordingly. The era of the empowered customer had arrived and the business ecosystem had moved to a new phase where the customer became the focus of the corporation, not the product any longer. Products were created to the specifications of the customer. The customer was no longer victim to the product. The days of waiting patiently for delivery of new consumer goods had pretty much gone the way of the Packard.

This customer-centric perspective moved quickly through the business landscape. By the late 1990s, the business world understood that they had to respond to this new order with something else. It was no coincidence that this knowledge coincided with the growth of CRM. All of a sudden companies like Siebel became hot because they were pioneers in providing the larger enterprise version of technologies that were focused on "customer-facing" activity. Business acquiesced to the realization that they had to respond to customers and had to do it quickly because customers were no longer consumerist patsies—though they continued to love "stuff." But "stuff" had to be delivered quickly, in a timely way, without defect, and cheaply, or customers would go somewhere else. CRM became the competitive edge that was needed to grab those customers and hold them. CRM was then perceived as the system and technology that worked to do this. Remember this paragraph as you go through the first three chapters.

How can you identify this change in the customer social-psychological state? Take a look at the telecommunications industry. Even though legislation broke up the AT&T monopoly years ago, the telcos had virtual territorial monopolies for an extraordinarily long period. But further legislation and customer empowerment generated a much more demanding customer base that required excellent service at low prices or they would simply change carriers. In 2003, 43 million people in the United States did just that. That is *14.3 percent of the entire U.S. population*. Scary levels of incendiary customer behavior, isn't it? Think about what the cost must be to the telcos to deal with that ongoing conversion tsunami. In 2004, the projected changeover, with the regulations allowing phone number transfer, is 77 million! That's the negative side. There were some very powerful positive effects of this ecosystem characterized by the incredible surge in e-commerce:

- ▸ A 2002 Pew survey showed that 32 percent of U.S. consumers, or roughly 37 million, now bank online, compared with only 17 percent in March 2000.

- ▸ By 2003 year end, worldwide business to business e-commerce revenue is expected to exceed $1.4 trillion; by 2004 year end, $2.7 trillion. Yes, trillion. *Emarketer* says so.

These are magnificent numbers when it comes to both sheer dollars and the knowledge that the empowered customer is not just flaunting that discovered power, but using it wisely (at least according to the vendors) by engaging in these online commercial activities. It is also a small bridge to the evolution beyond the customer-centric corporate ecosystem to what has been an essential transformation to a customer ecosystem.

From Customer-Focused Corporate Ecosystem to Customer Ecosystem

In the second edition of this book, in Chapter 18, I said the following: "The future of CRM is a part of this trend to convergence. This convergence is not just the marketing trick that some companies use to make their products 'bigger than CRM.' This is a DNA-level convergence where the processes are integrated, the information technology architecture is uniform, and the interactions and results are real time. Additionally, the standards are no longer proprietary but open, allowing any application to speak to any other application. In fact, this goes further—not just application to application, but corporate to corporation."

This is now reality. No longer is the corporation the fulcrum around which customer groups and suppliers revolve. In 2004, the customer is now the pivot point. Collaborative business that interlinks the supply chain with the demand chain (customer-facing activities) and forms an extended value chain, governs the success or failure of businesses, whether or not they perceive this.

There are signs that the change from a customer-focused corporate ecosystem to a real-time customer ecosystem is not just well underway but already here. Businesses that are intimately involved have changed their operating models, even as the economy remains ragged. For example, a significant number of consultants, software vendors, and systems integrators are merging their supply chain practices with their CRM practices since issues such as delivery, logistics, inventory management, and scheduling are actually now customer issues, not just processes in need of optimization. Think about it this way. If you're expecting something via UPS or FedEx at 10:00 A.M. on Monday and it's now 12:30 P.M. and it isn't there, how do you feel? Do you care whether or not they have accurately forecast the production schedules, materials needs, and shipment and delivery methods? Or do you just want your package? Delivery is a customer issue and a real-time one at that.

Field service, which had been historically seen as a function in support of finished products, is now emerging as a profit center and a critical component of CRM planning (see Chapter 8).

More than any of this, CRM is now entering the mainstream of business thinking. Despite the uncertainties and weak corporate spending, CRM is seen as the second most important business initiative, because during times of economic dislocation, customer retention—repeatable revenue—is a matter of survival. CRM is the method that businesses have to deal with the newly minted customer economy.

Why else do you think that CRM needs to be redefined once again? Why else is it no longer just seen as a system and a technology, but as a business initiative and strategy? Why else have all the CRM major players redefined their applications from applications that were data-driven to applications that work more like the businesses they are trying to sell to? All of this is because the pivot of the business universe is the customer, not the corporation.

Now let's look at that customer-individual-atom in this new business manifold.

"Every Day Is Mardi Gras and Every Fan's a King."

Bill Veeck, noted baseball entrepreneur and showman, elaborated about what his optimum customer experience would be with the maxim, "Every day is Mardi Gras and every fan's a king." Veeck's customer was the baseball fan who paid to come to the Chicago White

Sox ballpark, hopefully regularly. Mostly likely he would obtain the highest lifetime value from a season's ticket holder. The diehard sports fan was (and is) the epitome of a customer—providing repeatable revenue on many sunny summer days by paying for tickets, hot dogs, beer or soda, and souvenirs for his entire family.

With the economic slowdown of 2001 and after, the Mardi Gras ended, though the kingdom remains intact. Customers are reluctant to spend; they are reluctant to provide any form of value to business at all. Money is tight. Confidence is uncertain, as the economy teases its victims with recovery but never quite gets better. But the rollercoaster nature of the consumer spending throughout 2003 shows that customers are still willing to take advantage of bargains (such as the housing market).

They also know they own the marketplace. That is why the landscape has become so competitive. As we saw in the last section, the 21st century customer is empowered with high expectations, low tolerance, and thus, high volatility. As a consumer, the customer can leave your company with a single mouse click. Your business reputation can be cemented or broken with that very same customer's wrist movement. The social epidemic that Malcolm Gladwell identifies so brilliantly in *The Tipping Point* can be activated by these wrist movements. For example, the first popular success with "word of mouse" was the movie *The Blair Witch Project* in 1999, which became a mega-hit movie phenomenon through the use of marketing via the Internet. Millions of paying customers were drawn to the movie theaters to see a low-budget movie that had virtually no distribution, until customer demand was so high that it was released to thousands of screens over its life. All due to mouse clicks, Internet buzz, and clever marketing. But Internet buzz can now do what Madison Avenue spent an incredible amount of money trying to do: create demand. All because the customer is empowered to conduct business in real time.

That Customer Is Just so Twentieth Century

The historic customer is the paying client—that individual or entity that gave you money for goods and/or services. But that was before we reached the multichannel communications-driven world that we live in, the one that gave this particular grouping global reach. Most companies now realize that to effectively reach those clients, they need an extensive network of collaborators that actively participate in some way in the business processes you use to improve the overall experience for that hopefully profitable client. Each cluster within this collaborative confederacy is also a group that needs to gain something from its relationship to you. That means that, while pleasing the paying client is the ultimate objective, you need your collaborators to help you do that. In exchange for their help, you need to provide each of them with a value proposition that makes sense to them. So you are exchanging value with all the collaborators a.k.a. customer segments. While this complicates the CRM picture, it also means that a CRM strategy has to encompass the other members of the shared consortium. In a typical commercial environment, they could include:

- ▶ Paying clients

- ▶ Employees

- ▶ Business partners

- ▶ Suppliers/vendors

It gets even more complicated when you are involved in a specific industry that has specific processes that govern the way a company in the industry does business.

THE UNIVERSITY AS CUSTOMER AND THE CUSTOMERS OF A UNIVERSITY: A BRIEF EXAMPLE

Imagine that you are an admissions officer or registrar at a university with a mission to draw students to your fine institution of higher learning. You recognize that you have to have technology savvy prospects, technology savvy students, alumni with children, alumni with money, alumni and others who buy university-branded merchandise, grant providers, bequestors, participants in a sports program (especially football and basketball), a staff that provides an unparalleled education, and a staff that provides an unparalleled corollary set of experiences both on and off campus, and that supports non-academic services ranging from bursars to janitors to grant writers to an MIS department. You also have a surrounding community that supports the activities and existence of the university via social organizations and merchants and just interested third parties. From a structural standpoint you need a board of trustees and a superstructure that provides support for the multiple government regulations that drive you crazy.

Additionally, for a university, CRM is executed a bit differently than the typical commercial or non-profit venture. First, you are using a concept called "student for life." This recognizes that unlike the commercial world, you have to maintain a relationship to the student-customer that encompasses them from fresh young high school prospects to bequestors. The period to determine the lifetime value derived from those customers is almost literally their natural one.

Second, you've recognized that you have to involve all of these aforementioned groups in order to provide that lifetime experience in a way that maintains the relationship of those students to you over the course of their lives. That means:

- ► Students
- ► Non-faculty staff
- ► Faculty staff
- ► Alumni
- ► Individual donors (non-alumni)
- ► University trustees
- ► Government agencies
- ► Foundations and other institutional donors
- ► The community at large and its institutions, including merchants, student-focused community leaders, etc.

This is just one example of a distinctive, specialized set of customers characterized by industry-specific processes, rules, and structure. Now, multiply the numbers of potential customer groups you have by the dozens of verticals out there such as financial services, telecommunications, energy, public sector, and retail. Then break each of them down even further. For example, there are quite different processes that govern insurance and retail banking, though both can be lumped under financial services. There is a difference between the processes, regulations, rules, and structures for local, state, and federal government, yet they all are part of public sector. To add to the complexity, the interaction between the three levels of government is of mission-critical importance as are issues of jurisdiction and law.

This is not just some academic semantics. Your ability to appropriately define who the customer is can be of vital importance to the ROI that you will receive in a specific industry. Bain and Accenture did studies in 2002 and 2003 on how a 5 percent increase in customer retention significantly impacts profitability (more on that in Chapter 22). That 5 percent buys you a 28-percent increase if you are in auto service, a 35-percent increase in profitability if you are in retail banking, and a 50-percent increase if you are in insurance brokerage. This is no small deal. If you don't define who the appropriate customer in your specific domain is, you won't know whom to actually make happy and thus retain. Your profitability will directly suffer. How to get to this will be the subject of much of the rest of the book.

Learning from the Best: CRM from Its Leaders

If the customer is now the fulcrum of the business universe and the nature of the customer varies from industry to industry, how does a business actually capture the customer's commitment? If CRM is no longer just a competitive edge, but part of mainstream business activity, what does it now look like and how can it be used? Beyond climbing into the Himalayas, how do I figure out what is best for my company and who do I trust to tell me?

These first three chapters are the overview on what will be resolution of all of this by book's end. To start, I've enlisted some of the industry greats to enter the fray, with a diverse perspective and from a variety of domains:

- ▶ The head of the only MBA program in the United States that offers a CRM specialty

- ▶ The CEO of the largest enterprise application provider in the world

- ▶ A CEO who runs the most successful company in the most rapidly growing CRM sector, the applications service providers

- ▶ One extremely successful chieftains of CRM at one of the world's largest integrators

- ▶ An industry veteran who was named in the top 20 personages in CRM by CRM Magazine and has an illustrious history to back that up

- ▶ One of the best CRM analysts in the business from one of the most prominent analyst organizations

- ▶ Two of the best management consultants in the world

- ▶ One of the true CRM pioneers who is a key industry heavyweight with influence

Each of them writes with a unique perspective on how you might want to look at CRM.

John F. (Jeff) Tanner

John F. Tanner, Jr., completed his Ph.D. at the University of Georgia in 1988. Prior to entering academia, he worked for eight years at Rockwell International and Xerox Corporation in sales and marketing. Since 1988, he has taught sales and marketing at Baylor University's Hankamer School of Business, where he has also served as department chair and associate dean. Currently, he directs the first MBA program specializing in CRM and also serves as the research director for the Center for Professional Selling.

Tanner has published more than 50 research articles in top journals such as the *Journal of Marketing, Journal of Business Research*, and *Journal of the Academy of Marketing Science*. His research has won many awards, including Mu Kappa Tau's top sales study in 2000. An internationally known expert in professional sales, he has taught graduate studies and executives in Canada, Mexico, France, and India. He is recognized as a leader in the research of sales force strategy, particularly as it relates to the adoption and implementation of CRM business strategies.

Tanner Speaks on CRM

Three words that mean many things to many people when linked together, Customer Relationship Management has become something of an enigma. There is little doubt, it would seem, about what a customer is, though the term CRM is applied to "things done" to non-customers as well.

The key that makes CRM different from other forms of strategy or marketing is that it is about relationship management. That pair of words has two implications that may or may not be true: that the firm can identify the type or types of relationships it wishes to have with customers and that the customer will allow the firm to manage those relationships.

There are a number of dreams to which CRM software can contribute, dreams such as seamless customer interaction across multiple channels, one-to-one marketing, 360-degree knowledge of the customer, and so forth. The reality is that CRM often devolves into an endless stream of campaigns that may take advantage of better customer data, but do not really build or contribute to a relationship.

The most important step is to define what is meant, then, by relationship. Consumer package goods manufacturers, like Kraft or M&Ms, are not going to have the same types of relationships with their buyers as are business-to-business companies such as BASF or SAP. Moreover, Karr-Hunter Pontiac/GMC has different and more direct relationships with its customers than does the Pontiac division of GM. How each of those organizations defines relationship categories is going to be different. But what many pundits and experts fail to recognize is that simply dividing customers into "bins" (or whatever terminology they use) based on recency and frequency of purchase doesn't define the relationship. Having sex every night with the same person does not guarantee marriage—knowing that information might make for a useful prediction as to what will happen tomorrow night, but it won't predict what will happen next year, nor will it predict any other aspect of the relationship.

Why is it so important to define the type of relationship? Because what is left out of CRM, especially when defined operationally as campaign management, is the future. We are forecasting the future entirely based on yesterday's information. We are not building into our forecast anything about the buyer's commitment (or lack of) to us, nor anything about how much the buyer likes doing business with us or any other relational input. As such, we can't forecast our buyer's behavior any further than tomorrow night. That's why we lose important opportunities for product development, channel development, and more.

The dark side of how CRM is made operational in many organizations is how we train customers to play us. Years ago, the grocers complained about "deal-prone" consumers. The prevalence of couponing meant that grocers couldn't sell anything at regular price—coupons had trained buyers to look for deals and eroded brand and store loyalty. Now we are training consumers to use our "loyalty" programs in much the same way. What we are finding is that light users become stuck in loyalty programs, but they aren't the ones we really want anyway. Few vendors get all of the business of the heaviest users because we don't have a relationship with them; we sell loyalty as just another feature of the product/service mix.

With too much emphasis on customer management, we lose sight of what the CRM revolution is really about. We may think we're managing customers, but for every book on CRM, there are three books on managing suppliers. ✷

Marc Benioff

Marc R. Benioff is founder, chairman, and CEO of salesforce.com. A 25-year veteran of the software industry, Benioff has pioneered "the end of software," demonstrating how on-demand applications can replace traditional software to deliver immediate benefit at reduced risk. In May 2003, Benioff was appointed by President George W. Bush as co-chair of the President's Information Technology Advisory Committee (PITAC), a bipartisan organization of business leaders and academics charged to advise the President on how to maintain the United States' preeminent position in information technology.

In tandem with his technology leadership, Benioff has created and implemented a new model for integrated philanthropy through the salesforce.com/foundation, a recent recipient of the Points of Light Foundation Award for Excellence in Corporate Community Service (2003). Benioff has received a wide range of honors for his business and philanthropy leadership, including selection as a Global Leader of Tomorrow by the members of the World Economic Forum (2002), Ernst & Young Northern California Entrepreneur of the Year (2003), Computerworld Honors Laureate (2002), and Japan's SunBridge Entrepreneur of the Year (2001). *CRM Magazine* named Benioff one of the 20 most influential people in the industry (2002), and *Network World* magazine ranked him one of its elite 25 Most Powerful Vendor Executives (2001). Prior to founding salesforce.com, Benioff spent 13 years at Oracle Corporation. Benioff received a B.S. in Business Administration from the University of Southern California in 1986.

BENIOFF SPEAKS ON CRM

American cycling great and Tour de France champion Lance Armstrong called his 1999 best selling autobiography It's Not About the Bike. *As Armstrong makes clear, in competitive cycling—indeed, in life—success depends on the brains, foresight, and heart one brings to an endeavor. The equipment is secondary.*

As many enterprises are discovering today, the same applies to Customer Relationship Management. It is not about the software. It is about the people. Specifically, it is about sales, service, helpdesk, and marketing people sharing information about customers. Armed with more complete, timely information, these people can make better decisions and, ultimately, keep customers coming back to buy more products.

Like wishful contenders obsessing over the latest cycling technology, however, too many companies have spent too much time and far too much money focusing on the software. Software vendors and analysts have convinced many that the key to CRM is to license and deploy increasingly complex and extremely expensive CRM software packages.

Unfortunately, like most licensed enterprise software packages, CRM suites have proven difficult to deploy and difficult to use. One well-known software industry analyst has estimated that between 1999 and 2002, enterprises overspent by $100 billion to $200 billion on enterprise software—much of it for CRM—that has simply gone unused.

Another information technology advisory firm estimated that half of all new enterprise software system deployment projects have ended in failure. As a result, many CEOs have concluded that CRM—or at least CRM software—has been oversold and that returns have not justified the investments. Many are scaling back on CRM software purchases.

For example, banks, insurance companies, and other financial services firms were among the most committed CRM proponents. With rich stores of customer information, various methods of reaching customers and often multiple lines of business, financial services companies saw CRM as an excellent way to retain and sell more products and services to customers.

Recently, however, a prominent publication covering the financial service industry noted a profound shift in the way many banks are approaching CRM. According to an article in The American Banker, rather than CRM centered on complex software deployments, banks are "trying to achieve the goals of a well-functioning CRM system—cross-sales and customer retention—in a more collegial and less technology-oriented way." (from The American Banker, June 18, 2003.) Specifically, the article reports, many banks are focused on employee training and business processes that emphasize collaboration and shared customer information across lines of business.

This is not to imply that CRM and CRM technology have no future. Companies that are able to understand—even anticipate—customer behaviors and preferences and quickly accommodate them will enjoy a profound competitive advantage. And comprehensive, up-to-date, and easily accessed customer data along with applications that help reinforce collaborative sales, marketing, and customer support processes will continue to deliver important business advantages.

But technology must support critical CRM processes, not complicate them the way packaged CRM software so often does today. At its core, CRM is an important business methodology that helps companies quickly align their products, services, marketing message, and sales approach with customer needs and expectations. Technology should be, as much as possible, transparent in supporting that methodology.

There are alternatives to software complexity. One is to avoid licensing and deploying CRM packages altogether. Growing numbers of large, medium, and small companies are beginning to buy CRM technology as if it were electricity, water, or another commodity available from a utility. Using this utility model, a service provider creates and hosts CRM applications into which business users can *tap on a subscription basis. For $50 per user per month, businesses can get online access to the same type of sales force automation, marketing automation, and customer support functionality they get from licensed software. But they do not have to license software. Nor must they employee a large IT staff to customize software, test it, deploy it, support it, and upgrade it when a new release comes out.*

While using the Internet to deliver software as a service is a relatively new idea, it is beginning to take off, particularly as service providers prove they can keep customer data secure and private. That is particularly true in the CRM space. The same Aberdeen report that predicted CRM software license revenue will continue to slide through 2006 also said the CRM market will "rapidly transition to a … subscription-oriented model." By 2006, the report predicted, subscription revenues for hosted CRM application services will have grown to $2.8 billion.

There are reasons a software-as-service approach makes sense for companies launching CRM initiatives. Sales people, who have often resisted using complex CRM software, have an easier time adopting hosted CRM services that they access from their already familiar Web browser. In addition, the model supports easy and low-cost integration with other critical systems via Web services, erasing the cost, length, and risk that has characterized software integration and application development projects.

But, more importantly, by tapping into hosted applications that are already up and running, companies start seeing the benefits of CRM immediately. That is particularly important to top sales, marketing, and support executives, who often have been stuck paying for under-used or even unused CRM software. And, more than anyone else, they understand that CRM is not about the software. It is about the people. ✦

Don Peppers and Martha Rogers

Recognized for the past decade as world-renowned experts on customer-based business strategies, and individually named to Accenture's global list of "Top 100 business intellectuals," Don Peppers and Martha Rogers, Ph.D., continue to set the standards in Customer Relationship Management by demonstrating how to reap customer value in a global marketplace. *Business 2.0* magazine named them as two of the 19 most important business gurus of all time. In addition to being acclaimed authors and speakers, they are the founding partners of Peppers and Rogers Group, the world's leading customer-focused management consulting firm, headquartered in Norwalk, Connecticut. Their firm, first established in 1993, now has a network of 12 offices positioned on every continent throughout the world, and an impressive array of Fortune 500 clients representing a wide swath of industry verticals.

Peppers and Rogers have co-authored five best-selling books to date, focused on customer strategy, building the value of the customer base, and related subjects. This includes their seminal text, *The One to One Future* (Currency/Doubleday, 1993). Now celebrating its tenth year in print, this publication was heralded by *Inc.* magazine's editor, George Gendron, as "one of the two or three most important business books ever written," and is widely acknowledged as the industry standard for the customer strategy revolution. Their second book, *Enterprise One to One*, received a 5-star rating from the *Wall Street Journal*. Every one of the Peppers and Rogers books have been international best sellers, including their latest, *One to One B2B*, which made the *New York Times* Business Best Seller list within a month of its publication. The global demand for Peppers and Rogers books and presentations has resulted in translation to 15 languages, with over a million copies in print.

Peppers and Rogers Speak on CRM:

We wrote our first book, The One-to-One Future, *in 1993. Back then, we referred to the strategic phenomenon caused by new technologies as "1to1 marketing." But by the time our second book* (Enterprise One-to-One) *appeared four years later, we already realized that building the value of the customer base is not something that could be accomplished in the "marketing" department, and would in fact require the integrated efforts of all parts of the organization. Since then, we have referred to "1to1 Learning Relationships" and "CRM" more or less interchangeably, although we recognize the drawbacks of the term "CRM."*

At the root of the problems with the term "Customer Relationship Management" is the fact that the software vendors have used the term so much that many business practitioners equate "CRM" with "CRM software." Technology is a very important, enabling first step, but we have seen a variety of firms spend vast amounts on the installation and integration of technology without moving the needle on their bottom line at all as a result. Usually, this is because of a "ready, fire, aim" approach which puts the technology horse before the strategy cart. We've met officers at very large companies where tens of millions of dollars have been spent on "CRM" technology who did not know how that technology was going to contribute to the value of their customer base.

And that's the point. We are in business because we have customers. Those customers are variably and predictably valuable to us now and potentially. They have different needs from us, which we can fulfill in different ways. The way we can grow the company's bottom line, ultimately, is to reduce the cost of serving each customer, or to increase the revenue received from each customer, or both. That means we differentiate our customers by value (fairly common these days) as well as need (almost unheard of, effectively speaking), and then we change our behavior toward each customer in order to encourage the customer to change his behavior toward us.

That's why it's misguided to think of "CRM" as personalizing the email, or getting more sophisticated about the segmentation, or generating better lists, or training the CSRs to run a more efficient call center. CRM is not better targeted harassment. *CRM is not even the same as better customer service, because customer service doesn't have a* memory. *While it's a good idea to teach our frontline personnel to be more polite, there is no "relationship" until the good service a customer gets today can be replicated without his having to ask for it again.*

So what is CRM, or one-to-one customer strategy? Plain and simple, it is this:

▶ *Building shareholder value by increasing the value of the customer base*

▶ *Enterprise-wide*

▶ *Using information about each customer to make each customer more valuable to your firm, and your firm more valuable to each customer, while decreasing the cost of servicing each customer*

▶ *Applying more resources to more valuable customers, and more resources to keeping valuable customers, rather than to acquiring new customers of unknown value*

▶ *Recognizing a customer as that customer through any channel, at any time, across product purchase and service lines, and over time*

▶ *Remembering things for and about customers*

▶ *Deciding what each customer needs from the firm next, based on the customer's feedback (even more than on demographics, zip code information, or other traditional third-party data—after all, your competitors can buy the same third-party data, but only your firm has the information the customer gave you herself)*

▶ *Using information from a customer to do something for that customer that no competitor can do who does not have information from that customer*

▶ *Treating different customers differently*

We are bemused by those who discount the term "CRM" because it's some-how wrong of us to try to "manage" relationships. Customers don't want that, right? Of course, that's literally true. But we should think of "CRM" as the hun-dred managerial decisions each of us makes in business every day, and making those management decisions from the perspective of increasing the value of the customer base, and using the best tool we have—relationships—to do just that. ✶

Bill McDermott

As CEO and president of SAP America, Inc., William R. "Bill" McDer-mott is responsible for all SAP business activities in the United States and Canada, including sales, marketing, service, customer support, finance, business consulting, and administration.

Prior to joining SAP, McDermott served as the executive vice pres-ident of worldwide sales operations for Siebel Systems, Inc. He also served as president of Gartner, Inc., where he led both the company's core operations and its worldwide sales and client service organiza-tions. Prior to joining Gartner, McDermott spent 17 years at Xerox Corporation, where he became the company's youngest corporate offi-cer and division president. In 1997, through his leadership, Xerox received the Baldrige Award, which is considered America's highest honor for performance excellence.

McDermott's accomplishments have been widely recognized. In Jan-uary 2003, *InformationWeek* featured him as one of the country's fore-most IT experts. In December 2002, *Network World Magazine* named him one of the "Fifty Most Powerful People in Networking."

McDERMOTT SPEAKS ON CRM

There are many ways a business responds to individual customer needs that cre-ate value for its customers and itself. They call that value creation CRM.

Companies benefit from CRM when they use information about their cus-tomers to operate more efficiently or bring products to market more quickly. For instance, a company yields value when its call center automatically routes high-value customers to special, high-capability agents. In addition, a business may use CRM to save money by eliminating duplicate mailings or to focus on a new service or product based on customer feedback its sales force has captured.

To benefit fully from such customer-specific activities, companies must iden-tify and remember customers individually, understand customer differences, interact with them, and tailor those interactions to particular customers or customer segments. CRM thus unites a company's customer-facing side with its production or service side. Put another way, effective CRM connects a company's demand and supply chains.

CRM Business Objectives

The push toward better CRM technologies is a natural result of the search by businesses for greater productivity and efficiency in customer-facing operations like sales, marketing, customer service, and support. For example, in sales, companies need IT systems that provide greater control and efficiency. This means improved forecasting capability, greater visibility into sales performance across a variety of channels, increased productivity by external sales forces, and reduced sales costs. Meanwhile, companies must meet customer demands for better quality, timeliness, and customization in the service they deliver.

Companies also need technology that helps them approach customers in a rational way. A company must, for example, remember a customer's address from one transaction to another and carefully choreograph contacts between its sales force and customers. In addition to being wasteful and inefficient, pitching a new product to a customer who has just bought the same item makes the company look incompetent to the customer.

The Internet has dramatically accelerated the focus on CRM by making customer interactions more cost-efficient. In addition, the Web has established a new, more direct sales channel that supports rapid customer interaction and short sales cycles. Using Internet technologies, customers can interact with information from a wide variety of sources without special training.

The Financial Benefits of CRM

Most companies can easily document the financial benefits from CRM technology by the costs they saved from greater efficiencies in sales, marketing, and service. More importantly, CRM can increase the true economic worth of a business by improving the total lifetime value of its customers. Successful CRM strategies encourage customers to buy more products, stay loyal for longer periods, or communicate more effectively with a company. CRM solutions with robust analytics can help companies identify and take advantage of winning business strategies.

All too often, however, a CRM implementation falls short of expectations, triggering debate about the costs and benefits involved. After supporting hundreds of CRM implementations, at companies large and small, at SAP, we've observed that successful implementations must:

▶ Support the company's business strategy

▶ *Integrate information and process to deliver key insights*

▶ *Encourage adoption by users*

Supporting the Company's Business Strategy

Whether a company uses CRM for greater cost efficiency or for profit and revenue growth depends largely on the company's competitive strategy. Many CRM initiatives fail simply because management teams have not aligned their CRM goals with their business strategy and the customer demands that support that strategy.

Business strategists agree that companies confront difficult choices in deciding whether to control costs, offer products that are more innovative and useful, or provide services that are more comprehensive.

A company's primary competitive strategy determines both the type of financial benefit it will seek from a CRM initiative and the features that the initiative must include. A service-oriented company may use CRM to increase the value of its customer base, while an operationally excellent firm may use CRM to minimize costs and align its resources more appropriately.

As more companies use technology to reduce barriers and improve customer relationships, however, more customers are demanding excellence in product, service, and price. This means that most companies must have individual departments that address a particular area. An effective CRM implementation must seamlessly connect all of these departments and coordinate their various goals with the company's overall business strategy. Additional integration is necessary when a company aligns itself with other firms to enhance product, service, or price.

Integrating Information and Process to Deliver Key Insights

Key to this integration is the smooth flow of customer information among the various company players. The information must help the company treat every customer consistently and rationally, in all interactions and all sales channels. Too often, a company launches its CRM initiative by upgrading one part of its customer-facing processes. This might mean improving the contact center, automating the sales force, or introducing a self-service web site. It might also involve an analytical CRM application, such as campaign management. All too soon, the company sees that the technology cannot get key information to the right people at the right time. The result is often a CRM program that is irregular and even in conflict with itself.

CRM solutions that simply use the front office to receive and record information will eventually fail. Such a solution can actually harm a company's reputation with customers by highlighting the shortfalls of its back-office processes.

CRM only achieves customer loyalty and profitability when contacts with the front office prompt a beneficial back-office response.

Companies can enhance such coordination by practicing connected CRM. *Connected CRM leverages the relationships that customers have with the entire enterprise. For an enterprise to maximize its resources for serving customers, it must coordinate all of those resources in the following ways:*

- ▸ *There must be full integration of the channels for sales and customer interaction.*

- ▸ *The company must align its financial systems and metrics.*

- ▸ *Activities must be synchronized throughout the value chain.*

To serve the specific needs of individual customers in each of these areas, a company might collaborate with its distribution partners or other third parties. Just as a collaborative CRM solution must serve the various competitive strategies of an enterprise and its business partners, so it must harmonize the flow of information among all of the parties—both within and outside the enterprise— that deliver customer value.

In an effective collaborative CRM implementation, such cross-boundary integration lets customers serve themselves in increasingly sophisticated ways and helps channel members configure, order, install, and service products as individual customers require or prefer. This collaboration demands processes that are both flexible and robust.

In the future, the most successful competitors will form ecosystems of interconnected enterprises, channel partners, and customers that unite in a seamless way to execute product and service orders. For such an ecosystem to communicate efficiently, the participants must have easy access to interaction technologies that support information connectivity and process collaboration among a host of individual players, in multiple industries, from one end of the value chain to the other. Ecosystem members must be able to reach into each other's internal systems to execute processes, frequently in an automated way. At the same time, an enterprise must be able to restrict access to information and process to the most appropriate partners. The technology platforms that facilitate collaborative CRM must thus provide compartmentalization, access control, and security that is both complex and multi-level.

The specific characteristics of such CRM solutions tend to vary by industry. As a result, industry-specific CRM *applications have developed around different industry models. A cursory review of web sites for major providers of enterprise-level CRM software reveals more than two dozen separately identified, industry-specific offerings: from aerospace to wholesale distribution.*

Industry-specific CRM solutions must also support collaborative activities between industries. In the financial services industry, for example, consumer-oriented companies share customer information and collaborate in other intimate ways with firms in the automobile manufacturing, homebuilding, retail, and health care industries.

Encouraging Adoption by Users

The adoption of a CRM solution by a company's employees and value-chain partners is another factor in its success. CRM typically involves many more people from a wider variety of professional and clerical positions than business disciplines like supply chain management or product life-cycle management. In addition to marketing and sales management employees, users of a CRM system may include contact center reps, sales reps, and other customer-contact employees from both the front and back offices. The system must also work for a company's business partners and, of course, its customers. Each of these players has a different role and information need. An effective CRM solution must account for the varying ways that its users will be affected and how users will react to new tasks and responsibilities.

Addressing these issues requires a fundamental shift in approach for many stakeholders. Given the large number of multiple-role, customer-contact employees, and business partners involved, managing the adoption of new processes can be particularly challenging with CRM.

At the same time, users must clearly see the advantages they gain from the system. An installation that automates a sales force, for example, should be introduced as more than a tool through which sales reps collect additional information. For a sales rep, this translates into extra work for possibly fewer sales. Who would sign up for that? Instead, the company should create a value proposition for the sales rep. This might entail providing customer information that the rep could access just before a sales call or adding software or demo support that can make the rep more effective.

Such people-centric CRM solutions typically involve portal technology. Intelligent portals that expand upon Web-based user interfaces are the most important new medium of the immediate future. Using portals, companies can communicate more efficiently, integrate inter-company activities more effectively, and facilitate an ever-increasing level of customer self service that allows direct intervention at all points in the value chain.

A portal can give employees personalized information and support specific tasks and transactions with a natural, intuitive working environment in which they can easily interact and collaborate. In addition to desktop-based workstations, portals can reach mobile workplaces. Portals are destined to be the accepted *infrastructure within an extended enterprise for all employees, partners, and stakeholders involved in customer interactions.*

CRM: The Next Level

Going forward, companies will increasingly demand comprehensive, end-to-end CRM solutions that give senior managers the data and insight they need for crucial business decisions. With enhanced insights about their customers, executives can pinpoint the strategies most likely to gain the company market advantage. Examples could include a more effective sales pipeline, tailored pricing, right time fulfillment, or tiered service programs.

Today, many useful insights are hidden in the vast amounts of proprietary data companies already collect from customer activities in disconnected systems. Companies can easily take advantage of these insights by using advanced, fully integrated CRM systems that offer analytics, modeling, and reporting.

The CRM revolution is in full swing, leaving companies to decide not if, but how they will participate. While a company can embrace the revolution one step at a time, CRM eventually transforms the entire business. Savvy managers are already using CRM for critical insights and decision-making across the enterprise.

Bob Thompson

Bob Thompson is CEO of CustomerThink Corporation, an independent Customer Relationship Management research and publishing firm, and founder of CRMGuru.com, the world's largest CRM industry portal. Thompson specializes in CRM strategic planning and research. Since 1998, Thompson has researched the leading industry trends including how CRM concepts can be applied to business partners in the extended enterprise. In January 2000, he launched CRMGuru.com, which has become the world's largest and fastest-growing CRM industry portal, with more than 200,000 members.

Thompson is frequently quoted in industry publications such as *InformationWeek*, *ComputerWorld*, and *Computer Reseller News*. Throughout his career, Thompson has advised companies on the strategic use of information technology to solve business problems and gain a competitive advantage. Prior to founding CustomerThink, he had 15 years of experience in the IT industry, including positions as Business Unit Executive and IT Strategy Consultant at IBM. Thompson earned a Bachelor's degree and an MBA from the University of California, Irvine.

Thompson Speaks on CRM

In July 1998, when I launched my CRM email newsletter, I defined Customer Relationship Management this way:

Customer Relationship Management means taking great care of your prospects and customers, using information technology.

Other names you may have heard:

- ► *Sales Force Automation*

- ► *Technology Enabled Selling*

- ► *Customer Asset Management*

- ► *Total Customer Management*

- ► *Enterprise Relationship Management*

... and a few dozen more.

There are over 500 CRM solutions on the market, from contact managers like ACT! to enterprise-wide information systems costing hundreds of thousands of dollars. Whatever the size of these solutions, the goals are similar: to improve the effectiveness and efficiency of marketing, sales, or customer care.

Since then, it's become a bit of closet industry to define and debate the meaning of CRM. Is it as-old-as-business philosophy—"Customers Really Matter"— or just the latest management fad to line the pockets of high-priced consultants—"Consultants Reap Millions"?

With the industry's sometimes-painful experiences of the past few years, it's clear that CRM is far more than front-office efficiency. Simply put, CRM is a business strategy to get, grow, and retain the most profitable relationships. However, making CRM work well is not quite that simple.

Roles of Information Technology

Can automating sales and service help? Sure, if focused correctly. On the other hand, sales automation can enable companies to be stupid faster by selling to even more unprofitable customers. And automated support systems won't help a surly support rep create a positive impression with a customer.

Over the past few years, we've put the spotlight on CRM tools when the real challenges are with people. That's like the once-popular TV show Home Improvement, where Tim Allen as Tim "the Tool Man" Taylor loads up on the all the latest gear, but puts his life at risk in each episode because he's not trained to handle more power.

To better understand current market perceptions, we conducted a major online survey and found the definition of CRM continues to be fragmented.

Selecting from five choices, only 9 percent said CRM was "automation of cus-tomer business processes." However, none of the other responses gained a major-ity (see Figure 1-2).

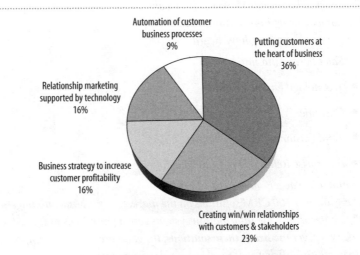

Source: CRMGuru Online Survey, 4400 Responses, July 2003 **CRM**guru
.com

Figure 1-2: "What is CRM?" survey results

Still, looking at the top two answers, "Putting customers at the heart of busi-ness" and "Business strategy to increase customer profitability," reveals that being customer-centric is part of the answer.

Why is being customer-centric important? Because, as loyalty guru Frederick F. Reichheld said in a May 2003 speech, "Loyalty can be earned only when lead-ers put the welfare of their customers and partners ahead of their own self-serv-ing interests." Reichheld found that loyalty leaders grow at 220 percent of the industry average, at 15 percent lower operating costs. It doesn't take a mathe-matician to understand why loyal customers are having a positive impact on the bottom line of companies like Harley-Davidson, Enterprise Rent-A-Car, Cisco Systems, Dell Computer, Lands End, and Intuit.

Bottom line: If you want customer loyalty, you have to earn it.

What Drives CRM Success?

While it's great fun to debate the meaning of life and CRM, the more critical issue is this: what determines whether CRM projects succeed or fail? We learned in a CRMGuru study of 448 projects that putting customers first is indeed good business.

First, survey-takers defined in detail the kinds of activities they performed in planning and implementing their CRM projects. Then they rated benefits received in the following areas, which collectively determined the ROI of the project:

▶ Increasing customer acquisition rate

▶ Decreasing churn (defection) rate

▶ Increasing share of customer

▶ Improving customer satisfaction

▶ Decreasing front office staffing costs (See Figure 1-3.)

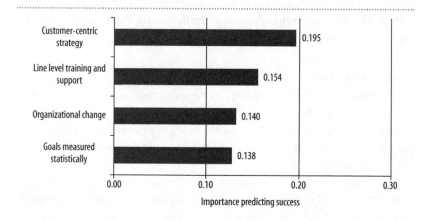

Source: CRMStudy of 448 CRM Projects, 2002 CRMguru.com

Figure 1-3: The drivers of CRM success

We found that about two out of three CRM projects are delivering a return on investment, from modest to outstanding. Four major factors accounted for 72 percent of CRM project success.

The number one driver for achieving ROI was "customer-centric strategy," which included using customer satisfaction and attrition data and getting customers involved in the planning process. In general, it meant driving the CRM project from an "outside-in" approach. First consider what's good for the customer, then how to make money doing so.

Next, "frontline training and support" and "organizational change" were tied for the number two spot. Companies tended to get a better return on their CRM investment if they proactively explained the value of CRM, providing training on *the new skills required, redesigned work processes as needed, and changed roles and responsibilities.*

The fourth key driver was using metrics effectively. Higher performing projects tended to invest considerable effort defining customer metrics, establishing a baseline performance, developing specific goals, and tracking against those goals.

What was even more interesting was what factor didn't make the list of key drivers: technology. By and large, companies are doing a good job selecting and implementing CRM solutions, whether from major software vendors, hosted services, or in-house development. In our research we found no correlation between the choice of software and achieving ROI.

Does this mean technology doesn't matter, or all software vendors are the same? No. What it does mean is that there are plenty of great CRM tools in the market. The difference between success and failure lies in the hands of people, not the tools they're using.

CRM: A Means to an End

Some companies succeed by building a better mousetrap, some by selling at lowest costs, and others by creating "better" customer relationships than their competitors. If you don't have the best product or lowest price in your industry (and not many companies do these days), odds are you're thinking about CRM and what it can do for your bottom line.

If you want CRM to deliver value to your business, you'd better start by figuring out the "win" for the customer, then getting your organization on board to make it happen. Otherwise CRM will be just another fad or software tool with unfulfilled promise.

Bruce Culbert

A seasoned professional with more than 20 years experience in delivering ground-breaking information technology solutions, Bruce Culbert has been called an e-commerce visionary by Forrester Research, described as a "charismatic leader" in *InformationWeek*, and has been recognized by *CRM Magazine* as "One of the 20 Most Influential People in CRM for 2002." He led BearingPoint's Global Customer Relationship Management Practice as senior vice president until late December 2003, when he became the Executive Vice President of Services at hot ASP salesforce.com.

In 1994, he started Interactive Media at IBM in Atlanta and expanded the unit to a team of more than 800 professionals worldwide, recognized as a global leader in interactive and new media development. After the proven success of Interactive Media, IBM named Culbert Vice President of e-business Services, Global Services. In this role, he led the largest end-to-end e-business solution provider in the United States.

Culbert received an MBA and a BS in engineering and commerce from Drexel University. He regularly speaks at a variety of industry events and currently serves on several corporate boards.

Culbert Speaks on CRM

Since the writing of the first edition of this book, I have seen and heard so many different definitions for CRM. It seems now that every logical grouping of people, (suppliers, employees, and shareholders) is included in some of today's contemporary interpretations of Customer Relationship Management. Supply partners and employees do play significant roles in meeting the needs of your customers, but they are not the big "C" Customer, the primary individual or entity that we are engaged with for a commercial commerce relationship. The last time I checked, the only way my employees, partners, and I got paid is by offering some product or service that had value to a prospective or current customer. In exchange for these valuable services and products I will receive something of value in return. In today's global market that usually means some form of currency or debt instrument, however, a customer transaction could also include barter and service in kind in consideration for the value received.

So with this definition of the customer, CRM is then a customer-focused business strategy designed to optimize customer satisfaction, revenue, and profitability. These strategies and tactics shape a company's people, business process, and technology infrastructure around identifying, acquiring, retaining, and growing profitable customer relationships. In today's customer driven economy, it is important to recognize that a consistent plan for continuing your relevance to your customer is paramount. For CRM strategies to be effective they require an enterprise-wide commitment to understanding your customers' wants and needs, creating compelling and relevant value propositions to offer them and delivering these value propositions profitably to the customer in their channel of preference (the Web, in store, through a distributor, and so on).

Where Are We Now?

Much has been accomplished in the past 5–10 years in leveraging advancements in process and technology to improve the effectiveness of what is referred to as operational *or* functional CRM. *Sales force automation (SFA), improved marketing effectiveness, and service consolidation and automation initiatives have been deployed to some extent in every industry. Many leading companies have taken actions to integrate and synchronize one or more of these operational initiatives in an attempt to deliver a superior customer experience and increase the ROI of their investments.*

Today the customer has an increasing expectation to interact in real time or near real time. The organization just can't react in real time, but must already be prepared to respond because they are committed to knowing their customers and anticipating their needs. By using the data and information obtained from the integrated functional areas—marketing, sales, and service—and tactics derived from customer intelligence and business analytics, companies have significantly increased their ability to know the customer and anticipate the customer's needs in ways that reinforce a company's relevance to their customers while sustaining and building profitable relationships.

Companies who are able to retain their relevance while understanding the needs of their customers and take action quicker than their competitors will be the ones that lead their industries.

Keeping customers, growing market share with current customers, and adding profitable new customers are the imperatives today. It is no longer appropriate to invest blindly and disproportionately without knowing your customer's value to your business if you expect to achieve top line revenue growth. I believe we are at a fundamental paradigm shift in how companies create and sustain value for their customers. I think moving forward, it will be imperative that companies accept the evolving nature of CRM. Opportunity can be derived from the time you start to learn the value of your customers and learn from the needs of your customers. This will provide the valuable insights needed to keep companies in front of their customer's changing needs. If you are in business and currently have customers, you want to learn as much about them as profitably possible. It may not be worth going through the expense of collecting information and knowledge of your customer if you cannot or will not use it to shape your offerings to the market, service your current clients effectively and efficiently, and build loyalty for your company's goods and services.

Fortunate for today's business, the CRM market for solutions has continued to evolve. Just as the consumer has never been so empowered, businesses have never had so many tools and techniques available to them, enabling companies to think "customer first." Thinking "customer first" may require a cultural shift in the business from product or service strategies to customer strategies. The impact of these changes should not be taken lightly. For most organizations, this will require a strategy and plan to change the company's focus, behavior, organization, compensation, training, and incentives. While this may seem to be an over-whelming task, in most cases it should not be undertaken all at once. An incre-mental approach incorporating lessons learned and best practices has proven to produce the best results.

Seven Tips for Highly Effective CRM

The CRM market and our collective experience have matured. Whether we are embarking on an enterprise-wide strategy or a specific functional point solution, we have learned to apply best practices and lessons learned to help ensure success from our CRM investments. As a result, I would recommend that each organiza-tion consider the following seven tips for highly effective CRM prior to imple-mentation and deployment of any initiative:

- ▶ Align to corporate strategy, ensuring that CRM initiatives are in com-plete alignment with the organization's overall business goals.

- ▶ Create an overall CRM vision for the company. Develop and communi-cate the CRM vision to the organization and key constituents, such as customers, employees, and partners.

- ▶ Changes in process, people, and technology should be evaluated and the business impact should be quantified and prioritized, supported by a solid business case and tangible return on investment (ROI)

- ▶ Secure the commitment and buy-in of senior management to the overall project vision, project objectives, and measurements of success.

- ▶ Develop an iterative and incremental approach focused on addressing the highest value opportunities first—think big, start small, and deliver results quickly.

- ▶ Recognize the organization change and motivations required to achieve full benefits, and create the action plans to achieve and sustain the future state of organizational readiness.

- ▶ Measure the effectiveness of your initiatives and create accountability for customer and business results. What is your baseline performance and what key performance indicators (KPIs) will you measure to know that you are getting results from your CRM initiatives?

Following these tips will not guarantee your CRM success. However, if your organization has a plan to address these areas, you will improve your chances of success and reap the rewards of profitable, customer-focused business strategies.◄

Steve Olyha

Steve Olyha is the vice president and general manager of Unisys Global Customer Relationship Management practice. He is the former executive in charge of Computer Sciences Corporation's CRM business, and previously held senior sales and marketing positions in several Fortune 500 companies.

The Unisys Global CRM organization, under his leadership, is focusing on a solution-oriented approach to the market based on solving the business problems of various industry segments, primarily within the public sector and financial services industries. Olyha's personal expertise and industry-recognized successes are in the area of business strategy development, particularly at the functional level, and the establishment of best-practice processes and enabling technology to ensure organizations achieve their business objectives.

OLYHA SPEAKS ON CRM:

Just about everyone has a definition of CRM—every analyst, systems integration firm, consulting company, business publication, and frankly, most operating companies. Most of those definitions make consummate sense when viewed individually, and many seem hard to assail for their accuracy as fair summations for what CRM is. The problem with them? CRM is no longer a "thing" that can be summed up by a short sentence that supposedly describes with great clarity this very complex topic. To be sure, there was a time in its early lifecycle that CRM was a thing. In fact, it was pretty simple—it was an application technology (at least the way is was actually and practically used and implemented) that was going to give sales executives a whole new view of their customers, and it was called sales force automation. From there, the CRM industry grew and matured into various functional areas such as call centers and marketing, and the new entrants on the technology side began to make claims of crossing functional areas by calling themselves enterprise applications (they aren't). Most recently, the focus has been on data, analytics, and development of a common view of customers across channels and organization touch points. Then the analysts stepped in and confirmed the self-promoting definitions that existed by proceeding to evaluate the success and viability of all the various participants in the space within these very segmented and discrete functional areas.

To be clear, there wasn't a whole lot wrong with these definitions, as they met the needs and actual operating practices around CRM—until recently. Today, CRM can no longer be summed up the way it once was. CRM is still all about getting as much profitable revenue as you can from new and current customers. You can wrap other words like acquisition, retention, churn, and so on around your favorite definition, but at the end of the day you're in business to make money and not much else matters. What is different about what CRM is today? It's that CRM is a complete business model and set of operating practices built around how to do exactly that: make money from customers. It's a philosophical, cultural, ingrained approach that crosses functions and technology infrastructure to the way your company behaves, and everything else about CRM is there to support that business model. It can no longer be viewed or described in the functional terms that have been used until now. In fact, real CRM even crosses other typical domains like supply chain management.

The compelling evidence for this is obvious and all around us. For example, one can look at all the recent documentation and analysis that point to the common causes of failure, or at least lack of resounding success, for many CRM implementations. What always comes somewhere near the top of every list? One item is change management, which is at the core of developing a culture of customer-centricity, yet most CRM project dollars are spent elsewhere. Another is the problems around data integration, almost always driven by a functional, not cross-functional, approach that leaves only partial views of the customer and painful costs for downstream integration.

There is also the common-sense obvious: if CRM is about driving profitable revenue, how in the world could it be done without the entire business model being involved? Not necessarily integrating everything, but at least the process touch points involved in meeting specific customer needs. Let's face it, can one be customer-centric just by selling without delivering—that is, integrating or creating a business model that meets every priority customer around a transaction? No.

So back to the definition. CRM is an integrated business model and set of operating practices coordinated and aligned to maximize profitable revenue from targeted customers. It can start with an initiative within a particular area in an enterprise like customer service or a call center, but that's not really CRM, that is a functional initiative that is but the first step in developing a CRM model for the organization. It is not true that in order to say one has a CRM model or initiative the entire organization has to be "integrated." That isn't practical, realistic, or likely even attainable in most firms. However, what must occur is the integration of process and technology touch points that have any impact on a particular customer transaction. For example, in a consumer goods company, a process redesign and technology implementation for sales force automation isn't CRM, it's a functional initiative, a "thing." If that same initiative involves the integration of trade promotion spending, forecasting, and fulfillment, now, that's CRM. If that same integrated initiative has the appropriate level of data integration so every transaction can be fully viewed, and, if it is further supported by a comprehensive and ongoing change management program, that is CRM that works!

Michael Maoz

Michael Maoz is a vice president and research director at Gartner, Inc., the world's largest independent provider of IT advisor services. His research focuses on Customer Relationship Management applications and integration, and he is the research area leader for customer service and support strategies. Maoz has 16 years of international experience in Europe, North America, and the Mideast. He earned a Bachelor's degree in European history from the University of Massachusetts and a graduate degree in technical communications from Northeastern University.

MAOZ SPEAKS ON CRM

Although it is still an immature business strategy, Customer Relationship Management continues to evolve. The essence of CRM is about customers—their processes, their preferences, and what they want from you. Once that's understood, the technologies and tactics begin to fit into an overall picture. Customers will remain a business's most important asset. Strategies designed to attract and retain customers will yield long-term competitive advantages. CRM is no longer just a good idea, it is becoming a matter of survival, as customers increasingly demand greater control of and convenience in their transactions. Enterprises recognize that CRM depends on front-office coordination (that is, the sales, marketing, and service channels), as well as effective integration with the back-office functions. This has resulted in a rising level of interest from enterprise resource planning (ERP) vendors, as they begin to cast themselves as providers of cross-enterprise, process-focused business application solutions. These major ERP vendors have now recognized the emerging requirements and have begun to deliver solutions that address them. Their continued investment in linking front and back office, and extending key processes out to customers, will shape the future CRM software market profoundly.

CRM, like most IT strategies, was first embraced by leading edge organizations as a way to address the needs of the customer. As it moves more into the mainstream, the large ERP newcomers are developing broad, but initially basic, CRM functionality. The traditional CRM vendors have already begun to remake themselves to compete with the large, front-to-back process systems. The CRM vendors are focusing on integration and back-end independence, and many are beginning to push the concept of their place in the real-time enterprise (RTE), offering decision support capabilities, as well as increasingly faster access to customer information. The goal is to enhance the likelihood of sales and improve the levels of service. In many cases, this turns out to be more "right time" than real time, but for many enterprises, that is sufficient.

In reality, real time is the solution to a symptom, and not the key to a new generation of CRM products. Real time is not the real problem. And beyond that, it's a short-term stop for the CRM vendors. They cannot hold that ground forever, as the large-enterprise ERP vendors will also begin to incorporate real-time components into their solutions during the next two years and negate any advantage these vendors have achieved. So the real question is, what's next? What comes after real-time CRM, and how will the broader enterprise application space evolve?

To answer this question, it helps to look at the ERP side to see what is going on in those solutions. Gartner sees CRM systems evolving to become more process-oriented and less application-specific. If this is the case, then eventually the two areas of ERP and CRM will converge at a third, higher-level solution. And that's the key not only to CRM applications, but to the future business applications space.

This view of the market will also begin to take advantage of much of the technological advances occurring at the moment. Given a broad adoption of redefined enterprise application suites, along with the evolution of integration capabilities (such as Web services), a new generation of best-of-breed applications (and functionally oriented or process-focused suites) will emerge to complement and enhance the core capabilities of broad enterprise application suites. Leading enterprises will lead in the adoption of these new applications, but penetration will also trickle down as more enterprises look to develop or highlight differentiated competitive advantages.

The period 2004–2007 will be an exciting and challenging one for users looking to CRM applications for competitive advantage. The choice will not be between best of breed point application, CRM suite, or enterprise application suite, but one of designing a customer ecosystem supported by the appropriate combination of several applications that share data, business process flow, and intelligence to deliver a successful customer experience.✎

Okay, Folks, What Did We Learn?

Obviously, there are still widely varied opinions on what CRM is, as you've just read. But there are common themes that our pundits identified in the discussions:

- ► CRM is a strategic business initiative.
- ► CRM is an enterprise-wide program that can be implemented incrementally.

▶ CRM initiatives are aimed at treating each individual customer differently.

So, with common themes, a view of the CRM universe and the customer, we can now move on to the next street on this road to clarity.

Ever hear "Riders on the Storm," by the Doors? There are a few lines in it that go:

Take him by the hand
Make him understand
The world on you depends
Our life will never end.

If you're considering a CRM initiative, that's you, rider. Let's move to Chapter 2.

2

Whole-Brained CRM: The Real Metaphor

" **C** RM is a philosophy and a business strategy, supported by a system and a technology, designed to improve human interactions in a business environment."

> —Me (Paul Greenberg)
> *CRM Magazine*, Reality Check column
> "Making CRM Whole-Brained," February 2003)

The META Group Definition circa 2000

When the struggle to define CRM began back in the prehistoric 1990s, it was characterized most frequently with technological and functional terms. The mantra, "It isn't a technology, it's a system," actually came into vogue because of a reaction to the strong technological wind stirred by CRM and what was at the time the dot.com boom, primarily because of vendor marketing. After all, Siebel's big enterprise CRM application suites were hot stuff, and they would make the future relationship between business and its paying customers something to behold.

The industry standard definition was developed in 2000 by the META Group in "The Customer Relationship Management Ecosystem." Unfortunately, what the META Group defined as the components of CRM technology and functionality became all-encompassing CRM to the rest of the known world. All the literature that emerged at this time used META Group's definition very broadly, which had the effect of distorting CRM's actual value, though there was nothing inherently wrong with the definition. In fact, this particular definition stuck and to this day is the foundation for traditional CRM.

But in early 2002, perception of CRM began to change and with that, a new round of attempts at a definition emerged, as companies contended with a number of new factors that affected institutional CRM. Among them:

▶ The rate of and reasons for CRM failures

▶ The explosive tangible value of and reasons for recorded CRM successes

▶ The effect of September 11, 2001, on the world economy and the global psyche

▶ The ongoing transition of the business ecology from corporate to customer-centric

▶ The transition from a data-driven CRM model to a process-focused CRM (see Chapter 3)

The CRM Techno-Functional Big Picture

The META Group identified three CRM segments: operational, analytical, and collaborative. The technological architecture provides a directly connected link between operational and analytical. Operational CRM is the customer-facing applications of CRM—sales force automation, enterprise marketing automation, and front-office suites that encompass all of this simultaneously. The analytic segment includes data marts or data warehouses such as customer repositories that are used by applications that apply algorithms to dissect the data and present it in a form that is useful to the user. Collaborative CRM reaches across customer touch points (all the different communication means that a customer might interact with such as email, phone call, fax, website pages, and so on) and can involve a many-to-many relationships hierarchy (see Chapter 6) and could include modules that are part of applications such as partner relationship management (PRM).

Operational CRM

This is the CRM horizontal segment that is most identified with routine CRM. When you are first thinking about CRM, isn't it true you often think sales, marketing, or support? At a functional level, that is part of operational CRM, especially when revolving around a typical corporate structure. Operational CRM covers customer-facing transactions from the internal company. Typical business functions involving customer service, order management, invoice/billing, or sales and marketing automation and management are all part of this bandwidth on the spectrum. Integration with financial and human resources functionality embedded in the enterprise resource planning (ERP) applications such as PeopleSoft and SAP is one of the historic agenda items of traditional CRM. With this integration, end-to-end functionality from lead management to order tracking can be implemented, albeit not often seamlessly.

Part of the operational CRM universe includes the customer call center, which, with the integration of multiple communications channels, is now even more frequently called a customer interaction center (CIC) or a customer contact center. For more on this, see Chapter 7.

Analytical CRM

Analytical CRM is the capture, storage, extraction, processing, interpretation, and reporting of customer data to a user. Companies such as SAS have developed applications that can capture this customer data from multiple sources and store it in a customer data repository and then use hundreds of algorithms to analyze/interpret the data as needed. The value of the application is not just in the algorithms and storage, but also in the ability to individually personalize the response using the data. But the true value of the interpreted data occurs when it becomes actionable intelligence (see Chapter 9 for more).

Ironically, as CRM has evolved, even the purity of this highly delineated segment gets a little spotty. For example, most of the excellent enterprise marketing automation (EMA) packages have a strong set of analytical tools for customer segmentation. Yet EMA is ordinarily defined within the category of operational CRM.

Collaborative CRM

This is almost an overlay. It is the communication center, the coordination network that provides the neural paths to the customer and his suppliers. It could mean a portal, a partner relationship management (PRM) application, or a customer interaction center (CIC). It could mean communication channels such as the Web or email, voice applications, or snail mail. It could mean channel strategies. In other words, it is any CRM function that provides a point of interaction between the customer and the channel itself.

The META Group Definition circa 2003

Because they are one of the better analyst groups out there, the META Group is resilient and resourceful and always researching. Consequently, mindful of the new realities of CRM and the business spectrum, they have redefined CRM. Let's take a look at the META Group definition as of mid-2003. This is penned by Liz Roche, one of the META Group's CRM analysts:

(1) Customer relationship management is not simply a technology tool or business process to "delight the customer" or show how the organization "loves its customers." CRM is ultimately about driving bottom-line revenue through proactive management of the customer life cycle. It is about applying the right CRM treatments to the right customer segment at the right time to produce business results. The difficulty is in determining what the right CRM treatments are and to what segments they should be applied. Enter CRM pattern matching, where to realize return on CRM investment, organizations must think in terms of using customer information and CRM technologies to build exit barriers and switching costs into reusable CRM treatments. Each treatment, described as a three-layered CRM pattern called a "customer relationship anatomy" (CRA), will be differentiated based not just on what the customer wants (we all want to be platinum flyers on all airlines), but also on what the organization determines to be appropriate (based on the customer's current period and future predicted value). And we note that "value" is defined as more than just profitability, as unprofitable current period customers may turn out to be very profitable in the future.

(2) CRM is a business strategy providing a systemic approach to customer life-cycle management (CLCM). CLCM is a three-domain business system, aligning business processes, technologies, and the customer life cycle. This business system must integrate sales, service, and marketing processes and the CRM technology environment with the customer. To fully realize the potential of CRM, this business system must be optimized around the customer life cycle (engage, transact, fulfill, and service [ETFS]), where the customer is the design point (not the technology or process).

Note two things about the difference in the definitions. The original definition of CRM (operational, analytic, and collaborative) is not driven by business, but by CRM's technology and functionality. Here is what

CRM technology can do. Their newer definition is considerably richer, profoundly strategic, process-oriented, and customer-centric. Here are customer behaviors and here are the processes that are designed to influence those customer behaviors over a lifetime. There are systems that will support the planning of this program and there are strategies to match the planned results. The difference between their original outlook in 2000 and the current outlook is focused around that customer pivot point.

The META Group 2003 CRM definition is a good jumping-off point for beginning to move to a more complete look at what CRM is as we march through the new millennium.

Program vs. Project

To begin with, there is one principle that governs CRM and needs to be always permeating its infrastructure, its objectives, and its life. We are not just looking for that singular customer experience and value. We are looking to see that there are ongoing, continuous improvements in that singular customer experience which leads to increasing value. In other words, CRM is a strategic program of continuous improvements to that customer experience. It is not a tactically focused project with a single objective. That said, CRM programs can include a series of specific projects (see Chapter 20 on implementation).

The original notion of CRM was that you implemented a CRM project, much like you implemented an ERP project. You chose an application suite, you found some people to install and configure the applications, and that would be it. There would be a bout of end-user training. Maintenance contracts were signed, upgrades would be considered, and life would be automatically good after that. CRM was still seen as customer-facing ERP. The vice president of IT was often the owner of the project. CRM was seen as technology vendors like Siebel, Vantive (in those days), Clarify, and others. It was a software implementation that was the front-office equal of an ERP implementation. When speaking of change management then, it meant how both parties would contractually handle the project if it exceeded the scope of the statement of work (SOW). So change management was the change in the pricing, not the culture.

The irony is that when CRM was rolled out to the staff, since there had been no idea that processes were going to change or that the business thinking needed to be transformed, user adoption rates were extraordinarily low. That calls for a much different approach—a holistic one. Plow on.

Whole-Brained CRM

In some approaches, the left brain is considered the rational side that governs language, logic, interpretation, and arithmetic. The right brain governs geometry, nonverbal processes, visual pattern recognition, auditory discrimination, and facial skills (the intuitive side). This is the CRM that you know and maybe love, maybe not. It is why the initial CRM was defined as a "system, not a technology," back in the day. Much of what you are going to read here is going to be discussed in detail in Chapter 17 on CRM strategy. But to understand how to get your arms around CRM, you need to know why the elbow joints are engaged. So reach out and get set to grab.

The historic CRM was defined in a rather odd fashion. While there has always been talk of improving customer satisfaction, increasing customer loyalty, refining the customer experience, enhancing customer interaction—all subjective factors—CRM has been very much a mathematical/statistical and operational endeavor, with analytic algorithms segmenting data to better understand how to use the data to improve the relationship that you had with the customer. The proofs of success were the top and bottom lines of corporate revenue. Benchmarks and metrics were created to measure how well it performed against the planned return on investment. CRM was seen as a result, more than as an ongoing process. Nothing was wrong with that—except that how to get the result was actually what CRM is, not the result itself.

It has also been tarred as ERP redux. It was a big system that was data-driven and transactional. It cost lots of money to implement, was implemented as a project, and dropped to the end-user without regard to the end-user's thoughts on the matter. After all, ERP captured business actions and automated many, allowed cross-functional interdepartmental data views, and provided a central repository for data that made planning somewhat easier. CRM did the same thing but for customer data, didn't it? Well, if you saw CRM as a technology and a system, yes, that's what it did. Its value seemed to be related to lowering costs or increasing revenue. Not too bad. But it also seemed to fail a lot. We've already seen the failure percentages of 2001–2002 from multiple analysts: 55 to 70 percent.

The most common reasons for those failures have been the result of ignorance of the right-brained aspects of CRM. At this point, you might be asking yourself, what are "right-brain aspects, may I ask?" Well, the failure to understand that the corporate culture was going to undergo a dramatic change or the failure to engage the users, both internal and external, in the planning and execution of the strategy and the implementation. The failure to understand the culture of the chosen vendor. The disregard for the politics of the corporation. Over-concern for senior management buy-in and stakeholder participation to the exclusion of the users from that stakeholding team. In other words, a fundamental disregard for the human performances in this very human endeavor.

By making its definition predominantly left-brained, CRM direction was often skewed and distorted, notably when cultural transformation was at stake. That led to problems with how training was handled. The stakeholders were chosen in a one-sided fashion, senior management only passively supported initiatives, IT departments ran the initiatives, and user adoption rates were low.

The corrective key? A balanced "whole-brained" approach to CRM which acknowledges that we are dealing with human beings who have interests, concerns, their own agendas, and probably think somewhat differently than we do. We have to map those human performance issues and criteria to a strategic business initiative to make sure that CRM succeeds.

Left-Brained Elements of CRM

Let's start by looking at some of the traditional pieces of CRM:

- ▸ Senior management buy-in

- ▸ Total cost of ownership

- ▸ ROI

- ▸ Benchmarks and metrics

- ▸ Application selection

- ▸ Implementation planning

- ▸ End-user training

Senior Management Buy-In: Passive or Active?

The lack of senior management buy-in is often cited as a mission-critical factor in the high failure rates of CRM. Oddly, there is very little data that I can find to support this posture. Take a look at what's out there:

- ▸ In a 2002 DataMonitor survey of the financial services industry, only banking saw lack of senior management buy-in as even a significant issue (2 on scale of 4), while insurance and investment brokerage saw it as insignificant (below 1 of 4).

- ▶ In a study done by the Baylor University Hankamer School of Business among 99 consultants and staff who had been involved in the implementation of a CRM program, 59 percent thought that there had been adequate senior management buy-in.

- ▶ 94 percent of the respondents to a survey of U.K. companies done by PA Consulting, sponsored by the then Compaq, SAS, and Siebel, understood senior management buy-in as a critical factor in CRM success.

While by no means am I saying these surveys are conclusive, they are representative of what is out there to support the case. The results seem to indicate that while it is clear that senior management buy-in is a critical CRM success factor, senior management does often buy in, so it is not as big a problem as is often characterized.

More germane to this is that senior management, once they buy in, also often step away and the initiatives suffer. There are multiple cases of CRM failure that are attributed to a lack of strategy, a lack of benchmarks and metrics planning, or even a lack of passion for the program. These problems can be attributed quite often to senior executives who aren't driving the CRM initiative and who remain uninvolved.

Senior management just passively signing off on an initiative, while perhaps not the major problem, is not adequate for success of the initiative, because it leads to other problems. It is essential to have the decision-making officers and executives actively involved in the initiative as part of the stakeholding teams.

For example, one of my clients has all of their senior C-level executives involved in their CRM initiative with the leading light being the CFO. They actively meet and formulate strategy and have seen that CRM needs their support. They interact with users regularly.

Additionally, take a look at York International, a leading HVAC equipment supplier. They spent seven months picking their stakeholders so that they had the right mix of active participants, not just bodies. They understood what it takes to get active leaders, rather than passive paper pushers.

Total Cost of Ownership (TCO)

I cringe when I see a major CRM vendor with a marketing headline like this: "Lower Your Total Cost of Ownership with (Large Vendor Name)

HelpDesk." While TCO is an important factor in deciding whether CRM is a viable initiative, it is never a driver for CRM. Nor are cost efficiencies or reduction in expenses. Bluntly, CRM will cost you money. What is paramount is to determine whether the derived value is worth the cost, not how the costs will be reduced.

With the certainty that you will heed this, I'm going to identify what the factors involved in determining the TCO are and how they can be an important part of defining your scheme for CRM.

Total cost of ownership (TCO) is a model developed by Gartner Group to analyze the direct and indirect costs of owning and using hardware and software. It identifies not only the immediate costs of deployment, but possible future costs that can often be hidden. For example, Gartner Group did a study in 2002 on CRM software licenses and found that significant numbers of companies purchase more software licenses than they need, perhaps anticipating some future requirement or falling for a software sales pitch that seemed too good to pass up. "If you act now, we can not only give you an additional 200 licenses for the low, low price of $750,000—that's $500,000 off the original price—but we will throw in a server and a free vacation to Disneyworld Resorts in Orlando, Florida. But when I walk out of this room, the deal leaves with me."

While this is exaggerated, many companies grab the deal in the heat of the moment. By purchasing what becomes shelfware (remember that 42 percent under flowerpots in Chapter 1), the TCO increases by at least 20 percent and as much as 30 percent. While not directly germane, the lesson here is buy what you need now and you can concern yourself with the growth later. Stick to the plan. This will prevent future surprises, which is what research on TCO is for to begin with.

THE ELEMENTS OF TCO

The elements of TCO, especially when concerned with CRM, are typically the following:

- ▶ Numbers of users
- ▶ License costs
- ▶ Communications costs including website
- ▶ Integration costs
- ▶ Support/upgrade costs

- ▶ Implementation and customization costs

- ▶ IT infrastructure/hardware or hosting costs

- ▶ IT personnel costs

- ▶ Other labor costs

- ▶ Other related software costs

- ▶ The cost of business process change and redesign

- ▶ Training costs (admin and end-users)

That is the high level view. But for example, drill a little deeper into the costs of the server. That could include a web server, application server, and database server. It could then need to be configured for high performance with clustered servers and need to use hot failover to prevent or minimize downtime. (In the industry they call it maintenance of high uptime.) Perhaps you need to guarantee extremely high availability because you have such a heavy stream of incoming data that is constantly being analyzed. That might mean some hot swappable storage configurations that can handle terabytes. It is by no means easy to figure all this out. This is a very disciplined (there are other words for it, but they aren't suitable for a business book) exercise that could cost a company millions if it fails to cover all bases.

It's also very easy to miss some hidden factor that could ultimately hurt. There is one that is of the "it's hidden openly on the table" variety: the cost of changing systems as business conditions change, or as the processes and rules of the company are altered because of the ongoing improvements that CRM creates and demands. While these may seem obvious, they are easy to overlook.

As an example, one possible solution for cost containment here is to make sure that the architecture of the selected suite or application is flexible and the off-the-shelf features are usefully plentiful and configurable. That allows a lower cost to making the changes when they must be made.

TCO is a major tool for preventing surprise CRM expenditures, but is not a driver for CRM. *Please* don't forget that.

Benchmarks, Metrics, and ROI

Benchmarks and metrics are the performance measurements for objectives and goals against a standard that you set for your CRM program and for any individual CRM project you might undertake. Your ROI is what you'd like to see result from the CRM program. It would seem that I'm stating the obvious here, but, sadly, that's not the case.

Look at these rather startling stats: In a 2002 study, Giga Information Group found that only 30 percent of the companies surveyed have implemented, or are in the process of implementing, a measurement strategy for CRM. In the same survey, 55 percent plan to measure CRM benefits but have no concrete strategy to do so. That's outright scary. It goes back to the problem of misconstruing what CRM is. If you don't know what it is, you don't how to use it, and if you don't know how to use it, how can you measure it?

The most subjective factor is the ROI. Because each enterprise has a history and a constantly evolving set of business processes, there is no question that what a company wants to get out of CRM is usually tailored to the individual concern. It doesn't stop with the company's desires, but often is subject to the political desires of members of senior management who might have to answer to the board. While there are industry-specific processes that often govern the CRM rules and programs or are governed by them, the outcome planned isn't necessarily the same for all members of that industry. For example, if your company is in the toy business and owns 12 percent of the market and has nearly 90 percent brand recognition, you are going to want a different result from your CRM programs than if you own less than 1 percent of the market with 5 percent brand recognition. Wal-Mart's objectives are different than Target's.

However, if you are doing it right, you define what results you would like to get from the initiatives. AMR Research did a study of what metrics businesses used to define CRM ROI with the percentage of businesses that specified them:

- ▶ Customer satisfaction/retention rate: 78 percent

- ▶ Reduced cost of services: 71 percent

- ▶ Increase in sales and revenue: 59 percent

- ▶ New customer acquisition: 57 percent

- ▶ Reduced cost of sales: 52 percent

- ▶ Head count reduction: 50 percent

In Chapters 17 and 22, we'll take a look at the validity of some of these metrics and their appropriateness to a CRM strategy and its ROI. Suf fice it to say, these are the popular metrics, good and bad, that are utilized in planning a CRM ROI. We'll save the "how to" for later.

Application Selection vs. Vendor Selection: A Cultural Event

Think about it. You're finally at the point that you have to choose the applications that you are going to use to create this system for customer ecstasy. The packages you're considering have features and functions that are probably useful and definitely cool. You had a pretty solid strategy and thus were able to identify three or four applications from three or four vendors that seemed to meet your techno-functional needs. These application providers were heavily into promises of paradise or perhaps Las Vegas, depending on your deepest beliefs. Interestingly, though, the question that you need to ask is not just what application features are good for you, but does the software producer live by the principles of CRM that the applications are designed to enhance? Or do they genuflect to some truism about how their core values are customer-driven? Instead, they should be driven by a deeply embedded customer culture, one in which the principles that define that culture are aimed at creating happy customers—in this case, your company.

The problem is that the CRM vendor world is often misconstrued by how good or bad the functionality of the program is—a vestige of the premillennial product-driven world. Vendors will often provide lots of homilies to processes, people, and technology, but the reality is that most of them are driven to sell the software. The result? Many make promises to the customer that often can't be kept, because their sales team incentives are for just that: sales of functional software that can be customized for additional, very high cost. The senior management engaged in vendor selection is often looking at functionality-driven metrics or hard and quick ROI as their drivers, even when addressing the issue of culture internally by planning a change management program as part of the CRM implementation. Even the customer's package selection teams are not looking very far, often responding to the relationship they have with the sales team assigned to their account, rather than taking into account the culture that drives those sales teams. This sales team is only a reflection of the vendor's culture, but not fully representative, because it is also driven by its own personality and self-interest. Consequently, there is a features-heavy haze that lies over the entire selection process. The result is usually shelfware, broken promises, or a significant number of useless features turned on for applications that were delivered over budget, late, and incorrectly.

Implementation Strategy

This is a strategy within a strategy. A strategy within a grand strategy, if you will. Once you've chosen the vendor and the applications, how you go about installing, configuring, and customizing those applications bear heavily on your success or failure.

For example, you might have a vast number of servers devoted to legacy applications and third-party software. How you integrate all of that will affect your implementation. The number of sites that need the suite you've chosen, the communications media, the mobility of your workforce, all can affect what you are implementing. If your lead administrator gets the flu or one of your senior decision makers goes on vacation—that can bother your implementation. A poor strategic decision before the project piece even begins...you get the message.

We'll see a lot more of how to implement in Chapter 20, but once the implementation is underway, there is no looking back.

End-User Training or Learning Management Systems?

User adoption is an historic weakness of CRM. "I see the system. I understand its value to the company, but I see it as a disadvantage to me. It's also hard to use. Why should I?" Part of the reason for this lack of understanding is the approaches toward end-user training that have been the norm for CRM implementations.

"End-user training is the single biggest (CRM) implementation challenge," according to a 2002 report from Sage Research. "Customers want training resources to be Web-based, simple to read, and customized for different roles within the company." Interestingly, that is rarely the way that end-user training is implemented. It tends to be a knowledge dump at the end of a project: "Here's the system. Here's how it works. Go use it." Even so, most companies aren't spending enough on it, nor do they have a perspective that is iterative. Here are some of the costs factors that are part of the price of end-user training:

- ▶ **Number of CRM "modules" implemented** This is self-explanatory.

- ▶ **Breadth of CRM system** This means the number of processes, communications channels, and such that are supported.

- ▶ **Level of customer service offered by the company** For example, 24/7 or personalized service or multiple service level agreements can bump up costs because the scope is that much bigger and more complex.

▶ **The maturity level of the company implementing the CRM system** The more complicated the system, the more complicated the processes, the more complicated the training.

▶ **The level of importance placed on deployment of training** What kind of budget are you willing to shell out and what kind of time are you willing to allow your employees?

▶ **The strategy taken for deployment** Train the trainer, go to the vendor; e-learning, blended learning, or what?

The most important segment is the last one: the learning strategy. The right learning strategy can be a major factor in the successful adoption of your CRM program. If you just drop it on the heads of your users, they will just drop into the commode. Chapter 21 will concentrate on the appropriate programs and strategies, taking it far beyond end-user training and much more deeply into learning management systems that are appropriate to ongoing transformation, rather than just application knowledge.

Right-Brained Elements of CRM

Human beings are defined by their cultures and help define those cultures. The interactions between people and the end results are the key indicator of how successful a culture can be. On the grandest scale, the often quoted proof of the quality of human culture as a whole is the continuously expanding population and the escalation of the means to support those cultures at an increasing rate. On the much smaller scale, it is the change in business culture that can determine the success or failure of a CRM program.

If you are dealing with CRM from a strongly left-brained perspective, this is not something that you think you have to consider. But think again. Individual human thought, business culture, and human performance–dependent operational excellence are all part of CRM The Program. The success of CRM The Program is marked by the satisfaction derived by the 21st century customer—whether they are paying clients, employees, partners, or vendor/suppliers that you exchange value with (see Chapter 1). The success is measurable by those benchmarks and key performance indicators that you've established as indicative of that customer's happiness.

The aspects of CRM that impact the participants' business culture and thinking are not only significant but completely integral to understanding what CRM is. But be clear, we are talking about transforming business culture and not something that will save the world. It is well defined, not at all amorphous, and it is focused on specific business strategies and objectives.

CRM and Attitude

I have a dilemma. CRM is more than just an amalgam of linearity, algorithms, and statistics. Mix cultural transformation, customer behaviors, and dynamic real-time interactions with those statistics, add self-interested adoption, and you get the beginnings of the holism that CRM demands in its fullest definition. But definition (by definition) is "a putting or being in clear, sharp outline" (Webster's Dictionary). Rather than continuing to provide improved sharpened delimitations, a number of user forums and consultant discussions are throwing out the strange opinion that CRM is a shapeless nothing, a mere shift of attitude. Wrong. That is a pendulum-swing response to the idea of CRM as purely a technology and a system.

CRM is a *business* initiative, not a feeling. Happiness is a feeling. Satisfaction is a feeling. But customer satisfaction is a necessary condition to be created and maintained. It fosters a planned business benefit. While not entirely mercenary, it isn't charitable either.

Those of us who don't dwell on the Dark Side like making people feel good and would love to foster that in our personal lives and business lives—but for different reasons. In our personal lives, it is because we love our families and friends and helping them be happy is something that is essential for loving humans. For a business, the connection is not intimate, despite all the marketing jargon about customer intimacy and customer loyalty. Unless there are personal relationships involved, CRM's purpose is to benefit the business and the customer jointly for a classic win-win. Being sensitive to your customer's desires, agendas, and behavior is one thing—it is just the right thing to do. It is a good human trait. *But it is not CRM.* While knowledge of and actions on subjective factors, such as changes in human behavior and new interactions between individuals and groups, are part of CRM, making it into an amorphous attitude eliminates the clarity and the science that CRM provides in determining the best courses of action with varying customer groups. Developing definition, fine-tuning its philosophy, science, and art to make it effective, is the task at hand.

Human Performance Support

All that said, we are human beings first. As humans, we have individual interests, unique behaviors, personal agendas, hopes, desires, and dreams. The success of CRM is dependent on these very human attributes. If, as customers, we are happy with our suppliers, then we will continue to do business with them. If we are not happy with those we are exchanging value with, we might stop, continue until something better comes along, or continue to do business with a very high state of volatility.

If a whole-brained approach to CRM is taken, how to motivate and support the self-interest of individuals involved in the use of the system, internally or externally, is a major part of the plan. One of the reasons that CRM is often thought of as a marketing initiative is that it is a mission-critical component for influencing customer behavior. The transformation of customer behavior and the support of the new behaviors are the determining features of the whole-brained approach to user adoption and customer satisfaction. But to get there we are dealing with a complexity that goes far beyond what ERP provided and that most "systems" have provided. It is not merely technology, nor is it merely a system. It is a universal cultural renovation that needs to satisfy the individual user. It is both broad, sweeping terms and hard-core practical reality.

User Adoption and Self-Interest

CRM, if thought of properly, is the satisfaction of self-interest. As we will see in Chapter 9, personalization, which enhances the possibility of that self-interested contentment, is a vital part of any CRM success. If CRM benefits you, the tendency is to say, "Okay, I see its value; I'll use the system or engage with it in some way."

Think of this scenario, one that has been replicated in real life countless times. You are an employee attending a meeting with many other employees on the benefits of your new CRM system. Senior management is all represented. The system has been rolled out with few technical issues remaining; the users have been named and you're one of them. At the meeting, senior management tells you how CRM will impact their bottom and top line revenue, how it will increase productivity and profitability, and blah blah blah until you fade out. What is your likely response? Is it "GREAT! I can't wait to see the business results!" Or is it "Who cares?" Likely the latter. There is no indication of the benefit to you, so you see no reason to change your behavior.

Depending on the approach that your company takes to its CRM execution, you could be allowed to continue the way you have historically worked and thus throw glue into the CRM initiative. You could be fired, not a pleasant outcome for you, but it would allow the CRM initiative to breathe at the typically increased cost of finding someone to take your place. Or the company could try to reach you by making CRM useful to you directly.

The lack of attention to individual users is a major reason for failure of CRM. In 2002, AMR Research found that only 11 percent of the respondents in one of their surveys implemented CRM to improve performance and efficiency of individual end-users, and most of those were referring to customers. The most common user-related inhibitors AMR found were:

- End-users could perform their job and still meet their goals without using the system.

- End-users feel that providing knowledge into the system makes them less valuable and more easily replaced.

- Companies experience problems when they push business process changes with the software without first getting user buy-in.

Those fears reflect two significant areas of concern. One is the need to create a CRM initiative that doesn't simply map to the business objectives, but also fulfills the needs of the individual users. Unfortunately, it is impossible to provide a system that would appeal to every user, so the operant principle should be a "community of self-interest." That is a system that appeals to as many users as possible without distorting the business requirements. Be prepared to lose people in the attempt.

With the attempt to create this community of self-interest comes a simultaneous effort to transform the business environment to support and sustain that difficult transformation.

Culture Change

If you are considering a CRM initiative, you recognize that things have to change at your company. Thus, you know that the processes you use to do business have to change—perhaps adding some, eliminating some, and altering others. You know if you are changing the processes, then the way that individuals do business at the company has to change. If the way that the individuals do business has to change, the way that those individuals think about business has to change. If the way they think has to change, the environment to support that change has to be created by senior management. Thus, to create the environment, the way that senior management thinks about doing business has to change.

This is not just culture change. This is culture *shock*.

There is no CRM program that is not impacted in every department and every way. Keep in mind, too, this change is ongoing.

Think this is important? Well, most companies are unwilling to spend the necessary currency to make sure that change management initiatives are set and ready to go. Nor are they willing to develop the programs that support the changes in the company's atmosphere, such as compensating all employees for customer satisfaction. We will examine this in depth along with the best practices for change in Chapter 19.

Hopefully, with all these chapter references, I'm whetting your appetite. If not, think some more about Ashley Judd and Tom Cruise.

CRM: The Total Package

We are now at the defining moment. CRM is what? We've looked at its strategic elements from both sides of the brain, so to speak. The acronyms and terms scream at us—TCO, ROI, benchmarks, metrics, vendor selection, cultural transformation, process-driven, training, user acceptance, individual self-interest, continuous improvement of the customer experience, program not project, and many more. What do we come out with as an appropriate global definition of CRM that we can use throughout the life of our program? Here it is, without fanfare:

"CRM is a philosophy and a business strategy, supported by a system and a technology, designed to improve human interactions in a business environment."

In other words, CRM is a grand strategic business initiative that maps the transformation of business processes to the transformation of a business culture to satisfy the community of customer self-interest. That means it has a definable mission, vision, objectives, and performance criteria that if successful will get an expected result due to the improvement of the individual customer's experience. (That's customer as defined in Chapter 1.)

With that, we are going to start moving into detail. The reason that this is a brand new book is that CRM is now a brand new ball game. It is process-driven, not data-driven any longer, and we are going to see what that means.

3

Data-Driven CRM vs. Process-Driven CRM

Many of you may know that the opening line in Franz Kafka's *noir* humorous work *The Metamorphosis* is about Gregor Samsa waking up one morning and finding he had been transformed into a giant cockroach. While by no means am I equating the CRM vendors here, they had a similar miraculous, though not quite as funny, transformation in 2002. They woke up one morning and found themselves process-driven. In late 2002, Siebel and PeopleSoft in particular announced that their versions 7.5 and 8.8, respectively, were going to be released around a process-driven engine that would change the way the world looked at CRM. With the release of the now ancient 3.1 and the contemporary 4.0 MySAP CRM versions, SAP decided to emphasize their industry-specific process mapping expertise. Oracle, who had been organized to a certain extent around a process-driven conception from their Applications Suite release 11i, simply crowed that they had already established "accelerated business flows," Oracle's name for business processes. Other companies, such as Chordiant, said, "Told you so," and continued on what for them had been a well-traveled path.

But what's the difference between this process-driven version of CRM and its historic antecedent, the dear departed data-driven CRM? After all, data-driven CRM had served the CRM world (and the first two editions of this book) rather well. CRM customers wanted applications that were built around viewing and using data such as accounts, addresses, fulfillment requests, customer transaction histories, and the like. It had been the reason that the Holy Grail of CRM was described as the 360-degree view of the single customer. This is the premise that CRM customer data can be consolidated into a single, easily available customer record. It has been one of CRM's proudest achievements. The problem is that this Grail was found by Monty

Python, not King Arthur. By the time a 360-degree view was a recurring event, a new form of CRM application was needed because of the requirements to develop business applications that would work as businesses do. In other words, the applications would focus on the processes and rules that people use to make decisions about how they engage in commerce daily. This would be something closer to reality. What kind of business workflow do we need to make sure that customer problems are resolved? What regulations do we have to comply with? What do we do to sell a new product to a customer and how do we handle their order? There are infinite possibilities, because each business has its own combinations of unique rules and disparate processes, but the applications have to not just reflect them, but support their improvement as well.

Data-Driven CRM

If you have a data warehouse—a centralized place where your customer data is stored—you probably have the means through a tabular structure to query the data and call up reports (more on this in Chapter 14). Essentially, a data warehouse is a place to gather, store, and, when needed, extract data and then analyze it in some useful form. The value of the more recent data-driven CRM applications is that the data is collected and stored in a single database instance that is available to all users who need to see it. That means that theoretically (and technically) a single view of the customer information is available to what is typically the sales, marketing, and support personnel. This also means that it provides information to the user about a customer that allows that user to "know" that customer and plan a course of action based on this personal information. However, this is a passive result, allowing only the slicing and dicing of information based on transactions and interactions with customers. But it has its benefits:

▶ Uniform, up-to-date customer data is accessible regardless of user "location" (for example, geographic or departmental).

▶ Centralized data stores mean decent data quality after redundancies and errors are eliminated. Missing data is identified and rectified, data conflicts are resolved, and so on.

- ▶ Consistent customer experiences are possible, regardless of communications medium, so that customers have a single view of how they receive the company message.

- ▶ Analytic tools can be usefully applied to the data to help in the decision-making process.

What this can do in practical terms is provide sales management data, such as pipeline data, to the sales managers in any form they want to see it, or provide forecasts using CRM sales tools that allow managers to identify their potential successes more accurately. Implementing sales force automation (SFA) under a data-driven model is great for sales management (see Chapter 4 for more on SFA).

But this result was a 20th-century CRM outcome—use of lots of technology and a little process to automate business actions. It worked, but only to an extent. For example, by designing SFA to appeal to sales management, the majority users of SFA—salespeople—were almost ignored. To get salespeople to use SFA, it needed to appeal to the actual salesperson, which it didn't. It also needed to address the cultural issues, which it didn't. The processes that the salesperson used to sell were not part of these versions of SFA. It ran up against the limitation of data-driven models quite often, which was salespeople were asked to input data available to sales management, but saw no useful result for themselves.

Ultimately, the purpose of CRM is to create or retain customers. Data-driven CRM ran up against its limits by creating a customer profile that provided passive information that was useful, but didn't take into account the dynamic or real-time activity of the customer. Instead, it simply provided information to be analyzed, which was a useful but limited result.

That all changed in 2002. Twenty-first century CRM arrived.

Process: An Overview

When the term *CRM business process* is used, we are typically talking about a set of possible interactions that lead to a result from a customer. This is governed by business rules that are set by the company. These rules are based on anything ranging from regulatory necessity to available communications media to comfort zones. Thomas H. Davenport, in his book, *Process Innovation* (HBS, 1993), defines a process as a "structured measured set of activities designed to produce a specified outcome for a particular customer or market." He classifies business processes as "set(s) of logically related tasks performed to achieve a defined business outcome."

A CRM business process, as with any business process, has two critical factors:

- ▶ It must have either internal or external customers or both, as defined in Chapter 1.

- ▶ It must be cross-organizational, which is to say, it must have a workflow that occurs between units.

Those units could be individuals who have different functions within an institution, so don't be fooled by the quasiformal jargon. It simply means a set of interactions involving customers with an outcome. Of course, CRM's value is that the outcome is, as we say in the business process management (BPM) world, "good."

Best Practices

There is a difference between a best practice and a business process, though we'd like to think that all our processes are best practices. Best practices are proven methodologies for executing a business process effectively. Of course, one company's best practice is another company's worst nightmare. That said, there are some practices and procedures that have stood the test of time. Where they tend to be the best known is in the world of sales, where best practices and panaceas are often mixed. Salespeople are notorious for looking for the apocryphal magic bullet. Thus, there are hundreds of selling "methods" out there, most of which are just twists on one another. In reality, best practices have proven results that can be typically universalized but are not always appropriate. They can apply to any business process whatever. For example, typical CRM marketing tools feature customized offers to individuals during an inbound interaction online. They are available in what might be a "call to order" process. Think Amazon.com here. The system matches the individual's customer data and history to the person who is making the inbound call. However, a best practice would be "real-time offer optimization," which can develop or even change customized individual offers in real time based on the customer's online responses and apparent interests. In other words, this would affect not just the static customer record, but the dynamic customer behaviors as well. It can also set the offer based on inventory levels for specific items that fall within the purview of the customer's apparent interests. This is an example of a best practice that improves the customer's likelihood of making a purchase online.

CRM Business Processes: The Macro

At the thousand-foot level, CRM business processes are characterized by customer-facing activity. They include fairly far-ranging activities and outcomes. I'll throw a few examples at you so you can get a feel for what they are.

Some examples of sales processes are:

▶ **Call to order** From the first call into the sales center (or cold call to the potential customer) to the point where an order is placed by the customer

▶ **Opportunity routing** The rules that define who owns a specific opportunity (these could include geography, seniority, territory assignment, prior success rates, specific industry, size of deal, and so on)

Examples of support processes include:

▶ **Request to resolution** From the time a customer puts in a request for service to a customer service representative (CSR) to the time that the ticket opened by that request is closed due to some resolution—in other words, a final interaction with that customer on that request

▶ **Install to maintain** The steps that take place from the time a product is installed to the time that it has to start being maintained

Some examples of marketing processes are:

▶ **Marketing plan development** A combination of processes, best practices, and workflow rules that are involved in designing a specific marketing plan. For instance, it could mean the involvement of Department X and Y but not Z under one instance, but Z and X under another.

▶ **Campaign response to lead capture** The procedure used by the company to identify a marketing campaign response as a potential lead and once that is done, to capture and route that lead appropriately.

CRM Business Processes: The Micro

What do one of these processes look like? That's a little hard to say because each company has (or doesn't have) its own specific set of best practices and existing comfortable processes that apply to their corporate culture, their current needs, and their business rules (see Chapter 19 for more on best practices). However, with those caveats, here is a typical example of a CRM-related business process—call to order:

I. Cold call to potential customer

    A. Not interested

    B. Interested

        1. Literature requested

            a. Printed material

            b. E-mailed PDF files

II. Follow-up call made

III. Sales call made

    A. Not interested

    B. Interested

        1. Order entered

IV. Order received

    A. Information sent to Accounting

        1. Invoice issued

        2. Invoice sent to Shipping for inclusion in package

        3. Copy to sales rep

    B. Production receives request

        1. Quality check product

    C. Product sent to Shipping

        1. Shipping boxes product

V. Shipping sends product

    A. Sales rep notified by Shipping

Note the multitiered nature of the process and the fairly complex number of actions that take place. Each of these is associated with a workflow, such as Sales to Accounting and Production, or Accounting and Production to Shipping. Normally, this process would be represented graphically using schematics that are set by Unified Modeling Language (UML) standard.

Process-Driven CRM

Interestingly enough, data-driven CRM and process-driven CRM come at each other with diametrically opposed approaches. The more passive data-driven version doesn't have processes natively implanted. What this means is that each business process has to be customized to utilize the data that the end user needs and, at the same time, fit the company paradigm. That is a huge undertaking. Doing it is something akin to the way the pyramids were created.

On the other hand, process-driven CRM, built around existing processes practices and rules, uses data sources to enrich the processes. Customization is possible to tweak the rules and practices so that they correspond to the practices of the company that is implementing it. Additionally, lighter-weight configuration of the processes through tools that come with the applications provides a lower-cost alternative to customization. In other words, process-driven CRM dynamically mirrors the way that business is actually done, when executed correctly.

There are a significant number of advantages to this newer CRM model. First, it is contextual. When a customer interacts with a business, the applications will respond to the customer's interactions and the customer record in a real-time setting, using those business processes and best practices that are appropriate to the customer's history and activity at the time. It can use existing data sources or a new one, but doesn't synchronize data from multiple sources. Instead, it coordinates real-time customer activity with existing historical data across whatever interaction points are engaged.

Second, it is multidimensional—data-driven CRM is usually channel specific. In other words, information is consolidated into a single place, but that place is an application that serves that specific channel. So an e-mail from customer X is entered into an e-mail database and perhaps attached to a customer record. However, in a process-driven architecture, e-mail is one medium in a multichannel environment that maps to the processes and policies. So, in a process-driven environment, that e-mail from customer X is applied against processes and policies in real time, and each interaction generates a process both stored and responded to based on the policies established and workflow involved. This makes for a true dynamic single view of the customer record, not just a synchronized result of updated information.

Finally, it is real time. The customer profiles are continuously updated with data from multiple channels and multiple sources in real time, and the response to that customer can be in real time.

Industry-Specific Undertones: A Hint of Petrochemical

Process-driven CRM didn't emerge from a vacuum nor was it immaculately conceived. The transformation of the ecosystem in combination with the saturation of the enterprise marketplace with CRM initiatives dictated necessity. Companies wanted to have their specific business procedures, practices, and rules as part of their CRM initiatives. Each vertical industry—such as life sciences, energy, financial services, consumer goods, communications, and the like—had unique business practices applicable only to their industry. For example, it is highly unlikely that anyone in the life services industry cared about how to sell crude oil to refineries, but there are well-established specific practices for doing so in the petrochemical industry. These had to be captured and represented by the CRM applications that aimed at the industry. For example, SAP has spent countless dollars developing industry maps that are specifically geared to each industry they've targeted as a viable market (see Chapter 10).

The Vendors, Vendors, Vendors

The largest enterprise vendors have been the most enthusiastic, though not the first, proponents of process-driven CRM. In 2002, ahead of even the analysts and integrators, for the most part, they recognized that CRM had become a mainstream product. At the cost of millions in research, they "intuitively" grasped the transformation of the business ecology from a corporate ecosystem to a customer ecosystem. To the vendors, this meant that CRM had become a tool for business transformation, not just customer satisfaction. The way they architected their applications and marketed them had to change dramatically and quickly. Some of these vendors were more foresighted than others. Some came late to the game. All of the major players have either given this process focus lip service or have actually changed the nature of their business suites. With this process-driven direction, CRM became part of conventional business strategy, not cutting edge. From the release of these suites in 2003, interest had only grown, even though spending was down.

We'll take a very brief look at the major vendors' approach to process-driven CRM here. I also want to introduce the "Steppin' Out" segment. From chapter to chapter, I'll provide an expanded look at a single company (on occasion, two) that represents the subject of the chapter really well. Chordiant will be the first because:

▶ Chordiant has, in my estimation, the most sophisticated and elegant execution of process-driven CRM.

▶ Chordiant represents an excellent real-life example of how process-driven CRM can work effectively. Real-life examples make all of this a lot easier to understand.

▶ Chordiant's architecture is representative of architecture designed for process-driven CRM and is something useful to understand.

The Steppin' Out section is not aimed at getting you to use the vendors mentioned. Each potential CRM customer has to choose its vendors based on individual needs. However, you will never suffer by considering any of the vendors mentioned either. Well, okay. On occasion, you might suffer, but I swear I had nothing to do with it. In any case, these companies represent best of class in their particular Steppin' Out category.

Oracle: Going with the Flows

This is one place where Oracle excels. They had the foresight to "processize" parts of their EBusiness Suite well in advance of most of the major CRM vendors, as far back as the ancient days of 2000. They call their embedded processes "business flow accelerators," primarily because they provide prebuilt processes that can be configured to conform to the business practices of any company. They are a well established presence in this domain with such processes as:

▶ Call to Order; Click to Order; Configure Quote to Order (Sales)

▶ Call to Resolution; Click to Resolution (Service)

Note their business process style. They are often built around communications channels (call and click are the ones I've given you here). While these are certainly not the only processes made available, Oracle has one of the strongest multichannel focuses of any vendor.

Siebel: Best Practices

Siebel's approach to process-driven CRM is almost to be expected. They have embedded hundreds of best practices into their applications. Siebel focuses on two types of best practices:

- ▶ **Horizontal** These impact sales, marketing, services, call centers, partner relationship management, their branded "employee relationship management," and customer order management.

- ▶ **Vertical** These impact specific industries, notably automotive, communications and media, consumer goods, finance, high tech, insurance, health care, life sciences, public sector, retail, travel, and utilities.

The verticals demand interesting and sometimes esoteric best practices. For example, in the insurance industry, take a look at this best practice: "Profitability-Driven Policy Renewal Processing." It integrates individual profitability analysis so that segmented customer renewal strategies can be created and proactively executed. Aside from its mouthful of a name, it is actually a valuable method of approaching a policy renewal. As with all best practices, to embrace it wholeheartedly you have to see the value in it. Then you must have the means and ability to integrate it with the new business process schema you are planning on implementing to make your CRM initiative successful. We'll discuss business process management further in Chapter 19.

SAP: The Angel Is in the Details

As we'll see in more detail in Chapter 10, SAP has superior business process maps and perhaps the best understanding of industry-specific processes known to our species—that species being someone at least remotely interested in CRM. SAP's approach is to develop industry process maps that detail the specific, generally identifiable processes that govern a specialized vertical industry. For example, they have very comprehensive industry maps for such business categories as:

- ▶ Consumer products

- ▶ High tech

- ▶ Automotive

- ▶ Insurance

- ▶ Professional services

- ▶ Media and entertainment

- ▶ Public sector

PeopleSoft: Here, There, and Everywhere

PeopleSoft 8.8 embeds processes everywhere in the applications. They are embedded in their Enterprise Integration Points (EIPs), such as Telemarketing to Order Capture. They are part of their Pre-built Connectors, such as Engage to Cash and Install to Maintain. They are part of their sales applications, such as Target to Engage, or support applications, such as Request to Resolve. They are industry specific with multiple industries such as insurance (for example, fraud management). They also provide a means of constraining business process usage through their Advisor feature, which steps the user through collaborative selling processes. The depth of its integration is almost Dr. Seuss–like: "You can use them on a boat; you can put them in your coat…" The processes are deeply integrated throughout PeopleSoft 8.8, more broadly than any other vendor.

STEPPIN' OUT: Chordiant—The Process-Driven Porsche

When businesses changed their perspective and began focusing their CRM desires on a program that cohered with the processes that actually ran the business, most vendors began a mad scramble to comply with this brave new world. Chordiant yawned. They had known this for years. In fact, back in 1985 when they were J. Frank Consulting (a call center systems integrator), the idea of a process-driven architecture was nothing new to them. They were well ahead of the pack. They understood that from data-driven to process-driven, as David Bernstein, Chordiant's CTO, put it, "was the natural next step." Bernstein again: "Data is not the way enterprises think about customers. It may be how they deal with a customer, but not what the customer is."

Consequently, by the time process-driven CRM became a reality in late 2002, Chordiant had actually devised a sophisticated process engine fully integrated into a very flexible architecture for all of its applications. Heck, on their website, they don't even call it CRM anymore—they call what they provide "process-centric solutions."

It must work, because as of late 2003, Chordiant was reporting revenues of $17.1 million for the second quarter of 2003, an increase of 24 percent over first quarter 2003 and an increase of 15 percent over second quarter 2002. Something good must be going on here.

Chordiant applications are obviously process-driven. At the time of any interaction, Chordiant—having constructed a real-time customer profile and applied the appropriate business rules—initiates business processes so that the correct tasks can be automated and managed across the enterprise.

Their overall offering, the revamped Chordiant 5.5, is somewhat different than the normal CRM handout:

- ▶ Enterprise Marketing

- ▶ Enterprise Contact Center

- ▶ Retail Channel

- ▶ Straight Through Service Processing (STSP)

What is germane here is STSP.

STSP is Chordiant's core work management system. It handles the automation of all service and operational processes in the retail channel, contact center, self-service channel, and back-office operation. It can create and deploy process-driven business applications that automate the end-to-end process from systems that range from back office (such as financial) to communications channels with customers (such as e-mail). In other words, an extremely flexible framework that can be tailored to any enterprise system regardless of existing or future business processes or infrastructure.

STSP works in real time. It automates and manages work that begins when the customer contacts the business. STSP orchestrates the entire ensemble of processing steps and policy requirements across different systems and business units, until the inquiry or transaction has been completed. This means touching a significant number of different data sources, applications, processes, and communications channels. Each process is different in length of execution time from seconds to days. Scheduled events and process tasks can be called or executed at any time during the performance of the process. If timed tasks are used and not completed, for example, escalation, using rules and workflow, can move the process to another level internally or notify an external user for action.

The other STSP attribute is the ability to do all this changing and moving in real time. By developing reusable components (see the following section on architecture) and having an intuitive process designer as seen in Figure 3-1, the changes in processes and procedures or in groups affected by processes and procedures is in the hands of the business person, not the IT department. Using these objects, a universal change is quite easy to implement via the Web interface.

Imagine Leonard Bernstein in his heyday conducting not only the New York Philharmonic, but the Chicago Symphony Orchestra too. Simultaneously, he is conducting a different composer's symphony for each orchestra, each of varying length, tempo, and mood. The maestro's job here is to make them work harmoniously somehow. Multiply that scenario to the nth degree and you get an idea of STSP's remarkable capability to keep that harmony.

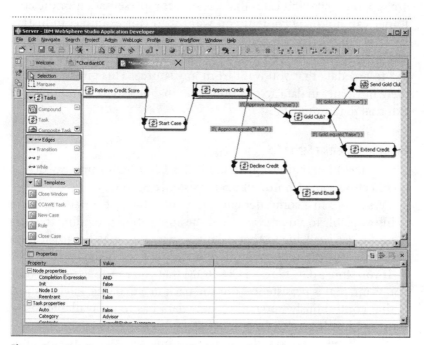

Figure 3-1: Chordiant Process Designer 5.5 is almost intuitive (printed by permission of Chordiant Software, 2003).

I consider Chordiant one of the more significant midsized players, one who can compete in the Global 1000 market, especially within their industry specialties: telecommunications, retail financial services, and consumer direct industries. Though considerably smaller in size, they battle most frequently with companies like Siebel and have alliances with the major integrators, such as IBM.

Chordiant Enterprise Architecture

What makes Chordiant's architecture unique is the full integration of process and policies into the platform itself. Unlike the data-driven architectures, Chordiant JX architecture based on XML and J2EE, rather than using a customer record per se, uses an object representation of an individual customer that operates like a store, able to accept new policies and processes based on the current, real time interaction. It then uses transactional semantics to link this object store to data. What this all means in plain English is that the content of the message to be sent and the information needed to send the message are separate. That indicates that the object representation of the customer can hold any content you want it to (for example, industry-specific rules or processes). That also means that the transaction semantics can be used to hook up the UML-compliant object wrapper to any data that you want from any source. This gives you complete flexibility in data acquisition from in-house data warehouses or external data suppliers.

Chordiant Persistence Server 5.5

The other thing that uniquely identifies Chordiant's process-driven architecture is the Chordiant 5.5 Persistence Server.

Persistence in a computer environment is the state of current data being available to a user even when the application providing the data is no longer available to that user. Connectivity may be down for a short while or the application used is simply done being used.

If you store a data file on a CD-ROM that you can access at any time you want, that is persistence. But the trick in a dynamic environment is that continuously updated or new data has to be available in the same fashion. If you think about what it takes to get that data, you realize the difficulty and complexity of providing persistence in a dynamic environment—and the value of it.

For example, you're on the road as one of 80 salespeople, six of whom are part of your sales team. You need the ability to see your account, sales, or pipeline data, the team's data, and competitive information at any time using your browser, regardless of whether the other salespeople or team members are online or are synchronizing, replicating, or entering data. The information has to be available to you, whatever channel you are using and whenever you need to access it, whether it resides in Chordiant Enterprise Marketing or PeopleSoft Sales. While this may seem a palpably needed feature to anyone reading this book, it isn't so easily accomplished.

The ability to do this with both newly updated data and no data loss even with breaks in connectivity is the value that the Chordiant Persistence Server provides. One of the reasons I actually chose these guys for Steppin' Out is that they have linked persistence to both processes and rich data environments with diverse architectures, something that other vendors like to claim but don't do nearly as well.

CHORDIANT SOLUTIONS: A BRIEF PROCESS VIEW

Given their financial services pedigree, their solutions integrate directly with existing infrastructure and core transactional systems such as savings accounts, checking accounts, mortgages, loans, customer information files (CIFs), statement files, investment services, credit history, credit scoring systems, and about anything that a retail bank can do.

One example that Chordiant uses: in many leading banks it can require "up to 25 separate screens" to change a customer address across all of that customer's accounts, though I don't personally know of any banks that are this clumsy. Chordiant's solution can reduce this process to a three-screen task and do it through self-service, making it rather easy.

In Conclusion...

By now, the definition of CRM at the height of rarified air should be apparent. If not, please go back and reread what has been written so far. We've established the universal definition of CRM, which now gives you an idea of what you're in for. But it's so, so much more. Read on.

PART II
The Modules

4

Sales Force Automation: Power to the (Sales) People

Salespeople *hate* CRM. If you are a salesperson and you love CRM, be prepared. You are CRM's unicorn—a mythical beast, ripe for capture and exhibition at the salesperson zoo. Don't worry; it's a natural habitat. You can live outside and pursue your client prey.

The sales staff intense dislike of CRM has been something of a conundrum for sales management. User adoption rates for sales force automation (SFA) are often terrible. CRM is more often the victim of sales virulence than just passive disgust. Yet, sales folks love contact management programs such as ACT! They wouldn't (and don't) leave home without it.

Contact Management vs. SFA

So why do salespeople love ACT! or Goldmine (well, actually, no one really loves Goldmine—contact management steroids can do damage to your system)? It is an issue of control. Salespeople often see their personal value as the account and contact data they "own." Having been a business development creature, I can speak from experience. The mindset is, "Just leave me alone and let me do what I do, and I'll sell. Don't bother me. Just look for the results when I have them." This bravado is often really just irritation and vulnerability. The vulnerability comes because of the intense pressure on salespeople to be accountable to their bosses. Salespeople hate CRM because CRM makes them transparent to accountability. Who wants to be accountable to someone else? Your life should feel like your own, shouldn't it? Why should the pressures of management sit on your salesy head? Well, my friends, they do.

Why do salespeople feel so uncertain, even though their function is perhaps the company's most important?

This is due to multiple factors, both social and psychological, and far deeper than this book will attempt to go. But let's delve into a few that are important to the rates of adoption of CRM/SFA.

Salespeople love to hunt. They are always circling their prospect, looking for the closing. But they hunt like cats, singularly, not in packs. They mark territories and are fiercely protective of their territory and the assets within that territory. Rather than mark it with the glands at the sides of their heads, they mark it with the possession of their network in a data file on their desktop. I reiterate, *their* database on *their* desktop. Regardless of who actually paid for that desktop.

The fierce protection of that database is also recognition that the database is not just data input. It is the flat file representation of the important relationships that they built up over their sales lives. Note, I said relationships. That isn't unimportant in how to think about the user adoption issues that salespeople have. They understand relationships, because it is inherent in their job that they do. But sales folks are limited in their ability to pursue and maintain those relationships because of the pressure to "make the numbers now" rather than establish a longer-term relationship. That's trouble with a capital T. Knowing that evolving relationships over time is the key to sales and that immediate healthy financial numbers are the key to management angst creates a nearly impossible to resolve conflict.

Management Eye on the Sales Guy

Yet conflict or not, management is management and the salespeople are self-described "peons" (though they really aren't). They often are left little leeway to do what they think is best, because of those quarterly pressures that management feels. Yet there is some validity to the revenue pressures. No sales means no company. No company means no jobs. So even though salespeople are subject to the vagaries of time and place like anyone else—meaning a bad economy affects them too—unfortunately, they are still given very little room for failure. New salespeople are often expected to learn the specifics of a company and begin to show some results in three months, which is a nanosecond in business development time. Newness isn't even a good reason for lack of sales. Regardless of circumstance, sales staff is among the few groups

of employees that have to achieve no matter what. Thus they have perhaps the most volatile, tenuous positions in any company. That's why
the turnover rates among salespeople are usually the highest at a particular enterprise. A study done in 2001 by Hewitt Associates shows
that the average turnover rate of participating sales organizations was
18 percent, considerably higher than the rest of the workforce, which
hovered around 8 percent. As the economy deteriorated so did the sales
positions. It's even worse in the hospitality industry where the average
sales turnover is 24.7 percent as of 2002. That's 165 percent worse than
the rest of the sales force. Yikes.

What causes this galactic turnover rate? Why are salespeople leaving at an alarming rate for any industry? By contrast, the employee
turnover for outstanding employer SAS from Cary, North Carolina
(see Chapter 9) is around 3 percent between 1998 and 2003.

It's not that hard to see. Aside from the dismissals for those non-
performers, salespeople have always known they are the most vulnerable to firing. They are in a damned if you do, damned if you don't
situation. If they win a significant contract, they are expected to always
win significant contracts and frequently. If they don't they are blasted
for not winning it. As a result, they are the least committed to the company—and rightfully so. They live a high risk for medium reward life.

Sales folks also know that companies that are struggling for profitability or revenue often impose ridiculous quotas per salesperson—
while justified as "what they need," they tend to be entirely unreasonable.
But no salesperson will ever object to it. Corporate politics dictate that
you accept it or you are "less than desirable." Firing might well follow.
I worked at a company where one of the CxOs rightfully refused to
accept responsibility for an annual dollar figure that was way out of line
for any realistic expectation. Someone else stood up and said that he
would accept the responsibility, was promoted to vice president and the
CxO was let go several months later. Needless to say, this revenue number was never even close to achieved, screwing up the company for more
than a year before it could get back on track. When salespeople see what
happens to a senior manager who stands up, what chance do they think
they have to object to something patently silly?

This chest-thumping approach is often supported by compensation plans designed to get the deal closed now, rather than to
develop a long-term approach to a relationship with the customer,
which would mean that services promised would have to be services

delivered, with the originator of the promise held accountable for delivery of those services. For example, in the retail world, often the salesperson is compensated for the sale so that commissions are earned upon payment. Delivery to the customer becomes considerably less important because payout on commission had been earned prior to delivery. This type of practice damages how the salesperson deals with the customer—making them willing to do what has to be done to close the deal, not satisfy the customer. There is a particularly virulent strain of this deal-closing mentality in the world of software vendors, which of course affects you if you're reading this book with an eye to a CRM initiative.

What does all this mean? The level of pressure on the sales force member is 20 Gs–heavy. They have to perform. When they perform successfully, they have to be even better the next sale. They are responsible for the revenue of a company. They only are rewarded reasonably well. Yet they love the hunt, even in an uncertain position in uncertain times. What does this do to the thinking of a salesperson day to day?

It means that salespeople are always preparing for their next jobs. Their "selling point" in an increasingly scarce job market is their personal network of possible clients. If it is 20 years of client associations in an ACT! file, it becomes valuable intellectual property. Having that network (the file) protected from the prying eyes of sales management is almost a moral imperative if they are to defend their jobs and their future elsewhere if they fail along the way. Often nonsolicitation and noncompete agreements are put into place as a condition of employment, such as, "You can't work for any competitor nor can you solicit a client for business if you aren't at this company, nor can you take the file, which is company property." Even with possible court action as a threat, there are many salespeople who risk that and take a copy of that file with them in some form. While this is certainly an area for plausible denial, it's a real truth. It's their relationships, whether it takes the form of a database or a little black book. Ultimately, it is something that the individual salesperson built up over time and can offer to a future employer.

Sales folks have a no quarter given or gotten relationship with their company—friendly or not, small or large. While this may sound hyperbolic, think about the turnover rates and, if you are in sales or know business development professionals, you'll realize that it isn't exaggerated at all.

Contact Management: The Good, the Bad— and the Not-at-All Ugly

That said, contact management suits this salesperson just fine, thank you, for many reasons:

- **They are aimed at the single salesperson.** If the company has no need to worry about whether they have visibility into the salesperson's data, this is nearly an ideal solution.

- **It handles contact records with individual flat file contact databases.** Flat file databases have the advantage of being no muss, no fuss when they are relatively small. There are few individual salespeople who would need a database that would individually handle terabytes of contact records.

- **Basic reporting tools are available.** Most contact management packages have basic reports available in a few formats, including reports such as a contact directory, task list, contact status, sales by contact, and a look at the sales pipeline either in list form or graphically. But note the simplicity of these reports.

- **Web versions don't need to be synchronized.** Often, if there is a web version of the contact manager, up-to-date looks at the contact data are available with a browser, no synchronization necessary. However, there are often issues when trying to see more than a single salesperson's database.

- **Personalized interfaces, personalized contact letters, and so on are easy.** There is little customized code necessary to make the desktop reasonably comfortable for the individual user. It is also easy to develop personalized letters to clients or client groups. No real IT background necessary.

Contact management is adequate for small businesses that are relatively undeveloped—it can do the basic sales lead and opportunity management functions. That means mail merge for larger mailings or targeted mailings; templated stationary and scripted e-mails or direct mails; calendar and task management for the individual; basic sorting, filtering, and reporting.

But it is not CRM:

- **It is software, not a strategy.** If you remember the lessons of Chapters 1 and 2, CRM is not just an application. It is a strategy and a philosophy. The software supports the strategy by automating actions that improve the human interactions. Contact management is nothing more than software that is there to help accumulate, store, and sort contact data.

▶ **It is primarily data driven, not process driven.** Look at ACT! and tell me what the sales processes of the company that is using ACT! are. I'll bet you can't. You can't because the focus of contact management is data. The processes that drive a company are not associated with the applications in any way, unlike CRM/SFA which is aimed strongly at utilizing embedded best practices to help salespeople do their jobs either better or at least the way the company wants them to.

▶ **The integration capability is weak to nonexistent.** For example, contact management systems are not designed to do billing, nor are they created to handle inventory or generate pricing. They do not integrate (speak) to the back-office financial systems without custom APIs or often expensive middleware, if at all. The same information is often entered and re-entered and entered again from one system to the next, creating duplicate records for the same contact, with the possibility of error greater with each entry. I know of nonprofits that use contact management software for their contact database, but have several of them ranging from volunteers to donors to grant providers to, well, you get the idea. There is little relationship between the contact management applications data and the customer support data, leading to a dangerous disconnect. For example, if one of your customers calls your support guy irate due to a major problem that the customer has with you, you don't want to have your salesperson inadvertently call on that customer at that moment. You might be one salesperson less, though with a really good ACT! database left behind! Are you able to determine the lifetime value of a customer using existing customer records and current customer behavior? Do you have the means to see anyone's pipeline but your own? Can you generate a proposal using data and best practices from a number of sources in the back office? Of course not!

▶ **It is not scaleable.** ACT! can generate around 50,000 contact records before it decides to leave its orbit. While this may seem to be a lot, just think of this. A MasterCard-providing bank owns millions of customer records totaling terabytes of data.

▶ **It is not very customizable.** Most of the contact managers are configurable, but don't have the authoring tools that more robust sales applications might have. They have software development kits (SDKs), but they are pretty basic. There is no real authoring tool at the code level to customize the application to levels often needed by larger enterprises (such as the workflow). These kinds of tools are what PeopleSoft provides with PeopleTools, for example.

▶ **The results are not real time but need to be generated each time.** Each time you need to see how you are doing, you have to generate a new report. There are no dashboards or no real time numbers that you can see the second you log on. There are a couple of add-ons that provide something akin to a real time report, but they aren't native to the applications and it shows.

▶ **There is no workflow.** If you have a complex contract approval process, you're out of this market already, since there is no real workflow built into any contact manager.

▶ **Analytics are nonexistent.** There is no way of looking at your data and sales information beyond the prepackaged reports provided. Tools to analyze your sales information aren't available.

▶ **Add-ons are very simple and only marginally useful.** For example, ACT! add-ons include de-duplication applications to eliminate duplicate records, a "migration" app that changes the paths of attachments (reconnects them if the links are broken because the attachment was moved), and links to and converters for Outlook, QuickBooks, or the Pocket PC. Not exactly an awe-inspiring group, is it?

▶ **It promotes a "lone wolf" culture rather than a team standard.** The data is not shared, it is hoarded. Because it resides on a personal desktop, it remains proprietary. Contact management is also not designed to handle either team selling processes or team selling coordination well, though groups can be created and managed to some extent. It is meant to maintain and access a single salesperson's network.

SFA: Sales Bourgeois vs. Sales Proletarians

Okay, so now we know the limitations of contact management, but also why the salesperson loves it. It's theirs and theirs alone—almost. But that isn't the end of it, because it ultimately isn't their decision to provide a sales force automation system to their company. It is senior management's decision, with sales management, of course, playing a critical decision-making role in this. What is the sales staff's decision is whether or not each of them chooses to use the system, with consideration of the consequences of not using it. So the battle for the sales force hearts and minds continues here.

The problem is that while sales management is often looked upon as not quite the enemy, it is not quite part of the team either. Consequently, there is a disparity between what is valuable to sales management and what is important to salespeople. However, traditionally, CRM vendors have focused on sales management features and functions simply because it is often sales management who is involved in the purchasing decision, either as the final decision-maker or at least as an influencer. The salesperson is rarely at that level, if ever. Since humans operate from self-interest, and that means vendors want to sell the product, the features that appeal to sales management are the primary features that have been developed over the past few years.

Those features are those that made the revenues and the opportunities for revenues visible and easy to access and increased individual salesperson visibility and thus accountability. Forecasting tools were also highlighted so that forecasting the quarterly pipeline was no longer a manual process, but a real time graph. If I were a VP of sales or a CEO, I'd want to be able to see what I'm going to be doing at a moment's notice, wouldn't you?

Let's look at some of the traditional sales force automation features—the ones that make management crave the system:

- ▶ **Pipeline visibility** This has always been one of sales management's favorite features. Most of the vendors have real-time pipeline visibility as they've moved to Web-based or Web services integrated thin client SFA applications. This lets the sales manager drill down by territory, sales rep, account, time frame, and multiple other ways to see the immediately current status of that beloved sales potential data. Most of them allow for graphic representation so that you can also view the pipeline by where it is in your established process—accomplishing two things, providing better forecasting capabilities and letting you know if your processes work. Monthly sales plans are possible and you can, horrors of horrors, see how well you or your salespeople are performing against the plan.

▶ **Data central for consolidated sales information** This is the SFA version of the single customer record. A consolidated data warehouse or other form of data store, where all customer data including history, activity, and sales information are available in a single place under a single record to a single individual authorized to view that data.

▶ **Territory management** This is always a dicey proposition for salespersons and management simply because good customers can often span geographic boundaries. What do you do when there are geographically distributed territories and the opportunities span offices in Indianapolis and San Francisco with a company that has a New York corporate headquarters? This is where territory management functionality steps in to help you deal with the knotty problem of determining whose sale it is or how to allocate the sales results for commission/bonus purposes. In fact, PeopleSoft 8.8 SFA provides drag and drop territory management in a tree-like metaphor that automatically populates the right salesperson's records with the new information should you make a change—hierarchically, of course.

▶ **Strong forecasting capabilities** This is where the difference between contact management and SFA starts becoming really blatant. The forecasting that SFA provides is in real time and can encompass thousands and tens of thousands of data points so that forecasts are as accurate as the data entered by the salespeople. *Caveat emptor.*

▶ **Solid analytic tools** The gulf becomes extensive. There is no analytics in baseball, er, contact management. But one of the hallmarks of the strongest of the enterprise SFA packages is an analytics facility that helps define the value of the performance of the salesperson or team or the company as a whole. For example, using PeopleSoft's Enterprise Performance Management (EPM) Sales Incentive Management (SIM) analytics, your company is able to design complex incentive plans that cross multiple and widely diverse business units. Based on the results generated by the analytics, you can create an appropriate rewards structure that will potentially maximize the sales results from your teams. The stipulation, of course, is that this is an aid to help you, not the be all and end all. Human decisions are still paramount, no matter how automated your information gathering and results are. We still have to use our brains to interpret the results and make the judgments that will benefit both the company and our individual employees. You'll be developing your own programs from the suggested possibilities based on the analysis of sales results that you carve out and look at.

- ▶ **Dashboards, reports** Another grand canyon of difference here. Reports in SFA are normally infinitely customizable, including what you want to see and how you want to see it (format it). Additionally, while the reports in Goldmine and ACT! are simple, SFA packages are capable of producing multidimensional reports. For example, SAS, which has perhaps the strongest analytics in the CRM world, uses its multidimensional database products to provide you with information that linearly would look like this: Product Line/Geography/Time/Sales Lag = Actual Sales. When done hierarchically, this can get very complicated, but then, that's what these packages are for. So that these reports are viewable by those of this solar system, Crystal Reports is often included as an embedded part of the CRM or SFA package.

Now for the Salespeople

Study after study in 2001–2003 showed appalling rates of sales adoption of SFA systems, often less than 35 percent. By 2002, the notable teeth-baring yawning of the sales force when it came to SFA made the vendors sit up and take notice. Salespeople weren't using the applications, turning those millions of dollars and thousands of man hours into a highly customized sinkhole.

But while all of them began to give lip service to the value of SFA to the blue collar sales human, the 2003 product literature was still geared to solving the problems of "your" sales organization (read: management's). For example:

- ▶ "Develop an overall sales strategy that gives your sales reps more customer-facing time." (PeopleSoft)

► "In today's turbulent economy, your sales organization must do more than simply meet revenue goals—it must also control costs and improve efficiency." (SAP)

► "Click on an area below to learn how Siebel Sales provides comprehensive sales pipeline management." (Siebel—more on them later)

On the other hand, while most CRM vendors were slow to move, a few of them began to make the effort, notably Oracle, SalesLogix with their sales automation upgrades to SalesLogix 6.1, and ASP Salesnet. In this chapter, I'm going to cover both Oracle and Salesnet in Steppin' Out. SalesLogix will be covered in the Chapter 12 Steppin' Out. But these three have been the ones who have taken the lead in providing true SFA for the actual salesperson.

"CRM has to be more engaging and more useful to the sales guy," explains Mike Doyle, chairman and CEO at Salesnet. "The new wave of online CRM solutions must deliver the functionality that makes it easier for salespeople to use it than to not. Sales-focused CRM must deliver real value to salespeople."

So what is that value? What differentiates the sales management–focused SFA from the new generation of sales force–focused (meaning both management and sales staff) SFA? Keep in mind, the features and functions I mention below are added to the traditional SFA, not substituted for it. There is a lot of value in providing the lead, opportunity, account, contact, and pipeline management functionality. But these additions distinguish the aforementioned vendors from the pack and should be seen as mission-critical features (in most cases) for increasing user adoption among the sales force members.

► **MS Outlook integration** Oddly, this is one of the most important sales-friendly features. There are 198,000,000 Microsoft-claimed users of Outlook in the world. That means that there is a wide familiarity with the features and with the interface of Outlook. Outlook is often used as a contact manager or the foundation of a more substantial sales-related program. It is no coincidence that Microsoft made its initial CRM offering, MSCRM, a very Outlook-friendly near clone in look and feel. Outlook integration is almost a universal necessity for an application to succeed with that volatile sales force. Think of it this way, you're more likely to eat an apple that looks like an apple than an apple that looks like a spider. Unless of course, you're a contestant on Fear Factor.

▶ **Better mobile applications** AvantGo, a notable wireless applications provider and a company that anyone with a PDA knows, did a study in 2002 that found that 83 percent of the sales folks surveyed would be more interested in adopting a CRM/SFA solution if it were mobile and PDA accessible. That was noticed and several of the vendors have included the following:

- **Offline versions** These are synchronized versions that allow you to make changes when you are disconnected. When you go back online, the changes are automatically added to the server's database.

- **Instant messenger integration** Again, a wireless feature that lets you use instant messenger to immediately correspond with your fellow salespeople—or your 14-year-old daughter.

- **Mobile versions of their applications with easy wireless web access** Transparently easy, browser-accessible thin client versions of the applications that can access needed information via a mobile device such as the Hewlett-Packard IPAQ or a Bluetooth or 80211.b enabled laptop or a cellphone with some PDA functionality. Most of the vendors have this capability now. Siebel has a separate Mobile Sales module that is compatible with Windows Mobile 2003 (the Pocket PC) or Palm's operating system and has a wireless component that provides real-time access to Siebel Sales data, including accounts, activities, calendar, contacts, employees, opportunities, sales orders, and correspondence via any one of the devices I spoke of. Imagine inputting your order via a Nokia 3650 phone with a ring tone that plays Avril Lavigne's "Complicated" when your sales manager calls in—to congratulate you on the order you just input via the phone.

▶ **Improved calendar functionality (appointments, tasks, sales process steps)** While this bit of functionality is still in its infancy, it enhances the calendar so that the salesperson can see where in the sales process he is with a particular client and when he is scheduled to reach the next stage.

▶ **Proposal and quote systems** This is a critical feature set, one that the salesperson who at any point has to prepare a proposal, quote, or proposal response in the private or public sectors can't do without. See the discussion below on Oracle and Pragmatech for how this can work in detail. Keep in mind, the discussions of what these companies provide in that arena are there so that you'll have an increased understanding of what to expect both as best practices in this complex domain and from any vendor you might be considering.

▶ **User interface suited to sales, not IT** This is kind of the "duh" one. Unfortunately, user interfaces have often been ugly. A good example of how an interface should be organized for a salesperson comes from Pragmatech's product represented in Figure 4-1. It is easy to understand without any real training and is intuitive. A salesperson won't be spending precious time trying to figure out how to use this interface. They just will.

▶ **Configurable personalized screens and interfaces** The way to call your sales screens "home." Basically, most of the leaders offer the easily malleable screens so that the person using the application can format their particular screens to the colors, shapes, and sizes they want and show the information that is particularly relevant to them individually—even though there is a single instance of the application being used enterprise-wide. The individual nature of the home-like interface is accessed through a portal with a single user sign-on and password.

▶ **Analytics and data access for the masses** For example, a sales rep on the phone is able to call up the lifetime-value score of a particular customer based on the analytics model and tailor an offer accordingly. Analytics move out of the realm of the mathematician and into the realm of the real-world user. Information interpretation becomes valuable to salespeople and helps them do their jobs better—rather than an exercise in advanced head-scratching. For example, NetSuite, an ASP you will be hearing more about in Chapters 16 and 26, released a commissions management tool in September 2003—for salespeople, not for sales management. This tool, near and dear to a sales heart, allows sales personnel to see their projected earnings from any particular deal on their personal (and secure) software dashboard. Having this information available with the ability to slice and dice so that you can forecast your personal income, provides particular incentive for the hunters to catch their prey.

Focus: Proposal Management Meets Sales Process

Proposals are a big part of the sales process. God knows how many weekends, calls to FedEx, gallons of coffee, cramped writing or typing hands, arguments, missing mission-critical information, ridiculous price quotes that had to be adjusted, nervous moments, and wasted supplies you had to go through doing proposals that you might not have ever come close to winning. But then you would win one and the process would begin all over again, hope renewed, until there were five more losses and you were back to dragging through the weekends, FedEx, coffee-slurping grinding sessions. Wouldn't it be nice to make that easier?

Pragmatech

If you took a look at Pragmatech a couple of years ago, you found a company that was small, smart, and specialized. Proposal management was their thing, Proposal Express their primary product. They were a great add-in to sales force automation products, but if you had to, you could live without it. But things changed in the CRM world and Pragmatech did too. While they are known, tracked, and lauded for their proposal management products, take a deeper look. In fact, glance at Figure 4-1. Notice something interesting? Pragmatech understands the nature of 21st century CRM and has become the streamliner and document producer of not just sales, but the sales process. They've gone from a star in proposal automation to a star in what they call "sales effectiveness." Good idea for a great product.

But why should you use them if you have a sales force automation product in place already? First, they do something that sales force automation doesn't. They provide both a document and knowledge management product that works along each step of whatever your sales process is. They escalate the look and content of a proposal or a presentation or any document that is necessarily engaged in a sale by roughly a zillion percent. They save time by having a library of not exactly best practices as much as "best writing" that can be shared and matched to appropriate proposals. For example, if you're bidding on a CRM project that involves the use of SAP's mySAP CRM 4.0 in a consumer packaged goods company, you can pull up the pricing information and proposal language and put it directly into a proposal shell that will save you countless hours of effort and hundreds of aspirins. You can also standardize your language and content, minimizing the chance of a major mistake. Plus the proposals look so much better.

Figure 4-1: Pragmatech knows the sales process.

You might not think that the look and feel have much of an impact, but look and feel sometimes have more impact than content in the immediate sense. For example, when you see a BMW 330i or a Lexus 430 and you compare it to a Dodge Ram minivan, which one do you salivate for? Style has meaning.

But let's look at some sales effectiveness stats on behalf of professional preparation. A survey done on Fortune 1000 companies concluded that developing selling materials with applications designed to develop them is responsible for turning 48 percent of the proposals produced that way into contracts, well above the 26 percent used by those manual laborers producing similar types of materials. Not only that, the same survey concluded that the development of the materials with the applications was done in 47 percent less time, with 20 percent less time in locating old documents. The tedium is eliminated and the timeliness increases. That is something that wins sales.

Pragmatech has moved by leaps and bounds directly from a good SFA add-on to a necessary part of any SFA solution. They can brag about a customer base that includes such companies as Hewlett-Packard (increase win rate by 30 percent over four years), Chase Merchant Services (RFP response time reduced from 43 hours to 27 hours), and DST Innovis (proposal completion time reduced from 5 days to 5 hours!) and even PeopleSoft, who used them to help effect the merger of the Vantive (former CRM major product acquired by PeopleSoft in 2000) sales force into the PeopleSoft sales force.

What does all this mean? It means that Pragmatech, by understanding as well or better than most of the SFA vendors what sales process is, is now part of that very same sales process, not just adding to it. Remember that next time you spend your weekend at the office working on the proposal from hell. Or, rather, the response to the proposal from hell.

Vendors to Watch

Because this has been the forefather of all CRM applications, there has been no dearth of vendors that are involved in this space. I'm going to mention a few of the notable before I get into the highlighted vendors for this chapter.

Siebel

While much of the CRM vendor world is struggling with features and functions that provide value to both sales management and the sales force, Siebel continues to develop increasingly sophisticated sales management tools. Siebel senior director of sales, Steve Apfelberg, when asked about "next generation SFA capabilities" in an ad sponsored by Unisys in *InfoWorld*, said the functions should include the following:

- **Pipeline analysis** The ability to slice and dice the pipeline from all kinds of angles.

- **Team performance/sales effectiveness evaluation** Slice and dice the performance of sales reps by individual, region, sales numbers, and so on.

- **Territory insight** Slicing and dicing territories for comparisons by salesperson or territory. In Siebel 7.7, this is called hierarchical territory management.

Is this a good idea for the newest generation of SFA? Only if you're Jason or Freddy with that much slicing and dicing. But given the generally identified issues of user adoption that have plagued CRM the last few years, the efficacy of this move is questionable. Perhaps it can provide a differentiator or two for Siebel, but they are bucking an important tide. Even with their recognition of this tide, let's hear from Steve again: "Unless the sales force sees that executives are also using the SFA solution, they are likely to view the system with skepticism." This is a serious misconception of how user adoption problems arise. Management adoption is by no means the answer to user adoption, though it, of course, has to happen. We'll see what the actual answer is throughout the book.

Siebel also embeds selling methodologies into their SFA applications, such as Solutions Selling or Targeted Account Selling. While I've never been a big fan of formal selling methodologies, they can have some real value to companies establishing consistent processes and best practices.

Others by Name Only

I'd be watching PeopleSoft with both their enterprise-level product and their J.D. Edwards EnterpriseOne Sales product, which is perfectly suited for the AS400 and upper end of the small and medium business market (see Chapter 24 and elsewhere through the book) and SalesLogix, the other of the three who are leading the next generation of sales force automation charge. SalesLogix would have been included in Steppin' Out in this chapter except that they are one of the Steppin' Out features of Chapter 12.

Note: I want to say a final little bit on "Stepping' Out" sidebars. I have some basic strategic criteria that any of the "Steppin' Out" candidates have to meet:

> ▶ *The vendor's application has to be process focused.*

> ▶ *It has to account for an extended value chain that integrates suppliers, vendors, employees, and partners as a collaborative unit to please that single paying client.*

> ▶ *The vendor has to have a "blue collar" or "proletarian" (for all you budding leftists out there) view as part of its thinking, meaning the ordinary user has to benefit by this application, rather than just the corporate dealmaker.*

STEPPIN' OUT: Oracle Sales—Working for the Working Stiff

If you have read either of the first two editions of this book, you'll know that I wasn't particularly an Oracle fan, though I gave them props for forward thinking. They've now carried this foresight into their overall planning and it is good for them and their customers. They have made serious leaps forward. While you can read considerably more about this in Chapter 23 on the Big Boys, I want to focus in on Oracle Sales and its features.

Suffice it to say for the purposes of this section, Oracle's development of grid computing has a lot to do with their overall outlook. "All things Oracle" has evolved into "the integrated enterprise"—a single instance of everything on a single system. The ultimate image is a computer dropped into the middle of your server room and it all starts working. Nice image. But the "integrated enterprise" is more valuable later in the book than now. Just have it in your cranium when you are reading this section.

This is an enterprise sales product that is actually aimed not just at sales management, but at the "blue collar" sales force with enough features and practices to make management happy too. Not only does it have the tools, it has the process. It is modeled on a "lead to order to compensation" sales process and handles each step of the way in a multichannel, multitiered partner approach so that it deals with not just your direct sales force, but also with your indirect channel. They've added the right features at the right time.

If you think about what makes a salesperson's job easier, it isn't visibility into the pipeline. That is not much more than a necessary angst-producer for the salesperson. Timeliness, accuracy, customer-friendly pricing, and service are what provide a differentiator that is meaningful.

What Oracle Sales has done is actually understand this perspective. Some of the salesperson (read: internal customer) friendly modules include:

- ▶ Proposals
- ▶ Sales Offline
- ▶ Field Sales
- ▶ Oracle Quoting

Oracle Quoting

I'm going to spend some time with this particular feature because it ties together Chapters 3 and 4 in an interesting way. CRM's current incarnation as it should be (not necessarily as it is) is encapsulated in Oracle's Sales application.

What makes Oracle Quoting particularly instructive is how it is accessed. Not only can you access through a direct Oracle Business Flow (see Chapter 3), but also through various points in multiple flows. For example, you can always access the quoting module directly from the Quote to Order process, but also as part of either Field Sales or Telesales in the Campaign to Order flow. If you use Quoting directly, you can link the quote back to an opportunity. If you do it through the Field Sales or Telesales modules, you can do it through the opportunity.

Preparing the Quote

Another notable Oracle Quoting feature is its ability to gather data to prepare the quote from anywhere. All of the current products and services information offered in a catalog (Oracle prefers it through Oracle Inventory) can be included, even the extended warranty packages. To make this even yummier, Oracle can provide a real-time inventory check to see about availability of the products, while you're producing the quote. It handles similar products and competitor trade-ins. It seems as if everything was thought of here, doesn't it?

Well, we're not quite done. Now that we've seen how it integrates with the supply chain (see Chapter 15 for more on this subject), let's see how the "extended value chain" works even more so. Once you've identified the products and services and possible trade-ups and trade-ins, it's time to take a look at quotes that not only account for the supply chain features, but are customer-personalized. That means customer record look-ups and customer-specific pricing—dynamically. That can mean standard pricing or promotion pricing based on specific customer characteristics applied to the quote. It can also mean volume discounts. It can also mean working from prior pricing history. It can also mean just about anything your little ol' sales heart desires when it comes to customizing a quote. What is important to note here is that you are engaging all resources to optimize the quote.

Internal Business Approvals: Going with the Flow

The workflow engine behind CRM processes is always a critical component of its likelihood of success or failure. Getting approvals for a quote (or for anything else that might need it, for that matter) is a must-have when it comes to timely activity that theoretically won't experience any difficulties and will provide what is needed to the sales.

Salespeople can apply standard terms and conditions to a quote without involving a contract administrator, by selecting an appropriate sales contract template. Oracle Quoting retrieves the contract templates from the central contract repository in Oracle's Contracts module. Through Oracle Quoting, salespeople can also request creation of a nonstandard contract and specify requirements to contract administrator.

Once the contract is created, it is automatically associated with the quote. The salesperson can review terms and conditions from the quote. Additionally, the customer can review the terms and conditions for Web-published quotes in online stores. The contract details are also included in the printouts of quotes that are eligible to be placed as orders.

Oracle Quoting supports service contracts as well as sales contracts. When services are purchased, service contracts are automatically created in the Contracts module.

RFQ? QED

This is an outstanding feature for the blue collar salesperson. Oracle Quoting is integrated with Oracle Proposal. For those of you who have ever participated in proposal development you know what a strain developing quotes puts on the effort. By being able to launch proposal creation for a quote from Oracle Quoting with Oracle Proposals automatically bringing in quote information such as customer name, products, and pricing into the proposal, sales pleasure seems only a keystroke away. It can be made automatically far more complex, of course, by the preselection of elements to be brought in through Oracle Proposal. That could include cover letters, executive summaries, and product descriptions among many other features. This is great stuff for the prole sales guy. Just look at how well this serves you in Figure 4-2.

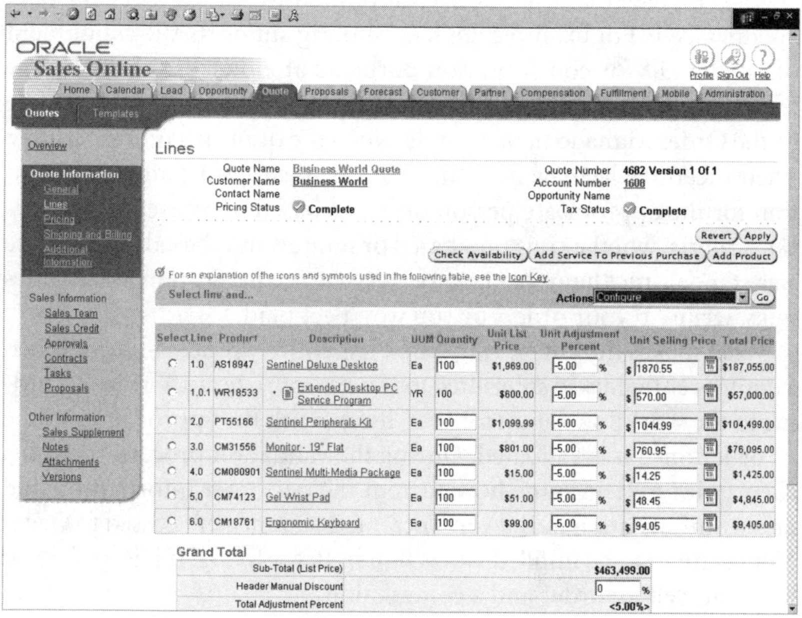

Figure 4-2: Oracle Quoting is a great example of the Gen S SFA.

Other features of Oracle Quoting include:

▶ **Sales Supplement** Templates with predefined quote-specific information and routing instructions.

▶ **Advanced Security** Access is allowed only to the appropriate personnel. Access is configurable down to a specific state for a specific role (such as read-only to sales associates).

▶ **Customer Credit Checking** Credit checks can be run from the application itself or externally if need be.

▶ **Quote Searching** Simple and advanced searches. It can be complicated, but it works and you can save the searches.

▶ **Advanced Printing** It allows output in either Acrobat or Rich Text File (RTF) formats.

Oracle Sales also has strong e-commerce features. Using Oracle iStore, quotes can be published online for the viewing pleasure of the customer. Self-service quote creation, customer response and entry, security and notifications, are all part of the e-commerce features.

Sales management hasn't been forgotten by Oracle either. Thank goodness, eh? For example, Oracle Quoting supports the assignment of sales credit for compensation purposes at either the quote or line level. They get passed through to the Incentive Compensation module by the Order Management module, when the quote becomes an order. Then Incentive Management determines the appropriate compensation for the appropriate person or teams based on preset compensation criteria, whether revenue-based or nonrevenue-based. If the quote was standalone, the quote creator gets the credit. So remember, sales folks, write up your orders or you won't get paid.

What makes this interesting is that it is entirely process-based. When a quote is entered and submitted to the appropriate authorities according to the workflow set up for that, it can, with the approvals, become an order once it is validated. During the validation process, there is a checkpoint to determine how current the customer information and pricing information is. If it isn't current, the quote isn't passed to Order Management to be fulfilled, but is sent back for fixing. If it is, voilà! You have yourself an order and a commission.

Steppin' Out: Salesnet—Bang for the Practical Buck

I like these folks. While you'll read more of them in Chapter 25, I want to emphasize that we have an ASP (see Chapter 16) that understands the value of business process and the value of the salesperson. Two of the hottest 2004 CRM values.

What makes this precious, especially to Steppin' Out, is that they are not only there to provide the processes that salespeople need, but they are building what they call "intelligent automation" into their solution. While there is something debatable about what seems to be an oxymoron ("intelligent automation") and, while I'd love to get into the weightier questions of real intelligence vs. artificial intelligence, suffice it to say that what Salesnet is doing is actually really good.

Before we go on to look at this exceptional company's sales solutions, keep in mind that about two years ago, the ASP market did not really seem all that viable. But under the able leadership of Mike Doyle, one of the nicest and most competent CEOs in the CRM world, and an infusion of funding from trusted sources, plus a few key larger seat deals—600 seats and up—Salesnet not only kept plugging away, but began to grow. As the ASP market became increasingly interesting to a very price- and overhead-conscious, economically shaken business world, Salesnet simply started to do better and better. Now Salesnet can boast of very large scale deployments, most with two to five year contracts. Their customers are Staples, Sovereign Bank, and Software AG, among others. That is amazing for a company that isn't supposed to be appealing to the larger enterprises. They are bringing into question my continued assertion that the ASP market can't handle the largest enterprises. Salesnet is quietly disproving me. More on all this in Chapter 25, but for now I'll say three things about their sales offerings:

- ► They have successfully aimed at both the upper and lower ends of the small and medium business market and spilled into the larger enterprises. Their lower end product is called Salesnet Express.

- ► They have the deepest sales process conception and functionality of any of the ASPs, and they understand and execute on sales process better than many of the standalone CRM vendors.

- ► They are one of the three vendors (with Oracle and SalesLogix) that "get it" when it comes to the next generation of working stiff sales force automation, and that is worth some congratulations.

The Features: The Future

Salesnet provides three versions of its product, each increasingly rich. Salesnet Express is aimed at the small business with up to ten users. It provides the basic functionality with some reports, e-mail management, and account and opportunity management. It also helps the novice small company build their sales process.

Salesnet Standard is all of that in a more substantial package that also includes embedded sales processes such as Targeted Account Selling and the fully customizable Process Builder. Outlook integration, sending and tracking outbound e-mail, centralized customer data, and a myriad of other features are part of this hosted solution for a larger company.

Finally they have Salesnet Extended, which takes all of the above and adds wireless and remote management and use and the secure offline edition. This is aimed at the Staples or Sovereign Banks of the world.

A TOUCH OF CLASS DISTINCTION

Salesnet is distinguished from its fellow ASPs and several standalone vendors by a clear-cut commitment to the everyday sales team and the sales process simultaneously. To translate this commitment into practice, they provide a technology called Process Builder (see Figure 4-3) that uses an authoring tool to graphically represent and embed into your workflow any sales methodology you want it to. It could insert the famous highly structured Miller Heiman sales approach or one of your own creation. I think that the Miller Heiman approach is when you get behind a client and squeeze his sternum to pop out the lite beer can they are choking on. They are then so grateful you win the deal. Or is that the Miller Heimlich approach? I can't remember.

However, what I *can* remember is that Process Builder is a masterful process/workflow design tool that allows you to customize the Salesnet applications to the best practices that govern your sales process. That is the way that SFA is supposed to be done.

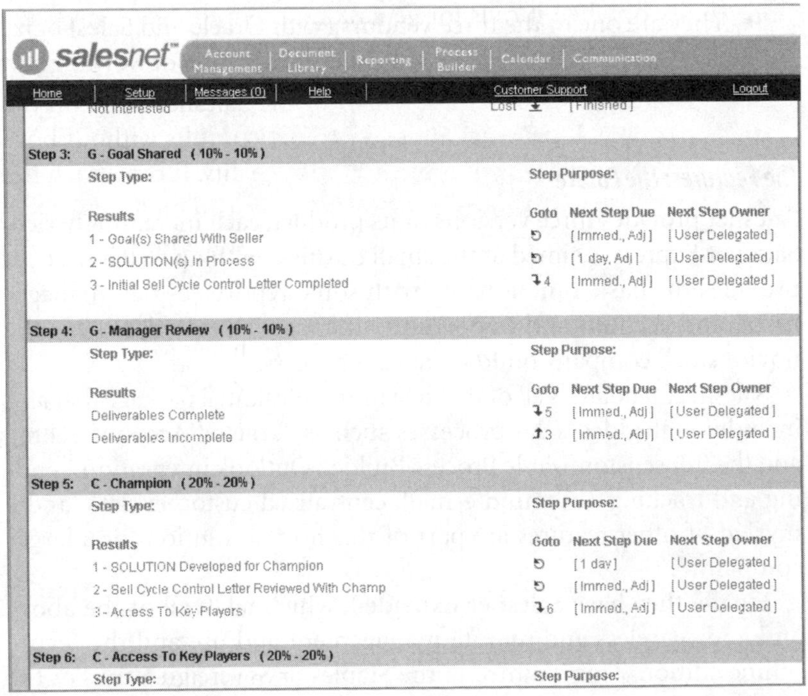

Figure 4-3: Salesnet's Process Builder is a beautiful tool.

Other features that make Salesnet a standout for the working sales guy:

▶ **Virtual Coach** Salesnet uses a wizard to guide sales reps through the sales process, embedded through Process Builder. This can give predefined results and outcomes to select at every milestone, but only after the previous milestone is reached. This system of process-driven constraints is superb for newbie sales rep training and for making sure that what we'll call "lesser performers" aren't at the lower level because of failure to understand how to sell. Virtual Coach also provides the consistency of methodology that many companies like to have.

▶ **Automatic lead qualification** This is a great feature for a salesperson. Once you've established the business rules that govern lead qualification, Salesnet can score those leads upfront—taking into account those criteria and the business history that is appropriate to the lead. Once that is done, specific business steps can be triggered at different stages of the lead process—for example, when it automatically kicks over into a viable opportunity or when it calls for generation of a proposal. The salesperson kicks back and says here, "Life is good."

▶ **Workflow tools** This is the heart of the Salesnet focus on the salespeople. It provides almost automatic results without bogging down reps with extraneous functionality. It can attach the steps in the sales processes that you've decided on to the actual responsibilities and roles of the sales (or other) personnel. So for example, a constraint can be created that states that any deal that is under 20 percent gross margin must be routed to the appropriate sales managers for approval. Then it goes ahead and does it. If that's what you want to do. The workflow tools allow for this granular customization. And sales managers like it because they can keep their fingers on the pulse of sales activities through fully customizable reports, dashboards, and charts. Salesnet offers add-on functionality for mobility, integration, advanced reporting, and enhanced process management.

▶ **Report Snapshot and Comparison engine** This allows you to compare any historic moment in sales with real-time data. No more guessing how current sales stand up to sales 60 days ago.

► **Microsoft Outlook Integration** I think I've said enough about this elsewhere. It is necessary. Salesnet has it. So do most of the competition. Salesnet does it very, very well and that merits notice. Their inclusion of it was driven by the need to eliminate copying and pasting of e-mail content by the sales rep into Salesnet's database.

► **Instant Messaging (IM)** No longer just the tool for your teenage daughter to blab with her friends online. It is now a serious communications tool for the enterprise—for salespeople to blab with their colleagues online. Actually, the ability to instantly communicate with your colleagues and even some of your clients via your desktop, notebook, PDA, or cellphone is priceless. Especially during football season.

The up tick in the number of sales reps using wireless technologies, like cellphones, wirelessly enabled laptops, and personal digital assistants, meant that Salesnet had to expand into the offline arena. Using the SQL Server and .NET framework, Salesnet's secure offline solution is a bit more robust than most of the offline solutions offered. Salesnet offline users can actually run reports and analytics offline, which distinguishes them from their competition. All in all, Salesnet is a distinguished company with a great set of solutions and a firm grasp on what's needed for this generation of salespeople: Gen S.

Rage Against the Machine?

Gen S, our current generation of salespeople, made it clear that they weren't going to stand for SFA tools that meant little to them and lots to their management. They were able to show how peeved they were by doing what they did best: rage against the machine by not using the applications or system when it was implemented. Now, with the newly process-focused CRM and especially its sales-related applications, there is some recognition on the negative side that the prior approaches to SFA were either only partially successful or paralyzing. On the positive side, if you provide salespeople with tools they see as valuable to themselves—meaning you treat them as your customers, too—then they will naturally go out and do what they do best: sell. That's a good thing.

5

Enterprise Marketing Management: Finally Getting the Message?

You can't get around it. Marketing is something that you have to live with. You do it every day of your life. How fair and balanced is your résumé? Does it outline all your screw-ups as well as your achievements? How about when you talk to someone else? What do you think that is? You are giving someone an opinion about something that you want them to agree with you on, aren't you? That is the essence of marketing.

I frequently deal with the marketing folks at many vendors. They give me "white papers" to look at, which are about ten pages in length. The first five pages are conceptual documents that have some good ideas, though usually obscured by buzzwords that only a marketing manager could love. The last five pages are "and this is why our solution is the best possible one for the concept behind this white paper," destroying any validity the concept had as anything but a blatant selling job. There are two problems here. The first one is that the "white paper" audience is not the planned target audience. The target becomes an internalized version of the marketing manager or director that the writer reports to, rather than a focused segment such as regional bankers. The appeal is not to the target group, but the writers appeal instead to their boss for a pat on the back. To make matters worse, there is no subtlety about the message. White papers are written to provide thought-leadership. They are not marketing collateral. A successful white paper elicits the following thinking in some form from a target audience member, "Hey, these guys are really expert in this subject or, at least, seem to be aligned with the experts in the domain. Maybe I need to contact them for my needs in this area." Companies like Accenture actually understand this value proposition in a sort of ham-fisted way—clumsy, overpowering by degrees, but at least they are smart enough to engage in it. I can't say the same for their consulting, integration, or vendor colleagues in the enterprise applications world, with the exceptions of Unisys, whom you will read more about in Chapter 23, and Quaero, who is my Steppin' Out choice for this chapter. I'm sure there are others, but none stand out that I can see.

To make it personal, when good marketing works, it is someone using your metaphor to get their idea across. As marketers, they are obligated to "know" you, to understand how you think, your metaphor, what makes you tick, and why you get interested in something. Preferably, something that their company can provide. Good marketing scions need to know that there is no point in selling water to a fish— unless it's out of water or they can figure out that the fish will be out of water sometime in a discernable future. But to sell water to that potentially flopping fish, they need to know how the fish's gills work and what the fish is thinking.

What makes marketing abhorrent to many of us isn't marketing itself, which is an honorable profession. It is bad or unwanted marketing.

Traditional marketing is ironically called "interruption marketing." When a telemarketer calls you on the phone, even though you have the right to not answer the phone, the very act of the phone call to sell you something that isn't particularly of value to you or is one of a million calls for the same item, is an irritating interruption in your daily routine.

But there is also good interruption marketing. It is unobtrusive, but still, it intrudes. When you see a good commercial on TV, usually an ironic spot, a spot with good music, or a constantly repeated spot, don't you appreciate the artistry of the commercial (if it wasn't just repetitive), remember the company advertising and the product, and talk about it with your friends? For example, if I say "priceless," what do you think of right away? That's right, MasterCard. Personally, I think that this is the greatest advertising campaign of all time. But I'm sure you have your own favorites. I hope "I'm lovin' it" isn't one of them. That's right, McDonalds. See what I mean?

But nobody has pushed these commercials down your throat. You saw it, it didn't force its way into your retinas. This is interruption marketing done well. You didn't request the commercial, but your expectation is that, in return for watching the rerun of that *Seinfeld* episode, you will have to watch commercials if you don't choose to get up and do something during those 60-second intervals. This is interruption marketing at its "finest."

So what does all this talk of advertising and marketing mean for CRM? Why bring all this up?

For those of you who are CRM veterans, you'll remember back in its application-focused horizontal days, sales, service, and marketing were the three pillars. Marketing in particular was the most difficult and least evolved of the areas. There were a few vendor experts—notably Annuncio (acquired by PeopleSoft), E.piphany and a few others. Typically, marketing was seen as a necessary evil that supported sales opportunity, but didn't sell directly, so was only worth a few dollars—and that during prosperous times. Enterprise marketing automation (EMA) systems, which were expensive ventures, often costing a million dollars or more for a basic implementation, were not really visible in the generally myopic purviews of senior management at many firms. Combine that with the bad economy in 2001 and 2002, and marketing budgets were the first to go (along with marketing staff). EMA sales sagged so badly that their vendors became something that looked like Sméagol/Gollum in *The Lord of the Rings*—a deformed, formerly humanoid half-creature that never can achieve its fully humanoid status again. Sales of the EMA "Precious" were wished for, but the market leveled to the point that most of the EMA companies were either acquired or went down.

But this is 2004 and the market is infinitely brighter. With the economy in recovery and business on the increase, and the fight for customers ever more cutthroat, money is being spent on marketing and advertising again. The Interactive Advertising Bureau (IAB) and PricewaterhouseCoopers (PwC) did a joint study and found that Internet advertising for the first quarter of 2004 was just short of $2.3 billion, the highest quarterly total on record since the tracking began in 1996. This is up from $1.6 billion first quarter 2003 and even up a little (3.9 percent) from the fourth quarter of 2003. Mind you, this is just Internet advertising. If you start looking at other channels used, such as direct mail, or media such as television and print, the numbers get staggering, over $263 billion in 2004. The Interpublic Group sees this increasing to $280 billion in 2005. Some of that will go to the technology, but the entire world of EMA is changing, much in the same way that CRM is changing. From system and technology to strategy and outlook supported by system and technology.

The Core Beliefs

How has EMA changed? Well, despite considerable debate as to differences and acronymic patrimony, 21st century CRM marketing is strategic, not tactical. It is multichannel, not siloed. It is permission-based and opt-in, not interruption-based and opt-out. It is based on a clearly defined customer/business value exchange, not just establishing brand loyalty. Let's start by spending significant time on loyalty and loyalty programs because it is perhaps the number one issue at the core of marketing and, to a large extent, the core of CRM.

Loyalty and Loyalty Programs

Loyalty is perhaps the most overpuffed concept in the CRM world. There are dozens of books on customer loyalty. There are multiple companies that make their livings on providing secret tricks to customer loyalty ranging from programs to feedback surveys. I was verbally and personally attacked in a letter to *CRM Magazine* by a guy who was COO of a loyalty feedback company because I wrote a controversial column in August 2003 that questioned the existence of customer loyalty. He called something I said "transparent, offensive, and ridiculous." I'm sure there are plenty of times I'm transparent and ridiculous, though I try hard not to be offensive, but this guy was totally off base because I was reiterating something that had been told to me in fact. It wasn't my opinion being posited. But hey, I imagine what I said threatened his livelihood, which is the only reason I can see for his excessive comments.

Loyalty in the world of marketing (though not the world of etymology, linguistics, or philology) really means consistent commitment from a customer to a specific brand or company. Clive Humby, the chairman of dunnhumby, a loyalty marketing company and the creator of the incredibly successful Tesco's Clubcard program, said it succinctly in an interview with Bob Thompson at *CRMGuru* in January 2004, "...what loyalty means is, I'm going to do stuff for you and show you that I care about you, and because I care about you, you will trust my brand, and you will respect my brand, and when I say to you, 'I've got a good deal for you,' then you will believe me."

Bravo. How right he is. Brand loyalty is decidedly not the profound emotional loyalty that you show your family and likely also show your country. It is not a loyalty that makes you willing to sacrifice beyond what is in your self-interest. In a business sense, it is a commitment to a brand value exchange. There are two criteria for maintaining that commitment to a productive value exchange. First, the company that you are committed to is providing you with sufficient value to retain you. Second, the cost of change to another potentially higher value company is too high for you to make the change when the possibility comes along. You know the latter feeling: "Yeah, it's a good deal, but I've been with Company X for so long and this effort isn't worth my time." If the two criteria are consistently met, then the brand holder can make the assumption that you will be of sufficient value to them over a lifetime as a customer.

So, if we see one of the results of loyalty being a reduction in customer defection, then we can identify the value in that. In prior chapters, I've identified the Bain and Accenture studies that said that a 5 percent increase in customer retention means a 25 percent increase in profitability. In 1990, the *Harvard Business Review* issued an article titled "Zero Defection: Quality Comes to Services," which set the standard for the concept. Their argument was a 5 percent increase in customer retention would almost double profits—a little more optimistic than Bain or Accenture. But more interesting was their long-term conclusion. Over five years, a firm with a 70 percent customer retention rate will have lost two to three times as many customers as a firm with a 90 percent retention rate. So keeping your customers committed makes a huge difference in your success. As I mentioned before, the cost of acquisition of a customer is typically four to eleven times the cost of retention of a customer.

Needless to say, I can't deal with all the issues of loyalty and commitment in this book. It's already bigger than McGraw-Hill wanted it to be. What I would recommend is that you read the industry classics—Frederick F. Reichheld's *Loyalty Effect* and its sequel *Loyalty Rules*. Despite my professorial fussiness, these are great books that really cover the social, psychological, and business side of customer retention and commitment.

Loyalty Programs

There are very few of us who aren't engaged with one loyalty program or another. In fact, Maritz Loyalty Marketing reports that, based on the 2,250 loyalty programs identified in *The Cowles Report*, the loyalty program business is a $5 billion baby. For most, it means "points." I have no doubt that a significant number of you reading this book chose your credit card because of the points that you could accumulate. How many of you who fly aren't members of a frequent flyer program, probably the most successful loyalty program of all time? Of those of you who are members of a frequent flier program or twelve, how often do you make the point of flying on your favored airline, even if it's a few (but only a few) dollars more? Again, the issue that runs through your head here is an issue that loyalty always engenders. "Is flying this airline for a few dollars more worth the value of getting more frequent flier miles for this airline, or should I watch for a bargain flight, regardless of airlines, because I'm a member of twelve different frequent flier programs and will get miles from this other airline cheaper, though it is less meaningful to my targeted points accumulation?"

Don't kid yourself—the airlines, hotels, car rental companies, and others providing the loyalty programs are interested in and fully aware of your psychological state, not just your customer segment. In fact, there is an entirely new form of marketing devoted to it called "behavioral marketing." It is of prime importance for their targeted marketing to understand the type of person you are. In fact, in March 2004, the Priority Club of the Intercontinental Hotel chain developed a survey with the help of Dr. William Emener, a psychologist, and then went out and found out what personality types were accumulating points and getting deals from their loyalty program. Dr. Emener came up with six behavioral types with clever names (see Table 5-1).

Table 5-1: Priority Club Loyalty Plan Psychological Types
(Source: Priority Club Rewards, Intercontinental Hotel Group, from *The Wise Marketer*)

Classification	Percent of Respondents	Attitude to Loyalty Schemes
Sherlock	32%	Bargain hunter, get the best value
Swinger	25%	Collects any points and miles
Stasher	22%	Hoards specific points toward a dream
Snob	10%	Goes for the perks and upgrades
Shepherd	6%	Goes for the double/triple point bonuses
Slacker	5%	Indifferent, doesn't care about perks

Intercontinental Hotels was pleased with the results. The bargain hunters (the Sherlocks) are exactly the type of loyal customer they are looking for because they actually will read the deals that are being offered by loyalty programs. "The inherent trigger that makes the Sherlock search seven different stores for the best deal on a new suit also prompts him to check the websites of each major hotel program for the best point promotion before the next trip," explained Dr. Emener in *The Wise Marketer*. How often do you do that? Do you take the time? What category do you fall in? I'm somewhere between a Stasher and a Slacker. I don't care about perks unless there is one that really interests me, and then I'll work like crazy to get it. That comes along once or twice a decade.

If you only did a quick interpretation (as I did) of the chart profiles, the Sherlock wouldn't seem to be the type of behavior that is optimal for getting best results for your company, because they are prone to a "better" offer from another vendor. But this is where the cost of change and overcoming "retention inertia" come in. If you are a member of Intercontinental Hotels Priority Club and are offered deal X, even deal X+1 from somewhere else might not be enough incentive to make you want to change. So the only thing that Priority Club has to do is to make sure that if they see X+1.5 out there, they provide a similar benefit in the same category—if you are a customer of sufficient value to them. That is where the concept of best customer marketing (BCM, another acronym) comes in. Suffice it to say, it is the marketing world's equivalent of customer lifetime value. Find out who your high-value loyalty respondents are and provide them with the appropriate deals to keep them.

The Loyalty Guide, a 470-page annual report and encyclopedia of marketing methods, found that to keep these high-value customers, your offers have to fall within a certain range of categories. Their top three loyalty enrollment reasons are:

- ▶ Rewards for products and services frequently used (54 percent)

- ▶ Greater discounts on products and services (49 percent)

- ▶ Special member-only perks (42 percent)

The Types of Loyalty Programs

There are individual sole-sourced loyalty programs and there are partnered programs in the world of loyalty programs. Within the partnered programs, there are two main types of multipartner programs that have proved their value over the unpartnered programs time and time again: single operator programs that include other partners and, best of all, coalition programs, which are the most effective both in cost and availability of benefits. How do they work?

Let's make it simple. Marriott Hotels has relationships with the airlines that give you both Marriott points and frequent flier miles when you stay at a Marriott. However, you can't use the frequent flier miles for the Marriott Rewards and you can't use Marriott Rewards points for free airline tickets.

Tesco's Clubcard, which has been called the most successful loyalty program ever, generates over £100 million in incremental revenues a year. Clive Humby, quoted earlier, wrote a book on it called *Scoring Points*, well worth the read according to those I know who have read it (I haven't). Tesco, a huge grocer in the U.K., launched the Clubcard several years ago, and it is a perfect example of a single operator program that involves other partners. Tesco is the brand holder. However, Clubcard holders can collect points when buying from various partners in the program, such as Alders, Beefeater, Marriott, and National Tyres. You can redeem your Clubcard points for Vidal Sassoon products. Imagine what happens if too much Beefeaters takes you to the nearest Marriott for a room. It's about time you can get something other than a hangover for one too many! Haircare instead of head care. But this is not a coalition, because not all partners are equal—they support Tesco, the holder of the points and the brand.

Coalition programs are partnerships that are almost entirely interchangeable. Take a look at Table 5-2 for some idea on the differences.

Table 5-2: Two Types of Loyalty Programs

Single Owner, Multipartner Loyalty Programs	Coalition Loyalty Programs
A sole brand holder whose points are the only ones given out	Multiple brand holders with a customer's choice of selected points from a single brand holder as the provider
Specific partner benefits, each individually given (for example, not all partners may be redemption partners)	All privileges are the same among the various brand holders
All programs revolve around the sole brand holder	Often provides overall coalition program benefits separate from the member-specific program benefits

Loyalty programs are effective because they provide value to a member. The more value, the more likely the member is to stay a member.

Permission Marketing

Loyalty is established over time. As dicey an issue as it is, commitment and customer retention are dear. To get to commitment, there has to be a period of engagement, where the new customer is initially captured and kept, even while being assaulted on all sides by not just your competitors, but company after company with all manner of products and services. A big old blur of mass marketing aimed right at that person you want for yourself.

Permission marketing might just be the answer to sharpening that blur. This is a strategic marketing approach that was developed over the last five years to replace the mass, undifferentiated, not requested, and most typically ignored marketing that had dominated the channel waves for an endless period. The thought behind mass marketing is very much the approach that direct mailings still use. Throw thousands of mail pieces out to a semi-targeted list and be thrilled with a response rate over 1.5 percent and just go into raptures if it exceeds 3.0 percent. Don't ask permission. Send the mailing. Hope for the best.

Permission marketing is a radically different strategy that has been adopted by the more foresighted companies. While some elements have existed for a long time, usually a promotion prefaced with the phrase "would you, in consideration for X, be willing to…" the actual structure was articulated and popularized by Seth Godin, Yahoo!'s vice president of direct marketing in his now classic book, *Permission Marketing*.

Godin claimed that the average consumer sees 1 million marketing messages a year, roughly 2,800 per day. That is almost beyond comprehension—and, in fact, some of the messages are beyond comprehension: subliminal. But one thing is not at all subliminal. If you are hit with 2,800 messages a day, you are going to have a black and blue psyche. Keep in mind, Godin's estimate was in 1999. Just to highlight some more, according to Jupiter Research, just the e-mail and web-based messages alone are going to be at 5.6 billion for every 1 million subscribers by 2005.

As a company, how do you deal with your assaulted customers? Godin makes that easy—you woo them. You court them. You love them. You show them they mean something to you, but only after you ask their dad for permission to date. Godin, in fact, uses "dating the customer" as his five-step metaphor for permission marketing:

1. Offer the prospect an incentive to volunteer to receive your e-mail or other marketing media.

2. Using the attention offered by the prospect, offer a curriculum over time, teaching the consumer about your product or service.

3. Reinforce the incentive to guarantee that the prospect maintains the permission.

4. Offer additional incentives to get even more permission from the consumer.

5. Over time, leverage the permission to change consumer behavior toward profits.

This is a courtship. If it is a successful five-step courtship, the customer will be a committed lover of your products and services. They (and their dad) will appreciate that you didn't try to take advantage of them on the first date. You courted them, sent flowers, took them to classy restaurants, were polite, but always pressed ahead a little more in an inoffensive way.

Once the commitment was there, then the marriage and keeping the marriage happy became of prime importance. What do you think when you hear that Larry King had seven wives or Elizabeth Taylor eight husbands? What do you think when you know that you have been married once and you are your spouse's first spouse too? Which, for every reason, seems to be the better situation? Seven or eight spouses over time, or one spouse for life?

The issue is how you keep those customers, once you've engaged and attained them.

Opting In, Opting Out

Opting in or out is the most frequently cited permission-based marketing concept. How many times have you gone to a website and downloaded a free book or white paper, or even entered your name in a prize-winning contest? Typically, for that, you have to register online with some basic data such as name, address, phone, and e-mail address. Much of the time there will be a series of checkboxes at the bottom where you see something that says, "Please check (or uncheck) this box if you want (or don't want) to receive offers from the company and our partners." Checking the box to receive the offers is opting in. Unchecking the box or checking to not receive the offers is opting out.

Opting out, while still a widely accepted form of permission marketing, is definitely second best to opting in. For permission marketing to be optimally successful, you, the consumer or the B2B recipient, have to have control of your own destiny. Then when you do receive something, it's because you wanted to, not because it was shoved at you. That feels so much better, doesn't it?

To put it another way, opting in means that for some consideration (for example, the contest, the white paper, the discount), you allowed the company you are interacting with to send a solicitation that they expect you to take interest in. Rather than just another e-mail address, you've become a potential customer with a real existence.

Opt-in e-marketing has two functions: intelligence and engagement. The first stage, even prior to clicking your mouse on the checkbox, is the forms you fill out with information about yourself. This information is stored along with your website activity, which is monitored as you meander your way through the site. After the form is filled out, at the point that you've clicked or unclicked the checkboxes, you are engaged. Congratulations!

The benefits of opt-in are measurable. Traditional banner ad click-through rates are 0.5 percent, and traditional interruption mail is 1 percent to perhaps 2 percent at most. Click-through rates for opt-in e-mail are 7 to 10 percent as of 2003, with about 8.5 percent being the accepted norm. This is in a world where 91 percent of those having e-mail receive permission-based e-mail. Even with the clear rules of customer engagement for opt-in e-mail, opt-out e-mail is still sadly the foremost approach, pre-eminent in retail, travel, media, and financial services as well as Europe, according to studies done by Jupiter Research.

Opt-in looks so much better. In a study completed by Forrester in October 2001, 41 percent of those who get permission-based e-mail think the e-mail is a great way to learn about a product. A substantial 36 percent actually read all the permission-based e-mail they get and 9 percent actually forward it to friends if it's interesting enough. That is powerful incentive for permission-based e-mail. In 2003, DoubleClick, owner of the SmartPath product, did its annual survey of consumer behavior and permission-based e-mail and found the following purchasing and information-gathering behavior: 27 percent of those receiving relevant e-mail offers clicked through and made a purchase during that same online session; 33.6 percent clicked through to find out more information, then purchased online at a later date; 12.2 percent clicked through to find more information and then purchased offline through catalog or retail. A whopping 72.8 percent did something that led to a purchase.

But note one thing: "relevant" is a concept in this study. Not only does the e-mail have to be permission-based, it has to be useful to the recipient.

Looking at a Special Case: E-mail Marketing

E-mail marketing is both increasingly successful and increasingly a nuisance. I'm not going to waste a lot of time discussing spam in this book. You know what spam is, and what spam I'm talking about—the spam that makes you millions due to the availability of funds after the overthrow of an third-world dictator, increases your prowess in ways that this PG-13 book can't discuss, and provides you with over-the-counter drugs nearly free. We know the amount of time and effort that is being put into stopping spam, ranging from anti-spam programs and filters to proposed legislation that will hopefully have the effect that the Do Not Call list has. So enough on the nuisance side. Let's look at the actual benefits for a change.

E-mail marketing is a channel that is highly effective and increasingly so as analytics are applied to it so that the messages are increasingly personal. In fact, it is so improved that Bigfoot Interactive, in its quarterly vertical benchmark analysis for e-mail communications, found that in the first quarter of 2004 the click-through rates (CTR), one of the key measures of e-mail marketing success, for permission-based e-mail were up 21 percent in the financial services sector among others, over the fourth quarter of 2003—a remarkable jump. What makes this even more chops-licking is that personalized promotional campaigns, which might include, for example, a special price at a local outlet of a national chain, saw a universal 4.9 percent return in the first quarter 2004, up 96 percent. That's success, my children.

But it doesn't stop with CTR. Delivery rates, the measurement that identifies the successful receipt of the e-mail message sent, are at the highest ever in verticals like retail, financial services, and media. For example, in media the first quarter delivery rate was 93.3 percent and in financial services during the same period it was 92.4 percent. That attests to accuracy of the e-mail address and the likely willingness of the addressee to read the e-mail.

What makes e-mail marketing campaigns increasingly valuable for their customers is exactly what is making the customer ecosystem dominant. Individualized messages to the customer are becoming increasingly refined and effective. For example, Jupiter Research released a report in early 2004 that identified the increasing value of e-mail alerts in the online banking world. The expectation is that over 35 million American households will do some online banking by the end of 2004. By the end of the year, personalized e-mail alerts are expected to become the financial services standard as a customer service. I currently get an alert from Quicken if my personal checking account amount falls under $3,000 at any time. I get it as a pop up on my PC screen because I have 24/7 broadband coverage, but it could be just as easily an e-mail alert. The idea that I can personalize what alerts I want is immensely appealing and genuinely useful. By the way, please tell your friends to buy lots of this book so I never get that alert message again.

It is no different on the media side, with e-mailed personalized newsletters increasingly being utilized. In fact, the use of those individually specific newsletters of the "MyWhatever" genre, were up 26 percent from the final quarter of 2003 to the first quarter of 2004. So the use and value of the e-mail marketing campaign increases as the ability to personalize the messages increases.

But even though these trends are indicating an increasing success rate, that doesn't mean this is a matter of writing an e-mail or even getting your marketing department to write an e-mail and then shipping it out to a large list. There are things associated with doing marketing through this particular channel that are complicated and hair-loss inducing.

The Challenges

Because of the increases in spam and the amount of effort that each of us has to make to control it, frequency tolerance (discussed more in Chapter 9) is a prime concern for all e-mail marketers. How many times can your hopeful respondent receive an e-mail from you or, more common, a similar e-mail from competitors in combination with yours, before they get irritable and turn off all together? There are two answers to this challenge: legal compliance and best practices.

LEGAL COMPLIANCE: THE CAN-SPAM ACT

On January 1, 2004, the Controlling the Assault of Non-Solicited Pornography and Marketing (CAN-SPAM) Act became law. In the March 2004 report, Jupiter Research tracked more than 50 leading e-mail marketers in a variety of industries, including retail, travel, media, and financial services, to measure how well companies in those industries complied with the act. The majority provided a working opt-out mechanism, but a substantial amount didn't comply with all the provisions. Only 64 percent of the commercial e-mails tracked included the street address of the sender—part of the law. Over 25 percent of the marketers sent e-mails after opt-outs were submitted. In a separate study done in May 2004 by MX Logic, they found that only 1 percent of all companies were in complete compliance.

It's not just legal compliance that creates issues, though. There is a major controversy brewing around GMail, the "free" e-mail service from Google providing 1 gigabyte of free storage, far more than any other ISP offers. But in return, you have to allow relatively unobtrusive, but still visible targeted ads that get their personalized content from a scan of all your e-mail content inside and out. There is a huge debate about whether or not this is a violation of privacy, with the very privacy-conscious Steve Bass of *PC World* supporting GMail nonetheless, while privacy advocacy groups are going nuts over what they see is a violation.

For an intelligent look at some of the representative issues, I turn to Karl Wabst, CISSP and president of Eagle Mountain Computing, a superstar Internet security specialist organization:

> Even though Google says that they do not currently index the "to" or "from" fields, the amount of personal, potentially embarrassing material that exists in the body of e-mail is mind numbing. Even if we take Google's claims that the user's privacy is protected seriously, what about the privacy of those discussed in the user's messages?
>
> Another issue in the debate is the lack of clear intent regarding scanning of e-mail received by GMail users. Sending a message to a GMail user could effectively opt-in the sender without their permission. Their e-mail address or content can also be harvested and analyzed. Given 100MB of free storage, many people, ignorant of the possibilities for abuse if Google sells the business or is itself bought one day, will potentially cause problems for themselves or others.

See how complicated this gets. Even opting-in, the bastion of permission marketing, is not a safe concept with Google's approach.

BEST PRACTICES: E-MAIL MARKETING PERMISSION

There is a well-established series of best practices for permission-based e-mail marketing that cut through the mind-numbing, irritating both legal and illegal efforts of many companies:

- **Permission must be granted.** This is where opt-in is far superior to opt-out. Let's face it, those who use opt-out as their primary "permission granted" approach are actually doing two things. First, they aren't getting permission, they are not having permission withdrawn. They often survive the opt-out because the parties don't see it. It is passive and sneaky. Opt-in is active and requires an interaction from the customer to get permission.

- **There must be value to the recipient.** All business relationships through any channels are value exchanges. So self-interest, whether on a phone call or through an e-mail message, must be met.

- **Permission should be revocable.** The ability to leave the fold has to be made clear. You've seen it: "If you want to unsubscribe, click this link."

- **Permission is "privately held."** If you have permission to send e-mails to someone, you don't have permission to either give or sell that e-mail address to anyone else, including even an associated subsidiary, partner, or even a relative of the recipient.

- **The request for permission must be clearly stated.** No interaction automatically grants permission unless it is clearly expressed in writing that the act does grant permission and that the intended recipient is made aware of those terms. Opting in on a website when you download something is a good example. The address is not fair game unless the website says that downloading documents constitutes that and it is clearly visible to the downloader.

- **Opt-in should be the gold standard.** "Click here if you would like to receive our e-mail newsletter." This is the standard, and most common, method of permission. Note I'm not including opting out as a best practice.

▶ **Double opt-in should be your cutting edge approach.** This is a very good way of guaranteeing that the recipient giving you permission didn't change their mind and is the actual person. The most commonly seen version of this is when you get a verification e-mail to "activate your access" to a website. That is double opt-in. You signed up and you verified.

Enterprise Marketing Management (EMM)

The last generation business ecosystem's CRM related marketing tools were called enterprise marketing automation (EMA). EMA was the creation of personalized marketing efforts that not only engaged the customer or prospect, but also engaged the entire enterprise in the effort and provided a single view of the activity to any department or segment of the company. Not only were the subjective issues of campaign planning and management a core function of EMA, but so were the technology issues of increasing data for each customer, as were the analytics that are used to design targeted promotions at reduced cost, with increased effectiveness.

Superficially, EMA methods didn't seem very different from traditional marketing's methods. The analytics were (and are) the core difference. The tools for campaign design, execution, and real-time feedback and modification are the capabilities that bring marketing to new levels of effectiveness. EMA tools also provided a consistent, continuous representation of a value proposition across multiple channels. The field, the call center, the Web, and internal departments all saw a single view of the customer due to the tight integration between the front office and the back office.

But with the evolution of the customer ecosystem, and the increasingly expectant customer and improved economy, the costs of marketing were on the verge of skyrocketing as the conundrum of improving that individual customer experience became a core need for marketing. How do you generate the quality leads that can create opportunity for customers? And how do you provide the type of customer experience that keeps a customer interested? Needless to say, if the approach was to target every customer with a promotion without differentiation, the cost would be abusive. The ability to segment customers wasn't the only analysis that had to go on for targeting. Both the psychological types and the value of the individual customers had to be determined. It was far better to know that the plumber in Cleveland you were selling a pipe wrench to was not just a plumber in blue collar areas of Cleveland, but was a customer of multiple tools that he bought at multiple locations and a bargain hunter who could stay committed if relevant deals came his way monthly.

That's why EMM—a more strategic approach to campaigning, analyzing, and operations—is becoming a more pre-eminent way of handling the customer-driven marketing of this era. Campaign management is still its core, but a more comprehensive version than has existed in the past. Table 5-3 shows a comparison of the elements of EMA and EMM. There is no direct correlation between rows. EMM is more complex.

Table 5-3: EMA and EMM

Enterprise Marketing Automation – 2001	Enterprise Marketing Management – 2004
Identification of the prospect	Online and offline planning and execution
Generation of the lead	Integrated planning calendars (for both internal and external resources)
Prospect and customer information capture	Planning for resources, budgets, and overall departmental goals
Campaign planning	Multistep campaigns
Lead qualification	Segmentation and list management wizards
Distribution of leads to appropriate segments	Marketing event management
Campaign execution (such as promotions, events planning)	Automated response modeling (from sample segments)
Response management	Campaign test tools
Refinement	Partner/affinity program management
Channel management (for example, joint marketing campaigns)	Message broker
	Central creative repository
	Internal/external workflow and approval structure, based on roles
	Synchronization engine
	Direct connection to existing data sources

Marketing Metrics and Models: Same Old, Same Old? Nope.

Marketing analytics are not just standard customer segmentation and traditional customer valuations, although that is certainly part of the package. In the current process-driven CRM world, a look at results, for example, that show you how your leads generated by marketing campaign X led to a response rate of 4 percent and that, when drilled down, the deal closure rate was 3 percent of the 4 percent and it generated you Z revenue dollars. That gives you the chance to focus in on that segment which was responsible for 70 percent of the 3 percent of the 4 percent next time with a similar campaign. And you can run "what if" models to see how likely it is to be effective.

But unique to marketing are the loyalty indices and models that are used to measure the quality of the customer's behavior and attitudes. They can enrich the indicators of the customer's predicted value when combined with the traditional customer lifetime value measures. (See Appendix.) Here are two of the nine or ten most interesting loyalty models.

Loyalty Metrics and Models: The Enis-Paul Index

This is defined by as a consumer's inclination to patronize a given store during a specified time period. It takes into account things like the inclination of the customer to shop at a single store, the level of purchases comparing customer purchases at one store with customer purchases at another store, the inclination of the customer to spend at your company in relation to total purchases in the industry segment, and other like numbers. Totally loyal is 100 percent; totally "promiscuous" (not my term, I swear) is zero percent.

Loyalty Metrics and Models: The Hofmeyr Conversion Model

This is an analytics model that is focused on customer behaviors and attitudes. Its approach is to find out how to identify the commitments of the customer based on expressed satisfaction levels and actual repeat purchase behavior. The elements it looks at are brand equity, demographic and psychological differentiators between the customers and the noncustomers, satisfaction levels, and ambivalence. One thing that makes this model interesting is that it does a form of scenario building by using tools to anticipate the effectiveness of marketing strategies—yours and your competitors—on your customers.

The Players

The players in the EMM/MRM market are numerous, but the quality players are not. There are myriad companies that specialize in one facet or another of EMM/EMA, including campaign management, list management, database marketing, e-mail marketing, and any number of smaller niches. There are some notable ones that I will briefly mention. I'm not going to cover the enterprise-level players who have marketing modules for their suites in any detail here. Suffice it to say that Oracle, Siebel, SAP, PeopleSoft, and E.piphany all have powerful marketing modules. In fact, PeopleSoft's was Annuncio, an early millennium market leader that they acquired. All of them are solid, with E.piphany's marketing analytics worth singling out.

SAS Marketing Automation

When SAS gets it right, they get it right. There has never been any question of the quality of their analytics—they were always the best in the industry. But there had been a question of their usability. Great results, but it took multiple Ph.D.s to actually figure the product out. They spent millions on usability and released Marketing Automation 4.0. Check out Chapter 9 for more detail on this product in the Steppin' Out section, but even I can use this one. Great job by SAS. However, the SAS product is not a full EMM suite, but focused on developing deep analytics and campaign management strengths. That they do admirably.

Unica Affinium Suite

Unica's Affinium Suite 6.0 is the best EMM suite on the market. They cover the full spectrum of functions—lead generation, multichannel personalized campaign management, data mining capabilities, predictive modeling, and even a centralized marketing resource management solution, all packaged with this really easy to use, nearly intuitive interface. The interface is in fact world class, on par with PRM vendor ChannelWave's as a model for all enterprise applications. Additionally, they have a fully web services compliant platform that integrates well with other applications. A couple of years ago, a large enterprise applications vendor did an internal study of all the marketing automation vendors—Unica won hands down and they've only improved. No surprise.

DoubleClick SmartPath

When DoubleClick purchased SmartPath in March 2004, they completed the EMM cycle. Even Gartner saw this as a tremendous positive and in a note issued shortly after the acquisition said that "DoubleClick will move onto shortlists after buying SmartPath." What makes the acquisition complete is that the capabilities to automate planning, budgeting, and managing multichannel campaigns will be available with perhaps the strongest process mapping and workflow engines in the EMM world. This is where they really shine with the ability to include vendors and managers and anyone you want in the workflow requirements. The first full integration of SmartPath will show with DoubleClick Ensemble 7.0.

Aprimo Marketing

Aprimo was named the only "leader" in Gartner's February 2004 look at marketing resource management companies. I don't debate their leader slot, only whether or not other companies weren't as deserving (Unica, for example). What I also don't debate is the depth of their applications suites and the range it carries to. They are the strongest in the vertical markets such as financial services, technology, media and entertainment, pharmaceuticals, and manufacturing. But they are also incredibly process-strong in "horizontal" ways, with the only set of solutions that cover divisions that are involved in marketing. For example, they cover marketing and communications, finance for marketing budgets, what they call "customer dialogue," which is really their customer analytics and personalization applications, and, of course, the more traditional lead management, all in an XML-compliant framework. They are heavy-duty and just plain good.

STEPPIN' OUT: Quaero

Typically, I've covered companies that are vendors in my past selections. Oracle, SalesLogix, Chordiant. This is going to be the first of several deviations from that in this edition, because CRM applications are no longer data driven and CRM is a strategy, so any company that best represents the concept that I need to get across and is best in class (in my view) in doing this is going to be a Steppin' Out selection. See Chapter 11 for a different type entirely.

In marketing automation, I love SAS and Unica as applications, but Quaero is my choice for Steppin' Out. Quaero focuses on strategic marketing solutions and does them very well with a uniquely successful approach and a client list to die for. They are also up and coming on fast.

Quaero, founded in 1999 by marketing thought-leader and fellow CRMGuru Board of Experts member, Naras V. Eechambadi, was a classic solutions and projects company from its beginning. But when they diverged was when they became better than their competition. Dr. Eechambadi, because he always had a thought-leader's outlook, saw that changes had to be made: "Quaero was designed as a unique firm that could bridge the gap that often exists within many companies between IT and marketing. We started off by focusing on building world-class customer information infrastructure for large companies. However, we found out that the best infrastructure, well designed and well implemented, is not good enough if the organization is not capable of leveraging it sufficiently. As result, we now put as much emphasis on helping our clients align their measurements, processes, and organization to their strategies as we do on the data and technology side."

The culture of the company is based on customer value, but through execution, not just words. They actually rejected venture capital pretty regularly during the dot.com boom so that their financial success depended on clients paying them on the delivered value. Because of this, during the last couple of lean years, they doubled and tripled in size when most were cutting back.

Full-Service Model

Quaero provides all the services that an aspiring market share-grabbing company could want. They range from what Quaero calls Marketing Effectiveness Consulting, which covers readiness assessment, needs assessment, customer strategies, and educationals, to marketing automation and integration services, which are end-to-end implementation services such as architectural development, tool selection, customer analytics modeling, and marketing operations design and implementation. They also have MarketReady, a service devoted to the creation of the technology, systems, and training for marketing campaigns. As full scope as this is, though, none of these are the crown jewels. Quaero SpringBoard is.

Cutting Edge Services Model—Quaero SpringBoard

Quaero has a full-service approach to marketing automation that also allies them with what they consider the best-of-breed applications vendors: Unica and DoubleClick SmartPath. But what makes them interesting to the 21st century ecosystem (and me) is Quaero SpringBoard.

SpringBoard is a web-accessed, hosted relationship marketing service that provides business managers and marketing teams with solutions for managing customer and prospect information and executing effective and measurable marketing programs. This is coupled with their strategic planning services to provide an incredibly intelligent and elegant approach to a very complex part of the CRM marketplace.

SPRINGBOARD PIECES

SpringBoard is no slouch when it comes to robustness. As long as you have a clearly defined strategic plan (worked out with Quaero consultants, of course), SpringBoard gives you the means to execute that plan effectively:

▶ **Marketing Knowledge Center** This is a hosted marketing database, custom configured to handle requests and needs regardless of the channel that is used for the query.

▶ **Report Builder and Data Miner** This is a powerful, Web-based business intelligence tool that both extracts and organizes selected data and provides strong enterprise reporting tools to make the data intelligible and then turn it into actionable intelligence.

▶ **Predictive Modeler** This is a sophisticated modeling capability that programmatically selects the best fit algorithm and then automatically applies it and scores a designated file.

▶ **Campaign Manager** This provides a powerful campaign management solution to help develop, execute, and evaluate multi-channel marketing programs.

▶ **Web Portal** The user interface and central hub is an integrated web interface that accesses SpringBoard capabilities and assembles, organizes, and shares marketing knowledge.

This impressive strategic solutions approach won Quaero one of the most impressively high caliber customer lists I've seen. For example, they number Bank of America, Johnson & Johnson, Reader's Digest, Apple Computers, Starwood Hotels and Resorts Worldwide, Wells Fargo, and St. Supéry Winery among their clients. Wow. Wonder if I could meet the folks at St. Supéry?

Marketing calls for some entirely innovative approaches, as I hope I've made apparent throughout this chapter. Quaero is up to the challenge.

Okay, folks. This was a tough one. Marketers are rarely given the credit that they should get for their hard work. Maligning them is just so much easier and sometimes more fun. But the reality is that when they do good work, their creativity approaches sublime levels and I applaud them for that. When they don't, well, as I said, maligning them is just so much easier.

But it's time to move on to something that has a lot more clearly defined location in the new customer ecosystem: collaborative CRM, a.k.a. partner relationship management. The return on PRM will be obvious, so let's re-turn the page and start the next chapter.

6

....

CCRM = PRM: Not Just a Name Change

This one is important. I'm not saying everything else I write isn't important. But this is a chapter of possibly pivotal consequence. Partner Relationship Management (PRM), which had been just another category of CRM, is now becoming a core business need and one of the most important facets of a CRM strategy—if you understand where the business environment is. Important enough for me to suggest a name change that reflects the importance. CCRM. Collaborative Customer Relationship Management with the emphasis on the C.

The Basics Are Really Basic

If you are unlike me and have no short-term memory issues, you will remember that in Chapters 1 and 2, I established the business environment as a "customer ecosystem." This has its most far-reaching consequences in how business has to be conducted to work. As a well-known noncandidate for the Democratic Presidential nomination stated in her book, "it takes a village" to please a single paying client. In order for a company to meet the standards set by the multichannel savvy customer, the complex demand chain involving not just the products and services offered by the company, but the suppliers, vendors, partners, and employees must be involved to keep that customer close throughout a time when the economy is uneven and the choices for those same goods and services are wide.

The New Breed Customer

These are not your father's customers. (Unless, of course, your father owns a company and they are.) What you are dealing with here is a highly volatile customer base that holds no particular loyalty to you or your product lines or your service offerings. They have multiple choices and multiple ways of accessing those choices. They have incredible amounts of information at hand to understand what they are, or aren't, getting. They are tighter with their money. Give it up? Sure, if you can prove to me why I should go with you and not that other place a mouse click away. Think about it. Thirty-three million customers changed phone vendors in 2002. More than twice that will change carriers by the end of 2004. That's an incredible number. But let me throw more at you. In Jeffrey Gitomer's book *Customer Satisfaction Is Worthless, Customer Loyalty Is Priceless*, (Bard Press, 1998), he argues his title and then promptly disproves himself by saying that "the customer could care less (sic) about you, your company, or your company policy and EVEN LESS (his emphasis) about 'why you can't give them what they want.' They want YES or help in getting to yes and if you can't help them, they'll go somewhere else." That's a pretty accurate description of the current state of customer volatility and expectations. That's hardly a loyal customer or one that will be, though.

While my statements denying the existence of customer loyalty are incendiary to many, the fact is that loyalty is defined by the willingness to do something that may not be in your own best interest on behalf of another. That is a personal matter and tends to be defined by personal relationships. Do you know any company that you would stay with if it didn't provide you with sufficient value for you to stay? Arrangements of customer to company are defined by the exchange of value that each provides to the other. You remain a customer while that exchange is sufficient. When the company ceases providing the value that you require or when another company provides you with enough value to outweigh the costs of change, then you make the change. There is no company that isn't willing to fire you when you no longer provide them with the value they expect or to release you due to the vagaries of meeting shareholder expectations, your personal value notwithstanding. There is no company that wouldn't drop you as a paying client if they saw your value as unprofitable. This is one of the reasons that the metrics for Customer Lifetime Value (CLV) exist. It's important to know which customers are the most profitable. But it's also important to know which customers are least profitable, so they can be either cut or put aside. As a supplier, your relationship with the company you supply lasts as long as the value on your price and your ability to supply their demand in a timely way is ample. You have to make sure you provide price, product, and services in a timely and cost-effective way or the only thing you will be providing will be the crumbs on the table, because you'll be toast.

The new highly volatile customer demands that the entire value chain works in harmony to make sure they are satisfied. If there is a failure somewhere along the chain, the blame isn't on Federal Express or one of your employees. It is on your company if you haven't delivered. Another customer lost.

PRM is now a key part of making sure that the value chain doesn't lose links.

An Example of the Village

What does a channel look like? How does PRM or Collaborative CRM solve its problems? I'm going to use the example of Arrow Electronics, one of the premier national distributors of high end servers and other computer related hardware. As you know, I try to make my thinking on why I do something pretty transparent, so I'm going to briefly explain why I'm using them. There are two reasons:

▶ They are an important and significant national distributor with a well defined and easily represented channel.

▶ They used my "Steppin' Out" choice, ChannelWave, to automate their channel and they are a prime representative of how it can actually work.

Figure 6-1 shows what their channel looked like pre-ChannelWave (see Figure 6-1). Figure 6-3, later in this chapter, shows what Channel-Wave did for them. I'm going to outline the process that Arrow uses to show you what it takes to get a Hewlett-Packard server into the hands of a user via a value-added reseller (VAR). Arrow has a sector called the SBM Division that handles all Hewlett-Packard enterprise system sales. First let's see how tricky this whole process really is.

1. The VAR calls the sales and marketing rep (SMR), typically an inside sales person for pricing and configuration for an opportunity they are bidding on to run SAP.

2. The SMR uses a configurator to build the system and to price it. The configurator verifies each part's ability to work in the custom configuration. If the SMR finds something more effective, he or she may recommend another option. Once the system and pricing are complete, a quote is generated. This is turned around to the VAR in four hours.

3. The effort could take between one week and six months with up to twelve separate configurations. Continuous discussions and reconfigurations and repricings are going throughout the process. Engineers may be involved for technical issues that may arrive or for verification to the customer and the end-user.

4. As the process is being completed, Arrow works with the VAR to find the appropriate vehicles for financing, either directly through the VAR's credit or through Arrow's financing options.

5. Since 70 percent of all the opportunities have special pricing at some level, Arrow works with the vendor to secure the special pricing so that business is either won or the sales process is accelerated if it isn't competitive.

6. The VAR closes the deal.

7. The VAR submits a purchase order to the SBM division.

8. The SBM division verifies that configuration and the costs are correct—which is very inaccurate because of the lengthy sales cycle. With that lengthy process, the prices and the parts may change over the time. Some quotes may be price protected, but if the price goes up Arrow can often go back to vendor for special pricing.

9. Once this happens, the SMR works with Hewlett-Packard's field rep to get that special pricing.

10. The SMR then works with HP's customer service reps (CSRs) who receive the purchase orders, make sure the order is entered correctly, make sure that the order is included in the manufacturing schedule, get the SMR a ship date, and stay on top of it until it arrives at destination's door. Arrow can also track it directly, because the VAR ordinarily checks with Arrow, not HP. The SMR gives the VAR a heads-up that it's on its way. Arrow uses an internal system called iTrack to do this.

11. If the customer needs it sooner than the HP ship date, Arrow gets involved in expediting the shipment.

12. HP then builds to order and ships to either the VAR (to integrate) or even to the end-user so that the VAR can integrate the hardware, software, and/or the network on the customer site. Sometimes Arrow will do the integration (though more frequently for IBM and Sun) at its Phoenix integration facility.

13. The VAR ships product to the end-user, if it has been shipped originally to the VAR.

14. Arrow registers the warranty for the end-user with HP and gets service registered (for telephone support, software support, and so on).

15. Arrow invoices the VAR.

16. The VAR invoices the end-user.

17. Arrow collects from the VAR.

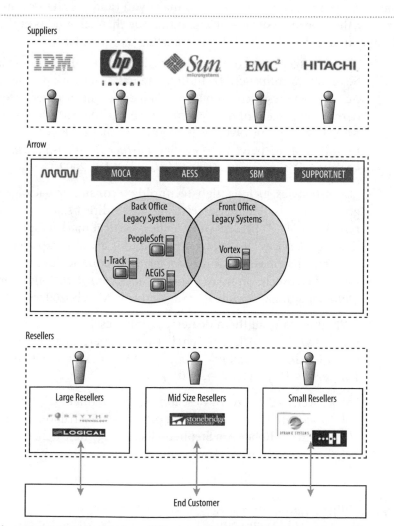

Figure 6-1: Arrow's channel prior to PRM strategy and implementation

Think through what you just read. This is what it takes to get a server into the hands of an end-user through a channel that engages a distributor, reseller, manufacturer, integrator, a set of internal departments (finance, engineering, and so on), and a lot of automated fire power. Imagine if there is one glitch in the chain. A multimillion-dollar bid could be lost.

Channeling That Energy

It's clear that it takes an extended value chain of partners, suppliers/vendors, and employees to make you (and me) happy. But frankly, that's been no surprise to either the true channel pundits or the bean counters. Look at the following startling comments:

- ▶ "By 2010, 65 percent of revenue for Global 2000 enterprises will be driven or influenced by indirect demand-network partners. According to research from Booz Allen & Hamilton, enterprises derived 40 percent of their revenue from partners in 2000—up from 15 percent in 1990. By 2010, this number is likely to grow to as high as 65 percent." (Gartner. *Partner Relationship Management: Optimizing the Demand Networ.* May, 2002.)

- ▶ "In industries such as high-technology, consumer packaged goods, and discrete manufacturing, the indirect sales process represents 60–70 percent of revenues. Vertical markets such as financial services and telecommunications are also experiencing a rapid increase in the percentage of revenue achieved from indirect channels." (Yankee Group. *The Bottom-Line Impact on Optimizing Your Channel Partner Network.* March, 2002.)

- ▶ "Whether you call them dealers, agents, resellers, or brokers, indirect sales channels represent between 40 percent and 70 percent of many companies' revenue." (AMR Research. *Channel Partners for Profit.* October, 2001.)

- ▶ "Moreover, by 2004, AMR Research expects indirect sales channels to account for 70 percent of a projected $5.7 trillion in B2B eCommerce." (Robertson Stephens Technology Research. *Channel Commerce Software.* April, 2001.)

Look at those numbers, forty percent, sixty-five percent, seventy percent. The most fantastic is the last: 70 percent of a projected $5.7 trillion in B2B e-commerce. That's roughly $4 trillion.

With the blatant dependence that the business world has on indirect channels, you would think that PRM is the largest CRM segment. It isn't and doesn't seem that it will be over the next few years. However, it is the pivotal CRM segment if enterprises that are part of the $4 trillion have even the slightest inkling of what it takes to manage the value chain that is going to produce that extraordinary and business life–dependent volume of revenue.

Let's drill it down a bit further, so you can see how important the channel is to a single industry.

Industry Examples: The IT World, Familiar, but Not Warm or Fuzzy

According to IDC and industry media, indirect channels will play a growing role in a company's short- and long-term financial success. For example, industry data for the information technology sector indicates that:

- Worldwide, 40 to 60 percent of all IT spending flows through indirect channels.

- By 2005, more than $100 billion of all servers, nearly 60 percent, will be delivered via indirect channels.

- By 2005, sales of server and storage devices delivered via indirect channels will have a three-fold compound annual growth rate (CAGR) versus direct channels.

- 69 percent of networking equipment is supplied through indirect channels.

- By 2005, more than $123 billion—more than 40 percent—of all software spending will be through indirect channels.

- 59 percent of all software sales in North America are *influenced* by a third party.

Influenced. That is a very important, increasingly recognized value in the world of channel management and partner cooperation. In a study done by Ed Keller and Jon Berry in their excellent book, *The Influentials*, it is noted that when buying computer equipment, 40 percent of their survey respondents depend on people they know (the highest percentage), while only 18 percent are influenced by advertising. In fact, Bill Gates said it very well: "The key to any phenomenon in personal computing is word of mouth." Measuring the influencers' indirect value is important because, as any of you considering a PRM solution know, both referrals and collaboration among partners is an essential revenue source.

Gartner Dataquest says, "On average, channel partners influence 66 percent of all specific brand or product purchases bought through the channel." CMP Media found even more startling results: 70 percent of high-tech purchases go through resellers and the end customer accepts 96 percent of the resellers' recommendations. This increases the complexity of managing the partner organization. The relationships alter significantly. How does the brand holder, the organization that owns the products and services the channel is selling, handle influencers as opposed to those doing sales directly?

To situate PRM even more effectively, let's examine it from the other end of the customer, the brand holder that the partner works with. Keep in mind that a partner might be working with the brand holder and five (or twenty-five) of his competitors. It isn't uncommon to see large and small integrators, for example, working with PeopleSoft, Oracle, SAP and Siebel, and perhaps smaller vendors.

Microsoft's New Partner Program

I'm sure that at some point, you've dealt with Microsoft. If you haven't, do me a favor, and install electricity in your home, because it's been harnessed for the good of mankind.

One way or the other, at work, most of us have used Outlook, Word, Excel, PowerPoint, MSN Messenger, Windows ME, XP, 2000, Mobile 2003, or their small business solutions like Great Plains, Navision, and of course, MSCRM. Or, if we are IT professionals, we've used Exchange, SQL Server, Sharepoint Server, Small Business Server, and dozens of administrative and development tools. If we're computer illiterate or semi-smart, as consumers we've logged on to www.msn.com, played with the Xbox, or listened to MP3s on MS Media Center XP. At the very least, we've watched MSNBC. In other words, they are omniscient and omnipresent.

What you don't know is what kind of channel Microsoft depends on to get those products and services to you. Let's look at the cold hard facts. As of late 2003, they have 775,000 business partners—300,000 in the United States. They have 33,000 certified partners globally, of which 11,000 are in the United States. They have 6,000 certified business solutions partners—those who are qualified to bring you MSCRM (see

Chapters 12 and 24). They have 2000 gold certified partners (600 in the United States) who have met the criteria of being certified in all major categories. Now the real shocker. Ninety-five percent of Microsoft revenue is from this channel. Of their $32.2 billion in fiscal year 2003 revenue, they depend on the channel for $30.6 billion of it. Think about it. If they depended strictly on themselves they'd be a mere stripling of $1.6 billion—in fact, that is pretty much the amount they spend on their channel programs.

Now imagine how unwieldy it is to manage these 775,000 partners with the 2003 number of 54 different partner programs. As of 2004, they are moving to consolidate that to one program over an 18-month period, but with partner numbers of that magnitude, it is going to be a daunting task. I'm sure they're up to it.

How Does the Microsoft Spider Do It?

Microsoft's new partner program is intelligently based on the needs of customers, rather than the revenue produced by partners. For example, Microsoft developed a competency framework that allows the partners to individually define their own areas of expertise, such as Microsoft Business Solutions, Advanced Infrastructure Solutions, or Learning Solutions. There are 11 competency areas that the partner can choose from, each with a unique set of requirements and each differentiable within the competency. The partner can define their proficiency with each domain they associate with. But it doesn't stop there. There are multiple certifications that are required for the higher level partner programs, and they vary and are applicable within the competencies. Some examples:

- ▶ Microsoft Certified Systems Engineer

- ▶ Microsoft Certified Solutions Developer

- ▶ Microsoft Certified Applications Developer

- ▶ Microsoft Certified Trainer

- ▶ A large variety of Microsoft Business Solutions certifications (such as the soon to appear MSCRM certification or a Great Plains certification)

This is only a small sampling of the possible individual and business certification Microsoft makes available, and each is applicable (for the most part) to each competency.

To add fuel to the flames, there are three partner levels that go beyond competency ratings or certification levels. They are Microsoft Registered Members, Certified Partners, and Gold Certified Partners, who have met the requirements for specific solution competencies. So imagine this. You have 775,000 partners of which 33,000 are certified and 2000 Gold Certified. In between there, you have hundreds, perhaps thousands, of partners going through various certification processes so they can move up a notch in partner status. To complicate it even more, you can enroll an entire enterprise as a single entity or break it down into multiple partnerships under multiple IDs. Or you could enroll a single office of a multioffice company on behalf of the entire company or just that office, depending on how you want to have Microsoft treat you.

To make it even more spider-web enabled, among other things, Microsoft has to track the program status of each partner, the revenue numbers, the lead distribution, the collateral distribution, the product inventories, the appropriate related customer accounts, the use of co-marketing funds, Customer Advisory Council activities (available for certified and Gold Certified partners), the training both online and offline, the applications use for the Microsoft Action Packs, which provide you with usable not-for-resale software, the contracts and service level agreements associated with those partners, the performance metrics associated with the partners' sales activity, and the cooperation between partners. It has to distinguish between the partners providing direct revenue and those influencing sales, yet reward each of them. It has to make sure that partners have specific information made available to them based on these multiple criteria, but at the same time, protect the information of each of the partners from the others. So visibility and opacity are both important facets of a collaborative CRM strategy. It has to provide all these services through multiple media such as the Web, direct mail, print, e-mail, fax, in person, and phone. In fact, one of the benefits of both certified and Gold Certified partnerships is the (as they call it) "at least phone based management" that Microsoft will supply to their elite partners.

In other words, we are dealing with a huge volume of partners that each have individual needs, desires, concerns, information, and requirements to sustain their partnerships, all of which Microsoft must micromanage without micromanaging—because if they don't, they have micro-revenue.

This doesn't even account for how they handle their partner account managers or their suppliers or vendors.

So not only does it take a village to deliver products and services to businesses and consumers, it takes a kingdom and a substantial global administration to make it even feasible. And when 95 percent of your revenue depends on this complicated spider web, believe me, you'll do what you have to so that it does work.

But there is more than just this extended, beautiful web of spun greenbacks working effectively.

Many to Many Does Not Equal Mano a Mano

The complexity of this vast partner network doesn't stop with the brand holder-partner-customer relationships. It goes considerably deeper than that one-to-one or one-to-many focus identified in the prior sections. When it gets down to its deepest recesses, it goes to the many-to-many interactions. What are they? Let's start with Chris Heidelberger, president of PRM industry-leading applications provider ChannelWave:

> A many-to-many architecture supports the highly complex and fast-changing nature of partner collaboration and must enable direct, spontaneous interactions among numerous partners. In addition, a many-to-many architecture allows partners to initiate collaboration with complementary partners to dynamically form teams spanning multiple organizations while providing vendor visibility into partnering activities.

So, what I hear in this is that it allows not just brand-owner-to-partner, but partner-to-partner relationships within the brand holder's matrix. That means we can establish partner teams for appropriate tactical selling to a single opportunity or strategic partner relationships for providing a long-term complementary service. The latter could be something like the 2003 IBM/Siebel partnership that created the hosted CRM service for the small and medium business market called CRM OnDemand.

But there are a number of other strands that come into the many-to-many web besides this. For example, each partner not only teams with other partners within the universe of the brand holder, but they could actively be involved with the same partners or others within a different brand holder network. For example, IBM has a relationship with Onyx for CRM services also.

Additionally, they could have permanent relationships or temporary alliances with direct competitors to the brand holder. For example, IBM has PeopleSoft, SAP, Oracle, and Siebel practices.

They could be a brand holder themselves. IBM has a vast partner network of its own—more than 90,000 global business partners and 17,500 in just their distribution channel. They have brand-holding relationships with companies that have their own channels. So they will ally with companies like Siebel or Accenture or Bearing Point or PeopleSoft. They also ally with companies that are smaller and aggressive on specific bids or in specific implementations without bringing them into their formal alliance structure.

Welcome to the world of many-to-many in the channel. But it doesn't stop there.

Is There No Rest?

To add one more step, the emergence of the business value chain from the 21st century demand and supply chain coupling makes the channel even more complicated. It now is not just the partner network that provides you revenue enhancement directly and indirectly, but also the logistics network, the company's suppliers and its delivery networks (such as Federal Express and UPS) that can be part of this comprehensive enterprise.

Take it one final step, and many-to-many adds another level of flavor and becomes even more perplexing. Some partners will provide direct revenue. Other partners will provide product add-ons. Other partners will provide distribution channels for other partners. While the programs and metrics for measuring the success of these types of partners are clear-cut, how do you measure the important value of the influencer partners?

Isn't this a daunting structure? How can you strategically, technically, and functionally manage the incredible process and structure depth that would be needed to do this? That is what PRM or the new generation Collaborative CRM is for. So be of good cheer. It all becomes clear by the end of this chapter.

How to Succeed in Business by Really Trying Hard

Clearly, this level of business complexity involves a collaborative effort—the development of a set of strategies that are supported by applications deeply embedded into core CRM processes: sales, mar-keting, and support. So, *qui bono*? Who benefits—or more correctly, who could benefit—from PRM and a collaborative strategy?

Issues? Sure, We Got Issues

Companies have problems. They have business problems, they have relationship problems, they have broken processes, collection issues, and, most important to PRM, they have dysfunctional channel rela-tionships, which given the revenue-codependent status that most of the Global 2000 and others have, can be deadly. Some of the most bla-tant indicators of the PRM-needy are:

- ► Lack of collateral and collateral access to partners who always need it

- ► Failure to offer training to partners on the products and services they sell for you

- ► Poorly motivated partners—no incentive or reward for influ-encing sales, developing add-on products, taking advanced train-ing, or successfully teaming with other members of the channel

- ► Failure to co-sell or co-market with the partners in any system-atized way

- ► Failure to provide partners with benchmarks, metrics, compet-itive information, or tools that will benefit them either strategi-cally or opportunistically

- ► Inability to clearly measure partner performance

- ► Inability to provide your partners with appropriate visibility into your customer network and vice versa

- ► Poor communication with partners with few avenues

- ► Obvious partner favoritism that is more ad hoc than it is pro-grammatically determined

There are certainly other signs of the channel-challenged, but these are good indicators of a dysfunctional channel.

Now that we have some of the issues on the table, who are the can-didates, with or without these issues?

The Candidates

The candidates for PRM are pretty much everyone who deals formally with companies outside their own company, a.k.a. a channel. That means partners and, in the current incarnation of the business world, the suppliers and vendors are all part of a complex network of relationships that needs to be managed, one way or the other. For example, McDonald's has a combination of both owner-operated stores and company-owned stores, each of which has regionally defined menus, promotions, objectives, and programs. While the overall theme has to be consistent nationally, it still has to reflect the regional themes and "cuisine" such as lobster rolls in New England or saimin, a fish cake noodle soup, in Hawaii. At the same time, owner-operators work differently than company-owned stores and are held to a different set of objectives, though the same overall standard. McDonald's is a serious candidate for PRM.

Other possible PRM-ripe channel-focused organizations:

▸ **Insurance companies that use independent agents across the country** What makes this particularly intriguing is that the agents often don't just represent a single insurance company but multiple different companies for multiple products (see the earlier discussion on many-to-many relationships).

▸ **Car manufacturers with thousands of dealerships** Each dealership has multiple products, extensive delivery, logistics, and warehousing issues. Think about the value of PRM here. There can be huge margins on the servicing and maintenance of automobiles. In order for that to remain a margin-happy endeavor for a dealership, there has to be a close relationship with the manufacturer over at least a five-year period so that the customer satisfaction remains strong and the brand association with that satisfaction remains "top of mind." This smacks of a channel that needs to work as well as a luxury car.

▸ **Product companies with both sales teams and manufacturers reps** This makes for a similar situation to McDonalds, a combination of corporate sales and independent representatives who carry the banner for other companies too. One example would be a company like Maytag, which sells directly to larger retailers and also has a series of smaller retailers and will sell directly online.

▶ **Value-added resellers** An important part of any industry, VARs are the companies that not only buy products, but provide additional services and products that they develop related to those they sell. For example, they might make a connector to Siebel that ties in the SalesLogix applications from the front end and provide the product and the services for that. Each of the VARs isn't necessarily connected to just one company. They each could have a network of value-added resellers of their own, making the relationships quite intricate. For example, companies like Data Management Group (DMG), sell multiple business intelligence products (Cognos, Crystal, etc.) and services.

PRM Strategic Thinking

PRM strategy is similar to CRM strategy, which is covered thoroughly in Chapter 17, but has a few distinguishing characteristics. PRM needs more than just an internal strategic effort. Its stakeholders don't only include the CxOs and power users; it includes the partners, more than just as opinion givers. So when we talk of a PRM strategy, we're talking about a channel strategy for the value chain. You can't ever think of a PRM implementation before you plan for a successful effort with your channel. *The purpose of a PRM strategy, and please pay close attention here, is to utilize partners to provide a satisfactory brand experience from end to end for the customer.* That means enriched products and services in combination with opportunistic sales activity. It means that your customers in this effort are your paying clients and your partners. You may be the brand holder with the keys to the kingdom. But your partners are your generals and supporting armies that will provide you with the scope and strength to provide the great customer experience you need for your business to boom—or survive.

Collaborative Grand Strategy = Strategy and Tactics

There are both strategic and tactical reasons for a PRM collaborative strategy.

First example (tactical) META Group did a study in 2003 that found that for enterprises that depended on channel partners, almost 70 percent of the leads that were distributed to the partners were not pursued at all. That means that lost opportunities abounded, even if a few percentage points panned out, and a likelihood of millions of dollars were lost because the brand holder was unable to follow through on the distributed leads until it was too late or maybe even never. Products companies that have inventory are particularly vulnerable here because inventory management costs and excess inventory can be a crippling expense. If some of the leads became opportunities which then became sales, those costs are reduced and the inventory is cleared and revenue is up.

Second example (strategic)   There are often problems managing the existing partner network. Stretching it a bit, it could be called partner retention problems. An IDC study found that 36 percent of all the problems that resellers have with their partners are related to poor sales and technical support and the difficulty of doing business that can engender interpartner conflict. By using program management features that are the core of PRM, these issues can be avoided, though a clear-cut partner program strategy has to be in place prior to the use of the technology. The corollary issue here is the highly fragmented nature of many of those same partner programs. Microsoft is an indicator of that very issue. Think about it. While Microsoft is making a heroic effort to consolidate their programs to a single program with multiple facets, the fact is that they had 54 programs prior to this Herculean consolidation. Unfortunately, it's a lot easier to defragment a hard drive than it is a partner program. But the value of doing it is huge and is recognized by companies like ChannelWave, Comergent, Siebel, and a very few others. Oddly, there are only a few players left in this market that could become a $4 or $5 billion market by the midpoint of the 21st century's first decade.

The Shadchen Strategy: Doing More than Feeling Good

Shadchen is a Yiddish term for matchmaker. Back in its heyday, it was actually a profession—a pro who would match a potential bride with a groom. It was honored and honorable and pretty lucrative for the *Shadchen*. Now, who knows a *Shadchen*?

The *Shadchen* Strategy matches potential partners with brand holders and other partners. While this may seem to be an easy or almost automatic process, it isn't. It is a channel strategy that recognizes not just services, products, and demographics of a channel partner, but also their cultural characteristics. When done well, the criteria are flexible guidelines for cultural alignment of partners with the brand holder and each other. They are not rigid, because no two cultures are identical. They can only be compatible.

When cultural characteristics are taken into account with the channel strategy, future partner churn is minimized, because the chances of a successful relationship have been qualified by the strategy.

This approach suggests programs and incentives once the culture and business model that the brand holder is looking for is identified. For example, in 2001, Cisco revamped their channel program when they realized that one of the planned objectives for the partner program needed to be support for a sustainable business model that could deliver high value services, not just products. So they established a mandatory certification program, a customer satisfaction index that partners had to participate in, and specialized training in several areas that was geographically granted so that Cisco had the most effectively dispersed value for its customers. Part of the strategy prior to implementation of this new value-added program was to identify the existing highest value partners, extract their best practices, and make them available to the partner community at large. This way, the relatively underperforming partners could see the cultural and business values that the top players were using. It is very successful.

Features and Functions

There is an industry complaint (not an uncommon occurrence) that PRM doesn't provide the levels of sales, marketing, and support functionality that the pure versions of those CRM-related systems do. True. But they provide enough to make the overall CRM capabilities of PRM a contender because of the many-to-many related functions that it provides. Frankly, you could implement a PRM solution and if you didn't need a lot of customization in sales, marketing, or support, you could be perfectly happy with it. Though if you aren't using the PRM capabilities, you've overkilled, my friend.

For example, some of the more common functions include:

- ▶ **Lead management** This is the place where the sales pipeline opens. Lead generation and distribution start from this module. Actually this is an extremely important and well thought-out part of most PRM applications due to the complexity of the workflow associated with proper partner lead distribution.

- ▶ **Opportunity management** Opportunity management is not just a simple jump up from lead management but also encompasses metrics to measure, and the means to monitor active sales. This provides visibility for the brand holder into the partner pipeline. Important, indeed.

- ▶ **Marketing** Here is where the partners participate in marketing campaign management and to their great joy, marketing funds distribution. Again, notice here the additional richness of the classic application. Comarketing funds distribution and closed loop campaign management get complicated when you are dealing with thousands of partners. For example, ask the question, which partners should be involved in this campaign and at what level? Should they be included by name? Should we reach their lists? Should they be cosponsors? *Ad infinitum.*

- ▶ **Planning** Planning for partner networks is aligning the business and revenue goals one partner at a time with the overall revenue goals. It requires an understanding of each partner's business model and level of participation in your partner program and their ability to align them with your corporate objectives. That's just to begin to think about the planning.

- ▶ **Reporting** This is one of the mission-critical features of PRM, as much as or more so than "standard" CRM. Improper reporting means missed opportunities, lost revenue, unreaped rewards for the partner. It is not just badly formatted paper. It is an organized means of tracking partner performance which can then be weighed and found either useful or wanting.

- ▶ **Analytics** Demographic and partner analysis are essential features. For example, by segmenting Microsoft's partner base, Microsoft knows which partners are available for what and how to weigh their value in any particular opportunity so that the opportunity is provided to the best team for the maximum chance of closure and success.

- ▶ **Services and support** At one level this means automated and other centralized call centers and technical helpdesks. The value to partners for both internal purposes and for their customers is incalculable. But more specifically, it involves how to handle training and certification, how to distribute the co-op and development funds for marketing or how to make sure that crucial collateral is in the hands of key teams of partners.

Other one-to-many classic, but more specifically PRM functions are:

► **Partner recruitment** Applications, qualification, and program selection are the hallmark of this important facet of PRM. Pick the wrong partner and what you saw watching *The Ring* was not half as bad as what you will see with the partner you incorrectly choose. PRM can automate the selection process and provide tools that can help you choose intelligently.

► **Content and document management** Getting the right collateral and information to partners and providing them with the access to the appropriate internal information means substantial workflow to set the rights and permissions. It means available libraries that have audit trails so that the actual document flow can be traced, partner-by-partner. It means finding the information via multiple communications channels. Imagine the body of work that Microsoft turns out between itself and its partners and paid collaborators in any given year and you can begin to see the value of this feature set.

► **Training and certification** Training sounds reasonably simple, right? Wrong. It is a very complex piece of managing partners. First, considerations have to be given for whether the partner qualifies for the training, either due to the nature of the partner, the level of the program they are engaged in, or some incentives they've earned. Then the type of training that the partner is taking is important. Clearly, if the partner is a specialist in Microsoft Business Solutions, training in systems administration for its sales teams isn't too swift. The next concern is what the partner company or individual earns once the training is completed. In fact, the results can affect the partner profiles and attributes associated with the workflow in a way that makes changes in the kinds of leads or campaigns they receive. Especially if certification in products or services is involved, the automation of those processes isn't easy because the qualifications often differ. The testing mechanisms and tests themselves have to be administered and feedback provided. The means of delivering the training (online or offline) is another issue. If offline in person or via direct mail? This is a very complex and very important part of partner relationships.

▶ **Targeted partner-communications** If you enter a well-designed partner portal under your designated ID and password, you will find messages and information in several categories. How well you are performing to plan and what needs to be done about it. The latest program incentives. And if you call now… How much is that doggy or any other product in the window to the partner and what price point is the sale? General news that fits the partner's profile. Specific news for that partner alone. Requests for meetings. New collateral available to your organization because of what you do and how well you've performed. In other words, targeted partner communications. Imagine what kind of analysis and history must be extracted and addressed to make these determinations. Now imagine it for Microsoft's 775,000 partners—each as a separate entity.

▶ **Contract management** Now take those 775,000 partners and have each of them sign a contract that differs depending on the program level they commit to, the type of company they are, and any specific terms they have negotiated. Imagine tracking the compliance to that contract. PRM once again to the rescue, if it's done well.

But PRM functionality extends beyond CRM, potentially far beyond as the PRM applications market matures and redefines itself. In a mature model, PRM has the capacity to provide a coordinated many-to-many experience so that customers and partners are interacting with the brand holder and each other productively in areas such as planning, relationship management, reporting, marketing, sales, and collaborative forecasting.

PRM is a rising star in the world of managing cooperative models. Its ability to enable multitiered and complex business relationships eclipses its more established brother, CRM, here and provides what CRM misses in the dynamic world of the many-to-many.

For example, where program planning, development, and execution might seem to incorporate one-to-many functions (that is, enterprise to partners), in PRM it is based on a dynamic collaborative model because of the fluid relationships between partners. While partner goal planning involves developing appropriate benchmarks, metrics, and incentives to measure individual partner performance against objectives for the brand holder, it also needs to develop metrics, benchmarks, and rewards for collaborative partnering efforts. CRM can't do this without massive customization, but PRM vendors often can, sometimes out of the box. It provides the means to set up reward systems for multitiered partner cooperation. It handles monitoring presales, sales, and postsales activities in a structured way. *PRM is designed for a successful collaborative business model.* Traditional CRM is not. Period.

The Architecture

That's all well and good from the functional side, but what about the technical? The business model that drives Collaborative CRM (CCRM), a.k.a. PRM (and thus begins the transition), is the customer ecosystem. That means that the paying clients and the partners (and others) are treated as customers. What kind of enterprise architecture makes this work (because classic CRM architecture supports a one-to-many business model, not a many-to-many version)? CCRM's business model is a distributed network of partners who are involved in multiple networks themselves, where they are seen as part of an extended sales force and technical community. The partners are providing value-added services and products to this entire distributed network, not just the brand holder. How does one provide an enterprise technical framework to handle this rather complex milieu?

Clearly the core issue is both data and process integration and communications between the data, processes, and the companies themselves. Think of it this way. Partner A has business model A and a PeopleSoft Human Resources System along with PeopleSoft Sales CRM. Partner B has business model B and an SAP Financials back office with Siebel Call Center. Partner C has business model C and is small so they use Great Plains and MSCRM for support. The brand holder is standardized on Oracle.

By using a standardized web architecture increasingly integrated with web services, a common data format can be established to take advantage of the data that the different systems provide. This cross-system data exchange is a necessary component of a many-to-many collaborative architecture so that partners can communicate with brand holders and other partners in standard, recognizable, and easily integrated data formats. XML is currently the standard most frequently employed.

Because the integration issues are so dicey, web architectures are the frameworks that most contemporary PRM packages worth paying attention to are using. They are ordinarily XML-compliant, J2EE-compliant, and often .NET-compliant, as the new Microsoft web services framework gains traction. Many of them are SOAP-compliant too. They should have enterprise application integration (EAI) tools that allow the customer or integrator to build connectivity to other CRM applications or the back office such as SAP, PeopleSoft, or Oracle.

But this many-to-many architecture also has a compound set of specialized requirements, not the least of which is siloed security. Each partner's data and intellectual capital must be protected, while still allowing the brand holder to contrast and compare the data from multiple vendors. This is accomplished, by the better vendors, through a combination of permissions-based collaboration, governed by the brand holders, which exposes only specific information to specific people or groups who have the rights to see that information; secure single sign-on, so that the user only sees what he or she is authorized to see via the enterprise portal; and the use of secure protocols such as SSL or HTTPS or both.

Portals: Gateways to Partner Paradise

Perhaps the most effective way to manage the shared and siloed information that each partner is privy to is through partner portals such as those provided by ChannelWave and Onyx. In a study on partner lifecycle management, Gartner found that 52 percent of all the enterprises surveyed had adopted portals as their communications center. What is striking is that 48 percent *didn't*. How did those particularly shortsighted brand holders present their information to their partners? A mystery wrapped in an enigma to say the least.

By having a single point of entry with a specific ID and password, each partner is able to see a customized individual view of information that is relevant to them and not viewable by others, except of course permitted things such as a common library of available collateral. The interface, if done well (see Figure 6-2 for a glimpse of the interface) is an easy to navigate and use, information-friendly entry point for real-time updated information that helps the partner do what they are there to do: move services and product. The partner is the customer that the brand holder's portal serves.

Obviously, because of the complexity of the many-to-many relationships and the partner programs levels, the workflow engine must be virtually magnificent to do the job right. It has to handle multiple and flexible roles and permissions and be able to segment the partner community, partner by partner. But the partner has to be shielded from this automated power and, in fact, needs to have an enjoyable experience with the effort. There is actual value in a little bit of wow-like sex appeal with the ease of use of the interface. Frankly, given that partner companies are composed of the same species as most companies (with a few exceptions)—human beings—there is no harm in making sure the experience of using the portal to access the relationship between the brand holder and the company is enjoyable. This portal is not meant to be a passive gateway to static information. It is a dynamic reflection of the relationship between the brand owner and the partner. It should be a major consideration when choosing a PRM solution.

PRM Then

In its early incarnations, PRM's primary benefit seemed to be improved efficiencies of various stripes and hues:

- ► Cost reduction
- ► More efficient use of resources—in other words, partners
- ► Streamlining of channel-focused business processes
- ► Improved product distribution effectiveness
- ► Improved communications
- ► Optimized channel program management

Initially, PRM was seen as a "horizontal" CRM application lumped into the same class as sales force automation (SFA), enterprise marketing automation (EMA), analytics, and others of that categorical ilk. What became increasingly noticeable was that PRM offerings were typically missing from the major multisuite CRM vendors. It was left to best-of-breed upstart vendors to meet the functional needs of the potential customer base. In a conversation with the then general manager of one of the largest enterprise vendors, I asked why he hadn't acquired a PRM company to fill the clear hole in the suite. His answer was telling: "PRM is so absolutely integral to the overall processes of any company, we're going to have to build it from the ground up to make sure that it integrates well with the rest of our applications." That statement reflected the awareness that PRM was different from the other horizontal applications. SFA, EMA, and such could be implemented without necessarily impacting every business process of a company. However, that wasn't the case with PRM—it is more than just another CRM subset. PRM's value proposition promised to be unique. It was.

PRM had something that traditional CRM didn't: the ability to handle many-to-many relationships, which is essential to managing partners or collaborators of any kind. That is now a really big deal in the new customer ecosystem. PRM is one of the few applications that can handle this very difficult matrix and also be reasonably assured of handling the more traditional one-to-one and one-to-many relationships.

Collaborative CRM Now

However, the combination of a PRM model simulation done by Gartner Group in 2001 and some eye-popping results from an AMR Research study in early 2002 burst the "efficiency bubble"—in a good way. Despite wildly disparate methodologies, both studies proved that PRM's major benefit was revenue enhancement, though all the benefits of PRM cost savings and process optimization remained intact.

AMR's research was straightforward. They found that in the companies they studied, 40 to 70 percent of the revenues were driven by the channel. This is a very significant number and reflects the value of having a channel. Specific early adopters of PRM such as Cable & Wireless, PTC, and Cisco saw a significant increase in their overall revenues through the use of PRM. Cisco's order error rate went down from 40 percent to 6 percent, and productivity increased by 15 percent—a direct impact on the bottom line of the company. At Cisco, 92 percent of their revenues is channel-driven, making this productivity increase extremely important to their bottom line

After deploying a global PRM solution, Cable & Wireless, the telecommunications giant, increased its partner sales pipeline by 50 percent and reduced its lead close time from weeks and months to days and hours. Partners say the PRM deployment "differentiates C&W from other carriers." PTC, which manufactures product development software, used its PRM solution to grow from supporting one channel partner to 175 active partners in one year, without hiring additional staff, and increased channel-based sales revenue from 15 percent of total to 23 percent. The company has also cut its partner recruiting costs and reduced the time to sign up a partner from one week to one day.

Gartner's PRM model simulation was considerably more complex, but equally as telling. They assumed a manufacturing company with 50 partners. Without going into too much detail, they found that of the total PRM benefit, 21 percent was cost savings and fully 79 percent was revenue enhancement.

ROI Means King in French and Bottom Line in English

PRM is the single most quantifiable value in the CRM world. According to an April 2003 Gartner report, companies deploying PRM solutions are receiving a much stronger return on their investment than those deploying *any other* CRM application. Sixty-six percent of all executives surveyed identified a clear ROI from their PRM deployments. This compares for example, with CRM sales suites (see Chapter 4) which had 48 percent of the executives waxing enthusiastically.

In mid-2002, Accenture commissioned a survey that found that over 80 percent of the executives responded that the channel would be a major source of their revenue. This viscerally confirmed both of the above-mentioned AMR and Gartner studies.

The ROI on PRM is also eminently quantifiable. Each partner's revenue number or their improved lead to opportunity numbers are easy enough to measure and PRM provides the tools to do just that.

But when managed well, the results can be similar to those achieved by PTC and Cable & Wireless. There are dozens of other scenarios that could be spun, such as:

- ▶ At 30–40 percent less than the cost of selling direct, channel partnerships can help vendors rapidly achieve superior market coverage and increased revenues. (Frank Burkitt and Associates)

- ▶ Several statistics show the financial impact that a well-executed PRM program can have on a company. Eighty percent of the companies that use a PRM program see revenue growth, with 30 percent seeing growth beyond 20 percent in their channel. (OnDemand, 2001)

- ▶ The same percentage sees a decrease in costs, with 57 percent experiencing a decrease of over 20 percent. (OnDemand, 2001)

- ▶ Other estimates show that PRM-enabled firms can save 32 percent annually on dealer support costs while increasing revenues by 17 percent. (Hayes & Ref, 2001)

- ▶ If order-processing time for Toshiba Canada was cut in half with a PRM system, twice as many orders could go out in the same time. This is measurable, real ROI.

- ▶ Cable & Wireless can now manage 25,000 leads with 700 partners with a lead distribution efficiency increase of 100 percent.

▶ If a computer manufacturer projected a 60 percent increase in revenue from higher lead conversion rates, due to closer collaboration with field sales and the channel, then ROI is quantifiable.

▶ If the same manufacturer estimates a cost reduction of 40 percent for its call centers due to offloading some of the functions to web-based self-service for the channel, then the return is something tangible.

▶ Finally, if, as AMR's PRM analyst Louis Columbus states, cutting reimbursement time from two weeks to one effectively doubles revenue turns to the channel, "...that's where PRM really makes sense. As long you can infuse cash, you'll be better off because they'll be paid and loyal. And the channel will have more cash to invest in your business."

The PRM Vendors: CCRM or Merely PRM?

Besides my Steppin' Out winner, ChannelWave, there are only a very few vendors worth their channel salt in this vendor diminished market. These include Siebel (once again) with their enterprise PRM module, Comergent, Amdocs with their release of version 5.0 of their PRM platform in June 2003, and strong competitor Click Commerce, who bought what was perhaps the number three PRM vendor, Allegis. In the last two years, two of the most promising companies in this space, Partnerware and XChange, lost their promise and went under, leaving a handful of first class companies remaining in this tremendously potent marketplace. Let's take a brief look at one of the most important of the PRM gladiators, Click Commerce. Of the Big Four, Siebel has a mature PRM application that competes as one of the best in class. As this book was being published, PeopleSoft released what promises to be a solid PRM application as part their PeopleSoft CRM 8.9.

Click Commerce (In Name Only)

Click Commerce, a company that had (note the past tense) specialized in enterprise channel management, did something very smart in 2003. They acquired Allegis and its eBusiness Suite and positioned themselves to be one of the most significant remaining PRM studs on the market. They have a smart management and with the release of Allegis eBusiness Suite 7.0 are ready to rock in the marketplace. While there are more than 40 components to the Allegis suite, there are a few notable tools and features which are indicators of the direction they are aiming at and the parts of the suite they are attempting to bolster. Besides support for seven new languages, the 7.0 suite is aimed at providing much deeper partner participation in both planning and execution of sales. The two features that reflect that are Channel Forecasting and Enhanced Channel Sales.

▶ **Channel Forecasting** You might think that involving the channel in forecasting sales is no big deal—just ask them to help—but it is a daunting task. How many separate databases in how many disparate systems are there to capture the information from? Each partner has their own data, style, storage system, and business model for forecasting. To provide a channelwide coherent forecast using automated functions is a significant step. Channel Forecasting captures units and revenue information with a centralized, integrated environment so the data can be stored and accurately assessed. New opportunities can be dynamically submitted. Accuracy can be assured through regional rollup and management review. Using Enhanced Channel Sales, the forecasts can be validated against the actual sales and inventory.

▶ **Enhanced Channel Sales** New workflow-enabled business processes characterize this core piece of functionality. Partner performance monitoring, automated routing to the appropriate programs or training, and integrated external data are all tied to a stronger analytics engine than has characterized Click Commerce or Allegis in the past. If you need to identify your best or worst performers, you can and then you can trigger appropriate workflow. Using Enhanced Channel Sales, companies can now proactively reward strong performers while incentivizing poor performers to do better.

▶ **Sarbanes-Oxley Compliance** In Chapter 17, I'll cover Sarbanes-Oxley, but suffice it to say here, compliance with it is a major headache and concern. Allegis 7.0 meets the requirements of the dreaded Sarbanes-Oxley Compliance Act by using the following to address financial transactions within the indirect channel:

 ▶ Marketing Funds Management

 ▶ Enhanced Configurable Workflow

- ▶ Reporting

- ▶ Warranty Management

- ▶ Returns Management

- ▶ Price Management

- ▶ Forecasting and Sales Data Reporting

The approval processes are documentable, and are created via the strong workflow. The use of these modules can be tied to controlling and recording the financial transactions, reducing the possibility of fraud and noncompliance.

Watch these guys. They are smart, and with the combination of Allegis and Click Commerce, they are going to continue to be significant players in this important market. The only gripe I have with them is that Allegis sounds like it's a cold capsule.

STEPPIN' OUT: ChannelWave—Wave of the CCRM Future

I've known these guys since I discovered them at the time of the first edition of this book. They have never ceased to amaze me. Since their founding in 1998, they have become the best that PRM has to offer. While they certainly have some high caliber competitors such as Click Commerce and Siebel, and more limited challengers like Amdocs and Comergent, they consistently provide superb applications and a great culture.

They have what I consider the best of the best in the PRM market, made only stronger by their merger with Aqueduct in 2003. They have a strong and very friendly management team run by Chris Heidelberger as the president and Rob Hagan, the CEO; and strong financial backers including blueblood Lazard Technology Partners and Mobius Venture Capital, one of the more creative funding organizations around. Get this: they have virtually no debt. Don't we all wish we could say that?

They have more than 40 clients as of late 2003, including Arrow Electronics, AT&T, BEA Systems, Cable & Wireless, Hewlett-Packard, Legato Systems, PTC, Qwest, Toshiba, and Verizon—a blue chip list.

They have a strong presence in the industry and significant mindshare. They are, in fact, the frontrunner, growing stronger as the number of players diminishes.

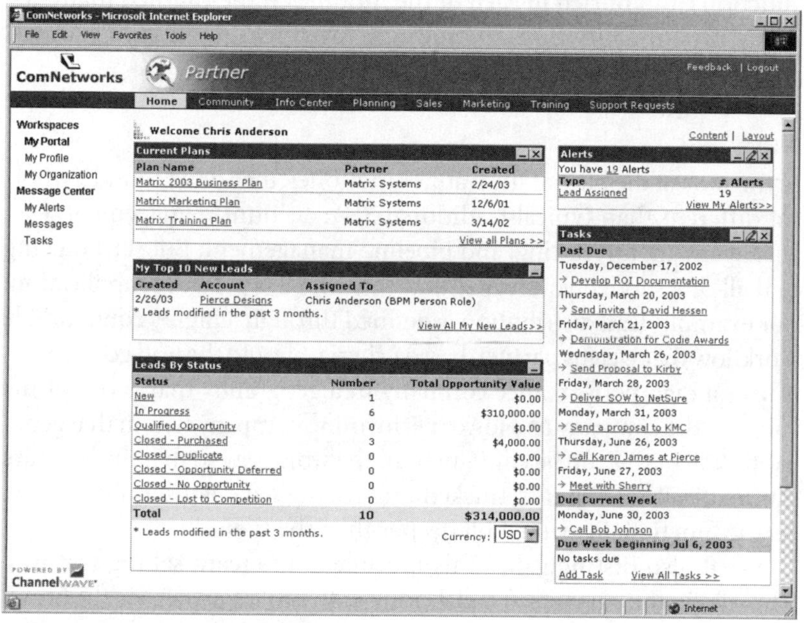

Figure 6-2: The ever-friendly ChannelWave user interface

Oh yeah, they have an awesome product too. With the release of ChannelWave 6.0 in September 2003, they have moved to a new generation of entirely user-friendly, superpowered channel management tools, features, functions, and analytics. Best of breed. Best of group. Best in show.

ChannelWave appeals to my whole-brained cranial peaks and troughs. They have always had a serious concern for user friendliness and for usability. For example, their user interface (see Figure 6-2) is not just the best in PRM but perhaps in all of CRM. It is a model that all enterprise applications vendors should consider.

ChannelWave 6.0: The Product

ChannelWave's product is classically presented (in a CRM sense). It has two editions, Enterprise and Mid-Market, to handle the appropriate company size. Each edition has four modules: Sales, Marketing, Service, and Partner Lifecycle Management. On the surface, the first three seem to be traditional operational CRM modules with traditional functionality such as lead and opportunity management, pipeline management, campaign management, and various support functions. But buried in each of the modules is the vaunted many-to-many functionality that catapults CCRM/PRM purveyor Channel-Wave into a whole new venue.

SALES

If you look at the titles of the features they offer, they don't sound a whole lot different than typical traditional SFA: account management, lead management, forecasting, and pipeline management. But start digging and all of a sudden you realize that this isn't a typical SFA application. For example, lead distribution is defined through a highly configurable workflow that weighs partner-based criteria. Should the lead go to someone at a high performance company in a geography that is out of the range of the company or a lower performing company within that geography? All of this can be configured in the workflow so that the leads are automatically distributed, tracked, and reassigned if it just isn't working. So the functionality runs a bit deeper than the typical.

What also distinguishes this module is the team selling features. This allows the partners to collaborate with other partners or the brand owner's direct sales force. Plans, tasks, incentives, pricing, rates, and tracking all are part of this important differentiator.

MARKETING

Again, it covers the traditional such as campaign management, personalized campaigns, and the usual bag of marketing module tricks, with the ability to monitor campaign effectiveness and closed loop ROI. But the many-to-many tosses its handsome mane here with several unique features, such as:

- ▶ **Co-Marketing Funds Manager** This module automates the management of funds, including such processes as co-op and marketing development funds (MDF) requests, approvals, and usage. It allows the partner to view account status and the brand holder to see how well the entire fund is being used. It tracks the individual partner usage of the funds by specific initiative and can handle the payment runs for that partner. An all-purpose feature.

- ▶ **Information Center** This actually spans much more than just the marketing module. It is the library, the marketing materials repository, and the business information center. All formats are stored here, including PDF, PPT, DOC, and just about any other suffix you can muster. It is where you can pick up a user guide to a product, a collateral piece for a customer; read a service bulletin, or find a related web link. It can be managed so that the appropriate content is visible to the appropriate partners and no one else. It can provide information based on the technical skills of the requestor. It is a true information hub and one of the finest features of ChannelWave.

SERVICE

Service in the world of PRM is not the same as support. It is how to best service partners' needs for communications, information, problem resolution, and, best of all, training. ChannelWave manages to provide a Training Manager that not only provides all of the above mentioned features, but also the registration for courses and the ability to develop an online course catalog.

Additionally, they add a Problem Resolution Advisor to the Service module that takes the form of a wizard that can guide you through the resolution of problems online with expert advice and best practices.

PARTNER LIFECYCLE MANAGEMENT: VERY COOL, VERY DIFFERENT

This is where ChannelWave CCRM begins to seriously deviate from traditional CRM. The foundation for true collaboration between brand holders and partners rests with this module. This module governs the life of a partner from the initial inquiry into partnership through the time you throw them out for nonperformance. Just kidding—unless you're Siebel or Computer Associates. Initially, partner recruitment is done through the Program Manager, which is where the applications and the criteria for the different channel programs are stored. If necessary, the Recruitment Advisor is available to provide a wizard to handle the registration, qualification, and possible enrollment of the partner prospect. The background information collected is entered into a Profile and Community Database, which operates as the central repository for history and information about each (profile) and all (community) of the partners. The Program Manager is summoned when membership is up or changed, or the partner is tracked, meaning there is a change in resource allocation or targeting has to be improved.

To handle the strategic planning with the partner and the creation of the Key Performance Indicators (KPIs) that measure the partner's performance against the plan, there is a Planning and a Metrics Manager.

So all you executives can see this, ChannelWave provides a colorful executive dashboard with graphic representations of the metrical success of your partners. That way when you see red, it's a good thing, not a bad thing.

ChannelWave 6.0: The Architecture

ChannelWave architecture is based on J2EE and XML and is open and accessible to multiple platforms and databases. If you're looking for a pure .NET solution, look elsewhere. But it has near-universal applicability and a strong integration framework using a Novell product called exteNd Composer (hey, don't blame me for the spelling). While one may question alliances with the always shaky Novell, there is no issue with their products, which have always been and remain strong.

ChannelWave relies on three-tiered servers. There is an applications server, an integration server, and a database server. Here's a quick look at each:

▶ **Application server** This server integrates data directly from external sources, manages security, and translates external requests into the appropriate database requests to update or retrieve data from the ChannelWave database. This is where the XML requests are handled, using HTTP or JMS transports. In fact, ChannelWave's API is a native XML interface. SOAP and other web services can extend those XML-native web services, as will future standardized web services.

▶ **Integration server** Starting with ChannelWave 5.0, Novell Extend Composer became the integration agent. It can handle any integration from enterprise applications such as PeopleSoft or Oracle, CRM applications such as Siebel, legacy systems written in COBOL or other mainframe systems, and other possible platforms and frameworks. ChannelWave leverages a large set of adapters that provide business logic and data mapping capabilities so customized integration needs can be handled. It can also handle translation between formats.

▶ **ChannelWave database server** This is where the data accessed by ChannelWave application resides. Where else? It's the ChannelWave database.

ChannelWave 6.0: The Benefits

One of the best ways to see the benefits derived from using Channel-
Wave is to refer to Figure 6-3. These are the results derived by Arrow
Electronics after ChannelWave was implemented.

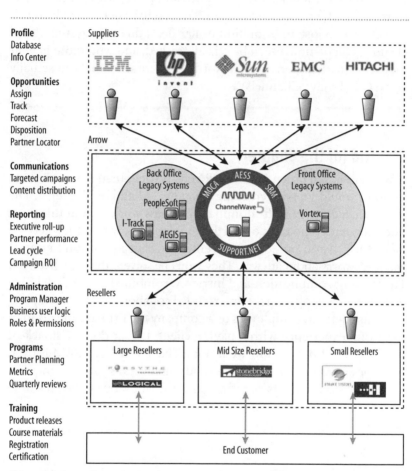

Figure 6-3: Arrow Electronics: Note how well organized it is after ChannelWave has been
implemented.

What is the ultimate benefit? First, I would recommend you look at
Figure 6-3 and read the margins. All of that bears out as true. It is an
organized effective collaboration between Arrow, VARs, manufacturers, integrators, and a set of internal departments using that automated
firepower. The system? It is a system that can tie the systems of Arrow's

suppliers such as HP with Arrow's internal systems; for example, PeopleSoft. Yet the VARs that Arrow deals with will just see Arrow's portal to the products they need and the status of those products. They see the information they need, such as the status of an order, or get the technical tools they need to configure and price, without having to worry about the engine underneath. The results? There won't be much of a chance to lose multimillion dollar deals due to a dysfunctional channel. Opportunities can be seized, tracked, and won more in a far more effective manner. In other words, collaboration that can actually work. Good show, ChannelWave.

The End (of the Chapter)

If you still haven't seen PRM/CCRM as pivotal, then I haven't done my job. I would suggest rereading Chapters 1–3 and rethinking it. The customer ecosystem is the dominant business worldview at this time. There are few companies on earth who don't know that they need to focus their vision on customer-centrism. Those that don't know, I wouldn't worry about anyway. They won't be solvent that much longer. The levels of complication and intricacy, combined with the delicacy of customer volatility, make an extended collaboration between partners, suppliers, and employees of a company the primary means for a successful experience with a paying client. If that doesn't smack of PRM/CCRM, I don't know what does. That's why I say, PRM is over. With the extension to the suppliers and employees as partners and customers, let's call it by its rightful name: Collaborative CRM. It's time for a change.

7

Call Center, CIC, Potato, Po-tah-to: Customer Service Can Be Good— Whatever You Call It

Pop quiz. If I say &!#&@#*!, do you think of:

1. Customer service representatives (CSRs) and being on hold

2. Your boss

3. Your life right now

4. Your ex

5. All of the above

Odds are pretty good on a bad day, it's all of the above. If the day isn't so tough, number 1, the customer service representative, is still one of the choices, isn't it?

How do you make number 1 go away if you're a business person who has to concern yourself with that? Developing a strategy for your call centers can not only cement the relationship the customer has with you, but can be quite profitable too. As far as 2 through 4, on a bad day, they won't go away, so fuggedaboudit. Just have good days.

From Call Center to Customer Interaction Center

I don't know about you, but when the national "Do Not Call" list became a reality, I was thrilled to death. The number of telemarketing calls I got daily dropped from about 25 to about 2 or sometimes none. The evening phone silences were palpable. After awhile, (about five minutes) I realized, "Hey, I don't miss those horrid telemarketing calls at all. This is good."

The dialups from the call center in New Brunswick may no longer be irritating your eardrums, but one of the disadvantages of the current advances in the technologies and business processes is that the call center is no longer the place you get harassed from. There are multiple other ways to do it: via calls from a virtual private network (VPN), but also by e-mail (spam), the Web, fax, and direct mail. Harassment knows no boundaries as we leave the era of the traditional call center and enter into the era of the customer interaction center (CIC).

While this paints an obviously negative picture, I mean it with love. In fact, the CICs or call centers or contact centers, whatever stage of evolution you're at, are vital to many businesses. In a 2003 survey, Aberdeen Group found that 83 percent of businesses they surveyed found customer support centers of real importance.

What that means is that the call center or CIC is not only still a vital part of a CRM strategy but gets increasingly important as CRM moves from edgy to conventional. Even as it moves to conventional, its edge— IP call centers that can use web services and are architected to integrate data and phone services—are becoming increasingly visible on the radar screen of the CIC future, though I won't be covering them beyond what you just read. Just keep an eye on this market, though they only represent 4 percent of the call centers currently according to a 2003 report issued by Datamonitor.

Just a brief housekeeping item. You're going to see call center, customer interaction center, and contact center used interchangeably throughout this chapter. While nitpickers could argue the whys of that, I'm not a nitpicker. The assumption, for literary purposes, is that any one of the three terms can be used, but they all mean a CIC since most call centers, contact centers, or customer interaction centers use multiple channels.

CICs Can Be Complicated, Can't They?

To begin to cover everything when it comes to customer support strategies or the technologies and processes that are engaged with customer support would take a book or two unto itself. So, of course, I'm going to condense it all into a single chapter and try to make it comprehensible. To begin, let's look at a typical call into a CIC that uses live agents and Siebel Call Center, which along with KANA's iCare Service Resolution

Management solutions (part of their iCare Suite—see Steppin' Out in this chapter) is best of breed.

Making the Call

The customer, who works for Seabiscuit, Inc., a company that produces small heartwarming thoroughbred race horses, phones into the service center on his first day of work. He punches in a corporate configuration ID which is then automatically matched against a table that shows the customer's company has a Kryptonite service level agreement (SLA). That means that this caller needs to be afforded the highest level of service offered by the customer center. Because this is his first call on his first day at work, he is a little tentative, but the automated menus carry him through the necessary one-time setup steps so he can have a unique ID on the corporate account—which would still afford him Kryptonite SLA services, but would begin to build a separate customer history. So he gives his name and other necessary information and is assigned a unique configuration ID (called a config ID for short) that is attached to the config ID of the company. After he is set up, his unique config ID will be used for individual call recording and logging and for monitoring the call through the Siebel Audit Trail. That has three purposes. First, to make sure that the levels of service afforded this company's representative are met. Second, to meet any compliance requirements that the call might require. Third, to maintain a corporate service record that can be analyzed after hours for its overall success based on pre-established key performance indicators that are run against the Siebel analytics applications algorithms created expressly for this type of call center analysis.

The other setup information, which includes his corporate role, will constrain his access to that allowed by that role. For example, because he is a manager, not a director, he can call or e-mail or get Web access to certain SLA-driven services, but other services that the CIC provides that he might attempt to access (such as FAQs with specialized information) will trigger a business rule that will automatically route a request to a senior director via the workflow for permission to allow the caller to access the documents he is interested in. When the permission is granted, the open ticket request for information is completed, the info is sent, and the ticket closed.

In this case, once the setup information is completed, the call is routed to a service representative who is at a level that can handle your SLA.

The customer service representative (CSR), who, after consideration by the Greenberg Political Correctness Meter, I'm going to continue to call a CSR anyway, then asks the customer what level of
urgency the problem has. The categories are typically low, high, or
urgent, though you could easily customize that to any number of categories—from sub-basement to yikes. Whatever the categories, they
are available to the CSR through a pick list. But it isn't just a marker.
Each category has business rules and workflow attached to it accordingly. When the choice is made, the workflow and rules automatically
kick into gear. For example, if the call is categorized as Urgent, there
are three people, including the CSR who answered the call, who are
responsible for getting the question resolved within an hour. This is all
part of the business rules that are determined by the Kryptonite SLA.
If it is marked High, there might be four people who get serial rout-
ings, depending on where the call has to go, and who have 12 hours to
resolve the question. Conversely, if they have an Aluminum SLA that
provides for the same categories, an Urgent request might be four people solving the open ticket in eight hours.

In any case, the status field is automatically flagged as open when the
call and config ID are logged. It remains open until it is marked as
resolved, and the information is then logged and stored in a table that
is attached to the customer's corporate and individual config IDs, thus
providing new data and an amended customer record.

The workflow is a very important part of the Siebel (or PeopleSoft
or KANA) call center operation because it handles the automatic routing (see below for more on automatic routing) that is critical for timely
resolution of problems. In the previous example, if the first assigned
engineer fails, the problem is escalated automatically to a specific person called the "backline"—really the level 2 support—and this goes up
the designated chain until the problem is resolved or there is final failure to resolve it. If the issue is closed successfully, screens pop up for the
CSR who solved the problem that ask him questions to be answered,
such as what the problem was and how it was resolved, and who else
might have helped resolve it. The name of the person answering these
questions autopopulates the Assignee field, under the assumption that
the final resolution lay with that person. There is a date and timestamp
field that is autopopulated once the "resolved" flag is checked.

Should the same person from the same company call in with the
appropriate config IDs later, several things occur. The information that
was entered into the system at resolution (and along the way) will pop

up for the use of the CSR now dealing with the newer call. Additionally, there is the capability for a query to find like defects that may have occurred either within the customer's company or from other companies that are being serviced by the same service provider. The fields with this information are attached to a business object, which is attached to a table with the information that answers the query. Plus the status of the SLA or analyses of success and failure rates, or whatever else the agents need to do their job all are available to the agents with the screen pop, if it's configured that way.

Keep in mind, you could be doing this via the Web or via e-mail or fax too.

Following It Through: The Planning, Processes and Best Practices

In order for the call center or CIC to be successful, there are two considerations—planning and execution. How do you plan for successful customer support centers and what practices have succeeded in being the best for the job? Brad Cleveland, president of the Incoming Calls Management Institute, and Julia Mayben in their book *Call Center Management on Fast Forward: Succeeding in Today's Dynamic Inbound Environment* have a nifty group of planning steps and practices that make sense in a 21st century customer environment. The running commentary with each of the emboldened steps is mine.

1. **Choose a service level objective** In the old days, this would be something like figuring on answering 95 percent of the incoming calls within two minutes of the time they come in. More germane now would be a process-driven objective such as time taken to close an open trouble ticket, from problem presentation to resolution.

2. **Collect data** This would be taking a look at information that was relevant to the service level objective. For example, how many calls were received that led to open tickets, how long did each of them last initially, what have been the changes in customer needs and interests?

3. **Forecast call load** Once the objective is set and the data gathered, then forecast the average talk time, average after-call work, which is the amount of time that the agent spends in closing the call after the purpose of the call is fulfilled, and the volume of calls expected within any given time frame—to the half hour

seems to be what much of the industry looks at. Given that we're now in the world of the CIC, forecast other loads such as e-mail, web interactions, and faxes, since the reception of and the responses to will take up agent time.

4. **Calculate base staff** This is a complex set of algorithms. The classic algorithm to determine how much staff will be used at what times and with what volumes is called the Erlang C algorithm, which is detailed a bit more below. However, simulations are being used as are neural networks to make increasingly more accurate assessments of not just the agent numbers needed at a time and place at a certain call volume, but the skills of the agents needed at those times, places, and volumes.

5. **Calculate hardware needs** This means phones, trunk lines, switches, PCs, vending machines, whatever the needed systems are to handle the volume and successful resolution of customer issues.

6. **Calculate rostered staff factor** Once you have the base staff determined at whatever level of sophistication you need and you have the hardware in place so they can do their jobs, you have to see what factors will interrupt the untrammeled time of the agent in taking and resolving calls. That means normal, measurable, and identifiable circumstances like absenteeism, breaks, training time, and other non-customer interaction related work.

7. **Organize schedules** If you've gotten this far, it is time to begin to plan the scheduling of the agents based on the volumes, times, skills, non-interactive circumstances, and the like so that by the end of the day, you'll know who has to be where and when for at least the week ahead, if not more.

8. **Calculate cost** All of this will cost you big time. Figure out the costs of meeting agent quality and service objectives.

9. **Budget for a higher and lower level of service** Break down the costs by looking at three budgets: optimal service provision, normal expected service provision, and marginally successful service provision, meaning the lowest levels of service that are provided to "get by" without any major damage control necessary. The highest levels are where you begin to see the customer support centers as profit centers, because it could include a budget for training

agents to spot up-sale and cross-sale opportunities and could include money budgeted for a commission for agents who successfully provide a lead that becomes a closed opportunity, for example.

BEST PRACTICES ARE BEST REALIZED

Okay, so we know the steps to plan, but what in the world would be some of the best practices that could enhance these steps, once implemented? Here's a couple of them so you get the flavor. You'll have to talk to the industry stars in this area if you want to do more than taste the cake. They charge. I don't (except the cost of the book, of course). They're worth it. Hopefully, so's this book.

▶ **Next best activity** Case-based reasoning (CBR) is becoming a popular technique for more effective troubleshooting. Systems that can handle CBR match current problems with historic problems by inputting the situation to a database and case files, often using freeform text retrieval. The idea is to return case solutions that were used to solve those cases that had similar histories. Then, through a question and answer session with the agent, the CBR engine narrows the number of possible cases, until the most appropriate solutions are found. This is a way of using descriptive analytics (see Chapter 9). There are four "re-s" that are often quoted from Aamodt and Plaza, two CBR specialists: retrieve the most similar cases, reuse the cases to attempt a solution to the problem, revise the solution if necessary to solve the problem, and retain the modified solution as a new case. This, of course, increases the efficiency of the retrieval engine next time. CBR is used as the foundation for a best practice called "next best activity." The idea of next best activity is to figure out what should be done once the case is closing, rather than just wrap up the call. CBR provides the basis for understanding the details of the case in addition to what was learned. So what might be the next best activity would be an attempt to learn more demographic information, or get more detail than was originally needed to troubleshoot the problem, or provide some information to the customer for an up-sell or cross-sell opportunity that would not only resolve the problem but provide new features. The specifics would be provided by the customer record in combination with the information from the CBR system. The idea is that it wouldn't just be "get the problem resolved," but see where opportunity lies. From cost of doing business to chance to do more business. All because of best practices.

▶ **Optimize profitability, not just the cost, of service interactions** Typically, when you are dealing with customer support, you are making the blithe assumption that what you are doing is retaining a customer at some cost to you. So, more often than not, you are looking at supporting that customer as cost-effectively as possible. But if you see your objective for service interactions being how to optimize profit, not reduce cost, then the way that your customer support proceeds is entirely different. The best practice immediately above this one—next best activity—is a perfect example of institutionalizing a best practice/process because of a best practice implemented in strategic thinking. Remember one thing: when a customer's problem is solved, they are often happier with your company than they were before the problem was found.

Following It Through: The Technology

Have you ever thought about the technology that a customer interaction center involves when it is a "full service" version? Of course you have, but only out of frustration. First, what happens is that the voice menu gives you a substantial number of automated choices with the warning, "Please listen carefully, the menu has changed." You are asked to enter some ID or another that will apparently personalize the call and identify you to the presumed future human you will be talking to. Then you are asked a series of questions that seemingly are narrowing down the options so that the CSR can handle the call with all the details necessary. By this time I *know* you've had this thought: "I wish I could talk to a human being already. This voice menu is driving me *nuts!*" Then finally, after about five minutes of button pushing, a human comes on and asks you for your phone number or the same ID that you punched in when the call started and he then says, "What can I do for you?" Which is a polite way of saying all that button pushing for the last five minutes was a complete waste of time, designed for a nefarious purpose only known by the Illuminati in *The Da Vinci Code*. What's driving you nuts is a CIC organized for the convenience of the CIC and for efficiency, not effectiveness. However, when the technology is used in support of a process, it can be an enormous help. Here's a brief guide to some of the processes and the associated technologies available in real life to you at a technologically sufficient CIC.

Computer telephony integration (CTI) These are the technology applications and interfaces that allow data integration with telephones. For example, CTI-enabled functionality allows both Internet-based information and phone-based information to be gathered and sent to a particular agent or routed to a particular desktop.

Automatic call distribution (ACD) This is phone call workflow, which is how a call gets routed based on the defining characteristics of the call.

Automated voice response and interactive voice response This uses an interactive voice response menu (IVR), you know, the "Please enter your 10-digit phone number" menu that we were just cursing. However, when it is a 24/7 multilingual menu that handles speech and text-to-speech technology, it can be tremendously useful for native language speakers, non-native language speakers, and speakers with disabilities. Its real benefit is to handle easy transactions without the need for a live agent, such as finding out your current bank balance (which is probably close to zero, so why call?).

Voice speech recognition This is a natural language interface that has a self-learning technology embedded so that recognition and response accuracy is being improved in near real-time and continually. If done well, it supports VoiceXML.

Text-to-speech services This uses word, phenome, and bookmark support with an extensive dictionary in combination with speech synthesis, especially with its markup language, SSML (you can figure this acronym out yourself, I presume). The obvious advantage here is that it can be a huge boon for the blind.

Fax services This would include both auto-fax and fax-on-demand services. Auto-fax is the "hit the button and get the information faxed to you" menus that you've run into once in awhile. Its strength is that it's self-service. Fax-on-demand is usually run through a customer service representative and will get you what you request.

Automated callback Leave your information and you are immediately given an estimated callback time. This is routed to a CSR who is available to call you back and your number is auto-dialed. This information can be left via the phone or the Internet.

Automated appointment services Typically, this is a self-service function that is designed to set or cancel appointments via a telephone push-button system or a Web-based form. It is available 24 hours a day, 7 days a week. For example, you would enter your information, including your zip code so a local branch of the agency or company you called can be located. This is tied into an integrated scheduler that has all employees who are appropriate in the calendaring. Once you find the appropriate local branch, you enter the times and the appointment is set. It is routed through workflow to the right person at the right branch so that when you go there, they are ready for you. If the system is created right, it can handle concurrent users. It can also issue reports that are analyzed by agent, or number of daily appointments, or cancelled vs. confirmed appointments, and so on.

Hosted FAQ services The importance of knowledgebases to contemporary editions of the CIC can't be overstated. The idea here is to provide a knowledgebase to customers that is available to them each and every hour of each and every day. That way they can resolve some problems or settle an inquiry through an online lookup. Who hasn't used one of these or wanted one in some instances?

All of this technology and process is geared to the interaction between the caller and agent. But we haven't really dwelled much on the agent. What about that agent?

The Agent Can Be Your Friend

The biggest conundrum in this equation is the agent. After all, as bad as your image of the agent is for a call center or CIC, you also know that good agents are worth their weight in gold and can make or break the relationship you have with a company. For example, how many times have you called a company with a customer support issue and been outraged because of either poor call handling (a technological issue) or poor call handling (an agent issue). A long wait followed by an agent who either doesn't know what to do about your problem and is poorly trained or an agent who has the phone-side manner of the Beastie Boys can irritate you beyond ordinary human limits. But an agent who gets your call in a timely fashion and is able to solve your problem with an attitude that is clearly of good cheer makes you happier with the company than when you had no problems. Who doesn't want to know that they will be taken care of, for better or for worse?

This is both subjectively (emotionally) and objectively (statistically) obvious. In early 2004, Purdue University's Center for Customer Driven Quality did exactly this study and came up with fascinating results—fascinating because they bore out what you already know. When the respondents were asked "How important was the overall call experience in shaping (your) image of the company?" the answer was overwhelming. Forty-nine percent said very important, 43 percent said somewhat important, and the rest either were myopic or lied outright and said not important at all. Yeah, sure. Equally interesting were the results of the question "After a bad experience, would you stop using the company?" Sixty-three percent said yes.

Yet, the agent is a shaky proposition. These are often under-trained individuals who are agents only as a whistle stop on their career ride. William Mercer did a research survey in 2001 of agent turnover and if you think sales turnover is high, wait until you get a look at this. Overall, entry level agents have a 73 percent turnover; managers have a 78 percent turnover rate. These aren't the highest numbers, either. In centers described as "outbound with selling"—telemarketing, in other words—the agent annual turnover rate is, get this, 187 percent! That means that for each agent hired in January, there are nearly two more hired—one after the other—to that spot by the end of the year. Utterly nuts. In inbound/outbound centers, which would be like technical support or helpdesk as examples, the turnover was 97 percent. The lowest level of turnover was at account management centers at 25 percent. Can you imagine, it's all so horrible, that 25 percent becomes an "oh, that's not so bad." Something like New York real estate. I've been reading the *NY Observer* for the last seven years. They have a very entertaining real estate section, so I read about New York City real estate each issue. I see a 1500-square-foot condo for $875,000 in the upper 70s (for you non-New Yorkers, that's one of Manhattan's tonicst neighborhoods on the east side of the city), and I think "Hey, that's cheap!" That's not cheap and 25 percent is a lousy rate, but not by comparison in this brutal, discontinuous job category.

Yet we're beginning to see a significant trend toward making your customer interaction center into a profit center. How in the world do you do that in an industry where a single bad agent experience can get the company the customer is dealing with "fired" and the customer rarely deals with the same agent twice?

The answer is a combination of best practices, technology, and of course CRM strategy for these CICs. Same answer you always get, just under different circumstances with different practices.

Workforce Optimization: The Value Is No Secret, Agents

Call centers see the need to improve the quality of customer service and they realize that one of the ways they can do that is through increases in both effectiveness—meaning the agent's successful resolution of the call—and efficiency, meaning the agent's and the call center's ability to handle the call in a satisfactory time frame. This can lead to an improvement in the quality of the customer experience.

The idea that an agent has to be good hasn't escaped any of the industries that need them. TowerGroup did a May 2004 study, entitled "Contact Center Performance Optimization: Getting Better at Getting Better," focused on the banking industry, that claims that U.S. banks will spend $1.9 billion this year on contact center technology, while spending $5.2 billion on personnel, up 4.5 percent from last year. In other words, nearly three times as much on agents as technology—a righteous ratio.

Workforce optimization, supported by workforce optimization technology (WOT), may just be the ticket for this improvement. WOT aims at the increase in efficiencies of the call center using technology, processes, and training. That means agent performance, use of the human resources such as agent distribution at peak and nonpeak hours, and capturing data and phone interactions between the customer and the agent to improve the depth of the customer record and to monitor and analyze the results for better performance. It also means making sure there is a strategy for the utilization of the better-performing agents and increased training availability for those in need of it.

Because you can see performance improvements and ROI in six to twelve months, the value of what is effectively an agent optimization strategy is now being seen. In 2003, $695 million was spent on WOT software and this is estimated by Datamonitor in their report, "Workforce Optimization in the Contact Center," to be a total of $1.2 billion by 2008. The bulk of the dollars spent will be on quality monitoring with about $414 million, but agent analytics and e-learning technologies will be the fastest growing, with compound annual growth rates

(CAGRs) of 26 percent and 19 percent, respectively. By 2008, agent analytics expenditures will be more than triple 2003's $39 million, and the 2008 e-learning estimate is $294 million, over twice that of 2003's total.

Not bad, if Datamonitor is right.

Workforce optimization strategies encompass four elements: quality monitoring, workforce management, agent analytics, and e-learning. TowerGroup says that no vendor has a full suite that is all that good yet. I'm leaning a little toward Blue Pumpkin and Envision as providing the necessary functionality and processes.

The market for workforce optimization is not nearly penetrated if the mid-market, meaning CICs that are between 30 and 75 agents, are included. These are complex products that are geared to the Fortune 1000 of call centers, which have been nearly 100 percent penetrated. They see the value. The midmarket doesn't quite yet but is getting ready.

Quality Monitoring

Quality monitoring is the recording and analysis of telephone and data interactions between customer and call center agent. Interestingly, it is here that Datamonitor and other corroborating surveys see the largest investment interest. It's the way to find the answer to the simplest but most crucial question: how well is the agent doing? This isn't that easy an answer. Imagine that the customer is interacting with the agent in multiple ways—via the phone, e-mail, the Web, and any other way to communicate possible. Good quality monitoring applications and processes allow agent supervisors to use multichannel recording, online evaluations, and desktop delivery. The accumulated information allows them to provide some pretty sophisticated feedback to the agents like "Great job!" Or "You stink!" Actually, they can do a lot better than that. There are typically rules-based engines, intuitive interfaces, and skills-based scheduling machines that can organize schedules easily. The software can record randomly, scheduled, or triggered. The triggers are where this stuff gets good. It can be event driven—say, a 25-minute phone call to a Level 2 support person that has a problem identified that typically takes 10 minutes. It can be done through what is called Automatic Number Identification (ANI) which means that when a certain number shows up on a caller ID screen, it can start a recording, or, by the same token, when an outbound number is specifically dialed the same thing can happen. It can do it with word prompts or even stress levels! The agent can initiate the recording too.

When a "recording session" is scheduled, the software records and allows users to review the telephone conversations, multimedia interactions, and screen captures resulting from interactions between agents and customers. These recordings are subsequently stored in a database and replayed for evaluation, training, compensation, and performance management purposes.

The problem that can easily arise (and does) here is the obvious one. If you're an agent, do you really want to be monitored? It seems to be a possibly punitive action, doesn't it? If you fall down on one call, you could be penalized. If it's set to randomly select agent calls, you're always looking over your larynx in fear of someone catching you doing something you probably aren't doing. Even less conspiratorially, it can be seen as something used to make sure that you keep to a time limit for a call.

Obviously, paranoia isn't going to make quality monitoring acceptance easy. The agents will need to understand the value that the applications have. There are two things that can be done. Agents should be able to see the data and should understand the performance metrics so they can see how they are being evaluated. Second, the quality monitoring should be seen as agent improvement, which is why it needs to be coupled with e-learning and with compensation benefits so there are processes that prove it is beneficial and not punitive.

Workforce Management

Workforce management is perhaps the old school segment of the workforce optimization components. It is for the efficient scheduling of human resources in call centers. Typically, schedule optimization, queue management, call routing, and other efficiencies are the focus of workforce management. But there are some changes afoot in workforce management, some around agent empowerment, which means improvements in agent self-service so they can control their own schedules both as CSRs and as people in need of a day off every now and then. They can even control their own breaks. Remember the planning process from the ICMI above—this level of agent involvement would allow the agents to be part of schedule organization and could provide, if managed with constraint, a happier agent organization. The tradeoff is the point where an individual agent's scheduling involvement starts to complicate the overall scheduling. So there must be constraints.

However, equally as interesting and more directly germane to this section are the advances in both technology and best practices that lead to not just intelligent call routing but intelligent call routing that accounts for customer value. This is a fundamental change and improvement in workforce management.

AUTOMATED INTELLIGENT CALL ROUTING

Why in the world should we single out call routing as a technology to be concerned with? It's not something that you would ordinarily care about, since, if done well, it's taken care of automatically, isn't it? But did you ever think about what it takes to get you from your initial call to the appropriate place without having live operators route you to the place you need to go? It sounds easy—hit button, get to person. But think of it this way. Ping'An, the second largest insurance company in China, is highlighted below. Their national call center, 95511, got 14.27 million calls in a year in 2003. Presuming even distribution, which is a ridiculous presumption, but will make the point, you are dealing with 14.27 million calls over 365 days over 24 hours. That works out to an evenly distributed 39,096 calls per day, 1,629 calls per hour and 27 calls per minute, presuming everybody waited their turn in a queue in an absolutely consistent world. But start to set it up in volumes that are more accurate and you are dealing with a function that could be doomed to failure and destroy credibility. Remember &!#&@#*!? That is the result of that failure.

Intelligent inbound and outbound traffic direction can make or break a call center or CIC. When you have multiple channels including the traditional telephone call, but also voice over Internet protocol (VOIP), which allows you to make a phone call via the Web, then routing can get really difficult. Throw in different working hours for the agents and different volumes based on time and geography. Managing this meant using call-routing software that could handle increasing volume, geographical dispersion of the CSRs, multiple channels, and workflow. The software automatically identified who is calling, used the customer database to identify their history, and then found the appropriate party available for the caller at the time they called. The software ordinarily integrated IVR so that some of the processes could be routed to auto-response systems. It used multiple channels to both gather information and route calls so the architecture was open and scalable. Good routing software was typically Web-enabled so that

Internet-based routing to the appropriate menus could occur. It allowed live collaboration on the Web. It provided remote agent support so that branch offices and small office/home office (SOHO) agents could be utilized in the problem resolution. That means that the home agent and the branch offices accessed most of the functionality provided to the HQ agent. This eased the weight of the high-volume days without tying up valuable HQ real estate.

The software had strong scripting capabilities and an open interface. This meant the interface controlled IVR scripting governed by applied business rules. Finally, it integrated workforce management tools with its call-routing capacity so that the CIC's agent capacity and scheduling forecasts were integrated into the use of the call-routing functionality in highly specialized ways if needed.

Note I've spoken about this advanced call routing technology in the past tense. Yet, much of it is still around. Why the past tense? Because there are technologies that have begun to supersede it that actively not only handle the call routing and multichannel interactions, but take customer value into account while doing so. Additionally, the medium for the call itself is beginning to change for the contact center. That is a huge step forward inside a customer ecosystem.

UNIVERSAL QUEUE AND CUSTOMER INTERACTION MANAGEMENT

Interaction management coupled with automated intelligent call routing leads to something that is called the universal queue (poetically known as UQ). What makes this an important new generation of technology is its ability to handle interactions with the callers in real time based on the caller's customer value and through any channels that they access. It is the CIC toolset to provide what Unisys calls "differentiated customer treatment."

UQ's benefit is twofold. It integrates all channels customer interactions and the results into a single customer record, whether the interaction occurred via phone, fax, Web, e-mail, direct mail, or person-to-person. Once the history is gathered, the record can be analyzed through the use of advanced algorithms to come up with a customer value. The UQ can:

- ▶ Identify customers and interactions and attached unique values prior to resolving a communication.

- ▶ Manage customers and interactions according to their assigned value to the organization—meaning is this a high value or low value customer or a customer assigned a differentiated value—and thus has courses of specific action to be taken according to the assigned value.

► Manage customers and interactions for their propensity to generate additional revenue. This is how a CIC can be a profit center. What are the possible up-selling and cross-sale opportunities for this specific customer?

All of this is based on the multichannel history established in the customer record.

Leading vendors in the UQ domain are Apropos, who have fully integrated their UQ version 6.0 into PeopleSoft CRM 8.8 and beyond, and Avaya, who have used their Gplus adaptors to integrate their UQ technology with primarily Siebel Call Center, but also several other call center players.

This becomes of major significance in the world of commerce we now live in, my friends. Customer value identified is customer value given is customer value returned.

ERLANG C: AN ALGORITHM, NOT A VITAMIN WITHOUT ROSEHIPS

Erlang C, the old standard algorithm, has become a little controversial. Its value is being questioned by parts of the call center community because it wasn't developed to handle the new multichannel customer ecosystem we live in. But, even with that, it remains the standard to this day.

Because the customer empowerment is magnitudes greater due to multichannel communication, customer volatility is very high. These changes in expectation of quality service and minimal waste of time are dramatic. What was an acceptable level of frustration on the telephone patiently waiting for responsive service is no longer acceptable. How agents handle phone calls becomes multifaceted. It involves how long the caller waits, how long the actual call is before the problem is resolved or the request answered, how much time is spent after the problem is resolved or the request answered, and ease of getting to the appropriately skilled agent, among other things. There is actually an algorithm called the Erlang C equation, developed early in the 1900s and refined in recent years, which finds the optimal number of agents required to handle call loads. Its recent incarnations not only take into account historic call reception and agent skill sets, but also busy signals and call abandonment. So what, you say? Well, nonbeliever, think about it this way. If you have 1,000 agents and only receive enough calls for 650 agents daily over a three-month period, and receive calls for 800 agents for four months and for 1,200 agents for the other five months, you are spending a lot of money on agents who aren't needed at times and not spending enough other times. Now get down even deeper. What if you receive 275 calls in the hours from 10:00 P.M. to 1:00 A.M., 130 calls from 1:00 A.M. to 6:00 A.M., and 2,415 calls from 6:00 A.M. to 10:00 A.M.? What's the right number of agents, since you can't move agents' numbers around every hour or so. Most people like working a consistent number of hours. Also, if you underestimate the number of agents, including during the call spikes that are expected as part of a given time period, how are you going to handle the overload? You'll have lots of unhappy customers—again, a cost you can't afford.

Agent Analytics

Using data from call center sources, agent analytics aim to empower call center agents through greater understanding of their own performance. Vendors in this area even offer systems whereby agents can be rewarded for improvements and better than average performance.

The analytics fall into three categories:

- ▶ Call statistics that you can find from phone switches, such as call volume and average speed of answer

- ▶ Quality monitoring—how many cases opened or closed, how quickly trouble tickets were resolved, and how satisfied the customer was with the resolution

- ▶ Agent performance—also related to quality monitoring—which agent had the highest customer satisfaction score or helped the most customers in a month

All this set against benchmarks and relative performance of the center gives you an idea of how the individual agent is actually performing. For example, let's say the agent you are reviewing opened only three tickets and closed two of them in a two-day period from Monday through Tuesday. That seems to stink. But then you look at the performance of the other agents and you see two things—first, that this is comparable to the other agents, and second, that the norm for a five-day period is twelve a day and closure of nine. What does this suggest? First, that there is something universally wrong here, not just wrong with the particular agent. That would then indicate that the investigation of the problem not be an investigation of the agent, but an investigation of the causes of the slowdown, which could amount to anything ranging from a terribly slow day to hardware failure, a deliberate agent slowdown for increased wages, or a vast coincidence of one-time poor performances.

The key point is that the data analytics become useful when they are a guide to action. But as always, the actions are open to interpretation. The analytics have to eliminate as much room for interpretation as possible. The analytics results are there to provide acumen and limitations.

E-learning

E-learning is the online delivery of training. In the case of workforce optimization it is self-service training delivery for call center or CIC agents to improve their performance. Typical contact center e-learning solutions can create content that either can be delivered to the agent desktop via a network or provided to the agent via the Web. The actual training is usually given or accessed during either specifically scheduled periods or times that are identified with low customer contact volume. These solutions are often integrated with the other workforce optimization solutions that include scheduling, analytics and the data provided to the analytics, other workforce management functions, quality monitoring solutions, and automated call routing capabilities.

Some of the typical online training an agent might get includes:

- ▶ How to build rapport with a call center customer
- ▶ How to reduce escalated and repeat calls
- ▶ Understanding the legal side of call management
- ▶ How to handle upset customers
- ▶ How to spot up-selling and cross-selling opportunities

Sounds pretty silly, doesn't it? It does until you think about the CSR you were yelling at the other day, and how well it all turned out. Then it isn't so silly, is it?

WOT Beyond the Contact Center

There are other possible locales where WOT can be beneficial. It tends to be in the areas that are similar in dependency to CICs or call centers. For example, a bank branch, ticket office, and hospital are all dependent on wait times, speed of service, and quality of service that depends on the customer representative. Field service (see Chapter 8) is another area that uses workforce optimization, particularly workforce management. Government agencies such as the Department of Motor Vehicles in any given state are also subject to the vagaries of speedy high-caliber service requirements. Workforce optimization is a candidate for those areas too. No stretch of the imagination necessary.

Qui Bono? Benefits and Stories

One of the oldest and most baffling expressions (as to origin) is "the proof is in the pudding." It means it is the results that count. So let's see what the benefits of CRM and its corollaries are in the CIC:

- ▶ **Cisco** Implementing e-learning solutions in 2002 that reduce the time the Cisco call center agent spends on a successful call have meant savings of $9 for every dollar spent on e-learning solutions. That is a 900 percent return on investment.

- ▶ **State of Washington** Call center handles between 30,000 and 50,000 calls per week. They implemented the Genesys call center technology in combination with Verizon call center services. The results? Average agent talk time is reduced from 805 seconds to 504 seconds. The value of this is $27,000 per month. The number of calls answered immediately increased from 16 percent to 45 percent; they reduced calls with defects from 84 percent to 18 percent.

- ▶ **Admiral Insurance** Implemented quality monitoring and training programs in 2001. The results for the 900 agents responding to 28,000 calls per day were lovely. Agent evaluations which took a half-day each now take two hours. Administrative time to fill out evaluation forms, which was 12 minutes each, is now four or five minutes each. Cross-selling opportunities for ancillary products are up to 10 percent from a less than 4 percent number.

- ▶ **Northwest Airlines** Uses agent coaching through e-learning from Envision for agents receiving 100,000 calls per day. The direct ROI was 2.5 percent increase in sales, with an extrapolated revenue gain of $23.5 million across contact centers. There was a two percent decrease in call time, which extrapolates to $1.8 million across contact centers in a given year.

▶ **Southern California Edison** Used Witness Systems eQuality tools. They got results that achieved customer satisfaction goals every year since implementation (2002) and reduced average call handling times.

There are countless examples of extremely quick ROI when implementing the new versions of customer service solutions. But you have to work at it. There are a lot of customers and a lot of agents waiting to meet each other. In a nice way.

Case Study: Let a Million Calls Succeed—Ping'An Insurance

Every now and then, CRM succeeds with a nearly breathtaking perfection. To do so, strategies have to be formulated, processes examined, changes in culture made, communications established, learning done as learning and not just knowledge dumped, and the CRM program needs to be heartily embraced by the entire value chain. One of the least likely places for highly successful CRM is the call center, because the high volume of transactions and interactions are often paired with minimal training and poorly thought-out analytics. A lot of the problem lies in the need to deal with the customer *now*, not later. That makes speed often as important or more important than triumphant problem resolution. Reduction in queue time becomes the measure rather than time to resolution because it looks better on daily reports. The overtaxed, usually underpaid CSR is not equipped to take on the more complex role of both problem solver and trained ferret for cross-selling and up-selling opportunities.

You would think that if we were to find a beautiful example of CRM success, it wouldn't be in a call center environment and it would most likely be in the United States, where CRM initiatives are at their most mature. You've probably figured out by now, given the obvious leading statements, you'd be wrong on both counts.

Welcome to Ping'An, China's second largest insurance company and one of China's most successful CRM initiatives to date. It's a beauty, it's not in the U.S., and it's appropriate to this chapter, because it's a call center, or more directly, a CIC. It is also a model of how to think and act on a CRM initiative in this environment—regardless of where you globally or locally plant your posterior.

Ping'An's national call center, 95511 (yes, that is the name) was launched in July 2000. The services it covers are not just claims filing but insurance consultation, specific policy inquiries, sales opportunities, and general policy issues among other services. When they created 95511 in 2000, they received 31,000 calls. In 2001, they received 312,000, and in 2002 they received 815,000. In 2003, there were more than 14 million phone calls to 95511, with over 10 million of them handled by the more than 600 Ping'An employees. With this 24/7 customer service, comes not just the Ping'An staff, but also 36 partner and contractor organizations and their subsidiaries so that Ping'An can ensure national blanket coverage.

The 3A Service Principles

Ping'An saw that to handle this huge call load effectively and within a customer's universe, they had to develop a strategy and then execute. They went about it the right way.

3A's statement of principle: "Anytime, Anywhere and Anyway, you can always get satisfactory services from Ping'An Insurance Company." (By the way, the capitalizations are theirs.) This was not some vacuous marketing statement, but a statement of profound importance to the business future of the company. This was the principle that they would breathe and eat every day from the time it was formulated. Unlike many companies, they refreshingly took the time and made the investment in planning and then building the institutions and the organizational support necessary to make this a customer-focused reality.

The results were the 3A service network that took into account the multiple touch points where their customers were likely to intersect them. That meant the creation of not only a national call center that also functioned as the hub of the 3A service network, but an Internet center, a salesperson direct sales group, and a store-based service center where customers could meet with live and real customer service representatives, not just disembodied voices. But their strategy took this even a step further. They created regionally specific units that accounted for cultural and business practice differences. They divided China into three areas—Northwest, South, and East. Each of the areas included metropolitan centers. For example, Northwest included 18 metro areas, the best known probably being Chengzhou and Chongqing. The East had nine centers, including Shanghai and Nanjing, and the South also had nine, including Beijing. Each of them has specialized treatment and personalized services based on their region.

The range of services that the 95511 network provides is strategic. Not only are the Ping'An leadership providing customer value, but they are seeing 95511 as a potential profit center too. Thus, they are looking to both solve problems and up-sell or cross-sell products to their customers.

Calling In and Out, Manual and Auto

Because opportunity knocks but once, Ping'An takes full advantage of the chance to have human beings speak to their customers. But they also understand the value of customer convenience. So they provide both automated and "manual" call center services. Using interactive voice response (IVR) 24/7, they provide customers with a service that can give them policy information on the general products that Ping'An can provide to them or secure access to individual policy information. Their inbound services use live, well-trained consultants who can provide information on insurance policies, changes in the policies, claims, other inquiries, appointments, and complaints. There are financial consultants who can help customers determine the best mix of insurance products for both protective and financial reasons. This is a crucial component for Ping'An because it carries the possibility of new product sales to existing (and new) customers.

Ping'An also provides outbound call services so that they can maintain regular contact with their customers. Customer satisfaction plays a huge part in the strategy for this activity. Over the phone and by mail, they do surveys on the quality of sales personnel, and follow up on any inquiries or complaints. They even do customer birthday visits and annual visits to make sure their relationship to the customer is actually personal, not just the automated IVR. To Ping'An, IVR is a true customer convenience, not a convenient excuse to avoid personal interaction.

But make no mistake. They fully understand the principles of CRM in a customer ecosystem. Provide value to the customer and the customer will provide value in return. They are not putting all this effort into a cost center. They fully expect that their efforts will be rewarded with customer retention and increased product sales to those retained customers. Look at Figure 7-1 to see how the 95511 call center is structured. Customer-centric, to be sure, but sales is never forgotten.

Wearing the Voice of the Customer

We've spent a lot of time in this book on hearing the voice of the customer. Well, Ping'An does the same thing using a different set of body parts. They speak of "management based on the perspective of being in someone's shoes." I'm going to quote them directly here on their two management styles as they presented them at the extraordinary Greater China CRM Conference in April 2004.

Human-oriented management...The management should take into account "human beings," this being the call center's service target. Therefore, in addition to providing analysis and guidance to staff in the manner of factory-like workflow, management should be based on empathy and understanding. Through improving the hardware conditions of the workplace environment, we can ensure that staff will enjoy their work.

Vivacious management...Since young females form the majority of the call center staff (78 percent, of which 60 percent are college educated and 86 percent between 20–24 years old), a vivacious management style will help to increase staff satisfaction levels and boost morale.

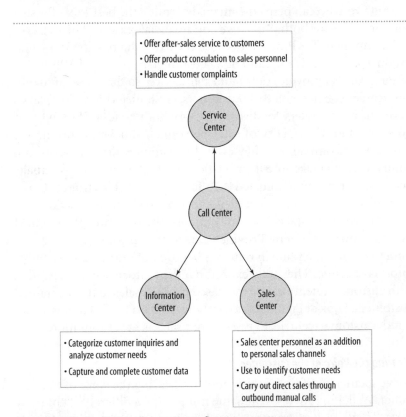

Figure 7-1: Ping'An 95511 call center is a profit center, not a cost center.

Besides those of you who will get into a politically correct snit about vivacious management, try to see past the terminology and look at what these two management methods take into account. Human-oriented management says treat the customers as people, not assembly line parts. Vivacious management says the employees are customers too and because most of those employees are young, college-educated females just starting out, a management style that appeals to them will make them happier and more likely to provide the service necessary to the customers. In other words, they've segmented their workforce and identified the specific types of services that should be making them happy as employees. If I remember correctly, isn't that what you're supposed to do, you CRM gurus out there?

The Future Calls

The future beckons to Ping'An. They are looking to improve the multichannel capabilities of the 3A system and add highly personalized services to the overall mix. That means that not only will you be able to get either personalized representative service or self-service, but you'll get it all in one place regardless of the channel that you use— phone, e-mail, web-call, fax, or any other channel your heart desires. If you qualify, you will get VIP services that will handle your case or needs with a special effort. In other words, not only is the present looking good, but the future looks to provide complete customer value, in a way that any company should envy or emulate.

STEPPIN' OUT: KANA Reaches Out and Touch Points Someone

KANA is an excellent product-driven, high-caliber company. They have a flair for products that you don't frequently see in CRM, though there are lots of poseurs. Not KANA. They produce genuinely good applications. They have been a lean and mean company for a long time, with a very intelligent management team. Thus, they are smartly effective in what they do and what they produce. They know their job more so than most companies that play pretend CRM and even more than some of their fellow CRM real deals. That is why they are a Steppin' Out choice for their service resolution management applications, the support side of their iCare suite. Their flagship product, the KANA iCare suite consists of Service, Marketing, and what they call Commerce Analytics. Normally, if I had any confidence that they were going to release the SFA applications they purportedly have, I would include them in my enterprise apps companies in Chapter 24. Sadly, I'm not sure they will, so I can't include them. If they do, I have no doubt that it will be of the same high quality as the other applications. Their customer service solutions are top of the line. While they originated in the e-mail response marketing world, they have had a carefully chosen and well trod path since their founding in 1998 through a build and buy strategy. They have acquired companies like BEI, NetDialog, and SilkNet and at the same time continue to build many of the components of the iCare suite on their own. In May 2004, they announced their attendance in the on-demand world, by releasing a hosted version of their applications. They didn't change the on-premises version whatever, since it has had a web architecture as long as or perhaps longer than anyone else in the industry. They now have the best of both worlds. They also have industry specialties in health care payers, telecommunications, consumer financial services, high tech manufacturers, and government with a state and local bent.

All in all, you are dealing with a sinewy heavyweight champ when it comes to KANA.

Customer Service Solution

We're going to focus on the technology here so you can see what kinds of customer service technologies are typical of the high end contact center solutions.

FEATURES AND FUNCTIONS

There is a constant overwhelming certainty when it comes to seeing the thrust of the KANA service resolution management solutions. They are oriented toward making contact centers profit centers and the agents the drivers of those profits. The features are designed for customer visibility to the agent in all areas and not only speedy call or problem resolution but opportunity identification.

- ▶ **Agent and staff knowledgebase** This organizes corporate knowledge and provides intelligent, guided search, and retrieval that speeds up inquiry resolution. The knowledgebase includes the successful (or not) resolution of prior calls so that inquiries will have current and useful information on what to do, what to say, or how to do something as well as what not to do.

▶ **Web self-service** Self-service is one of the crucial features of customer satisfaction. Customers are finicky folks. How often have you said, "I wish I could just speak to a person?" But how equally often have you said, "I just want this information. I don't need to go through the hassle of speaking to someone." KANA web self-service offers personalized, secure web portals and knowledgebase access so that customers and partners can resolve inquiries on their own.

▶ **Unified agent desktop** This is the call center version of the 360-degree view for the customers, but it does it dynamically. Bringing real-time customer data and a complete cross-channel history together at the desktop, it helps agents quickly answer all types of inquiries across all channels using that knowledgebase mentioned a couple of bullet points ago. It also can provide agents with one-stop access to data contained in back-end systems, and create and manage all accounts, contacts, tasks and staff from a single interface, among many other things. It consolidates a significant number of the features you are reading about in this part of the chapter.

▶ **High volume e-mail management** KANA is just so incredibly strong in this area. This is their history. They can intelligently automate routing, auto-acknowledgement and auto-response to reduce handling time for high volumes of inbound e-mail, Web form and chat messages. All from a single place.

▶ **Confidential messaging** Confidential messaging doesn't mean that you can send love notes to your darling, though technologically you could. This delivers secure online communications to help organizations ensure the privacy of interactions with customers and partners.

▶ **Proactive notifications** This engages workflow and business rules to automatically deliver event-triggered messages to provide information before customers call the contact center.

CONTACT CENTER

Another best of breed application, KANA's contact center is organized around the unified agent desktop, so I won't reiterate what it does. But the contact center also handles automated request management by customizing the workflows using best practices, the ordinary business processes that govern the center, and necessary business rules to handle requests across any channels both internal and external—meaning partners, employees, suppliers, or customers.

SERVICE RESOLUTION MANAGEMENT

KANA gets very interesting here. They take things out of the realm of just applications and put the idea of customer support into the realm of process-driven solutions. Good move, KANA.

- ▶ **KANA Self Service** This is one of the courses of action that leads to customer empowerment. KANA Self Service allows the customers (or the agents) to access the knowledgebase via the Web, and then use e-mail and other collaboration tools to provide escalation, if need be.

- ▶ **KANA Assisted Service** This is agent country. Assisted Service gives CSRs access to the knowledgebase or any other source of current information instantly. It provides tools that allow the agent to communicate the appropriate information to those customers.

- ▶ **KANA Proactive Service** The automated crown jewel. It allows for planning, automating, and scheduling the delivery of outbound customer service messages via event-driven notification. It can provide highly personalized dynamic communications with individual customers. Campaigns built around these messages or events can be created and triggered so that service resolution can be released. For example, though not a KANA example to my knowledge, update notifications to fix security holes in Windows XP are a good example of a campaign built around a proactive service plan and automated triggers. With KANA's advanced e-mail management features, the proactive campaigns can use e-mails to route messages to work queues, priority queues, or even departmental queues, create auto responses to the campaigns, and run analytics reports to see how successful the campaigns have been.

SERVICE ANALYTICS

KANA provides sufficient embedded analytics for determining customer service resolution, without a separate business intelligence or datawarehousing application to do it. There are more than 40 packaged reports and analytics, which is not a large number but will likely do the trick for most businesses. KANA can handle service analytics measurements such as:

- ▶ Accuracy of automated responses
- ▶ Success rate of knowledgebase sessions
- ▶ The number of self-service to agent-assisted escalations
- ▶ Agent e-mail response productivity for specific time periods
- ▶ Volume distribution by specific communication channel
- ▶ Inquiry volume by inquiry type

In the second edition, in this chapter I covered both contact centers and field service. Each of them changed. Each matured. Each went from a slim combined, efficient one-chapter cost center to a fatter one-chapter-each profit center. All because the customer ecosystem took over. So let's move to the other fat cat, (possibly) profitable field service CRM.

8

Field Service:
Not Just Your Maytag Repairman Anymore

Jesse White was the actor who sat around. His job, on Maytag® commercials, was to show that Maytag washers and dryers never needed to be repaired. The fact that he had this horribly boring, listless job was a good thing for the customer because it meant that the customer never had to worry about the sparkling clean, crisp, warm dry clothing that resulted from using Maytag products. Though certainly not mentioned in the commercials in the early '70s, it was good for the company too, because they didn't have to spend the money that field service cost them as the price of doing business. Back in those days, field service was seen as a necessary expenditure to keep happy customers buying products. It was a cost center, but hey, do what had to be done for moving products, products, and more products out the door.

Field Service: Welcome to the 21st Century

But along comes the 21st century, a customer ecosystem, and a transformation of the business climate, and all that changes. Field service is no longer just a necessary business cost, but has become a potential revenue-generating monster. But to make the move from cost center to profit center is not cheap. This domain cuts across all aspects of business and each segment of the extended value chain "village" is impacted by field service. It overlays finance and human resources—all ERP functions. It rips through inventory management, parts maintenance, scheduling, delivery, and logistics—all supply chain management. It impacts customer service, marketing, and sales through service level agreements (SLAs)—all CRM features. In other words, field service, historically the vessel containing the people with the worst jobs (having to deal with irate customers, spending a good deal of their life on the road), is now not just a vital function, but actually a means of providing your company with revenues and profits and effective valuable relationships with customers.

Integration of field service functions with this value chain can drive the conversion of field service operations from cost center to profit center, even with a poor economy. The value chain provides the end-to-end communication and information infrastructure that are needed to make field service operations a tool for customer retention, in addition to its already well-established maintenance and repair functions. But myopia still exists among field service executives. While most see the value of field service, few are willing to invest in it. Yet, if it is essential to respond to customer demand in real time, then field service needs the information available in real time. No more six to eight weeks' assessments of asset status before corrective measures. Now it needs to occur quickly. No more, "I'll get back to you on the status of that part," from the field service technician. Now the service tech needs to check his handheld and tell the customer about the availability of that part instantly or the company could lose the customer. All of that costs money that field service executives are reluctant to spend. Yet if they do spend it, it will be well spent.

Form Follows Function

Louis Sullivan, early 20th-century Chicago's great architect, made the now famous statement, "form follows function." For architecture, it meant that you had to know what you wanted the building for, prior to designing it. In the CRM world, it means you need to understand what you want to do with field service before you decide how you want to implement it. Once you've identified the objectives and planned a strategy, you can begin to see what processes you need to improve or add or subtract. Then you can decide how you want to frame those processes and design the system to implement those processes. It doesn't seem that complicated, but when it comes to field service, it can be. The objectives and approach seem straightforward. Field service CRM, effectively implemented, provides great service in a timely fashion. This retains customers and that enhances revenue. But the actual customer process is quite complicated. So even if ongoing customers getting great service will lead to incremental and sometimes larger increases in revenue and, through cost reductions, increased margins, it is not easy to get to. The levels of functionality available in field service applications are perhaps the most rich and interwoven of all CRM applications (with the possible exception of call centers in a multichannel environment).

What I'm going to do here is examine some of the components of field service that are most necessary. In order to understand them, it is important to remember that field service extends across multiple domains and departments and involves the cooperation between suppliers/vendors, employees, and partners to succeed. All the functionality in the world won't make it work otherwise. That said, onward to features.

Contract Management

Service level agreements (SLA), warranty management, pricing, and delivery all fall under the aegis of contract management. If the contract management lifecycle can be captured and directed, revenue opportunities can increase dramatically. For example, one lucrative source of revenue has been the re-up of warranties. However, one of the weaknesses of field service tracking has been the inability to track warranty expirations with sufficient knowledge to make sure that the time is there to get the warranty renewals completed. This is minimally a marginally lucrative income source and potentially a substantial one.

Service Level Agreements (SLA) Tracking

Depending on how they are handled, service level agreements can be among the most important pitfalls or windfalls that any company can manage. Each SLA is individually tailored and is generally associated with extensive performance measurements (KPIs) and acceptable service levels. Nonperformance means financial and other penalties. Conversely, overachievement means premium payments. In any case, they can get highly involved and it is quite easy to lose track of what you have. York International, one of the leading domestic HVAC equipment providers, found itself losing money on SLAs, which should have been generating substantial revenue. After analyzing their situation in 2002, they found that many of the contracts signed by their sales representatives for the SLAs were actually negative revenue producers because of the committed service levels versus price. Using Siebel Field Service by early 2003 they were able to add business rules that put constraints on the acceptance of SLAs. If the SLAs didn't meet certain financial criteria, the system prevented them from being accepted or signed. End of negative revenue story.

The problem with any SLA is that it is crafted at a particular moment for a particular purpose. That's fine, but the nature of most companies, I hope, is dynamic. Even though you have a SLA that identifies baseline service levels, the needs of the signee might be very different less than a year from the time the SLA is signed. Now, of course, while this can be problematic, it is also a major revenue opportunity, if the flexibility to upgrade the SLA with new value-added services exists in the agreement. If there is sufficient planning aforethought, the pre-existing knowledge of the corporation about its customer's processes, events, and assets can provide for both the long range changes that are likely and still build in sufficient "future-proofing" to allow for both costs and profits currently and down the road.

Let's take a look at a common example. SLAs of corporate Internet service providers (ISPs) often include the amount of guaranteed uptime and a guaranteed amount of time for the service necessary to get a downed network up and running again. A typical number for guaranteed uptime is 99.5 percent. What happens, though, if the number falls to 97 percent in a single year? While that 2 percent might not seem to be much, it can amount to 3,700 lost hours of uptime in a year! So it is of vital importance that the time to get up and running be short. Suppose the guarantee for the Gold Level SLA customer is four hours. What can be done to handle this is that there is a penalty built into the SLA for hours over, say, five hours, and a premium built into the agreement if it is less than perhaps three hours.

That means that problems or events can be anticipated, planned, solved, or scheduled. The costs of service are controlled. Since the SLA is a proposition for managing risk, sharing pain, and mutually benefiting from success, it can be a solid incremental revenue producer. For example, if a company providing network maintenance services is sourced to make sure that the networks are up and running continuously and the SLA calls for problem X to be fixed within two hours, it is possible to provide a rewards system that financially benefits the network maintenance company for returning network services within less than one hour. *Ad infinitum.* By using field service applications, much of the time to get the problem in hand and the technicians to the site can be significantly reduced so that the rewards can be earned. Again, it is incremental but very real revenue. Additionally, the cost of service is reduced because of the elimination of wasted time and service redundancies, making the

SLAs more profitable for the company and improving the quality of service for the customers, which, in turn, keeps them customers.

Dispatch and Scheduling

Dispatch and scheduling are among the most dangerous and complicated field service tasks. There is no question that if scheduling/dispatching best practices are instituted in support of a system, scheduling can be an important delineator and a source for cost effectiveness, profitability, and customer satisfaction and retention.

Think of it personally. It's July and your air conditioning is out. You deal with a major HVAC service provider and you have a warranty that gives you parts and services for a year. Luckily, this unit is only six months old. Unluckily, it's six months old and broken in the middle of July in Alabama (which is where you live, incidentally, in this little yarn). You've set up the service call for 11:00 that morning and you're waiting at home, sweltering.

To set up the call, you called into a service center where a CSR (see Chapter 7) took your information. He called up your customer record, took a look at your warranty, your service history (zero so far), set up a trouble ticket, and gave you a ticket number. In the meantime, you're at home waiting, sweltering. Hot.

He then forwarded the trouble ticket through the system workflow to a scheduler who used the scheduling system they had to decide who would be the best technician to come to your house. This could be an employee or a contractor they partner with for your area in Huntsville (by the way, it's Huntsville, Alabama). While you waited, you sweltered. Hot and sweating.

The criteria that were used to determine this simple scheduling for that technician were things like:

▶ Geographical proximity

▶ Specific skills to deal with your problem effectively

▶ A determination as to what level of service you were due according to your warranty or your SLA

▶ An optimal route for the technician, who had to have available time that fit your schedule also

▶ Parts replacement that needed to be shipped and delivered according to your needs (the customer) and the service tech's schedule as the specialist with available time on appropriate dates

▶ Inventory that then had to be replenished based on the parts that were shipped to you from a warehouse location that would minimize shipping time and possible missing parts

So we have priority, location, parts availability, skills, and technician availability all involved in scheduling this single visit.

If scheduling optimization and best practices are involved, the likelihood of you continuing to swelter, hot and sweaty, beyond the 11:00 appointment time are minimal. But if they are not embedded in the activity or the activities around this scheduling and dispatching are still fairly manual, then the cost to the company and the likelihood of a very angry, very hot customer goes up exponentially. Labor costs, parts replacement costs, and the cost of lost customer satisfaction are the difference between profit and major negative revenue impact.

You can automate dispatch and scheduling optimization, even if you don't incorporate best practices, and there is a significant cost savings. Let's look at the models for that first and then we'll look at some of the results numbers with the institutionalization of best practices.

Scheduling Models

There are three models that are usually constructed. In the order from least effective to most effective, they are:

▶ **Decentralized scheduling** The call center representative (CCR) receives the call. Another CCR or a system that has a good workflow allocates the job ticket to a field technician. The field technician reviews the request. The field technician calls the customer and schedules the visit.

▶ **Centralized scheduling** The CCR receives the call, and the request is entered into a centralized system. The dispatcher picks up the request from the system (based on geography). The dispatcher reviews the request, makes the scheduling decision, and chooses and sends the technician based on location, time, and skills.

▶ **Optimized scheduling** The CCR receives the call. The request and all other customer information (including existing customer records) is accessed and entered into a centralized system. The job is booked and the technician visit scheduled by software system. The field technician is notified through the workflow routing build into the optimization system.

In large field service environments, optimized scheduling is a necessity. The technician can concentrate on the job, without worrying about the scheduling, saving labor time and optimizing billable utilization. Customer contact with humans at the other end occurs at the first call and at the service technician's visit and that's about it. The dispatcher is the central point of deployment. He handles multiple technicians' schedules simultaneously, which makes the number of dispatchers necessary very small. Engineering productivity, according to many studies, increases by about 10 percent. This is good for cost controls and labor effectiveness, but it is only the beginning of the real value of field service—the profit center.

Scheduling Best Practices

In 2002, D.F. Blumberg Associates (BAI), one of the premier field services consulting organization in the United States, and the Association for Service Management International (AFSMI) did a fascinating study called "S-Business Optimization" which examined the results of the implementation of best practices throughout a services-based company and the differences with those companies that didn't embed those practices. While I'll be referring to this report throughout the chapter, let's look at the results of implementing dispatch-related best practices throughout companies by comparison to those who didn't:

- ▶ Customer satisfaction rates increased 100 percent

- ▶ Service quality levels increased 80 percent

- ▶ Service profitability increased 60 percent

- ▶ Service revenue increased 40 percent

- ▶ Response time improved by 20 percent

The numbers speak for themselves.

Customer Relationships

The human side is always a factor. If your company has a number of HVAC units that need maintenance or repair, you depend on that field service technician to not only get there on time to fix it, but to have the tools and parts to take care of the problem and to have a demeanor that doesn't get people at your company mad about whatever the problem or need is. That means it is imperative that the field service technician:

- ▶ Understands your company's service problems and needs

▶ Understands your account history

▶ Knows contact-specific information

▶ Is aware of the service level that he is required to provide

▶ Arrives on time and with the appropriate parts and tools

▶ Has the information that he needs dynamically at hand

From a practical standpoint, that means that the scheduling, logistics, mobile facilities, knowledge bases, and field service systems have to be in place and working. Otherwise, you might not be very happy with the human beings you are counting on to take care of whatever ails you.

Inventory, Logistics and Parts Planning

Supply chain issues, right? Nope. Customer issues. What if with all that scheduling and dispatch planning, the technician in Huntsville didn't show up at 11:00 and left you hot and sweltering because he was unable to get parts he needed to fix your air conditioning? You wouldn't have cared less why he didn't get the parts. You'd only have known that you were really very hot and sweaty. And mad.

Regardless of the cost of the item, the broken delivery promise is one of the most debilitating failures for the relationship between the customer and the company. Logistics and delivery—heretofore a supply chain management issue—become a CRM issue, or more appropriately, a value chain issue. How does this affect the top and bottom lines? Some of the value of implementing parts planning and inventory and logistics functionality includes:

▶ Shipping and receiving costs can be managed.

▶ Parts replenishment can be automated.

▶ Parts ordering can be done effectively, not just haphazardly, especially with Web access to availability.

▶ Analytics can help control inventory costs by identifying which parts are chewing up costly shelf space and which parts need to be stocked more substantially.

In that same BAI/AFSMI study, the best practices companies who used parts planning and service logistics improved 21 percent in total calls per repair completion (1.1 for best practices; 1.4 for the ordinary firm). The repair turnaround days went from 5.8 for the regular companies to 3.2 for the best practices firms (45 percent improvement). Finally, most interesting to those of you with a CFO's head, logistics operating costs as a percentage of total cost went down from 13 percent for the ho-hum company to 10 percent for the best practices company, a 23 percent improvement.

Other Things to Keep in Mind

There are other potentially important functions to consider when thinking about getting a good ROI with field service:

- ► On the financial processes side, quote to cash functionality such as billing, invoicing, order issuance
- ► Remote diagnostics
- ► Analytics
- ► Cost tracking
- ► Asset management
- ► Repair management

These processes are examples of potentially essential functions that make sure that you service your customers well and keep them with you as clients. It takes an extensive network to do that as the demand becomes greater for better service.

Service Cycle Management: The Indus Industries Example

What would it be like if field service CRM worked the way it was supposed to? Interestingly, there are companies out there that do it the right way. Indus Industries, which serves the utilities world, is a good example of successful field service. Let's listen here to Steve Roth, vice president of marketing for Indus International:

You are new to the Atlanta area and are moving into a new home. One item in the long list of moving day to-dos is to call the local gas utility to establish new service. You're dreading the call because you just know that somehow, someway you'll be inconvenienced.

Unbeknownst to you, the utility has just implemented a new service delivery management (SDM) solution which combines functionality of Customer Relationship Management (CRM) (CIS), workforce management (WFM), and enterprise asset management (EAM).

You speak to their call center or customer service rep (CSR), and through their Indus Banner CIS system they ask you a few personal questions—name, address, phone, credit information, and so on—and establish you as a new customer. The physical address, unless it's a brand new home and you are calling for first-time service, is already part of their records. GIS, a partner function and integration touch point, would provide a graphical rendering of the utility's entire infrastructure, including your home, to the CSR so that they can establish which assets/infrastructure, if any, are associated with your address. If any new infrastructure (such as piping) is required to support your installation, the CSR would be notified at this time so that the downstream work could be planned.

You've asked that the gas be turned on today and your call to the gas utility was not a scheduled event for their workforce. Through the Indus WFM module, the CSR has visibility into the entire field service workforce's schedule and availability. You tell the CSR that you would like to be at home when the work is done and the CSR asks what time would be convenient. You respond with, "Are you joking?" and then after a pregnant pause you respond with 11:00 A.M. The CSR enters your request as a high priority and the system then runs a real-time rescheduling exercise, using a multivariable optimization problem based on priority of work, the workforce's current location (Global PositioningSystem (GPS)), current workforce availability, estimated time to completion of work being done in the field, tools and equipment on their truck, lunch breaks, and so on. The system responds back and it turns out that John B. can do the work, has the parts, and can be there at 11:00 A.M. The CSR commits John B. so that he can no longer be reassigned and the appointment is set. The CSR asks you if you would like to be called or e-mailed when John B. is ten minutes from your home. After falling off your chair, you ask that an e-mail be sent to your Palm Tungsten. The CSR thanks you for the call and then hangs up.

Back at the gas utility, the Indus enterprise asset management (EAM) module now creates a work order. The work order and any supporting information or documentation (special information, maps, safety info, required parts, and so on) required for this work are wirelessly communicated to John B. If a stop is required to pick up parts from a parts depot, John is notified at this time. John is also wirelessly sent detailed driving instructions to your home (using a GPS)—another system touch point. John arrives at you home and installs a new meter. That asset is now put into service and its life-cycle (cost, repair history, and so on) is tracked through the EAM module. John B. has connected you, the work order is closed via his wireless device, and you are now part of the CIS billing process. You receive a welcome e-mail from the gas company. You smile and think, this is how the rest of the world should operate.

That's a compelling story that should make you think about the true benefits of field service both as part of a CRM strategy and as a profit center. It's there, but you have to be bold, creative, and smart.

Strategic Considerations

First and foremost, as in any CRM program, a clear strategy has to be developed. I won't detail it here because I do so in Chapter 17, but there are a number of possible field service strategic initiatives that might be worth investigating. Let's look at some of the hypothetical scenarios:

- ► Creating a best practices–based company that provides high levels of service that utilize service management models such as the BAI/AFSMI S-Business Optimization model.

- ► Increasing productivity by incorporating a series of best practices into a standardized business process model. For example, closed-loop product defects tracking, which isolates the single corrective action that can fix similar defects. The business process that holds this best practice is the installed base quality management process. One other example: continuous contract profitability tracking— this very important best practice allows your service managers to assess the profitability and value of a contract in any format that you want, by service, contract, product, or product line.

- ► Increasing the identification and closing of opportunities from warranty expirations or up-selling higher level SLAs to the client. These opportunities could be generated through the field service technicians.

▶ Increasing the overall profitability of field service sales through increased pipeline visibility and managed margin constraints. This one holds for any CRM business objective, actually.

▶ Increasing productivity and reducing the cost to the customer by optimizing schedules and routing, minimizing technician downtime.

With each of these come the considerations that can be particularly volatile with field service operations: geographic distribution of service technicians, warehouse locations for parts, issues related to scheduling, and logistics, among many others.

Mobility: Onsite, Outta Sight

One of the more important numbers to know when thinking about field service is that 28 percent of all mobile workers are field service technicians, according to a study done by Yankee Group in 2002. But considerably more drool-worthy is the following statement in the same study: "The Yankee Group predicts that over 2 million U.S. field service workers will use software solutions that combine wireless data capabilities by 2008. Additionally, U.S. revenues associated with wireless field service solutions will increase from $700 million currently to more than $2 billion by 2006." (Source: Mobilizing Field Service, Yankee Group, 2002) That is a big market, a lot of clout and a substantial gap in 2002 reality and 2006 forecast.

The Basics

Mobile field service is a tricky field. The reason is that there is a wide array of hardware choices, software choices (though not good software choices), carrier choices, needs, wants, and desires when it comes to functionality and features, and confusion over what is actually the best way to go about this Neanderthal-level effort. For example, here's just a few of the hardware platforms available:

▶ Pocket PC (Hewlett-Packard, Toshiba, and so on)

▶ Palm (Palm, Handspring, Sony)

▶ Ruggedized PDA (Itronix, Symbol Technologies, Fujitsu, Panasonic, and Melard)

▶ Tablet PC (Acer, Toshiba, Compaq)

▶ Notebook (myriads)

- ▶ Ruggedized notebook (Panasonic and others)
- ▶ Xybernaut Hybrid PC (hip-sized)
- ▶ Pager (fast fading)
- ▶ Cellphone
- ▶ Radio

To make the hardware choices even worse, the standards for each of these platforms are different, both in operating systems and in approach. For example, the PalmOne handhelds still operate on the Palm OS, the Pocket PC on Windows Mobile 2003, and many ruggedized PDAs on the Symbion OS. Yikes.

Next, consider the software that needs to be used. The software application vendors are myriad with such key players as FieldCentrix and Astea, Siebel, SAP, PeopleSoft, Oracle, Wishbone (acquired in early 2004 by Indus International), and MSDI, all of whom have full-featured versions (Siebel, PeopleSoft, and FieldCentrix), industry specific foci (Astea), or horizontal specialties such as contract management, costing, or parts sourcing (Metrix). But that's just a few of the major players. Within each of them and among others lies a mobile application set that varies in strength. For example, Siebel mobile services are good; SAP's a bit weaker though much strengthened with version 4.0 of MySAP. Once features, functionality, technical strengths, and mobile applications value are determined, the carriers that will provide service to your service areas have to be chosen. Those are often the standard carriers—AT&T Wireless, Verizon, or Cingular through its Mobitex network—but if your service areas are rural, the choices become dicey. Which carriers provide the most guaranteed uptime for the connectivity? How are you going to handle multiple carriers for national service areas that are urban, suburban, and rural and don't necessarily overlap? Then you have to think back on what applications can handle spotty or lost coverage during service calls. How do you regain connectivity for your handheld when coverage is dropped?

Another barrier is the actual network that the carriers provide as it is today. As of 2004, you are still dealing with CDPD networks that only provide 19.2 Kpbs speeds, far slower than even a dialup connection on your PC. While the promise of future 2.5G and 3G networks is great, it is just beginning to make an impact in the United States through AT&T Wireless and others. But for now, things are really turtle speed.

Because communications are remote in many instances, it is also the area most fraught with danger of failure. Technical issues become customer issues quickly when there is a problem that is to be resolved and contact is via cellphone, laptop, ruggedized PDA using voice, or e-mail or SMS or some other form of exchange. The room for human error and technical difficulty is frighteningly wide. Even if the scheduling is optimal, the downtime for the technician is minimal, and all parts are available, a simple technical transgression such as a PDA that can't remotely synchronize with the office or the inability to access a knowledgebase can lead to a disastrous result with the customer.

Even York International, my field service poster child, with a picture-perfect CRM project, had trouble with their chosen handhelds and is looking to replace them with better devices for 1,500 traveling technicians. It can mean the difference between profitable margin-happy work and a negative investment. Care must be taken in choosing appropriately. Capital and revenue costs involved are things like:

- ▶ Mobile terminals

- ▶ Telecommunication networks

- ▶ Internet servers

- ▶ Network service charges

For example, if you are using an 802.11b network, it is important to know where T-mobile might have an access point. If you are using satellite networks, it is a different story, with (most likely) greater accessibility, but also a likely greater expense. Be careful.

All of these are important considerations when trying to configure a mobile field service network. But that's just the beginning of the ride, folks. It's never easy.

Strategic Value

The strategic value of field service is short-term, mid-term, and long-term. There are wins that are available tomorrow morning, so to speak, and several that will occur at the point when you see your grandchildren off to college.

The Short Term

Often, when trying to get the support of senior executives who have been either lukewarm or clueless for a CRM project, it becomes essential to win a few small tactical victories to warm things up. In field service those kinds of wins are usually derived from cost reduction or improved efficiencies. While these are not the real advantage of CRM in the service of field service, they can be valuable because of some cost benefit and because of the political implications of the victory. Often, these efficiency victories are derived from traditional supply chain domains such as inventory planning or warranty management. For example, using analytics to determine the level of demand geographically for parts. The results will indicate whether the stock for the low-demand parts should be reduced or shifted to warehouses in other parts of the country where the demand is higher. Reducing the stock means shelf space costs and maintenance costs are reduced. Or perhaps, if the demand was higher elsewhere, planning the geographic dispersion of parts to specific local warehouses so that the time to delivery to the field technician was reduced, thus reducing service call cycle time.

Remote diagnostics provide almost immediate benefit. Technology has reached the point that the self-analyzing systems are not only cool, but have a strong ROI attached, because the costs associated with machines saying, "Hey, come fix me" or "I'm at capacity, get me another one of me," are not nearly as expensive as they once were. For example, Coca-Cola has equipped thousands of its vending machines to wirelessly transmit inventory, cash, and repair data back to local distributors, eliminating that arduous human step. Coke uses CDPD (cellular digital packet data) to transmit 1 KB per day at a cost of eight cents per transmission. Estimate what just the labor cost of a manual entry would be and you can see the benefit. Plus, eight cents buys Coca-Cola optimized schedules and logistics, with the distributors dispatching trucks to only the machines that need to be restocked or repaired. Not only cool, but also it means that Diet Coke is cheaper than bottled water—though not as good for you, kiddies.

The short term does have a lot of cost savings that can often be in the realm of 5 percent to 15 percent with tactical initiatives that succeed in the short run.

Other short-term benefits of field service are cross- and up-selling opportunities that are identified by service technicians in the field and are immediately registered in an opportunities database by the field service representative. Routing moves the opportunity to the appropriate salesperson. The appropriate person is automatically determined due to the workflow's embedded business rules. Baker Hill Corporation generated $750,000 in referred business from their service techs in 2002, a previously unfathomable result.

The Mid Term

In this region, the lines between the supply and demand chains get the blurriest. The cycle here for results is considerably longer—somewhere between two and five years for significant returns. However, it is here, by developing strategies to link automated processes to strategic planning, that the real revenue returns begin to show. Internet-based services or satellite services are one domain that can provide a mid-term benefit. For example, some of the features available in 2004 Acura's models features include XM satellite radio, an eight-speaker DVD-audio system, and a voice-recognition enabled GPS system and OnStar (though only in the RL). Note that there are three satellite-based systems that can be linked to each other. The mid-term value proposition is not the products such as the GPS system, but the services that OnStar can provide, which are not just remote diagnostics through real-time live interactions with the driver, but remote technical (field service that doesn't require the technician to be in the field) services that are subscription based. To get to this point with OnStar, as Honda and other auto manufacturers have, there had to be a considerable investment in satellite and wireless infrastructure that took two to five years of both strategic planning and infrastructure spending and setup.

The value proposition at this level is increases in the revenue stream directly due to the provision of premium services, detailed service level agreements, and increased customer intelligence that is used to make better decisions on customer value.

The Long Term

This long-range investment cycle is only for those decision makers with cast iron stomachs. This can be a cycle that outlasts the employees who began to implement the long-term changes. Mark McCluskey of AMR Research, one of the foremost field service analysts, says the SLAs associated with this cycle hold the manufacturer totally accountable: "power by the hour." This is a daunting, high-density, high-intensity risk that can provide dramatic returns.

For example, contractually guaranteed upgrades or replacement of parts and systems every x number of years is a continuous revenue stream that is planned and accounted for. The parts and labor costs are controllable because they are known in advance, the inventory can be well managed, the scheduling planned well in advance, and so on. In other words, good planning provides a cost-controlled ongoing revenue source. In fact, the long-term effect of centralizing customer data is seen here, because the longer the history and more consolidated the data, the better the services company can serve its customer. If the customer is given a means of tracking their own service and parts requests on the Internet, the cost of labor is reduced and the customer can enter the data needed to plan the time and place of a profitable service call. For example, Siemens Medical, over time, improved its technician utilization rate by 10 percent, reduced travel time 5 percent, reduced overtime costs 15 percent, and increased workload by 50 percent without adding resources. This is a long-term benefit since the investment here is frontloaded.

The Ultimate Benefits

In the 2002 BAI/AFSMI study mentioned above, the long-term results of the implementation of enterprise-wide best practices were examined. What happened when best practices were applied to strategic visioning, planning, automation, process optimization, and real-time data capture? They did benchmarking of industry averages against best-in-class service parameters to see how the results shaped up. They then isolated the factors that led to the most successful results. There were smart conclusions and interesting results.

The conclusions? With a focused strategic vision and plan, supported by technologies, processes, and a strategic marketing approach, there can be significant improvement in both top line and bottom line revenue. The internal improvements need to focus in call management, logistics support management, and field communications.

The results? The "best practices" companies had a mean improvement of 23 percent as a result of field service implementations. When best practices implementations were applied (such as tracking key metrics like revenue per service employee or per field service engineer), the revenues of those sterling enterprises were 43 percent higher—an average of $254,000 per best practice employee to $178,000 per "nuthin' special" company. The pretax profit was even more impressive: 41 percent to 18 percent (128 percent better), and the utilization rates of those field engineers were spectacular at 86 percent to 55 percent. The cost per call? Only $143 per best practice company engineer to $208 for a "regular" company.

What Could They *Possibly* Be Thinking?

Here's something I want you to know that seems to be anomalous. To help you understand it, I'm going to draw a conclusion first and reverse-engineer it.

Conclusion

Chapstick sales are way up in the world of field service executives.

Reverse-Engineering

In this neo-CRM world order, executives who own field service profit and loss centers recognize that it is now an important part of their sales, marketing, and customer retention efforts. Note: I'm talking about recognition, not action. Hold the thought.

Astea, one of the longest-lived field service software vendors, did an influential study of 1,900 field service decision makers in November 2002. The results were shocking:

- ▶ 56 percent of all CEOs interviewed saw field service as vital to their sales and marketing missions and thus revenue, either as a direct profit producer or product differentiator.

- ▶ Only 42 percent of the CEOs were going to increase their field service budgets in 2003.

- ▶ Of the 42 percent, 40 percent of those will do nominal spending of less than $250,000, which is tantamount to no spending at all, given the high costs of parts and labor maintenance and associated processes.

Further, Aberdeen Group in 2003 corroborated this thinking at a more tactical level: corporate executives were unwilling to spend more than $6,000 per year per field service–related mobile user. That wouldn't even cover the annual overhead and direct costs of the purchase use of a ruggedized laptop or tablet PC much less infrastructure creation and hardware maintenance, software, connectivity charges, associated labor time, and so on.

This is why of that 28 percent of all mobile workers that are field service–related, not even 5 percent are automated and wireless. Contrast this with the fact that 40 percent of all U.S. adults are using mobile telephony services (that is, have cellphones). What an amazing lack of thought and foresight on the part of these executives.

The irony is that this could be immensely profitable for those manually dexterous, automation-clumsy service operations. The Association for Service Management International (AFSMI) has put out statistics that support an average gross margin of 30 percent for service operations (as opposed to 21 percent for sales). But AMR saw that services expenditures were no more than 20 percent of an IT budget, despite the 40 percent plus increase in gross margin, proven through the might of AFSMI statistics.

Let's look at this in even more stark statistical terms. AMR in another study said that the field service divisions of manufacturing companies that provide parts, maintenance, and other services post-product sale account for 40 to 50 percent of the company's profits and fully 25 percent of its revenues.

Let's get even more down and dirty. Gartner Group CRM vice president Michael Maoz, one of the most respected analysts in the business, estimated in 2002 that "profit margins can be improved by 20 to 60 percent through improvements to field service operations and field logistics." (Source: Customer Service and Support Strategy Key Issues, 2002, Gartner Group)

What makes the Astea survey executive response almost surreal is that 56 percent of those executives have figured out the imperative nature of field service to their revenues. They gave it lots of lip service, but they won't do anything about it. Amazing. So, for their lip service only...

Conclusion Restated

Chapstick sales are way up in the world of field service executives.

STEPPIN' OUT: Siebel Field Service

All other concerns about Siebel aside, they are number one when it comes to field service applications. They understand its complexity and that field service is perhaps the most sensitive customer direct interaction that a company can have. Consequently, they've actually spent a good deal of time crafting and refining their field service applications and have thought through this intricate and confusing process. They've even figured out that field service for insurance works differently than field service for HVAC. I don't know about you, but I'm glad for that. I don't think I want my insurance agent working with my air conditioning.

Siebel Field Service—Definitely Not too Much of a Good Thing

Siebel Field Service is one of the applications where Siebel's huge scope is a good thing for all those considering field service. The individual modules are feature rich and complete. I'm going to detail them because this is one instance where that level of sophistication is not just bells and whistles but actually works to the customer's benefit.

THE GOOD THINGS: SIEBEL FIELD SERVICE MODULES

- **Customer** This is the centerpiece of Siebel Field Service functionality. Not only are you able to access the account information that you need for any particular corporate account and the individuals involved, but through a centralized customer record you can view and manage the service events and activities associated with those events. You can also schedule service activities, develop best practice activity plans, manage complex tasks, and track service costs. In other words, a genuinely singular and dynamic customer view. Cool stuff and invaluable. Plus you can sync it to whatever gadget moves you—Pocket PC (my favorite), Palm, Outlook file, whatever.

- **Service requests** Siebel Field Service provides full call management and resolution capabilities, allowing users to create, assign, and manage customer service requests. Field engineers, no matter where they are standing, have immediate access to a customer's complete profile, including existing open issues, related product issues, service agreement information, and information pertaining to the customer's operating environment.

- **Contract and warranty management** This is perhaps one of the most important revenue-producing pieces of the Siebel Field Service application. First, it identifies and controls the value of service level agreements (SLAs) and handles the constraints built into them via the underlying application workflow. This is the most important part of field service–related contract management. It's usually called service delivery execution. Typical IT functional geek speak, but actually one that really affects your business. When it comes to the warranty management, it handles defective parts recovery and return. It works to track and recover service costs, using a closed-loop warranty management system that I won't explain here.

▶ **Service automation (proactive)** This is where you track assets across accounts. That means that each asset that is registered with a particular client company can have its warranty tracked so that you can determine whether that asset is under warranty or out of warranty. This is regardless of whether the warranty agreement has a single tier or enough tiers to put a bride and groom on top. This is interesting because you can manage both your own internal assets and those of your customer from this single module. It fits well with the "neo-CRM" that is defined by the extended value chain links between CRM-ERP-SCM (see Chapter 15). You can even associate the single asset with a preventive maintenance plan that activates based on time interval, usage, threshold, or event triggers. That means scheduling, which segues to...

▶ **Dispatch and scheduling optimization** The visual centerpiece of this segment is the Dispatch Board. This is where you can view schedules by region and drag and drop new service technicians' activities onto the board for automatic optimization. Running behind this is an Assignment Manager that assesses the skills and experience of each individual technician plus the availability of those self-same folks to make sure that the right person is going to the appropriate job at the right time. Then the scheduling, depending on the priority assigned, can be transmitted via varying wireless devices to the technician and the dispatchers in real time. Additionally, future scheduling according to contract provisions. The schedule optimization engine optimizes deployment schedules using a business rules–based engine that takes care of rules like minimizing travel and labor costs, while ensuring that contractual commitments are met. It doesn't get any better than that. Except maybe if you win a lottery and then don't even have to worry about things like this.

▶ **Knowledge management** What makes this interesting is that it is a repository. Siebel likes to call this problem resolution and service management. To me, this is where you can use sophisticated search techniques on knowledge bases that contain technical documents, videos, product specifications, operating procedures, FAQs, Web pages, and known customer service solutions. It is also the location of the Service Encyclopedia, which holds all the collateral that you need for pricing, products, and processes, plus libraries of best practices, which segues again...

▶ **Best practices** Aside from the best practices that are built into the system, there are a couple of very cool and effective features that Siebel provides here that make field service life a lot easier. The best of them is Service Assistant, which takes predefined activity plans and automatically triggers activities in their appropriate order. That means a service request can be driven to completion. Imagine the possibilities here. No longer will you have to rely on the inexperience of your younger staff, because the events will be preordained and one step cannot occur with the occurrence of its prior one. Imagine if you could apply this to having your teenager do household chores.

▶ **Optimized parts and logistics** This can do the following: Produce and process internal orders to transfer parts internally. Create purchase orders to buy parts or services from third-party partners, if they are needed. Generate service orders to ship parts to a customer. Check it against sales orders and apply appropriate discounts. It then can inform the customer of the activities. It can also handle the logistics necessary to get the parts where they have to go using algorithms and business rules to identify preferred inventory and fulfillment location, replenishment relationships between the different locations, and allocation and substitution rules at multiple levels. If that weren't enough (and believe me, in the field service world, it isn't), it can handle the returns of defective parts by issuing RMAs associated not with just the defective parts, but with the service level agreements that the parts-returning party has with the parts provider. If that was overwhelming, get this. It can also handle logistics through line level parts management. This means that it can identify and handle parts shipment and replenishment of diminished parts stock based on whatever customized rules are embedded into the system. Then it handles the shipping and receiving, too. Wow. Who needs people?

▶ **Service inventory management** Using a parts locator, inventory is tracked in real time and at any level you'd like to see it, down to the warehouse, the service center, or the supplier. It is accessible in real time to the CSR or engineer or logistics manager. You can get the real-time info from anywhere using either fixed or mobile hardware.

▶ **Analytics and reporting** Siebel Field Service builds in more than 140 reports. It uses an executive information system to identify trends and potential problem areas in a graphical way (for example, most customers are not renewing warranty agreements when they have a strong SLA) and a specially configured datamart for analysis of field service operations and customer satisfaction, among other facets.

▶ **Away from home: mobile, wireless, handheld, and remote** Interestingly, despite a pretty darn wide range of mobile and wireless capabilities, this hasn't been a particularly sexy thing for Siebel Field Service potential customers. Siebel still has only a handful of wireless customers. Pretty much the entire gamut of mobile platforms including cellphones, Pocket PCs, Palm devices, pagers, laptops, and whatever you can think of are handled by Siebel Field Service. The communications methods are remote synchronization for those of you who want to exchange information between laptops and corporate servers, wireless messaging through your handheld or phone, and an offline solution for those of you who can't be online all the time. Having all these platforms and communications means doesn't mean Jack unless there is something to communicate. In this case, access to complete customer, site, and asset histories is available on whatever medium or platform you wish to use, as is the corporate knowledge base, and even time and expense reports, service requests, and inventory availability. Not bad for something that you can view from your palm (your real hand palm, not your device).

Other Leaders in the Field (Service, That Is)

There are a few other solid competitors worthy of mention. All the major players such as PeopleSoft, SAP, and Oracle have solutions for field service, with SAP in particular showing a considerable leap in their application functionality and quality with the release of MySAP 4.0. But if you are looking for a field service–specific vendor, the two to look at are Astea and FieldCentrix.

ASTEA

Astea is an old timer, having been around since the prehistoric late-1970s. It is a keeper, even with some financial issues that have burdened it. Somehow, while finances are always an obstacle, this hasn't prevented them from providing excellent applications and some of the best research done on this fledgling profit center domain. Gartner, in fact, ranked them as the field service management leader in the niche player sector of the Magic Quadrant during first quarter 2004. That, for those of you uninitiated, is the lower left (as opposed to the regal upper right) quadrant for the market leader. However, being ranked as the leading niche player is no mean feat and should be at least understood as a good thing in your assessment of various vendors in this marketplace.

Astea's specialty is providing high quality field service solutions to capital goods manufacturers, though they have other customers, too. While not particularly strong in mobile solutions, with the release of Astea 6, they have perhaps the most comprehensive solution set with field service–related marketing, sales, and support products. So you can see how comprehensive this solution is, here is a list of the product titles, all preceded with Astea, then the title and then 6 (for example, Astea Marketing 6): Marketing, Sales, Field Service, Depot Repair, Professional Services, Contact Center, Mobile, Portals, Alliance Contact Center Analytics, Alliance Depot Analytics, Alliance Field Service Analytics, Alliance Marketing Analytics, Alliance Practice Analytics, Alliance Sales Analytics, Alliance Studio, Alliance Links and API, Alliance Collaborate, and, last but not least, Alliance Global Database. That is as comprehensive a field service solution as exists in the marketplace today, with everything ranging from the classic CRM solutions to the centralized data store and those features and best practices needed for a complete field service operation.

Additionally, Astea was responsible for that killer research that I mentioned earlier in the chapter. It created quite a stir and gave Astea more visibility than any time in their 25 years of existence. Unless superb mobility needs to be part of your portfolio, I'd treat these guys as a big-time competitor for your field service dollars.

FIELDCENTRIX

FieldCentrix is a fine small ten-year-old company that is just beginning to see an increase in mindshare in the field service space. They are incredibly strong when it comes to mobile, wireless, and Web-based solutions—perhaps none stronger in field service. They have a strategy based on solid, reliable applications and effective partnerships with major players such as IBM, Microsoft, and PeopleSoft/J.D. Edwards, and wireless carriers such as AT&T Wireless, Cingular, TMobile, Nextel, and Verizon. They are smart enough to associate themselves with hardware providers like Panasonic, producers of the Toughbook™ ruggedized notebook, an important piece of hardware for the weather-susceptible, concrete-looming field technician.

One of their core applications is the very cool FX Mobile. FX Mobile supports all major mobile communications protocols, including dynamic IP networks, concurrently on a single server. It can run on a PDA, a ruggedized (or regular wimpy) notebook, or a handheld device using Windows CE. It is the mobile platform for FX Service Center, the base product that FieldCentrix provides. FX Service Center captures service call information in real time from customers calling in and then automates the scheduling and dispatching processes that are transmitted through FX Mobile to the field technician. Using FX Mobile, the onsite field technician can look up the equipment he's servicing and find out what the most common problems are, accessing a centralized knowledgebase back at headquarters. Then using their patented ServiceFlow technology, the service technician is guided through the steps that will take care of the problem. Very slick.

To make it even better, FieldCentrix provides FX Interchange, the integration framework for legacy systems or CRM systems.

This is good stuff for a ten-year-old company that virtually introduced the mobile platform to field service in 1998. I'd keep an eye on them and seriously consider them for your vendor if you're looking into field service solutions that need a high degree of wireless connectivity.

Up and Coming: Passport

In 2002, I didn't know these guys. I should have. This Massachusetts-based firm has been around for 12 stable years and has been quietly and effectively developing a mobile field service solutions platform that is better than good. They've built up a strong customer base, including AT&T, American Airlines, Con Edison Communications, Exxon Mobil, and GE, with blue chip names that you don't find even in their competitors' customer assortment. They have a great portfolio of strategic partners, including Verizon Wireless, Hewlett-Packard, and EDS.

They've got some investment capital behind them and small, but strong boards of directors and advisors. Yet, until 2003, I hadn't heard of them. More my fault than anything else, because what they have is worth knowing about and it's time they were on the map.

I met with Todd Richman, their senior vice president of strategic development, after receiving an e-mail based on an article on field service I wrote in *CRM Magazine* (April 2003 issue). They demonstrated a very effective mobile framework for field service that could be easily configured and yet had a rich depth. The levels of connectivity were spectacular. Even when the connection would drop on occasion, it picked up where it left off seamlessly, a major boon in areas with weak wireless receptivity. That's called session persistence in the industry. I was impressed by what I saw in action.

I like these folks. Their products are based on a dynamic real-time mobile model. They have a significant future on the CRM side of field service, at least from where I sit with my PDA at the ready. Their only sin is that they have senior management who are Red Sox fans.

Products

Passport takes a parfait approach to their products. They are layered upon each other from the most elemental to the most complex, depending on the business requirements your mobile workforce has—both industry and company specific. Do you need disconnected access or not? What kind of fields need to be in the applications? What operating system do your handhelds work on ?

"Passport is all about connecting mobile workers into the real-time enterprise, allowing companies to serve their customers better, utilize their resources more productively, and process revenue-generating transactions more effectively," says Richman.

▶ **Passport inField** This is the most elemental of their applications. It provides the framework for customized field-side applications that are server-based and provide instant wireless connectivity. For example, let's assume that you are a property and casualty claims adjuster sent out to an accident site. Passport inField provides you with the means to enter all the relevant information into the claims form, including digital pictures, and have it immediately available for possible action on the server at the corporate headquarters (see Figure 8-1).

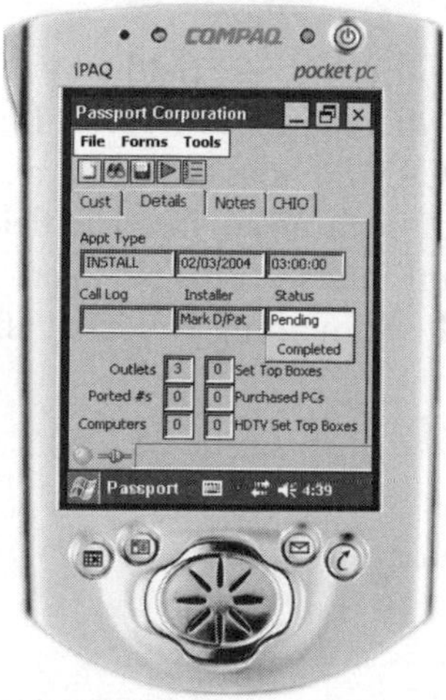

Figure 8-1: Passport inField on an HP Compaq handheld

▶ **Passport inForm** This is the next layer of the parfait. Let's take that same claim. There is a reasonable chance that the claims adjuster who filed it doesn't have the power to approve it. So what inForm provides is the ability to act on the claim from the desktop via the Web. Validation, approvals, and review actions are all possible, though more complex workflows are left to...

▶ **Passport inOrder** This is the actual ice cream in the parfait. inOrder is a full-fledged business process management system that is specific to field service. The business process that it captures and conveys is from request to resolution. It handles order routing, work queues, exception handling, and real-time status reporting and performance metrics. This is a complete system for any field service company that needs the mobile and desktop capabilities combined. It is particularly effective with a complex system that handles service orders or trouble tickets both on a large scale and with a good deal of intricacy.

Don't do what I did and ignore these guys for too long. They have a solid past, a growing present, and an expansive future. Hop on their bandwagon. Especially if you're a Red Sox Nation member. Passport or the Patriots are the best you can hope for.

Waiting for You

Hopefully, those of you who are field service executives will read this and decide, "Hey, where did I go wrong? I have to invest in this very important area of CRM." Those of you who aren't, while you didn't go wrong, please heed the same advice. The field is one of the most sensitive and important intersections between you and your customers. Field Service CRM is something you can't afford to be without.

9

Analytics: I Never Saw a Purple Cow, but if I Did, It Would Be a Demographic

"From true premises, it is not possible to draw a false conclusion; but a true conclusion may be drawn from false premises—true however only in respect to the fact, not to the reason." —Prior Analytics, Aristotle

"Since what is known without qualification cannot be otherwise, what is known by demonstrative knowledge will be necessary." —Posterior Analytics, Aristotle

So, class, what conclusion can you draw from these two statements? No, it doesn't mean *that* posterior.

Aristotle is saying that from premise to knowledge takes demonstration. You may make a certain assumption, hoping it is true. You then have to create the proof of its truth. But it also can be that in the course of examining this premise, which may be false, you come up with a true conclusion because you uncovered facts that are incontrovertible. That is demonstrative knowledge. In order to develop a strategy or impact a group or make a point, you have to prove it.

While these quotes are translated from (I falsely or truthfully presume) Greek to English, making it Greek to many of you reading this, the fundamental principles here are the governing principles of analytics. Use information that is examined in multiple ways and interpret it to come to a conclusion on how to make that information benefit, in this case, your business. In knowledge, there is power. But not just in information or data. Neither data nor analytics stands on its own.

What Are Analytics?

Analytics, in the enterprise applications sense we use it here, are the collection, extraction, modification, measurement, identification, and reporting of information designed to be useful to the party using the analytics. This includes multidimensional online analytical processing (OLAP) techniques as well as calculations, logic, formulas, and analytic routines/algorithms against data extracted from operational (OLTP) systems (the "T" stands for "Transactional," where the data is too granular to be useful for analysis). This is the slice and dice engine that is used to determine why you should be given a 10 percent discount on your next purchase of an Amtrak Acela ticket to New York from Washington D.C. where you live. When you drill down from the offer you received for this, you find that you live in D.C., make 7–10 trips per year via train or plane to New York, you are between 45–54 years old, have an income level over $100,000, and are a professional with a college education. That puts you in a segment likely to take Amtrak with some carefully offered incentive to do so. Especially, the high tech east coast corridor train Acela that gets you where you want to go in two and a half hours.

What magnifies the value of analytics is the real-time nature of many of the products such as those offered by E.piphany or the products that are early stage, but beginning to show up, offered by companies specializing in price, revenue, or offer optimization for online purchases. Each of them is available to capture the moment almost literally. If you go online to buy something, you might get an offer for something else related that pops up on the screen while you are still in the web session. That is because of an optimization engine which is working to compare your customer history with your current online activity and then "thinking through" what would be the best possible up-sell or cross-sell opportunity on the spot. These real-time analytic engines are just maturing now and can make a valuable difference in transforming customer behaviors or improving customer experiences.

But there are hundreds of products that use it and picking one is like walking through a (data) minefield. The wrong one can destroy you. The right one can provide you with the value you need to succeed. To begin to make the right choice, we have to understand how analytics work.

Analytics Types

There actually are analytic "types." No, not psychologist, psychotherapist, and psychiatrist, though writing this book over ten months qualifies me for a few sessions with any one of the three. Those are analyst types. The analytic types are descriptive and predictive. Here is a brief description of them both, which I predict that you'll appreciate.

Descriptive Analytics

This is the analytics for "as is." It is an historic look at a customer's behavior, organization's performance, or customer segment's habits. For example, if you run a marketing campaign, how effective has it been? Have the CSRs been improving their call-to-resolution time? Since you completed the implementation of your SFA system, how has the sales team performed in each city that has it? If there are cities that don't have it, how does sales compare there? Are the logistics and delivery up to the task, now that sales have increased? These are some of the possible uses of descriptive analytics, also known as operational analytics.

Predictive Analytics

This is the analytics for the "could be if," rather than the "to be." This is where developing models of the possible and scoring the likelihood of achieving that possibility by individuals become an important part of the analysis. Predictive analytics take customer data and identify customer segments or individuals and forecast possible behaviors based on historic performance and other factors introduced into a model. They then try to figure out how to utilize the likely outcomes for the benefit of the company. For example, if you reduce the sales team's administrative time by 12 percent and provide them with the means to get information this much more quickly, what is the possible impact on cost and on your revenue? Or if you promote a specific price cut on a product to 18-year-olds with driver's licenses in Arkansas, what is the likely increase in responses and in sales based on that promotion?

Got it? Now let's get to the engine.

The Analytic Processes

What goes on under the hood in analytics is something that you as a business person should understand, though you don't need to worry about the micro-details. There is a reason CRM analytics are so hot these days. It's because they are being used to make business decisions that impact the present and future of a company and its customers. In fact, the interpretation of the information presented is often the determinant of what kind of future the business has. Wrong decision, wrong information and the result is either business doom or job death. But, like any other instrument, don't you feel more comfortable understanding how something works before you have to use it? It just feels better.

Analytics Provides Actionable Intelligence

I saw a definition someone gave of analytics as "actionable intelligence." My nitpicking side notwithstanding, I see analytics as the means for providing what you need to turn data into actionable intelligence. Unto itself, it's a process that has multiple steps that result in information that can be used to create a plan to attack a certain segment of a market or even a single customer if that's the desired idea. But the technology and the processes to extract and present that intelligence are dense and complicated.

The Process: Segmentation

Customer segmentation is one of the earlier steps in creating actionable intelligence from data. It's a pretty straightforward idea, even if it isn't a simple process. To understand what it actually takes to begin to refine data so that it's meaningful, imagine that you're a bank with 3 million customers. You have all kinds of specific information about your customers, ranging from the basic name, address, and phone to birthdates, preferences, bank products owned, reading habits, income levels, investment success (based on your own confidential records) or not, employment history, risk profile and much more. You've got about 100 data fields that are completed for each customer—meaning that there are 300 million data points that are available to you. Now, tell me something. You've decided that you want to target a segment for the sale of a new product that you're bringing in that will provide them with a fairly high interest rate but over a long term. Obviously, this is a low risk instrument that isn't going to be particularly appealing to those who are willing to take high risks or those who are elderly—say, over 65—since long-term instruments really aren't their thing, when retirement is now the case or soon to be. It also might not be the instrument for someone who makes under $250,000 a year, though I'm not sure why it wouldn't be. Plus whatever else. On the other hand, it might be a good investment for the age group from 40–54 who are a bit more conservative than their younger brethren, because they might have children and are in more fiscally conservative states with better individual tax benefits and also have a while until they retire.

We can make the profiling anything we want, since this is pure speculation, but the point is, do you think that you will manually go through all 300 million data points and try to list them with a pencil to find what would be the best, second best, and third best target groups, and which groups you would make no investment in a campaign to sell this to? I don't think so. But analytics applications like SAS Enterprise Miner, one of the tried and true industry standards, can do this for you automatically and in a reasonable time.

Customer segmentation is the identification of attributes and behavior patterns that provide companies with the means to group its customers into identifiable and marketable segments. Once the segments are established, the company can weigh the value and potential return from a particular size of investment in that group. The key to segmentation, using a multidimensional model, is that it can be any set of attributes or behaviors that are identifiable from the data that you already have. Once the common behavior with these chosen attributes is identified in the group, you can then make decisions on how to achieve optimal results from either the intersection with the customer behaviors attributed to the particular segment or when you change the behavior attributed to the particular segment. This is profiling a customer.

Better analytics applications can pull in data from multiple sources, including your datawarehouse, your suppliers' data marts, and third-party data that you purchased and mapped to the system last night.

What makes segmentation particularly daunting is while attributes might be both dynamic and static, the behavior is continually changing due to changes in the market or to events beyond anyone's control. Think September 11, 2001. That changed all kinds of social behavior forever. Less dramatic or more dramatic events beyond our control will take place and change behavior again. For example, a 31-year-old entrepreneur with a pipefitting business making $245,000 revenue in 2003 will do one thing in year two and another in years three, four, or five, depending on all factors imaginable. Thus, just segmenting the data isn't enough to make a final judgment. It simply refines how you are going to look at the data to ultimately make your decisions.

The Process: Modeling and Scoring

Modeling and scoring sound like the fantasies of several single women and men I know. While there are multiple approaches to modeling and scoring, none of which take place on a catwalk or at a bar, ultimately, whatever the definition, they do the same thing. Modeling uses data mining techniques (see Chapter 14) to identify customers that fit optimal (and less) profiles for planned campaigns. This means finding relevant customer characteristics in segments that are targeted for the best chances of a successful campaign. Scoring is the process of applying the model, a complex arithmetic equation, to your target audience and associating a number (weighted score) with each individual.

MODELING

Modeling is not profiling, though they are associated. Puzzling statement, isn't it? A customer profile is a historic picture of a customer. The customer is 55 years old. The customer retired from his position as a retail banker at Fleet Financial Services and now lives in Pompano Beach, Florida, where he enjoys surfing and tanning. He has an income over $200,000 per year. His purchase history is geared toward high tech gadgetry such as HP IPAQs and Wi-Fi 80211.g routers and access points in addition to being a big consumer electronics guy. He has visited your A/V equipment website five times in the last two months, though he hasn't purchased anything.

That is good detail and historic. It is a continuously changing snapshot of a single customer. It is descriptive.

Modeling, on the other hand, is focused on predictive behavior. Modeling takes this profile, compares it to the behaviors of similar profiles, and then makes a weighted prediction as to some of the likely outcomes based on factors that are introduced into the model. So, if you took this profile and found that 13 percent of the customer profiles within a certain range of similarity responded to specific offer A and that 56 percent of the customer profiles within that same range responded to specific offer B, the customer is likely to respond well to specific offer B. If he doesn't respond within 5 days, then he is more likely to respond to specific offer A if you follow up. All this is dependent on any number of variables that can be part of the model.

There are several modeling techniques that are used by the analytics gurus. One of the most commonly used models for marketers in particular is RFM—which stands for recency, frequency, monetary.

This is not too difficult to understand, though it can be a complex model.

Recency is the method of looking at the timing of a customer's action. For example, how recently did a customer log in to a website to view something for purchase? How recently did they download a fact sheet on the items they were interested in? How recently did they actually make a purchase of those items? The historic trends according to those who place a lot of credence in this model are that the more recently the customer took an action, the more likely they are to repeat an action. In other words, act before "out of sight, out of mind" becomes the reality. So if you order an insulated jacket from L.L. Bean online, you are likely to see the L.L Bean catalog in the mail with the purchase because you are more likely to order something else either impulsively or at least shortly after you've ordered the jacket. Credible? Use yourself as an example, When you do something on a website related to a potential purchase, are you likely to go back and do that something again or even escalate to the next level? Are you likely to do that pretty soon after the first time? Or not so likely considerably later? Absence doesn't always make the heart grow fonder when it comes to purchasing. Inertia rules as time drags on.

Frequency is the number of times the actions have been taken. If you've logged into the website five times over the last 30 days, you are more likely to log in again then if you've logged into it once over the last 30 days. Some also advocate stickiness—the length of time that you spend in any one place. For example, you go to www.buyany-car.com and linger lovingly over that Audi A6 that you wish you could buy. You whip through several screens of promotion for Chrysler Sebrings and Chevy Malibus. But then you linger over the BMW 5 series cars for a long while, and finally, whip through the Saturn ads. What does this tell you? Either that you are seriously interested in a luxury auto or that you fantasize a lot because you have a Honda Civic income. If they have your customer profile, they will be able to make a more accurate guess as to which it is.

Monetary is the amount of money that a customer spends on a purchase or type of goods, or at a particular location, and so on. It can vary, but it is a determinant used in the RFM model to see if you are a high value customer willing to spend money who needs to be targeted.

RFM models are both the simplest and the quite ordinary models used for predicting customer behavior.

Scoring

Scoring individuals or groups is part of the criteria applied to get results from predictive analytics. The value is in risk management or opportunity management in particular. For example, companies like SAS (see Steppin' Out in this chapter) provide applications that handle credit scoring for banking or telecommunications which is primarily risk management. By looking at customer histories, behaviors, and other factors that could be "environmental" or even more global, such as the state of the economy or current interest rate, an agency can determine whether a individual customer applying for a loan is a good credit risk.

The best example of this is the one that we all either dread or love whenever we are refinancing or financing something—the scores that a credit agency provides to a mortgage company or an auto dealership to see not just how creditworthy you are, but what kind of interest rate applies to you. The less of a credit risk you are, the better the interest rate you qualify for, if you qualify at all. Take a look at Table 9-1 to see what factors actually go into scoring your creditworthiness under the universally accepted FICO (Fair Isaac Corporation) rating.

Table 9-1: Criteria that Determine Your Credit Score (Source: MyFICO.com)

Payment History
Account payment information on specific types of accounts (credit cards, retail accounts, installment loans, finance company accounts, mortgage, etc.)
Presence of adverse public records (bankruptcy, judgments, suits, liens, wage attachments, etc.), collection items, and/or delinquency (past due items)
Severity of delinquency (how long past due)
Amount past due on delinquent accounts or collection items
Time since (recency of) past due items (delinquency), adverse public records (if any), or collection items (if any)
Number of past due items on file
Number of accounts paid as agreed

Amounts Owed
Amount owing on accounts
Amount owing on specific types of accounts

Table 9-1: Criteria that Determine Your Credit Score (Source: MyFICO.com) *(continued)*

Lack of a specific type of balance, in some cases

Number of accounts with balances

Proportion of credit lines used (proportion of balances to total credit limits on certain types of revolving accounts)

Proportion of installment loan amounts still owing (proportion of balance to original loan amount on certain types of installment loans)

Length of Credit History

Time since accounts opened

Time since accounts opened, by specific type of account

Time since account activity

New Credit

Number of recently opened accounts, and proportion of accounts that are recently opened, by type of account

Number of recent credit inquiries

Time since recent account opening(s), by type of account

Time since credit inquiry(s)

Re-establishment of positive credit history following past payment problems

Types of Credit Used

Number of (presence, prevalence, and recent information on) various types of accounts (credit cards, retail accounts, installment loans, mortgage, consumer finance accounts, etc.)

Weight is important to scoring also. Not all criteria are equal. In this case, in the broad categories, Payment History is 35 percent of the total; Amount Owed is 30 percent; Length of Credit History is 15 percent; New Credit is 15 percent; and Types of Credit Used is 10 percent. The vast weight rests on payment history and amount owed—not all that surprisingly. So pay your bills on time or you will be judged—and scored.

In effect, scoring is the comparison of the existing customers against the model. Those who come the closest to matching the model's characteristic behavior or ideal profile are most likely to respond to the targeted campaigns. So a customer is rated numerically in comparison to both the model's characteristics and all other customers in the target segment or segments. Your 800 FICO score (don't you wish?) is your credit record against the ideal model credit record, in the example above.

VALIDATION

Validation is used to learn from the results of the modeling and scoring. Validation tests the predicted results from your model to ensure that a random sample was not accidentally biased. Then, depending on how successful the model was, calibration and tuning are done to improve the model for future use. Additionally, by looking at the various response rate changes, recurring and nonrecurring costs, or factors such as new types of previously unidentified customer behavior, this could give rise to new customer segments or brand new models that will work with the existing or new customer segments that are accounted for. Surprise results do account for something.

Whatever methods are used to model, score, and validate, analytics are attached to test campaigns that expose a sampling of the population that has been identified through the initial profiling to a given campaign. Valid statistical samplings of specific groups are used and then predictive models are applied to the results.

The Process: Risk Analysis

Even presuming success, there are risks and they have to be accounted for. While risk management these days seems to be the prime purpose of corporate America and sometimes seems to be their proprietary bailiwick, the reality is that risk analysis is a big part of all that we do and has a very serious role to play in analytics. Possibility of serious disease, bankruptcy, walking down the street and collapsing, and eating a banana with an adverse reaction all pose a certain amount of risk, albeit at different levels.

You look at the choices I just mentioned and you probably mentally categorized them something like:

1. Risk of serious disease

2. Bankruptcy

3. Walking down the street and collapsing

4. Eating a banana with an adverse reaction

I know you did because I categorized them that way—look at how I listed them in the first paragraph. But what were your risk criteria? The gravity of the result? The likelihood of occurrence? Both evenly distributed? Both, but heavier on result gravity than likelihood? I'll bet you don't really know. There may be even some other criteria you are using. Global nature versus specific nature of the event?

As much as the ranking you gave seemed to be intuitive to some degree, it wasn't. It came from your mental database and stored history. Risk management is not an intuitive science. It needs to be precise. For example, what if the individual you are talking about has a serious potassium allergy, but has an income over $400,000 per year and $3 million in the bank? All of a sudden, number 2 is 4 and 4 is 1. With risk analysis, this is what you need to know for potentially millions of people you never even heard of. Information that is much more precise is needed to determine the specific risk. On the other hand, you are making these partially intuitive risk assessments every waking hour of every day. If I do this, rather than this, I'll get this result—won't I? It's the "won't I?" that is the risk factor. As a thinking human being, you're attuned and accustomed to making these risk judgments instinctively all the time. You don't walk into brick walls because you know that solid brick walls hurt, and therefore if you walk into the wall, the risk of getting hurt is very high. As obvious as this sounds, you're actually judging risk factors. This is not a foreign concept to analytics or the applications that apply the analytic algorithms. Think about the quotes from Aristotle at the beginning of the chapter. He didn't have SAS or Cognos to help him. He was developing the philosophical foundation for the human actions that use analysis.

Contemporary risk analysis applied to CRM takes two prominent forms as we saunter through 2004 and beyond. It is the risk of losing customers, and it is corporate governance—the risk of violating a government statute. While we discuss corporate governance several other places in this book, customer risk a.k.a. customer retention strategy is perhaps the most important risk factor for a CRMer to be concerned with. Risk begins the minute you acquire the customer. If you have 'em, you can lose 'em. It is that simple. The risks that you have to determine are those that will erode the customer's confidence in you over time and cause them to ultimately move on to a competitor or, even more dreadful, simply leave you, whether there is an alternative to you or not. What creates the risk is what you have to identify. Then you have to reduce the likelihood of failure or the possibility of that.

For example, if you are a telecommunications company, you are looking at a churn rate that industry-wide will lose you 77 million customers in 2004, as I have mentioned elsewhere. Since the general confidence level in customer service of the telecommunications industry is low, the volatility (the ease with which a customer might leave, in this case) of the customer is high. So, where in some industries, it would take several incidences of bad customer service to make a customer leave a company, it might just take one in the telco world, because of the low satisfaction levels that most telcos suffer with. That call might have to create a significant instance of dissatisfaction or perhaps it is a small event like several attempts on the same call to reach the right person that could trigger the churn. The risk factors could include the overall dissatisfaction with the industry; the dissatisfaction with the particular provider; the quality of level one customer service; the ease of use of the customer service system; the volatility of the particular customer segment that is involved and on and on. In fact, AT&T lost a goodly number of customers when an upgrade to their CRM system made it impossible for thousands of customers to log on to the AT&T Wireless site and for thousands of customer service representatives to access customer records for weeks. A bad upgrade process blew thousands of customers away from AT&T Wireless—prior to their purchase by Cingular. If AT&T Wireless had been able to assess the risk appropriately and looked at customer factors such as individual customer values and commitments, they would have assessed the risk to their high value customers and taken appropriate prophylactic measures, saving their "more important" customers in the process. They didn't, and they didn't.

The Process: Measurement and Tracking

1. Did you know that Britney Spears "Oops I Did It Again" album sold 1.3 million copies in its first week, making it the fastest selling album in history?

2. Did you know that the Chicago White Sox and the Milwaukee Brewers played a game lasting 8 hours and 6 minutes on May 9, 1984? The Chicago White Sox eventually won 7–6 in the 25th inning. This game lasted the longest time of any single game played in baseball history.

3. Did you know that the best-selling "bad breath" detector was the Fresh Kiss HC-201, released in Japan in 1999? It sold 800,000 units. Really fascinating, huh?

Needless to say, these scintillating facts are here to make a point. Human beings are stats freaks. We love measuring things. The "best of," the "top 10," the highest and the lowest. We even have a book that is hundreds of pages long that annually updates nothing but the records for almost anything imaginable—the *Guinness Book of World Records*. People enter eating contests just so they can say they hold the record for eating the most Brussels sprouts in a minute—which happens to be 43. What other purpose would that have? While you may not want to be known for that, you want to be known for being exceptional in some way, and numbers prove it. I love the fact that *CRM at the Speed of Light* is in eight languages—operant word here is "eight." Cool. That's a lot. Wow. Eight. That makes me cool. I'm cool, aren't I? Eight.

Human decision-making also mirrors analytic behaviors and modeling and is as dependent on numbers as an analytic algorithm is. We look at the history of something, we decide what is the best possible course of action under the circumstances, and then we see if the course of action works. We tend to measure the success or failure of the value of that information or performance by a preconceived measurement of some kind. How do we know if something worked? In business, the bottom and the top lines improve or don't. In football, you are the number one quarterback if your statistics add up to the highest number after a formula is run. How'd you do? I came in first! I had the highest evaluation. I had a 95 average or a 3.6 for the semester. I ran the marathon in 4 hours 15 minutes. I did really well; my SATs were 1431, better in English than math. If the numbers aren't good, we fix the cause of the bad numbers, not the numbers themselves. Analytics automate a mimicked version of some cognitive functions. Analytics are decision planning. They provide us with information that makes some sense to us so that we can make rational decisions on how we want to do something.

We can see that measurement and tracking are a significant part of the analytics process. Using analytics, how do you measure results and track the success or failure of that measurement?

I'm going to repeat an example I used in this book once already. *CRM at the Speed of Light* (CRMSOL) was used for a lead generation campaign. The value of white papers versus books as incentives was looked at prior to the use of CRMSOL (my acronym) as the promotional item. The potential value of the campaign was analyzed looking at factors like cost of the production and mailing of the direct mail piece, cost of the book purchase with different rates of return on the direct mail piece, cost of response to the lead, and so on. Then what would be a successful expected number and percentage of leads based on the targeted segments was determined. Typically, a response rate over 3 percent would be well over the industry average result for a direct mail campaign. Imagine their pleasant surprise when the return rate was 4.35 percent. That led to thousands more books being purchased. Then the marketing analysts tracked the success rate for leads to the success rate for opportunity closings. It was also extremely high and the results were further purchases of the book.

However, this is a particularly simple form of measurement and tracking, useful for a quick overview and for some PR for me. But what if it gets more complex?

Scorecards.

BI and scorecards go together like Starsky and Hutch or biscotti and cappuccino or a shot and a beer. But careful preparation is paramount to making sure that the measurement and tracking done through scorecards are useful. Again, we're dealing with garbage in equals garbage out. Even more germane, garbage that seems to be possibly important in equals garbage out. Choose what data needs to be measured carefully. Don't let IT determine it, since to them data is data. To you, it's potentially useful strategic information that needs to be analyzed. By prioritizing the information that needs to be mined, you can save a lot of time and money and get the right returns. Make sure that the data is high quality—cleansed and standardized. I discuss this issue in Chapter 14 much more thoroughly. Then determine what data would benefit from an OLAP solution/multidimensional analysis. Not all data does. Sometimes you have data that is useful in its nearly raw form or simply doesn't need to be attacked by algorithms. Know which data does need work and which doesn't. The dollars you save may be your own.

Keep in mind, the use of these scorecards for measurement and tracking, or the use of analytic applications results or the creation of enterprise reports, are for the purpose of knowledge. It's just what the knowledge is used for that can vary. If you were targeting a particular result that needed a behavior change to get to the result, you would use analytics and scorecards to find out the existing state of things relative to the expected result. Norton and Kaplan, in their groundbreaking book, *The Balanced Scorecard* use Mobil Oil as an example. Mobil was analyzing service station gas sales of their product. But they wanted to increase the sales of premium gas to the public, not just know how well their gas sales were going at the pumps. So they changed the criteria to measure the sales of premium gas. What that did is begin to drive the behavioral changes that would increase the premium gas

sales. Why? Because the premium gas sales became the key performance indicator. Thus improving the premium gas sales—meaning,
meeting the specified performance goals—became a strategic driver,
because it was a visible measurement. So the focus on the specific measure became as much a proactive driver as a passive result. Thus, the
KPI became strategic, not static.

Suppose, for example, that you are reviewing your sales numbers
for the third quarter of 2004 for your IT services business. The scorecard, which indicated a target of $27,000,000, shows that you fell short
by $4 million. If you were looking at the results without a strategic
view of your criteria—in other words, you had simply had a revenue
goal and not much other thought went into it—you could see with
more granular information available to you that you sold $13,000,000
in enterprise applications services of your targeted $13,500,000, and
you sold $10,000,000 in desktop applications and helpdesk services of
your $13,500,000 target. You could also see that you had trouble reach-
ing your targets in southern states, but exceeded your targets in the
northeast. You could deduce certain things from this. You might think,
"Well, next quarter, we'll target more heavily into the northeast and
aim more at enterprise applications services." But if you were using a
scorecard that relied not just on some form of OLAP-driven results
but also the relationships between the key performance indicators in
marketing, sales, legal, and supply chain related departments, you
might learn a lot more. If you drill deeper, you find that the marketing department hadn't succeeded at any campaigns in the south at all
and there was a major problem in your call centers that led to a big
backlog on solving technical support problems related to your helpdesk
services for the desktop applications. All of a sudden the solutions are
somewhat different because the causes for the failures in the south and
with the overall desktop applications work become explainable. That
is the different between pure play analytics and the use of scorecards.
How you decide to measure and track is up to you. Use scorecards if
you want to or don't. But plan on how you're going to do this, regardless. Good thinking in, good things out.

Analytics Technology

Most of the technology applied to CRM and business related analytics is covered with its own chapter in this book—Chapter 14. However, I'll provide you with a really quick overview of the technology to

give you a big picture before you delve that much deeper into the depths of this very complicated technological minefield.

According to Dave Schmidtknecht, vice president of delivery at the Data Management Group, "The most important aspect of analytics technology, particularly that of business intelligence, is a commonality of the data—having everyone go through a standard front end to access a common backend. This will provide one version of the truth."

The Technology: The Software

There are three types of software tools that are needed to make analytics work:

- ▶ OLAP tools are software that give the user the opportunity to look at the data from a variety of different dimensions.

- ▶ Query tools are software that allow the user to ask questions about patterns or details in the data.

- ▶ Data mining tools are software that automatically searches for significant patterns or correlations in the data.

These are discussed in considerably more detail in Chapter 14. However, OLAP isn't.

The Technology: OLAP Dance

Online analytical processing (OLAP) is the analytics workhorse. It is the engine that generates the interesting information you will be looking at. OLAP vendors out there are fruitful and multiply with regularity. But no two OLAP engines are alike and that is a problem. Consequently, for the OLAP engine to generate intelligence responses and views usefully there are a significant number of considerations and a basic standard that has to be met by those selfsame engines or they are not going to be effective products. I've found that the OLAP Report (www.olapreport.com) has what appear to be the most process and user friendly standards for OLAP. I'm going to summarize what they call their FASMI criteria here so that you can understand it.

F is for FAST This means that the OLAP application can deliver most of the responses it needs to within five seconds of the query. The acceptable range for the simplest response is one second to the most complex around 20 seconds. Research from the Netherlands according to the OLAP Report says that users consider the process as a failure if there is no response within 30 seconds. This can lead to distraction and thus lower quality interpretation of results. So the five second mark is actually really important. Never thought "usability" of a query engine would be something to consider, now did you? Answer me within five seconds or I'll…something.

A is for ANALYSIS This is also a question of usability. What this means is that the system can handle any kind of business logic, business rules, statistical analysis, and so on and present it in a way that a user can understand. Once again, an intuitive result from a complex engine is the standard. This can vary, depending on who your target user is. For example, the results will be different for a marketing manager than for a statistician. Unfortunately, in the past, analytic applications were often geared to the statistician, which led to some really ugly interfaces and highly complicated results that, as we say in Yiddish-English, "you shouldn't want to know from."

S is for SHARED This is actually the security model. That means that when the data is entered, queried, or returned, that confidentiality down to the cell level if necessary is guaranteed. The trick here is when the data is being written by more than one person simultaneously or the same data is being queried in a different way from more than one person. How do you handle both confidentiality and access? They call it "update locking" in the vernacular, but what that means is that even if you are dealing with a single instance of data, it can be used by multiple sources for reading and writing.

M is for MULTIDIMENSIONAL This is the one that all the analytics guys love. Even the OLAP Report says, "If we had to pick a one-word definition of OLAP, this is it." What it doesn't mean is your ability to travel to alternate universes, whether you speak Klingon or not. What it does mean is that you can slice data cubically or volumetrically or left, right, up, down, through layers. For example, you have a spreadsheet you are staring at that has a number of columns. The columns are name of product, name of producer, local address of producer, city of producer, state of producer, product rank by analysts in numerical order, and revenue. You're interested in sorting the column by revenue from the product, so you hit the sort button and it sorts in order. But what if you want to sort it by revenue and you also want to find out how it is doing with revenue by state and by analyst rank? Not as easy as clicking a Sort button. Multidimensional analysis lets you do that and a heckuva lot more complicated operations than that.

I is for INFORMATION This is all of the data for when, where, how you need it, and get it taken care of. While an apparently simple concept, it takes into account how the data is presented, how the data is stored, where the data resides (a datawarehouse, data mart, or wherever), how much space the data needed takes up, how complex the data is, and how you view the data, among other considerations.

Put it all together and you get Fast Analysis of Shared Multidimensional Information (FASMI). These features are the components for OLAP. If the OLAP applications incorporate these features and meet these standards (not all specifically outlined here), then they qualify as a valid OLAP engine.

Business Intelligence

Once you have a feel for OLAP and understand how analytic processes work, you can begin to think about business intelligence, perhaps the hottest segment linked to CRM that exists in this part of the millennium. I'm going to answer questions that came from readers over a long period of time.

What Is Business Intelligence?

Business intelligence is the use of an organization's disparate data to provide meaningful information and analysis to employees, customers, suppliers, and partners for more effective decision making. It is a critical component of a CRM strategy.

Is Business Intelligence Strictly a CRM Thing?

Customer intelligence is not the only BI that exists in the business world. Other BI that is frequently found is product, services, supply chain, financial, and human resources intelligence. In fact, BI extends along the entire enterprise value chain and, even though that value chain is organized around customers, the BI can be broken down to specific links in the chain. BI has applicability, though in different forms, to both commercial and government enterprises and has undergone a technological evolution that mirrors the increasing complexity of the analytics world as customer records grow into the millions and customer value rises to the top of the corporate objectives hierarchy. The more information you have on each customer interaction throughout all steps of the value chain, the clearer and more innovative thinking you can do on how to treat those customers appropriately, either by segment or, if your information is granular enough, down to the individual.

Isn't BI the Same as Enterprise Reporting?

In a word, no. Enterprise reporting is the combination of multiple reports from multiple systems using a standard reporting tool and a common delivery platform. It reports the "as is" data that you want it to report from multiple places. It is an impartial information aggregator that grabs already analyzed and interpreted data from multiple sources and neatly (if it's working well) ties the data together in a format that makes it readable. It's not more than that.

The analogy is sort of obvious. When you wrote a paper in college, you handed in a Word document or if you're as old as…my colleagues, a typewritten one. Are the actual physical pages the same as the thought and content? Nope. The physical pages are just the delivery vehicle. When I write a white paper, I usually have a clause in the contract with those hiring me that states that they own the work product, but I maintain my rights to use the ideas elsewhere. If I couldn't, there are parts of this book that couldn't be written. The book, the white paper, the college term paper are all delivery formats to present the ideas. The ideas are not the reporting of them.

Is BI the Same as Predictive/Descriptive Analytics?

Not exactly. It uses both predictive and descriptive analytics, particularly the former, but isn't the same thing. The analytics features of business intelligence help present that actionable information and help you make decisions.

Business intelligence takes raw data and turns it into information. It uses complex algorithms on captured data in the "as is" state and makes some interpretive sense out of it. The algorithms can provide you with information that you can actually use. The information, once mapped, interpreted, and identified, is then presented through an enterprise reporting tool in a way that makes it intelligible to those of us with ordinary mathematical skills. That information provides tremendously valuable input for developing the innovations and approaches to improve customer experiences. Some of the general uses of business intelligence according to the OLAP Report are:

▶ Data warehouse reporting

▶ Sales and marketing analysis

▶ Planning and forecasting

▶ Financial consolidation

▶ Statutory reporting

▶ Budgeting

▶ Profitability analysis

The purpose of business intelligence is not really any different than any combination of predictive and descriptive analytics. The purpose is to provide you with a set of results that can help you make a smart business decision. Perhaps the most lauded and most commonly stated business intelligence result in the service of CRM is customer lifetime value. What is the value of a customer or a segment over his, her, or its lifetime with you? Is the value going to vary in different time periods? Other possible BI benefits are to help you determine what you are going to sell to whom and when that sale is going to occur. For example, financial services companies might want to see what products will be appropriate for what segments during a certain time of year. You might be interested in creating a scholarship related instrument that would be sold to 35–49 year olds with children during a school year while their children were between 3–15 years old. The BI engine would help you decide whether or not this was a good time of year, a good segment, and/or a good product.

What Are BI's Challenges?

The implementation of a BI project is not without challenges. Although the selection of the BI product is important, many of the major challenges remain internal. The number one major nonproduct challenge is company politics. Experience has shown that single department implementations are less challenging, but often result in fragmented, nonintegrated approaches that, in the long run, increase interdepartmental issues instead of simplifying them. Experience also tells us that, as with many enterprise projects, those projects crossing department boundaries typically yield a greater value than departmental specific projects.

As with any project, the user is very important and the interest of the user must be considered key to project success. The factor of ease-of-use for users is critical in both product selection and overall success. The OLAP 3 report indicates that the inability to get users to agree on requirements is a common problem with BI implementations and if the requirements are agreed upon, staying the course without changing the requirements proves difficult.

There are technological challenges too. The dispersion of the data sources, the "dirtiness" of the data and lack of standards for a common data format, the disparate technologies that are being used, the availability of web services—or not, the sufficiency of the hardware and software to do the job, the sheer size of the total data available—all provide significant challenges to the application of those pesky and complicated analytic algorithms.

For example, First Union has a 27-terabyte database with 16 million customers. They use both SAS and Microstrategy for their analytics. Their ideal, which they've pretty much achieved, was to determine what to up-sell and cross-sell to profitable customers. That meant centralized, normalized, and clean data just to get to the point where the data was useful. That's 27 terabytes of data. That's 16 million customers who had to be ready. Then they needed to determine the relevant criteria for the data so that the analytics engine could do its number(s) on the customers. That meant that the data that needed to be there had to include the account information, sales and purchase data, demographic data, profile data, service/support records, shipping and fulfillment information, campaign responses, and finally, web and other touchpoint data. The level of effort is immense. The results are really good if you take the time, as you can see in the next section.

BI Well Done, Customer Value Received

If you meet the challenges that BI presents in a CRM environment, then the value of the customer intelligence returned can be immeasurable. It helps you identify four basic customer value categories:

Customers to retain These are the high value customers that should get the most attention because they will provide the highest profitability.

Customers to acquire These are the customers that have high value potential based on their segments and the relevance of the products or services of the offering company.

Customers to grow These are the future high value customers that will become the company's and its partners' long term investment. These are strategic accounts.

Customers to harvest These are the low value, low margin customers or product/service offerings that can be gathered to the bosom of the company by optimized services or pricing with a minimum of effort and investment.

Once you have this information, you have to plan to do something with it, not assume it is another notch in a belt or a thing to be catalogued and forgotten. Bells and whistles have to be rung and whistled. Use what you have received as valuable customer intelligence you now can act on. Other than that, it's just another way to look at data, hardly worth the million or two dollars you spent on it.

The Marketplace Grows as the Return Increases

The value of BI is becoming apparent to those interested in gleaning customer intelligence as part of their overall CRM initiative. BI is perhaps the hottest segment of the CRM market in 2004 and promises to be for several more years. It is a market that is expected to be $6 billion by 2005, up from $2.5 billion in 2003 according to a 2004 survey by IDC. Why the intense interest? The value of the tools is that they help companies understand and influence behavior. What kind of value will BI give you in return for the work and effort it requires? After all, business is a value *exchange*, not a charitable function. Luckily, for you, the hardworking mother's son, BI's return is fairly easy to see. In 2003, IDC did a study called "The Financial Impact of Business Analytics" that showed 49 percent of all companies that had invested in business intelligence produced a return in less than a year, and 63 percent in two years or less. More pleasantly startling, the median return produced was 112 percent of that cost in that time. The lowest return was a positive 17 percent, the highest 2000 percent! IDC also found that over a five-year period, the returns for applied business intelligence were 431 percent of cost. Wow.

More data. Aberdeen Group found that approximately 19 percent of companies implementing BI claim they have met or exceeded their business goals. More than 60 percent state they have at least largely met their goals. As always, soft nonmonetary benefits were more easily obtainable, and even quantifiable, than hard revenue bearing benefits. A detailed look at the types of benefits and the percentage of companies with BI initiatives realizing them reveals the following improvements as discovered in the highly recommended 2003 OLAP Report 3 annual survey shown in Table 9-2.

Table 9-2: The Return on Business Intelligence Investment (Source: The OLAP Report 3)

Business Intelligence Benefits	Percent of Respondents with Realized Benefits
Faster, more accurate reporting	81 percent
Improved decision making	78 percent
Improved customer service	56 percent
Increased revenue	49 percent
Savings in non-IT costs	50 percent
IT savings	40 percent

You can't get a whole lot clearer than that—or can you?

AMR Research Inc. did a study released in April 2004 that said that CRM investment will grow to $10.8 billion in 2004—a billion dollar increase from 2003. Laura Preslan, a research director at AMR, saw that a substantial part of this increase would come with spending on analytic tools. Companies that had the data collection tools seemed to be willing to spend between $1 million and $2 million on these analytic applications. The results they found for those who had already deployed them were staggering. Those who were using them for making real time adjustments to marketing campaigns could see between a 30 percent and 70 percent improvement in response rates.

Business Intelligence Begins to Verticalize

In the world of CRM-agnostic business intelligence, Business Objects, especially with the 2003 acquisition of Crystal Decisions and its product lines, is perhaps the BI industry's most significant player, only challenged by Cognos as an all purpose vendor. Always savvy, Business Objects has introduced a substantial number of industry-specific business intelligence applications that cover consumer products, communications, energy, financial services, government/public sector, healthcare, manufacturing, pharmaceuticals, and retail. No coincidence that the CRM-centric analytics-strong companies like E.piphany, PeopleSoft, Siebel, and Oracle all follow similar industry-specific patterns in their offerings, including analytics. This is the 21st century battleground for business. The idea of vertically smart BI would be to have algorithms that deal with processes that are faithful to their industry only. The most obvious are the anti-CRM analytics that can match foreign student behaviors to their travel patterns, school attendance records, and other factors, or the algorithms specific to financial services that can trace anomalous patterns that could indicate possible illegal activities.

Business Intelligence and a Real-Time Future

There is a BI Holy Grail. The vast majority of BI applications are not real time at this stage. They run their algorithms at some predetermined time interval and then slice and dice appropriately. While well suited to long-term planning and identifying customer segments, they are not suited that well for personalized real-time interactivity that most competitive companies want to maintain or gain an edge. The current generation works well with both identifying the state of the current customer database and evaluating the appropriate segments for targeting campaigns. It works not quite as well but still okay for compliance such as the 48-hour window provided by Sarbanes-Oxley to correct any regulatory exceptions discovered in the accounting system. With a workflow, it can almost approach near real-time execution, but it isn't the Holy Grail, merely the traces of the trail.

Personalization = Real Time

There are few among us who haven't ordered a book on Amazon.com at some point. We appreciate its ease of use, responsiveness, and particularly its personalized approach to each customer. But few of us (about eight in total in my queries of tens of thousands of people) have ever spoken to a human being there. That is where personalization comes in. The human touch without the actual interaction with a real human. The best personalization engines are those that provide you with a "warm and fuzzy" experience and an associated good deal during your sojourn with a company through some communications medium.

There are a few vendors that are approaching this sacred vessel. E.piphany, in the CRM space, has without a doubt the best real-time engine, its Interaction Advisor, one of the few that reached for the grail and grabbed it with both hands.

E.PIPHANY E.6 INTERACTION ADVISOR

The Interaction Advisor is an inbound marketing machine driven by a real-time self-learning analytics engine. The analytics engine looks at the customer who is interacting with the touchpoint and uses predictive algorithms to maximize the value of each interaction by providing a customized message to the individual customer. The real-time analytics monitor the response and results of the interaction and then fine-tune the future interactions with that individual customer based on the history and the results. But it is not just offer optimization or price optimization (see the section immediately below on price optimization). They have an offer arbitration function that helps companies determine which of the messages have the highest statistical chance of success with a particular customer. What makes this so cool is that that determination is made at the time of customer contact. It is a complex cocktail of real-time algorithms, business constraint modeling, and automatic targeting. Once the appropriate message is identified, it is deployed to any one of a number of channels—the contact center, an e-mail, a phone call, or even a web interaction. This can be done to the tune of several hundred thousand real-time decisions per hour, which means activities of several thousand service reps or web visits or combinations of those. The architecture is web-services based—SOAP, Java, HTTP, COM, MQSeries, and the usual band of suspects.

This is the future of analytics—only it's in the here and now, not the there and then.

Price Optimization

What is some of the realized value of personalized targeted campaigns as business intelligence and other analytics are used to create this information? The newest desire in CRM analytics is price optimization. To achieve this, engines and tools provide real-time targeted offers to customers who might be shopping online or who are engaged in direct contact with the vendors. There is cold, hard measurable business value to achieving this objective successfully. Customers accept the offers they are given on the spot, be it online or on-premise. The idea behind these optimization tools and engines is to provide them with the *right* offers, so that the odds of success increase dramatically.

Let's listen to Nachi Junankar, vice president of RetailIQ, a provider of price optimization engines to the online and retail world:

Imagine a product you are selling for $10 that is consistently a top 10 percent seller. The last time you made any adjustments to this product (pricing or otherwise) was back when the Celtics dominated and Larry Bird was de facto governor of Massachusetts. But if you had the capability to test out tiny price changes and adjustments to this product and, say, increase the price to $10.25 (a 2.5 percent increase) and measured if the demand for this product changed, that 2.5 percent increase could go straight to the bottom line, couldn't it? What if you also were able to pinpoint the price range in which customers "don't care" about the price? What if you found out those customers would pay $11.50 for this product without even blinking? Now combine this idea with the entire top 20 percent of your products. What if you could do this to all of those (for example) 100 products?

And what if this was done on a real-time basis? Meaning, a customer shows up on your web page and clicks on a specific product. Then that web page goes back to your optimization system and says, "Pass me the price for this product for this customer profile," and the optimization engine then does it. In the background, calculations related to the parameters for profit, inventory, promotions, loyalty, and such are being made by the system—based on the parameters that you had just entered into the system at 10:00 A.M. The customer then sees a price of $10.39 for this product and chooses to buy it or not. If she does buy it, you've got a price optimization slam-dunk! Now you just made 39 cents for doing nothing (the system does it for you).

Price Optimization Requirements

The most important requirement is good data, but what else is new? Everything under the analytics sun requires good data. But price optimization in real time requires a slightly different handling of the good data. The real-time data gathered as the surfer is surfing the Web creates an ephemeral customer profile that disappears the moment the customer logs off, but the data results remain, available for analysis in combination with the more permanent customer data. So the pseudo-profile will have data on shopping cart abandonment rates, or conversion rates or other things that might reflect failure but is valuable to learning to how to reduce the failure rates. The price optimization tool takes all of this data and "interprets" it into actionable components resulting in price adjustments for each specific customer interaction.

But the data alone doesn't finally determine the pricing. The pricing is also the make or break component in any deal ultimately. For example, recently my wife and I decided that we wanted to get library bookshelves built in, with a work desk also built in. This would replace our existing "we put them there ourselves" shelves. The first quote we got was $25,000. That was so absurd, we ended the relationship with the company immediately. We were prepared to pay well and had a number in mind. That wasn't it. How often do you find yourself bargaining on something? Oh, come on. You are always bargaining, looking for sales, using coupons—whether you can afford to do without it or not. The fact is that human beings love deals. They love the idea that they are getting what they perceive to be a break on a price for something that is still going to be profitable for the seller, break or not. Ever go to a bookstore and see books in the bargain bins? You see them marked down from $24.95 to $4.99? Unless there is an inventory clearance going on from the publisher over a discontinued book, the odds are even that $4.99 is turning a profit. But rather than being outraged that a publisher is making a significant profit on a $24.95 price on the book, instead you are happy that you could get the book for $4.99, rather than $24.95—profit notwithstanding. You love the deal. Price is the deal maker or breaker.

What the price optimization gurus do is identify a "price insensitivity band," which simply means the bottom and ceiling range within which customer behavior does not change significantly despite price changes. A change in price within this range does not affect demand. The question then becomes, how do you find this "insensitivity band"?

Once this band is identified, you can begin to look at the historical sales and product information, test out various scenarios of combinations of price, presentation, commitment, and customer. You—or more likely the system—will find the specific scenarios in which the customer is insensitive to small changes in price. Price optimization engines do that for you. This is an early-stage venture, though. Several vendors have price optimization engines, but it can be a pricey, not all that optimal experience in terms of the cost accrued in getting things set up and running. The value proposition is excellent, though the price dear. The results can be juicy good.

250 CRM at the Speed of Light: Essential Customer Strategies for the 21st Century

A couple of vendors you might want to watch out for here are the CRM agnostic RetailIQ and the CRM heavyweight E.piphany.

Vendors on the Move

Analytics players who are pure plays or CRM vendors who offer analytics as part of their suite are easily found. Cognos, Business Objects/Crystal, Microstrategy, Microsoft, IBM, Hyperion, and PeopleSoft through their Enterprise Performance Management applications—all excellent. PeopleSoft's CRM 8.9 stands out with an exceptionally good analytics package that has extended the envelope when it comes to user-friendly customer segmentation, especially for a CRM package.

For example, using PeopleSoft 8.9, a few clicks segments your customers into those purchasing your higher end software applications—spending over $500,000 for delivery and logistics software and services. Then you can use the integrated functionality in PeopleSoft 8.9 CRM to take this information and offer a promotion for those willing to upgrade to a new maintenance release of that higher end software. PeopleSoft has added SmartView so that users can see the customer segments after you click them into existence and how profitable they are or aren't. You can develop the strategy for that upgrade promotion using their integrated Strategic Account Planning product to design it on the fly. They have even integrated a real-time optimization engine of sorts into the overall functionality by providing a technology that can automatically recommend promotions or sales opportunities to customer service agents or salespeople as they interact with customers in real time.

This is a significant and very slick upgrade to PeopleSoft CRM 8.9's analytics.

Steppin' Out: SAS

When it comes to overall analytics scope, size, and quality, no one in the discovered cosmos comes close to SAS. They are the King, with all due respect to Muhammad Ali.

What else can I say about SAS that hasn't been said? Well, first, they are *not* the SAS Institute anymore and shame on you if you call them that. They are just plain SAS (pronounced "sass"). They are one of the best employers in the world with a turnover rate a little over 3 percent a year, even in good times when churn is higher as employees with options available to them seek the Seven Cities of Cibola elsewhere because the cities are made of gold. But SAS treats its employees like they are human beings with souls, not cogs in a revenue-generation burr grinder and the employees gratefully stay.

SAS covers almost all the needs of employee heaven. They have full-time doctors and nurses, a gym, a day care center, allow the employees to do what they need to do to balance their family lives. They are a pleasure to work for and with and apparently have been since 1976. I spoke at one of their events in New York in April 2004—a group of financial services executives—and was thrilled by the professionalism and warmth their staff showed throughout the event and by the quality of their input into the events. In other words, they are a class act.

They also have 94, count 'em, 94 products that are associated with analytics and intelligence. They range from the highly sophisticated Enterprise Miner application to the Interaction Advisor for Telecommunications to data quality management tools to tools for pharmaceuticals development.

This is a company that had over $1.2 billion in revenue in 2003 and yet remains the world's largest privately held company—though they did flirt with a public offering in 2003.

They have 3.5 million customers at 40,000 sites. Another wow factor added to many. They even have begun to clear up the one problem they have always had—tough to use interfaces that were rocket scientist hardened. With the release of their newest product generation in 2004, the user interfaces are now being seen as easier to use by, surprise, users. This is especially evident with the release of their marketing campaign management version 4.0 products. More striking is their concern for the actual skill levels of the user. For example, they released SAS Report Studio 9.1 for tech savvy users. They simultaneously released SAS Web Report Studio 9.1 for the ordinary, not too technical human being. This is one of the first products on the market that is released with the skills of the user in mind.

Not only are their products superb, but so is their post-sales service. Here's a comment from Linda Coffey, the information development manager for Maytag's customer service operation in an article from *Information Week* in 2003: "They promised excellent support and they delivered excellent support." What a company.

Marketing Automation 4.0

You probably saw a brief reference to this product in Chapter 5—you know, the one on enterprise marketing management. Even though SAS wasn't the Steppin' Out choice in that chapter, the fact of the matter is that

SAS made such extraordinary advances with this product with the user interface (see Figure 9-1) that they deserve some love. This is a great product that carries what might be the best of the analytics engines available in the EMA market stamped with the SAS standard of excellence that applies to all their analytics products.

The product is aimed at the Fortune 3500 enterprises, particularly the financial services, telecommunications, and retail industries. They spent a quarter billion dollars on research and development in 2003, a significant part of that on this product. They completely overhauled and re-engineered the architecture. Part of the architectural change was a much tighter integration with the analytics engines. They also spent time ripping the old interfaces to shreds and then spent thousands of hours revamping and developing new interfaces that use the most advanced data visualization capabilities—which you can see reflected in Figure 9-1. They even built in compliance capabilities such as control over business rules, metadata, and data management logic, so that customer privacy legislation (a very touchy and regulated subject) could be complied with. So a shout out to SAS here for doing something valuable and actually, gasp, nice looking.

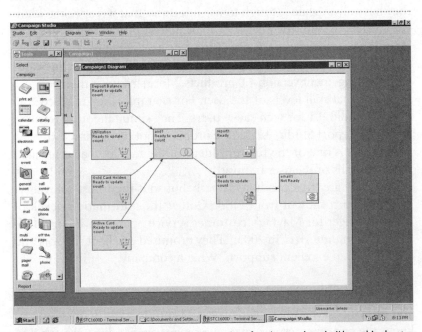

Figure 9-1: The SAS Marketing Automation 4.0 user interface. I never thought I'd say this about a SAS interface, but it's really very friendly.

SAS 9.1—Intelligence with Intelligence

SAS has a tendency to outdo not just its competitors, but itself. When you have more than 90 analytic products, you have to be thinking about the underlying platforms that govern each of them. Or do you? SAS 9.1 takes a big step forward and provides a single platform—conveniently, although not particularly creatively, called SAS 9.1 Intelligence Platform. This is a significant update that reflects the needs of the customer ecosystem with both highly integrated and integratable functions and concern for the actual users of the platform. It also is aligned with the needs of the contemporary business ecology.

To get this baby out, SAS had to account for everything from processor speeds and scalability on the architectural side, to user interest on the "customer" side, to quality and function of analytics for each point in its intelligence value chain. For example, they are the BI providers for Amazon.com. The scale and immensely dense level of action that Amazon requires is almost incomprehensible. Millions of catalogued items that have to be applied to hundreds of thousands of customers across six or more multilingual sites is just an astonishing thought, much less something that has to be actually done each day. SAS 9 was their platform of choice to do this.

With this release, SAS also begins to directly compete with the CRM vendors who have BI capabilities and the CRM-agnostic BI vendors like Business Objects or Cognos. They've introduced the more traditional BI products, ranging from OLAP to enterprise reporting interfaces and even understandable dashboards that are customer-friendly.

SAS has established a whole new set of capabilities. For starters, their straightforwardly named Enterprise Business Intelligence Server is designed to not only deliver usable high caliber content to business users—not just analysts—in an enterprise, but to do it in a familiar way. It adds an easy to use reporting capability through Web Report Studio. They also included a really smart idea—an add-in for Microsoft Office which gives SAS analytical strength to the "comfortable-as-two-year-old-New-Balance-hightops" Microsoft Office applications, especially Excel and even Word. This is a really smart move, akin to the now *de rigueur* Outlook integration that no CRM application can leave home without. Use the familiar to become more familiar is the operant principle.

The new version also enhanced the flagship data mining tools such as Enterprise Miner and Text Miner. Enterprise Miner now has a nearly intuitive and certainly easier to use Java interface that allows tech-savvy business folk to pull data from across multiple storehouses and create results that are integrated into existing systems. Text Miner does the same thing from text documents such as surveys, call center tickets, patents, and standard text sources such as Word documents or even the ever-popular .txt files—in multiple languages.

SAS also completely revamped their Enterprise ETL Server with this release. What is interesting is what was targeted: data quality. How smart is that? They spent an incredible amount of time on fine-tuning their ability to cleanse data, to normalize it, and to standardize the formatting in a way that can communicate the data and the queries to the data across multiple platforms, multiple applications, and even multiple enterprises. They actually targeted something that should be targeted.

So integration is better, portals are improved, interfaces are clear and targeted to specific user groups, algorithms are refined, data quality jumps to a new level and maybe, perhaps, it could be that there is a Santa Claus. If all these other things can be done by SAS 9.0, why not?

Okay, chums and chumettes, we're done with the horizontal versions of CRM, now let's move on to the vertical—the industry-specific versions. There are as many versions of CRM now appearing on the market as there are industry segments. We're going to have a lot of fun with some of these as we tool through the next few chapters.

PART III

The Markets

10

Going Deep: Verticalizing CRM

In mid-December 2003, IBM made a quiet announcement. That is, as quiet as a $100 billion company can. They are reorganizing their research, consulting, technology, and sales groups around 12 industry-specific groups. Not only are they going to invest countless dollars into adding industry-specific capabilities to WebSphere, but they are going to do the same with their business process units (the former PricewaterhouseCoopers dudes). They are going to use their 3,000-strong research arm to develop new applications, processes, and tools for industry-specific business transformation, and they are going to train 13,000 sales people in explicit industry-relevant knowledge. Some of the more evolved industries served will be health care, banking, insurance, and automotive. So this announcement was about as quiet as Hurricane Isabel.

IBM is squarely in the middle of a trend. As the processes that govern businesses begin to appear on center stage, moving the data-driven focus to the stage back door, the increasing desire to make those processes useful to specific industries begins to emerge as a big time need and big time drive. But what does that mean? What does "verticalizing" mean to you (or me, for that matter)? As Bob Dylan said, "The answer, my friend, is blowin' in the wind." So follow the breezes throughout this chapter.

Industry-Specific, if You Please

There comes a time in every CRM initiative when the business processes are mapped to the customer's needs. You saw much of that in Chapter 2. But what you saw in Chapter 2 was generic—or more appropriately, universal. The processes could apply to any business in the pantheon of commerce

But, there is another increasingly visible layer emerging as CRM continues its process-oriented transformation. It is characterized by particular industries with specialized processes that are applicable only to that industry, as you'll see in the discussions around higher education and insurance in particular.

This industry-specific customer focus isn't only private sector. Competition for dollars drives the nonprofits too, even though their motivation for those dollars may be very different.

Here's what Randy Bunney, director of development research at the University of Minnesota Foundation, has to say about nonprofit CRM:

> Fundraisers have long-known that their business is about building relationships. David Dunlop, formerly of Cornell University, in the 1970s was among the first to document the process of relating to donors in a series of deliberate moves or strategies designed to result in a major gift. Now, more than a quarter-century later, the concept has matured. One would be hard-pressed to find any major nonprofit without a mission statement referencing "donor-centricity" or "donors first."

> Yet the race to achieve ever-larger campaign goals (billion-dollar campaigns are passé for some large nonprofits) threatens to shove donor-centricity aside. After all, the purpose of fundraising is to raise money. Indeed. Yet donors have choices where to bestow their generosity. Nonprofits that maintain a product instead of a customer focus will fail to optimize their share of philanthropic dollars, now totaling some $260 billion annually in the United States. Instead, fundraisers have to figure out how to add value to donors in order to remain competitive. Nonprofit initiatives require a specific knowledge of how the nonprofits work.

However, every industry's CRM ventures are at different levels of maturity, partially due to when they realized the value of CRM. The financial services industry is perhaps the most sophisticated—especially the retail banking industry. In fact, very few major bank groups haven't initiated CRM in some capacity. But things in this industry get a little dicey when it comes to what is often necessary collaboration with other industries. Retail financial services companies already collaborate with a number other industries such as automobile manufacturers, homebuilders, retailers, and healthcare companies. For example, they provide loans for a new car or a mortgage for a new home. What complicates matters here is that each industry is at a different level of maturity with their CRM infrastructure and their customer initiatives. Yet they have to provide an integrated experience for the customer. For example, given that there are a number of financing vehicles for financing vehicles, how upset would you be if you didn't have a seamless, trouble-free experience in arranging these car payments for your new BMW or Mercedes? Or if you were subject to different perspectives and rules and kludgy interfaces when dealing with the car dealership and then the financial services company? It would be upsetting, to say the least. In the worst case, customer records could be so different that the auto dealership was sure you would get financing, but the bank said no. Bad news. So the idea of making sure that industry-specific processes and CRM initiatives are still governed by universal technology, workflow, and process standards and business practices is very important. It is why vendors like SAP play well in vertical CRM, as we'll see in Steppin' Out.

It gets even more complicated when you are dealing with a substantial channel in a particular vertical. For example, the partners for that automotive company are dealerships, but they are also parts companies. They are possibly companies that are hybrid in that they sell automobiles, boats, and other transportation. They could be services companies that handle automobile servicing. In late 2003, Channel-Wave (see Chapter 6) merged with Aqueduct to provide some of their CCRM/PRM solutions for specific industries because of this need. For automotive, they have a Service Information System that applies to the channel-related processes associated with the automobile's service cycle. It covers:

- ► Technical service bulletins
- ► Special service tools
- ► Labor time standards
- ► Electronic troubleshooting manuals
- ► Diagnostic trouble code guides
- ► Dealer management systems
- ► Training/learning tools
- ► Maintenance and warranty data
- ► Campaign circulars

▸ Policies and procedures

▸ Feedback forms

Note that while SIS handles the automobile industry and its dealers, it could be tweaked to apply to other industries too, such as machinery maintenance.

CRM at Different Theaters: The Show's the Thing

Few industries don't have ongoing CRM initiatives. In this chapter, I'll give you a piece of the rock with my focus on insurance—an industry that is in the midst of CRM initiatives, though it still has a way to go—and a piece of the Rock (a.k.a. Dwayne Johnson, star of stage, screen, and the WWE) with sports, which is not only in their baby-steps stage (with two exceptions) but is also a lot of fun. I'm also going to let you have a peek into the nonprofit CRM world of higher education—because nonprofit issues are so different than commercial vertical issues.

Insurance: Not-so-Passionate

In 2002, Doculabs issued a study that said that consumers lack passion about insurance and would rather not talk about it. Because of the complexity of the subject, the public would rather leave it to the experts. Well, we're going to bust the taboo here and talk about it—as an industry in the throes of passion—for CRM. But don't get ready to smoke that satisfied cigarette yet—not only is there a long way to go, but your premiums will go up if you do.

What makes insurance an unusual vertical industry is that it is a statistics-driven world that scarfs data like we down water. Ironically, it is those very stats that show you the industry's state when it comes to CRM. Analyst firm Aberdeen Group did a benchmark study in mid-2003 entitled "CRM and the Insurance Industry: Room for Growth." Their significant findings place insurance squarely in the middle of industries that have interest in CRM. Of the insurance companies surveyed, only 43.4 percent used CRM products in their industry, and of those, only 50.8 percent developed benchmarks that they used to measure their results. That shows a significant interest with room to grow, but a true lack of strategy when CRM is on the table. Other significant aspects of the Aberdeen findings were that the respondents spent less than $100,000 (52 percent) even though over 82 percent felt that CRM was either as important as or more important than any other IT initiative, and the plurality were going to increase their budgets in 2003.

When I interpret these numbers, here's what I can conclude. The knowledge of and desire for CRM is clear. But there is tentativeness about what to do about it. Why? As in many CRM programs, there is no clear-cut thinking about how to measure what the success is going to be. There is still a tendency to view the initiative as technology-driven, especially when you are dealing with a heavy emphasis on analytics. There is a real irony about a numbers-driven, risk-aversive industry that is increasing its risk by not figuring out the metrics it needs to measure CRM success.

Granted, most of the companies surveyed were smaller, with under $500 million in direct written premiums and 500 or fewer employees. They were relatively evenly spread over property and casualty, life, health, and commercial, with property and casualty with a slight edge at 58 percent of the respondents. The competitive pressures on the entire industry and especially these smaller players are huge as financial services companies look increasingly to add insurance as an offering in their portfolio. Issues of customer retention are greater than ever as these full-service, one-stop-shop companies make insurance with them appealing due to competitive policies, offerings, and rates, as well as the advantage of sticking with a single vendor for all your financial services needs.

CRM implemented at insurance companies can have an obvious and fast ROI. In 2003, I had the distinct displeasure of being dropped by State Farm Insurance for my homeowners insurance because I had filed two claims for a garage accident and a burst boiler and had made another inquiry without filing a claim. Again—two claims and one phone inquiry—and my risk profile was too great for them.

But imagine this scenario: State Farm is smart enough to implement CRM and thus has a 360-degree view of a single customer. Rather than being the policy-focused, customer-unfriendly company they seem to be now, they would be able to view my entire relationship with them. They would see I have auto insurance with them, homeowner's insurance with them, and a $1 million life insurance policy with them. They might have let the cancellation slide. (Of course, I have no policies at all with them, but you get the idea.) By providing that kind of customer-centric data, CRM allows an insurance company to weigh the value of the customer against the effect of its actions on that customer, rather than just automatically acting on the business rule set up in their system. CRM personalizes the insured—and humanizes the insurer.

Insurance: Actuarially, It Is Analytics

Insurance's prime concern is selling its products. It provides them for sale using both direct sales teams and independent agents. To do this, interpreting data is vital to the success of insurance's CRM initiatives. The investment it makes in gathering customer intelligence and centralizing its storage has dramatic effects on the insurance company's culture and its ROI. For example, a customer record for insurance isn't only going to show the history and transactions associated with that customer, it will also identify the claims and contracts that are associated with that customer. In the health and life insurance industry, the need to associate knowledge of specific health issues with the particular customer is paramount. Ultimately, life insurance is going to pay out on all active policies, so the healthier the customer and the more products the customer has, the better it is for the life insurance provider.

Analytics play a critical role in insurance. For example, the ability to know that the coal miners who are insured in West Virginia are more likely to get black lung disease than a resident of Tampa, Florida, is rather important in setting the premium for that coal miner or that Florida resident.

Companies like SAS (see Chapter 9) provide applications such as their Insurance Intelligence Solutions, which combine analytics built on insurance industry algorithms, a data warehouse, and embedded processes and models designed to improve marketing, to increase opportunities for cross- and up-selling products, and to mitigate risk. It is a solid solution for an insurance company focused on the analytic engine.

The Culture

Insurance is risk aversive and statistics driven. Here is a quote on retention that I think best reflects how the industry "thinks" as a whole:

> Retention is the act of keeping the possibility of loss with no attempt to control or transfer that loss to another party. This method, when used as the sole or primary risk management approach, may be appropriate when the risk of loss or the loss exposure is either too small to fool with, or too great to be able to do anything with. Each of us practices loss retention every day to some extent. The mere act of getting up out of bed is an example of loss retention. We accept

the possibility that we may trip over the dirty clothes strewn about the floor and injure ourselves (risk too small to do anything about) and we start the day with the expectation that the world won't end (risk too great to do anything about). Retention is actually what people are doing when they say that they are "self insuring."

—J. Alan Johnson, CPCU, ARM, AIS,
"Issues in Insurance and Risk Management"

A typical reason for retention in most industries is increased revenue and profitability. Insurance sees retention (in addition to the above reasons) as decreased risk of loss. Insurance CRM is aimed at shifting the culture from policy-centered to customer-driven. However, what CRM means to the insurance culture is what it means to any industry.

For example, one major change in a customer-centered culture could be the efforts of the insurance companies to become health thought-leaders. If it were still a policy-centric culture, policy administration with an eye to risk mitigation is the focus. But risk mitigation in a policy-centric universe is something like what happened to me with State Farm. Plug in the business rule, crunch the numbers, and reach a threshold. Then dump, dump, dump—or retain.

Risk mitigation in a customer-centric insurance culture is thought-leadership. For example, Blue Shield of California (www.mylifeplan.com) has a large online knowledgebase on health issues. It also helps the customer find a drugstore if they need one in their area. As part of their Lifepath Decision member offering, they provide a means of asking a pharmacist a question or asking nurses questions online, or even guides to compare hospitals and find treatment options. They have an extensive health and wellness database online as well as a drug database that you can search for drug information. In other words, they are providing you with information that could maintain or improve your health. The twofold benefit is that they are insured-friendly and are reducing risk by providing you with this important health information.

Taking it a step further, it is in the interest of the insurance company to see that a diabetic customer has regular checkups for blood sugar. Consequently, by institutionalizing CRM processes, the alert will show on an agent's or other appropriate CSR's screen that diabetic customer A should take advantage of a free test being given in his area over the next month. Aside from any humanitarian concerns that the insurance may (or may not) have, keeping that diabetic customer healthy is in the insurance company's interest, simply because if the diabetic is healthy, no one collects and premiums are paid for a longer time. The insurance vendors can also track whether the diabetic took advantage of the free blood sugar test. The response can create the need to adjust the level of risk associated with the diabetic. This is a step better than even the thought-leadership that CRM-driven insurers can provide and is a major step to reducing risk without the cold-blooded approach characterized by State Farm.

The Customer Is Not Only the Insured

The insured is the end client. But there is usually a national network of independent agents who represent the insurance companies who are every bit as much customers as the clients. There are also the employers who have insurance as part of their employee benefits programs. They have benefits managers who handle the insurance for the employees who are policyholders. If it is auto insurance, the auto companies are customers who have to be serviced too.

Hartford Financial Services Company services the agents online. They can develop a quote, request issuance of a policy, file claims, and ask billing questions via the Web. Blue Shield of California has separate gateways for employers, providers, and producers, since they are all customers with specifically different needs. On the whole, insurance purveyors understand the nature of the 21st century customer very well. The end client—the insured—is only one piece of a complicated puzzle.

Processes and Workflow

Let's drill down even more. What would a simple insurance-specific process set look like? Here's the process map that SAP uses for policy management:

1. New business

2. In-force business

3. Manage group contracts and coinsurance

4. Support claims process

5. Support commission process

6. Support collections process

7. Link to business intelligence

How does this tie to the workflow and the technical architecture? Figure 10-1 gives you some idea of what is involved in the effort to bring CRM to this industry, at least in industry leader Chordiant's view.

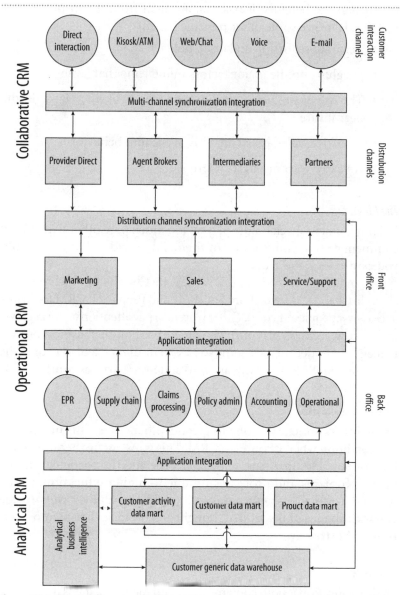

Figure 10-1: The Chordiant view of CRM in the insurance universe represents what is typical of this vertical.

Benefits

Ultimately, for the insurance industry to adopt CRM there has to be some real benefits that are apparent to its rather tight culture prior to the change in the culture. Some are mentioned elsewhere in this chapter, such as the benefits of risk management from the insured's perspective. Here are some other possible benefits:

- ▶ Accurate reporting on lapsed policies

- ▶ Insights into the major factors influencing that lapse

- ▶ The use of predictive analytics on who is likely to lapse in the near future

- ▶ Proactive, rules-based analysis of account behavior

- ▶ An early-warning alert system

The Players

I'm not going to dwell on the players too much here other than a brief comment so that you're aware of them. I'll provide a URL for each if you care to look them up.

The industry's two best in this vertical are Chordiant, which you read about in Chapter 3 (www.chordiant.com), and PeopleSoft CRM for Insurance (www.peoplesoft.com). Other players to pay attention to are Pegasystems (www.pegasystems.com) who are focused on the business process management side, but have some success in insurance, and of course, the always present SAP (www.mysap.com) and SAS (www.sas.com).

Higher Education

I'm going to present this one in great depth, because it is in a primitive condition when it comes to CRM. This is instructive because of the level of obstacles that have to be overcome and the particular nature of the problems and processes unique to higher education, which reflect the difficulties in the nonprofit world. Hopefully, it will provide you with an idea of the level of thought and obstacle that go into a vertical CRM strategy.

Overview

Higher education is both contemporary and medieval. If it is doing what it is supposed to, it is providing a student with the skills and training to enter the contemporary world. But it operates as if it was a 13th century town and has the technophobia to support that. Certainly, it operates like a business. It has processes and functions. It needs money to sustain itself. But its operations are more like a municipality that is integrated into a larger municipality. It's no coincidence that the University of Michigan is often called Ann Arbor. It is also no coincidence that when a student considers a university, part of what they consider is the life of the community that it resides in. There is a symbiotic relationship between the town and the university/college.

Yet with all the interaction between the two, the university environment is insular. If you look at the organizational structures of many of the most prominent universities in the United States, what is astounding is the lack of influence those very same communities have on deliberations of the university. In multiple discussions I had with university officials on CRM, it was evident there was a lack of consideration for the external customer beyond a community liaison and lip service. For example, in the excellent book *The Strategic Enrollment Management Revolution*, edited by Jim Black and published in 2001 by the American Association of Collegiate Registrars and Admission Officers (AACRAO), perhaps the most forward-thinking higher education trade association, there are a dozen charts for Strategic Enrollment Management (SEM) organizations that reflect the lack of community integration into the thinking of the universities with no external community liaisons. The only even partial exception is Chicago's DePaul University. SEM is the CRMish (but not CRM) strategy that is used for increasing enrollment by many schools.

The Customer, University Style

This group is quite different from the classic CRM customer for reasons you will see later. It's not just the usual client-partner-employee-supplier grouping. In university terms, the customer could include:

- Students—on campus, commuting, or distance learning

- Prospects

- Adult learners

- Parents—often ignored in university CRM initiatives, but mission critical

- Alumni—passive, participant, or donor

▸ Institutional trustees

▸ Event attendees

▸ Purchasers of university logo products

▸ Staff—nonfaculty and faculty

▸ Community at large—merchants, residents, or social institutions

▸ Academic advisers, guidance counselors

▸ Vendors/suppliers

▸ Other educational institutions

- Government agencies, compliance agencies

- Grant providers

- Nonalumni donors

Higher education CRM planning has to include all of these groups, especially given the approach that needs to be taken to break the insularity and to serve the academic world "end client"— the student for life.

Student for Life

The student is a pivot point in the academic ecosystem, though not the only one. What makes the student unique is that, unlike commercial CRM customers who come and go, in the world of higher education, if done well, the student always remains. With a long view of CRM—the student from cradle to grave—the returns can be significant. This seems to make some linear, rational sense: track a student's existence from prospect to, put delicately, bequestor. Ah, but that's not all the student for life is.

CRM's student-for-life value proposition is the ability to *enrich and track* singular student relationships over time and to identify the value and possibilities of return at each stage of that singular relationship. Tracking alone does not provide an effective value exchange—which is what CRM is all about.

The student has a profoundly interesting relationship to the university. If you think about it, a student usually attends his or her university for four years. But that same student remains at least somewhat committed to the university most of his or her adult life—even if the commitment is limited to rooting for the football team. The university shapes the student's career, legacy, and biography. But the university is unaware of that fact most of the time, except abstractly or during adversity. For example, one coach of a major college football team was forced to resign after only days on the job because he lied about his academic degree on his résumé. Would that affect his coaching ability? No, not really. But to lie about your degree is serious stuff. The university community took notice.

How does the university shape the student's life after graduation? To answer this takes interaction, data, infrastructure, outreach, a strategy, cultural change, visibility, a mission, vision, and lots of patience. It's an uneven return on the relationship that could take between 40 and 70 years, depending on the state of medical science and the health of the alumnus.

Student-Centered CRM: Different How?

There are a number of differences in a student-centered CRM from any other type. It has to consider the community. It has to establish a long-term relationship with each student. The long term relationship will yield different kinds of returns in different stages of the student's life. For example, in the early stages tuition, in the years right after school probably nothing, many years later money and perhaps a child matriculating at the university. It has to recognize the dramatic improvement in the choices of communication media that have arisen due to the impact of the Internet over the past decade. How do you deal with an Internet-savvy student body that will graduate to a world considerably more technologically focused than it was 25 years ago? Multichannel strategies for a university are important, even if incrementally implemented. The options for other types of CRM can include even only one or two channels as we will see in Chapter 11 on the public sector. For the university ecosystem, all channels are needed, because it's the way students and graduates communicate. To provide a consistent lifelong experience, the university must make sure it has the infrastructure and culture (hardware, software, and plan) to handle it and the strategy to develop a singular view of the student across the enterprise. So we are looking at the following:

- ▸ A multifaceted, student-centered university ecosystem that involves multiple types of customers, both internal and external.

- ▸ Ongoing, lifelong relationships with students that are tracked and that take into account the change in the nature of the social matrix of relationships each student has as he or she moves through life. This information is then used to enrich the interactions of the student with the university.

▶ The larger revolution in communications that necessitates appealing to a technology-savvy student body and the provision of infrastructure and culture to handle this multichannel world.

Obstacles

All that sounds great, doesn't it? But let's take a quick glance at the obstacles in the way of this primitive CRM ecosystem:

▶ **Institutional politics** As with any institution, politics are a determining and often defeating factor. With issues of faculty tenure, institutional power, trustee appointments, among others, the politics of student relationships can destroy an initiative.

▶ **Rudimentary student information systems and lack of funding** In the 2003 survey by EDUCAUSE, a nonprofit association whose mission is to advance higher education by promoting the intelligent of information technology, IT funding challenges were identified as the number one problem and the problem most likely to get worse. This is on top of the often-primitive nature of existing IT infrastructure at many colleges and universities.

▶ **Lack of mindshare about CRM in the university community** The same EDUCAUSE 2003 survey lists the second most pressing issue as implementing administrative/enterprise resource planning systems (ERP). CRM doesn't appear in the list of top ten issues at any kind of institution, from small to large, from public to private.

▶ **Lack of technological sophistication of the staff** Sadly, the world of higher education is often noted as being anything from technologically indifferent to technophobic.

▶ **Information redundancy and fragmentation with decentralized data** Multiple databases exist in multiple locations and departments that have entirely repetitive data and no consolidated records. For example, the admissions office, bursar's office, and athletic department may each have a different record with different information on the same student. If each department could see a single consolidated student record, it could alter the way the department treated the student. To make an example rather extreme if the athletic department didn't know that the student was failing because that was in the bursar's database, the student could remain academically eligible to play his sport until the bursar chose to tell the athletic department. If the athletic department saw the same information as the bursar, then academic ineligibility would scream out to him immediately. No verbal lateral necessary.

▶ **Insularity** There is rarely representation from parents or community leaders when discussion of CRM occurs. No engagement of those constituents as stakeholders occurs when the programs are planned. There is little thought concerning the dynamics of the relationships between the student, community, and university, given the already existing level of integration of the three.

Given these difficulties, is success possible? Yes. Two pioneering initiatives in this primitive industry's Cretaceous Relationship Management efforts have succeeded dramatically. The first is mentioned later in the sports section: the Arizona State University Sun Devils. The second is the University of Dayton.

The University of Dayton

Normally, I never recommend a home-grown effort. But I have to admit, in the case of the University of Dayton, their baby is brilliantly conceived. Their system is a Web-based portal with single user sign-on that can route you to an alumnus or student website or elsewhere. The student website regards you as an existing or a prospective student. The strategy they developed was simple: engage the student for life. That means interactions with the student whether they are high schoolers looking at potential admission or alumni looking at potential donation or simply looking for their former classmates. For example, on their portal (www.udayton.edu,) click on "Admission," then "Undergraduate," then "Customize this site." They have a three-step personalization process, based on concepts of permission marketing, that provides increasingly detailed information about the prospective student:

▶ **Join the mailing list** Very basic information—name and e-mail address and a little more.

▶ **Customize your experience** More details related to academic and extracurricular interests; this provides a deeper engagement and thus commitment.

▶ **Receive more information** Demographic and sensitive information such as SAT/ACT scores, actual mailing address, grades, and other more intimate information that fully engages the Internet-savvy prospect.

When all of this information is pulled together, UD provides an individual website and a single user sign-on that supplies personalized information for that student identified through a user ID and a password. They have a floating "To Do" list that is tailored to the individual student's profile.

One of the more important prospecting processes is "Inquiry to Applicant," essentially a procedure that starts with a communication with a university indicating a prospect's interest. Hopefully, this ends with the prospect submitting an application. There is an extended version of this process called "Inquiry to Deposit," which starts with the same initial communication, but ends with a financial deposit, indicating a serious commitment to matriculation. By taking the approach that they are engaging the student more deeply with each interaction, UD got spectacular increases in successes relative to opportunities (see Table 10-1).

Table 10-1: University of Dayton Results from Using CRM

Process	Yield (Not Personalized)	Yield (Personalized)
Inquiry to Applicant	14.7%	53.4%
Inquiry to Deposit	3.3%	17.1%

In addition to these extraordinary numbers, the site traffic increased 738 percent over a four-year period. The cost per application dropped from a high in 1996 of $473 to $380 in 2000. Expenses were reduced, productivity increased, and admissions were significantly improved.

UD didn't stop with admissions. They developed an alumni gateway that went live in 2001 with the following goals: getting 20,000 alumni (25 percent of their total) online by 2005; increasing online donations; decreasing printing and postage costs; and providing an exciting experience for alumni, keeping them connected to the university and their classmates (that is, student for life). By early 2002, they had already registered more than 13,000 alumni and had received $41,000 in online donations, including single donations of between $1,000 and $5,000. They saved more than $190,000 in printing and mailing costs. Less than one-tenth of 1 percent unsubscribed to this resounding success.

The Student for Life Lesson Plan

What does this say? Generally, it says that CRM works in specific industries with specific processes. Even with unusual requirements such as student for life, CRM can establish a track record in an industry, provided the strategy for that particular industry is designed to the processes that govern that industry.

Specifically, it says that despite the fact that higher education is among the most technophobic of environments and the most insular, CRM remains a viable way to bring the academic ecosystem into the greater world and provide its denizens with the long-term successes they need to survive in their increasingly competitive environment.

Fascinating CRM? Sports Is the Ticket!

What red-blooded man or woman isn't a sports fan? You aren't? Get out of my book! Just kidding.

Sports are usually ignored as an industry with CRM concerns. After all, the fans are ordinarily loyal to their team, right? Why would you need CRM? Yet, there is a growing knowledge in the sports business that CRM is an increasingly important strategy.

A sports franchise has unique characteristics. It engenders civic pride and thus true loyalty. The same type of loyalty associated with loyalty to one's country is loyalty to one's team, though to a lesser degree. That team most often represents the municipality you live (or lived) in or the school you went to. It is an emotional loyalty, far deeper than typical business commitment. There certainly are always exceptions to the origin of the loyalty. For example, Lots of the upper part of the age bracket of the baby boomers root for the New York Yankees in baseball because they lived out in the boonies and didn't have a major league baseball team as a local market. They saw the Yankees all the time on the Game of the Week—the only televised baseball in their market.

But loyalties are part of the business of sports. Look at the stakes here. We see hyperinflated salaries for sports stars because they bring in fans, not because they catch twelve touchdown passes in a year for the San Francisco 49ers or they average 28.0 per game for the Chicago Bulls. The $252 million, 10 year deal for Alex Rodriguez of the Texas Rangers (now of the New York Yankees) was signed because calculations were done on his lifetime value—at least 10 years—as a revenue producer in ticket sales, merchandise and any other value that the Texas Rangers needed to make the determination and it was very high. Though the Rangers forgot that to get fans excited enough to give away oodles of money for their entertainment pleasure, a winning team is also usually necessary. That's why he's now been traded to the Yankees. (Yeah!) Even his fan appeal and his ability to sell merchandise wasn't enough to sustain the financial burden of a last place team. It's quite telling that the first statistics out about Alex Rodriguez of the Yankees—three days after he joined the team were about the 104,000 ticket sale increase over the prior year and how A-Rod (his nickname) number 13 (his number) shirts were flying off the racks—nearly all the first consignments sold out in the three days. To heck with home runs and batting average!

All that was said to emphasize one thing: sports is a business. Businesses, regardless of their unique twists, need CRM as part of their strategy. Sports are perhaps the most uneven vertical of all. Some of the most advanced CRM (albeit not always under that rubric) is present. There are limited edition loyalty programs present in sports, and most barely even think about it—probably also incorrectly presuming that fan loyalty only needs that winning team. Look at the Florida Marlins. During most of 2003, they averaged 16,290 seats sold per game (contrast to the Yankees 42,785). But during the playoffs, they averaged more than twice that. Does that mean they don't need CRM? Only if they think short term. They are world champions for one year and then they start all over in earning that right to the moniker back. Bad year? Look at the Marlins 2002 numbers—they averaged 10,039 fans per game. Good year? The Kansas City Royals saw a 40 percent boost in attendance based on their (unsuccessful) run for the American League Central Division title. But it is only a year. Heat of the moment is meaningful in sports. But the ideal is to capture that heat and warm the team in good or bad years—for many years to come.

With the price of attendance at a professional sports event exceeding $200 for a family of four, the need for fan retention is not lost on major league and collegiate teams. The National Basketball Association (NBA), Major League Baseball (MLB), the National Football League (NFL), and the National Hockey League (NHL) all have teams that are using CRM effectively (see Table 10-2). While the table is by no means complete, it gives you an idea of what is actually out there. This is not including those who have fan loyalty programs only.

Table 10-2: CRM in Sports

Sports League	Teams Using CRM
Major League Baseball	San Diego Padres, Chicago White Sox, Texas Rangers
National Basketball Association	Phoenix Suns, Golden State Warriors, Seattle Supersonics, Miami Heat, Boston Celtics, Indiana Pacers, Charlotte Bobcats, Philadelphia 76ers,
National Football League	Green Bay Packers (whether they know it or not), Jacksonville Jaguars
National Hockey League	Carolina Hurricanes, Philadelphia Flyers, Nashville Predators, Columbus Blue Jackets, Dallas Stars
Collegiate Sports	Arizona State Sun Devils, Vanderbilt, Baylor

The Sports Customer: A Different Kind of Passion; A Different Kind of Folk

If queried, you would find that most fans and most sports management and players think the fan would be the customer. Well, in sports, the fan is a customer, but not the only one. There are a couple of unique aspects to fan definition in sports because of the loyalties and passion that govern the attachments to teams and the symbiotic relationships that the media have with sports.

It would be dangerous to consider fan loyalty programs CRM programs. The fan is the ultimate customer—the significant other that drives the symbiotic relationships that define sport's other customer/partners. The most interesting of these customer groups is the media who operate both as customer and as influencer. For example, the reason for the incredibly hyperinflated salaries that are being paid to sports figures today is not fan tickets and merchandise, but billion dollar plus TV deals. The networks make these deals because their customers—the advertisers—see it as a way of reaching millions of fans to buy the products that their favorite players endorse and that are advertised on TV. Yet, TV, radio and print journalists influence the fans when it comes to their teams and its players. Civic pride, childhood nostalgia and comfort, govern what team the fan roots for. The media enhances or reduces that influence by its commentary. So the media are customers, the fans are customers. the players are customers, the other teams are customers when it comes to revenue sharing and the agents of the players are customers. All of this overlain with a patina of intense loyalty to someone or something. Ironically, they call all of this entertainment, but it is a huge business and knowing the customer is critical in sports—and complicated.

The Green Bay Packers: When Is "Not-CRM" CRM?

Most sports CRM is focused on fan loyalty programs in one form or another. Keep in mind that fan loyalty tends to be focused geographically, not as much across sports. The Seattle Supersonics basketball team competes with the Mariners (baseball), the Seahawks (football), and collegiate athletics more than they do with other NBA teams. Loyalty in sports tends to be based on civic pride.

One of the most interesting long-term CRM initiatives is not actually a CRM initiative. It is the relationship between the Green Bay Packers and the citizens of Green Bay. This dynamic is the paradigm perfect CRM program:

- ▶ **Long-term, strategic, and ongoing program rather than a project with an ending** It has been going on since 1919 and is seen as something permanently part of the Green Bay community. It is no coincidence that there are streets with names like "Packerland Avenue," or a school called "Vince Lombardi Middle School." This extends to restaurants, field houses, businesses, practice fields, and a myriad of other institutions and roadways throughout the town.

- ▶ **Fully integrated customer and company collaboration on making both sides successful** But there is still a strong focus on success for the company. The Packers fans are owners of the team. There are thousands of stockholders in the Packers who see the success or failure of the Packers as their success or failure. Look at this paragraph on the Packers website: "Presently, 111,507 people (representing 4,748,910 shares) can lay claim to a franchise ownership interest. Shares of stock include voting rights, but the redemption price is minimal, no dividends are ever paid, the stock cannot appreciate in value, and there are no season ticket privileges associated with stock ownership. No shareholder is allowed to own more than 200,000 shares, a safeguard to ensure that no one individual is able to assume control of the club." Now look at this one: "The initial response to the recent stock offering was staggering. In the first 11 days, roughly one-third—or $7.8 million—of the total amount transacted was sold. Paid orders poured in at a rate of 3,500 per day during this early period, generating about $700,000 each day. The sale hit its high point during the first week of December as fans purchased shares as holiday gifts." This is for stock that has no financial value, as you can see from the first paragraph. CRM at its best, indeed. Ultimately, this 1997–98 offering raised $24,000,000 from the citizens of Green Bay.

► **Commitment to the long term from the customer, regardless of how well or poorly the company does either for itself or on behalf of the customer** The Packers have been sold out for decades. Right now, the waiting list for season tickets is 60,000 people and the wait time is 30 years. There are rules and regulations related to inheritance rights for Packers' seasons tickets.

► **An extraordinary interest in purchasing the goods and services provided by the company** This is not only highly lucrative to the team but is also usually too the customer's continuous and complete satisfaction. Packers merchandise sold all over Green Bay or given away as a promotion is prevalent. There is no place you won't see townspeople with the omniscient, omnipresent green and gold Packers' colors—jackets, keychains, sweatshirts, cars, calendars, bobbleheads, beer bottles. Color neutrality means green and gold in Green Bay.

► **Involvement of the customer in the day to day life of the company** The discussion of the fate of the Packers is all consuming and preoccupying year round, not just during football season. I spent a weekend in Green Bay to attend the Packers-Bears game in December 2003 and I heard conversation about nothing else all weekend. Nothing else. "How are you? Don't you love Bret Favre?" was pretty much the way the entire weekend went. I loved it.

► **Detailed customer and employee profiles** Did you know that Packers running back superstar Ahman Green loves deviled eggs for Thanksgiving and greens for Christmas? And talented place kicker Ryan Longwell loves cornbread casserole for the holidays? Bet you didn't. The Packers release the personal details of their players' lives (with the players' permission), and the players get involved in the lives of the fans and know them very well. Their involvement can't be beat. It's easy to meet and greet individual Packers on the street.

▸ **Nearly 100 percent brand recognition** C'mon. This is the Green Bay Packers.

▸ **Intense corporate involvement in the community—business, philanthropic, personal** The festival of love never ceases. The members of the revered Packers teams of the 1960s, such as Ray Nitschke, Willie Davis, Herb Adderley, and Willie Wood among many others, never left Green Bay. The explayers own businesses and restaurants, stay active in the community. The current team members often live in Green Bay in the off-season. The team involves itself in the local area Special Olympics, Pop Warner Leagues, elementary school classes, Salvation Army, Feed the Children charity, cystic fibrosis fundraising, Boys and Girls Clubs, among others. They donate millions of dollars through the Green Bay Packers Foundation and provide signed items (4,000 of them) for auction.

While you may find this a bit stretched as an analogy to CRM, let me assure you it isn't. This is the paradigm of CRM for sports, whether it has been called that or not.

THE ROI?

Green Bay has more than 106,000 hearty souls living there. The Green Bay Packers projected 2004 revenue is over $168,000,000 in the smallest NFL market. That is more than $1,500 for every man, woman, and child who lives in the city. There is nowhere else that you'll see numbers that even approach these. The sources of revenue range from merchandise to game attendance to stock sales. The customers participate in this bonanza unblinkingly. Brown County, Wisconsin, supported a stadium referendum for increases in their taxes to improve Packers home Lambeau Field. Where else will you get this level of integrated customer relationships for what is a business, whether viewed as more than that or not?

Arizona State University Sun Devils

This is the best and most well thought-out sports-related CRM program in either college or professional sports. Under the leadership of Steve Hank, director of CRM and marketing for the Arizona State

University Sun Devils, their program is centered around the sinister-sounding Devil's Domain website (www.devilsdomain.net). This is a multichannel, multimedia program that not only envelops and immerses the Sun Devils fans into the culture of the ASU Sun Devils, but also can capture the customer information needed to constantly improve the individual fan's experience with the Sun Devils. It is also the first of its kind for a collegiate athletics department anywhere.

Steve Hank recognizes the value of fan engagement in the market he serves. The market is Phoenix. His competition is sports represented by the University of Arizona, the Phoenix Suns, and the NHL's Phoenix Coyotes. In other words, sports in his geographic market.

His research into the market showed that the fans wanted three things:

► Exclusive information about the team.

► The chance to feel important and wanted by the Sun Devils—their school, their team.

► An opportunity to have some sort of unique experience.

These abstract desires were translated into practical efforts. This is the moment where human interpretation and determination in a CRM strategy is critical. If Steve Hank had either misinterpreted this research or not come up with appropriate rewards and plans geared toward a particularly well understood and defined audience, this could have been a major failure. His analysis of his audience and his research data, plus his ingenuity in determining the right mix of channels and programs, laid the grounds for the major success it became.

To capture their hearts and dollars, Hank developed the Devil's Domain as the strategy's centerpiece. He reached the fans on nearly all communications channels. By early 2004, the fans had the following channels available to them from the Sun Devils:

► **Website** Not only could you root around and read information on whatever ASU sport interested you, but starting in 2004, you could watch game webcasts directly on the site.

► **E-mail** Aside from promotions, "The Insider" newsletter was pushed to subscribers (free). Typical content was the game results, features on players or history, and promotions of the week exclusively for the use of the Devil's Domain subscribers. Often buried in the e-mail are clandestine offers of tickets or merchandise, exclusive to the e-mails.

▶ **Video and audio clips** As of 2004, streaming media and web-cast games are part of the offering to interested fans. As a member of Devil's Domain, you'll be able to see the football or basketball game live online. Installed to your system is "The Communicator " which provides these clips daily.

Hank isn't afraid to try mixing media either. For example, they have a promotion that is designed to drive traffic to the Devil's Domain and provide the fans with a benefit that they will appreciate. He calls it "Online to Offline/Offline to Online." An attendee at a game will receive a promotion coupon with a code on it. To redeem the gift that the code promises (without revealing the nature of the gift), you have to register with the Devil's Domain and enter the code on the site. This attaches a personal customer profile to the redemption of the code—which is a meaningful code. That means there is some event attached to the code that adds personal information to the profile. An e-mail is generated and sent to the new Devil's Domain registrant. The recipient of the e-mail prints it out and takes it to a merchant or wherever to redeem it for a gift. So the mix of Web, personal interaction, and e-mail leads to a happy fan with a prize and a useful customized fan profile for the Devil's Domain and the Arizona Sun Devils.

It goes beyond that. Any future interactions that a registered member of the Devil's Domain has with the site are captured and placed in that customer profile. Say I go online and check out the news related to football and soccer for last week. Then I watch a video of the game highlights. Then I order a Sun Devils sweatshirt. All of that information is captured and added to my customer profile so that personalized offers and information can be generated and sent to me.

The program even takes advantage of what has been known as "push" technology with "opt-in" features (see Chapter 5 for a discussion on "opting in"). What this means is that (with the permission of the fan) a small client applet called "The Communicator" is downloaded to the fan's system. Each day at some measured interval, Sun Devils sports information—text, audio, and video—is captured and uploaded to the fan's system and scrolls across the screen in some corner of the fan's screen. If you click on the scrolling text, it will take you to the text or audio or video to fill out the details (see Figure 10-2). With 2004, special offers are embedded into the scrolling text that one merely has to click on to get.

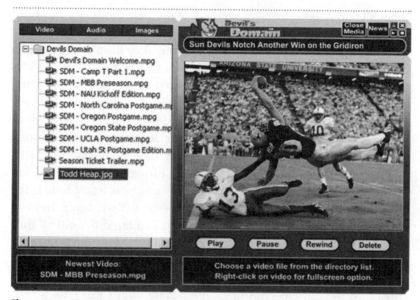

Figure 10-2: The Communicator is a very cool multimedia tool for the fan's desktop. It engages the fan with Sun Devil's content as the fan chooses to view it.

How successful have they been? In 2003, on the football field, not as successful as they'd like to have been. Twenty-second ranked in the preseason polls, they had a disappointing 5-7 record. But in the hearts of the fans? Despite the disappointment, their average home game attendance went from 45,837 in seven games in 2002 to 54,248 in six games in 2003. Even their desired projections for 7,500 site registrants were wildly exceeded with 15,743 members as of October 2003. I'm one of them. Not only that, the Devil's Domain CRM strategy made me a fan of a team at a school I didn't even attend.

Think about it. Major disappointment like a poorer than expected season's record normally reduces fan attendance. But not when you've identified and executed a brilliant CRM strategy well. The fans are engaged, 18 percent attendance increases occur, and revenues climb. Welcome to the world of CRM, sports business, and the Arizona State Sun Devils.

The Vendors

While E.piphany, Onyx, and even MSCRM have penetration into the world of sports, the most interesting and significant player in this venue is not all that well known—SmartDM. With their products, they hold the franchise with 12 major league sports teams. Starting out as a company that specialized in database marketing, they have evolved into a company that remains focused on the back end, but with CRM applications added to their arsenal. Not only do they handle Arizona State, they have been able to corral both the Philadelphia Flyers and Philadelphia 76ers, opening the way to a creative cross-fertilization of prospective fans. Under the aegis of Comcast Spectacor, they have combined the databases of the two teams and several other Comcast Spectacor venues to create unique uses of the data for promotions and fan involvement. Clearly, if you know a fan is a season ticket holder for both the Flyers and the 76ers, with club boxes (or whatever they call them in Philly) for the Flyers, you will treat that fan differently if they have simply bought a 76ers Iverson jersey. SmartDM products not only are able to help the teams do that, but can "de-dup" the data, cleaning out the duplicates even if there are Bill Smith and William H. Smith entries for the same person in each database. All of this data is centralized to a single warehouse that the teams share.

I would watch for these guys. They are clever and are making waves in a domain where being clever might end up an extreme sport. They don't have it to themselves, with Onyx and MSCRM providing some serious competition, but they are focused strongly into this venue. Though I haven't seen it yet, judging from the response of 12 teams to it, their package DirectTR@K 2.0 seems to be the real deal for the world of sports. I'll reserve my judgment until I see it, but I'd give it a serious look if you're in sports. Though I haven't tested it, it has a good reputation which should count for something, shouldn't it?

The Vendors and the Verticals

To give you a flavor of how deeply the big guys are into specific industries, Table 10-3 covers the verticals the big four cover. Oracle does it a little differently than the other three. They embed industry-specific processes in their e-business Suite 11.9, but all customers get it and turn on the functionality or turn it off depending on what industry they are in. This can be awkward, but certainly reduces the production costs of a pure industry-specific play.

Keep in mind that J.D. Edwards is part of the PeopleSoft enterprise suites so their verticals—midmarket style—are also represented here.

Table 10-3: Big Four Vertical Offerings as of December 2003

Vendor	Vertical
SAP	Automotive, chemicals, pharmaceuticals, engineering, construction, consumer goods, high tech, industrial machinery and components, leasing, media and entertainment, oil and gas, professional services, retail, telecommunications, utilities, public sector, aerospace and defense, mining, engineering, construction and operations, chemicals, higher education and research
PeopleSoft	Financial services, utilities, higher education, insurance, communications, public sector, high tech, professional services, staffing, homebuilders, paper, real estate, wholesale distribution, life sciences, construction, chemicals, industrial products, automotive, energy
Oracle	Manufacturing, telecommunications, consumer goods, high tech, public sector
Siebel	Life sciences, financial services, healthcare, communications, high tech, consumer goods, energy, automotive, complex manufacturing, hospitality and travel

This list is not exhaustive but is indicative of how far CRM has come in creating the processes for specific industries at least 80 percent out of the box—though you can expect to have to do some customization no matter how hard you try to avoid it.

STEPPIN' OUT: SAP Maps to the Best of Them

What do the automotive, chemical, pharmaceutical, engineering, construction, consumer goods, high tech, industrial machinery and components, leasing, media and entertainment, oil and gas, professional services, retail, telecommunications, and utilities industries have in common? C'mon. Just look at the title of this section. That ought to give you a big hint.

If you haven't figured it out by now, the answer is: SAP. When it comes to vertical industry specialization, there is no one even close to their expertise. I remember once being at an SAP conference (they call them Sapphire) in Los Angeles. I went over to the area where they had set up kiosks for all their verticals. I was lost for days. There were so many industry-specific kiosks to choose from.

SAP's vertical solutions are not just CRM. They are enterprise-wide solutions that have CRM components. That means the processes are fully integrated into the overall applications, which extend from the customer-facing sales applications through the accounting functions to the supply chain functionality such as inventory management or those more nebulous applications that can't be placed on the spectrum, such as order management.

What characterizes them with SAP is that they have an exceedingly deep understanding of how each industry's end-to-end processes work. They meticulously put together these maps with a truly impressive level of research and development. It might be useful to follow the research process they use so that you can understand what a vendor does to get the expertise that you need to make an industry-specific CRM initiative work.

SAP's R&D—Don't Even Go There, Because SAP Already Does

In 2000, SAP bragged about how they spent $1.2 billion in R&D. I remember thinking that this was more spent on R&D than most of the ERP companies made in a year. At the time, I wondered if it were necessary to spend this kind of money. After understanding how they research, I now am convinced. I've seen the light. I understand how it works. It is meticulous. It is thorough. It is effective.

SAP undertakes five major steps when identifying an industry-specific CRM strategy:

▶ **Planning** This is the longest and deepest segment in the development of strategy. Through both formal and informal interviews and meetings, with scrupulously designed questionnaires and notes taken on hallway conversations, SAP experts start piecing together the explicit needs of the industry in question. Stakeholding organizations are created and are the coordinators of the effort. The effort incorporates discussions with and formal feedback from numerous groups of experts—including thought-leaders, analysts, partners, customer user groups, industry groups, ramp-up customers, the SAP field organization, and the SAP industry organization. Additionally, during this first phase SAP "scientists" are conducting competitive benchmarking. Other experts normally associated with SAP's strategic alliance partners (for example, Accenture) develop projects aimed at creating these industry practices, maps, and competitive strategies.

▶ **Development/testing** Once the prototypes for the industry are developed, they are tested for their veracity and effectiveness. It is at this stage that specific requests for development projects will come from SAP industry customers who are looking for answers to their questions. These ideas will benefit the overall knowledge of and improvement in strategy. For the most part, the SAP field stakeholders (such as those customers) are involved in this stage.

▶ **Production/assembly** The research and prototypes are then assembled into a draft product that is reviewed by analysts and in-house SAP industry experts. Data input never stops even at this production stage.

▶ **Production ramp-up** At this stage, the product is delivered to some of the SAP strategic partners for "field testing" to see if the customers in the industry are happy with what partners are providing them. Additionally, key customers receive these "release candidate" level products to see how they can work with them. Then the press is informed that the product is undergoing its final workout before the general release.

▶ **Mainstream rollout** The product is released to market, and the industry practices and maps are made available and ready to go. SAP in-house expertise—consulting, training, implementation, sales, and so on—is active and in gear at this phase.

Time consuming, expensive, and fastidious. The results are the best vertical maps and processes in the CRM and enterprise applications world. I wouldn't ever rule them out as a candidate if you are looking at industry-specific CRM and they cover your vertical.

Moving On

Now let's sashay into a segue to the more technical side of CRM—though not so technical that you won't understand it.

11

"Of the People, by the People, for the People":
CRM in the Public Sector

I'm going to make a bold statement in this chapter and then prove it. CRM initiatives in the public sector, especially through the federal government, can ennoble a population. Lest you think me mad, I'm going to show you how.

CRM in the Public Eye: More than Just a Good Initiative

When Abraham Lincoln spoke at Gettysburg in 1863 and entered that immortal phrase "of the people, by the people, for the people" into history, he wasn't exactly trying to explain CRM, despite the resemblance. He was reminding a war-weary populace that they needed to remember why they were so committed and loyal to the cause of the Union—that all humans were, as the marvelous Greek philosopher Philo Judaeus called us, "miniature heavens," and there was to be no degradation of the human spirit, even during a war. The phrase "of the people, by the people, for the people" summarized the principle that Americans had fought and died for during the American Revolution and the same principle that Americans fought and died for in wars ever since. It is the credo that Americans have lived for in their daily existence, though there have been enough grounds for them to rightfully forget it—but they don't. That we are all equal in the eyes of both human and divine law is a profound manifestation of what shows all humanity at its best. This deeply engrained conviction reflects a beauty that has a humbling effect on how an individual acts in a moment of importance—whether it is a life-threatening situation or simply an event of meaningful interest. But it can easily create a cynic, when the institutions that were created to uphold the principle and create the environment to foster it through the generations don't meet the expectations of the populace that these institutions are required to serve. "Of the people, by the people, for the people" unfulfilled not only remains a vision on someone else's horizon, but becomes the object of disgust in a more profound way than any anger at failed expectations in a business deal can engender.

Americans—in fact, citizens of most countries—have a love/hate relationship with their government at multiple levels. It tends to vary widely, dependent on whether the government is showing its citizenry that it is responsive to its needs in an appropriate way. But the appropriateness is not just organizational or institutional. Because we are dealing with firmly rooted beliefs, it is also emotional. We identify strongly with and respond to both the strengths and weaknesses of the U.S. government and how it reflects on us and in the world. That means when our government and its agencies are unresponsive, we feel as if *our* government and *our* country are letting us down—not *the* government and *the* country. The actions of our government are a personal matter. You don't believe this? Take a look at how Americans get treated for being Americans overseas. The nationals from other countries will map America good or bad right or wrong smack onto your *tourista* swimwear. So whether you believe it or not, the rest of the world acts in concert with that belief.

Think about it. For those of you old enough to remember, what was it like during the era following Watergate and the resignation and then pardon of President Richard Nixon? It was hardly a love fest in this country. The level of cynicism about not just the Nixon administration but the *institutions of government* reached unprecedented proportions. It had been eroding since 1965 and the Watergate break-in capped it. When JFK said in his inaugural address, "The energy, the faith, the devotion which we bring to this endeavor will light our country and all who serve it, and the glow from that fire can truly light the world," Americans believed him. That was in 1961 when fully three quarters of the American population believed that they could trust Washington to do what was right, according to multiple polls taken from 1958 through 1964. But after Watergate, in 1974, that percentage was 36 percent, and in 1997, according to a poll done by CNN/*Time* magazine, it was 32 percent.

However, the principles that were embodied through the U.S. Constitution, the Declaration of Independence, and the Federalist Papers continue to hold and remain the expectations of the population. That means that the most important thing that a government can be in this post-9/11 world is responsive to its citizenry and to work together throughout agencies and among federal, state, and local jurisdictions in the way that the citizenry imagines they should. That is what CRM in the public sector is for, especially at the federal level. The stakes are high. For if it succeeds, those historic ideals and the contemporary reality begin to align and confidence increases. The population feels increasingly ennobled when they see that what they believe in actually works. If it fails, then 32 percent becomes a high number.

Interestingly, the federal government is coming to the same conclusions on CRM that I have, though without my particular twist on the subject. The U.S. government is saying that it is now time to transform its agencies to customer/constituent-friendly institutions and refocus on improving those processes which support that perspective. This, rather than simply improving business methods through streamlining institutional transactions for cost-saving. Reducing the size of government, while perhaps devoutly to be wished by some and a noble objective to be sure, is not the answer to the rejuvenation of faith in our institutions. As the government is beginning to recognize, what can help toward the revivification of that faith is the institutionalization of CRM.

Bringing CRM to the Electorate

One of America's real visionaries, at the time U.S. Office of Management and Budget's associate director of information technology and e-government chieftain, Mark Forman publicly recognized the need for a federal CRM program as part of his Quicksilver initiatives. In an article that appeared in *Washington Technology* magazine in October 2002, Forman saw that the U.S. government needed to be prodded by commercial businesses that have had CRM success. "We need industry to be a catalyst," Forman said. "As consumers, citizens have become accustomed to high levels of service that, in the past, government hasn't been able to provide. The president has made it clear that the federal government has to become more focused on better serving citizens."

That said, there is a long distance between desire and execution. Accenture completed a study in March 2003 that showed the marathon that still remained, despite a strong commitment. Interviewing 140 government agencies in 15 countries on all major continents, the results were eye-opening though not particularly shocking. Over 90 percent of the executives polled saw that increased customer service should be and was the imperative driver of service delivery initiatives in the various governments. But only 28 percent claimed any degree of significant effect in succeeding at that effort. Even more telling, in our increasingly multichannel world, only half the agencies used more than two channels. Only one third had a contact center of any sort that could handle multichannel transactions and that led to only a self-described, self-flagellating 40 percent efficiency rate for resolving customer requests appropriately. This isn't particularly good, but the government recognizes the gap—and that's important.

Even with limited success, national, state, and local governments across continents are changing the way they think. They see CRM as an imperative though in its infancy, for many reasons that I'll look at throughout this chapter.

Public Sector: CRM Stands for Constituent Relationship Management

It isn't good enough to call public sector CRM, "Citizen Relationship Management." Companies that glibly do that don't understand the nature of CRM in the public sector. While clearly the relationship between the citizen and the federal government is of paramount importance, the reality is that 53 percent of all government interactions and transactions are interagency—between the agencies of the federal, state, and local governments, not between the individual citizen and the government department. If you are looking at calling CRM something other than customer relationship management when it comes to a public sector version, then it's more appropriate to call it constituent relationship management.

What does that mean? What could be characterized as "agency-driven" models, which are operational and internal in nature, have to be replaced by constituent-centric models aimed at revamping and remapping all of the government business processes toward processes and workflows that have "customer value" attached. It means identifying the specific constituents associated with the specific agency or department, but remembering that there is an overarching view of the "enterprise"—the government as a whole—which has to be accounted for in the thinking. It also means that each process has to be shown to have some purpose that will enhance and engage the constituencies identified and served.

Who Are the Constituents?

The constituents/customers of the public sector do not at all resemble the typical private sector business customers. Of course, the "end client" is the citizen or the legal resident. But constituency becomes a much more complex weave when the beneficiaries of specific agency largesse are identified not just with the citizenry, but among other agencies and the private side of the public/private partnership.

An Example of a Constituency: Government Style

One of my Steppin' Out choices for this chapter is the Defense Logistics Agency (DLA)—the organization responsible for supplying the military and its personnel with all expendable/consumable supplies from food to weapons system parts. You'll read more on them later, but let's look at who their constituencies are here so you can see the differences between the private and public sector. This is their early segmentation prototype model, designed to help DLA develop its overarching CRM strategy:

- ▶ **Unified combatant commands** These are the command organizations that have operational control over U.S. combat forces. They are typically organized geographically. The current commands are Central Command, European Command, Joint Forces Command, Pacific Command, Southern Command, Space Command, Special Operations Command, Strategic Command, Transportation Command, and Northern Command.

- ▶ **Deployable operating units** These are the existing military divisions, brigades, special operational units, task forces, air expeditionary forces (AEFs), marine expeditionary forces (MEFs), and carrier battle groups.

- ▶ **Military installations** These are permanent or temporary locations these units operate from—the forts, bases, camps, stations, ports, and so on. This is a worldwide group.

- ▶ **Branches of the military** This constituency includes all military services from the Army and Navy to the Coast Guard.

- ▶ **Private sector suppliers and partners** Often these are characterized by strategic supplier alliances with companies like Honeywell, Hamilton Sundstrand, Northrop Grumman, Parker Hannifin, General Electric, Sikorsky, Pratt & Whitney, Fairchild

Fasteners, AVIBANK, Dresser Rand, AM General, GM Defense, Raytheon, Textron/Bell Helicopter, Eaton Corp, BAE, Canadian Commercial, Oshkosh Truck, and so on.

- ▶ **Individual service members** For example, DLA handles all the clothing items for all ranks of all services.

- ▶ **Other military agencies** This might include ROTC, National Guard, Air Guard, Army Reserves, Air Force Reserves, Navy/Marine Reserves, and so on.

- ▶ **Civilian agencies** These are the agencies that intersect the DLA supply chain, such as FEMA, DOT, FBI, Department of Education (milk programs), and Veteran's Administration (medical supplies).

Each of these has specific requirements and needs. Extrapolate that to a separate though overlapping constituency base for each of the departments associated with the federal government, and then for each state government and then each local government. You get the idea that there is a daunting task ahead for government CRM to be effective.

Different Objectives, Different Benefits

I trust you'll stipulate to further differences and the complexities of government constituencies. That said, isn't CRM pretty much the same though the constituencies are different? Let me answer a question with a question. What corporate CRM venture when successful ennobles a population? The answer? None.

CONTEST #1

From time to time, in fact, three times all told, throughout the book there will be contests that if you can answer there will be some sort of prize—at least in my view a prize—attached. In this case, if you can send me an e-mail with a corporate CRM initiative that can have or had an ennobling effect, I'll give you two free hours of consulting to be used anytime in 2004 or 2005 over the phone. That's a $750 prize, all for proving wrong the following statement: "What corporate CRM venture when successful ennobles a population? The answer? None." Make a very compelling case for something that hasn't happened or show me a real-life example. E-mail your entry to paul-greenberg3@comcast.net.

Actually, the purpose of a public sector CRM effort is very different than the private sector as Table 11-1 shows.

Table 11-1: Differences in Approach and Results for the Private and Public Sectors

Private Sector	Public Sector
Revenue enhancement is the key ROI.	Improving the quality of service to constituents is the mission.
Key value-add is improved customer retention.	Key value-add is improved constituent interactions.
Well-established set of business practices (or not).	Business practices and regulations are intertwined.
Subject to regulations.	Regulator, though subject to strict guidelines.
Case management is not as much a private sector concern except in call centers.	Case management is of paramount importance.
Marketing.	Outreach.

Benefits

What the government looks to for its ROI is very different in most respects than the private sector. Cooperation rather than competitive edge is more the speed of a government agency or entire department. Think about it. What kind of agency is trying to "beat" another agency? There are exceptions though. Gartner Dataquest did a 2002 study and found that 80 percent of state and local officials interviewed were looking at increases and improvements in customer service, 55 percent for improvements in data sharing (for example, interagency collaboration), 45 percent in enterprise-wide government (for example, centralized and more effective institutions), and only 15 percent were looking for revenue enhancement and 10 percent for competitive advantage.

While the least desired public sector CRM benefits happen to be the most desired in the private sector, there are opportunities on occasion for revenue enhancement and competitive advantage. Perhaps the best example of this is the U.S. Postal Service, which survives on its revenue and competes each day with Federal Express, UPS, and other couriers for a piece of the worldwide delivery market. In fact, they have a multi-channel strategy and a CRM director to handle their initiatives So what are governments trying to get out of CRM? Some possible benefits:

- ▶ Improves the quality of service to the individual constituent

- ► Improves interagency cooperation at federal, state, and local levels

- ► Changes in the business structure of agency or departments make them more effective

- ► Improves multichannel access for the constituents

Let's take a look at these in more detail.

IMPROVES THE QUALITY OF SERVICE TO THE INDIVIDUAL CONSTITUENT

Remember, this is where ennoblement occurs. What it entails is a strategy to create a customer service–oriented culture in the government. One of the most notorious examples of this lack of customer service is the Internal Revenue Service (IRS). Not much has to be said about their unfriendly, adversarial history with the American taxpayer. It was to the point that just hearing the term "agent of the IRS" created a shivering cold fear ordinarily reserved for a hired killer. An audit was a fiscal assassination, not a check of the books for accuracy. To reach the IRS was a nightmare with busy phones and hostile and defensive employees trying to get you off the phones as fast as possible. Imagine 115 million phone calls annually. In their defense, that was quite a burden to handle.

But despite some well-publicized glitches that have occurred through 2003, the development of a multichannel phased CRM strategy, with PeopleSoft CRM at its center, has had some excellent results. Calls were at 800 answered simultaneously, now they are at 1,500 as of 2003. The call centers route the callers automatically to the appropriate agent, depending on the level of need and a substantial number of other variables gathered when the caller calls in. The future holds the integration of phone, fax, e-mail, and Web-based responsiveness and even VOIP (see Chapter 7). It will no longer take all that much of an effort to deploy the call centers since they will not need the trunk lines and tangle of hundreds of telephones—just the VOIP-enabled Web.

Perhaps the most important characteristic of a government initiative that is designed to improve constituency services is personalization. If successful, there are multiple results:

- ► The image of the government as cold, unresponsive, and impersonal is shattered.

- ► The individual user is getting the most effective information for him—as an individual.

- ► Access to all things government is made easier.

For example, hypothetically as a private citizen, you could go to the state government website and with a single sign-on (meaning a unique user identification name and a password) through a portal, you could access a personalized set of links, news, accounts, and services that are visible only to you in the particular configuration that you have set. If it is a highly effective analytics engine, the view you have of the offerings could be determined by what you personally and manually configured, but also by the site's engine following and identifying your active behaviors, mapping it against your constituent record, and finding suitable services that would make sense to someone like you with your transactions and interactions. Additionally, you could get newsletters customized to these interests. You might get an e-mail that states that its time to renew your license plates and registration. Click on the link to the state DMV embedded in the e-mail and you are taken to the appropriate screens for your specific registrations. Online, you enter some data, give credit cards, change the personalized license plates you had to ILUVU (if you're under 30), and print out the registration receipt and registration for your glove compartment. The plates come through the mail. No fuss. No muss.

We're actually close to this technology and much of this is being done in states like Virginia among many others. But there is a problem that impedes further progress. In order to easily identify an individual, a Web interaction needs to set a "cookie"—a small file that resides on the client computer with the individual client's personal information. If done legally, it is for identification only for future trips to the site. When you see a box on a login screen that says if you check it you will allow the login information to be kept on the computer, that is a cookie—not as tasty as an Oreo, but probably more useful. Probably.

Due to privacy restrictions, the federal government is unable to place cookies on your system, which hinders personalization, since, in effect, each visit to the website becomes not continuous but unique and "first time." It's a big deal. There is a raging battle between those who advocate personalization and effectiveness and those who want to protect privacy. The balance is delicate and legally lands squarely on the side of privacy, at least when it comes to the citizen's compact with the federal government.

IMPROVES INTERAGENCY COOPERATION AT FEDERAL, STATE, AND LOCAL LEVELS

This is a direct and indirect CRM benefit that can't be underestimated—especially since the permanent jitteriness of 9/11.

The stated key performance indicators (KPIs) for this are something of both the tangible and the intangible. They are response time and quality of decision-making. While the first is a straightforward measure, the latter is a complex determination because it could include not just how to move troops in Iraq, but the way the TSA handles your baggage down to the individual baggage handler at the airport. For example, one of the e-government initiatives is a disaster-preparedness portal. There are multiple departments and agencies involved in disaster response and preparation. Typically, it's been very convoluted for state and local government to deal with federal disaster recovery agencies, especially during a crisis. So there is a lot of simplifying to make it easier for state and local governments to get access to the federal resources they need to deal with a crisis. It deals with a number of things, ranging from "How do you put together a disaster preparation plan?" to "Whom should you involve in your planning?" That's different if you're out west and dealing with the southern California forest fires, or you're in the mid-Atlantic and southern states and dealing with Hurricane Isabel. To get an idea of the mind-boggling number of agencies and institutions involved in such an effort, here's a brief and very partial list of the federal, state, local, and private agencies involved in some way in the murderous fires in California in October–November 2003:

▶ **Federal** Federal Emergency Management Agency (FEMA), Department of Transportation, U.S. Forestry Service, Department of Labor, Department of Commerce, U.S. Natural Resource Conservation Service, the office of the President, the Small Business Administration (SBA), the Department of Agriculture, a special team from six agencies called the Burned Area Response Team

▶ **State** California Department of Forestry, California Department of Transportation, California Office of Emergency Services, the office of the Governor of California, firefighters from local venues in Arizona and Nevada dispatched by the states of Arizona and Nevada

▶ **Local** At least the counties of San Diego, Los Angeles, San Bernardino, Alameda, and Ventura; dozens of local fire and police departments and transportation authorities; San Diego Resource Centers; water districts from dozens of municipalities; county and city departments of environmental health; local chambers of commerce; locally sponsored food banks; county Departments of Public Works; San Diego Development Services Department; the quasi-public San Diego Gas and Electric; San Diego Parks and Recreation; hundreds of school districts; county and city governments of all affected areas and all those volunteering services; San Diego Department of Planning and Land Use; San Diego Attorney's Office

▶ **Private** The Humane Societies and animal shelters; Habitat for Humanity; the San Diego Chargers (Qualcomm Stadium); Tzu Chi Foundation (Buddhist charity); Volunteer San Diego; all the media and outlets; hundreds of other volunteer organizations and corporations who gave dollars and time; thousands of individual volunteers

This is only a small part of the total. Imagine the level of coordination necessary to take care of this single (though massive) disaster. Imagine 9/11. Imagine simple day-to-day operational interagency transactions. Imagine CRM—quick!

CHANGES IN THE BUSINESS STRUCTURE OF AGENCIES OR DEPARTMENTS TO MAKE THEM MORE EFFECTIVE

This is required change for a successful CRM initiative, though in and of itself it is not the driver for change. For example, the Michigan Family Independent Agency used PeopleSoft to track how customers were using the services, to make better decisions on what services to provide those customers. The customers here were both the recipients of public assistance and family services and the 100 county agencies that handled the local traffic for these services. They tracked how the citizens and the agencies were using the services by distribution channel. This data was to restructure and streamline the business processes of the agency to improve support for the recipients with streamlined services and automated provisioning. It even provided the added benefit of compliance with federal reporting standards by reporting family aid allocations to the federal government, which saved them mucho dollars from fines for noncompliance.

IMPROVED MULTICHANNEL ACCESS FOR CONSTITUENTS: 311 SERVICES AND TALKING THE TALK

311 is contact center–based phone access for centralized nonemergency government services and information. A citizen or other agency representative calls in to a central phone number. After the caller gives the CSR who answers a detailed message on what the problem or inquiry is,

the caller is routed through 311 to the appropriate government agency. The inquiry is ticketed and tracked either on the phone or via the Internet with a reference number provided to the caller until the inquiry is satisfactorily answered.

Sound simple? Not. This is what is needed just to take care of this via a single channel.

- ▶ A centralized data store with customer records

- ▶ A contact center with trained personnel and appropriate technology

- ▶ Integration of legacy systems and other applications coordinated with other agencies

- ▶ CRM applications that are used interagency

- ▶ Revamped government processes and regulations

- ▶ Tracking, reporting, and auditing processes

- ▶ Mobile and desktop hardware

- ▶ A single service delivery model where multiple models existed

Keep in mind that this is for one single channel. Not e-mail, not Internet (except to monitor the inquiry), not fax, not direct mail, but only phone. But it is one of the more important federal multichannel access initiatives.

Does this constituent-centric thing really work? Well, yep, especially if you look at it compared to traditional governmental structure. In 2002, Deloitte Touche did a study of performance goal achievement in the state and local arena. Their comparatives were constituent-centric government results versus nonconstituent-centric government results. The differences are definitive. The results in Table 11-2 are the percentage of governments who felt they reached their specifically characterized performance goals.

Table 11-2: Constituent-Centered Government Pays Off at Any Level

Performance Goals	Constituent-centered Governments	Nonconstituent-Centered Governments
Fewer employee complaints	64%	8%
More customers served	75%	41%
Less employee time on noncustomer activities	77%	22%

Table 11-2: Constituent-Centered Government Pays Off at Any Level *(continued)*

Performance Goals	Constituent-centered Governments	Nonconstituent-Centered Governments
More agency recognition	79%	39%
Better operational information	84%	41%
Easier customer access	100%	46%

CRM: Federal Government

This is not small potatoes. Projected federal spending on CRM in the period from 2002 to 2007, according to market researcher Input, Inc., is going to increase from $260 million (2002) to $590 million (2007). If the Steppin' Out winner, the Defense Logistics Agency (DLA), is any indicator, we're looking at a $70 million CRM initiative just for them— a pioneering effort that will lead the way for considerably more investment in CRM from the feds. One of the challenges in selling to the federal government is that there are multiple layers of bureaucracy that have to be repeatedly wooed, and the level of effort required and amount of overlapping work is phenomenal. Yet, there is also a truly fine line to walk due to regulatory requirements related to anything involving contractor solicitation. Until a few years ago, you weren't even able to take a federal employee out to lunch that you paid for because of the seeming impropriety in the act. That's changed since, but the minefield remains.

Wisely, the federal government is responding to the movement of the business ecosystem in a surprisingly nimble way—almost light (speed) on their feet. E-government is integrally tied to CRM and other constituency based efforts as we begin our roll through this third millennium.

Is E-Government Actually CRM?

On July 18, 2001, Mitchell Daniels, then Director of the Office of Management and Budget (OMB), established an E-Government Task Force through OMB Memo M-01-28. The significance of this cannot be lost, because it was the first serious effort by the United States to recognize that the transformation of the perception, quality, and needs of its citizenry had to be met in an entirely new way if the government was to be responsive.

But does the responsiveness simply mean that these e-government efforts are CRM initiatives? There is constant confusion over this subject and I aim to clear it up in a word.

No.

But, they are potentially part of a CRM initiative. Conversely, CRM is also potentially part of an e-government initiative.

E-government is sparked by the President's Management Agenda, which is driven by citizen service, and the long-established, often-maligned-by-standup-comics Paperwork Reduction Act, which is aimed at improving efficiencies within the federal government. For example, in the latter category, e-government initiatives began in 2003 for reducing redundancies in six federal "business lines" as they so cheerily like to call them—criminal investigations, data and statistics, financial management, human resources, monetary benefits, and public health monitoring. Not one of them is a CRM initiative, though if they traverse the path to a cross-agency initiative, they begin to approach CRM.

It is fascinating to see how regulations and politics can be the cauldron of initiative creation.

ARCHITECTURE

What would the architecture of a CRM Public Sector initiative look like? It is similar to a CRM private sector initiative but with different emphases on the components. For example, security is a top priority for a public sector initiative, making the ASP hosted model at a federal level in particular less than likely. Portals are more important typically because of the need to provide a consistent experience to the public and among agencies and the likely volume of activity—both interactions and transactions—that the CRM initiative will engender. An empowered public will use the institutions of government if they have some hope that those institutions will be responsive. Look at the numbers of the FirstGov site (discussed later in this chapter) visits alone and you begin to get a sense of the sheer magnitude of response when it comes to government/citizen, government/business, and government/government activity. Thus, the scalability of the applications used and the interoperability of those selfsame applications via Web services or other standards become of critical importance.

All governments exist in an atmosphere of regulation. Regulation means that it is both legally and politically critical to track, audit, and report on all the activities that are endemic to the CRM initiative (see the discussion a little later on pharmaceuticals). When the government is thinking about its architectural and functional requirements, it has to think about deep reporting capabilities that would include customizable features. For example, Crystal Reports 8.5 is included in most of the major CRM packages and it provides the features that a typical CRM initiative might need. But does it support specific military specifications (milspecs)? That is no small thing. In the early 1990s, I was working as a contractor on a project bid with IBM. They were doing the project response in the now under the radar, page formatting program called Interleaf, perhaps the best of these production programs ever produced. In order to submit the RFP response, though, a template (which I built) had to be produced. This template was required to conform to Milspec 2167, a lengthy set of format rules developed and described by the Department of Defense. If the formatting was done incorrectly, in other words, not in conformity with Milspec 2167, the bid for the $11 billion long-term Army program, would not be accepted. The effort to build the template was long and laborious, but it was necessary—hardly the case in the world of commercial bidding, but always the case in the government. CRM applications that can't conform to these standards are no go.

If it is a CRM e-government initiative, ways to record citizen and interagency interactions without violating privacy are essential to the architecture that is required for a government venture.

Another architectural feature is a constituent-friendly user interface for the portals. For example, the Government Printing Office (GPO) spent time getting to know what could be called the "voice of the customer" (more on the VOC in Chapter 18). There had been complaints on the general unfriendliness of government websites. Another example: the GSA, in its continuous desire to revamp FirstGov to make it more constituent friendly, spent a good deal of time getting feedback from formal usability testing (more on this in Chapter 19) to informal feedback from their staff who travel the country teaching how to use the site. The site was reorganized so that it is without a doubt the most navigable site that the federal government has to offer.

The features:

- ▶ Multichannel integration

- ▶ Integration with existing back-office and third-party systems to protect government investment

▶ Consistency of interface and ease of access for constituents

▶ Use of portals that are citizen friendly

▶ Substantial monitoring, tracking, reporting, and auditing functionality (regulatory requirements)

▶ Very strong security/privacy processes in place

▶ Web architecture or minimally Web-enabled

▶ Scalable

▶ Very strong analytics functionality

▶ Flexible toolsets for customization that conform to mandated standards

CRM: State and Local

In the United States, there are 50 states, 19,000 municipalities, and 3,200 counties, all with relationships between and among themselves and their citizens who have relationships with several overlapping public state and local entities and the federal government. Each of those entities has unto itself a governing charter, a set of rules and regulations, and is subject in some way, depending on their level, to the rules and regulations of other governing bodies. They have relationships with corporations and with nonprofit agencies that either work in concert with them or are regulated by them.

Most states and many municipalities are developing CRM initiatives with an eye to improving the services provided to the state residents. One interesting example is Biel in Switzerland, land of chocolate neutrality. Using SAP MySAP CRM, they developed an extremely user-friendly website.

Dog license purchases and renewals are a good way of looking at this. Formerly, police officers would collect the fees due by visiting homes to sell the special stamps. Now, an owner can register their pet online. The police officer receives notification and confirms the information in the online application. The workflow then triggers the billing process. When the invoice has been paid, the stamp is mailed to the dog owner. Because it is integrated with the accounting processes and is easily navigable on the front end, this makes Biel dog owners happy petizens.

Never Underestimate the Locals

This is also a market. According to Gartner Dataquest, by 2005, state and local governments are expected to spend close to $57 billion, budgets having grown at a rate of 8.2 percent from 2002. There is a lot of power in them thar agencies when it comes to potential CRM initiatives.

But what do the locals want in CRM and what are they focused on?

On July 8, 2003, a study conducted by IBM and the Robert H. Smith School of Business at University of Maryland was released that reviewed the information technology investments of more than 412 state and local government representatives. The study found that 62 percent of the initiatives had focused internally, while 22 percent were to improve customer service. The results? The primary benefits across all initiatives were better information collection and distribution and improved customer service.

Looking at It from the Other Side: CRM, Regulation, and Compliance

I've spent most of my time on the government, also known as the regulators. What about the regulated? One of the more important functions that CRM serves is to provide a framework for regulatory compliance. Think about it. What public company hasn't had some regulatory dealings with the Environmental Protection Agency (EPA) or the IRS or the Justice Department or the Securities and Exchange Commission (SEC)? Most of them probably have. They are regulated and must comply. How does this work? Check out the Patriot Act.

The Patriot Act

The Patriot Act brought forward a new generation of CRM applications, much in the same spirit that Superman brought forth the Bizarro world—meaning, a highly unlikely, peculiar, petulant relationship between the two. Typically, CRM is for the improvement of customer interactions. In the new breed of Patriot Act–compliant software, it is for detecting suspicious customer transactions, especially detection of money laundering or INS violators. Find the customer transactions you can't trust and investigate them. For example, if someone starts to buy $500 money orders in sequence strings (ostensibly so that the $3,000 reporting limit can be bypassed), sophisticated algorithms from SAS's antimoney laundering product go into action and flag that person and their activity, according to the statutes of the Patriot Act.

Most sophisticated in this regard, though obviously somewhat chilling, is PeopleSoft's Patriot Act SEVIS Solution that PeopleSoft provides for free to its higher education customers. The software captures data about the students housed in the PeopleSoft human-capital management module. Regardless of how the information is entered, the new program will format it in a manner to be transmitted to the INS over the Internet. PeopleSoft says the data can be transmitted to the INS real time. With the data, the INS can quickly determine if a foreign student should have his student visa withdrawn because, for instance, he dropped out of school or if he should be monitored because of his suspicious attendance pattern.

The Vendors: How Are They Doing?

Vendors jumped into this market and you can now find purported CRM "solutions" for all your compliance needs from Sarbanes-Oxley financial compliance to the FDA scrutiny of pharmaceuticals. For example, RWD Technologies has a product they call OTIS which is an integrated compliance platform that uses Siebel Pharma on the front end and Documentum (for a highly sophisticated document management and audit/tracking capability) on the back end with connectors integrating the two.

There are a lot of pretenders to the throne in the government CRM world and if you're a public sector official seeking a CRM solution, you have to be particularly careful, even with the bigger vendors. Heed the words of Steve Monaghan, CIO of Nevada County, California, in an article on SearchCRM in June 2002: "There's a lot of hype around CRM in the public sector but when it comes down to it, the options aren't ideal. The e-government label is thrown around too loosely. There are a lot of vendors promising support, but all they've done is add little ticket systems to an existing package and renamed it as 'government CRM.'"

He goes on to blame the big ticket vendors, singling out Siebel as geared to the Fortune 500 and not particularly to the government—federal, state, or local. In fact, his crew went with the e-mail routing package provided by Metastorm, a business process management (BPM) software.

The Public Sector Major Players

Here's a brief snapshot of the Final Four of the enterprise-level software providers—the ones who can handle BIG GOVERNMENT.

ORACLE

Oracle's strength is that much of the federal, state, and local government's databases are Oracle databases. While there had been some much publicized problems with Oracle in the state of California in 2001, they remain a strong choice for public sector CRM work. The Oracle government solution is intriguing because rather than providing a point solution, they are taking a strongly process-driven approach to the government world. One of their most intriguing applications is their Citizen Interaction Solution. This is based on the 311 services (discussed earlier in this chapter) that Oracle is packaging. They are using multiple modules, including:

▶ **Citizen Interaction Center** This is where the calls come, the CSRs reside, and the 360-degree view of the customer is put on the silent PC screen.

▶ **Advanced Inbound** Sophisticated CTI and IVR with advanced queuing function to speed call resolution.

▶ **e-mail Center** The e-mail channel.

▶ **Scripting** Customizes the workflow for the call centers—for example, routing trouble tickets of varying levels to the skilled CSRs for that problem.

▶ **Mobile Field Service** Scheduling, dispatch, and delivery via the offline or online web capabilities.

▶ **Advanced Scheduler** Schedule optimization for the field agents.

▶ **Spatial** Handles sophisticated citizen queries and puts them in an Oracle data store.

▶ **Interaction Center Intelligence** Best practices intelligence gathering.

▶ **Customer Intelligence** Customer information viewer and customer intelligence gatherer.

▶ **Service Intelligence** Internal service intelligence—that is, how your department or division is performing.

Oracle's data consolidation and associated analytics provide powerful tools for constituents to get the right information at the right time, at the same time meeting the standards set by the governments providing that information.

PEOPLESOFT

PeopleSoft is the most cerebral of the vendors aimed at the public sector, with a serious attempt at providing both thought-leadership and some opportunity knowledge in the public sector. PeopleSoft integrates its CRM solution into its more generalized solutions for the public sector. The two government focused solutions that PeopleSoft offers are the Guardian Suite—Homeland Security applications that have a heavy emphasis on monitoring and tracking functionality—and PeopleSoft for the Public Sector, which not only encompasses CRM, but also their supply chain and ERP applications. Worthy of some serious consideration.

SAP

They are the up and coming CRM application in the public sector, primarily due to their strength in the ERP world public sector. SAP has always been a strong enterprise player in the state and local and higher education venues.

SIEBEL

They take the most drilled-down approach to the public sector of the four major players. For example, they have the Siebel Public Sector Unemployment Insurance Solution, which handles the claim management needs of the citizens, providing an integrated call center, e-mail and Web capability to file a claim 24x7 online. Another of their CRM solutions is Tax and Collections. Strong emphasis on collecting and doling out money, don't you think? I would seriously look at these guys for public sector CRM with strong financial overtones.

Enough with the vendors already. Steppin' Out this time is devoted to what I find to be the most significant military and civilian agency CRM programs. These are some of the genuine breakthroughs in the government on that path to ennoblement. These are world class efforts that are not only groundbreaking but provide good road maps for those of you who are looking at CRM in the public sector.

STEPPIN' OUT: The GSA's Office of Citizen Services

As those of you who deal with the federal government know, the use of acronyms can get downright funny. Only the world of information technology can go toe to toe with them for the highest percentage of a sentence dominated by initials. For example, a list of the civilian-side acronyms would run about 25 pages of this book with about fifty list- ings per page. The military acronyms and abbreviations would run about 115 pages. But with all the acronyms, bureaucracies, mysteries, and vagaries, sometimes the federal government can get downright heart- warming. As far as CRM initiatives go, this one is an actual story of ded- icated people who are truly CRM-centric, constituency-focused with a passion, and who reside in the halls of the General Services Adminis- tration's (GSA) Office of Citizen Services and Communications (OCSC).

If you lived through the late 1970s and 1980s, you'll remember the commercials for that strange government agency that sent you book- lets on how to lose weight or how to mail a package or how to find a Christmas tree or who to call if a whale beached near your house. That site founded in 1970 was the Consumer Information Center (CIC), and it was part of the Federal Citizen Information Center (FCIC) estab- lished that same year by an Executive Order of the President and placed in the GSA. Another separate agency, the Federal Information Center (FIC), was established four years earlier with a mission to direct citi- zens to appropriate Federal agencies to handle inquiries or problems. For twenty years, the agencies handled the publications and calls effec- tively and with enough fanfare to be recognized by the public.

But the world changed pretty dramatically in the 1990s and the GSA was foresighted enough to recognize that they had to not just change with that world, they also had to understand that the expectations of the baby boomers (which many of the staff were also) of their coun- try were not just dramatically heightened but were multichannel. Con- sistency of message and availability of information regardless of how it was accessed—via phone, fax, e-mail, web, direct mail—were now concerns of the GSA where they hadn't had to be a decade prior. To that end, there was consolidation of existing entities and the creation of new entities as the millennium was welcomed. In February 2000, the FIC became part of the FCIC and became known subsequently as the National Contact Center (NCC). Firstgov.gov, the A-list level federal website discussed next, became part of the FCIC in June 2002. The federal government understood the need to consolidate these citizen- focused functions into a single entity and proceeded to do so.

But most importantly, in September 2000, the GSA mandated the Office of Citizen Services and Communications which if viewed from a private sector set of eyes is a CRM Program Office nonpareil. Its mission was con- sciously driven by communications with those named citizens and by coordination throughout the federal government to meet the expectations of that citizenry. They were emphatically not driven by technology, which they saw as an enablement tool only. They are tied to the e-government slogan: My Government, My Terms. It portends some good things.

What is excellent about the OCSC and its personnel is that they understand that it is necessary to take an enterprise (read: government-wide) view of constituency-based cultural transformation to make it work. This is not a simple task since throughout much of the 20th century the federal government was a transaction-based, internally focused body of agencies. The OCSC is not just pivoting around a U.S. citizenry that when polled could barely name a single government agency (the most often named was 30 percent for the Department of Defense). It is also responsible to plan and prepare using large but chewable chunks, coordination of federal, state and local agencies to make sure that those perplexed citizens are satisfied. This means cultural change, which the OCSC leadership is thoroughly aware of. It means an effort that the indomitable staff wants to take on. To that end, OCSC has two organized initiatives: FirstGov.gov for the citizenry and USA Services for the interagency coordination of those efforts for the citizenry.

FirstGov.gov

FirstGov centralizes a massive agglomeration of information and services spanning 24 federal departments and their agencies, all 50 state governments, and over 180 million federal, state, and (soon) local government Web pages unified through a single set of constituent-usable portals.

There are four types of portals that can be accessed: Citizens, Business and Nonprofits, Federal Employees, and Government-to-Government. (See Figure 11-1.) An astounding 32 million documents per month are downloaded through the site. The visitor traffic in 2003 was more than 6 million per month—over 70 million users, up from 37 million in 2002. FirstGov does CRM with eloquence, speed, and currency, linking huge storehouses of information that are scattered across countless agency systems in a way that is constituent-loving. In fact, you can organize the site information by your constituent group (for example, seniors, kids, Native Americans, small business, and so on).

Equally as important, FirstGov relies on feedback from those self-same constituents. They get about 200 e-mails a day on the site's usability, which, in combination with surveys, studies, and information from their sister organization—the Federal Citizen Information Center—they are constantly improving what the site does. In fact, FirstGov has been so successful in providing services and information that they won the prestigious 2002 Innovations in American Government award among many others.

But FirstGov is not just FirstGov.gov. It's kids.gov, español.gov, it's relationships with the Recreation OneStop program of U.S. Parks and Recreation, the business gateway of the SBA, Exports.gov at the Department of Commerce, and it's all those government websites with the egov/FirstGov logo and link.

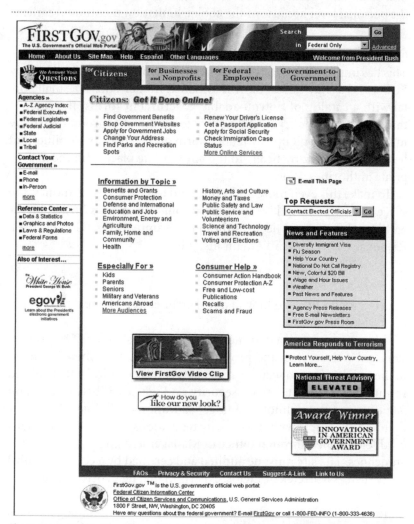

Figure 11-1: The FirstGov.gov portal page: The citizen's e-gateway to government

What it provides through these golden veins running throughout much of the government is consistent citizen-facing Web solutions using the same infrastructure for information sharing and interoperability. The efficiencies are obvious—maximum utilization of bandwidth by multiple agencies. More interesting is the ability to provide a timely and consistent citizen experience regardless of agency priorities and direction. It also means that important information from the citizens can be captured from multiple locales for use in identifying and understanding the citizen's needs even though they can't drill down to the personal level because of the cookie limitation mentioned earlier.

Responsive Government: Now That's a Plan

This has implications. For example, the SBA, through the FirstGov.gov Business Gateway, has an Eforms initiative. Initially, this is a small portal with a catalog of downloadable government forms. But later, if things go as planned, you will be able to go straight through FirstGov to this SBA site, pull up any federal form online, fill it out online, and have it routed automatically to the appropriate place with the appropriate authorities. Wow.

To make this even more appealing, and to save taxpayer money, the space to do this would be available through FirstGov's hosted bandwidth and the portal licenses though the unused FirstGov licenses. Responsive government. Ain't it just great!

FirstGov Architecture: A Brief Synopsis

This is a useful place to look at a real architecture of a real public sector CRM initiative.

It has analogies to a commercial site. It is hosted by AT&T. It uses standard Web services and protocols like HTML. But where it veers is in the weight given to security measures. Unlike a typical CRM-related venture in the private sector, security on FirstGov is between 30 and 50 percent of the technology budget allocation at all times. The site is required to comply with the security regulations and the security standards established through Office of Management and Budget (OMB) guidelines. The site must be audited and certified by a certifying third party such as Mitretek or Etelos, experts in that field, before it can ever go public.

To meet these standards and provide a common technology model, FirstGov uses BEA's portal tools and middleware for integration. Their content management applications are from Vignette, the best in the content management business. Between BEA and Vignette, they are providing sure-handed functionality, features, and information and technology security.

USA Services

OCSC is dealing with the citizens—the ultimate end clients—through FirstGov.gov. But what about the interagency coordination and inter-relationships? This is an extraordinarily difficult task because of the politics, different operating standards, varied constituencies, possible jurisdictional conflicts, significantly different missions and mandates, and finally, different levels of potentially unfriendly existing technology and systems—and of government.

On July 30, 2003, USA Services was created to coordinate these agency efforts for integrated case management and CRM for government. Perhaps the most important facet of this effort was the mandate to establish customer services standards government wide. Obviously, this standardization represents a huge cultural challenge because of the reasons mentioned above and because of the careerists who had a vested interest in the "as is" but were adamantly opposed to the "to be." Additionally, the technology and content standards at the agency and within departments were disparate, with every system known to man implemented. One would be hard pressed to find anything resembling best practices in all but a few departments. The mandate to change this is a major step forward.

Part of this mandate is to create a standardized common content model for all government websites. In fact, in 2003, an executive steering committee was created to accomplish this. The Office of Citizen Services and Communications plays a prominent role on the steering committee in this two-year effort.

BABY BOOMERS, BABY STEPS: THINK GOVERNMENT, DO AGENCY

In order to meet these significant challenges, the OCSC USA Services chose to take smaller first steps with an enterprise-wide perspective—similar to what you'll see later with the DLA. OCSC knew that the small victories could make a huge difference in the buy-in of the other government agencies. To that effect, their first foray was to do something which might seem easy, but is incredibly difficult: create the means to successfully redirect and answer misdirected communications from the citizenry. Think about it. "What do I do to get the raccoons out of my kitchen?" Okay, tell me who you should call? Wrong. Wrong again. Don't ask me. How would I know? Check in with the folks at OCSC. They'll direct you to…you catch my drift, don't you?

To prepare for this effort, OCSC engaged 14 partner agencies. The departments of Agriculture and Justice and the Small Business Administration (SBA) to lead the way in the redirection of the misdirected inquiries.

Look at the care that this "simple" task requires:

▶ Two channels are put into use—e-mail and phone.

▶ All misdirected queries that come to the U.S. Department of Agriculture (USDA) call centers are sent to the USA Services Center in Indianapolis, Indiana. For example, if the USDA gets an inquiry asking, "What do I do if I catch a small-mouthed bass?" Rather than arbitrarily being told to stuff it (take it any way you want to), the call is routed to the FCIC, which then directs it to the Department of the Interior's Fish and Wildlife, who might tell you how to stuff it or not, but you will get an answer within two business days.

▶ To do this requires training. OCSC staff travel from call center to call center under the aegis of the 14 agencies, training each CSR on how to handle the misdirected calls. This has the added benefit of fostering interagency cooperation and extending the OCSC customer-centric culture to the agencies. USA Services has a liaison/advocate at each of the agencies that operates as a "tour guide" for this effort.

▶ Each agency has a mailbox when the inquiring mind who wants to know isn't even sure of where in the agency they might mistakenly go.

This level of commitment has had direct and anecdotal results already. Perhaps the most interesting and important anecdotal result was a call that occurred from California during the fires there in November 2003. California law enforcement officials had been unable to find the phone number of a refuge that they needed to evacuate as the fires swept near to it. They called Fish and Wildlife's 1-800-344-WILD—not the right place. But because of the USA Services program, they had the right number in plenty of time to evacuate the refuge and save lives.

Importance of the OCSC

How successful has the OCSC been in this effort? Do the simple math here. In a scorecard on responsiveness in federal agencies and departments to the citizens, 28 agencies/departments received failing grades of 35 (of 100) and below. The OCSC got a 95. This is a big A+ in anyone's scorecard. End of story.

ACTUAL END OF STORY

Well, not quite. Remember, CRM initiatives are driven by people—breathing life forms that make differences. The OCSC staff makes that difference each day, driving the CRM initiatives to ennoble and to educate the citizenry—and to transform the culture of the institutions of government. As Teresa Nasif, Federal Citizen Information Center Office of Citizen Services and Communications, says, "At the end of the day, you really think you helped people." CRM, as it lives and breathes.

Feeling ennobled yet? You should be.

STEPPIN' OUT: Defense Logistics Agency (DLA), First in War, First In Peace, First in CRM

The Defense Logistics Agency supplies goods and services to all the military and then some. It oversees a staff of slightly less than 22,000 civilian and military employees who work in all 50 states and 28 foreign countries. As they state in the description of their own work: "It supplies almost every consumable item America's military services need to operate, from groceries to jet fuel. In short, if America's forces can eat it, wear it, drive it, shoot it, or burn it as fuel, chances are that DLA helps provide it." The DLA director reports to the Undersecretary of Defense for Acquisition, Technology, and Logistics through the Deputy Undersecretary of Defense (Logistics and Materiel Readiness). They are the military's lifeline.

A Huge Business

Without the DLA, the United States combatants in Afghanistan and Iraq don't eat and don't have the fuel they need for combat. In other words, the DLA's success is mission-critical. Error is failure—something that has no room in their mission statement.

They are also a huge business that, if placed on the 2003 Fortune 500, would be number 65. Their fiscal year 2003 revenue was around $25 billion, with the single biggest chunk—$10.2 billion—going to troop support. They have a medium-sized business line that handles foreign military sales to friendly countries—124 to be exact. They handle 4.6 million products in their catalogs. They have 22 distribution centers to handle those items and that number is growing. They secure 8,200 contracts per day and issue 45,000 requisitions per day. Also, don't forget those 22,000 employees, who do all this.

Their constituents are highly diverse and serving them under pressure poses an inordinately difficult challenge.

Table 11-3 is a prototype segmentation model that gives you an idea of what the broad constituent segments identified in a prior section of this chapter require at different levels. It's a remarkably intricate and delicate operation. What you should picture here is an enormous business that handles noncritical and life and death issues every single day of the year—and not only has to deal with regulations from the government, but is the government and has to operate as the federal agency to civilian companies—a dual, demanding role.

Another Daily Requirement: Being Extraordinary

The CRM initiative that the DLA is undertaking is part of a complete revamp of all their enterprise processes and technology and a conscious transformation of their culture. Historically and not terribly surprisingly, they have been a supply-chain focused, transactional and operational culture, an agency that saw its objective as getting the products to the customer. Like most government agencies, they have been agency-driven and internally focused—looking for constant improvements and tweaks in how the business of the DLA was done.

But with the transformation of both the Department of Defense around the requirements for contemporary warfare and peacekeeping and the exigencies of the expectations of the citizenry, foresighted key players at the DLA knew that their way of thinking, not just operating, had to change to meet these requirements. They also understood that a collaborative customer ecosystem was the new paradigm for business. They knew that, overall, the military would be skeptical of the dramatic changes that this implied, but a $25 billion revenue producer for the government has a lot of clout.

Table 11-3: DLA Customer Needs Across Segment Reflect Strong Supply Chain Components
(Source: Defense Logistics Agency LMI Expert Interviews, 2003)

	Combatant Commanders	Deployable Operating Units	Industrial	Installations
Delivery Needs	Advance planning; contingency support; 24x7 support	Real-time need 24x7 support; most emergent items are critical	Time-definite delivery is more important than instant delivery	Time definite delivery; short lead times
Service Receipt Requirements	Complex; often changing delivery sites; changes quickly	Complex; often changing delivery sites; changes quickly	Fixed delivery sites; may be scheduled; critical items may require alternative delivery	Simple; fixed locations; planned and scheduled
Price Sensitivity	None	Little to none	Critical items: sensitive; sensitive: metrics based on cost	Mostly commodities; price is negotiated from vendor
Internal Inventory Management	N/A	Limited on-hand and safety stock; on-demand fulfillment	Replenishment of stocked items; non-stocked items may be critical	Limited on-hand stocks; third-party re-supply
Planning Requirements	Long-term contingency planning	Pre-deployment planning	Forecasting of scheduled maintenance activities; demand planning on item level	Predictable planning for maintenance and consumption needs
Information Requirements	High need, for both historical and current information	Consumption information; status of requisitions	Technical info; consumption patterns; trends	Technical info; consumption patterns; trends

Translation? The DLA Must Change

From the DLA's perspective, it became apparent that simply improving the operations of the supply chain through more efficient product delivery wasn't going to do the trick. Rather, what was becoming necessary, as you saw previously in Table 11-3, was to provide integrated logistics solutions, rather than just goods, that met the needs of the specific customer segments. They had reached their transactional limit at about the FY2003 $25 billion and to go further it would take not just improved processes but a change in the culture of the DLA and eventually, through that, a change in the military's culture.

To begin the process of transformation around a CRM initiative, the DLA developed a balanced scorecard so that they could define the customer segments, the metrics associated with successful execution and customer satisfaction, and the key performance indicators (KPIs) that would let them know how they were doing along the way. (More on the balanced scorecard in Chapter 17.) Ultimately, they saw this tool as a means to educate not just the staff personnel but the various customer segments on how they wanted to do business in the future. One practical result was the use of performance-based agreements with their suppliers—agreements that shared risk and reward, depending on predetermined KPIs that were embedded in the contract.

But there was another major dilemma. They are not a typical "business." They are a government agency that deals with life and death logistics every day. That means that immediate requirements that are truly urgent step in the way of the long-term strategy that this CRM initiative requires. In the commercial business world, one of the greatest problems that any company that attempts a CRM initiative has is their ability to follow through. While their desire and "gung ho-ness" is strong, their commitment to sticking with it regardless of the needs of the day-to-day (which aren't all that mission critical most of the time) is poverty-stricken. So how could the DLA, in a far more deadly environment, handle the long-term requirements without the daily necessary distractions? Private sector, take note here. They created five teams that roll up under the leadership of Renee Roman, staff director for Policy Programs and Requirements. These teams are dedicated to nothing other than this initiative. It is the government equivalent of a CRM Program Office. Of the five teams, three of them do nothing but move the initiative as part of the culture day to day.

- ▶ **Team 1: CRM and customer strategy** Creates a strategy for a constituent-centric culture at the DLA.

- ▶ **Team 2: Change management and organizational alignment** This also includes knowledge transfer and learning management systems.

- ▶ **Team 3: CRM Blueprint** These are the business process re-engineering folks. They are looking at the DLA processes "as is" and developing the blueprint for the processes "to be."

A fourth team deals with the legacy CRM programs such as the customer satisfaction assessments they have historically done.

Step by Step, Inch by Inch

This is clearly an enormous strategic initiative. In fact, when the DLA bid the CRM initiative, I saw the RFP and was tremendously impressed by the scope of the effort. It not only accounted for the integration of the supply and demand chains, but was the first RFP I ever saw from a government agency that fully understood the dramatic transformation of culture that had to be undertaken *and* the need to plan for it.

One of the most characteristic pieces of this entire effort is the planning itself. This effort has a truly "think enterprise, work modularly" strategy—unusual in any CRM initiative, much less a government effort. In fact, this has a series of well-developed phases that will be carried out over time. Phase 1, about eight months, will be to flesh out the strategy and will end in 2004. The next step will be the discovery/learning phase where 200–300 customer interviews will be conducted initially to hear the voice of the constituent. By roughly October 2004, the next phase will begin—the idea is some quick CRM wins to accelerate buy-in, aid the cultural transformation, and solve problems.

This is a remarkable effort. The DLA is trying to both accommodate and lead the conversion to a constituent-centric government. As Col. Leonard Petruccelli, the DLA's Deputy Director, Customer Operations and Readiness (J-4) said in an interview I did with him and his colleagues, "This will provide better information, help make better investments, and provide actual customer services. I can't think of a more exciting thing to do."

Neither can I.

12

CRM and the SMB: Small Is Beautiful

For years, the little guy in business looked up to the big guy. "Gosh, someday, I'll be just like him: big, powerful, lots of employees, and lots of cash." As we pass through 2004, all of a sudden being like Enron or Halliburton doesn't seem so great. Nor does having to comply with Sarbanes Oxley whether an honest big guy or not. Being a small business is now cool. It gets you a walk on the red carpet when it comes to the vendors who want your business. Small and medium business is a beautiful thing. Ask a CRM software supplier.

SMB Is More than an Acronym

SMBs are the great untapped market. Small businesses are becoming increasingly sophisticated due to the exigencies of surviving and flourishing in a complex economy. Yet, when it comes to personnel and revenue, they are still pretty miniscule. Nearly three quarters of all U.S. business firms have no payroll at all. My company—The 56 Group, LLC—has 55 fewer employees than its title. What makes small and midsized businesses so attractive to the CRM industry? What makes CRM so attractive to these businesses? How does it differ from the enterprise CRM deployment? What do you have to do to make sure you can effectively use CRM if you're a small venture? Check it out.

Small Business: The Standard Definitions

According to statistics released by the Small Business Association in 2003, there are more than 20 million businesses officially classified as small. Typically, though its definition varies by industry, the official SBA definition is a company of 500 employees or less and revenues of $6 million or less. Gartner

Dataquest defines the small business as a business that has between 50 and 100 employees or less than $50 million in annual revenue. Most of the 20 million small businesses are closer to 1–50 employees than over 50 employees.

I've spent a lot of time on definitions in this book so that confusion on what is what in CRM can be cleared up. What makes small business difficult to pin down is the variances among what is defined as small business by different sources, plus the possible confusion over how to link the different components of the definition. For example, are you a small business if you have 75 employees and $7 million in revenue? If you are the SBA, the answer is yes and no in that order. If you are Gartner Dataquest, the answer is yes and yes in that order. If you use my criteria, which is based on the potential users of CRM, the answer is yes, but one that probably has more employees than it can handle.

For CRM's purposes, the companies that have between 1 and 200 employees fit the definition of small business well. I would suggest if you are considering a small business CRM solution, you use these numbers and recognize that there are significant differences between a 10-user and a 100-user system. I would also suggest using the revenue numbers of your company only as guidelines for your CRM strategy and to determine whether or not you can afford to do it.

Midsized Business: The Standard Definitions

We're starting to get to the vendors and integrators' mouthwatering territory here. The midsized domain is their sweet spot, though both unwisely and hilariously in some instances, as I'll show you shortly.

Gartner Dataquest defines these businesses as in the range of $50 million to $500 million in annual revenue and between 100 and 999 employees. AMI Partners is considerably more precise in their numbers, though not in their definition. They see it as any company between 100 and 999 employees, but they don't attach a revenue number to it. This makes sense, since the amount of potential users is far more valuable a measurement than the amount of money that a company makes in any given year. What AMI Partners points out, however, is that the average annual revenue for a midsized company is $70.3 million, pretty much on the lower end of Gartner Dataquest's numbers. With these numbers, AMI Partners estimates that there are 103,000 businesses at the midsized level in the United States. While a tasty morsel, nothing by comparison to the more than those 20 million small businesses in the U.S. Though it's still not too shabby since the 103,000-company expenditure for IT in 2003 was an estimated $69.3 billion—a large dollar amount of that low-hanging fruit that CRM vendors so love to pluck.

Small and Midsized Business: The Software Vendors' Take

Far be it from the software industry to accept those standard definitions. They border on the ridiculous in how they redefine small and medium business pretty much every two weeks. Because it suits them to do so, they attach a revenue number that reflects what size company they've sold to this week. For example, PeopleSoft caps the SMB market in the ranges of $200 million one week to $500 million the next. For the big vendors, PeopleSoft seems almost reasonable. SAP caps the market with a ceiling of *$1 billion*! Wouldn't you love to have a $1 billion business that qualified for help from the SBA? Know what size the bottom rungs of the Fortune 3500 businesses are? It's about a billion dollars. Small business, SAP style.

Perhaps the definition that is meaningful to those of you considering a CRM solution in the world of the small business is the one that Microsoft has for its MSCRM product. They are defining you as a small business from 5 to about 100 users. Users are a far better standard for defining small and medium sizes than revenue. Revenue is a software vendor's wishful thinking, not a legitimate measure of the viability of a small or midsized company or the value of a CRM initiative to the people of the company. Note CRM's value isn't to the revenue of the company. Revenue upticks are a *result*. CRM's value is to the people—*the users*.

The upside is that the CRM vendors and integrators now understand the need to get into the real SMB market and to stop spinning their erotic fantasies. They have become single-minded in their focus to penetrate it. Historically, they have failed miserably in this arena. In the 90s, when small companies became a sexy target due to the dotcom boom, the CRM vendor's approach was "Let's dumb down our enterprise software and call it midmarket." The largest vendors didn't want to give up their pricing models which simply were impossible for a small company to handle. The model for and the problems of the SMB are very different than the larger enterprise, but to recognize that didn't seem to be lucrative enough so the vendors simply adjusted reality. Consequently, rather than trying to actually understand the SMBs, the enterprise applications vendors simply crippled the features that the SMBs weren't likely to use in a smaller environment, such as highly developed analytics or complex workflow features and toolkits. They then scaled down the "size" of the pricing and implementation length to the small and medium businesses—treating them like Photoshop images, scaling the proposal down but keeping the pixilated proportions. So where it might be $10 million and 18 months with 100 percent functionality for the enterprise customer, for the smaller company it was $4 million, 8 months, and 40 percent of the functionality. While this is a bit of an exaggeration, this Dr. Doom and Mini-Me approach was actually the way they developed their midmarket programs. There was no understanding that the SMB had an entirely different set of issues, approaches, processes, and cultures.

For example, a company I worked for was a partner to one of the CRM vendors in this market in the late 1990s. The vendor's approach was to give the partner the implementation work but keep the project management themselves and tie the partner to a fixed price negotiated by the vendor. If there was a scope change, well, tough luck. In the one project my company got from this vendor, the project manager promised an upgrade to the customer for free without any consultation with my company because the customer was unhappy about the major changes in the applications so soon after they had contracted for the prior version. In order to honor the agreement and keep the customer happy, my company ended up eating the cost (over $167,000). The client was unhappy because of the way the vendor sales reps had sold the project to them; we were unhappy because we weren't given any consideration at all in the discussion. All in all it was an utter failure. We lost money, the vendor lost credibility, and the client was left in a shambles.

This assumption led to the failure of all of the enterprise players in the 1990s and early part of the new millennium to penetrate the SMBs with any great success. The requirements for the SMBs were vastly different and the ignorance shown by the vendors was appalling. However, to their credit, they are all developing a different approach to the current SMBs, learning from their mistakes of the past. (See Table 12-1.) While most of the offerings of the 1990s were failures, the offerings of 2004 are aimed with the lessons of the immediate past locked and loaded.

Table 12-1: Finding CRM Solutions for the SMBs

Vendor	Prior Offering	Current (2004) Offering
Siebel Systems	Siebel Midmarket (fired 246 midmarket partners for failure to perform).	Siebel Midmarket, Siebel CRM OnDemand (with IBM), Siebel Upshot (acquired ASP in 2003).

Table 12-1: Finding CRM Solutions for the SMBs *(continued)*

Vendor	Prior Offering	Current (2004) Offering
PeopleSoft	PeopleSoft Select: Specialized program that allowed SMB-sized partners to implement the applications for a fixed price with PeopleSoft managing the projects.	Acquired J.D. Edwards; developed EnterpriseOne Suite; heavily hosted applications.
Oracle	Small Business Suite	Small Business Suite
SAP	None	SAP Business One: New product developed from a framework acquired with SAP's acquisition of Top Tier in 2002.

SMB vs. Enterprise: What Are the Differences?

Business life in the SMB is entirely different than business life in the Fortune 1000. There was an abortive attempt by the Fortune 1000 companies to "adopt" SMB characteristics when SMB was being equated with dotcom in the late 1990s. "Nimble" and "quick" became highly desired business characteristics though most Fortune 1000 companies, when trying to do that, become impaled on the candlestick, rather than jumping over it as they had hoped. Departments were mandated to be more flexible, dress codes relaxed (one of the few continuing holdovers), and creative thinking became a mantra, rather than a process. When the dotcom bomb exploded, businesses got really quick—quick to run as fast as possible from the dotcom's not-so-nimble-footed collapse.

Failure of the dotcom business aside, SMB characteristics are dramatically different than the largest companies and thus the approaches to CRM are also quite different, both functionally and technically. The failure of the potential vendor to understand this can wreck your company if you're not alert, so Table 12-2 is here for your perusal.

Table 12-2: Differences Between Bigger and Smaller Businesses

Small and Medium Business	Fortune 1000-Level Enterprise
Multiple roles for individual employees	Highly defined responsibilities by title
Underdeveloped or nonexistent business processes	Either libraries of best practices or inflexible business processes (or both)

Table 12-2: Differences Between Bigger and Smaller Businesses *(continued)*

Small and Medium Business	Fortune 1000-Level Enterprise
Nimble but not big	Powerful but often inflexible
Modular CRM strategy	Enterprise-wide CRM strategy
Undeveloped corporate policies and procedures	Manuals defining specific policies
Spending is more "intuitive"	Spending is highly regulated
Employee is often quite near the senior executives through past relationship or nature of the company	Senior management has a group of direct reports, indirect reports, and never know most of the employees

The Culture Shift

Drama defines the growth of a small company. What is an incremental number for a larger enterprise is a massive business transformation for a smaller entity. There is a point at which the smaller company which had gotten along quite well with ACT! now has to make the move to CRM. Does the following scenario seem familiar to you small business owners?

The scene opens at a small office that is being expanded. Construction and associated noise is going on as the president of the small growing company is pacing the floor, and there is a good deal of hubbub and chatter going on in the background. The company president is watching the scene unfold as a Muse speaks to him:

Sales have become more complicated because you have more opportunities to manage. Forecasting is now important because there are considerably more mouths to feed and expenses to handle. That means there is more data that reflects processes you need simply to do the forecasting and fulfill customer needs. The business world you are engaged in has changed dramatically since 9/11, and you need to be able to approach it differently as you move up the opportunity scale. You can no longer provide all the services that your bids and RFP responses require, so you have to begin to collaborate formally with partners who can provide what you can't, extending what had been a simple value chain. The complexity of your service needs is increasing as just a few packages have changed to hundreds of orders a week—not gigantic, but enough to place intense pressure on "the way you always do it." No longer is it possible to just drop the order off at UPS each night. The level of customer expectations and volatility has gone up since the Internet became such a good source of comparative shopping. Of course, this means that pricing schemes and discounts and catalogs are getting more complex, as is the competition to keep a customer. It isn't just the customers that you know personally any more. You're lamenting that, but you're kind of glad too, because it's time that you grew enough to get a little impersonal. But you still want to take care of those you have known for several years.

With more than 40 salespeople and six offices, your geography has left the room at the identity suite it used to reside in. You need to do revenue forecasts now, because you are hiring, and your expenses are that much higher and more complicated, with computer leases and air travel and lots of insurance costs and training and salaries plus bonuses and taxes.

The six offices mean territories and the 40 salespeople mean territories within territories and teams and managers to manage all of these folks. You want them out on the road, too, don't you, so they can do what they hopefully do best—meet customers and develop relationships? PDAs, cellphones, laptops, and handshakes are all part of their arsenal. Also, maybe some of your salespeople are underperforming and your sales managers have noticed that a team selling approach works well with the underachievers and fits the corporate culture. You might as well train the new salespeople on it to prevent underachievement and provide some process consistency so your sales managers and staff can see where they stand.

You've also reached the point that when someone is a director of something, they actually have to direct, and they don't have four different business cards, each with a separate title for a different kind of customer.

You're not quite at the point yet where you need to know more than the 80–20 rule for your customers, but you can see the day coming where how you allocate your funds to each customer will need some differentiation. "John Smith" is still the way you address your key customer, not "45 percent profitability." A smile and hug is not quite cutting it anymore for a customer satisfaction benchmark, though.

Know what else? Terms like "market share," "top of mind share," "differentiator," and "rate of return" are all creeping into your vocabulary and you recently found out what EBIDTA means and that Sarbanes-Oxley is not a law firm.

Marketing means campaigns and use of e-mail, and you always hated that, didn't you? Who the heck needs more spam? But you're not spam; you're e-mail marketing with a response rate that matters. A colorful brochure done with Microsoft Word is no longer enough. And you need organized customer support for your services and products because they've gotten so complex and there are so many more customers..."

(The Muse's voice trails off into the ether with the point well made and the stage goes dark.)

This is a successful small business that is reaching the exact point where contact management is heading out and CRM is coming in on the agenda. I'm sure that many of you successful SMB folks recognize the "symptoms" of growth. While I might be mentioning this in a humorous and more readable vein, the fact is that you need to consider CRM at this stage of growth and these are real points that you might well reach or have reached, requiring a business transformation to reach that omnipotent next stage.

Now I'll elaborate on a few of the differences between the SMB and the large enterprise issues and strategies.

Multiple vs. Defined Roles

I grew up in the small business environment, having worked for companies that ranged from $300,000 in revenue and about 25 employees as chief recruiter, business development person, internal HR, father figure, mother figure, strategist, and occasional accountant, to $35 million and nearly 400 employees as vice president of marketing, which was really a business development, practice leader, and alliances chief position. Of course, this is entirely the point. In the world of the entrepreneurial business, the roles and responsibilities of the employees have little to do with the job description. As the company grows in size, job responsibilities get naturally differentiated and more procedurally rigid. When you went to a particularly small company, how many of you got an offer letter that said "and any other responsibilities that might be necessary from time to time"? That meant always. But as you hit the larger (but still not major) companies, that "from time to time" actually meant from time to time and eventually disappeared from the offer letter.

In the large enterprise, that level of loose description is looked upon as appalling. There are specific job responsibilities attached to specific titles, as are specific compensation packages. They are not flexible because any sign of gelatinous thinking about the job description can mean a lawsuit in this litigious age. "He made me do something that was outside my job description" is a real threat that a larger enterprise can't overlook. However, in a small corporation, multitasking is positive and pretty much required, not negative and a pending court case.

For example, if you are the VP of sales and marketing at a small company, your role may require that you have to handle human resources matters in lieu of the director of HR if you have such a person. Or you may have to make financial decisions for the entire company that are out of your area of expertise, but the president is on vacation and you're the most senior person there. Often not only does senior management wear multiple hats, but they know everyone at the company and have for years. Each person has an open door to the entire management team at any time and management hangs out after hours with the staff. Differentiation is minimal. Grab a technical guy and take him on a sales call with you. I've done it. It can work or it can be a nightmare. But it is the life of a small company.

Small Business Processes

As we will be seeing in Chapter 18, business process transformation is such a functionally critical piece of the business plan, it's hard to underestimate it. But the way that a small business looks at processes and a large one looks at processes varies perhaps more than any other divergent view in this pantheon.

Often when I speak to a crowd of small business people, I ask them a question that goes: "How many of you have a library of best practices?" So far, in the many thousands of people I've spoken to and with, only one has said that they do. This isn't surprising. Typically in a small business, there are routines and habits, but they are either not documented or formalized as processes or often even seen as processes. Salespeople sell as they learned or they wing it. There is no particular adherence to anything but the final revenue objectives and even they are subject to change with or without notice. But as the company grows, so does the need for an organized way of doing work—in other words, processes. For example, metrics and KPIs get attached to how a support person gets paid as a business grows and as the use of capital gets more formal and judicious. That means that because you now have 55 support staff at your call center rather than you and two full-time CSRs fielding the phones, it no longer is so easy to dole out a bonus here or there as you please. Expectations of the CSRs are that they will be treated similarly and uniformly. Consequently, a compensation structure that depends on each of the 55's performance is created. This is both good and bad. It is bad because it means that the individual relationships that had characterized the "mom and pop" environment are now part of the past. The company is getting "corporate." It is good because, since the company has evolved this far, there needs to be standards for all employees to be treated fairly. It is the right thing to do when a company reaches a breakout size. It can also prevent a lawsuit that can be filed under any number of federal entitlements.

Constant process adjustments characterize small and medium sized businesses. You know this if you are in that environment. Something doesn't work, it's dropped and then something else is tried. Contrast this with a larger company where a change in procedure involves multiple sign-offs and even committees, and of course, attorneys.

What makes the transition point for the SMB to go from contact management to CRM difficult is that the processes are continuously in flux. For example, Prophet 2004, produced by Avidian, takes a very sophisticated approach to contact management—in fact, it falls somewhere between contact management and SFA. It places all of this within Outlook, using Outlook for its contact files, making it very convenient to use and allowing you to tailor sales processes within the application. It provides simple pipeline management tools, opportunity, account, and contact management. It works directly with Outlook so the learning curve is virtually nonexistent. It has an easy-to-use interface. In other words, it is very slick. But it doesn't have workflow or embedded sales processes or back-office integration. It doesn't pretend to, positioning the application competitively with ACT! more than SalesLogix or MSCRM. It lies in the ethereal in-between. Should you use this on the way up to SFA or a fuller CRM package? Sure. Should you call it CRM? No. It is good for the company that is evolving to the level of the scenario above but hasn't gotten there yet, or those who are still in the realm of contact management. Think about that, packages for contact management, then the transition, then the fuller CRM. Whew. Being an SMB is a daunting task.

The Vendor and the SMB

Historically, the CRM vendors have drastically misunderstood the SMB. That means that if you aren't a savvy SMB purchaser, you're going to allow the assumptions of the vendor to determine what you will likely need and likely not, and, if you still have your job a year later, you will be seeing a therapist due to feeling inadequate. While I will cover vendor selection in Chapter 17 on strategy in a considerably more detailed fashion, for this section's purposes, there are several SMB-specific mental notes that you need to take when you deal with them.

The vendor needs to provide you with:

▶ **Flexible applications and terms** Most vendors will provide you with what they call their "accelerated solutions," a silly euphemism for short-term implementations at a fixed price using a specific methodology that varies little among them. For that "accelerated" price, you get basic functionality implemented in a fixed time frame. Unless you've planned well and mapped what you are going to need, customization that you need along the way will drive your price up and considerably extend your time to rollout. The best way around this is to determine what you need in advance and when you are interviewing vendors, give them scenarios to demonstrate what they can provide that you know you need right out of the box. That way, whatever vendor you select will have minimum customization requirements.

▶ The "accelerated methodologies" usually promise to have you up and running in 30–70 days. Don't assume that this is going to be the case. Make sure the vendor takes on some of the risk with that fixed time frame and that level of risk is detailed in the contract and/or service level agreement you sign with the vendor. That means that after a certain time frame within some limits, the vendor assumes the cost, not just extends their end point.

▶ **Limited cost by thinking modularly** Because you have limited funds as a small company, figure out your area of pain and cure it. But never forget that whatever you do in the short term in a department has an impact throughout your entire company over the long term. For example, let's assume that your sales force is not being that productive. Implement SFA and even turn on the embedded Solutions Sales methodology, but recognize that increased sales of goods means that production, inventory, shipping, and delivery of the product has to be able to handle the increased sales of the product or the backlog will kill you with the success of the sales staff.

▶ **Actual knowledge of the SMB world** Don't assume that the vendor knows anything about the SMB world you inhabit. The failure of the large enterprise vendors in the late 1990s and the early millennium with companies like yours is proof that they had little inkling of what the differences between the larger enterprise and you were. Make them prove their knowledge by showing you benchmarks and metrics that are useful to smaller companies. They need to show you the love you deserve, which means have some concern for what your SMB actually needs and not what they can sell you. For example, you might love the colorful dashboard with all the complex graphics based on the huge analytics engine working to provide you with high end predictive analytics, but you don't need that for your 50-person business. The money you save may be your own.

You've Got Leverage

If you're an SMB, I'm going to get inspirational on you for a minute. You've got enormous leverage right now and you should use it. In 2003, *VAR Business* published a study indicating that while 75 percent of the largest enterprises were going to either maintain or reduce their spending on IT, 76 percent of the small and midsized companies were going to increase theirs. That is significant given that ultimately over $86 billion was forked over by SMBs for computer-related services in 2003. You are also a vastly under-penetrated market with roughly 30 percent considering CRM initiatives and around 20 percent actually implementing or having implemented CRM in some form. There are some vendors who are positioned well and have strong SMB customer bases and histories. Best Software through its excellent CRM product SalesLogix is one that comes to mind. There are some who have lots of money and penetration with other products in the SMB market like Microsoft, who has 30,000 Certified Partners and 198,000,000 users of Outlook. Within the first six months of their release of MSCRM 1.0 in February 2003, they had more than 1,000 customers and a 6 percent market share. Phenomenal numbers for a rookie—though more of a rookie in the manner of Japanese baseball veterans Hideki Matsui for the New York Yankees or Ichiro Suzuki for the Seattle Mariners. Microsoft had plenty of prior experience in playing the software game, just not specifically in the CRM leagues.

There are some who are positioned well because of their back office products, like ACCPAC (now owned by Best Software) or even Oracle through the Small Business Suite and their database. However, these are actually rare. There aren't too many highly placed CRM vendors or integrators with histories in the SMB space and this makes them drool for what is otherwise known as "corporate quals." These are case study–level success stories with customers that the customer has given permission to tell, often for some consideration in return, such as discounted future pricing or free maintenance for a time. This way the vendors can point to their dramatic successes.

Since these stories are few and far between, and this is virgin territory for most and these initial partnerships between the customer and the vendor are so critical, the vendors are willing to cut very promising deals as of this writing because it is such a new market.

Simply stated, use your leverage while you have it. You have the vendors drooling for your business. For now.

The Vendors

It's time to take a look at those vendors who want to cater to your every whim—sometimes to your detriment, on occasion for your actual benefit. These are the leaders or the newer entries worth noting. What is absent from here are those purveyors of contact management—ACT!, Maximizer, or Goldmine. One I would like to note, and advise caution with, is Intuit's QuickBooks Customer Manager, a highly touted $80 small business version of what is claimed to be CRM. It isn't. It has merits as something that can track customer history. It provides additional functionality to QuickBooks. But that's about it. It is missing much of what distinguishes CRM from contact management and is by no means a substitute for SalesLogix or MSCRM. It is devoid of workflow, and much of classic CRM functionality (such as pipeline management). As an add-on for QuickBooks, it's not bad. As CRM, it is bad. There is no such thing as a cheap substitute for CRM, regardless of who tells you that. CRM is a business initiative, not software, remember?

What is also important to note is that while the ASPs are becoming an increasingly important competitor to the standalone CRM vendors, they are not listed here because they have their own chapters (Chapters 16 and 26). However, not only can't they be ruled out, they are often the best alternative for the small and medium business. But they are not the only ones.

Midsized Doesn't Fit All

There is a segment of the SMB market which is "in between." That means in between the small and large enterprise—the midsized company. For example, one of my clients, David's Bridal, is a company that fits this description perfectly. They are the leaders in wedding apparel and are one of the great business success stories of the past five years, growing out of nowhere to become a $450 million, 210-plus stores empire with no end in sight. I have to say, it is nice to have a client that is figuring out how to continue with success, not how to get there. They are the perfect example of a part of the market that is not quite a Fortune 3500 enterprise, but is large enough to begin to differentiate job descriptions, business processes, and customer management approaches. They are not the small business that Microsoft is currently aimed at, for example, but there is an entire class of vendors that are aimed squarely in their market. These vendors have the sophisticated levels of functionality necessary to meet the midsized companies' needs, but they are overkill for the smaller business. One of the midsized vendor problems is that they constantly were lapping up the waters of the large enterprise well. Sadly, it was poisoned water for them, because they can't compete with PeopleSoft, SAP, Siebel, or Oracle, despite their temptations and fantasies. They thought there was something to the idea that bigger is better.

Without further ado, it's time to take a quick peek at the best known of the vendors who cater to the midsized companies.

ONYX

Success becomes Onyx. They have been largely based on a portals-focused model that plays extremely well with the largest of the midmarket companies. If you look at their model, there are three "customer" specific portal solutions they provide—customer portal (the paying client), employee portal, and partner portal—all of which have specific functionality built in. Originally focused on a Microsoft

.NET solution that worked with SQL Server, in 2003 they expanded to take advantage of Oracle's strengths and developed an architecture that generates SQL code regardless of what database is being used. More importantly, their portals provide the features that each customer set needs to function quite well. They provide a top of the line experience for the midmarket CRM customer.

For example, through the Employee Portal, their Support capability provides you with features that are aimed at helping the CSR and the call center management handle large volumes of incoming calls and queries from multiple channels. So you see features like Service/Support Request Management, which handles and documents incoming support and service issues, or Service/Support Escalation, which automates and routes problems from any channel in any center to the appropriate party at any level. There is also Queue Management, E-Service, Knowledge Base, Online Service Inquiries, and Online Chat, which are geared toward making sure that customer problems are resolved as easily as it is to resolve any customer problem. Then you have Call Center Performance Analysis, Reporting and Analytics, and Quality Management to see how you're doing and to monitor and correct things that you're not doing so well. Finally, to make sure that it integrates with your existing phone system, it supports Computer Telephony Integration (CTI). Now, if you're a customer, through the Customer Portal, you get support functionality that is primarily aimed at self-service, an often touted but very tricky area of CRM thinking and execution. (See Chapter 7.) Notice the focus:

- ▶ Web self-help

- ▶ Online surveys

- ▶ Knowledge base

- ▶ Online profile management

- ▶ Online service inquiries

- ▶ Product registration

Each of these is related to inputs from a customer online in one way or the other. Each can be tracked and added to an individual customer record. If you go to the Quicken (Australia) support side of the website, you'll register yourself and your product, look up details on the product in a knowledge base, perhaps ask an online representative through either their online chat function or an e-mail query about an issue with Quicken's integration with QuickBooks (it doesn't), and then fill out a survey on how well you were served—and maybe you could even win a $25 gift certificate for Foster's, mate! This can be done without leaving your keyboard and using the Onyx Customer Portal.

PIVOTAL/TALISMA

Pivotal is a bit self-serving when it comes to their definition of the midsized company. They see it as between $100 million and $3 billion, a nice wide swath that takes them out of the SMB market as you head toward the middle of their range. But their merger with top flight CRM vertical specialist Talisma and acquisition of marketing automation vendor MarketFirst made them a truly formidable for midsized companies, especially in healthcare, financial services and insurance. Where they are exceptionally strong is in the sales and selling applications. Not only do they provide the standard functionality, but their embedded Miller-Heiman selling processes include excellent templates intended to engage a larger sales force. Pivotal takes it a step further with their Assisted Selling module, introduced in 2003 with Pivotal 5.0, which provides the novice with the tools for product configuration, pricing, and quote generation for proposals, whether you are mobile or at the office. They even have an Interactive Selling toolset that adds wizards to guide your salesperson through whatever sales processes and configuration need to go on. Where I wouldn't really give them the time of day is in partner relationship management, where they don't even come close to companies like ChannelWave.

E.PIPHANY

This software provider remains a formidable player in the midmarket space, despite taking some hits in 2002–2003. Their analytics and real-time applications provide a high level of value for the larger end of the midmarket. Their strength is in marketing and analytics, but they do offer a complete suite of applications that cover the gamut of CRM traditional suite modules: Marketing, Sales, and Support. What makes them exceptional for the midmarket upper end is the E.piphany Interaction Advisor. This is one of the few truly real-time applications in the CRM world. While there has been fealty paid to the so-called "real-time enterprise," few companies have much more than frequently updated analytics-driven dashboards for various types of managers. E.piphany provides the real-time deal. Their Interaction Advisor uses a combination of historical, personal, and contextual data to create a real-time customer profile, and then applies real-time analytics and predetermined business rules to deliver the highest-impact offers at some moment of customer interaction—a form of optimization that bears on and uses the customer's buying behavior. It then measures the results and continuously adjusts itself to improve effectiveness over time. If you need it, this is fantastic stuff. But make sure you need it. Coolness is not need, and desire doesn't mean fulfillment.

PeopleSoft/JDE

This is intriguing for two reasons. First, PeopleSoft acquired and absorbed J.D. Edwards in 2003. J.D. Edwards was the leader in the AS400 hardware market, a market typically serving the upper end of the midsized companies. Second, PeopleSoft, announcing their PeopleSoft/J.D. Edwards hybrid product, placed a great deal of emphasis on their hosted services for what they call their EnterpriseOne suite. This is the former J.D. Edwards One World product. The PeopleSoft EnterpriseOne "suite spot" is the integration of significant learning and eLearning tools to make the adoption process considerably easier for the larger midsized companies. PeopleSoft quotes META Group on this subject with the following useful numbers: "eLearning provides 30 percent more learning content in 40 percent less time at 30 percent less cost than traditional classroom learning." Good numbers.

Small Business

What this vendor class provides is quite different than even the midsized CRM vendors. In most small market applications, what is missing is what is notable. The vendors provide all the basic functionality you get with even the enterprise-level applications but much more simply. Additionally, you rarely will see any analytics engines in the small business packages like the up and coming ACCPAC, and its front end brother, the well-established SalesLogix, Best CRM, or the always popular Microsoft MSCRM. While they provide forecasting and reporting tools, they are nowhere near the sophistication that E.piphany or SAP Business One gives you. If you're a small business, you don't need it. Your cultural paradigm is considerably more intuitive and direct than a larger or midsized company. Decisions are formed from discussions, Google research, and gut feelings more often than not. Your customer information is centralized if you are using CRM, but you don't have millions of customers and terabytes of data to deal with. You are dealing with dozens of customers and gigabytes of data. Simpler needs mean simpler solutions.

SAP: Goliath Loves David

You would think that this behemoth didn't quite get the idea of the SMB. For many years, in fact through the second edition of this book, you would have been absolutely right. But no more. With the release of SAP Business One in 2003, SAP finally began to get it right, aiming at the 10-user to 250-user market. Goliath realized that there was more to David than just a slingshot. Rather than what they (and every other large vendor) had done historically—dumbing and dumbering down—they created a new product from scratch, using technology developed by TopTier's Shai Agassi (now SAP board of directors' superstar and SAP heir apparent) with TopManage. They then integrated the best of SAP adaptable enterprise technology—Drag&Relate and SAP business maps—into the programmatic mix, coming up with a powerful product. Drag&Relate allows users to drag information from disparate data stores and link them on the desktop. It really doesn't matter whether the data source is PeopleSoft, SAP, or some homegrown legacy system. Well, it matters, but it still works easily.

Additionally, as we saw in Chapter 10, SAP is a specialist in vertically and process-specific solutions maps, with the most detailed and deep process maps in the entire industry. For SAP Business One Sales, Marketing, and Support, they have provided solutions maps that cover, for example, Contact Management, Opportunity Management, Pipeline Management, and Service Management. Take it a step deeper and beneath Contact Management you get Contact and Contact Overview. Beneath Contact you get the ability to document a phone call or any other channel-driven connection to and transaction with a customer. You then can attach this to the customer record. While this may be simple (it is), what is interesting is that with Drag&Relate, you can take this transaction and move it into whatever other data source you want to and it remains part of that overall customer record.

While the business maps that SAP provides with Business One are far simpler than what they do with their industry maps, they need to be because the level of complexity is simpler. However, these are not just dumbed down and disabled features, they are developed toward the SMB users. That is their value, since the processes of a small company are simply not as well formed. SAP, in alliance with American Express has reached more than 1,000 small business customers with this product. In November 2003, they released an enhanced version of Business One adding service management and service sales components and a newly honed Software Development Kit (SDK) to allow the SMBs the ability to tailor their solution as precisely as they want to their own needs. All this for a reasonable (as of this writing) $3,750 per three business user licenses. SAP is also offering industry-specific, stripped down templates of its core R/3 software as mySAP All-in-One, with implementations promised from as low as $250,000. This is aimed at the higher end of the midmarket. In 2003, SAP formed an alliance with Sybase to give the Business One small business user an increased number of platform and database choices.

Notice one thing. I never mentioned that SAP Business One was CRM. It is, but only as part of an enterprise-wide front-office and back-office suite that incorporates that "one big value chain" I've mentioned in previous chapters. When we look at the future of CRM in the final chapter, we'll see why it's becoming increasingly difficult to separate CRM from that overall value chain.

MICROSOFT'S MSCRM: GOING STRAIGHT FOR THE HEAD

Microsoft always seems to have an amazing story to tell. Ubiquitous Microsoft (UM) is a fitting phrase, not just a marketing term. What area of technology in the home or the business don't you see them either dominating or at least capturing a large chunk? Consumer electronics, PC/entertainment convergence, software, hardware, wireless world, television, large enterprises, midsized enterprises, and now the small businesses out there with their MSCRM release. What I find amazing (and actually, classically typical) is that they captured 6 percent of the market share in SMB CRM in the space of the first six months of their release 1.0, which didn't even have a marketing module and still doesn't. They had more than 1,000 customers and 1,580 certified MSCRM partners by November 2003 after a February 2003 release date. At the release date, their competitors pooh-poohed them, especially those in the highly opinionated ASP community. How wrong they were (and are).

I presume that whoever is reading this book is most likely familiar with Microsoft Outlook. If you are, then being familiar with MSCRM is a piece of cake. The interface looks the same as Outlook's, but of course, has very important differences both under the hood and even in the chrome. Lead management, opportunity management, the single view of integrated sales and service individual customer records all are available in what I have to say is one of the simplest interfaces to understand and use that I've seen in the CRM world. Through Outlook directly or as an Outlook-look-alike, you have account, product, quote, order, and content access. Your contacts, appointments, tasks, and e-mail are all integrated directly with Outlook. Needless to say, the integration of MSCRM and Outlook is seamless.

From the standpoint of features and functions, keep in mind that MSCRM is not a full CRM suite as of early 2004. It is sales and service, but there is no marketing nor are there any analytics to speak of, though you can sort or filter more than 100 embedded reports. Customization is not an option yet. But, frankly, if you're a small company falling under the purview of MSCRM—meaning about 10 to 100 users—then how many customized reports are you going to need, if any? The likely answer is none, but there are always exceptions. What MSCRM provides is definitely enough functionality for their target market, despite the "there isn't enough functionality" routine you hear from various analysts and competitors. Here's a brief look at some of the functionality and features. You tell me if this isn't enough.

- ▶ **Complete customer view** Pretty much all the account information you could imagine up to and including payment histories, but not including transaction histories except those manually entered.

- ▶ **Lead routing and management** This one is so easy. It is a button on the initial Outlook screen saying "Escalate to Lead" if that's what you want. From there on it's workflow.

- ▶ **Opportunity management** Same as lead management. You can hit a button and escalate the lead to an opportunity with one click. That will automatically attach workflow so that the opportunity is appropriately routed.

- ▶ **Sales process management** This is not a commitment to any formal selling process such as Spin Selling or Miller-Heiman, but instead is more workflow-focused routing and tracking a stage at a time.

- **Product catalog** You can build a product catalog that handles complex pricing levels and schemes, units of measure, discounts, and pricing options.

- **Order management** This is where orders and invoices are generated and can be directly engaged through the back-office financial system—in Microsoft's view preferably Solomon, Great Plains, or Navision, but they've conceded integration with others.

- **Quotas** Something that warms the hearts of all salespeople. This is where you can benchmark performance of individual salespersons against their quotas.

- **Territory management** Another sales management feature that helps the manager determine how both individuals and teams will work with specific geographies or product lines or solutions or all three.

- **Reports** There are roughly 100 reports that come with the package, but customization is not an option here.

- **Sales literature** This is a collateral library for .doc and .pdf files that is not only good for information storage, but also for making sure that the appropriate collateral gets to the right customers.

- **Competitor tracking** If you can find the information on how well your competitor is doing, you can track it here.

- **Workflow** This is the most powerful feature of MSCRM. They have an exceptionally good workflow that can handle tasks as simple as notifications and as complex as escalations and lead routing. Entirely customizable and excellent for the SMB side. But don't try this in your home. Professionals should develop the business rules and sales processes that you are going to provide.

- **Correspondence and mail merge** You can use customizable templates to create and send e-mail to targeted prospects and customers.

The one place that MSCRM falls down is in its server requirements, which are pretty heavy for SMB customers. To make MSCRM do its thing, you need Active Directory, Exchange, SQL Server, and the partner version of BizTalk Server. That virtually requires a full-time administrator. Even without it, what seems to be a very reasonable cost of ownership is driven up by the hardware and server side.

With the release of MSCRM 1.2 in December 2003, Microsoft added support for all their 2003 version products such as Windows Server 2003 and Exchange Server 2003 and made it a little easier to install and maintain. It also provides a common development environment with Outlook and Office. Rather than waiting for 2.0 to make the hosting easier, Microsoft recognized the bandwagon that the hosted CRM market is providing for jumping onto and improved the hosting capability in MSCRM 1.2. This makes it easier for companies like Surebridge, which derives 40 percent of their revenue from MSCRM, to handle the online services. Finally, you can speak MSCRMese now in international English, Spanish, French, German, and Italian.

Microsoft is doing a very good job, early edition or not. Chances are pretty good that they will only continue to do better and prove the dismissive pundits wrong. But what else is new?

STEPPIN' OUT: SalesLogix Is the Best

Best Software's SalesLogix, Best CRM is warm and fuzzy. That's a strange way to talk about a CRM package, right? But not this one. SalesLogix has been around since 1997, far before the SMB love-in began. They were founded by Pat Sullivan, a true pioneer in the industry, creator of ACT! and one of the members of *CRM Magazine*'s CRM Hall of Fame. Their métier has been the knowledge of small business processes or the lack thereof. They are comfortable. That means they are so familiar with the SMB marketplace that you can rest assured they are providing you with applications that get it. While there is much more to be said in Chapter 25 about their corporate life, SalesLogix is one of the well-established, highly successful CRM vendors with a true track record in the market that doesn't need the corporate quals—they have them big time. They also have a strong base of satisfied customers. In fact, in the very valuable study, "The State of Customer Relationship Management Software: 2003-2004" (HYM Press, 2003) by Dick Lee of High Yield Methods and David Mangen of Mangen Associates, SalesLogix had the highest 2003 customer satisfaction ratings, as they had in the 2002 edition of the report. I quote, "Customers like SalesLogix for being easy to install, affordable, adaptable to their individual functional requirements, and quite well supported." Comfortable, like that (fill in your favorite NFL team) sweatshirt you always wear on the weekends in the fall.

The Full Monty

SalesLogix, Best CRM is a full-featured CRM suite and well deserving of the Steppin' Out trophy (well, okay, there is no actual trophy). It has three major modules—Sales, Marketing, and Support—which are aimed at providing a good deal of the necessary functionality for the SMB out of the box. While by no means as feature or function rich as the large enterprise suites, it is what is supposed to be: sufficient out of the box and much of what you need when you customize it if you fit into the SMB skin. It has substantial workflow and a process architect that provides you with the ability to create a sales process or marketing process flow. It also has embedded sales processes, the time-honored methodologies such as Solution Selling and Miller-Heiman, built right into the applications, in case you see the need to use them as your company begins to grow to the point where a consistent sales approach becomes valuable.

What makes the Best CRM folks so intriguing, aside from their name change, is that they aren't resting. As of December 2003, they introduced a dramatic change in their CRM model with the introduction of a hosted/rental version. It is an extension of their core belief that not just sales management should benefit from a CRM initiative. The users need to be satisfied. Let's hear Kevin Myers, the former vice president of SalesLogix Regional Sales on this subject:

> SalesLogix must steadfastly continue to improve in areas of comfort, ease, mobility, and effectiveness. These areas of our software are the reasons we win with voting constituents that matter, the end-user! Our charter is to create WIIFMs (what's in it for me?) for the end-users, but these same WIIFMs must have a "quid pro quo" effect that provides management with the needed insights into their businesses. Herein lies the conundrum. Users prefer to use their own black books like ACT, Outlook, and PDAs, while management needs that customer data inside corporate rolodex systems like SalesLogix. The WIIFM for management is to get data from individual users that represents all the *interactions* that have taken place over the life of a customer's relationship with salespeople. The WIIFM for salespeople is to use the data in their black book as a trade to get access to the rich information contained within the data from back-office systems. This back-office data is the documented life of all the *transactions* that have taken place over the customer's buying experience with the company. The joint

WIIFM is to marry these data sets (interactions plus transactions) in what we refer to as a customer scorecard. This scorecard not only lets the salespeople gain more knowledge about the customer's buying, credit, and customer service experience, but also feeds their need to not look foolish in front of any customer due to a lack of knowledge. The real lesson here for anyone trying to automate sales professionals is to understand and address the following:

► Systems *must* be easy, intuitive, and help users to be more productive.

► Systems must be win/win. Translation of this idea from a user's perspective is "If you want to win, create a win for me!"

► Feed the sales attribute of ego: "The smarter I am in front of the customer, the happier I am to be there!"

By adding a hosted offering, they do three things. First, they extend their own user-friendly thinking into a domain that makes them not just user- or management-friendly but business constituent–friendly overall. Second, they recognize that the hosted model as a low cost, reasonably simple alternative is here to stay and they're not trying to buck the tide. Third, they take industry concerns about their architecture's retrograde nature seriously and do what they have to so that they continue to be best of class.

But what does this mean for their applications? Not a lot when it comes to features and functions but a lot when it comes to architecture and workflow models.

The Architecture

SMB architecture resembles the enterprise-level CRM architectures. This is not a hosted architecture, but rather, the standalone version for SalesLogix and is typical of its type. It consists of:

► A common customer data repository to serve as a consistent customer memory.

► An extraprise network architecture to span the internal (employees) and external (partners and customers) stakeholders that must interact with the system. This would include the necessary APIs to integrate with the legacy and third-party systems. The model for the architecture could be hosted, standalone, or hybrid. Interestingly, there is a preponderance of .NET architectures in the

SMB world due to the dominant use of Microsoft-related products. However, J2EE and mixed architectures do exist (NetSuite is an example of a J2EE; SalesLogix itself is a mixed architecture).

▶ A common business logic that ensures consistent customer response across all customer touch points.

▶ Diverse platform capabilities to enable a rich, multidimensional user experience. This includes traditional record-keeping capabilities as well as capabilities for communication management, knowledge management, document management, business intelligence, back-office integration, and portal services.

▶ Process workflow capabilities to seamlessly carry front-office work across organizational boundaries.

▶ Broad presentation services to enable productive system access by internal and external users, casual and production-class users, connected, remote, and disconnected users. This could require LAN, Web, remote synchronization, PDA, or phone access clients.

The Applications

The core applications are very different than they were when the second edition of this book was written. Integrated deeply into the foundation Sales, Marketing, and Support applications are customer service–focused processes. This is not a module, but part of the systemic offerings. To make this clear, that means that issues of the user interface and ease of use are paramount to the way the system looks, feels, and operates. For example, with the new suite, there has been serious consideration given to automated alerts that are pushed to your Outlook screens or your Blackberry or your varieties of PDA. The dashboards for management and for "ordinary" users are considerably easier to understand and to configure so that the information you want is the information you get. Interactions between the CSR or the salesperson and the customer become part of the customer record so you are dealing with a single, complete, and dynamic customer record— not the real-time enterprise (RTE) but just the medicine an SMB needs. The SalesLogix products, which had been revenue focused, are now service driven. This is a highly intelligent change because it is in sync with the evolution of the customer ecosystem that is now a part of the business fabric.

How is this manifested? All transactions, front and back office (for example, financial or human resources), such as orders, back orders, inventory, and invoices are fed directly into SalesLogix systems and across all product lines. That not only means SalesLogix products, but transactions recorded by PeopleSoft EnterpriseOne (J.D. Edwards), Microsoft, Epicor, or whatever your little heart desires and your little business has, can be integrated into the SalesLogix framework.

Now that's for connected users. What about the disconnected user? Note here that when I say disconnected user, I mean disconnected from the system or offline or mobile, not disconnected from reality. SalesLogix, with its hybrid architecture has been historically focused on developing a sophisticated synchronization process for the disconnected, mobile user. Instead of depending on synchronization, SalesLogix is developing its own application program interfaces (APIs) that will provide the data pipelines between transactions and interactions whether you are disconnected or connected, or using the hosted or standalone system. Combine that with the customer scorecard that Kevin Myers mentioned in our conversation with him and you have a genuinely user-friendly blue collar link into the next generation of CRM that still recognizes the needs of your business.

But it doesn't stop with that. One of the biggest issues of user adoption was characterized by implementing massive CRM systems at the cost of 18 months and $5 million. After the system was rolled out and imposed on the employees, the employee response was "fine" and they went straight back to Excel.

Well, SalesLogix says to the Excel user, "Okay, Excel it is." In fact, they have integrated Excel with this new generation so that the user can be familiar with the system from the beginning. The data can be output in an enhanced Excel spreadsheet with pretty pivot tables. What this means is that the data from the scorecard is integrated with the tools that people actually use. What a strategy! Don't try to bulldoze the users into the new system, let them have a transparent new system that also uses the tools they already use. Transitions to acceptance become so much easier. That is an insight that other vendors might learn from.

Vertical SMB Applications

"Build or buy" is a term that you will often see in the CRM industry. It is the expression of a dilemma on how to deal with the additional processes, features, or functions that the CRM vendor needs. Should you put a team of programmers on the case and have them develop the new processes or features? Or should you simply acquire a company that already has the features and processes you need. The advantage of the latter is that you don't have to spend the time to build them and you have a ready market position. The disadvantage is that the architecture of the acquisition and your architecture require integration, which might be a daunting task.

SalesLogix is moving into key vertical domains with their applications—areas where they already had strength: construction, manufacturing, high-tech, and financial services. Their approach? Build and buy. They acquired Timberline Software in 2003 because of their strength in construction. Just like "Intel Inside," Best is looking for "SalesLogix Inside." Keep Timberline's software intact, but add SalesLogix functionality to the application framework. That means that the quoting and forecasting for construction that is done well by Timberline remains, but they add opportunity management or whatever else they decide to add. That is directly in line with their philosophy of keeping what works for the user. SalesLogix, Best CRM, becomes the core with the verticals. As far as the other verticals mentioned, only time will tell whether it is "build" or "buy."

On that note, let's move on. We're going to get as technical as we will be in this book with the next several chapters. Be prepared to go a little further technically than usual, but I promise you won't be bored.

PART IV
The Modules

13

Web Architecture for Enterprise Applications: Why Learn THAT?

For the next four chapters, I'm going to make the technical part of the CRM equation transparent—something that I'm assuming most of you reading this book are never going to care much about in your day-to-day activities. As primarily business people and possibly students vying for "businesshood," you are probably focused on the strategy and the philosophy parts. But you have to have a bit more than a vague recognition that there is technology and a system involved in a CRM initiative. Despite the always popular disparagement of "CRM as a technology," knowing what is going on under the hood and how the system works is important. In the next four chapters, I'll give you just enough information on the technology to make you a nuisance for your technical support folks when it comes to CRM. I'll cover the architecture (this chapter), datawarehousing and business intelligence (Chapter 14), integration of CRM with the supply chain and ERP (Chapter 15)—though this will be a bit less technical and more strategic—and finally, the sexy stuff, the application service provider (ASP) model (Chapter 16) and how it works. If you've been looking for a technical book, get your money back—this isn't it. These chapters are the equivalent of what we called in college "Physics for Poets." It should be enough for all you interested in what CRM has become.

Widescreen Architecture

CRM has been in the midst of a long transformation. As Michael Park, a CRM leader and vice president at SAP said to me in 2001, "Someday, CRM will just be an on-ramp." As 2004 moves along, this is more the case than less.

CRM is now an all-encompassing collaborative "customer-voice" strategy (see Chapter 18). It is a wrapper that surrounds enterprise-wide processes, be they business processes or Web services, supply chain applications, or CRM applications. This applies to a large company or a small one. It doesn't matter. With the customer permeating the pores of the entire value chain, the company is only one of the pieces of the puzzle—though, as a business person or future one, perhaps the one that you consider the most important.

There are implications for CRM architecture. Contemporary CRM architecture is by no means separated from the overall enterprise, but it includes a set of customer-based components that involve multiple communications channels that customers use to interact with the company—often a Web browser, but also a fax or phone. It involves hardware that is not tied to the corporate center, whether it is a mobile unit or the server of a channel partner. That means not only are you dealing with your internal legacy systems, you are also looking to conform to external applications, protocols, services, and frameworks.

Standards, such as XML (see below for definition), need to be formalized and approved by a neutral body that is composed of the companies who need to implement the standards. Sounds good, doesn't it? Well, that is easier said than done. For example, while XML is being standardized by the W3C consortium, it doesn't mean that Siebel or PeopleSoft or Sun or Microsoft are looking to make it easier on each other. So standardization is tempered by competition, though standardization is winning the war as the collaborative customer ecosystem begins its march to world domination and total victory.

Think about it. You log onto a website. You've been there before. You've set up a personal profile. You have your own user ID and password. You have a history on the site, having purchased information that you've downloaded more than once. You've read .pdf files on the site without downloading. You've surfed the site, looking for things that you linger on for a longer time than typical. You've even taken advantage of a couple of pop-up "special deals" that made sense at the time. You've done these things in the normal course of a day or evening. You've spoken with the customer service representatives from the company to return an item more than once, but overall you're satisfied with the quality of the purchases you've made.

Now slap on those thinking caps to imagine what it takes architecturally to do all of that.

First, you are interacting in real time. Those pop-up offers you get are tailored to you at that moment because of the real-time analytics and perhaps, price or offer optimization engines that the applications driving the site use. It has to extract the appropriate data from not only your customer record stored somewhere in a datawarehouse, but use the information gathered in real time from your current activity on the website. It is then using algorithms to identify and interpret your purchasing behaviors and interests and history and coming up with offers designed to entice and tantalize. Hopefully, all unbeknownst to you until you receive the offer onscreen.

Additionally, it has to identify you uniquely from among what are likely at least tens of thousands if not millions of customers who have used the website. That means that when you log in, not only is the system finding you from among all the other possible visitors, but it is providing you with your specific information, while protecting all the others from seeing that information.

When you log in, you are logging in from what is most likely Internet Explorer 6.0 or some other Web browser. You are logging in from the outside by using the Internet. You are logging in with nothing more than a cookie making your login easier. There is no client software that is being used—just the Web browser.

In the meantime, you've taken advantage of the site real-time special deal and ordered something. You've filled out a form on the site for the order and used your MasterCard—all at a secure section of the site. The data from the form is moved into order management and accounting systems. The item you ordered is prepared for shipping when the information is routed to the shipping department and flagged for action. The item is also removed from inventory records so that it isn't sold again online when someone else wants that particular thing.

All of that was driven by CRM applications with embedded business rules and workflow. It possibly used a price optimization engine. You might be working from a PeopleSoft system while the system you logged into was Oracle Small Business Suite which was using an Oracle database and an SAP financial system.

Most of these processes, whether on your desktop, on a network, or through the Web, are routed through a system that uses multiple applications, possibly several operating systems, and certainly a variety of protocols and standards. To make all this work seamlessly is a daunting task and a lot to consider.

But it isn't you doing the considering. All you know (hopefully) is that you paid for something that seemed like a great deal and it's going to be delivered to you in a timely way.

Given the infinitely increased complexity of the "it takes a village to please an end client" ecosystem you have to deal with, what kind of architecture can handle this? I'll let the mystery hang for a few paragraphs.

Evaluating Architecture

I'd have my IT department working with me on this if I was you, but I'm not you, so I'm going to give you just enough information on evaluating a customer-driven architecture to make you want to have the IT department work with you.

Web Services

Web services are a nearly mandatory part of the architecture supporting any CRM initiative. Yet, there are competing platforms (.NET and J2EE—see below) that address them a bit differently. But Web services are now available in all the newer CRM applications working alongside the old but always popular Internet protocols and transport mechanisms such as HTTP.

A Web service is defined by the official standards body for Web services, the W3C consortium, as "a software system designed to support interoperable machine-to-machine interaction over a network. It has an interface described in a machine-processable format (specifically WSDL). Other systems interact with the Web service in a manner prescribed by its description using SOAP-messages, typically conveyed using HTTP with an XML serialization in conjunction with other Web-related standards." That doesn't seem to be a very sporting definition, does it? In English, that means that Web services provide a common way of "speaking" between computers via a network so that the action of one can be understood by the other and a response to the action that is understood by all concerned can be sent. If I send a requirement from a salesperson to fulfill an order generated through the PeopleSoft Sales system, the Oracle Order Management system and the SAP R/3 Billing and Financial systems will understand that requirement and take appropriate actions, such as generating an order number and an invoice and filling in the financial information automatically in the customer's record. These actions will activate a workflow to track the order until it is delivered through actions taken by the Supplier Relationship Management system, also by PeopleSoft. This is done via a browser, regardless of physical location. The five Web services pillars are:

▶ **Extensible Markup Language (XML)** XML is a "meta language"— a language with which you can write other languages. So, if you want to write a series of Web services that are applicable to the retail clothing industry, you can create the vertically specific instructions using XML. The advantage is that XML is universally understood by different environments and machines. The disadvantage is that there is an XML standard for every single vertical imaginable, which creates a Tower of Babel that still speaks the same language!

▶ **Simple Object Access Protocol (SOAP)** SOAP (most current version 1.1) is a series of procedures written in XML to allow objects and procedures to pass through from one operating system to another using HTTP as the transport mechanism. That way, system administrators don't have to take down firewalls so other ports can be accessed beyond the standard port 80 that is commonly used. Even though reusable objects are ordinarily platform specific, SOAP allows them to call and respond to each other regardless of platform, port, or firewall.

▶ **Web Services Definition Language (WSDL)** This XML Web service is used for describing the interfaces between Web services (the endpoints between the services). Current version is 1.1.

▶ **Universal Description, Discovery and Integration (UDDI)** The UDDI is a registry that an enterprise uses to publish its Web services descriptions so that other parts of the enterprise can discover and use those Web services due to the common descriptors. The current version is UDDI v.2.

▶ **Business Process Execution Language for Web Services (BPEL4WS)** BPEL4WS, also known as BPEL for short, defines both business processes that use Web services and business processes that externalize their functionality as Web services. It is usually a tagged XML message that is sent between partners or links partner to activity. The current version is 1.1.

But Web services alone do not an architecture make. They are brokers for moving messages and actions within the overall framework. But what of the framework itself?

The Earlier Architectures

In just a few short years, we've already reached the stage where we can talk about "traditional" n-tiered architectures. Amazing. That architecture combined (ordinarily) a business layer, a presentation layer, and an applications layer to do its stuff in a CRM implementation. The business layer handled the business logic, the presentation layer handled the calls and procedures and message transmissions between servers, and the applications layer handled, usually through an applications server—the software technology. Often there were Web servers and database servers involved. When messages and data were being passed back and forth between layers, middleware such as WebSphere was used to move the information between places. Applications were accessible through Web browsers. Integration brokers, connectors, translators, and APIs were part of the architecture so that the different systems could speak to each other. It worked, but it was awkward, and as complexity increased so did the number of necessary components.

By 2003, something had to change. CRM had changed from a data-driven endeavor to a process-driven one. The architecture needed to follow.

Service-Oriented Architecture (SOA)

With the increasingly complexity of CRM process-based models, the levels of customization, configuration, and integration have increased to something that could befuddle even the most razor-sharp IT architect. This sea change calls for a different, more flexible architecture with an enterprise-wide scope that can manage ongoing business change. That's service-oriented architecture (SOA). This is not a small change in thinking or a cult-like worship of the latest and greatest. ZapThink, an analyst firm, released a study in December 2003 that not only sees the SOA subsuming multiple other architectures and pieces of architecture such as applications servers, but sees it as a $43 billion market in 2007. A large chunk of change, but one that is indicative of the importance of the SOA in the near future for customer-based initiatives.

SOA is replacing the early Web architectures and the remaining client/server architectures. They are being increasingly considered as the new enterprise architectural standard. Gartner thinks they should be more properly called interface-oriented architectures for reasons I have yet to fathom. But you decide after you read this entire chapter.

Service-oriented architectures tie specifications such as J2EE with components like Enterprise Java Beans (EJB), Microsoft's competitive platform standard .NET components, or Simple Object Access Protocol (SOAP)–related web services with business processes using business process management (BPM) tools (see Chapter 18).

In its simplest definition, an SOA is a collection of business services and IT functions that are constantly evolving along with business requirements. These services communicate with each other. The communication can involve something as simple as data passing from a sales force automation system to an order management system. It could also involve two or more services coordinating some activity. For example, you are providing a just completed, authenticated document compiled automatically as an Adobe Acrobat file (.pdf) to a person registering on the website for the first time. His registration, when completed and submitted, extracts the document from a data store somewhere on the system and then time and date stamps the extraction and e-mails the document to the new registrant. The data from the new registrant populates multiple data sources. Some means of connecting these services to each other is needed, most often through provided connectors or customized code. Each component involved is interoperable without being dependent on the other components.

Developing an SOA involves planning the integration of business processes with applications. What distinguishes the SOA from any other layer is that the services it provides are business services that represent core business logic, not presentation logic or data services. So as Ryan Ireland, director of product development for WingateWeb, states so articulately on SearchWebServices.com, "As such, services may utilize business process management (BPM) in order to fulfill their designed purposes. BPM systems are technologies that manage business processes. These processes can then be incorporated into enterprise applications as services within an SOA. The SOA publishes the services (and the business processes they incorporate) to be made available to interested clients." You'll hear more on BPM and its tools in later chapters.

Building and Maintaining an Enterprise SOA

How would you evaluate this apparently complex architecture? Some questions for you to ask yourself and any vendors you might run across in your hunt follow.

The Enterprise Service-Oriented Architecture

Traditionally, when assessing an enterprise architecture, you are considering the

- ▶ **Environment** What platforms and databases might be of value?

- ▶ **Organization** Should the architecture be the now nearly defunct two-tier client/server or the n-tier architecture that is so favorable to Web architectures? Or should it be the au courant SOA?

- ▶ **Infrastructure** Should your architecture be object-oriented with reusable assets? What standards are applicable to your architecture? What measures for authentication and security are appropriate?

- ▶ **Applications** What applications should be used to execute your business rules or to implement Web services?

- ▶ **Need for customization** How much customization will be necessary? What kind of tools are available to do the customization? Should you, for example, standardize on PeopleSoft and customize using PeopleTools? Or find a universal tool for best of breed implementations?

- ▶ **Integration** How many third-party and legacy systems must the applications integrate with—internally and externally? Will you use middleware, Web services, or something else to integrate data, business processes and workflow?

But when developing a service-oriented architecture, how to handle dynamically changing business processes and the shifting IT structure is also a consideration. Chanting "interenterprise on the move" is probably the right mantra. However, massive overhauls aren't necessary for IT to begin implementing an SOA. What is most important is developing architecture flexible enough to handle changes in IT functions and business processes as they occur—not all at once.

Now let's roll into what the SOA has to look like when you build it.

Build and Maintain a Platform-Independent SOA

The SOA is built around a strategic business initiative and appropriate business processes and services. IT functions interface with the business functions, so as the business processes evolve and change, so do the services and the IT environment. What makes this interesting is that you will be able to ascertain the state of IT services and functions through the business actions being taken by the system. While maintaining platform independence, recognize that you will be running across multiple platforms in multiple environments as you develop this architectural model.

Develop in Increments and Use the Reusable

Iterative methodologies are often effective because they are prototype-dependent and always involve the user in each completed production cycle. That allows changes "on the fly," so to speak. When developing your prototype SOA, remember that the idea of a reusable asset is to use it again. That means you don't have to throw out code that didn't absolutely apply in a particular instance. As you are developing the pieces of the architecture and testing them, you can use the assets in more appropriate places or even rework the code so it can be used elsewhere. Again, the SOA idea is IT functionality in the service of business processes.

Encapsulate Existing/Legacy Functionality

Rather than create connectors and adapters or use middleware per se to integrate legacy and third-party systems with the newer system, develop Web services interfaces to meet that requirement. Those Web services will be available even as the functions and processes change over time.

Shoot for Standards-Based Interoperability

Historically I've been a fan of enterprise suites and less of a fan of best of breed approaches. But I have to admit, the advent of Web services and the tsunami of interest in developing standards for data and messaging interchanges are sowing the seeds of doubt. Best of breed can be very valuable if the BOB applications can speak a common language. I know I can reach an audience in English, but when I have to wait for simultaneous translation, the flow is interrupted badly and I lose time and momentum. If XML-compliant applications can speak to each other in "XMLese," then who cares who makes the applications, as long as they work well together? SOAs create the framework for this level of painless interoperability.

Functionality vs. Usability

The more things change, the more they remain the same. One of the timeless arguments in the world of CRM vendors is functionality versus usability. While customers often buy their applications based on the coolness of the functions and features, they only use roughly 10 to 40 percent of the available functionality. The same argument goes for the SOA and Web services. While it is good to have an SOA with Web services of varying stripes and hues, they are only clutter unless someone is using them. So that means the SOA has to be designed with the ever-popular user in mind.

Harmonia Mundi: SOAs Are Flexible, Ever-Changing and Fit the Ecosystem

One of the conclusions that you might draw from reading Johannes Kepler's masterwork *Harmonia Mundi* is that there is an evolving orderly principle that governs the universe and all its creations that is coherent with each of its creations. Viewing things from a more pragmatic vista, it is no coincidence that the development of the SOA coheres with the needs of the business ecosystem as it becomes increasingly customer focused, process-centric, and transmutable. As the business ecosystem becomes more attentive to the voice of the customer, the continuous changes in business processes demand an IT architecture that is as flexible as the changes themselves. Service-oriented architectures fit this rather nicely. SOAs take reusable assets and libraries of assets and modify them, piece them together, and rewrap them so that they fit a new business process or changing business rule or requirement as the change occurs. That is why object-oriented models work. The architecture doesn't require complete overhauls to meet the needs of the changing business world. It simply requires the use of different or modified independent assets and the appropriate user interfaces to make that asset viable. It also requires the strategy to determine how to configure those assets and the common standards to make sure the messages can understand each other's actions

Applications on What Platform, Please?

The two specifications that applications and services architecture are ordinarily built around are Sun's J2EE and Microsoft's .NET. Both of them provide the framework for the components, services, and processes that service-oriented architectures require. J2EE is still industry dominant with companies like E.piphany being strict J2EE shops, but .NET is making serious advances, perhaps most importantly the standardization of Siebel 8.0 on .NET in 2004. This doesn't mean that Siebel isn't compliant with J2EE, but that they are trumpeting their .NET compatibility while whispering their J2EE friendliness.

The irony of the battle between J2EE and .NET is that it is another example of Microsoft versus the rest of the development universe and is more based on marketing musculature, rather than the value of one of the platforms over the other. Each of them can provide an appropriate framework for the architectures of the new generation of process-driven CRM, but with different emphases.

.NET

This is a relatively new platform, out only since 2002, but it is not as new as you might think. In fact, elements of the .NET framework existed as far back as 1996 under Microsoft DNA nomenclature. But as far as the unadulterated .NET framework, MSCRM 1.0, released in February 2003, was the first application built purely on the .NET framework.

The .NET platform/framework is designed for Windows-based desktop and Web-based applications. Microsoft calls .NET desktop applications "smart clients" because they are desktop applications built using Web services, though I'm not sure how that makes them smart. Microsoft, always on the lookout for the users, is even trying to do the developers one better by providing tools for nondevelopers to create schemas on the desktop that use XML services. One of these toolsets is InfoPath. It is part of the Office 2003 Professional suite. It is a smart, easy-to-use tool that allows a modestly proficient user to take applications developed with Office 2003 and enable them for Web services. As in all smart client applications and .NET developments, the components are reusable, so an XML component written for use in Excel can be used in Word, too. Because the Web services–based smart clients are built using open Internet standards such as XML, XSL, and SOAP, they are compatible with any applications using those same standards. That means, for example, if you have a smartphone that uses Windows Mobile 2003, your smart client on the desktop can interact with that smartphone. Why you'd want to call your desktop, I'll never know.

.NET architecture is not programming language–dependent. It is, however, operating system dependent—Windows, of course. On the other hand, J2EE and its Enterprise Java Beans (EJB) components can only be written in Java, but are operating system neutral.

What .NET theoretically creates is a seamless flow between client- and server-side applications, so, for example, MSCRM and Word 2003 or Excel 2003 can interact without carpal tunnel syndrome repetitiveness when it comes to entering or re-entering data. Populate an Excel spreadsheet and the data magically appears in your CRM application in the appropriate fields.

That means if you are a field service technician out in rural America with no online access, you can still enter data into your smart client CRM application. When you connect to the network at the office, the data is uploaded directly into the corporate database even if the corporate and field systems are built on different platforms or with different languages. Hooray for Web services.

Of course, the interactions' seamlessness is only theoretical. See Figure 13-1 for a look at the .NET architecture.

The .NET framework consists of two main parts: the common language runtime (CLR) and the .NET framework class library.

▶ **Common language runtime** This is the foundation for the .NET "virtual machine." Regardless of whether you wrote your programs in C or C# or Visual Basic—or even FORTRAN—you can run Web services if you have the CLR installed.

▶ **.NET framework class library** There are no books to take out here—even if you live in Redmond. This is a library of components that were built using object-oriented languages such as C++ or C#. The three most important parts of this class library are:

- **ASP.NET** This piece is for building Web applications and XML-based Web services. This is for server-based components that can generate HTML, WML, or XML to the desktop or to a mobile unit. Each of these components can have a separate user interface wrapped around it since it maintains separation between the application logic and the user interface.

- **Windows Forms** This facilitates smart client user interface development. Combining this with the Web services generated by ASP.NET and the database services generated by ADO.NET, Windows Forms provides the wrappers for the components.

- **ADO.NET** This helps connect applications to databases. ADO.NET provides consistent access to data sources such as Microsoft SQL Server, and data sources exposed through OLE DB and XML. Data-sharing consumer applications can use ADO.NET to connect to these data sources and retrieve, manipulate, and update data. It is an integral part of the .NET Framework, providing access to relational data, XML, and application data.

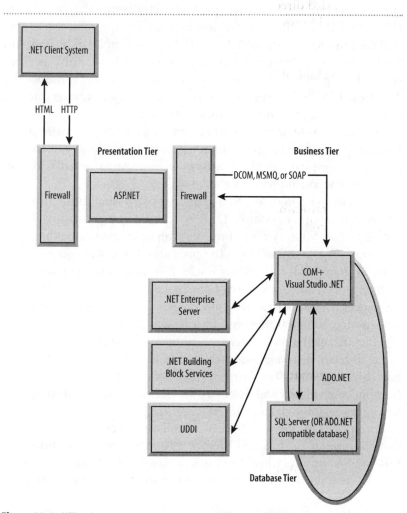

Figure 13-1: .NET architecture embeds Web services within its framework.

J2EE

Most of you have had some experience as a consumer with Java and J2EE already. If you've ever gone to a website that uploaded a small piece of code to your machine called an "applet," odds are this is a Java applet. Java applets allow you to interact with the site via your browser. For example, when I was a kid, I used to play a game called APBA Baseball, which had individual real named baseball player cards that recreated the prior season's batting average, home run totals, and so on for that individual. We would play leagues. I found an APBA card "creator" on the Internet where you plugged in the numbers, like .311, 31 HRs, 110 RBIs, 22 SB. Once the numbers were plugged in, you generated the numbers for the APBA "card." This Java applet only works on the Internet. I couldn't move it to a normal desktop. But it uses an embedded algorithm and number generator that could reproduce the APBA card. With the Java Virtual Machine on my computer and the small piece of code, I could see the APBA card.

I'm sure you've seen Java in action. If you see a website using E.piphany's real-time engine and marketing applications, you are seeing a J2EE-compliant set of applications—more germane to CRM than APBA. Not as much fun, though.

Where the paradigm for .NET is a series of products united around a framework with standards, J2EE is actually a specification that is owned by Sun Microsystems. Products can be created using this specification, but Sun doesn't own the products. It has stronger industry traction than .NET with IBM, Oracle, BEA and others supporting it with products like IBM's WebSphere, based on the J2EE specification. This specification is used to build object-oriented components that are reusable, such as Enterprise Java Beans (EJB). It provides a series of APIs such as the Java Database Connection (JDBC), which is used to access relational databases such as Oracle or IBM's DB2. To handle asynchronous workflow, Java Message Services (JMS) are available. Naming conventions and directory services are accessed through the Java Naming and Directory Interface (JNDI).

Enterprise Java Beans are J2EE-compliant server-side components that encapsulate the business logic of an application. For example, an EJB might contain CheckCustomerRecord, which would allow a mobile salesperson to check the record of the customer he is visiting, or the server could automatically do that to provide a real-time offer to the customer surfing an e-commerce site.

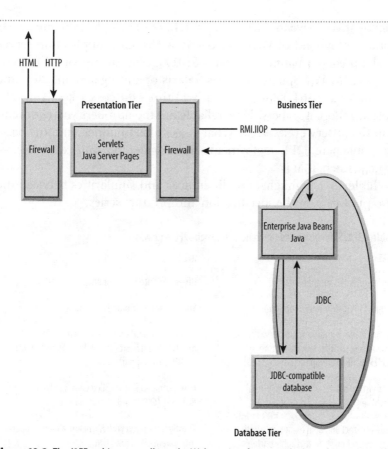

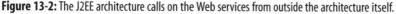

Figure 13-2: The J2EE architecture calls on the Web services from outside the architecture itself.

See Figure 13-2 for a look at the seemingly less complex J2EE architecture.

What's a CRM Business Person to Do?

If you have to choose between .NET and J2EE—don't. Leave it to someone in your IT department or a group at your company that knows what it is talking about. But there are some reasons to choose one over the other. For example, if you are heavily invested in Microsoft architecture, it would be wise to continue to invest in it through .NET. If portability to a non-Microsoft operating system is important, by all means, go J2EE.

.NET is gaining some credibility as the framework of choice for smaller business because of the cost differences. .NET is cheaper to deploy if you have to start from scratch. For example, estimated costs for a deployment of Web services on a 1X8 CPU application server under the .NET banner is roughly $6,000. With the use of J2EE-compliant IBM WebSphere on Sun's Solaris operating system, the same machine runs $64,000. That's nearly 11 times the cost. Yikes. How reliable are those numbers? How reliable are the numbers you choose to win the lottery every week? What is useful is to understand the basic principle here. J2EE deployments are considerably more expensive—from scratch, that is.

Table 13-1 highlights the differences and similarities between the two platforms or the specification and product series.

Table 13-1: Similarities and Differences Between J2EE and .NET

J2EE	.NET
Object-oriented components.	Object-oriented components.
Support for distributed computing.	Support for distributed computing.
All applications and components written in Java. Access to other languages through outmoded CORBA interoperability.	Applications and components written in C or C++ or C# or Visual Basic (Visual .NET). Even supports COBOL. Also supports Java.
Uses virtual machine called Java Virtual Machine (JVM) to run applications, etc.	Uses virtual machine called Common Language Runtime (CLR) to run applications, etc.
More abstract and able to integrate with more operating systems. Highly portable, vendor neutral.	Tightly integrated with Microsoft Windows operating systems. Windows ONLY.
Web services are seen as APIs added to applications servers. Thus, an EJB is hosted in a server container, which needs a separate Java-based wrapper. It also means a protocol bridge because application server containers don't accept HTTP as native. Adds extra steps to integration or development.	Web services are integrated directly into the .NET architecture. Web services are treated as client and server technologies. The CLR hosts the Web service components.
Web services: XML, SOAP, XSL, HTTP, WSDL support; no UDDI support.	Web services: XML, SOAP, UDDI, XSL, HTTP, WSDL support. eCollaboration model based on UDDI.
Legacy integration through: Java Messaging Service (JMS) for existing messaging systems; Web services; J2EE Connector Architecture (JCA)—a specification for plugging in resources to communicate with existing systems such as SAP R/3 or Siebel.	Legacy integration through: Host Integration Server; BizTalk Server; connectors to Siebel, SAP, Onyx, PeopleSoft; COM Integrator; MS Message Queue P(MSMQ), etc.

Table 13-1: Similarities and Differences Between J2EE and .NET *(continued)*

J2EE	.NET
Scalable but not cost efficient. According to benchmarks, 5–10 times more expensive than .NET.	Scalable and more cost efficient if you believe the .NETiphiles. Shorter deployment time.

Vendors: Short Shrift

Despite the fact that all the vendors claim to be moving toward service-oriented architectures, the claims fall into two categories: true and partially true. Each vendor has a slightly different spin on the approach to their architectures. Each of them is either more or less advanced than the next one. Table 13-2 is a partial breakdown of what various architectural components are used by the vendors.

Table 13-2: Fundamental Architectural Components of the Vendors

Vendor	Applications Architecture (Client and Server Side)
PeopleSoft	Java, J2EE compliant, C++, Tuxedo all used for applications development. People-Tools is the configuration tool. Runs on J2EE applications servers—IBM or BEA. Thin client ("no code on the client"). Java Server Pages (JSP). Enterprise portal available, works with other portals.
SAP	NetWeaver platform. Enterprise Server Architecture. Interoperable with .NET and J2EE. Works with IBM WebSphere. Still can use proprietary SAP ABAP code, which can be turned into Web services through WSDL. XML, WSDL, UDDI, SOAP compliant. JDBC-compliant; EJB 2.0 support. Leans to J2EE more than .NET. Portal available.
Oracle	Oracle grid computing paradigm (dynamically shared resources across a network via multiple servers with single database instance). J2EE. EJB 2.0. Java Server Pages (JSP): Oracle Call Interface (OCI)—small client code to access JDBC compliant databases. PL/SQL support. XML support via Java APIs.
Siebel	SmartWeb architecture. Unified Application Network (UAN)—integration framework. J2EE and .NET. Siebel 8.0 to standardize on .NET.
Onyx	Enterprise application server, proprietary. Support for XML, SOAP, COM+, C++; .NET.
E.piphany	Highly efficient service-oriented architecture. J2EE. Each service is an EJB. Java Message Service compliant. .NET compliant. XML, SOAP compliant. Web Service Business Process Execution Language (WS-BPEL) compliant.
SalesLogix	One of the last surviving successful hybrids. Supports XML, Internet protocols like HTML, WML, DHTML, and of course, .NET
Microsoft MSCRM	.NET only. XML, SOAP, Dynamic HTML, multiple languages, etc.

In the second edition of the book, I spent a lot of time identifying the CRM architecture du jour (2002). What you saw there is still a prevalent structure. The messages hold strong, but the new wind a-blowin' is service-oriented architectures using Web services, an organization far more suitable to the ever-raging customer ecosystem that each of us will be faced with in the next year or two.

You'll note as we depart the premises that there are two significant omissions in this chapter—data and portals. I didn't forget, oh ye of little faith. The next chapter is on data and datawarehousing in CRM. It deserves better than a footnote or two in this chapter. Portals will be covered in Chapter 15 on "A Big Enterprise Value Chain, Gang."

14

Data Mining, Datawarehouse, Data (Just Not Star Trek's)

I f I ask you what you need when it comes to dealing with your data and gave you the following multiple choices, could you tell me?

- ▶ Datawarehouse

- ▶ Data mart

- ▶ Corporate information factory (CIF)

- ▶ Data vault

- ▶ Operational data store (ODS)

- ▶ All of the above

- ▶ Some of the above

- ▶ None of the above

I didn't think you could. In this chapter, we're going to take a quick tour through that customer data that you've been hearing so much about in CRM. You heard how to analyze it in Chapter 9. Now, you'll see how to find it. Hopefully, by the end of the chapter, you'll be insistent on what you need: a consultant to tell you what you need when it comes to data. Leave it to the experts. You're an expert in business or a budding one. You don't need to be expert in data management. You simply have to know what it is.

Data: It's Good for You

Don't confuse data with information. Don't confuse data with knowledge or understanding. Don't make data anything useful until it is put in context. It isn't. Data is a fact or multiple facts or a set of values that is raw material stored in a structured manner. Out of context, without interpretation and human intelligence applied, it means nothing other than it is a nugget. With interpretation and human intelligence applied, it becomes (possibly) useful information and thus, valuable to your business. But collecting data and storing it somewhere is not particularly beneficial unless it is part of a strategic plan. For example, if you have a customer record that has a complete history of the purchases of the customer and the complaints of the customer and the other interactions of the customer through various channels, what does it mean unto itself? Nothing. It is a listing of events. But what happens when you begin to interpret details? You determine that certain customer purchases were followed by a complaint and a return of that item. You also see that some of the customer's interactions indicated that there was an interest in purchasing items that were entirely unrelated to the class of items that were returned. That suggested that you gear your marketing material to this new set of potential purchases. Perhaps you took it a bit further. You mapped the customer's age and geography to buying patterns of the same age and geography. That suggested some purchasing possibilities that were not obvious until you did this analysis.

Note something very important here. When human brainpower is applied by studying the details, interpreting them, and identifying patterns that are determined to be useful, then data becomes valuable information. Until then it is a structured fact but out of context.

Okay, cool; that's data. Now, what's a database?

A database is a set or collection of these structured facts stored in physical files and managed by a database management system (DBMS). It is a collection of facts potentially valuable to a business when organized and interpreted. The DBMS is the system that handles the data so that you have access to it in a variety of ways. For example, using a relational database such as Oracle allows you to query the data to find out patterns that the data suggests dependent on the components of your query. There is a query language called SQL that is used by most databases for these requests.

So far, it seems easy to understand, doesn't it? Well, easy is over. We're not quite at the head-scratching stage, but we're going to be getting there fast. Now that we've identified what data is and its potential value, we can look at the micro and see how data is structured in the information technology universe that you inhabit at least in an avatarish kind of way.

Data Structure

How data is structured is not something you have to remember as a business person, but it does pay to know at least the basics. The structure becomes important when you begin the difficult but potentially rewarding process of deciding what is important to you in that data nugget. For example, when you are collecting data from online registrations you usually see the same-old-same-old to start the process. Last Name, First Name, Address, City, State, Country, Phone, Fax, E-mail. But after that, the questions tend to vary widely. In CRM, they usually take the form of "When are you planning on buying CRM software?" or "Do you want a representative to contact you?" Sometimes they are survey-type questions asking about your interests and hobbies, occupation, or other personal identifiers. At this initial stage, the data collected is captured and stored but not much is done with it. How data is structured has some importance in the capture and storage, so we'll take a brief look at it.

Entities and Attributes: The Linear

Entities are data defined by a common group of characteristics that are of interest to the business. It could be person, place, thing, concept, event, or any other number of general classes of objects. So "customer" could be an entity. Attributes are the descriptors of particular characteristics describing the entity. So, for example, an attribute attached to the customer entity would be "number of years that the customer was associated with the store." So it would read something like "years_as_customer" if placed in a CRM data model. Entity = general data object; Attribute = descriptors attached to entities.

If you were viewing this in a relational database, you would see the entity as a table and the attribute as a column in the table, as shown in Table 14-1.

Table 14-1: Example of a Relational Database Table

Customer

Last_Name	First_Name	Phone_Number
Cruise	Tom	212-555-3221
Kidman	Nicole	312-555-5678
Judd	Ashley	650-333-2222

This table can be broken down by definition:

- ► Entity: Customer

- ► Attribute: Last_Name, First_Name, Phone_Number

- ► Instance of entity: Cruise, Tom, 212-555-3221

In order to make the data point unique—meaning Tom Cruise is different than Ashley Judd—there is a unique identifier created called a key that distinguishes this instance of the entity from that instance of the entity. Most often, it is a number associated with the instance.

CRUD Matrix: It's Not Sludge, It's Non-Linear

Business begins to rear its handsome head here. As we have been discussing throughout this book, CRM is no longer data driven. But that doesn't mean that data isn't important to CRM. It is, in fact, of essential importance, which is why I'm even writing a chapter on how data looks and acts. But what makes the data important is the association it gets with business processes and rules that are governing the approach to business that your company takes.

Developing a CRUD matrix, once the entities and attributes are defined, is the first step in linking business and data. CRUD stands for create, retrieve, update, delete. It is an important step in creating the omniscient 360-degree view of the customer as defined by his or her customer record. It is a matrix that shows how the business processes are identified with the entity types so that the business process model is linked to the data model. It is a set of rules that identify which business processes are responsible for the creation, retrieval, updating, or deletion of the different entity types.

This plays two vital roles. When the functions are mapped to the data, the useful relationships show on the matrix. Missing business

processes or data entities are uncovered, as are data and process relationship redundancies. For example, if you are mapping the billing
processes to the suitable data elements, what might show is that a data
element necessary to complete an invoice is missing. You then have to
create that data element.

This has got to be one of the few times that CRUD is good.

What Happened When You Metadata?

Once you have these structured facts, and you've mapped them, how
do you access them as a business user without worry? How do you
describe them? How do you communicate them in a way that can be
understood by a system to make it interpretable to the business users
of an organization?

That, my friends, is where metadata comes in.

Metadata is the information about data that enables intelligent, efficient access and management of data from creation through long-term
use across an institution. One of the primary purposes of organizing
the metadata is to be able to describe and communicate business and
technical information to persons within the organization. Effectively,
metadata is data about the data. For example, Last Name, First Name,
Phone Number is metadata. Greenberg, Paul, 571-213-6988 is data.
These are classes that are used to group data in organized and understandable fashion. A CRM class would be "customer." The value of
metadata is incalculable in CRM. Suppose you were undertaking a
CRM initiative in sales and defined your data classes in self-serving
sales terms. That would be valuable to your sales business unit but not
to the company as a whole. Now suppose, shortly thereafter, your CMO
rolled out a CRM-related marketing initiative but had a different set
of classes for marketing so that marketing customers were not the same
as sales customers. Confusion reigns supreme. That is where metadata
comes in, defining the customer as a specific type that can be understood by all. All customer data is the same as defined by the metadata
related to customer. What you have defined with metadata is either an
enterprise or interenterprise standard for naming data classes that can
be used and reused across the enterprise or enterprises.

But wait—am I saying that customer can be metadata and customer
can be an entity? Right. Metadata is a class of data that has entities and
attributes contained within the class. The best example I can think of
is a library catalog. The library catalog—a collection of descriptions

and attributes of multiple individual books with a unique identifier for each (the Dewey Decimal System)—is metadata. The individual books referenced in the catalog are entities. The metadata describes the class without you having to have knowledge of every book in the catalog. The book itself, including its descriptors, is the entity and the attributes describing that entity.

Data Quality

Now that you have structure and definition, you have to begin to concern yourself with the value of the specific data that you have. That means "good" data rather than "bad" data.

Good data means accurate and not redundant. Inaccurate and repetitious data (bad data) can clog up your system, waste your precious work time, and slow down the physical IT infrastructure. While desire for good data is obvious, how to get it isn't so clear. Even though deleting the redundancies seems easy enough—after all, we have the delete key—it isn't so simple, especially when you have hundreds of gigabytes or even terabytes of customer data. Think about the following scenario:

> Are William Smith, Bill Smith, and Will Smith all married to Jada Pinkett? What if Will Smith has a Pasadena address, Bill Smith doesn't, but his address is two years old, and William Smith is listed as a "rapper and movie star" as occupation, but not living in Pasadena. What if they are all listed at 33 years old? How many real Smiths are there? One, two, or three distinct entities—all or none of whom might be the star of *Men in Black*?

Is this serious? Absolutely. In a 2001 survey conducted by PricewaterhouseCoopers, 75 percent of 600 companies reported significant problems because of defective data. Over 33 percent of those surveyed indicated that because of these data problems they had failed to send a bill or collect an invoice, thus losing direct revenue.

Even more staggering, the Data Warehousing Institute (TDWI) did a study in 2003 that estimated that defective data (including incorrectly spelled names like "Paul Greenburg" —a regular event for me) costs U.S. industry a mind-blowing $611 billion in overhead for mailing costs and wasted labor time that could otherwise be saved with high rates of data quality. High rates of data quality are equal to about 98 percent accuracy levels.

TDWI identifies seven areas that characterize data quality. They are:

- **Accuracy** Does the data accurately represent reality or a verifiable source? For example, is the name spelled right? This is one of the prime "what can go wrong" areas, because simple incorrect data entry is one of the major problems with data quality. Data defects are common when data migration occurs from one system to another or an ETL (extract, transform, load) tool is used to grab data from one system to bring it to another. Conversion doesn't always work so smoothly when the data is migrated but not the business processes that the data is mapped to.

- **Integrity** Is the structure of the data and relationships among entities and attributes maintained consistently? This means is "Last_Name" the structure used across the departments at the company or is "Last Name" used and "last name" used and…you get the picture. When integration between disparate data systems is attempted, mismatched syntax and formats is often a real problem.

- **Consistency** Are data elements consistently defined and understood? Is a "customer" for sales defined the same way as a "customer" for marketing when it comes to data? Imagine the problem when a new field is entered into one system that is connected through several others and the database administrator forgets to let everyone know there is a new field. Or, if "net sales" in department 1 is calculated differently than "net sales" in department 2, there is a difference in definition as a result.

- **Completeness** Is all the necessary data present? For example, the Center for Data Quality does audits on data quality. In one case, it found an insurance company that was missing the required Social Security number for claims in 82 percent of the audited records. A securities firm had 300,000 records that had at least one blank (but required) field. That was 30 percent of their total records.

- **Validity** Do data values fall within acceptable ranges defined by the business? For example, a phone number of 90000-234-1235 is not valid and falls outside the range of acceptable phone numbers. Lack of validation routines is one of the most common mistakes in the land of data cleanliness.

▶ **Timeliness** Is the data available when needed? Real-time datawarehouses are a contemporary answer to this question, though not the traditional one.

▶ **Accessibility** Is the data easily accessible, understandable, and usable? This is defined by the intelligence of the team in charge of the data and data quality. If they understand the user is most likely a nontechnical business unit representative and not one of their own, then the data will be usable and accessible. If they don't, heaven help you all.

Migrations, Mergers, Migraines

This is the age of acquisitions. We CRM guru types just spent 2003 talking about Siebel buying Upshot, PeopleSoft buying J.D. Edwards, Oracle trying to buy PeopleSoft, ChannelWave merging with Aqueduct, and a myriad of other mergers and acquisitions. Differences in corporate culture and approaches in defining data can create a huge problem with the integrity and validity of data as each merger occurs. Your customer might not be my customer—at least as far as our converging databases are concerned.

But data quality is a science now, so never fear. There are methods of vastly improving data quality that are long established and effective. Many of them mimic any CRM project that you might be aware of. Some are software-driven. All involve judicious human behavior, a task unto itself.

The Data Quality Program

Good data quality programs resemble tactical versions of good CRM programs. There are executive sponsors and program managers involved. Project planning is part and parcel of the effort. Education, metrics, ongoing communications, process and data element assessment, establishment of change management policy and operations, and the development of ongoing internal processes are all critical to the effort.

Where it differs is in the level of scrutiny given the actual data and its structure and storage. For example, a typically important part of the effort is a data audit. A data audit is sometimes internal, if the skills are there, or sometimes done by an external firm such as the Center for Data Quality. It is a systematic review of the data for the identification of common defects. Once they are identified, metrics to detect the defects as they enter the datawarehouse or the other data stores are created as are rules for fixing the defects. If the work is systematic, then defects ranging from missing data or incorrect data to duplicate records or business rule violations should be discovered. What kinds of defects are found? The British Columbia Ministry of Advanced Education found defects that led to students who were over 2,000 years old (Mel Brooks, I wonder?) or not yet born, among other things.

Another aspect of the program that is unique is data cleansing. This is usually a rules-based software solution to providing good data that is bereft of duplicates, missing information, and invalid ranges. There are four methods used for cleaning the data:

▶ **Correction** This is the fixing of defective data elements and records. It could involve modifying an incorrect value to conform to the company standard or filling in a missing piece of information. It could involve merging duplicate records—often called by consumers "deduping." I use deduplication software for ACT! that merges duplicate records for me. It's modestly efficient but it depends on the fields that ACT! defines as duplicable—up to three of them. I change that so I can merge more duplicates. It is not complex, though. It won't find that Will Smith and Bill Smith might be the same person. It is looking more for identical, rather than similar, records to merge. Correction in the world of data cleansing is far more complex and more painstaking a process. Typically, the data analysts fixing Oracle or DB2 are using a data quality tool such as those provided by Trillium Software to correct the defects.

▶ **Filter** This data cleansing method involves deleting duplicate, missing, or spurious data elements that might occur as the result of some bad software process occurring.

▶ **Detect and report** This is for data that has little business value. It is simply what it says. Find the problem and let someone know, but don't fix it.

▶ **Prevent** This is, of course, devoutly to be wished, but not always the case. This means that data entry people are trained in proper data entry given the company's business processes. It also means that codes are up to date and stay that way, that when it calls for changing business processes or data models, the changes are made.

Benefits of Good, Clean Data (and H_2O)

This seems like pretty time-consuming stuff, doesn't it? So why do it? What are a few million data errors? Well, bud, the ROI is so clear and the benefits so material, not doing it seems to be a serious *faux pas*.

There are tangible benefits to your bottom line, and top line for that matter. Customer satisfaction is perhaps the most important one for purposes of this book. In a TDWI study, 19 percent of the companies queried said the most significant benefit was improved customer satisfaction. I'd rather be Paul Greenberg than Paul Greenbert, so I get that one. Nine percent saw increased revenues, twelve percent saw reduced costs. Having "a single version of the truth" was the result for 19 percent, tying customer satisfaction improvements as the number one reason for doing this (TDWI Survey on Data Quality, 2001). In that PricewaterhouseCoopers report I mentioned earlier, they said it rather bluntly: "Companies that manage their data as a strategic resource and invest in its quality are already pulling ahead in terms of reputation and profitability from those that fail to do so." (Global Data Management Survey, PricewaterhouseCoopers, 2001)

Data Models

I think that you can appreciate the need for high quality data. Now, how about the data model that should be used to contain this high quality data you've invested in?

There are several stages to get through to complete the design of a valid data model. I'm going to describe very briefly the various data models that data architects use in their planning. There are several that you can glance at and keep upstairs as a reference, but I wouldn't get into this too much.

- ▶ **Conceptual data model** This model is essentially the first thinking about the data in the early phases of system development. Data requirements are scoped from a business standpoint here, not from a pure data architecture. Technical details are not part of this design at all. This is the stage where the CRUD matrix is developed.

- ▶ **Logical data model** This follows the conceptual data model. The technical theories of data architecture are used here. Normalization is an example—this is the process of constraining the definitions of data to prevent redundant data definitions.

The relationships established at the conceptual level get absorbed as attributes called pointers or keys within the entities that the logical data model identifies. However, there are no constraints or restrictions that imposed by the database management system at this level, so no database can be created yet.

▶ **Physical data model** Once the logical data model is completed, the next step is the mapping of database design data groupings into physical database areas, files, records, elements, fields, and keys while adhering to the physical constraints of the hardware, DBMS software, and communications network. This is the physical data model and is the immediate predecessor to the database itself. The database follows.

But what happens once you have the data structures, and the database and the data itself? Datawarehouse, here we come.

No Reason for Homeless Data: The Datawarehouse

When it gets down to it, the datawarehouse is the single most important place to be when it comes to data. It is what it sounds like. It is a specialized data structure that contains data. But that is where the simplicity and resemblance to a real warehouse ends.

The term "datawarehouse" was coined by Bill Inmon in 1990 (a collaborator of Claudia Imhoff; see the discussion of data vaults later in this chapter). Over the years, it has come to mean an enterprise-wide data collection that is organized around subjects, collected from multiple sources and centrally merged into a coherent body over time.

If the data store is a single specialized subject, it is a data mart. Piping data from several data marts to a consolidated store can be a datawarehouse. Because data is now so voluminous, usually a datawarehouse has a time period associated with it. For example, if the time period is five years, then data that is one minute old is rolled into the warehouse, but data that is five years and one minute old is rolled out of the warehouse.

To function, datawarehouses have several technologies that are actively involved. Data is extracted from operational databases. It is processed and cleaned up to eliminate incorrect and redundant data or add missing data. It is then loaded into a relational database such as Oracle 9i or IBM's DB2 database. Once in the database, analytical operations are run on the data using analytic tools (such as those provided by SAS), online transaction processing (OLAP) tools (such as PeopleSoft's PeopleTools), or data mining tools to provide some historic patterns and interesting results. On the other hand, the analyses could be as simple as a report on 18–49 year olds' viewing habits in prime time: network versus cable. That takes tools like Business Objects' Crystal Reports Enterprise. If you are looking across dimensions and analyzing a matrix such as zip codes and the relationship to return rates on direct mail campaigns, then OLAP is for you. The most complex reports come from the data mining tools that can also identify individual historic interaction patterns and their relationship to demographically valid data.

Datawarehouses are a necessity for CRM. Think of it in the simplest terms. If you get five letters about the same thing or get "personal" letters that misspell your name constantly, what kind of trust are you going to have in the company committing the snafus?

If you are a retailer, a datawarehouse provides you with the data to discover customer demographics, specific shopping patterns, successes and failures in marketing campaign results, and so on. A financial services company can use the nice, clean, accurate data to find the most profitable and most committed customers. Telcos can do the churn analysis that is discussed elsewhere in this chapter. The value of the datawarehouse is incalculable.

But there are obstacles and dangers along the way to dropping the ring in the volcano.

Possible Problems

Architectural and human issues can turn a datawarehouse into a place ready for repossession and dismantling. Given that this is the repository for what is likely to be all the customer data that is needed for that gorgeous, 360-degree perfect circle of a view of the customer, failure is not an option, but it is a possibility. A very expensive possibility. Here are some of the known problems with datawarehousing:

- ▶ Eighty percent of time is spent on extracting, cleaning, loading—no time for applications

- ▶ Incompatibilities in the systems that are feeding the datawarehouse

- ▶ Data not being captured turns out to be important

- ▶ Query and reporting tools that are so easy to use everyone actually uses them and creates "report request overload"

- ▶ Conflicting business rules among users—same calculation performed differently

- ▶ Data homogenization

- ▶ Heavy overhead

- ▶ Security not assignable without process-driven approach

- ▶ High maintenance system

- ▶ Lack of knowledge of customer management against over concern with resource optimization (effectiveness, efficiency)

Currently, the dominant method of replenishing datawarehouses and data marts is to use extract, transform, and load (ETL) tools that pull data from source systems periodically—at the end of a day, week, or month—and provide a snapshot of your business data at a given moment in time. That batch data is then loaded into a datawarehouse table. During each cycle, the warehouse table is completely refreshed and the process is repeated no matter whether the data has changed or not. Using the ETL tools can create data discrepancies, particularly if the data is being refreshed and hasn't changed.

Reasons for Failure

Datawarehouse failures are not unknown. In fact, the Cutter Consortium issued an early 2003 report that stated that 41 percent of all datawarehousing and business intelligence projects fail outright or at least don't meet the business objectives of the company that is implementing it. This is a dangerous place to be. Fully 25 percent of all the companies implementing datawarehouses don't trust the concept, which is a nightmare in the making.

Some of the reasons for failure:

- ▶ **Design** A bad architecture; a data-driven methodology rather than a business-driven plan; no definition of metadata, creating confusing data definitions; ignoring configuration by the user or providing too much capability to configure.

- ▶ **Technical** Ignoring the obvious issues related to query volume and network traffic; installing the wrong components; not paying attention to issues like scalability (using terabytes of data is possible—how can the system handle that much?).

- ▶ **Procedural** Always a thorny issue for customers and vendors; poor scope management leading to scope creep (e.g. increasing the feature set constantly); using a methodology that doesn't involve prototypes or proof of concept; ignoring an iterative approach and isolating the users from the design process; operational and management procedures at data center not measured against the warehouse environment; poor training.

▶ **Sociological** The politics of datawarehouses are intense since he (or she) who controls the data controls the world (or at least the company); failure to investigate vendor product claims or vendor culture.

All of these can be reasons for failure, as can others. In order to provide a likely success, it is important to approach a datawarehouse implementation as you would a CRM project. If you check Chapter 17 on CRM strategy and Chapter 20 on implementation, you'll get a good idea (with some modifications) how to go about a datawarehouse related project, too.

Real-Time Datawarehouses

Customers run their own universe. This isn't a case of the inmates running the asylum, but of empowerment. As I've established, that means customer volatility is on the increase. That also means that the customer information that a company has needs to be as current as possible to allow that company to make the appropriate and timely decisions regarding that customer as close to real time as possible. Imagine this: you are a pharmaceutical company and you didn't have knowledge that the customer who is buying your medicine recently developed an allergy to something that is in the medicine. The results could be devastating to the customer and to you as a pharmaceutical company. Most cases of the "need to know real time" are less dramatic than this, but the contemporary nature of the information is often the difference between retention and loss.

Datawarehouses are storing customer information. This is good. But when the datawarehouse is replenished in real time, it empowers users by providing them with the most up-to-date information possible. Imagine the ability to have the data available in the datawarehouse as soon as the data is written and captured. Wow. If done well, real-time datawarehousing provides the data record image prior to and after the new information is gathered. Analysis becomes interesting and very valuable. Think about that pharmaceutical example. Knowing what changed and when becomes important to the health and well being of the customer and the company.

In the Internet era, more people are beginning to realize the limitations that snapshot copy replenishment presents and demand better alternatives. Snapshots do not involve entire database movement but simple captures of parts of database tables—for example, specified columns. In addition, not each individual change is made to a record between copy processes. In this light, the snapshot process can be likened to looking at last week's newspaper or using last week's stock market results to trade stock today.

Data is a perishable commodity: the older it is, the less relevant. Businesses need tools that can provide real-time business intelligence and an absolutely current and comprehensive picture of their organization and their customers—not last week or last month, but right now.

Other States of Data

Stopping at the datawarehouse is the equivalent of buying everything you purchase at Wal-Mart. Other (data) stores provide other value that might rival datawarehouses, but just might be a complement to the datawarehouse, too.

One of the most popular and often mentioned is the data mart. Where the datawarehouse provides you with all your enterprise data consolidated, the data mart is focused around a single subset of the enterprise data. For example, it may be the repository for all the data related to product sales for the company, while you might have another data mart with all the customer data. You can use the data singularly via the data mart or consolidate the data from both data marts to do analysis that might be valuable to you. It could cover a specific area such as products or be organized around a line of business such as sales or marketing. Data marts are smaller and use software to summarize, store, and analyze data that might be useful to you someday. The architecture still has to be characteristically the enterprise architecture so that the designations for entities, attributes, fields, and so on are consistent with those of other data marts and the rest of the company.

Operational Data Store (ODS)

Operational data stores have been made analogous to "short-term memory" in more than one instance. They are an interim area that is used to store continuously updated recent data gathered through the course of a business day. They are designed to hold small amounts of current data that has simple queries performed on it. For example, when you give Federal Express or UPS your tracking number and then see where your package is, that could well be data from an ODS. A few days after your package is delivered, that short-term memory is wiped out.

There are several classes of ODS. Each of them can handle more and more complex transactions in a closer to real-time manner. CRM-related ODS systems are Class I systems that provide synchronous or near-synchronous updates for customers receiving validated information. When the legacy system is updated, so is the ODS. There is either no lag or only a few seconds lag. So if I enter an order online and it is captured, its data appears in the ODS about the time I finish and submit the entry. Class II and III use a store and forward approach. That means every few hours (in a Class II system) or every day (in a Class III system), a new file with the new information is captured at the legacy system. Then once an hour or once a day, the file is dumped to the ODS and refreshes the data. Not nearly as effective as the Class I ODS that is most frequently used for CRM.

Corporate Information Factory (CIF)

The corporate information factory (CIF) is a logical architecture, developed by CRM and data management guru Claudia Imhoff and datawarehouse god Bill Inmon. Its advantage is that it concerns itself with the business processes of a company and drives its results (business intelligence) using data provided from business operations. It could equally as well be called a customer information factory because it combines the producers of data and consumers of information into a single architecture. It is a primo example of a decision support system for any CRM or enterprise strategic data architecture.

The CIF uses datawarehouses or ODS as the assembly point for data captured from the operational systems and business processes of the subject company. At the datawarehouse or ODS, the information is assembled and presented in a useable format for the ultimate user of the data. The users then acquire the newly formatted data so that they can slice and dice it and then assemble the new reports into useful information that is available in their own environment—using their interfaces.

According to Dr. Imhoff, four operations and administration functions must be implemented to maintain a CIF effectively:

▶ **Systems management** These processes manage the changes to new versions of databases, upgrades to software, and installation of new hardware components.

- **Data acquisition management** These processes monitor and maintain the programs that capture, integrate, cleanse, transform, and load or update data in the datawarehouse or operational data store. They are typical data acquisition processes.

- **Service management** These processes register, prioritize, assign, and track the disposition of all requests for service coming from the business community.

- **Change management** This is classic change management. When the environment changes, so does the culture. These processes make sure that the culture change is managed effectively with minimal disruption and maximum adoption.

All of the above are typical operations in an enterprise environment. What makes the CIF important to the new generation of CRM is the information workshop. The data and processes integrate here for the business community. Data is mapped to the appropriate process and presented in a way that the business users find easy to understand. PeopleSoft's analytic capabilities use this "workbench" idea with their Enterprise Performance Management (EPM) engines. Workbenches, rather than provide you with a hammer and saw, provide you with visual information tools that help you conceptualize your planning or understand the results of your search for some kind of knowledge. So if you are looking for patterns related to employee activity and customer satisfaction, you can not only derive them but see them as relationships using a workbench.

When it gets down to basics, though, the CIF is only as good as the datawarehouse at its heart. If the datawarehouse design is flexible and can adapt to the changes in business process and in the overall business ecosystem, it can work. If it can remain stable and use the data structures it contains already, regardless of the change, it can work. Finally, if it can handle the different forms of analytic processes that exist from straightforward simple SQL-based queries to complex data mining, it can work.

Becoming a Devotee of the Data Vault

To accommodate these complex requirements, Dr. Imhoff recommends the data vault. I'm not enough of an expert in this particular domain to say yea or nay. However, Claudia Imhoff rightfully deserves the respect she has in the CRM community because of her achievements and intelligent presentation of important ideas. Consequently, I'll defer to her thinking on the data vault. She sees it as the "next evolutionary step in data modeling." From what I see, it provides the appropriate model for the process-driven generation of CRM data too.

The early steps in building the data vault are linked directly to the business processes that move the company. First the functional areas are identified, such as financial or marketing, then the unique subject areas within units such as billing or campaign management, then the topic areas such as invoicing or direct mail. Once these are identified, the components and processes that link these are specified visually. So for example, if you are the accounts receivable manager and you are getting information from the billing clerk related to invoicing, you figure out what information you are receiving and how you receive that information—including any workflow that is needed to authorize the information officially if necessary. This is standard business process modeling with the addition of identifying the actual information that traverses, not just the process needed to let the information flow. Once you've identified the topics and its components—the topics become the "hubs" of the data vault.

Then you begin to drill down further. For example, if you are invoicing, what are the identifiers needed to make that invoice unique? Is it a contract number or account name or even a serially generated invoice number that is attached to that account name? If there are several of those, each of them becomes a topically related hub too. That means that invoice number or account name is a key identifier in its own hub.

Following the identification of hubs, you find a further level of description such as the date of the invoice, the amount of the invoice, or the terms of the invoice and group them in a "satellite." So you have a dimension of sorts here that is part of the hub. Keep in mind this satellite generates outward from the hub. The hub is the invoice, for example, and the satellite is the date, amount, and terms of the invoice. Then you can connect the hubs to each other according to processes— such as invoice to customer to sales process closing.

While this is a vastly simplified way of looking at a contemporary data structuring, its importance lies in not the details, but in the approach. It is a business approach to a data model. By identifying how the customer is related to the invoice, you can identify the relationships of the components of business and data in terms that a business user can not only grasp but can also not worry about, once the data vault is built and the CIF established.

You know what? I just talked myself into this approach. My reading, research, and a few conversations that went into this brief set of paragraphs prove to me that the concept of the data vault is coherent with the changes in CRM and business that created the need for a complete rewrite of this book to begin with.

Data Mining Finds Gold in Them Thar Hills

Data mining is not all that complicated a conception. In fact, its idea is very 21st century: eliminate massive clutter and overwhelmingly clunky information and go minimalist by finding lean data patterns. These patterns can range from purchasing behavior to customer "churn" rates, as we'll see below.

Data mining uses statistical modeling techniques to predict a customer's response or purchase based on the combination of transactional and demographic variables known about the individual. These can also measure customer values such as revenue obtained or profit derived from the customer.

For example, consider the plight of the poor telecommunications company. Now that customers can carry their phone numbers with them, the numbers of customers willing to change providers is expected to be over 77 million in 2004. In 2002, that number was 43 million. This changeover is called churn. You would think that there is nothing more dangerous than losing customers. That's sort of true but not entirely. Nothing is more dangerous than losing customers who have a high annualized or lifetime value to you.

Data mining can help you identify those high value customers who are likely to leave, through using customer records that are stored in your data central. Data mining is the acquisition of the data and the creation of the statistical model that can do that.

How does that work? I'm glad you asked.

To use data mining to create a "churn model" the company would look at data with a dependent variable. That variable could be something like "did not renew a contract." Then data is extracted to balance that of customers who did renew their contracts in the same period that the statistical model covers. Then you add the demographics, mix with transactional variables and voilà—you have a possible group of predictive models. Using this method, the models could identify up to 80 percent of the possible churners, based on the variables you included in the data mining exercise. Keep in mind, when doing the data mining, you are weighing the variables in order of importance. These are not plain vanilla calculations. For example, the various ways the customer received personalized attention could be one set of variables that are more important than the period from the time of purchase to the present might be. What may show up is that people who had signed up 24 months or more ago and received at least five communications through a variety of media are more likely to stay than those who didn't get the five communications and/or those who signed up less than 24 months ago.

But now that you've identified the individual customers or demographic cuts that are going to leave you, do you want to retain each and all of them? Nope. The next step is to create a model that can predict future revenues against each of these customers—in other words, customer lifetime value (CLV). The model can identify which segments will generate the greatest revenues against the average revenues across all customers. You can then apply the two models against each customer. You first identify whether or not the customer is likely to leave, and if they are or aren't, what kind of revenue you can expect from that customer over their lifetime or their average annual revenue if you prefer. So if you find a high value customer likely to leave you, you can plot and plan a strategy to keep that customer or cry as you wave goodbye to them.

The weakness of data mining as such is that it tries to identify trends based on past behaviors, and that can be risky in periods when there is a sea change. Generally, using what the military calls HUMINT—human intelligence—prevents it from being all that much of a risk. For example, if you tried to apply an historic statistical model to airline passenger behaviors in October 2001, based on customer histories prior to September 11, 2001, your likelihood of getting an even reasonably reliable behavioral suggestion ranges from about 0 percent to about 0 percent. But I would have to assume that you were smart enough without software to realize that airline passenger behavior had already changed so dramatically you wouldn't waste your time or your company's money modeling such a potential outcome.

A Little Bit of Vendor

This is going to be quick. This is a short list of the best of breed software vendors that are providing data-related tools. No explanation. You'll have to take my word for it.

Data Quality: Trillium Software

Datawarehousing: SAP Business Information Warehouse (BW)

Data Mining: SAS Enterprise Miner, NCR Teradata Warehouse Miner

Databases: Oracle, IBM's DB2, Microsoft's SQL Server

Okay, it's a wrap. This chapter is meant to be a sketch on data, not a mural nor even a watercolor. The basics that you need to be aware of are here and that's all. More importantly, it provides you with information—meaning that human intelligence has been applied to facts to give you perspective.

15

Supply Chain + Demand Chain = A Big Enterprise Value Chain, Gang

Back in the days when CRM was CRM in a manly way—big, beefy, and flabby—and the business ecosystem was a customer-focused corporate ecology, integration usually meant application integration. How did you conjoin those data-driven CRM applications with the legacy systems that your company had invested gazillions in and the third-party applications that you just didn't want to give up? But with the sleek new multi-channel customer ecosystem, our neo-CRM has a different place in the value chain and thus integration means very much more than it did. It is now how the front and back offices, the supply and demand chain all are interlocked as a unified customer-centric business effort. That includes the traditional CRM departments like sales and marketing or support. It includes the old ERP functions like finance and human resources. It even includes those mundane supply chain activities like inventory management, scheduling, sourcing, delivery, and logistics. All working together for a common cause—customer insight and customer "pleasure." In other words, business integration, not just application integration. This is not only applications communicating at the application level, but business processes intertwined and coordinated.

A pure application integration framework will look at how to make SAP Financials communicate with PeopleSoft HR communicate with Siebel Sales. The business integration will be interested in making them communicate but more along of the lines of having someone enter closed deal information in Siebel sales. This will generate an order which will then be booked in the financial system. This order will be applied to a compensation program that is part of the human resources system tailored specifically to the individual salesperson who closed the deal. Additionally, the order management system will generate a lookup of the available product inventory and send the information to the logistics team. That team will pack and ship the product, while an e-mail is being generated to the buyer on the expected ship date and delivery date, based on how he handled the shipping. None of the integration points and process integration will be of interest, nor will it be apparent to the salesperson doing the entry or the buyer receiving the e-mail. It is an application-agnostic approach, though the specific applications that will be engaged will matter.

The new ecosystem demands a collaborative strategy, both internally and externally. Where one company could John Wayne it in the past to reach and satisfy their paying clients, that is no longer possible. In reality, it was never possible, but the idea of strategizing with competitors or suppliers was not much of a universal thought in the 1950s through 1980s except in rare instances. Then in 1994, Adam Brandenburger, a professor at the Harvard Business School, and Adam Nalebuff, the Milton Steinbach professor at the Yale School of Management, came out with a groundbreaking book called *Coopetition*. *Coopetition* stressed the changes that were driving the marketplace into the arms of the customer. This demanded that competitors with complementary offerings begin to cooperate without guilt. Here's how these creative authors put it: "If business is a game, who are the players and what are their roles? There are customers and suppliers, of course; you wouldn't be in business without them. And, naturally, there are competitors. Is that it? No, not quite. There's one more, often overlooked but equally important group of players—those who provide complementary rather than competing products and services. That's where we'll begin this chapter. We'll see how complements can make all the difference between business success and failure." While they put the entire book in terms of game theory and game players, the principle was not only sound, but foresighted.

As we romp through the millennium, the need for the creation of an enterprise value chain supersedes the idea of mere integration among CRM, SCM, and ERP. It is a network that extends beyond the corporation per se and into the world of partners, suppliers, and others who provide the complementary goods and services that make the value proposition of a company exceptionally strong. That is a necessary condition of modern business. Reaching out and touching a customer is a multifunctional requirement to keep them in the fold and to provide them with the value they require so you get the value you require in turn. As Michael Park, VP of CRM at SAP, said to me back in 2002, "CRM is going to become an onramp to the enterprise." It now has become just that.

The Realization Is High, the Interest Deep

According to the Yankee Group's 2003 Edge of the Enterprise end-user survey of 78 companies, 71 percent increased spending on applications to improve interactions with customers, suppliers, and service providers during 2002–2003. While I can't imagine that most of them were hoping with Zen-like desire to get in harmony with the customer ecosystem, there is growing evidence that the business world is seeing customer strategy as the overarching strategy for their entire corporate value chain—end to end—back to front. META Group, in fact, was foresighted enough to detail the coming of this change back in 2001 in their report, "Integration: Critical Issues for Implementation of CRM Solutions." This report identified an enterprise ecosystem that linked supply chain management, enterprise resource planning, and CRM beneath the transactions and collaboration layer. They saw it from the standpoint of a customer driven *corporate* ecosystem, though. Even before that, in 2000, the very smart META Group analyst Steve Bonadio, in his short piece, "Exposing the CRM/ERM/SCM Intersection," wrote "Organizations can no longer afford to view customer relationship management (CRM), enterprise resource management (ERM), and supply chain management (SCM) initiatives as separate. Synchronizing front-office, back-office, and supply chain activities is critical to attracting/retaining customers, fulfilling demand, and improving cycle times." Bonadio was quite the oracle, wasn't he?

The interest in this topic is high as everyone tries to come up with a name for this customer-colored initiative. Collaborative Supply Chain, Demand Driven Supply Network, Extended Value Chain, and one of the better names from SAP and Peppers and Rogers, the Customer-Centric Adaptive Network (CCAN). Whew. The terms make me dizzy. I'll call it value chain integration and an enterprise value chain. Because you're reading this book, listen to me.

Supply Chain Management: Looking Out the Front of the Back

SCM is so well defined, its components are almost a chant: plan, source, make, deliver, return. Repeat forty times and fall into a stupor. Despite its soporific powers, these five components are a mantra to any company that delivers product to customers. They have the power to make or break your relationships with these customers. These five components are as clearly marked and well known as they are due to the SCOR model developed by the Supply Chain Council. SCOR—the Supply Chain Operations Reference model—as of this writing is at version 6.0 and is a highly refined, well-optimized standard that combines supply chain–only business processes with key metrics and benchmarks, and comes up with a set of best practices that have been put to practical use by the Supply Chain Council's members.

They Create the Model, They SCOR

The procedure the Supply Chain Council uses to create the model is interesting on the face of it, and worth understanding as one that is useful in developing any standard. The steps:

1. Identify the "as is" state of a supply chain related business process

2. Identify the "to be" state of the same process

3. Quantify that against the operational practices of existing similar companies (usually members)

4. Extract a series of world class processes, a.k.a. best practices

5. Characterize these management procedures and the associated software solutions that result in the best practices

Voilà! A model is born. There might not be a catwalk, but it is a model.

I am going to use the official definitions of the SCOR 6.0 model as provided by the Supply Chain Council document "Supply-Chain Operations Reference-Model: Overview of SCOR Version 6.0." This breakdown of each of the components is lifted straight from the document because it is a concise and clear description of the facets that go into SCM. Plus, it's official—the one that is widely used in supply chain.

Plan

Planning is exactly what it sounds like. Make determinations how to build, extend, define, or determine the supply chain and all its components.

► Balance resources with requirements and establish/communicate plans for the whole supply chain, including return, and the execution processes of source, make, and deliver.

► Management of business rules, supply chain performance, data collection, inventory, capital assets, transportation, planning configuration, and regulatory requirements and compliance.

► Align the supply chain unit plan with the financial plan.

Source

This is all the pieces needed to find the optimal suppliers that will provide you with the appropriate goods and services.

- ▶ Schedule deliveries; receive, verify, and transfer product; and authorize supplier payments.

- ▶ Identify and select supply sources when not predetermined, as for engineer-to-order product.

- ▶ Manage business rules, assess supplier performance, and maintain data.

- ▶ Manage inventory, capital assets, incoming product, supplier network, import/export requirements, and supplier agreements.

Make

Again, straightforward (if only the entire IT world were as clear and simple as the supply chain definitions). How to produce the goods that you need to get to the customer.

- ▶ Schedule production activities, issue product, produce and test, package, stage product, product to deliver.

- ▶ Finalize engineering for engineer-to-order product.

- ▶ Manage rules, performance, data, in-process products (WIP), equipment and facilities, transportation, production network, and regulatory compliance for production.

Deliver

We all know this one. What does it take to get the planned, sourced, made goods to the customer?

- ▶ All order management steps from processing customer inquiries and quotes to routing shipments and selecting carriers.

- ▶ Warehouse management from receiving and picking product to loading and shipping product.

- ▶ Receive and verify product at customer site and install, if necessary.

- ▶ Invoice customer.

- ▶ Manage deliver business rules, performance, information, finished product inventories, capital assets, transportation, product lifecycle, and import/export requirements.

Return

We all know this one too. What does it take to get the planned, sourced, made, delivered goods back to the producer or supplier?

- ▶ All return defective product steps from authorizing return; scheduling product return; receiving, verifying, and disposition of defective product; and return replacement or credit.

- ▶ Return MRO product steps from authorizing and scheduling return, determining product condition, transferring product, verifying product condition, disposition, and request return authorization.

- ▶ Return excess product steps including identifying excess inventory, scheduling shipment, receiving returns, approving request authorization, receiving excess product return in source, verifying excess, and recover and disposition of excess product.

- ▶ Manage return business rules, performance, data collection, return inventory, capital assets, transportation, network configuration, and regulatory requirements and compliance.

I don't want to call the above a process map, but it is a clear definition of what concerns supply chain and how the supply chain works. What is interesting, though unspoken, is that this is a highly customer–sensitive set of actions. Think about it. Plan (by employees), source (suppliers), make (employees, suppliers), deliver (to paying customers, partners), return (from paying customers, partners, suppliers). No matter how much you automate a so-called back-office set of processes, the ultimate target is the 21st century customer. SCM is a customer issue, not just an anonymous back-office process, there for the streamlining. There are live people involved in the creation and movement of inanimate products.

MINI-CASE STUDY

Patricia Seybold did a 2003 case study on Fairchild Semiconductor that shows the best results in how optimized supply chain planning can have a significant effect on ROI.

In 1997, Fairchild Semiconductor relaunched itself as a company breaking its shackles with National Semiconductor, its home since 1987. When they became independent, they used primarily manual planning for production activities and for product planning. To make this worse, each product group managed its own planning processes and was isolated from the other product groups. Each group tracked its own orders, production, and demand forecasting, and even scheduled its own product runs. Even inventory maintenance was manual. Seybold says, "Fairchild had difficulty linking its marketing and regional planning activities, which developed estimates of customer orders, with the business unit planning activities, which created the manufacturing capacity and revenue plans, and the factory planning activities that determined production schedules. Sales groups, in turn, relied on separate demand fulfillment systems to track product delivery schedules and inventories, and determine when they could promise product deliveries to meet customers' orders." To make this approach to planning even more knotty, the departments and product lines shared the same manufacturing facilities even though their planning and processes conflicted!

The numbers? Four to six weeks of finished goods in inventory (bad forecasting) at any given time. Revising a production plan took 10–14 days and never was current. Typically, in a best practices run business this was a one-day process. Nightmarish for Fairchild. So many chips sitting around in inventory, you might as well get some beer, watch a ballgame, and eat the reserves.

By working with IBM Global Services and i2, Fairchild Semiconductor developed an Advanced Planning Solution (APS) initiative that would centralize their planning and forecasting organized as a cross-functional, enterprise-wide effort. This covered demand planning, which gathers information globally and then analyzes customer orders and market trends in order to create a picture of future demand. It also covered master planning, which is based on optimizing product cycles based on forecasts, delivery scheduling, and inventory. Fairchild APS then can identify and forecast product lifecycle from how much and where the product is going to be produced to the actual delivery schedules. For example, they can look at the inventory, the products in progress, and capacity. They can match the inventory or products-to-be to customer orders based on specific business rules that have been embedded. This, in combination with multiple other functions, is likely to provide a 10 percent incremental improvement in customer service level, which, as Seybold states, "[Fairchild] believes will lead to a 1 to 8 percent revenue uplift."

The Sweetest Thing: Value Chain Integration

Value chain integration is the evolution from a series of linearly inter-linked processes that had historically been isolated from each other, to a smoothly functioning integrated business model that is effectively a single link from multiple parts of the enterprise. CRM, SCM, ERP, and a strategy for product lifecycle management (not covered here) will provide a complete "system" for a refreshed look at the new enterprise and what it needs.

Imagine this scenario. You made a decision to take your company to new revenue heights. To do this, you decided that you had to move from a product-out-the-door sales plan to a voice-of-the-customer strategy. You formulated a CRM strategy and included all the right elements. To gain some early credence among your colleagues, and to solve some immediate issues, you took care of the first damaged area: sales. You developed new compensation plans based on customer satisfaction ratings for the salespeople. You implemented a new SFA solution which reduced administrative time and improved the real-time access to customer and competitive information. Pricing customization was now easier.

You had amazing results. Your product sales numbers improved by 45 percent. Your sales teams had 17 percent more time with customers, gratifying the customers, because administration and attention was that much more efficient. Things were going great, weren't they?

Sure. CRM strategy aimed at the front end alone worked wonderfully—for a little while. But where were those products to be delivered coming from? How fast were they getting out the door? Did you and do you have sufficient inventory to meet the demands of the increased sales? How were you going to schedule the delivery of those products so that customers who ordered them received them in a timely way? If the sales numbers were that improved, the strain on the supply chain had to be enormous, because it is likely you didn't make any fundamental changes to the organization of the supply chain. After all, this was a CRM sales force automation initiative, wasn't it? Backlogged orders needed to be entered into the financial system, but they were straining the staff because no new employees were hired to enter the data properly. Employees had to work overtime to meet the load created by the success of the CRM strategy and the application of the SFA tools.

As time moved on, you began to fail to follow through on orders, delivery was late for your items routinely, and orders fell off precipitously as customer satisfaction with your company declined, even though the customers liked the salespeople personally and admired their effectiveness. Before long, the success kills you.

The lesson: Don't be successful! (Just kidding.)

The real lesson is that a CRM strategy in the new world customer ecosystem is merely the forward facing part of an encompassing collaborative enterprise strategy whether you are a behemoth or a mosquito-sized company. If you are in business, there is a value chain that runs from end to end. You sell product or services, you deliver product or services. That's simple enough. To sell and deliver the product or services, you have to buy products and services from a company that sells and delivers products or services. Straight out of *The Lion King*: this is the circle of (business) life.

CRM, ERP, SCM Integration Challenges

The challenges of linking the demand and supply chains are substantial. In fact, the problem is so large that AMR Research, while studying "current order management systems, business drivers, and approaches," found that 60 percent of the 400 companies it surveyed in 2003 have no CRM/SCM integration or partial integration at best. Not only that, it is seen primarily as tactical and as more of an application play. The results are a very fragmented bunch of companies. For example, the average company has 5.2 order capture applications and 4.3 order fulfillment applications, meaning nearly 10 applications just for order management. To make it even less customer friendly, 45 percent of their customers place orders in more than one system. To make that even more confusing, 50 percent of the companies have little or no product or customer standards at all. This is one disjointed mess.

The most formidable problem is that the supply chain and the demand chain are each seen (and thus organized) as a discrete set of processes and practices that are uniquely optimized. The relationship between them has been parallel at best, not integrated. For example, supply chain management has been touted as the organization and optimization of production and performance, including delivery and logistics. CRM has targeted the identification of and improvement in the customer experience, leading to improved top and bottom lines, SCM has been associated with efficiencies and cost controls; CRM has been associated with effectiveness and revenue increases.

The irony, of course, is that the supply chain's entire purpose is the efficient delivery of the products and services to *customers*, so how well that delivery is executed is vital to the pulse rate of those customers The ability to take that pulse is something that CRM delivers. The need for integration of the two couldn't be more apparent, could it?

It must be "in your face" apparent, because the vendors, who are normally myopic by embedded practice, are very aware of this integration need. Companies like PeopleSoft, SAP, Manugistics, and other vendors are all aware that CRM/SCM integration is the way both the present and the future are shaping up. It's very much in their self-interest, so they are providing solutions for that integration. Of all the vendors, SAP is taking the most intelligent direction when it comes to this important area. Aside from developing excellent products, platforms, and frameworks to facilitate integration, they are collaborating with Peppers and Rogers to grab thought leadership with an admirable, albeit too dense, piece entitled "The Pathway to Profit and Competitive Advantage." It is a 35-page in-depth look at the benefits of CRM/SCM integration. I would highly recommend you go to the SAP site and get it. While several other vendors have written on the subject, this document is a couple of miles down the road from the others.

If you remember my reference to ERO in Chapter 1, it was a PeopleSoft supply chain product that drove the recognition and articulation of the customer as the new owner of the marketplace. They saw the supply chain as the vehicle that had to respond to the customer. This was in 1996, not recently. But the need to integrate the demand and supply chains has become ever more critical, not just noticeable in 2004. Not only is there the possibility of serious breaks in the practices and processes of a company when the two aren't integrated, but it is an important competitive advantage.

Gartner sure gets this. In a study that they did in 2002 entitled "The Product Value Chain," they said, "...enterprises that develop a PCM (product chain management) strategy by integrating PLM (Product Lifecycle Management), SCM, and CRM processes and technologies will see a 40 percent improvement in effectiveness and value chain visibility." Those companies that do the actual integration of CRM and SCM will see a 50 percent gain in customer satisfaction measured against those that don't. All in all, whether their numbers are accurate or not, the idea is clear. CRM and SCM need to be integrated to prevent disconnects and to increase efficiencies and customer satisfaction, not necessarily in that order. How to do this is the burning question.

Frameworks for Integration

In Chapter 13, I covered the architectures that CRM needs to function and converse with the rest of the information systems it needs to chatter with. But the integration frameworks provided by the leading vendors are much more than just application integration. They are the baseline for integrating the business processes and the systems at multiple levels among multiple enterprises. Despite the marketing thrusts that all of the larger enterprise players put out there about one integrated system being best (though often, it really is), they all recognize the simple fact that companies have invested in other systems and they aren't interested in giving up those investments. At the Gartner CRM conference in Baltimore in March 2004, Gartner revealed that one of the primary returns that interests customers is getting more out of their existing infrastructure through integration. This is confirmed by a study done by Morgan Stanley in April 2003 of chief information officer priorities. Of the ten possibilities offered to the CIOs, 51 percent chose application integration as their primary concern. The traditional ways of integration, point-to-point or integration server–focused, haven't been that successful. Point-to-point integration requires a common interface for each pair of applications connected. So if you have 20 applications to connect, you have 190 integration points to connect. It increases exponentially for each additional application, because each addition has to connect (most likely) to the other 20 or 21 or 50. When you upgrade, you have to reconnect everything.

Integration servers are a huge step up since the server provides a common hub for all the applications. Where it gets problematic is when a CRM process needs to be working across the supply chain in conjunction with human resources, for example. That means custom development work. Deadlines aren't met and the cost increases. It is no wonder that in December 2002 *Computer Weekly* noted that Standish Group did a study that stated that 88 percent of data integration projects have failed. Imagine the difficulties in enterprise-wide integrations, where data isn't the only concern. Of course, that is what Siebel, SAP, PeopleSoft, and Oracle have been working to solve with their integration frameworks.

To deal with this is to make the business processes independent of the underlying applications. That way they don't have to be mapped and specially formatted for each application, they can simply be used.

That is the benefit of a service-oriented architecture (SOA) as outlined in Chapter 13. That is the benefit of web services such as BPEL4SW, the common business process modeling language that is XML-ish in approach and in syntax.

That said, let's take a quick peek at the different business integration platforms provided by a couple of the major vendors. We're not going to investigate WebSphere, BEA, or Tibco because they are by design software (and CRM)—agnostic. We're also not going to look at all the major CRM vendors because they have similar though not identical frameworks. Just remember that SAP, PeopleSoft, Oracle, and Siebel all have integration frameworks. We're going to view the current incarnations of two major CRM vendors who had to develop vendor-agnostic strategies against their own originally perceived "best interests." One is SAP, representing the enterprise applications vendors, and the other is Siebel, representing the only one of the big four that isn't an enterprise application vendor in the truest sense of the word. Just for the record, PeopleSoft's is AppConnect and the Oracle integration framework is AppNet.

SAP NetWeaver

It took SAP until March 2004 to even announce a version of NetWeaver, their business integration platform which would be accessible by mySAP CRM 4.0, their current CRM suite. The newest version of their platform will integrate a high-speed search engine that will allow users to segment customer data. The analytics capabilities will allow users to design analytics processes that map to the enterprise business processes. Software agents will lurk in the background, looking at the data generated by applications involved in running business processes and then feed it back into the call center or the marketing applications as planned and needed.

These rather cool features sit on top of a very capable, urbane framework that is aimed at making complex interactions and transactions available to the average Joe. SAP, using its strong R&D focus, had 9,000 developers with about $1 billion a year, much of whose time is spent improving NetWeaver as the driver of all the CRM, ERP, SCM, SRM, product lifecycle management products that SAP now produces.

NetWeaver is J2EE and .NET compliant and is a fully interoperable framework that works with other integration frameworks like WebSphere. It provides interfaces, preconfigured business content, preconfigured portal content, and built-in business intelligence analytics. What sat in the datawarehouse (SAP's BW) is now available in this comprehensive system that can provide all the agnostic integration you might ever need. Like all of its competitors, it combines service-oriented architecture with an integration broker that uses XML and SOAP to communicate between diverse sources. There is an interesting reflection of SAP's strong development heritage with a lifecycle management element that manages the design, development, deployment, implementation, versioning, and testing of software's lifecycle.

Besides the business process management and enterprise portal, the other mission-critical facet of NetWeaver is what SAP calls Master Data Management. It is the capture and consolidation of data from disparate sources that is then centralized into a single data store. Coupled with the new search engine that can search millions of records from multiple sources in a matter of seconds, we are talking about an extraordinarily powerful, ultra high speed (theoretically, of course) analytics engine that can provide you with critical customer analysis in a matter of those same seconds and a place to store it.

Siebel UAN

When Siebel announced the Universal Application Network (UAN) 1.0 in 2002, all the CRM pundits thought, "Hmmm, I wonder if Siebel is going to produce any back-office applications," because it was clear to all of us that this is an area where they just couldn't compete with SAP, PeopleSoft, or Oracle. Then in 2003, they announced version 2.0 of the UAN, which apparently was to appear with Siebel 7.5 at that time. It added 50 embedded industry-specific process applications that were concentrated in nine industries ranging from insurance to media. Then they announced version 3.0. But not only didn't anyone see UAN in action, there seemed to be, even by Siebel's reckoning at the time, only about 20 customers for at least what passed for UAN version 1.0.

But this "UAN vaporware" early press didn't really deter Siebel. They continued to build UAN and establish partnerships with the EAI world such as IBM, BEA, SeeBeyond, Tibco, Vitria, and WebMethods. For example, with IBM, Siebel licensed prebuilt business process templates and common object models so that integration costs could come down. A wise move, but not definitive.

What is definitive is what distinguishes UAN from the other frameworks. Unlike other frameworks, UAN decouples the XML and other web services–based processes associated with business from the other vendors' transport and routing services. In plainer English, Siebel provides the content; the other vendors provide the infrastructure. The enterprise vendors with their frameworks are providing the content and infrastructure.

The real UAN takes an approach to data that is somewhat like NetWeaver. There is a master customer record that is shared among all applications, regardless of whose application it is. The information is communicated along with the business processes via BPEL4WS (see Chapter 13), which is designed explicitly for business process integration and is used by almost all the significant vendors in 2004. Interfaces are organized around those same processes such as Update Order or Create Invoice. The common business objects, also provided by Siebel, that would be appropriate to these two interfaces are order and invoice. Siebel also provides a UAN engine called Business Integration Transformation, which reconciles data differences so that there is a translated format that fits the appropriate data model. For example, if the currencies in data model one is dollars and data model two is euros, then the differences between the data model, based on the business rules embedded in the transformation, are settled so that each model is reconciled with its format. So one dollar in model A is 0.65 euros in model B, or whatever the rate is that day.

By the way, Siebel in March 2004 had 50 customers, with 6 live for the UAN. Slow-going, but going.

A Word on Portals

The integration of multiple parts of the value chain can be pretty daunting and certainly confusing to the ordinary user. Let's say I am a business partner and I need to see the number of Louisville Slugger baseball bats that Hillerich & Bradsby has in stock that are Model MM7—a "Vintage Mickey Mantle" 34-inch bat for the use of the Babe Ruth League in Texarkana, Arkansas. If I can provide a good price, all of Texarkana will be happy and also buy balls, gloves, and helmets from me. All I want to be able to do is log on to H&B's system via the Web and see the catalog, the volume pricing, and the available bats in inventory. I also want to know what dates they are likely to ship. I want the ability to order them over the Net. Rather than log into separate sales systems, product catalogs, order management systems, inventory management systems, and delivery and logistics systems, I simply use an enterprise portal to log into the system. The system I log into has not only aggregated all these systems into a coherent whole, but also has my corporate history and preferences available to me only through a single sign-on and secure password.

Portals Love You and Only You

In 2003, Jupiter Research found that 80 percent of the enterprises they polled had portals. That's great, but the issue is what kind of portal doing what? Frankly, a good deal of what passes for portals these days is a gateway to a news feed or a company announcement on this year's company picnic, where bobbing for jobs is the primary activity besides eating. Not anymore. Where a lot of portals were really visits to the companies' digital library in the past, the newer portals that are being developed are not only aggregated applications centers, but highly flexible, easily configurable gateways and user interfaces that are constructed by the users. That means that the portals must lend themselves to verticalization. For example, SAP's Enterprise Portal, sitting on top of NetWeaver, uses the SAP specialized vertical experience and can provide business processes for more than 20 industries that will reside at the portal server, a server that resides between the actual portal and the application server. Portal servers, common to most portals, hold the processes and data associated with content management, document repositories, CRM, identity management, process modeling, collaboration services, and business intelligence, among other things. The portal servers are where the applications' activities are aggregated and then applied to the appropriate processes, logic, and interfaces so the user can transparently do his or her thing inside the portal itself without worrying about which application to use or which processes are active.

The other portal component of note is the portlet. Portlets are flexible constituent parts of a portal architecture. They are graphical objects that can be integrated with specific application processes by the users. These are very much like applets that you might use on your web browser, but they integrate with the portal and applications servers.

For a portal to be successful there are four questions that have to be addressed:

Is the portal environment standards-based? Yes, there is a standard for portals and languages to support it too, no matter how tired you might be getting of acronyms. The acronym for the portal protocol is WSRP—Web Services for Remote Portlets. If it is a J2EE portal environment such as Plumtree provides, it also needs to support JSR 168, which is the Java portlet specification. Plus you have to be concerned about security and verification standards. All in all, a tricky proposition, only mitigated by the fact that most of the portal providers are adopting one standard or another for their environments.

Are security and authentication sufficient to protect the single user? Access is granted to a portal. That means when I log on with my ID and my password, I'm not going to get your views and applications. It also means that I can only do what my role and responsibilities say I can according to what the workflow and the authentication procedures identify. Additionally, I should be unable to see anyone else's applications at any point whether inside or outside the portal. That means that specific interfaces have to be created with this tight security and identity management in mind. How is the information on me gathered? Is it pulled from Active Directory or does it have its own integrated administration of the security and authentication system? For example, Plumtree, the leading vender-neutral portal-only provider has its own security but can also integrate other identity management systems.

Is business logic integrated to the portal? Again, this is a weak point with most portal environments. The tools that are provided by the portal vendors are often pretty poor and will provide for the most part scripting languages rather than true business logic integration tools. Watch for this.

How effective are the interfaces? There is no easy answer to this one. While the portals often provide interfaces, your legacy interfaces from your content management systems, your CRM applications, your workflow and BPM engines all will have to be integrated with the portal interfaces. You will have to choose your portal provider very carefully. Clearly, if you have SAP CRM and SCM, the SAP Enterprise Portal is most likely your best bet, but you also will have to be using NetWeaver. While it's still your best bet, this can be a very expensive proposition.

Portals are a central part of integration strategies. Business integration is useless if your users still have to hunt for the applications associated with their tasks after they go online. Portals aggregate applications, centralize the environment, and provide useful individualized intelligence, thus making work easier, thus providing higher adoption rates. But they are difficult to define, develop, and implement. Be very careful in your selection and you'll be rewarded. But mess up...well, don't come crying to me. I warned you.

The best portals are Plumtree's Corporate Portal, Vignette's Application Portal 4.5 (acquired independent portal provider Epicentric in 2003), PeopleSoft's Enterprise Portal (especially their government portal), SAP's Enterprise Portal (newest version supports Unix and flexible integration), BEA's WebLogic Portal 8.1 (comes with one of the best development environments, WebLogic Workshop), and Oracle's Application Server Portal 10g (despite the clear applications specificity, it comes with strong business process modeling and applications development tools).

Supplier Relationship Management

If you subscribe to the premise that an enterprise value chain is the real deal, you probably realize that the end client is not the only customer that exists. The suppliers are customers as much as the employees and the business partners in your channel. All of them collaborate to make your end client cry tears of joy while they do business with you. As this has evolved over the past two years to the au courant model we are engaged with now, we've also seen the interest in and growth of both ERM and SRM—employee relationship management and supplier relationship management. The former is a construct from Siebel that Siebel swears will be a $20 billion market. I have seen no evidence of that whatever. Do I write it off entirely? No. But I'm not taking a $20 billion write-off either. To me, ERM is making sure that your employees are fairly compensated for providing quality work. Treat them with respect and make them accountable, reward them for success. Remember that they're human. That should do it for ERM. Granted, I'm being glib, but I also don't see the need for it when you already have human resources strategies, applications, and compensation strategies and the applications support it. SRM is another story altogether. This is an important component of the customer-centric universe.

Comparing SCM and SRM? C vs. R?

SCM is the actual processes and practices that govern production and its delivery. SRM governs the relationships between suppliers and the producing company. It resembles CRM strategically, and certainly resembles partner relationship management or channel management down to its practical level. In fact, it is so close in nature to PRM there is no reason not to include SRM as part of the CRM subset universe. If I describe something as "the software and business processes that create collaborative communications and align an enterprise with its _____," what would you think it is? Put "partner" in the blank space and it's PRM. Put "customers" in and it's CRM. Put "suppliers or vendors" in and it's SRM.

There is a difference between SCM and SRM besides the middle letter. While SCM supports internal processes to external customers of any variety, SRM supports collaborative networks that are integrating their mutual supply chains. The components are very different. SRM deals with the human interactions between the suppliers and the company or companies that use them. It uses automation to make the relationships more effective, rather than making the processes more efficient per se. The most advanced SRM solutions, such as PeopleSoft's SRM, are 100 percent Internet applications that use portals for supplier (and other) access.

So if you were to dissect the SRM machinery, you'd probably come up with a map that includes sourcing, contract management, procurement, presentment and payment, and perhaps spend analysis. Solutions that are more sophisticated throw in catalog management, trading partner management, order management, product configurators, ports, and a host of analytics beyond spend analysis that can track supplier performance.

GOING DEEPER

It pays to look briefly at the more common components of an SRM solution. Like any other solution of its ilk, it always should involve planning a strategy for how to execute an SRM initiative (if you are doing it separately). The only notable thought beyond the strategic planning norms outlined in this book is that SRM strategies require thinking about the vendors and suppliers as both customers and partners involved in making the ultimate revenue-producing customer happy. That means they are part of the collaborative chain and have to be happy themselves so the chain that leads to revenue creation doesn't break. Beyond that, read Chapters 17–22.

I present to you the major components:

▶ **Procurement** SRM solutions can lead to a number of important benefits in the procurement process. By bringing the processes under control, out-of-control spending is reduced. How often is it that you find some departmental budget monkey going wild and spending on the basis of departmental and not enterprise need, no matter what the damage? This can bring the spending under control and reduce the procurement cycle, increase contract compliance, and reduce the per transaction cost of procurement. In the more advanced places, catalog management is improved because of the improvement in the overall procurement processes. Solid workflow routing is introduced so that the orders can be more effectively managed and approvals assigned more quickly. Shipment notices can be issued automatically. Imagine your weary desire to do some requisitions at 3:00 A.M. because you can't sleep due to your inability to adjust to the time difference in Nepal. You go online, access a catalog and the supplier sites that are tied to the items in the catalog. Built-in business rules govern how the procurement requisition is created. You do all this—in Nepal—at 3:00 A.M. The requisition is created and entered into the system for action. It is secure. You can sleep now. The world is as one.

▶ **Sourcing** While choosing the right suppliers for a quote or proposal seems to be a matter of both knowledge and the heart, SRM can make this process so much more satisfying and effective. This is not easy. You'll see that when you see what SRM sourcing modules contain. For example, attribute weighing is a way of defining the important criteria that you set for seeing the value of a prospective bidder or an active one based on algorithms that I can't begin to comprehend. Another feature is event scoring and award. These are comparisons of multiple vendors and their responses to a proposal so you can evaluate and choose the winning bidder. Supplier performance is a set of provided or customized metrics that can measure how well a supplier is doing against plan. This can have a real effect on whether you award him a certain piece of business at a certain time. Some of the most commonly used metrics are quality, cost, responsiveness, and delivery speed. Finally, collaborative negotiations have a direct impact on the deals that are going on with spot buys, reverse auctions, or just plain auctions. Negotiations are real time and have to be done that way. The rapid dissemination of the negotiations information has to be handled through multiple organizational levels for both bidder and buyer. SRM sourcing provides the real-time workflow and knowledge management tools to do this.

▶ **Payment** Who doesn't know how touchy payment processes are? They are the most sensitive of subjects, the foundation for lawsuits. Those processes when flawed create bad communications and/or late payments and that leads to those lawsuits and highly irrational behaviors between the persons owed and the scofflaw company. All make this a thin-skinned and critical function within SRM. Paying the suppliers isn't just the use of your financial applications purchased from an ERP vendor. We are talking about managing relationships. If you pay in a timely fashion through an ordinary and comfortably repeatable routine, you don't have a lot of relationship worries. But what if there are conflicts? How does the settlement process, that which comes between procurement and check to your supplier, get handled? Never fear, SRM is here. SRM uses workflow to enable alerts that are triggered when payment disputes are initiated. Perhaps it's a mistake in invoicing or a payment discrepancy. It doesn't matter. If you are using SRM's best practices, all the invoicing, dispute resolution, and payment issuance are done online via secure portals with unique IDs and passwords for each supplier.

▶ **Analytics** Commonly, the most important analytics for SRM are analytics that help you control costs. For example, there may be a price increase in goods that you regularly order that is not apparent because the ordering process is automatic or automated. You don't want to see this for the first time after it hits the books. By doing what is often called spend analytics, you can carve the procurement process into tiny or big or diagonal pieces and see what's going on with the costs of each part of the procurement. But SRM-related analytics don't stop there. You can monitor employee spending patterns or analyze purchase data, for example.

STEPPIN' OUT: PeopleSoft SRM to the Nth Degree

This Steppin' Out bears a short explanation because I've ignored SCM as part of the choice for the vendor selection I've made here. If I were to choose an SCM solution, I'd choose i2 or SAP, and perhaps People-Soft. But the one thing that I want to reiterate is that this book is about how *CRM* has evolved in this new customer ecosystem. So the relationships between a supplier and the supplied are more important than the efficiencies of the actual production and its logistics that have been part of this chapter too.

PeopleSoft SRM comes with a royal lineage. It is the grandchild of Red Pepper and the child of PeopleSoft manufacturing. Red Pepper was a supply chain management suite that was acquired in 1996 by People-Soft and was responsible for PeopleSoft's elegant representation of the state of the customer market place, Enterprise Resource Optimization (ERO). Red Pepper begat PeopleSoft manufacturing, not exactly the success it was touted to be (they were looking for a 45 percent market share and got 4.3 percent), but it begat a highly successful applications suite, Supplier Relationship Management (among other grandchildren). Interestingly, PeopleSoft has been holding on to the thread of ERO since 1996, and it is fascinating to hear the contemporary version from Carol Ptak, vice president of manufacturing at PeopleSoft in an article in *CRM News* in March 2004, "Instead of focusing on inventory as an asset, now the focus of a manufacturing plant is to have a minimum amount of inventory and yet respond quickly to consumer demand." Shades of ERO! That is what they articulated so well in 1995 and continue to do today.

PeopleSoft's SRM offerings, SRM Enterprise and SRM EnterpriseOne 8.10 (the former J.D. Edwards upper midmarket), are organized around two portals that put most other SRM products to shame. The first portal is their Supplier Self Service Portal, which is aimed at collaborative efforts between suppliers and manufacturers. It allows the suppliers to share schedules. It provides direct visibility into the supply chain of the manufacturer including the inventories available to the manufacturer of products that would interest the supplier. It can clear up possible supply chain bottlenecks in real time utilizing the strong PeopleSoft workflow to alert the appropriate parties to the problems. It allows for forecast and demand sharing among the suppliers.

The other portal is also for Enterprise and EnterpriseOne. It is the Buyer Workspace and does what it sounds like. Buyers can streamline inbound supply chain transactions and handle multiple suppliers. It can prioritize those suppliers automatically and according to both pre-set and dynamic criteria, so purchase orders can be tracked in real time. Buyer Workspace also maintains performance histories and it can handle alerts, once again using that excellent PeopleSoft workflow.

These are the cornerstone pieces of PeopleSoft SRM. Who ever knew a relationship could work so smoothly?

Support Chain Management

Normally when I run across a potentially new acronym, I pooh-pooh it as something that is just a marketing ploy by a vendor desperate to differentiate itself in the morass of vendors that roams the CRM fields. However, my friends at ChannelWave have done something truly interesting with their next-generation CCRM, a.k.a. PRM product (see Chapter 6). They have extended the value chain even further with a new look at the intelligent link to the demand and supply chains, with their presentation of the support chain and support chain management. This is the services channel that supports the demand and supply chains as represented in Figure 15-1. To complete the value chain for the enterprise, manufacturers must extend their customer care solutions to the network of partners who are responsible for the overall customer experience. While this resembles a traditional channel or even a VAR arrangement, it isn't quite that. It is far more complex, combining multiple channels, including field sales, e-commerce, dealers, agents, distributors, VARs, and retailers to deliver consistent and positive customer care.

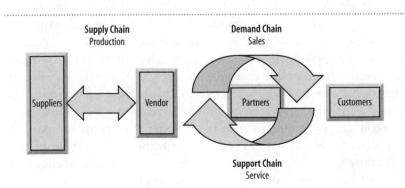
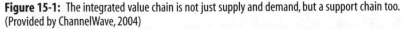

Figure 15-1: The integrated value chain is not just supply and demand, but a support chain too. (Provided by ChannelWave, 2004)

For example, product repair costs to vendors are about 1.2 percent of total product revenue. They can average as high as 8 percent. The cost of the field technician for the repair, the parts needed to repair the problem item and other labor and materials costs can easily erode your margins—as slim as they already are.

So how do you maintain the margins? One approach is to reduce the liabilities through improving service and increased partner use. Another possible approach is to increase the aftermarket, meaning partner/supplier, sales of parts and services, which reduce per item cost and direct overhead. The network that provides these parts and services is the support chain. It supports the supply chain and the demand chain. If field service teams are collaborating with the customers and the business partners or suppliers, then the effectiveness of the overall enterprise value chain increases. It can:

- ▶ Strengthen customer maintenance and retention

- ▶ Lower support costs per customer

- ▶ Reduce costly equipment and system downtime

- ▶ Increase revenue from spare parts, peripherals, and extension products

- ▶ Reduce warranty liability and costs

Rob Hagan, CEO of ChannelWave, situates it within a customer-centric strategy, "The support chain has been around for decades, but it was impossible to manage efficiently with telephone calls, spreadsheets, faxes, and printed manuals. The Web now gives us a platform to extend customer care through the support chain partners who actually own the end-customer experience."

What makes this interesting is that it treats suppliers as partners and partners as service units to the suppliers while the brand holder continues to hold the brand. But the hub of the supply, demand, and support chains is the customer, not the brand holder. A significant evolution in the overall process of enterprise integration.

To see this service platform in more detail, please take a look at Figure 15-2. This is the ChannelWave version of it and it provides an explicit look at how the integrated support chain works. The big picture was shown previously in Figure 15-1.

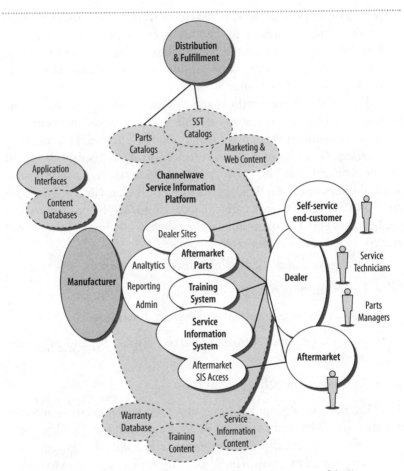

Figure 15-2:   This is the ChannelWave Service Information Platform—part of the New Enterprise Value Chain.

ERP: Trigger to Enterprise Integration History

Despite our concentration on the supply and demand chains here, we would be remiss if we forgot enterprise resource planning (ERP). After all, the initial thinking about integration with CRM was around ERP as company after company began to like the idea that they could link their human resources and financial functions to their sales, marketing, and support engines. In the late 1990s, ERP was led by the familiar players SAP, PeopleSoft, and Oracle with customized and integrated business processes and a growing middleware or enterprise application integration (EAI) market. It became the pioneer in attempts to integrate CRM applications and functions with the back office. The desire for this CRM link began to increase in the late 1990s when the major ERP players were raking in the bucks and feeling rather cocky about it. For example, PeopleSoft, in 1995 a $227 million company, became PeopleSoft 1999, the $1.4 billion company, giving them the capital and the leverage to purchase major CRM player Vantive in 2001, vaulting them to near the top of the CRM marketplace. SAP, though, became the 800-pound gorilla, becoming the fourth-largest software company in the world by 2000, after Microsoft, Computer Associates, and our friends at Oracle.

The giants didn't ignore supply chain management either. The successful acquisition of the very strong supply chain provider Red Pepper by PeopleSoft in 1996 triggered a three-year binge of supply chain acquisitions and investments by the major players in the supply chain world. For example, SAP invested in three supply chain companies— OKEF-tech, ILOG, and Catalyst International. J.D. Edwards acquired Numetrix, which became the foundation for their supply chain applications, all of which are now being integrated in the PeopleSoft SCM offering with JDE's acquisition by PeopleSoft in 2003. Oracle licensed i2 technology for use in their Oracle applications, and PeopleSoft, not content with just Red Pepper, two years later bought Distinction Software, a provider of a product that handled high-volume demand planning activities associated with consumer products companies. This is merely a glimpse of the edge of a huge binge of acquisitions, joint marketing agreements, agreements to embed licenses, and investments that went on as ERP, SCM, and the new child, CRM, began to show some real spunk in the market. In 1999, optimism was running high for what was then perceived as parallel systems that could possibly be linked in some fashion.

But ERP, as the most hyped and probably the most mature system, began to run into trouble during that period. Several things affected it. The implementation costs were running as high as $100 million and taking as long as 36 months to implement, when they were being planned for 12 months. Going over budget and overdue delivery dates for project completion, were all affecting the ERP market, which had been boosted because of their Y2K compliance when many other applications weren't. Well, Y2K was over and the ERP cost and implementation wasn't. Jobs were lost and careers of promising senior executives were cut short because of endangered ERP implementations that had no discernable ROI in acceptable time frames. Unfortunately, as with all quasi-revolutionary applications and changes, ERP ROI had no metrics at that time. CFO trash bins were filled with the remnants of vice presidents of finance or human resources or information technology who had pushed the ERP implementations as the savior of the company.

Unfortunately, CRM and SCM had the same taint during later eras, especially in the post-9/11 economy. The comparisons were drawn to ERP—too big, too expensive, too slow to implement, no results that we could measure quickly. The hesitance to spend in the downtimes of 2001–2002 and most of 2003 became a rush backward from spending on the big ticket enterprise value chain applications.

But, interesting enough, something that hurt ERP at first became a boon for the CRM and SCM evangelists. The establishment of the Internet as a global communications medium led to globalization and the dramatic escalation of transaction speed. That irrevocably changed the way the customer looked at the supplier. Customer demand for immediate response to inquiries and rapid shipment of orders, increasing competitive fervor, and the "need for speed" to market created a new form of customer demand. Personalized goods and services should be deliverable almost instantly upon request nearly anywhere in the world. In the meantime, with the business ecology shifting to customer attentive, the need for collaboration between CRM, ERP, and SCM became of paramount importance. How to devise systems to deliver effective business value to a customer, specific to each company and customer relationship, became the increasingly loudly chanted question heard 'round the business world.

ERP by itself wasn't very well suited for this. It was not designed for rapid, nimble action; it is made for integrated functionality. SAP R/3 is a good example of that. Throughout the late 1990s, there were complaints that SAP R/3 versions from 1.0 to 3.0 were inflexible and forced you to adapt to their business rules, rather than provide you with applications that could be customized to those business rules you used as your best practices.

SAP retooled and by 1997 came out with SAP R/3 4.0, an object-oriented version of the product that allowed the flexibility, but it remained a client/server application well into the millennium until the release in 2001 of MySAP.com. The architecture was not appropriate to the changes in the world of either business or information technology. XML was becoming a possible standard for communications between unlike applications from any company, obviating the need for the expensive connectors and EAI applications that dominated the client/server market. ERP was Galapagos turtle–like in its move to the more contemporary Internet-based architectures. CRM and SCM were much more adaptable.

Companies like PeopleSoft, especially with the release of CRM 8.0 in 2002, and i2 with its acceptance of web services integration, were able to bridge the gap without a lot of fallout. But companies like SAP and Siebel were slower to embrace the new technology of integration because of their heavy investment in client/server architectures and their "bigness." SAP has done a commendable job of getting on track. Siebel is getting to it now with the creation of the UAN.

As this book is being written, integration is the watchword of the enterprise value chain and customer strategies. An unscientific but nonetheless telling survey done by NetSuite and *CRM* magazine at one of their webinars (Web-based seminars) in 2004 entitled "Save More with On-Demand CRM Linked to Order Management" found that when asked the question, "Why is integration important to your CRM initiative?" the answers were fascinating. An overwhelming majority of attendees (65 percent) said, "For a holistic view of customers." Finally, senior management is beginning to get it. Finally.

Integrated Processes, Infinite Value

What would "integrated" processes even look like? Are they linear, where you just link a CRM process with an SCM process such as, say, sales with inventory management? That would mean that a salesperson can find out the availability of a product easily. Crank up your imagination and think about the following scenario.

Your marketing department purchases a large number of *CRM at the Speed of Light, Third Edition* copies—2,000—to use for lead generation. (This is a visible subliminal suggestion.) They get a great response rate—4.35 percent on a mailing of 45,000. Of those 2,000 leads, they generate 10 opportunities and 4 of them close, garnering a giant return on the investment. The new business generates a series of products and pricing configurations that lead to the new customers orders.

In that scenario, what CRM/SCM integrated processes were used?

Integration of marketing and sales This is distribution of the qualified leads from the marketing campaign to the appropriate salespersons in the appropriate territory.

Promotions management Promotions management provides the ability of the sales team and the marketing staff and the suppliers to see the costs of the lead generation campaign and to determine the most profitable of the campaigns and promotions.

Demand forecasting Based on round one of the lead generation campaign, demand forecasting when integrated can provide a look at the possible desire of the customers for more books or other products. It also provides a look at available inventories and production dates of new orders of the products so that an accurate assessment can be made about the actual demand and ability to fulfill it.

Product configuration If the customers want a complex product that involves multiple items, volume pricing, possible cross- or up-sales, and specific services, the product configurations and visibility into the supply chain for those complex products and multiple items are provided by this integrated process.

Available to promise This is for visibility into the inventory and for accurate knowledge of availability. Available to promise means available to fulfill delivery promises to the customer.

Order management When integrated, orders from multiple systems can be aggregated and then provided through a single source no matter what channel, what system, or what database the order is captured from.

Embedded inventory Rather than just a supply chain inventory management application, embedded inventory includes billing, shipping, and payment information.

Each of these is an integrated SCM/CRM process that may have been used somewhere along the "lead generation to closing" process that is outlined above. These are only a few of the benefits of integrating business processes in our brave new world of contemporary customer commerce.

Working Across the Value Chain, Gang

So, is there any value in cleaning up the supply chain and linking it to customers the way it was meant to be? Sure. According to Benchmarking Partners, inventory being held by retailers at any single moment is approximately $1 trillion. This is based on U.S. Department of Commerce data. If planning, forecasting, and replenishment were improved, the inventory could be reduced by $150 to $200 billion (in other words, 15 to 20 percent). That's just for the SCM changes. Imagine if you were able to forecast customer demand and understand customer behavior, making far more sophisticated analyses.

But the return doesn't stop there. CRM/SCM integration provides a measurable return on a number of key indicators that don't apply to just CRM or just SCM. AMR Research identified them in a report on the benefits of this integration in March 2003:

- ▶ Shorter order cycle times—decrease up to 65 percent

- ▶ Increased order accuracy—up to 100 percent improvement

- ▶ Incomplete orders—reduced by 20 percent

- ▶ Fewer order status calls weekly—up to 86 percent

- ▶ Inventory costs—10 percent reduction in sales inventory days

- ▶ Enterprise spend—5 to 10 percent savings on the cost of goods

These are a few of the possible results when the customer meets the supplier happily. The value of CRM/SCM integration and an enterprise value chain is both measurable and immeasurable.

16

The ASP Model: Sexy, but Utilitarian

If you look at the past two editions of this book, you can chart the rise and fall and rise again of what has been called (in a rather arcane and ultimately unsatisfying way) the hosted CRM model. The first edition had an entire chapter on it. The second edition barely mentioned it in passing. This edition has two chapters on it—this one and Chapter 25, which covers the application service providers (ASPs), company by company. How the mighty have risen again! It's like Joe Gibbs coming back to the Washington Redskins. The ASPs are the saviors of CRM. Hallelujah and amen!

Without the hallelujahs and amens, this probably isn't all that far from the truth. The ASP net native model is actually among the most important CRM breakthroughs of 2003 and beyond. It is one of the answers for how to deal with CRM's historic issues—long implementation cycles and high prices. In an executive white paper, Denis Pombriant, president of Beagle Research and CRM analyst, called the net native model "the disruptive innovation." He defines the idea of a disruptive innovation as something that "displaces a technology from a niche with something that accomplishes the same thing but at a very different price point and with a very different business model." I would add "and provides the potential to alter the existing paradigm." The hosted/ASP model can do this—and at that very different price point. It is significant and, to make it more interesting, it has some panache, a bit of the flair of the good old days of the dotcom, without all the ensuing stupidity. You'll read much more about the styling that the ASPs do in Chapter 25.

This market is here to stay and booming. In *Worldwide and U.S. Application Management Services Forecast and Analysis 2003–2007*, IDC said the ASP market was $2.3 billion in 2002 and is expected to have a compounded annual growth rate of 28 percent over five years, bringing it to an $8 billion monster.

"This has tapped into a desire customers have to move more quickly, with less risk, and more cheaply," says Laurie McCabe, Summit Strategy's well-respected chief ASP analyst. "They fit all checklists as a category with a great business case."

A Host by Any Other Name Would Work Just as Sweet

It's tough to come up with a name for this model because of the large number of permutations and the relative newness of the paradigm. Its current *nom de plume* is application service provider. Aberdeen Group calls it application hosting. It has been generally called hosted solutions—a singularly unproductive name. META Group calls it managed hosting. The Yankee Group calls it hosted CRM. A portion of the market is called strategic outsourcing. Salesforce.com came up with the best description—at least of their segment—christening it an "on-demand utility." For example, you don't buy electricity when you pay the power company. You buy services that provide electricity to you. Otherwise, you'd be cranking your own generator to power your house. The net natives work within the same model. You don't buy software; you buy subscription services that use software not residing on your system. The other value of this service model is that, like other utilities, there are few upfront installation costs, if any. When was the last time you remember a power company charging you to install the meters to read the power usage? It's the same with most of the net native models. More on the ROI and TCO later.

But questions remain, even with these promises of overhead-diminished nirvana.

Wait. I've been saying "net natives." What in the name of Gibbs is a net native? A citizen who wears mesh? A local fisherman?

The Net Natives

All the news is being generated right here. Unlike their conservative older cousins, the hosted solutions, these guys act like they are living at the edge. They tell stories in bars about their latest conquests and they are always trying to prove theirs is bigger. Story after story hits the wires (and my inbox) on who they have been beating head to head in CRM client competitions and what client they stole from whom. They are as competitive as 20-year-old males in a singles bar. Frankly, because those of us profoundly interested in this market are probably considerably older than 20, we don't really care about whether or not they are the biggest and baddest or what their latest conquest is. What we care about is: do they deliver the goods?

You know what? They do. The net natives can put meat behind their sometimes excessive claims. I spent the better part of 2003 doing intensive research and writing on this segment and it is impressive. I heard happy customer story after customer story which confirmed very high satisfaction rates, particularly with two of the ASPs—Salesnet and salesforce.com. The only company-specific complaints I heard more than once were about Upshot, though nothing dramatic.

This is a market with a new paradigm, pizzazz, and some real value. Aberdeen Group did a study of what turned out to be primarily small and medium-sized businesses in September 2003. That study, entitled "Hosted CRM Popularity Continues to Grow," found that 35 percent of their respondents were already using a hosted solution and 85 percent were willing to consider one in their deliberations. This when their CRM budget was increasing in 2003–2004. That was up from a February 2003 study also done by Aberdeen Group that had 52 percent of the respondents willing to consider this solution as a possibility.

Gartner Group is not as giddy about this model as Aberdeen, Yankee Group, and Summit or many other analysts and commentators. Wendy Close, Gartner CRM research director, conducted a survey in August 2003 that found that by the end of 2004 more than one quarter of small and mid-sized businesses will choose hosted CRM. More than that, she also found that during that same time frame, CRM will have been integrated to the back office by more than 50 percent of those same respondents.

While this seems positive, she saw this as trouble for the ASPs who only host CRM. "The ASPs are still pretty new," Close said in an interview with SearchCRM's Barney Beal. "A lot of companies are using the hosted [providers] as short-term solutions until they go with the bigger vendors like Siebel." She then went on to predict that the economy's recovery will lead to more to spend on larger CRM deployments, and hosted vendors will suffer for it. But, this is in contradistinction to the Aberdeen findings.

While I often like what I read from Gartner and trust some of their key analysts (such as Michael Maoz) more than most, I don't agree with the Gartner interpretation. Paradigm shifts or "disruptive innovations" don't really allow for the return to the older paradigm. There is no reason to turn back to something that has been superseded or at least is competitively challenged by cost of ownership and price considerations, all other things being equal. The line has been crossed.

The Software as Subscription Model

At the stratospheric level, the business model for an on-demand utility dovetails with the current business ecosystem. It is focused on business processes that are aimed specifically at hearing the customer's cries and then actually meeting their needs and desires. In geek-speak, that means you are building a multitenancy, shared services model that relies on the service-oriented architecture to provide you with the customized business processes that you need. In English, this means that the costs to you are reasonable and the concerns you have for both IT infrastructure and business management are being answered in a way that you can live with. Will you always be happy with it? No. Nothing is as good as the hyperbolically effusive net natives make it sound. But it is good.

How? Multitenancy means that the host can handle numerous clients securely and independently on its infrastructure without disruption. In other words, multiple tenants. That means if you are up and running on infrastructure system #1 at Salesnet, you can continue operations without interruption even though a new 500-seat customer can be put up by them the same day at the same time you are running. In the meantime, the host doesn't have to buy new hardware or software to handle the new client, thus keeping their operating costs and own upfront investment down, and keeping the price and costs down for you.

The architecture supporting this infrastructure is typically a form of the service-oriented architecture (SOA). All of the net natives use a web services–based model. Salesforce.com's web services schema (see Figure 16-1) is an archetypal model for ASP web services architecture worth looking at. Where their model differs slightly with the net native norm is their use of Intellisync at the API level. If you own a personal digital assistant (PDA), you are likely to use some form of Intellisync. Pumatech, the creators of Intellisync, provides you with the service to synchronize your data to a PDA, cellphone, or other small mobile device. They have special editions built for your Blackberry or your HP iPAQ. But it is not often seen in a web services architectural schema. It is smart since synchronization between devices is one of the key facets of a successful mobile strategy for a company using on-demand utility services. Intellisync is the best at that in the business.

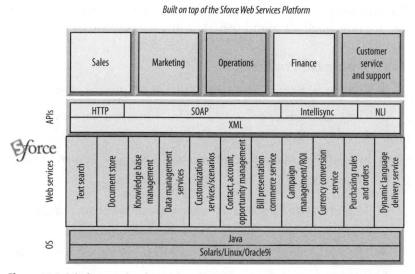

Figure 16-1: Salesforce.com's web services architecture is typical of a robust architecture for the ASP on the move.

What About the Data: Fear Factor Tamed

What's going to happen to my data? That's been a bigger, more frightening issue than anything else when it came to the location of customer data. I remember in the earlier days of hosting, it was impossible to break into the higher education market because they didn't want student information behind anyone's firewall but their own. During that era, the levels of security were still pretty infantile, so it was a real concern.

But what about now? Hackers are stealing credit card and Social Security numbers every day. Identity theft is the number one crime in America, and that is data theft when it comes down to it. Not only that, but hackers are getting increasingly sophisticated in their abilities to penetrate firewalls using worms and other hacker tools to seize control of even federally secure systems. Why shouldn't you be afraid of having an ASP holding your data on their systems? Not only that, but what if you decide to terminate your relationship with that ASP? They have your data hostage, don't they?

As they say in Italian, *calma, calma.* This is considerably less a cause for concern than you think. First, let's take a look at comparative security. Your system is no more secure than the system that the ASP has, and, in fact, is likely less secured. Let's look at all elements of security for this chapter's Steppin' Out champ salesforce.com so you can see how safe and sound your data and transactions actually are:

Physical Security at Qwest Data Center

▶ All their hardware is housed in a $10' \times 40'$ private cage.

▶ They have onsite security guards 24 hours a day, seven days a week.

▶ Indoors and outdoors security cameras monitor the private cage.

▶ Access screening is via picture, ID, and biometric.

▶ To go to raised floor areas within the data center requires an escort.

▶ There are trap door designs for access to the raised floor areas.

Internet Security

▶ Highest level 128-bit Secure Socket Layer (SSL) encryption is used for *all* Internet traffic (this is the same encryption used when you make a purchase on the Internet from Amazon.com or eBay or through PayPal).

▶ Global step-up certificates ensures full 128-bit encryption is used regardless of what country the user is in.

▶ Verisign certificate ensures site is not being spoofed. (Spoofing is when a site is accessed by a particular IP address, but a fake IP address is what shows up when checked.) Verisign is the premier digital certification authority in the world.

Network Security

▶ Cisco PIX hardware firewalls are used.

▶ They use minimal routable IP addresses

▶ Network address translation (NAT) for all servers minimizes points of possible attack.

► Separate subnets for marketing content servers and enterprise application servers keeps traffic from corporate website separate from the applications.

► Denial-of-service (DoS) protection automatically detects and shuts down DoS attacks.

► Centralized proactive log monitoring automatically scans for unusual activity. Using advanced pattern matching algorithms, they can correlate firewalls and intrusion detection system activity.

► Logs are stored in the datawarehouse for historic comparison. The application monitors itself for violations of either the multi-tenant security design or nonstandard URL access.

OPERATING SYSTEM SECURITY

► The Unix and Linux operating system is hardened and streamlined with all unnecessary ports and services shut down.

► Secure services avoid native code where possible to prevent hackers from exploiting security holes.

► Root services are not touched.

APPLICATION-LEVEL SECURITY

► All passwords are stored in MD-5 hash, which is a highly secure encryption method. End-user passwords can never be decrypted and displayed.

► There are several optional and even more restrictive password security policies that can be enabled, ranging from password length minimums and complexity to the ability to remember the last few passwords to prevent reuse.

► Invalid password lockout is used.

► Restricted access can be set by user profile or role. This is granular to the point that IP ranges can be set to limit where the user can access the system from. Login times can be set the same way.

► There is yearly security validation.

I hope that soothes your worries. But wait…what about the *ownership* of the data?

I checked into this while researching an article on the ASPs in summer 2003, because it does seem like that can be a problem. If you decide to dump the ASP, how do you get your data back? The ASP policies varied a little on this, but the general concern is unfounded. Upshot, prior to its purchase by Siebel, charged $25 for a copy of the data in SQL Server. Salesforce.com didn't charge you and gave you several options ranging from an Oracle database to an Excel file. Salesnet and Netsuite didn't charge and gave you a .CSV file to send you on your merry way. So your data is still your data. Really.

Just make sure you take care of this in your service level agreement.

Integration Challenges

Integration looms large when considering CRM, as you saw last chapter. One of the interesting questions facing the potential ASP customer is how to integrate their on-premise legacy systems, third-party applications, and business processes with the online "we-control-the-horizontal" systems that the ASP has at their data centers. Services-oriented architecture, because it is based on the common standard web services such as XML, is normally the way interactions, transactions, and messages between systems are sent. Each of the net natives has a slightly different approach, but fundamentally, they use web services to integrate to the back end.

'Twasn't always like this, lads and lassies. When the net natives began to emerge from the primeval slime, they often didn't include the back-office integration because CRM at that time was still the data-driven, traditional, front-office–facing island it came into the world as. But with the transition to the customer ecosystem and its process-driven version of CRM, the extended value chain which included CRM became the focus of the net native. Consequently, web services–based integration platforms became part of the architecture.

Salesnet has the most interesting approach to integration. Because they specialize in deep sales process functionality—the best in the market—integration is a particularly vital issue for them. They don't provide the enterprise functions that salesforce.com or NetSuite do. They don't pretend to either. So they know they are being included as part of the extended value chain. They aren't providing it. Consequently, they have had to come up with a solid framework for integration. They have done so, using what they call integration links and "integration as a service."

Integration links are configurable links that when clicked pass on information that is acquired in Salesnet to an external application for action of some sort. For example, if you are securing a sale and need to see the levels of inventory available for the product you sold, one click and the information is retrieved from your inventory management system.

They are doing the same thing when they provide integration as a service, except that they are doing it for you. They have built more than 200 connectors to commonly used applications that reside along the extended value chain. For example, the obvious—SAP, Siebel, People-Soft, Oracle, Lotus Notes, and Microsoft Great Plains. They use them at their locations to develop your integration links and then they work with you to configure them.

If you want to take it even further, they will provide you with web services APIs, as will most of the other net natives, to build your own custom connectors.

While integration is still by no means a slam dunk, the service-oriented architectures of the present and future make it a lot easier to handle integration than it has been.

What's My Line? Online, Offline...

What makes the ASP market even more interesting is the loose-limbed mobility that all the services seem to provide, especially the net natives. It makes sense, since they are premised on the web browser, that they have a good set of mobile applications for the road warrior you are or aspire to be. All the net natives mentioned have offline editions that provide you with a final snapshot before you become Internet-challenged (in other words, disconnected). The snapshots look identical to the online versions and will update automatically when you reconnect.

There is often confusion between offline and wireless editions. The simple way to differentiate is this: the offline edition is actually offline, meaning that you are disconnected from the Internet. You can enter your data into the offline version, which is usually on your laptop. When you reconnect, using synchronization, you can bidirectionally update all the data entered by you and your colleagues while you were offline. This makes you completely current with the online version.

A wireless edition is what it sounds like. It retains the Internet connection and allows for real-time updates through wireless devices. Those devices could be a Blackberry or a PDA or Palm device. It could also be a laptop that has a wireless 802.11b or 802.11g capability either built in or available through a PCMCIA card. It is not a snapshot such as the one that the offline version provides. It is real-time connectivity through a wireless device. Data remains up to the minute. In the offline version, data becomes up to the minute when you get back online and only then.

The Missing Link Is Found: On to Analytics

One of the late blooming complaints about the ASP market was that they couldn't provide the sophisticated analytics that the enterprise independent software vendors (ISVs) and companies like SAS could in the on-premise environment. They can't. But they can provide probably the level of analytics that most companies who would be interested in them need. That's what counts anyway, isn't it? It is appealing to think that you can leverage real-time analytics applications that are included in your monthly service fee, rather than the always very costly purchase and maintenance of the analytics applications in-house.

"Now that companies have accepted that sales force automation, for example, can be safely provided as a utility service, they are beginning to view other, more sophisticated, functions—such as analytics—in the same way," Former Yankee Group CRM analyst Sheryl Kingstone told *CRMDaily* in an interview in 2003.

Interestingly, because of the increasing warmth of this idea, companies like Island Data and RevenueScience, who provide the analytics engines for the hosted services market, gained a substantial market share in 2003, rising from a 13 percent piece of the market to 22 percent in a year.

Each of the major net natives such as salesforce.com, Salesnet, NetSuite and RightNow have analytic dashboards so you can view whatever results you've configured in visually graphic real time through your browser.

Value Proposition: The Pluses and Minuses

The upside to the net native model is sizeable. Not only can you concentrate on your actual business and avoid the headaches that come with doing CRM yourself, but...

Chief Financial Officers Love this Stuff

What is the benefit to them? There is a lower cost of ownership, relatively insignificant upfront costs, and flexible pricing with considerably less risk attached. There are no cost overruns because you are paying for subscription services, not extensive consulting fees. The CFO can amortize the costs of the subscription. All in all a good deal.

The lower cost of ownership is dramatic. While the numbers are only as accurate as their source, I would at least view this as an approximation of what the reality is. Yankee Group is an analyst firm that has been supportive of the ASP space so these numbers are most likely skewed a bit toward that bias. However, they do provide some Wagnerian mental thunder when you see them. In Table 16-1, I'm giving you the numbers for a 150-person mid-sized deployment, which is where the ASP still is most popular, though there is movement to the larger numbers of seats. The vendor for the enterprise CRM ISV is generic or maybe Siebel in disguise. The ASP is salesforce.com. Salesforce.com can be used as a characteristic example for all ASPs, with the costs for the ASP at pretty much their maximum.

Table 16-1: Cost of Enterprise ISV Implementation and Net Native Configuration (Source: The Yankee Group, via salesforce.com)

Total Cost of Ownership (TCO)	Traditional CRM Generic Costs (150 Users)	Salesforce.com Enterprise Edition (150 Users)
Licenses and subscription	$300,000	$225,000
Support/upgrade cost	$54,000	$0
Implementation and customization	$900,000	$56,250
IT infrastructure/hosting costs	$125,000	$0
IT personnel support	$150,000	$0
Training costs (all)	$45,000	$22,500
Totals	$1,574,000	$303,750

The license and subscription fees aren't too far apart—perhaps around $75,000. But there are two things to note. First, the net native fees include upgrades, support, hosting cost and help desk—at least at salesforce.com. But also don't forget the subscription fee is ongoing and fixed, while the fees for upgrades and licenses for the upgrades for example depend on the customer's comfort with sustaining the product for its full lifecycle. While there are variables that aren't apparent in the table, ultimately, the conclusion to draw is that the TCO is considerably cheaper using a hosted model—whether the table is entirely accurate in reflecting the cost over time or not.

Chief Information Officers (CIOs) Love this Stuff

This is where the net native's multitenant architecture starts to strut its stuff. The big advantage of a multitenant architecture is its ability to securely host and segregate potentially thousands of customers within a single framework. If you are comfortable having your data behind someone else's firewall—and you should be at this point with the security available—then you can hand off a huge amount of IT overhead that would otherwise have gone to administering and maintaining this generally very complex environment. You can deploy your IT staff to do other things that you probably need more.

Once you've ameliorated your staffing overhead problems and related cranial pain, the value of an extremely rapid deployment becomes clear. While the ASP's universal claims of everyone in the galaxy under 30 days are exaggerated, there is a vast difference between the typical 15–90 day deployment times with net native services and the implementation times of 4–18 months for traditional CRM. In response to the ASP speed, traditional CRM vendors are all pushing much shorter deployment times and, to some extent, are succeeding. The reality is that their typical time and cost are much greater no matter what they try to do to improve it.

Of course, another headache that throbs in the CIO's skull is the need to educate and involve the end-users. This is easy. Staff and administrator training is online and often in a blended learning environment (see Chapter 21 for more on CRM learning management systems), and the systems themselves are fairly intuitive. When not intuitive, there are usually wizards to guide you through how to go about your daily tasks from lead management to forecasting.

If all of this wasn't enough to make a CIO salivate, this will. Upgrades—a word that sends images of the little child coming out of the crypt in *The Ring* shooting into CIO brains.

Upgrades are ordinarily one of the most brutal, time consuming, and costly aspects of a CRM or any enterprise-level application. Why? To kick this part of the discussion off, the words of Kaiser Mulla-Feroze of salesforce.com: "For many large enterprises, there is a two- to four-year product lifecycle. When it finally becomes time to upgrade, the upgrades are totally disruptive for the big boys."

Upgrades are often even more difficult than the original implementation. Not only does the upgrade have new code to deal with which might create conflicts with existing operating system and application code, but now there is a two- to four-year accumulation of data, customized structures, possibly custom code, and interfaces that have been configured to take into account. Additionally, because you are running your own instance of the CRM applications, you have to shut down the system (most likely) and begin installations and reconfigurations to make the upgrade smooth. There will be process changes necessary to conform to the new system. It is also likely that you are going to bring in consultants again to handle the upgrade. You know how that goes. Finally, the amount of labor time spent can be hundreds of man-days, especially if there are upgrade problems. You know what? Most of the time, there are.

The ASPs have the old-timers beat by miles in this department. Multitenant architecture can provide a platform for a universal upgrade to the entire system for all users and then allow each of the users to choose how they want to upgrade without a single second of interruption. Since the upgrade has already been executed, it is a matter of minutes or, at the most, hours until the individual company's entire system has been upgraded.

RightNow deals with the upgrade process very effectively, if not the most elegantly, through their Hosting Management System. They provide individuated and selective upgrading. E-mails with links and steps to the upgrade process are sent to each client. They provide a simple way to a complete nondisruptive upgrade if the client chooses to and when the client wants to.

Each six to eight weeks, there is a new upgrade for RightNow. Does that seem like an excessive amount of upgrading? If it does, when you get your e-mail with the links to the upgrade, don't do it. The links in the e-mail are to the new features that can be configured, release notes, computer-based training (CBT), and a schedule setup for time and date of the upgrade should you want to. Click. Click. Click. Click. Voilà, you are upgraded.

What happens backstage is that a complete copy is made of your system once you've accepted the upgrade. The copy is upgraded and sent back and becomes your system with full data integration and synchronization for any changes that had been made from the time between acceptance, upgraded copy, and the present. All the upgrades are done automatically with all new features and changes scripted. No human is involved on either side except to accept the agreement to upgrade—or not.

With salesforce.com's release of Spring '04, their upgrade process is not selective at all but perhaps certainly easier. All they do is push a button and all 10,000 users are upgraded. No muss, no fuss, no disruptions.

Vice Presidents of Sales Love this Stuff

What about the users and executives who actually use the features and are not concerned as much with technology or cost? The entire idea of using a hosted system is to make sales, marketing, and support easier and actually ubiquitous. Vice presidents of sales are always thrilled with the idea that their salespeople have the corporate data they need available to them, whether at home or on the road, via laptop or PDA. Plus it's not hard to use and can be accessed via a browser. But I would caution that regardless of the ease of use, salespeople are typically loath to adapt to a new way of doing business so there is some cultural transformation and training necessary to get the sales teams acclimatized to the new environment. Whether that environment is hosted or on your own servers is immaterial to the need to change but material to how to effect that change. With substantially intuitive (salesforce.com) and even comfortable (Salesnet) user interfaces, the adoption rate is going to be higher for the ASP because the pain involved is considerably lower. But you know how it goes. In order for something to be moved from lead management to opportunity management it has to be entered into the system to begin with.

The Negatives

No matter how strongly I feel about this exciting paradigm, there are some functional holes in their services and a few concerns that have to be addressed.

Be careful. ASP claims are more often the products of marketing and spin than absolute veracity. While the claims of lower cost of ownership are real, they are not as substantial as claimed. The accepted levels of actual benefit (at least as analyst thinking goes) are 25 percent over the license vendors in a four-year period, not the often larger claims made by the net natives. The four years is based on the lifecycle of a particular product release from any given CRM vendor.

Reducing all ASPs' value proposition further is their inability to provide the "right brained" services that many licensed CRM vendors do either directly or through channel partners and outside consulting organizations. If you go net native, realize you won't get deep strategic services, value creation services, change management, or any other human performance–related benefits. The best you'll get is what Salesnet provides with their business analysts. These companies are in the business of application management, whether they own the applications or someone else does. The TCO suffers a further hit by the omission of the strategic services that are ignored by the ASPs, but still necessary. CRM is a philosophy and a business strategy, supported by a system and a technology, not just a technology.

There are some attempts to begin to improve the business services provided by the net natives, however. Many of the improvements are already provided by Salesnet—business analysts who work with you to tailor your business processes or changes that you will make to them with their services. The idea is that when you are up and running, *you* are up and running, not the net native. However, these are not strategic services; they are tactically focused business process dissection services. Companies like salesforce.com are experimenting with developing a partner channel that can handle the implementation services, but that is in its youth at the time of publication.

Best Vendors: Salesforce.com (see Steppin' Out in this chapter); Salesnet; Netsuite; RightNow, Siebel OnDemand: Upshot Edition. Chapter 25 will examine each of these companies independently.

STEPPIN' OUT: Salesforce.com Is Hot, Hot, Hot

When the history of CRM is recounted around the post-apocalyptic campfires, long after the Orcs have been crushed, it will be said that there was a paradigm shift in CRM during the early part of the second millennium. CRM went from a traditional, very costly, and time consuming on-premise applications model to a low-cost, web services–based model. And, lo, it is likely that salesforce.com will be the name that is chanted as sculptor of that paradigm. For the most part, that is the truth.

It is an important company in the creation of this new and successful business model.

If you've read the second edition of this book, you'll note that I was critical of them. Not hypercritical, but critical. That led to a call from their CEO, Marc Benioff, who told me he loves to convince skeptics. He asked if he could try to convince me. I told him to take his best shot—he did, and he hit the bull's-eye. I'm now convinced that the hosted harbingers are the likely future of CRM, though, to hedge my bets, not the only future for CRM.

Salesforce.com's corporate strategy and culture and their services will be discussed in more detail in the last section of this book, but they are the Steppin' Out choice here for a good reason. At the enterprise level (read: extended value chain) they represent the best of breed. They have a successful business model that led to Gartner Group calling them number one in CRM customer satisfaction in 2003. I used a random reference check method I call References+ to check out the claim. It bore out. I found very happy customers. As a result of their achievement of these noteworthy heights of customer happiness, they have 10,000 clients and 150,000 individual users—a formidable number indeed.

Their business model is something that customers can easily get their arms around. You pay a flat recurring subscription fee monthly, annually, or whatever seems to be a good payment plan for you. There are no installation costs. A CFO has to love this. It's a predictable cost. Cost overruns don't have to be a concern—often a frequent issue in traditional CRM. Siebel implementations are notorious for their overruns.

What makes this an even greater customer benefit is that you get the customization/configuration tools at no extra cost too. That came after some balking from the customers in adopting salesforce.com due to the fears of IT losing its handle on the system.

"We spent some time gradually eliminating all the hurdles of technology control," says Kaiser Mulla-Feroze, "That had been a real concern of our potential customers' IT staffs over the last couple of years. They were reluctant to go with us because they felt like they were abdicating control."

To deal with this, especially with the release of customer-friendly Salesforce Spring '04, customization has become configuration. What that really means is that much of the technology is now developed by wizards that pop up and guide you through the process that allows you to develop workflow. They have released explicit workflow automation tools to allow the nontechnical hobbits among you to develop your own workflow by following pop-up onscreen instructions written in your native tongue, not C++. Customization of basic business functionality is no longer at the level of programming and coding. As long as you have rights and permissions granted, you can configure a workflow using your keyboard and screen wizards. The same can be said for the development of complex sales processes. While the Miller-Heiman sales process is embedded in the system, any of the sales processes you care to adopt or craft yourself can be configured to the system with no-cost tools.

Lots of Editions

With its release of its Winter '04 and then Spring '04 versions, salesforce.com increased the number and type of its offerings to a full complement that meets the needs of any sized or styled group of users.

- **Personal Edition** Hey, folks, this one is cost-free! Not a thin dime in cost. The only catch is that it is exactly what it says it is. You have a one-person edition that is good for yourself and no one else at all. Plus you'll get hit with ads for upgrading within an hour of downloading and installing this edition. I know that for certain, because I'm using it now. It's a very good tool to test the basic sales functionality that an individual salesperson or sales manager will be using. It's worth whatever aggravation you might get from the ads. This edition is a gem and a great quick test to see how well it works.

- **Team Edition** When this edition was announced for a five-user or fewer cost of $995 in early 2003, it was the first positive word I said about salesforce.com. I praised it in an article as an eminently affordable option for a small business. It provides a strong sales-heavy service to the very small user for a reasonable price. In fact, with its basic functionality, the total cost of ownership is about $3,000 for three years including everything imaginable from setup to monthly fees to maintenance to upgrades.

- **Professional Edition** This is the edition that most of the small and medium businesses will gravitate toward. It provides the basic services needed to run a successful business with a CRM strategy. That includes the standard SFA applications such as lead management, account, contact, and opportunity management, plus some forecasting capability. Additionally, the simplest marketing and services applications such as case management, solution management, and activity management plus mass e-mailing are packaged with this rendering. Reporting and some analytic tools are also provided. This is a good solution for basic business CRM needs. The price: $65 per user per month.

▶ **Enterprise Edition** It gets considerably more robust when you come to this version of salesforce.com. It is using this edition that allows a company like Sungaard to deploy over 1,000 seats. This is both deeper and broader in scope than the Professional Edition. For example, unlike the Professional Edition, this version provides full campaign marketing tools. It provides more sophisticated SFA tools, such as product revenue tracking, which allows you to develop creative pricing schemes and to track the opportunities associated with those schemes, as well as the product catalogs you need to determine price, quantity, discount, and so on. It adds such large scale functionality as document and file management and contract management in addition to integrating with back-office functions. Both the Offline and Wireless Editions are included at no extra cost with the Enterprise Edition. What has been particularly interesting since the Winter '04 Enterprise Edition is the addition of the workforce automation tools mentioned above, some very snazzy-looking and useful dashboards (see Figure 16-2), and response management tools that keep your service responses consistent regardless of how and when the customer accesses your service group. The workflow automation tools are easy to use, though not intuitive. The workflow engine is rules-based; the engine handles task routing; and uses triggers such as, "send this document to manager X for approval after it is approved by salesperson Y. If it is not approved in three days by salesperson Y, send him a reminder." You can use this level of workflow to set up rudimentary channel management capabilities, but that doesn't mean you can expect a full-blown PRM service.

The Enterprise Edition, in combination with Sforce 3.0, allows you to develop custom configurations for your company. For example, they can provide vertically specific business processes that link your CRM

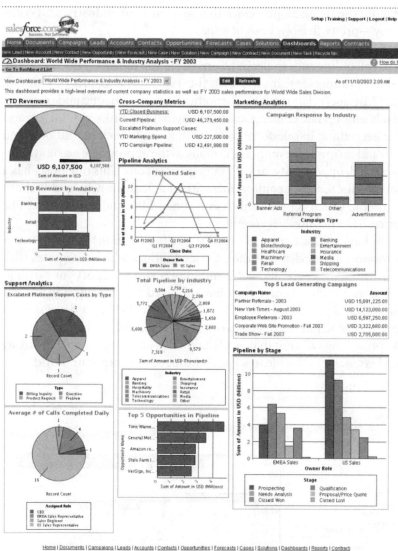

Figure 16-2: This salesforce.com dashboard covers a wide range of customized results for the entire value chain—in a very pretty way.

sales front end to your inventory management capabilities, which typically reside in the supply chain (see Chapter 15). Take a look at Figure 16-3—inventory management for the oil and gas industry. What makes this excellent is that you can actually develop what you need to handle the business processes that govern your industry and company—pretty flexibly, I might add.

Salesforce.com has Offline and Wireless Editions that do pretty much what all offline and wireless editions do. It also has an Outlook Edition, which promises integration with the 198,000,000 copies of Outlook that Microsoft claims exists. Theoretically, users can send and receive e-mails and update contacts, calendar items, and tasks in Outlook and log everything in salesforce.com. With a single click in Outlook, you can add incoming or outgoing e-mails to the appropriate account, contact, lead, opportunity, or case in salesforce.com. This obviously has a lot of value for those comfortable with or at least knowledgeable about Outlook, which is pretty much everyone in the known universe. The price: $125 per user per month.

In January 2004, using Sforce 3.0 (see next section), salesforce.com announced the release of their Office Edition, which integrates with Microsoft Office XP and 2003 and allows you to export your data to Excel and Office. Where they have showed real foresight is in their understanding of especially Microsoft Office 2003 as a development environment, not just a set of word processing and mathematical tools. Approaching Office at that level makes this edition particularly strong and eminently valuable to a good chunk of the corporate world.

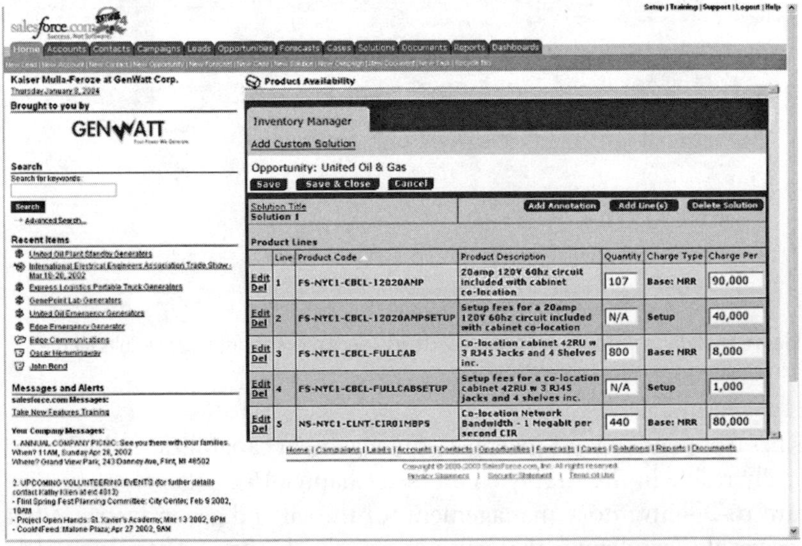

Figure 16-3: Saleforce.com gives you the means to link industry-specific business processes to the integrated value chain.

An Sforce to Be Reckoned With

Salesforce.com calls Sforce 3.0 "the first on-demand application server." To most of you reading this book, that either is meaningless or at least puzzling. However, Sforce 3.0 is important if you're concerned with building custom services and applications or making sure that your salesforce.com services are tightly integrated with your existing information technology infrastructure. Sforce consists of the following:

- An architectural framework

- A platform

- Custom objects that are reusable, extensible, and can be specifically created for individual business processes

- A SQL-like query language they call Sforce object query language (OQL)

- A set of web service–related APIs to make integration "easier," if such a thing is possible

- Controls that can be developed in the normal development languages for user interfaces and forms

In other words, an environment that is explicitly designed to create a highly sophisticated process-driven, web services–oriented platform and to solve those problems what ails ye—and just ye alone if ye so choose.

So pay attention to the salesforce.com model. Remember what I said about those post-apocalyptic campfires. They are one of the leaders of the present and will be remembered for it well into the future.

The Hosted Solutions: Old School, New Approach

Interesting. In the grand scheme of things, these guys—companies like USinternetworking, Corio, and Surebridge—seem to be lost in the shuffle. They are the quiet, conservative cousins who represent the older generation of ASPs. The ones that failed in the late '90s through 2001. All the buzz is around the net natives. Yet there are some viable companies that have a model that is not hybrid, but still sits in between the net natives and the standalone solutions. These solutions providers host applications from other CRM companies. They are priced differently, ordinarily hitting you with license and (fixed) implementation fees. On top of that, they can charge monthly per user fees too. They can be expensive to set up.

So what is the advantage of this kind of company? It's hard to see, isn't it?

Typically, the advantage is not a lot when compared to the net natives, but the reality is that they shouldn't be compared to the net natives. They work from a very different business model and currently target different markets, though that is rapidly becoming a thing of the past.

Keep in mind what they do. Companies like Surebridge, probably the best of the hosted solutions outfits, provide hosted and full-featured versions of PeopleSoft and Microsoft CRM. Where their solution becomes a distinct advantage is when the overhead required to configure and maintain a full-featured CRM product is high and the level of service necessary to develop the system is deep. For example, as noted in earlier chapters, one of the few weaknesses of the MSCRM product is the heavy server requirements for running the product. By using Surebridge's Microsoft CRM Online, you eliminate the heavy server requirements, because Surebridge owns the servers that your MSCRM "instance" sits on. Consequently, the value of MSCRM to a small or medium business is significantly higher because the server requirements and the hardware and overhead associated with it are gone, leaving the core CRM Sales and Service applications at your beck and call. Let's take a closer look at three of the best vendors.

USinternetworking

USinternetworking (USi) has strong SLAs that apply to the platform, hardware, connectivity, Siebel applications process, and security. In February 2004, USi officially announced the availability of payroll and payroll tax processing services that came along with May 2003's purchase of Interpath. Even though they have already offered these business process services prior to the 2003 announcement, the idea was to enter into a new market beyond just CRM, but responsive to CRM's new process-driven model—Business Process Outsourcing (BPO).

CRM packages offered include:

- ▶ Siebel

- ▶ Oracle (in conjunction with Deloitte Consulting)

- ▶ Specialized CRM applications services through their AppHost managed applications service

Corio

Corio is interesting because they not only provide a hosted solution in the old style, but also an on-demand version that is a fixed monthly fee. But they unlink themselves from the license sale that may be tied to the vendor's programs. That means you are still paying for the licenses, just not their monthly fees.

They also provide application maintenance services, but really aren't aimed at actually doing the implementation at the early stages. Their value proposition, according to studies, brings a 50 percent cost benefit to the customer, though I can't speak to what that comprises.

CRM packages offered include:

- ► Siebel

- ► PeopleSoft

- ► SAP

- ► Oracle

- ► E.piphany

Surebridge

Surebridge has what is perhaps the smartest business model of all of the conservative cousins. It calls itself an "applications outsourcing management" company because, unlike the net natives, they provide strategy, implementation, and maintenance services for their portfolio CRM applications. They actually are the premier provider of hosted MSCRM, Microsoft's highly surprising CRM product (see Chapter 4). Through their fixed price and fixed scope implementation of MSCRM, they transfer one of the biggest MSCRM headaches, its very significant server requirements, to their server farms, keeping it from yours. This comes from the acquisition of one of the earlier providers of hosted MSCRM, Managed Ops, and it has been a great source of revenue for Surebridge—40 percent of their CRM revenues the first year. This also means with MSCRM 1.2's release and its improved hosting architecture, it can only be a better service offered by Surebridge in the future. At this writing, Surebridge was being purchased by NaviSite, a company that has been acquiring hosted services since 2002. It will be interesting to see how Surebridge fares under NaviSite's ownership.

CRM packages offered include:

▶ MSCRM

▶ PeopleSoft

▶ Siebel

What ASPs Are and Aren't: Other Flavors

So that we can move on and so you are clear with what else is out there, I'm going to give you a small taste of the other hosted possibilities you might run across and their advantages and disadvantages.

One Permutation: Verticals/Specialists

There are a growing number of hosted services that provide either industry-specific approaches and solutions or a specialist application that has CRM ramifications. What they don't provide is the broader range of services that appeal to the larger marketplace.

The Vertical Version

RWD Technologies, not known for its online services, hosts a version of its OTIS application, a pharmaceutical industry CRM solution with a highly granular auditing and document management engine. It is their application of both Siebel ePharma, the best vertical CRM application for the pharmaceuticals industry, and Documentum, the leading enterprise document management system in the industry. RWD developed the connectors for the two disparate applications so they work seamlessly together and then developed a hosted solution that is at a rented data center.

The Specialist Segment

As you will see in Chapter 18, one of the key elements of CRM strategy in this increasingly litigious and suspicious era is compliance. The Sarbanes-Oxley Act in particular, imposing intense strictures on financial reporting and accounting to combat fraud such as Enron, sent the auditors and accounts of most companies into a frenzy. (More on the details later.) Many of the enterprise software vendors and CRM vendors see Sarbanes-Oxley compliance as a really lucrative market and they are providing dozens of solutions for accounting antifraud compliance. Most of the packages are from companies like SAS who provide analytic applications to identify potential patterns and areas for fraud. There are some leading-edge ASPs also providing these services, such as Concur, known for their hosted accounting solutions. But don't be looking for anything beyond the specialty.

In terms of value proposition pluses and minuses, it's pretty straightforward on both counts. If you need it specifically for your industry or for its specific features, it is valuable because it is a hosted service. But if you don't, it clearly is not even a consideration. A negative if you do consider it—would you want someone to host your potential accounting problems that isn't a certified auditor? Not me, bucko.

In this case, there are no best vendors to mention because the only thing that can be said is, it depends on what you need done.

Another Permutation: License On-Premise Vendors Go Online

Traditional CRM vendors are jumping on the bandwagon because they need to hedge their bets as the online market takes off. While it wouldn't seem in the interest of, for example, PeopleSoft to have an online subscription-based version, many have launched one of their own or have gotten in bed with the hosted solutions crew (for example, PeopleSoft and Surebridge) so that they can chew a chunk off of the anticipated large CRM online services market in ensuing years.

However, their online services are organized differently than the net natives. In fact, they are directly competing with the hosted solutions companies. They provide full-featured instances of their applications but at their data centers, on their servers, with their administration. Best Software's recently acquired ACCPAC International Inc. joined the online party in mid-2003, when it began offering a hosted version of its CRM application, called ACCPACcrm.com. Best Software also has a hosted version of SalesLogix (see Chapter 4).

What makes the ACCPAC offering interesting isn't that it has a hosted version of CRM. Its CRM offering is okay, but not as strong as SalesLogix, for example. But ACCPAC offers extensively integrated back-office functionality to the midmarket, and thus, like net native salesforce.com and NetSuite, could provide full enterprise services to their SMB targets. ACCPAC.com already offers an online version of its accounting application—where it made its reputation.

They are keeping costs attractive. ACCPAC offers free 30-day trials of its online software aimed at small and mid-sized businesses. Companies can start out paying as little as $995 up front for the sales force automation (SFA) software. The product ACCPACcrm.com Sales Team, which includes SFA with some marketing automation, costs $49 per user per month and $69 per month for the enterprise version.

Value Proposition: Plus and Minus

On-premise vendor hosted applications become useful to you if you need the full-featured applications and don't have a staff to support those applications. For example, PeopleSoft provides their entire enterprise solution and the former J.D. Edwards solutions via hosting services. That means you can get integrated CRM, supply chain management, and ERP solutions customized to your specifications. The variety of hosted applications available is mind-boggling. They provide a variety of SLAs to satisfy your requirements. The contracts can range from 24 to 60 months depending on the needs and the plan. The number of concurrent users can range from 100 to 500. They promise uptime between 99.5 and 99.9 percent depending on your plan choice. The more substantial plans support SQL Server, Oracle, and DB2 so you're never caught short in the choice of databases. Seems good, doesn't it? If you're a PeopleSoft or J.D. Edwards devotee, it can be good. It'll save you the headache of handling your own system. But there are negative aspects, which include:

▶ The upfront costs typically are still higher than the net natives.

▶ You have to buy into the vendor's specific applications and its vision.

▶ Integration with other vendor's applications is dicey.

Does this mean I think that you should never use this sort of system? No. If you are considering PeopleSoft, this is one of the viable options you have. It can reduce your total cost of ownership (TCO), by reducing overhead and labor costs substantially. But there are the other considerations specific to this model. Best vendors are:

▶ PeopleSoft

▶ Onyx

▶ ACCPAC (not as well established, but quality)

Another Permutation: Hybrids

Hybrids are interesting and possibly viable though they haven't been that successful in practice—yet. That is primarily due to the lack of customers so far for the hybrid solutions, which became visible in late 2003 with the creation of the IBM/Siebel solution CRM OnDemand.

Anyone who has Siebel 6.0 or later will be able to "rent" the online version and link it to the on-premise CRM they already have. That way, they can extend their existing licensed applications and add features and functions without purchasing licenses but instead paying for subscriptions. Cingular Wireless opens their rented "lead generation" features to their business partners so they can enter leads online rather than having them entered directly into the on-premises system, making it considerably more convenient. Synchronization occurs with Siebel CRM OnDemand provided connectors that automatically synchronize the data entered online with the on-premise system.

Value Proposition: Pluses and Minuses

The pluses here are straightforward. If you have an investment in Siebel or any other vendor offering hybrid models, you can extend your investment at a low cost. In the case of Siebel CRM OnDemand, a joint venture between Siebel and IBM, the cost as of the end of 2003 is $70 per user per month. This is a lot less than typical Siebel maintenance costs.

Siebel OnDemand in particular has become the only player in this specific domain at this time. Gartner analyst Michael Maoz, perhaps the most intelligent and astute analyst in the CRM space (see Chapter 1 for his CRM definition) said, "Siebel's large customers should re-examine the feasibility of extending Siebel to parts of the organization previously left out for budgetary reasons." According to Maoz, Siebel's OnDemand service has a number of improved features. The most prominent of these are the simplicity of the interface, the reliability of the hosting partner, rich functions and workflow, embedded real-time analytics and built-in connections to back-office applications. In other words, it is a valuable extension to their existing customers feature set.

I'm not a big fan of Siebel's corporate culture, so for me to say that this might be a valuable service is a major compliment to Siebel's effort. I rarely give them kudos for anything, but this hybrid model has some value.

On the negative side, the weakness of a hybrid is that you're more likely to have either paid for the already expensive licenses and services to set up the original on-premise system or you're going to, so while the system is extensible, you've already paid substantial upfront costs.

Synchronization between mobile clients and primary servers is often a problem even in the traditional CRM environment. Using a hybrid model, which doesn't have a consistent single architecture, creates both synchronization difficulties and some functionality issues. Siebel claims that their Universal Architecture Network (UAN) integration framework will take care of this, but the book is still out on the UAN (more on that in Chapter 23).

The only vendor worth discussing here is Siebel/IBM CRM OnDemand.

Yet Another Permutation: We Have Both, You Get One

RightNow, one of the core ASPs, offers a unique model. They provide you with either the online or the on-premise version, but not both. If you are unhappy with one but like the features and functionality, you can simply switch. That means that you can reclaim your data and bring it on home or you can ship it out to let RightNow data centers (one owned by them, one leased from AT&T) handle it.

Because both versions are built on the same architectures, this model works pretty well.

Pay Attention: Getting the Most from "Them"

If you're sold on the ASP model or at least are going to give it a serious look, it's time to figure out what you have to do to protect yourself from over-promises or the unavoidable *faux pas* that are likely to occur. Remember, one of the tradeoffs you are making is that you really do have less control over your system's fate than if it were in-house. The disadvantage of multitenancy is that if it goes down and there is backup failure—a highly unlikely scenario—you can't just call in someone to fix it. You have to let the ASP do that. You are at the mercy of their problems, which may not be caused by your system—unless you have some doofus who managed to breach them and do damage.

That means protection is in order. The key to your protection will be contained in the SLA, but before I go into detail, use the following broad guidelines:

> ▶ **CRM is CRM, not just software, not just services.** Many of the same decisions that you have to make for a standalone application

are decisions that you face with ASPs too. These include user-based strategies, allowance for cultural change, adoption issues, changes to your corporate business processes, as well as technical issues such as integration, data storage, and user interfaces. In the ASP environment, your relationship to them does not end with rollout, so your choice of vendor is mission critical. Are you interested in working with a vendor who over-promises? What is their culture like? Can you count on them to deliver their commitments over a lengthy time? This is not a small thing.

▶ **Integration isn't so easy.** Most ASP vendors use partners to handle many of the services they provide, so integration, touted as a no-brainer by most ASPs, can be a big headache. For example, several of them use Eloqua to handle their e-mail blasting or lead generation. Understand where the functionality that you are getting is actually coming from before you commit to it.

▶ **You get what you pay for.** The lower TCO and simple monthly subscription fees are tradeoffs for leaner functionality, simpler workflow, and lack of strategic services. Ignore the ASPs' claims that they are as robust as enterprise vendors. They aren't. There is no comparison between any net native analytical tools (notoriously lacking) and PeopleSoft's Enterprise Performance Management (EPM) tools.

▶ **Don't believe the hype, which is fast and furious.** In an informal study for an article, *CIO* magazine found that only one of the companies they spoke with managed to effectively roll out their ASP CRM in four weeks, despite the claims of multiple vendors. Salesforce.com makes the claim that 90 percent of their 8,000 customers have been rolled out in 30 days or less—a claim at odds with the *CIO* magazine unscientific, but interesting survey. Decide who you want to believe and act accordingly. I will say this, salesforce.com continually surprises me with their ability to actually back up their claims so I wouldn't just discount this one. But I would check it out before I gave it a carte blanche kiss of approval.

Your Service Level Agreement (SLA)

Your best protection is a very strong and detailed service level agreement. While you may personally trust the ASP executive team and its entire staff, this is still a necessity that you cannot ignore. Why? Like any other contract, the SLA is a set of guarantees in the event of problems. If things go perfectly, there is no need for contractual agreements. Life would be beautiful, uptime 100 percent, and you'd have all the access you needed to all the people you wanted anywhere in the world without cost. Plus you could get free stuff. But, as we all sadly know, that ain't the way it works. So the SLA has to be in place to do several things:

- ► Create a binding agreement

- ► Guarantee a scope and level of service

- ► Establish benchmarks and metrics for that level of service

- ► Handle problem resolution without room for interpretation as to how the problem is to be solved

Make sure the following issues are covered:

- ► **Uptime** The oft-made promise of 99.9 percent uptime (five minutes monthly downtime) isn't realistic, but 95 percent means downtime near 37 hours! Be careful on your downtime commitments. Make sure that you have guarantees for at least 99.5 percent uptime and more if you can get it. There are possible ASP restrictions on the uptime or on downtime (such as for maintenance). Review them carefully before you agree to them. They could well affect you, though with the multitenant infrastructure, this is less and less an issue.

- ► **Coverage** Make sure that you have coverage 365 days, 7 days a week, 24 hours a day. In other words, all year long with no off days or even off hours. Despite it seeming obvious, get it in writing.

- ► **Speed** Make sure that the time for page loading is written into the SLA—less than one second is a good benchmark. Less than 250 milliseconds is an optimal (and almost unattainable) number. Page load times can be as much as two to five seconds and there are ASPs who consider that acceptable. I wouldn't. Think about 300 concurrent users waiting five seconds each time a page comes up on the browser. That will be 300 highly frustrated users. Get a guaranteed time.

- ► **Problem resolution** Problems occur regularly. That is an inevitability you live with. Get in writing a short response time or time to problem resolution. Be willing to pay a premium for significantly shorter response times to resolution than the guaranteed. Outline times to resolution for specific problems, if you can pin the ASP down that far. Make sure that the means for detection and tracking are spelled out. Get the ASP to include regularized (such as monthly) reports on the system downtime and other problems so you are aware of how effective overall this system is. This is a way of measuring against the performance benchmarks that are included in the SLA. Contract for help desk support as part of the agreement.

▶ **Reimbursement** Include service or dollar credit for performance shortfalls. Make sure performance windows are involved (for example, different penalties for 2:00 P.M. and 2:00 A.M. downtime) with enforcement measures from escalated meetings to contract termination.

▶ **Services** The scope of services definition needs to be crystalline, despite the informal relationships you may have with the ASP. No matter how friendly or long term the relationship has been, get a detailed scope of services, even if the owner of the ASP is your mother.

▶ **Appropriate pricing** Don't pay for what you don't need. For example, make the response time definition exactly what is needed and make sure it costs what it should. For example, three days response time should reduce the overall price by X dollars if you can live with it, relative to a one-day response time.

▶ **Data transfer** Make sure you know how data would be handled if you terminate the vendor's services, or you could cut your own throat. Also see that clauses are included that stipulate that the data is owned by the customer, even though it resides on the ASP's system. Make sure that you get periodic copies of your data from the ASP. Include it in the SLA—either exact penalties and/or spell out procedures in the event of data loss or unauthorized data transfer.

▶ **Disasters** Make sure that there are provisions for disaster recovery in the SLA.

▶ **Security** See if you can get an included SLA on security—even if it costs you a premium. Minimally, make sure that the security measures that the ASP is taking are outlined in the scope of services. (See the salesforce.com security measures as a good example.) That should include possible restrictions you might face. Have them stipulate to both confidentiality and the integrity of their staff—meaning that they will state that the ASP staff will not commit any security violations. Again, it's not a matter of mistrust; it is a matter of security.

▶ **Termination** Finally, as in any good contract, make sure there are clauses for termination and remedies for breach included. The termination clause should include a smooth transition of data and all other cooperation that is necessary to make sure you regain complete control of all of your operations and transactions back with not even a shadow left on the ASP's system when you leave. Remedies for various breaches of the SLA should be spelled out clearly. They could be anything from refunds to liquidated damages to credits for problems or contractual breaches.

Obviously, the operant words here are "care" and "exactitude." Be very specific, leave nothing to interpretation or chance (as best you can) and you'll be very satisfied with your results.

Having CRM hosted is a significant cost-effective and valuable option if you can get past what are primarily psychological hurdles. Two years ago, I would never have said this. Now not only do I say it, but I would recommend it as a consideration when you are planning your CRM strategy.

That, my friends, segues us into the next chapter on—what else?—CRM strategy.

PART V
The Kernel

17

CRM Strategy: First in Plan, First in Implementation, First in the Heart of the Customer

"The anticipation was greater than the event." Has there ever been a truer statement than this? Think about it. Do you get excited when you're planning to go to Best Buy to purchase a plasma TV or getting ready for a long cruise to the Bahamas? Then you buy the plasma TV or you go on the cruise. Within a week or two of either event, you are planning the next purchase and the next vacation. This is the way life works, isn't it? Plan, execute; plan, execute; plan, execute—and plan again. We smack our lips in anticipation of what's next. When it comes to the big things in life, we love to dream and plan on how we are going to realize those dreams.

Then why is it that studies done by countless research agencies come up with the same conclusion? One of the primary reasons for outright failure in CRM is the inability to plan for it.

It can be even worse than just an "inability." There are numerous customers who actually think that they don't have to plan a strategy—just install and configure software. Remember the story in Chapter 1 of the company that bought all of the CRM modules of one of the enterprise vendors? Shame on the enterprise vendor for selling it to them knowingly. Sadly, this is not particularly unusual in the annals of customer brain cramps. Adam Golden, founder and principal of change management consultancy, Major Oak Consulting, has a long history in the strategic planning world. Here's what he has to say about this:

> While some companies struggle in developing a strategy, the issue is not just the inability to plan, but something much worse, the belief that a

strategy doesn't need to be developed. The reason can vary, whether it is because of a classic flaw in the project approach (driven by IT, fear of raising issues, limited budget, etc.) or because the sponsor already thinks they have the solution, but this happens in more cases than you want to believe. These companies that forgo the discipline and long-term thinking that a CRM strategy requires are the same companies that contribute to the disappointing CRM statistics such as limited sales force adoption and negative ROI.

The other problem that roams free range with lack of planning is poor planning. In fact, in 2001, Accenture and Wirthlin Worldwide queried Fortune 1000 executives and found that 74 percent felt that CRM fails due to flawed planning—too much reliance on technology and too little on basic business planning. Ironically, it's often the same complaining management who are the culprits in this particular problem.

CRM strategies and plans change as the bigger business picture changes. As the ecosystem goes, so goes CRM strategy. Steve Olyha, senior vice president and global general manager for CRM at Unisys, says:

> CRM strategic planning doesn't even resemble (when it's done right) what it did even five years ago. The difference falls in a couple of key areas. CRM is no longer as internally focused as it once was, where sales force automation was really just SMR—sales management reporting. It's much more multifunctional today, particularly relative to understanding process touch points across traditionally separated domains like marketing, inventory management, finance, as well as being a shared responsibility across the business and IT. Having a business case and key performance metrics is fundamental, and in fact is the basis for good strategic planning today.

CRM is one of the big things in life—business life. So planning well for it should be an imperative. If you don't think so, don't just skip this chapter; skip the book and skip CRM altogether. You aren't ready, comrade.

Prelude to a CRM Symphony

Trying to define CRM strategy is elusive. Look at these mini-definitions:

- ▶ "CRM strategy is about knowing your customers."
- ▶ "CRM strategy is about creating value for your shareholders."

- ► "CRM strategy is about the entire enterprise."

- ► "CRM strategy is about business process re-engineering around a customer-centric philosophy."

- ► "CRM strategy is about delivering tailored information sourced from contact management solutions or analytics."

- ► "E-CRM strategy is about enhanced customer service, interfacing with consumers the way they want."

The only thing these characterizations have in common is appalling English and their own agendas. What CRM strategy *isn't about* is poor language use or particular interests. Yet there is nothing inherently wrong with any of these statements.

Adding to the confusion, there are as many approaches to a CRM strategy as there are vendors, integrators, analysts, and consultants. To befuddle even the most sharply honed senses, there are also as many interpretations of what it is as there are approaches and definitions.

Each company will have a strategy that is tailored to their own thinking and exigencies. But there are certain steps in planning for our newly minted extended value chain that make universally good business sense in the early 21st century. They are not only classic best practices, but are suitable for the current CRM paradigms and processes.

The Overture and the Movements

Let's begin by looking at what you should know as you get seated into your orchestra chair. This chapter will be an overview of the elements of a CRM strategy. Chapters 18 through 22 will cover many of these elements in detail. The movements:

Chapter 18 Analyzing business processes

Chapter 19 The impact of cultural change on CRM initiatives

Chapter 20 Implementation strategies

Chapter 21 Communications and learning strategy

Chapter 22 Benefits, costs and their measurements (ROI and Metrics)

Think of Chapters 17 through 22 as an overall guide to CRM strategy.

Voice of the Customer

True CRM strategies begin with the voice of the customer. Classic business strategies start with the corporation and will reach out to the customer for its ultimate ROI. CRM strategies start with the customer and see how the business can do what their customers require in order to attain its ROI. The best strategies empower the customer to manage their own relationships with the company. In fact, it's the premise of an entire book by Frederick Newell called *Why CRM Doesn't Work: How to Win by Letting Customers Manage the Relationship*. While I can't subscribe to his entire premise, his core concept, that your business strategy has to be built around empowered customers who effectively manage their own relationships, is absolutely right. Ultimately, it is this "feel good" strategy that improves the value of that customer for your business. If the customers like what you are doing for them, they will remain with you. If they don't, they won't. What you have to determine is how to make them like you. The value exchange needs to be effective and sufficient enough to retain most profitable customers and to acquire new ones.

The first step in identifying the voice of the customer is to find out whose mouth that voice is emanating from. For example, if you were to look at the customer in the world of sports you would immediately think "fan" is the customer. You would be right, but only in part. Agents are customers. Players are customers. The media are customers and influencers, providing TV revenue and reporters who influence the fans about the teams and players. The obvious customer isn't always the only customer. So sit down and map the customer chain carefully. You can't listen to them if you don't know them.

Then, to succeed with this CRM strategy, you need to listen to those customers and to organize the strategy around what you hear from them. For example, if you have an organized list of business processes that will improve the customers' lot with your business, query these customers and let them prioritize that list in terms of each process and its importance to them. That will help you determine how and when to implement those business functions.

The voice of the customer is far more than that tidbit. It needs to permeate every facet of your strategy. For example, it could involve the customers as stakeholders; it could mean the change to a compensation plan to attach KPIs that are based on improved customer experiences; it could involve customer metrics attached to business processes.

It could take a more volume-based and automatic direction. A new breed of CRM tools can track responses to information requests which give you sliced information on specific customer segments. In other words, wherever you look, whatever you do, however you proceed with your strategy, the empowerment of the customer and the improvement of the customer experience stares you smack in the face and you hear the voice of the customer. Knowing the voice of the customer begins to help you understand what customer behaviors are associated and associable with the business model and processes that you profess.

The Movements Begin: CRM as Program, Not Project

Once you've established who the customer is both by definition and by behavior, it becomes time to figure out what CRM is. To begin, be cognizant of another often-overlooked and nearly always misunderstood CRM concept. CRM is a program, not a project.

Unfortunately, over the past several years, because of the belief that CRM was a technology, it was battered into submission as an IT project with lots of cool bells and whistles. Thus, even to this day, there is a strongly rooted misconception that you are planning to undertake a CRM "project." That is a surefire sign of likely failure.

Projects are finite. They are tactical missions that have a specific beginning and a specific end with a defined benefit at the end of it. When the project is done, it is done. The IT world has historically done projects. Anyone who has ever been in the software/hardware business or worked with or for an enterprise has been involved in applications implementations that have gone on for a period of time, were "rolled out," and that was that except for ongoing maintenance. If you were lucky enough to succeed at it. However, complex or simple, successful or failed, the project was characterized by that finite beginning and, eventually, that finite end. Some cultural change was probably necessary, but nothing terribly dramatic. It is possible that there was no change management initiative incorporated into the planning since change management is one of the most under-funded enterprise initiatives.

But CRM is different because it is an all-encompassing philosophy, strategy, system, and technology. Remember Chapter 2:

> *CRM is a philosophy and a business strategy, supported by a system and a technology, designed to improve human interactions in a business environment.*

Thus, CRM is decidedly not a project; it is a program. That means:

- ▶ It is an initiative to change the way a company operates at all levels.

- ▶ It creates a culture that can support those changes and that will continue to change and improve.

- ▶ It establishes a corporate focus on relationship-building and customer satisfaction, rather than operations and transactions.

- ▶ It provides ongoing commitments to incremental improvements to maintain and, in better times, expand the customer base.

- ▶ It encourages continued staff education from the point of initial commitment of the stakeholders to the program through an unforeseen end point.

- ▶ It establishes ongoing relationships with the vendors, integrators, suppliers, and, most importantly, the customers.

- ▶ It creates recognition that the fulcrum of business is the customer, not the company.

With the knowledge that CRM is "eternal," the priorities and approaches that you take are dramatically transformed. Tactics become an aspect of the bigger picture, and the implications of project results are extended to the entire enterprise rather than just the department or section that the projects were initiated by and for. Cross-functional and cross-departmental cooperation become the underpinnings of company success with customers, rather than something that shows up as a pleasant, unexpected surprise. In other words, the customers and company get with the program.

Building the Stakeholders Team

Stakeholding doesn't mean the job of those who carry vampire-killing weapons. Stakeholders are the team accountable for the success or failure of the CRM initiative (or any initiative for that matter). They can come from the ranks of senior management, the most important departmental leaders, external suppliers, partners, and customers. The glue that binds is that each of them has some important responsibility and represents some important interest that is necessary for the CRM initiative. Each of them has "skin in the game."

Here is Adam Golden on the subject:

What makes a great stakeholder team? Well, the key is to have the right people on the team both from a functional and behavioral perspective. That starts with understanding the far-reaching impact of a CRM project and getting senior management from each area involved. If you are considering an end-to-end CRM initiative, at a minimum you'll need the following stakeholders represented: sales, operations, finance, marketing, customer service, and IT. You'll also need a CRM expert and project management expert (ideally one person) to facilitate the team, whether it be an internal project lead or an external consultant. That group doesn't make the team great, it just makes them complete. What makes a stakeholder team great is active senior management participation, an open mind to change, enthusiasm to challenge the status quo, a willingness to demand excellence, and a commitment to meet frequently enough (every two to three weeks) to not only "govern" but have creative influence. You typically can't delegate this responsibility to the people in your organization who have more time (they usually have more free time for a reason). At the end of the day, you are changing the way you interact with your customers externally and how you conduct your day-to-day business internally, and that requires true stakeholders, not delegates. Stakeholders who realize that the long-term benefits the company will realize from a well-done CRM initiative are bigger than their individual functions. Maybe the best way to characterize the type of people you need on the stakeholders team is you need people who realize that the answer isn't going to come from just within the team. If you want to get closer to your customers, you need to understand what your customers want and how they'd like to interact with you in order to get it, and you can only figure that out by involving them. The stakeholder team needs to challenge everyone involved in the project to take that point of view.

Even when the various company interests are well represented, there is no guarantee of even minimal success. There needs to be a commitment from the stakeholders to create the strategy *and see it through*, not just a desire to have a CRM program. The stakeholders have an "eternal" obligation, not a short-term one. Remember, this is a strategic business initiative with a number of smaller projects to solve problems and create interest and support. It keeps going and going and going. While the enthusiasm is usually there with the stakeholders in the beginning, the tug and pull of the day-to-day vagaries of their jobs will begin to take its toll during the ongoing life of the program. The lust will fade, and we all know the road to true love is a rocky one. The stakeholders need to overcome their desires and make a commitment. If they can't commit, they don't belong in the relationship (the team relationship).

The Board of Advisors

Interestingly, this is an often overlooked part of developing the stakeholding team. There are two major benefits to a board of advisors.

One of the prime issues with stakeholding teams is that they are formed at the corporate headquarters. They are the core of the CRM program and by necessity have to come from HQ. But they are often insular and forget that the field is where the bulk of their employees and certainly their customers are. That means that they don't get the input from the very segments they are developing the strategy for. A board of advisors, without the decision-making powers of the stakeholders, solves that.

While there are multiple combinations of advisors possible, I would suggest at least the inclusion of:

Field personnel   This could include store managers or salespeople who work in the field offices; management from the regional headquarters; other personnel who have a possible interest or will be participants in the execution of the strategy.

Customers   These are the people you are trying to please, aren't they? Then involve them in helping you decide on the right strategic direction and the resolution of the problems that they've had with you. Bring in the most articulate ones and provide them with some form of "consideration" for their participation. They become more committed if they have a hand in solving your problems with you. This is how they (and you) benefit with an ROR—a return on the relationship.

Suppliers/vendors   These folks are an important part of your enhanced value chain. If they don't supply you with what you need in a timely way, lots of customers are potentially pretty teed off at you. They know their business and their relationship with you as well as you know your business. Involve them in the solutions and planning.

Finally, I would involve the "natural leaders." Let's chew on this one for a bit so you'll understand what I mean.

Natural Leaders and User Input

During World War II and after, Dr. Kurt Lewin, often recognized as the father of modern social psychology, did research at the University of Iowa on the influence of different types of driving and constraining forces on groups with different forms of organization. What he found (among far more than I could possibly cover here) is that there are role models—"natural leaders"—who tend to emerge primarily from groups that are nonhierarchical. When translated into everyday business life, you can easily think of people like this. The person in a department who is the mother or father figure for that department. The person people go to when they have a business, or personal, or technical problem—regardless of title. They are respected for who they are, rather than what position they carry. They are "one of us" but with a little bit more.

These are the natural leaders who, if they have a need to be somehow involved in your CRM program as a user, can articulate what their internal or external organizations or constituents truly think and want. If they are able to communicate that, they belong on the board of advisors. There are two reasons. First, by being on the board, their constituents feel empowered because one of them is protecting their interests (and at least as the thinking goes, their jobs) as a leader within the CRM program planning. Second, these leaders/role models become communicants and evangelists for the CRM program as the broader strategic vistas open up for them. They will bring this back to those same empowered constituents.

Don't underestimate the value of this. I will reiterate an important point. The biggest problem that is consistently found in failed or unsuccessful CRM programs is that the users don't see the value to them at all. If they feel powerless or uninvolved, they will do what they are comfortable doing—in other words, what they used to do. They will not do what they are mandated to do or what they can't see the importance of doing. AMR Research found that in CRM projects that failed, 47 percent cited "lack of user input at the beginning" as the primary cause.

Think about it. If your management comes to you and says, "We've implemented this new strategy and system and we want you to use it. Here is how it benefits the company's objectives. Blah. Blah. And it will do blather, drool, fizz for the company." What will you think? "Oh, that's really wonderful. I can't wait to benefit the company. You know what? If it changes my compensation or eliminates my job, but the company improves its profitability, well, hey, that's fantastic!"

Hardly. More likely: "So what? How does it benefit me? What does it do to make my work better, easier, more productive, more lucrative? How will it make my job more secure?"

If you have natural leaders on the board of advisors, those questions will, for the most part, have been answered by the time the strategy is settled and the system is in place.

Politics and Poker

Depending on its scope, CRM can be a career builder or a career buster. In any case, there are many individuals within a company at an executive level especially, but even among the ranks, who have a stake in the CRM program—or they don't and want to. There are "reactionary" elements within the company who have a fiefdom that they want to preserve, along with their hold on the serfs. CRM can dramatically alter the approach to business, and that threatens the existence of the fiefs, which depend on the existing infrastructure and practices of the company.

Don't underestimate the power of this to bring a CRM initiative to its knees. The internal results of CRM programs are every bit as threatening to someone with an ax to grind or a field to defend as a direct attack by a colleague. "The king is dead, long live the king" creates uncertainty about one's place and position. Even those who heartily embrace the initiative wonder about their future in this new surrounding.

If the politics rise to the level of senior executives, there can be serious problems. One set of practices that may help here are:

- ▶ Always map out the political situation prior to putting together the stakeholders' team—this understanding can be invaluable to identifying future bottlenecks. I never even accept a consulting assignment without a clear understanding of the politics of the company trying to engage me.

- ▶ If your opposition lies at the CxO level, neutralize it before you start. One bad seed CxO can poison the well and destroy the program before you ever start.

▶ Be mindful of company hierarchies when creating the stakeholders, but don't let them govern your choices. I was in a situation a couple of years ago where the head of the CRM program reported to a person who wasn't on the stakeholding team but their boss was. Think of the possibilities for ugliness here. They happened. It was solved by having the CEO announce to the company that the CRM program head no longer reported to that errant soul.

▶ The CEO's buy-in is indispensable. He must be visionary enough to understand the long-term implications of a CRM program and enthusiastic enough to understand that it will mean a dramatic change in his company. If the CEO is heavily vested in the present structures or tunnel-visioned and tactical, then there will be major problems. The CEO must be brought on board prior to the selection of the stakeholders, though the CEO doesn't have to be a member of the stakeholding team. He must be invested in the success of the program or it will fail.

▶ If you are a leader of the program, spend some time evangelizing prior to formal organization. While you are creating excitement, make sure that realistic expectations are being set, and the knowledge of what CRM is becomes clear. This minimizes the cynicism that will set in with unrealistic excitement about CRM possibilities. Sadly, there is always someone waiting to jump down a throat if the mouth is opened too widely.

▶ Whether you are an outside consultant or internal leader, be prepared to get involved in the politics. You can't hide from it. There is too much at stake in programs of this magnitude to make believe that everyone is wonderful, caring, and will love what you are doing. I love all living creatures, but we all have our own agendas. Sometimes CRM can be in the way of those agendas. Don't shy away from neutralizing the opposition.

Never underestimate the value of facing up to the stakeholder politics and realistically dealing with it prior to the evolution of the strategy. Listen to Reese Harris, managing director of Turnkey Client Care, LLC, express this:

A poorly defined and loosely articulated CRM project can allow those with political maneuvering skills to manipulate those who don't, and unless there is skilled intervention it generally leads to the project failure on some level. Politics often result in organizations with weak or inexperienced leaders since many top decision-makers evolve into leadership positions from roots as strong politically savvy managers. Often these managers lack the experience to recognize the damage and expense politics can cause and tolerate it since that is the way they got ahead. A new CRM system installation can also be intimating since many fear they will be left behind or look stupid in the process. Like a cancer, all levels of the organization contribute nutrients to the acerbic politics. The greatest challenge of a CEO or leader of an organization is to be crystal clear about the CRM big picture and what the expectation is, and that this could be the biggest change to the organization in its recent history. Communicate it often. It is a big deal.

Knowledge of the Known Universe

The earliest step in developing a CRM strategy is to see what you have already. The common parlance for this in the information technology linguistic wasteland is the "as is." It is also the requirements-gathering stage for the business, not the technology.

Steve Olyha again:

You need two things before a strategy is set: clarity of your business objectives and the issues or problems that need solving, and great knowledge of your customers' behaviors and their prioritized business requirements and needs. Because CRM should no longer be the functional and technology-driven approach it once was, a clear understanding of how that strategy fits into the enterprise strategy is critical. This will also insure that better process integration across other historically separated functions like supply chain is included. Lastly, there is a greater need than ever to establish key performance metrics and have good analytic capabilities to measure the progress of that strategy and its desired results.

Now, here is where the really good, customer-focused companies excel at strategic planning for CRM. While they look internally at the fundamentals of meeting their financial requirements to their shareholders as a starting point, they further align their strategies with the strategies and goals of their key customers or customer segments. In other words, their strategies are designed to help their customers succeed with *their* customers! For example, the paper industry has gone through a transition (well, the ones who have survived have) from being in the business of manufacturing all the wood pulp they can get into various paper segments, to one better aligned with their customer needs, such as creating value packs in the commodity category of cut-size paper. They no longer use their CRM strategy to just help their sales forces sell what they can produce, but align production and new product development with what the Targets, Wal-Marts, and Office Maxes of the world are selling to their customers. This kind of planning further drives enterprise alignment across the previously noted process areas for even further benefit.

Developing the Value Proposition

Team constituted. Political issues settled. Snapshot of the business as it is now taken. Now what does the team actually do? First, they develop their value proposition. That means creating a mission, vision, and a business case that the entire team buys into. That should be easy without the politics, huh? After all, mission and vision statements are just one or two sentences. That can be knocked off in a day or two, can't it? Yeah, right. First, tell me the difference between a mission and vision statement. Then we'll talk. Tom Terez, of Tom Terez's Better Workplace Solutions, Inc., defines the difference this way:

> In a recent study, conducted by the American Association of People Who Don't Mind and In Fact Advocate Long-Windedness in Their Communications, showed that the typical *mission* statement includes two semicolons, two dashes, and at least two business buzzwords, while the *vision* statement contains only one dash but makes up for it with at least one run-on sentence.

This is funny, but it's what you often get in mission and vision statements. Buzzwords, or a marketing message, or a departmental imperative, or something that reduces the statements to a few sentences that reinforce some existing corporate hierarchy or incomprehensible generalities.

In fact, the crafting of these two statements is very difficult because it is an entire company and its future encapsulated into a few short sentences, whether metaphoric, poetic, or straightforward. They are the foundation statement for your entire CRM strategy. Arguably, it is the most important phase of the entire strategic planning. The caveat is there are those who would argue over that. In fact, arguments over content are frequent enough to create the need for facilitated goal alignment on the stakeholding team, even though the mission and vision statements were crafted by those chosen by the team and reflect the corporate policies, practices, and thought.

Mission: The "As Is"

Mission statements give a clear concise couple of sentences on what your company is as of today and who the customers you serve are. It should encompass the foundation for the vision statement.

Here is a bad mission statement: "The mission of (name omitted to protect the guilty) is to provide society with superior products and services by developing innovations and solutions that improve the quality of life and satisfy customer needs, and to provide employees with meaningful work and advancement opportunities, and investors with a superior rate of return." (It was Merck's, if you must know.)

You know why this is bad? Because even with the name omitted, you should be able to get a clue as to who it might be or at least what constituencies they serve and industry they represent in the mission statement. This one is cliché-ridden and bland to the point of being valueless.

On the other hand, here is the picture-perfect mission statement— the Ritz-Carlton Hotels—"We are ladies and gentlemen serving ladies and gentlemen." That is a profound, almost poetic metaphor that says the Ritz-Carlton is dedicated to providing the finest service to their customers who will enjoy a refined customer experience. All in that one statement. Use this as a model.

Vision: The "To Be"

Once you've defined who you are, the vision statement is your "wannabe." This is vision-critical (couldn't rightly say mission-critical, now could I?) for any CRM initiative, because it is within this concentrated vision that the basis for your ROI is likely to be. But vision statements are not meant to be practical as mission statements are. They are meant to be usefully inspirational. That means that while the future objective may be relatively lofty and forward thinking, it is an admirable and achievable objective.

Once again, bad and good vision statements:

Bad vision statement "We live to give the world great products" This is so general as to be useless. Not particularly inspirational either. That could work if you are national and your products are pretty average or mediocre, but beyond that, there is little value in this ordinary vision.

Great vision statement "An Apple on every desk." Steve Jobs said this years ago, and while it didn't come to pass, it is the ideal vision statement. It inspires (within the realm of the company, that is), it provides an objective, and it states what the company is planning.

Developing the Business Case

This is the next step. While you might have a noble goal in mind, how can you justify an ongoing CRM program to the mavens at your company who are there to do little more than shoot down justifications? Often, the chief marksman is the CFO, though interestingly, when CFOs are onboard, they tend to be ardent program supporters and great allies, if such a blanket statement can be made.

The primary elements of a CRM business case are: how does it benefit us, tangibly and intangibly, and what will it cost us? That cost can be financial or the costs of risk.

For example, in his excellent white paper "Creating a CRM Business Case," Dr. Naras Eechambadi, president of Quaero, identifies the elements as both financial and strategic when making the case. The financial elements are sources of incremental revenue, reductions in cost, higher profitability, and incremental costs. The strategic elements are real but intangible benefits, sustainable competitive advantage, opportunity costs, execution risks, and barriers to success.

The business case doesn't just justify the reasoning for a CRM initiative, but it creates a skeletal framework for the elements of the initiative that have to be fleshed out and sets expectation levels. It can both identify how well prepared a company seems to be to take a CRM initiative on and can root out how prepared they are to do so—often not as well as expected.

Financially, it plans the return on investment (ROI) and identifies the costs associated with the effort and the likely TCO. This operates to both excite senior management and caution them. If the business case is accepted, senior management has effectively agreed to the risks that are associated with the program initiative. They have also accepted the metrics that are going to be attached to the results.

The strategic elements that cover the intangible benefits and the associated risks are probably even more important, in the long run. If there is anything that makes management sweat, it is intangibles. Most managers, because they are managers who live and breathe their company bottom and top lines, don't like things they can't grab. While you'll run across some genuine visionaries, that isn't characteristic of the vast majority—so sweat they do. Convincing them of the efficacy of intangible results is made easier by the creation of scorecards (for instance, the often used Balanced Scorecard) but still is not easy. However, intangibles such as customer satisfaction levels, more effective use of customer information, or increases in customer responsiveness are more important than the immediate financial impact in the current quarter or year. But convincing CxOs of this is easier said than done.

However, if you do, then you have an agreed-upon roadmap for the future effort, which is invaluable. So the business case is identifying both the drivers of success and the constraints that are present in the risks of that possible success. Agreement means that there is a common ground for building the actual initiative.

Start Small, Think Enterprise

Biting CRM off in small pieces is not a bad idea when presenting the business case and, later on, the program plan. Why? Not because senior management has attention deficit disorder, but because they can only handle pieces of the truth. However, that doesn't mean that your strategic plan and the subset business case shouldn't think enterprise-wide, because it would be a heart stopper if you didn't.

While some have labeled this limited project approach "the organic growth of CRM," I tend to go with NY Yankees manager Joe Torre and call it "little ball." You do the small things you have to do to win games, which win divisions, which win pennants, which win the World Series (hopefully). Those small things such as stealing second base, bunting, and scoring baserunners on sacrifice flies win the games, instill confidence, and build teams. CRM is no different. A small customer-focused project *in the context of the overall initiative strategy* can go a long way toward instilling confidence in the CRM program—as long as you don't forget to measure or plan for its impact on the overall program and business.

These small initiatives can be departmental; they can cure a problem; they can be a quick win with a strong business case for their future success so the funding is granted. But they need to be part of an overall business case and strategic plan.

CRM roadmaps are often used to detail these efforts. They are developed in the context of the strategy and they detail the nature of the "little ball" project, its timeline, the metrics including performance and ROI, and of course its business benefit.

For example, a retail company has reached that transition point where it recognizes that to increase its market share and move to Fortune 1000 status, it has to change the way the company is approaching its customers. The stakeholders develop a company-wide CRM strategy that integrates the front and back office in its approach. The buy-in is strong, but the cash for the program is still not forthcoming. They identify two pain points. The first is the need to understand their customers more and to develop and apply the marketing metrics that are "voice of the customer" focused. The other is to strengthen the supply chain so they can provide their products to the customer on time with an objective of 100 percent effectiveness and communicate the strength of their supply chain to the customers. They have been 97 percent effective, but that isn't good enough. They set an objective to reach 99 percent within 12 months and to make sure that the customers are regularly apprised of the status of their order until it shows at their door. They choose the supply chain–related CRM project, rather than the marketing metrics because it is achievable with tangible results more quickly and will bolster confidence in the overall initiative. But they are aware of that project's impact on the entire company and the CRM program. For example, the effort of informing the customers means they have to create a multichannel system (e-mail, phone, and so on) that they don't have. They have to base some parts of compensation on the successful timely product delivery and they have to redesign some of those programs. They might have to hire more personnel or change their SLAs with the delivery services such as Federal Express or UPS to make sure that timely delivery is reinforced and poor delivery punished. In other words, even this project, which can be done quickly, impacts the entire value chain. But it remains a piece that can be swallowed by senior management in a single gulp and has a high possibility of success with clearly identifiable returns. It is both a problem-solver and confidence builder.

Financial Elements: Return on Investment (ROI)

Determining ROI can be difficult, even when looking at its more tangible financial elements (profitability, revenue improvements, and so on). There is no real formulaic approach to ROI, so it can become somewhat whimsical. Usually the stakeholders are defining the initial ROI components, which is neither good nor bad. However, where it can get sensitive is making sure that the powers that be understand that the results are long term, not short term. Increased customer longevity, unit margin increases, better cross-selling and up-selling opportunities, faster time to market due to improved customer insight, and better pipeline management are all viable returns on investment.

Gartner Group did a study in 2002 on CRM and ROI. The result was staggering. Fifty-five percent of all CRM initiatives will fail to positively impact ROI. The reason: 45 percent of all respondents treated CRM as a pure technology initiative. Only 25 percent considered the business benefits, the processes, and the metrics that needed to be addressed in the strategic planning.

By contrast, when a CRM ROI is clearly defined, it is remarkably lucrative. Brother International planned on a reduction in the rate of return on their equipment. They achieved it—the annual rate of return was reduced from 11 percent to 5 percent. This reflected an annual savings of $1.6 million in revenue. Exactly as planned.

Financial Elements: Total Cost of Ownership (TCO)

What about calculations for what the entire program and its line items are going to cost all told? More on this in Chapter 22, but from the standpoint of strategy, remember one thing: while CRM often provides a successful reduction in the TCO, and it must be planned for, it can *never* be the driver of a CRM program. But it should be a factor. Don't follow the example of those Gartner respondents mentioned above—65 percent didn't allow for TCO planning as a factor.

But how should it be planned for?

Let's assume that part of your CRM initiative is to use e-mail and web interactions more frequently as a channel for customer communication than the historic use of print and direct mail. The plan needs to reflect that to give the customer a greater series of venues to interact with your company. It implies that a single message to the customer must be developed to make sure that regardless of which communications channel the customer uses, the message is the same. It also implies a customer record that documents the interaction regardless of media. While the plan called for this e-mail and web interaction jump to increase customer access, it very well may save you quite a bit of money in related costs. The University of Dayton lowered its communications costs in a year by $190,000 because the need for direct mail was reduced by the increase in e-mail traffic. But the reduction was not the driver of the initiative. Increasing customer access was. Again. Never a driver, but always a passenger.

Strategic Elements: Return on Relationship

But there is another facet to be planned for that distinguishes CRM from any other form of strategic planning. If you think about ROI, it is aimed at the best results for the company. There is another component that should be planned for and that is often ignored: return on relationship (ROR). The ROR is not just what the resulting benefits of your CRM strategy will be for you, but what kind of returns can you give a customer that will increase the benefits to them and thus, in return, to you. This way, the return on investment is planned for both the company and the customer, and the result is a magnitude greater than just planning for either.

Strategic Elements: Risk Management and Corporate Governance

Given the scandals ripping the corporate world from its formerly sacred perch to its current location roughly one ladder from hell, corporate governance has become the synonym for risk management. While risk management is far more "categorical" and broad than corporate governance, there is no doubt that fears of malfeasance are the most prevalent factor driving the need for compliance, a.k.a. governance.

Risk Factors

We look at the nature of risk in Chapter 9. The strategic value of risk management is our concern here. Risk factors appear from any number of places. Levels of risk can be assessed, values attached to that risk, risk mitigation and management strategies developed. All of that said and done, risk is something that you always live with. Often the activities or events that cause the problems are not necessarily those identified or planned for. The unexpected is a risk unto itself. The benefit of risk management is that you can contain much of the expected risk and identify its potential impact, weigh it against the benefits that are associated with the processes that have the risk, and decide on the value you give it and the willingness to take the risks.

Some examples of risk:

▶ **Lack of cross-functional planning** A failure to recognize the impact that CRM will have company-wide, not just on the departments that are implementing a project or developing a program.

▶ **Failure to include a clear-cut business strategy that leads to arbitrary approaches** This one is a risk that is almost always completely ignored.

▶ **Customer loss (or dissatisfaction)** In a study done in 2002 by the Information Systems Audit and Control Foundation (ISACF) with PricewaterhouseCoopers, this was the greatest concern of all the risks possible—over 27 percent mentioned it as important or very important.

▶ **Lack of support from senior-level management** That means there is no executive guidance nor is the funding kept as a priority. Senior management indifference can kill a project.

▶ **Lack of user support** This is a well-documented risk factor and has to be planned for, though oddly, of least concern in the ISACF study—only 2 percent mentioned it as very important. I have to say that the study points up the foolishness of the survey respondents.

▶ **Vendor misalignment** Purchase of an application suite that comes from a vendor who has little or no understanding of your objectives, processes, industry, or culture and thus your CRM plans

There are countless other risks, large and small—hardware failures, software bugs, change in the business climate, new laws passed by the Congress—all of which are possibly taken into account. For example, five years ago, would you have predicted something like the strict corporate governance and accounting standards that Sarbanes-Oxley calls for? I don't think so.

Complying with the Enemy: Sarbanes-Oxley

I presume that the majority of the readers of this book have heard about or been directly impacted by the dreaded but widely supported

Sarbanes-Oxley Act. It passed the U.S. Senate 97-0 and is designed to prevent egregious financial manipulations that companies like Enron have become notorious for. Of course, the problem is that even though, as the Jackson 5 used to sing, "one bad apple don't spoil the whole bunch, girl," Sarbanes-Oxley treats the corporate world as if it does. The costs are outrageous to meet compliance. Companies like Steelcase estimate 20,000 man hours necessary for compliance by June 2004, the first milestone date. That is ten people working full time for a year. Some companies are delisting themselves from NASDAQ so they don't have to bear the burden of compliance. The range of costs for compliance in dollars has been thrown around from $1,000 to $1,000,000 for a midsized company and much higher for the Fortune 1000. Yet the Business Roundtable, consisting of companies that have $3.7 trillion in total revenue, endorsed the measures even though they are draconian and potentially damage innocent companies.

How does CRM impact this? For example, Section 404 of Sarbanes-Oxley is aimed at validating the internal financial controls of a company in a way that can be audited by a third party. Customer-facing activities play a large part in that validation. Even more directly, there are requirements that sales figures be accurately reported for the prior year and any material changes to financial conditions, including the loss of a strategic account or even significant customer complaints that relate to defective products or services.

For example, if sales revenue is recognized improperly, it can nearly or actually destroy a company. Several CRM vendors were cited pre-Sarbanes-Oxley for improper revenue recognition. How cooperative marketing funds are applied is another potential sore spot.

A CRM system can help companies establish controls for the financial reporting related to these processes to support compliance with the legislation. In fact, in 2004, this is now a major industry with companies such as SAS coming out with applications that monitor compliance and, using analytics, detect potential irregularities or problems prior to their becoming issues. AMR Research estimates that 2004 Sarbanes-Oxley compliance-related spending will be $5.5 billion, with more than half—nearly $3 billion—in hard expenditures that could affect companies' bottom-line performance.

This is perhaps the most risk sensitive consideration of your CRM strategy.

Scenario Planning

It is exactly meta-factors such as Sarbanes-Oxley that make scenario planning, popularized as a planning tool by Shell in the 1970s, one of the most powerful weapons in CRM's strategic arsenal. It can be used for assessing the possible outcomes of geopolitical scenarios or down to the micro-level of use of particular software features in business processes.

Yet, scenario planning is rarely used in CRM strategy. With the exception of a few companies like Unisys, it remains outside the toolsets that are popular in determining CRM effectiveness.

To put it simply, it is the analysis of factors that can lead to a number of possible future results. There are methodologies and algorithms that vary from place to place, but the fundamentals remain the same, though the place it is used in CRM can vary. For example, York International, an HVAC equipment provider, used scenarios with the vendors they were interviewing, providing each of them with a similar possible situation and seeing how well the vendors could provide for solving those situations.

On the other hand, another scenario-building method is to examine the approaches that are beyond the reach of internal organizations. How will the upgrading of a terrorist alert status to Orange impact Your Choice Airlines and its relationship to its customers? What are the measures that might be applied to countermand some of the damage?

Back in 2003, Unisys successfully applied these meta-factors at a seminar with 25 major decision makers from Australia. They hypothesized a number of possible future scenarios and the impact of CRM on business and government. A few of the results:

- ▶ Collaboration with the customer is imperative in designing CRM systems.

- ▶ The concept of customer for life might be seen as arrogant by customers because of the amount of data about that customer eventually captured and stored by the supplier. This can lead to customer dissatisfaction and eventual breaks with the supplier.

- ▶ The tensions between the individual's desire for privacy and commerce's desire for more customer information, overlaid by security considerations, are nowhere near resolved.

- ▶ Meta-factors such as population growth and increased lifespan will influence the attitudes embedded in CRM. For example, the ability to understand and accommodate cultural nuances in the countries with increasing labor pools and increased business growth will become increasingly important as organizations expand their global customer bases and at the same time centralize their customer relationship operations.

In other words, scenario planning throughout the development of CRM strategy can help with the anticipation of catastrophic and not-so-catastrophic, but globally significant possibilities. Each of the conclusions can lead to a planned possible result that can turn a negative into a positive and a positive into a triumph.

But this isn't meant to be a broad or vague approach. The steps to scenario planning are specific:

1. Start with your "as is" assumptions about your own business and, if in a cross-industry venue, about the specific industry.

2. Look at the possible constraints and restrictions that might concern your business or industry.

3. Think through and present all the outcomes.

4. Weigh the outcomes by applying a methodology to determine value and risk.

5. Develop a decision tree that will outline possible outcomes and the resulting events and then identify the likelihood of each of the outcomes occurring.

6. Use the result as a model for a real-world prototype.

7. Refine everything and make the decisions that seem appropriate based on the risk, reward, possible outcome likelihood, and success of the prototype.

But before you go triumphantly into the night, learn what the tools are for scenario planning and how to use them for your strategy. The business you save may turn into the one that discovers the cures for many diseases. Possibly. But there are other outcomes, too.

Business Process Management (BPM)

When developing a CRM strategy, one of the most important facets of the effort is the dissection and reconstruction of business processes using increasingly sophisticated tools. The technology provided with

BPM solutions can manage processes, allow manual intervention, extract customer information from a database, add new customer transaction information, generate transactions in multiple related systems, and support straight-though processing without human intervention when needed. But those are the tools. BPM is also a critical part of your CRM strategy. Each business process that your company uses has to be examined for such features as:

► Its relationship to other business processes

► Its ownership

► Its viability as a process for the customer

► Its value to the customer experience (weighted)

► Its relationship to the workflow

► Possible changes

By no means is this all that has to be examined, but it gives you an idea of the detail. Dick Lee of High Yield Methods has one of the best methodologies for the breakdown of the processes and workflow. He calls it "visual workflow": "It decouples workflow (how work moves from function to function and stakeholder to stakeholder) from work process (how work is accomplished within functions or departments). It then couples workflow and information flow and analyzes and redesigns them as a single unit. The combined effect of these two changes from other process improvement methods—plus use of a "common language" mapping approach that's equally accessible to the business and technical/operations sides of companies—produces process improvement." (See Chapter 18 for more on visual workflow.)

Analyzing the business processes in terms of their benefit to your customers will suggest elimination of some, changes to others, and additions to fill holes that will become apparent. Don't forget, business processes and practices in combination with your culture is the way you do business. Benchmarks and metrics tell you how well you're doing it. But you need all of these elements to make a CRM strategy work

Benchmarks and Metrics

CRM success is seen in changes in customer behavior, and I love it for that. But if the success is measured by feeling and opinion, rather than benchmarks and measureable objectives, then it isn't really success.

While intangibles will always exist, results, in order to be meaningful, have to be discernable. Fortunately, in the last few years benchmarks and measurements have been successfully developed in the real world, using real practices, that can validate that triumph or defeat. Customer satisfaction, often seen as one of the behavioral measures of CRM success, is also one of the places where metrics have been developed through years of effort testing and tuning them.

The definition of the business case is also the place where you want to begin to define your benchmarks and metrics. What will be the expected results of the program at different points? What are the minimum thresholds for success and the optimal successful results? For example, if your benchmark is to reduce the queue time to less than 45 seconds per call with no increase in personnel over eight months, is 45 seconds over a year successful? Is 50 seconds a call in eight months successful? What are the subjective values attached to the benchmarks and metrics? Are those 45 seconds a call established as something that will make the customers happy? How will that reflect it tangibly?

Many companies use methodologies like the Balanced Scorecard to determine the value of and identify specific benchmarks that will reflect the CRM initiatives' impact on the company as a whole. There are dozens of possible options to choose from, and choosing none is one of the options. But what does have to happen is that these key performance indicators (KPIs) have to be established by the stakeholders and their advisors so that the results of the ongoing program can be measured against its goals, mission, and vision.

Customer-Based Metrics

David J. Mangen of Mangen Research Associates is the perhaps the leading expert on CRM-based metrics. When metrics are being defined, there is considerable confusion as to what customer-based metrics are. Dr. Mangen is here to clear the confusion:

> *Customer-specific* metrics focus on the client's needs and specific issues that drive their desire to do business with your company. Many companies too often want to only consider "hard" customer factors such the length of the client relationship, industry designation, number of employees, etc., as the most important characteristics of their customers. While this is, indeed, important information, the softer customer measures have to be differentiated from those harder factors. Ultimately, these softer customer measures are far more important

in specifying *who* elects to do business with you. Some examples of customer metrics might include:

> ▶ Customer desire for a partnering relationship with a supplier versus a transaction-based relationship

> ▶ Receptivity toward comprehensive solutions developed by a supplier versus the need to develop the solution in-house and maintain proprietary control of the final product

> ▶ A customer potential index, referenced by the number of products or services that the customer uses that a supplier is *able* to supply regardless of whether or not the customer currently uses that supplier as the preferred current vendor

Note that the first two of these metrics clearly focus of psychological willingness to develop an intense, comprehensive relationship, while the third is a bit "harder" in that it addresses client potential.

Performance Metrics

Some of the more common CRM key performance indicators (KPIs) are:

> ▶ Revenue per salesperson increase

> ▶ Ratio of administrative to street time in sales change

> ▶ Retention rate for customers increase

> ▶ Customer lifetime value (CLV)

> ▶ Response rate increase for marketing campaigns

> ▶ Queue time reduction in customer interaction center

> ▶ Increased up-selling and cross-selling opportunities from CSRs

> ▶ Increased renewal rate of service level agreements (SLAs)

Diagnostic Metrics

Erin Kiniken of Forrester Research, in a *CRMDaily* article, recommended that enterprises use diagnostic metrics to measure successful use of the actual CRM system. These could include such measures as the number of employees using the sales applications, the number of customer addresses in the database, the number of phone calls entered into the database, and the amount of time that it takes an employee to

access a customer record. In other words, measurements of the effectiveness of the system, not of the performance of the user.

Culture Change

I'm not going into detail about CRM and culture change here because
I'm devoting Chapter 19 to it. However, remember this: culture change is
the most significant and most overlooked piece of corporate strategy. The
dramatic impact of a newly established customer-based business practice
and lifestyle is no small thing. It is the lynchpin of any CRM program.
Since the way you do business is going to change when you establish a
CRM initiative, the corporate culture has to be restructured to support the
changes. But the resistance to those changes is heavy and that resistance
has to be overcome. Organizations and structures have to be transformed
to support the positive transformation. The factors that have to be taken
into account are social, psychological, emotional, organization, personal,
and dramatic. To take care of this, make sure that you have the change
management structure in place to direct and focus the changes. In with
the good things, out with the bad.

Alignment with the Customer Ecosystem

One important planning concern is the impact that CRM will have on
all your business processes and procedures, not just the obvious customer-facing ones. That means that CRM will affect your supply chain,
your mobile field force, your financial and human resources departments—pretty much all of your company. For example, the supply
chain, which has been an issue for optimization and physical management, is now a major customer issue and is part of that extended
value chain I keep talking about. Let's say you have a retail order that
is due in a timely fashion. If it doesn't arrive in a timely fashion, what
was previously a matter of managing the levels and distribution of
inventory is now a customer concern. What if the customer finds that
you've misread the available inventory or improperly delivered the item
so it was late? How likely is that customer going to continue doing
business with you when he's been blindsided? From the voice of the
customer, we hear two simultaneous musical notes:

> ▸ The company is changing the business processes and thus the
> thinking about the way business is done to a customer-focused
> approach.

▶ The business ecosystem is being transformed to a customer-pivotal ecosystem. That means empowered highly volatile customers with high expectations.

Which means:

▶ All your employees in all divisions that are along the chain that produces and supplies the product or services are affected.

▶ All your partners, suppliers, and vendors that are along the chain that produces and supplies the products or services are affected.

So what do you do? Develop plans to ensure that not only are the tools in place to make the users more "friendly" to the CRM program, but that compensation programs are in place that emphasize customer satisfaction. Initially, those programs will be needed for sales, marketing, and customer support, but don't underestimate the need for similar programs for human resources (employees = customers), field service technicians (often the first line of defense and face-to-face relationships with customers), and other traditionally back-office employees. Plan for programs that reward your suppliers and vendors for excellent product or services management that exceeds the standards agreed upon in your contracts. Penalize them for failures to meet the standards. Change even your partners' focus to customer-driven. Though these programs can be costly, don't underestimate their importance in your strategy.

Vendor Selection

Once you've chosen the strategy, vendor selection is on the table. Note that I didn't say "software selection" or "CRM application selection." That is the trap that companies often fall into when they begin to choose the system that will support their strategy. This is the point where it is easy to get star-struck. Bells, whistles, brass, gold, and silver finish all begin to float around your head when you see the things that CRM applications can do. Well, there are several things CRM applications can't do. They can't do your work for you. A CRM application can't solve its own installation problems, or customization problems, or configuration limitations. It is mute in the face of these. CRM software can't take care of a crash of itself. It can't work out financial issues when it goes over budget or over time. It is dumb, inanimate, lifeless code. But the company that provides that software can take care of those problems and solve those issues. That's why, as I've been preaching for a long time, "When you buy the applications, you buy the vendor." Knowing the core values of the vendor, the mission and vision and practices of the vendor and that vendor's culture are essential to your software selection process. The functionality of CRM whether online or in-house is about the same in each category. SFA is lead and opportunity management, forecasting, order management, and so on no matter who puts it out. The way it is executed is perhaps a little different. But functionally, the applications are 95 percent the same. It is your relationship to the company in addition to your examination of the software that is going to matter. It is an ongoing relationship that will not end after the first applications are released and running on your or their servers. I'll be covering this in detail in Chapter 20.

Implementation Strategy

This is tactical. Once you've implemented your strategy, chosen your vendor, picked the appropriate modules, decided which areas of pain you're going to cure or which quick wins are politically important as well as useful, then it's implementation time. It could take from thirty days to two years depending on what you've chosen to do and which model or methodology you've chosen to follow. The net native model transformed the big-dollars/long-time implementation cycles that have historically defined these enterprise whopper-sized projects. Now all the CRM providers are slimming down their cost and their times for implementation. Even so, there are specific things to do that are worth looking at. In Chapter 20, I'll compare the implementation methodologies of the net natives and the enterprise vendors (in their Atkins-slimmed new clothes) by going straight to the horse's mouth on this. Each will battle it out as to why they're the way to go.

Ongoing Learning Management

If I asked you, "How do you handle knowledge transfer and learning management in a CRM initiative?" most folks would tell me about end-user training, such as classes on how to use the software or meetings to describe the system. They would be barely partly right. Ongoing learning management involves the use of the same multichannel approach to communications with the ultimate participants in the initiative as you would use for actual day-to-day operations.

Some of the elements to consider:

- ▶ Communications planning

- ▶ Applications training

- ▶ Contextual online help

- ▶ Helpdesk and technical support

- ▶ Iterative involvement of the user in sculpting the appropriate system configurations and strategies

Dana Sohr, the managing partner of Attain Technologies, has 20 years in the learning management systems business. He cautions:

> People are often an afterthought, if that, in large implementations. In my experience, most technology implementations don't fail because of technical barriers but because the people side isn't handled properly. The project team successfully delivers a system that works, but the system doesn't provide the expected business advantage. In many cases, the system impacts the business negatively. People can't grasp the new system. It means more work for them. Frustrated employees, customers, and suppliers use it incorrectly or not at all. Even though you will find some pockets of success, more frequently you hear about employees resorting to workarounds that leave critical data out of sync with business reality. Employees are keeping data in rogue, ad hoc systems such as spreadsheets. Managers and supervisors can't get the data they need to make informed business decisions.

> Without enabling and driving changes in the associated human behaviors, you might as well flush your technology investment right down the drain. It's like parents buying a new piano for their children, setting it up properly in the corner, having it tuned, and then sitting back and expecting to hear Chopin from the kids. Savvy parents know that the kids probably need some motivation—some kind of gain to be realized—and they also need to acquire the right competencies through practice time, the right instruction, the right feedback. Those systemic changes are not easy to put into place, but without them, the parents will hear nothing but "Chopsticks."

> It's no different with CRM. Some of the employees will be highly motivated and will need nothing more than the new sets of CRM tools. But most employees need to be motivated by some ultimate

benefit to them. They also need to learn better customer-interaction skills, because an organization that doesn't put customers first can't expect a new CRM system to achieve that result. Finally, they need to learn the new skills required to use the new system. Getting adults skilled requires that they have opportunities to learn, that they can practice the new skills, and that they receive feedback on their performance.

Many organizations are now adopting learning management systems (LMS) as an answer to some of these issues. These technologies enable a more structured, consistent, scaleable approach to learning across the enterprise. They're a good way to manage and distribute content, to match required competencies with available training, and to keep track of who knows what. In combination with the required people skills and culture change, they can be powerful motivators for success.

Okay, enough of the overview. Now let's dig deeper into some of the tougher topics.

18

Business Processes Are Gender Neutral, Aren't They?

I recently saw a proposal issued by a government agency for a CRM-related project. Because this is a government agency I greatly admire, I'm only going to refer to it generally. I read the proposal and the more I read it, the more dismayed I became. The proposal, which was for customer interaction centers among other things, ignored something in its content. The customer. Imagine a CRM proposal that spent most of its time talking about how this process works and that process works. Here's how we do e-mail. Here's how we do phone calls. Here's how we do all the other multichannel things we do. It was business process–focused, but the processes were internal and, for this kind of proposal, simply missing the point.

That is often the problem when commercial or government CRM-desirous companies are developing their strategies. Business process transformation and management become an internal matter, not one focused on the customer. Best practices are developed that are primarily aimed at the most significant steps to some interoffice goal, but not to impact the customer so that their experiences improve. While there certainly is nothing wrong with improving internal business processes, they cannot be labeled with a CRM sticker because improving internal processes is aimed primarily at cost efficiencies, not improvements in customer experiences. Some vendors like Chordiant and Staffware (see "Steppin' Out" in this chapter) understand how customer-related business processes work, but they are not prevalent in the business process management (BPM) world, though it is a bit better on CRM's flip side. If only the customers saw the BPM/CRM intersection, life would be sweet.

BPM Gains Credence

BPM is gaining credence among the adherents of a customer-centric worldview. It is becoming an increasingly important part of strategic planning. After all, if you are designing a CRM initiative and changing the way you do business, your processes will have to change. Customers are just beginning to recognize BPM for what it is. In 2003, Delphi Group did a study where just short of half of the respondents identified BPM as an emerging software layer for building process-based applications. This reflects the fundamental shift toward cross-functional processes (across multiple applications) that come with a business ecosystem dependent on a collaborative value chain. It is no longer useful to have packaged software "islands," called silos in industry jargon. By providing common language to bridge the operational gaps, web services provide seamless interactions between the process/business layers and the application layers and between multiple business layers. They make the task of evolving appropriate processes a lot easier than it used to be, whether internal or customer-facing.

Changes to processes when made customer-friendly can have powerful benefits for a customer. Envision a mortgage company that saw its volume of work with loan origination increase by many times, because of the number of homes being refinanced to take advantage of the extraordinary low interest available. A seven-day decision-making cycle on loans was absolutely unacceptable, because of brutal competition for these home owners. By a thorough examination of the processes that were involved and a look at what benefited the customer for each step of the process, the mortgage company was able to reduce the cycle time to 48 hours, which in turn reduced the transaction cost from $250 to $60 per loan. This saved the company $50 million over a year, and the customer was thrilled with a 48-hour decision on the refinancing or financing of their house.

In Chapter 3, I identified what typical CRM business processes. Now it's time for how to identify these customer-friendly processes and manage them within your overall CRM strategy.

Business Process Reengineering (BPR): That Means You're Fired!

Back in the dark days of the mid-1990s, a famous book was written by business gurus Michael Hammer and James Champy entitled *Reengineering the Corporation*. This book was the clarion call for the streamlining of resources and processes within a company to provide the best means for maximizing revenues. Dozens of Fortune 1000 companies embraced this new technique. While Champy and Hammer recognized human beings as part of the production process, they saw them as about the same as the processes themselves—items to be reexamined and eliminated where possible. Bloodbaths from mass firings ensued as streamlining, cost cutting, and "increased efficiencies per unit of work" became the rallying point for multiple corporations. Big corporations—among them American Express, CIGNA, and Ford—all hugged this new approach to their heaving bosoms. The rallying cry? By any means necessary to boost shareholder value.

Productivity became a function of revenue or sales divided by the number of people required to generate the revenue. According to Hammer/Champy, BPR increases productivity by cutting costs. But it did nothing to increase the revenues or sales. Whoops. *Big* oversight. In fact, even changing business processes was a massive one-time "thing" you did. Processes and people fell as you slashed through them, making the company lean and mean. Downsizing and technology were the order of the day. Why have a human do it when technology might be able to? When the din of battle settled and the gore was wiped from the ax handles, you moved on to the next department. Eventually the bloated Roman Enterprise fell to the barbarian process reengineering (BPR) Visigoths, who were leaner and meaner. Companies that had been personnel-heavy were now just chattels to this new technique. As it worked out, firms that practiced it were often businesses on the cusp of disaster, not those trying to implement core strategy for actual revenue growth.

For years, BPR, still practiced today by those companies engaged in the process of discovering fire, gave business process transformation a black eye. Luckily, with the revitalization of business process management and a significantly improved knowledge of the value of incremental improvements and change management, this is now a useful tool for transforming businesses, rather than a Mongol Khanate slaughter of innocent villager-employees.

Six Sigma: Too Much Stigma

What about Six Sigma, if BPR is not going to do the trick in CRM?

Dick Lee, president of High-Yield Methods and member of the CRMGuru Guru Panel, says, "It pains me to see consultants contorting Six Sigma in attempts to apply it to sales and marketing functions. Sales and marketing together don't produce enough repetitions to get to one sigma. It's a solution in search of a problem. Like adjusting a door jamb with a baseball bat."

Mikel Harry and Richard Schroeder's *Six Sigma: The Breakthrough Management Strategy Revolutionizing the World's Top Corporations* is perhaps the best-known book on the topic of Six Sigma. The idea behind Six Sigma sounds great: process improvement. The fundamental premise is quite different than CRM, though certainly it has been successful for a number of companies. How do you reduce the defects per million (DPM) products or opportunities? The idea is to get to less than one DPM, which is achieved when six sigmas of process variation fit within the tolerance specification or quality requirement for the product. This is near perfection—99.9997 percent or otherwise seen as a failure rate of 3.4 parts per million.

In Six Sigma's universe, the world-class companies operate at a level of four sigma, which is about 99 percent defect free. Here is where it begins to diverge from CRM. The wisdom goes that to get to six sigma, a company needs to cut down on its high costs, which are seen as wasted dollars. Cost-cutting efficiencies are still the foundation for reducing the DPM. There is value returned as company after company lauds their results. It is seen as returning as much as $1 million per Black Belt to the bottom line every year. For those of you who are unenlightened, Black Belt is one of Six Sigma's karate-focused terms for someone who leads a Six Sigma project, as opposed to the Green Belts, who are the "backbone" of the project, as the Six Sigma scions politely state, to the Master Black Belt who knows the theory and leads.

Can it be a useful CRM methodology? At about three sigma, I would say. Honeywell Aerospace used it successfully. They identified four key customer-facing business processes that were causing them trouble, including tracking of customer service requests and issues, sales and opportunity management, campaign marketing management, and the measurement of customer satisfaction through their Voice of the Customer (VOC) program. They began using Siebel Sales, Call Center, Field Service, Campaign, and Analytics and centralized their customer data through a system called ATLAS (Aerospace Total Account System). They added real-time components to the datawarehouse. The overall results were on time closure of service issues up from 45 percent to 83 percent. Customer response time was reduced by 27 percent. Customer satisfaction increased 38 percent. Because of the centralized database and improved processes, opportunities from marketing campaigns were up 40 percent. Finally, the aftermarket for aerospace parts went from a $45 million business component to a $100 million business component.

These are good results, so clearly there is some value to the Six Sigma approach. But it has its limitations, best expressed unwittingly by Darryl Carroll, senior director of defense and space business operations at Honeywell. Overall, Carroll said, the system "helps us spot systemic issues so we can proactively address them. It's also improving opportunity management by helping us uncover opportunities that represent new trends or needs in the market, so we can beat the competition in putting together a solution to meet that need."

It is a good system if you are trying to improve the existing business processes in a production environment that has millions of repetitions going on. It is a good method when you are attempting to cut costs. It can provide some measure of increased customer satisfaction in some situations. But it is a measure of product quality if that product is a piece of equipment or a business process. It is not aimed at improving the overall customer experience to drive your ROI. It is aimed at improving the quality and efficiencies of your internal processes and production models. It was developed when the corporate ecosystem was still dominant, not the customer ecosystem. Its value lies in making what you have increasingly effective and providing a measurable discipline to do so. Carroll says that it helps Honeywell Aerospace spot systemic issues. But it doesn't provide a new paradigm for a customer-centric business model. It can improve the model you already have, not create a new model for you. Where it becomes valuable is in its ability to correct the imperfections of the existing model. For that, got to love that DPM. But it is not a substitute for a true redesign and re-creation of the business processes that are needed to change the way that business is done.

So what is?

Business Process Management (BPM) Ain't Six Sigma

Business process management (BPM) starts in a different time, from a different place, with a different rhythm (da.dada.da.dada.da) from BPR or any other business process "thing" out there.

Trying to manage customer-based processes is not the easiest task. Since it is not strictly an internal effort, all kinds of problems exist. Just dealing with efficiency improvements or deficiencies doesn't cut it in a CRM environment. When done well, customer-directed BPM links all of a process's internal and external participants—clients, employees, partners, suppliers, and vendors—through rules, workflow, processes, and hopefully, best practices. The payoffs are a smooth flow between all processes across departments and through applications. Manual and automated tasks work well together—at best, seamlessly. With the right framework, you can continually model new processes and test them easily, without disrupting workflow or the existing processes. You can measure (see Staffware in "Steppin' Out" later in this chapter) how effectively the processes are working, using the analytics that are present in the best of the BPM frameworks. Customer directed BPM can also:

- ▶ Standardize enterprise best process practices across all organizations

- ▶ Establish a powerful workflow that can move work to the appropriate next participant in the business process

- ▶ Gather, format, and present information applicable to each task activity in multiple formats

- ▶ Produce notices, correspondence, and communications to parties related to each process

- ▶ Manages services standard activity deadlines and constraints and automatically carry out the prescribed corrective actions when they have been exceeded

- ▶ Reduce process inefficiencies automatically by using business rules to eliminate valueless tasks uniquely, process by process

- ▶ Log, monitor, and report processing progress and logistics

- ▶ Automate and manage customer-specific process variations

As I'll show you, this isn't all that BPM does. But there is a lot of work that needs to be done to get the results.

BPM = CRM + 1 OR CRM = BPM +1

There is an almost silly discussion going on as to whether business process management (BPM) is a subset of CRM or CRM is a subset of BPM. It is clear that BPM is an enterprise-wide endeavor since business processes aren't limited to customer-facing ones. One example of an internal process would be a bookkeeping process used by the finance office. But it is also clear that CRM is a strategy that encompasses potentially enterprise-wide changes to existing business processes. BPM is a component of a CRM strategy, but can supersede customer-facing applications and processes, in particular. The end of the debate. Well, almost the end. See the section at the end of the chapter on Staffware. I debate them a little.

Business Process Management as It Is

Probably the most important lesson to remember in BPM is that most processes are executed by people. Those people are each responsible for the implementation of certain specific processes that when functioning well are linked tightly to the job descriptions of those people. You know it from your experiences with workflow as roles and responsibilities. The right metrics are the metrics that are associated with both the financial statement and the new business direction that the CRM initiative calls for. There should be strong feedback and support mechanisms in place so that any problems or changes can be not just noted but acted on quickly and effectively. In fact, those who are engaged in the processes should also be engaged in improving those same processes.

Once you've embarked on a good business process initiative for your CRM program and have the people part out of the way, get rid of the paper diagrams that you doodle the processes on. If you don't, you could ruin your company's order management system by spilling Diet Coke. Get your process model into a repository by using a business process modeling tool to organize them. If you're using good tools, you can simulate process models without damaging your actual system with a mistaken change. That alone is worth the cost.

By following these simple suggestions, appropriately characterized by the most clichéish of CRM clichés—people, processes, and technology—you're likely to do the right thing when it comes to making the changes in your business processes. People implement the processes that are best supported when technology is used.

Now we start to get a little more complicated. We're going to delve into the definition of business rules, how BAM is of real benefit to BPM, and what it takes to make BPM benefit you.

Business Rules

Business rules are not business processes. They are constraints that are placed on a business that might trigger processes. They will ordinarily reflect some business policy or practice that is institutionalized in the rule. In the world of BPM, they become variables or key points within the process. For example, there could be a business rule that triggers a 3 percent discount when the volume purchase that is entered into the quoting or order management system reaches a certain number according to the particular products. Or there could be a human business rule that constrains the way that a salesperson goes about his work. For example, at York International, a Pennsylvania-housed HVAC company, they were having a problem with the profitability of their highly complex service level agreements with some of their customers. Extensive analysis found that they were losing money on many of their SLAs. They created a business rule that was embedded in their sales process (through a Siebel sales application) that would not let the SLA proceed unless it met a profitability threshold.

This valuable process and rule has a drawback when you are attempting to change a business process. There are often multiple rules embedded in the large BPM processes and they have to be ferreted out in order to make the changes appropriately. They aren't necessarily so easy to catch. That's why there are dozens of vendors on the market that are attempting to create business rule technologies that can handle the ferreting and embedding as needed. With the technology, business rules can be implemented in a repeatable and consistent fashion and integrated with BPM and other applications that are being used by the company. As process management and change become increasingly real time, the ability to extract and change or re-embed or develop the business rules associated with those processes becomes increasingly important. BPM solutions will have to factor that kind of activity into their solutions. If they don't, embed the following rule into your purchasing processes: "If the BPM applications don't have business rule capabilities, don't buy." Though how you would embed it without those capabilities is beyond me.

In the technology that you will likely deal with, the business rules are part of a business logic that assumes constraints in the state or change of the state of data. It also constrains the use of data by individuals—an authorization constraint. It also will trigger when an action on the data occurs. Apply that to the volume discount discussed earlier. If you add, for example, that any variance from the 3 percent can be authorized by a specific group of managers, you can see how the technology can automatically trigger the workflow rules to route it to the appropriate managers.

By being able to see and steer the business rules that are in specific processes, you will be able to modify, subtract, or add rules to each process or even do a universal change to all the rules by some parameter or other criterion. Sleep will come easier if you can. Imagine doing it all manually? To err is human; to have business rules capabilities is, uh, good. Divine is stretching it.

Key Business Rules Vendors: Oracle CDM RuleFrame; Haley's Eclipse; Pegasystems; IBM/Versata

Business Activity Monitoring

I could have just as well put this section in Chapter 9 under the discussion on business intelligence, or in Chapter 15 under the discussion of integration across the value chain, or in Chapters 2 or 3 under the discussion of process-driven CRM. Business activity monitoring (BAM) is an acronym coined by Gartner a few years ago that refers to automation of the monitoring of business activities. Where most data-driven activities will grab the data from a datawarehouse, BAM takes its information from the actual applications—the order entry system, the CRM system, the ERP system—and reports it in multiple formats such as e-mail, dashboards, documents, and so on. If a BAM tool is working well, it will notify the end-user of the appropriate events and activities going on. These can range from the production of a utility bill that triggers an e-mail with a notification that they can pay online to a daily report to a CEO on how much revenue was garnered, how many orders booked, how many deals closed, and by whom. It can even send an e-mail to a sales manager that says Joe Smith hasn't logged in all day and you need to get on that, bud. In other words, by using powerful business logic, knowledge of a company's business rules, an understanding of its processes, and a customized set of metrics that are attached to a workflow, it can monitor any business activity. When thinking BPM, the BAM tool is a powerful supplement to your process planning and management.

BAM Tool to Love: Cognos NoticeCast

BPM Applications: Composition for a Busy Enterprise

While I'm not going to spend much time on the architecture of BPM, there are a couple of approaches to BPM that have been on the table in recent years that I'd like to briefly mention. First, automated processes, which tend to be the more primitive version of BPM. In this model, the business process is hard coded with all possible outcomes embedded into the branching of the process. Each step of a business process has to be defined in all its permutations and outcomes and then modeled and individually coded. For example, if you are designing a service request process, you'd have to allow for every type of service request ranging from technical repair to dispute, then the outcome or possible change in direction for each of those, and then a resolution process for each of them. That could be hundreds of branches and divisions. Automation insists on 1-2-3-4-5-6-7-8 in order all the time.

The automation model is "If-Then-Else" "If-Then-Else" "HUT 2, 3, 4!" Stay in step, no flexibility possible, soldier.

The more contemporary, even hip, version of BPM is an orchestrated process which allows the steps to be autonomous and not tied to a specific serial chain. The results are determined by the real-life runtime actions that are occurring. The model is much more context sensitive and based on real-world business activity. Processes become, as the Delphi Group calls them, "a set of atomic, goal-based activities with the enforcement of basic parameters (e.g., time limits, data variables), while separating the execution logic activities from the higher-level process definition." If an anomalous situation occurs, the flexibility is there to solve it. The dependency is on whatever the previous step was, but that could be 3-8-2-9, or depending on the context, 3-4-9-7. The automation model demands its 3-4-5-6.

Benefits of BPM Apps
The benefits of using BPM are substantial in a CRM environment, but to get the payback, you need the BPM applications to do some work. Let's look at some of the key factors.

INTEGRATION BETWEEN ALL PROCESSES ENHANCES THE FUNCTIONING OF THE ENTERPRISE VALUE CHAIN
Your processes are interwoven and well organized, working in real time. The execution engine is just humming along. They alert you to delivery problems in Cleveland that would otherwise wreck a major customer deal that one of your salespeople is in Cleveland working on today. You ship the items from a different location, they arrive tomorrow, and all is right with the world. If the processes (internal or otherwise) are integrated, you can get this kind of result.

Of course, this flawless integration is dependent on the acceptance of standards that can flow between not just the internal supply chain and CRM processes but between collaborators in the chain, for example, UPS and your company and the client. To this end, the Business Process Management Initiative is developing Business Process Modeling Language and Business Process Query Language. The first is an XML-like meta-language for modeling business processes, the latter an interface to BPM systems that will allow management of the system and querying of the processes as they execute. Additionally, an SOA (see Chapter 13) is necessary so that the discretely modeled processes can interact through an independent process layer and the application layer.

IN BPM, CHANGE IS GOOD, BUT IT MUST BE EASY

BPM changes made easier are effected through the business rules engines and a good user interface. We've already briefly looked at the rules engines. They are capable of steering the changes necessary as they occur. Business rules engines are dynamic when they do what they have to. But also important in the changes is the design environment. Because business processes are complex, whether automated or orchestrated, the environment to design the processes needs to be as graphical as possible. While Microsoft Visio is often used as a design tool, it has one big flaw. It doesn't execute the process. Design tools such as HandySoft BizFlow allow you to import the Visio diagrams or develop the workflow and processes natively and then execute them. In fact, BizFlow lets you change the workflows in real time if need be, while other processes are running.

BPM MUST REMEMBER THAT WHILE IT ISN'T HUMAN, WE ALL ARE

So-called "human factors" are a big part of BPM. While this sounds obvious to a CRM strategist, since culture and adoption clearly affect the success of the CRM initiative, when it comes to BPM we are dealing at a level where humans need to interact with technology, not just other people. For example, it is very important to have BPM that can handle long-running events with human intervention—manual events, in a manner of speaking. Any time you take an order, receive a payment for that order, approve the shipment of the order, and finally prepare and ship the order, there are going to be large numbers of human hands touching that effort. How easily the processes can handle the multiple human interventions is particularly important. In fact, applications like FileNet and IBM/Versata are strong in this, spending mucho dinero trying to identify how to make this a matter of ease of use.

But it doesn't stop with this. Since most reasonably savvy humans use e-mail to pass along notifications and alerts through their office e-mail systems, integration with that system is a big plus.

Good visuals are a plus. That means the process is that much more understandable. We've all seen the studies in information retention when the graphics are good. It holds that someone trying to see how a process works will see it more succinctly and understand it more clearly if they have it graphically represented through a BizFlow chart. It can even help in real time so that when a customer needs a status report on something, you'll be able to identify and see where that something is by the flow chart that is tracking the process and the object moving through it in real or near-real time.

Simulation tools are another human factor issue. Design the flow and test it without destroying the system. That's as good as Halo or anything you can throw up on your Xbox and worth a lot more to your company. Good graphic simulation and animation can provide you with answers.

BPM Needs to Work and Really Well

That's an obvious duh, but not when it comes to the technology of BPM. Have you heard the terms "state" or "persistence"? Ultimately, when you are dealing with loads of processes running concurrently, how well does the system maintain itself? If you are increasing the number of concurrent processes, how well does the system handle the scaling up? Those are what actually answer the "it needs to work and really well" questions.

Best Practices and Methodology: Visual Workflow

Okay, to recap. We've established a few things. First, people carry out most business processes and need to be involved in their improvement. Second, the processes need to be managed well and technology is a distinct help here. Third, business rules are not business processes. Fourth, BAM is not BPM but is an important addition to BPM. That said, how do we begin to examine the business processes in a CRM initiative? How do we use workflow to support those changes and to make them seamless?

Dick Lee, whom you heard from in Chapter 17, is the creator of a methodology to examine the processes and workflow and make the changes. He says:

> The first requirement for successfully redesigning business process in a front-office environment is splitting business process into its two components—workflow and work process. Workflow describes how work and information move from function to function (or department to department). Work process details how individuals do their jobs and use information. If you redesign workflow and information flow first, work process comes naturally. If you try to redesign them together—or worse yet, start with work process— you wind up doing something very unnatural. And it hurts.

Dick Lee calls this methodology Visual Workflow (VW). It decouples workflow from business processes; examines each separately and individually; identifies problems, potential modifications and additions, as well as those processes or workflow steps that need to be eliminated; and then recouples workflow and business processes appropriately.

According to Lee, there are four reasons that problems occur in workflow and processes, especially around CRM processes:

▶ **Bad hand-offs** These are the primary reasons why work outputs are often less than the sum of their inputs. Miscommunication, poor processes, or some other reason causes exchanges of work either between functional silos or between company and customers/suppliers (workflow) to introduce far more output-reducing defects than successful work (work process). For example, a salesperson takes a custom product order from a customer. They then communicate the order information to engineering either incompletely or inaccurately. The result: engineering designs an "off-spec" product.

▶ **Incomplete information** A customer service person receives a customer complaint about a late shipment, then e-mails logistics asking for follow-up without including the customer's routing instructions. As a result, logistics believes there's no problem.

▶ **Poor communication and faulty automation** A bank loan officer sets up a new car loan for automatic withdrawal, communicating a repayment date starting 60 days after the loan is issued, in order to give the customer a grace period. The loan shows as delinquent 45 days later, with the customer getting a bill collection call.

▶ **Manual labor and repetitive data entry** A sales rep records an order in a CRM system and e-mails the order as an attachment to order administration. Order administration has to reenter all the information into the order entry system (which does not communicate with CRM), and frequent errors result from the repetitive data entry.

In each case, the inputs (work) do not produce successful outcomes, which in turn require more work and cost to be invested before finally reaching a successful outcome. Dick Lee again:

Workflow and information flow are interdependent in nonproduction settings such as sales and marketing, professional services, and most forms of administrative services—all cases where work tasks and throughput are irregular. Work in these settings is based largely on information that passes from one function to the next, such as from sales to order entry. If we try to change either the work activity or the supporting information without changing the other, we usually create some manner of misalignment, where the information doesn't support the work or the work doesn't utilize information correctly. And misalignment creates the same effect as friction between moving parts. Additional energy (or work) must be expended to accomplish anything, and productivity suffers.

Production-based business process improvement methods designed for work settings with high frequencies of repetitive work don't transport well into nonproduction environments and don't square with CRM values. For example, Six Sigma, which is designed to use advanced statistical analysis to identify and minimize variability that leads to defects, is a fish out of water in field sales, where creativity and adapting sales approaches to suit individual customers is critical to success. Likewise in customer service, where interrupting the flow to coddle a key customer is hardly a "defect," even if it interferes with reaching call turn objectives. And Lean Business, with its heavy dependence on controlling and smoothing order flow in order to compensate for lack of inventory buffers, is very much at odds with the CRM principle of sellers adapting to customer needs, rather than pressuring buyers to do the sellers' bidding. That doesn't mean that Six Sigma and Lean Business are bad. You just need to pick your tools to the task at hand.

Hey, you can like both fishing and hunting, but you don't go fly fishing for grouse.

Visual Workflow Key Components

Visual Workflow is designed for the nonproduction environment, unlike Six Sigma. The primary components that a VW implementation provides are:

▸ **Strategic review** VW works by aligning workflow, process, and technology with strategy—making client strategic input essential.

▸ **Map "as-is" workflow and information flow** In cross-functional teams, VW is used to analyze current workflow and information flow. Session "marker maps" are converted into easy-to-read pictographs.

▶ **Design "to-be" workflow and information flow** In the same team settings, the workflows are redesigned to properly align with company values and strategies, and to take full advantage of new technologies now available. Once again pictographs are created to document and communicate the "to-be" state.

▶ **Reengineer work processes** Once workflow is redesigned, VW begins to do its magic on the work processes with workflow actually guiding process design. VW uses automation software, reducing the process mapping time considerably.

▶ **Define technology support: requirements** By leaving technology until last, VW can look at the systems support requirements for the "to-be" workflow and work process both—before technology selection and configuration begin.

VISUAL WORKFLOW ADDS A BIT MORE

In addition to its core contributions, there are three other more indirect benefits that come from Visual Workflow:

▶ **Change management** Even though this is no substitute for full change management programs, one of the tangible but indirect benefits of VW is that departmental roles and responsibilities often change. These have been worked out with cross-functional teams that are effectively designing their own change. Consequently, you see less resistance to the realignment that CRM necessarily entails.

▶ **Communication** There is a reason it is called *Visual* Workflow. The vocabulary is common, not geek speak. The pictographs are easy to read and intelligible, which isn't always the case for Visio-generated, UML-compliant process modeling. Most people could probably draw the pictographs used, much less just read them. Everyone can understand them.

▶ **Easy on staff resources and time** VW requires no prior training of team members, sparing companies the cost of pulling prime people offline. The time spent implementing goes easy on labor too.

What makes this a unique process is that not only does it work, but you'll actually understand it and participate in its success. While, like any other methodology involving business processes and workflow management, it needs an expert to do it, you'll actually be involved. And that, as they say at MasterCard, is priceless.

STEPPIN' OUT: Staffware: Not Exactly CRM

Staffware is a bit of an aberration. They are not a CRM company, yet they are getting coverage in a book on CRM and as best of breed. The thing is, they understand how CRM and business processes intersect and how one is intermeshed with the other, and they are without a doubt the strongest BPM framework that exists anywhere. So they belong here.

Staffware has been around long enough to have seen both fads and the longer lasting enterprise applications come and go. ERP, SCM, CRM have all crossed their radar screen. To their credit, since their founding in 1984 and the release of Staffware in 1987, they stuck with what they do extremely well: business process management. Their current product is iProcess, the best BPM engine and framework, which is part of Process Suite 3.0.

Staffware is headquartered in the U.K., has offices in 17 countries, and employs approximately 350 people. The Americas headquarters is located in the heart of New York. It is a debt-free, profitable company that turned $77 million in sales in 2003, up 10 percent from 2002. That breaks down to about 50 percent licenses, 30 percent maintenance (read: services) fees, and the rest, scattered among, well, the rest.

They've had this financial success because they are so good at what they do. They have a serious enterprise-level product that has been seen as the crown jewel of the BPM universe. Clients like Cigna, Vodaphone, the state of New Jersey, and Barclays love them. It's like Woodstock all over again. Process Suite 3.0 brings peace and love to your business processes and rules.

The Staffware Process Suite

Their Staffware Process Suite 3.0 addresses the full-spectrum of BPM requirements, providing a complete set of tools to create, transform, and streamline the internal and external processes and tasks of an organization. In order to facilitate the process transformation, the tools depend on the creation of an independent process layer that separates process from the application logic. This separation allows rapid facil-itation and development of new processes and the logic to support those processes. They use this framework to embed domain expertise to deliver industry-specific best practice process frameworks to expe-dite implementation and reduce development cycles.

THE COMPONENTS

The Staffware Process Suite 3.0 has all the standard components of a BPM application. A business rules engine, an execution engine, web services, a very advanced process designer with version control, a process relationship manager, a process administrator, process moni-tor, process engine, and a process client. They have a development envi-ronment, a PDK. They provide process objects—ready-made code for insertion into the process design when appropriate. But there are a few things that make them unique. I'm going to examine a couple of them to give you a sense of why they are best of breed in the BPM world. Staffware's Process Suite is a very good example of the orchestration model mentioned earlier in the chapter and I would think about it from that standpoint as you read this section.

THE STAFFWARE ORCHESTRATOR

The Orchestrator provides processes developers with the ability to dynamically assign process components such as subprocesses and web services to the overall business process, in context, depending on data content and external events. The system dynamically determines which subprocesses to execute based on the context of those events or on the communications with the external system. Thus, the processes become adaptive and responsive without knowing what the events are going to be, but as they meet up. Subprocesses allow the Process Definer to spec-ify the trigger point to start multiple other subprocesses. The Orches-trator can also enable external applications to initiate tasks even the Staffware subprocesses and then take what the external apps initiated and graft them to the appropriate point in the primary process. This facility recognizes that, while Staffware Process Suite does not neces-sarily own all of the decision-making, it can monitor and manage the outcome of decisions made by other components of the whole solu-tion, in conjunction with external applications and make this a con-tinuing and changing dynamic effort.

Do you understand yet? No? Hold on.

496   CRM AT THE SPEED OF LIGHT: ESSENTIAL CUSTOMER STRATEGIES FOR THE 21ST CENTURY

GOAL-DRIVEN PROCESS SELECTION

Using the Orchestrator allows for a much simplified design and a flexible response to actions along selected processes. But it needs one further step because, by itself, dynamic process orchestration is not able to achieve sufficient gains in agility, robustness, and scalability that larger business environments need. For example, in designing a process for getting a hit in the major leagues, the process developer may know that the batter needs to hit, but that is all they know of the process. Getting the hit is the goal, but the subprocesses are the means to achieve the goal, the variants of the goal, and the context that will determine which of the subprocesses to use. All of this is beyond the designer. These subprocesses may be changed frequently. All the designer knows is that a goal (to get a hit) is to be achieved.

Goal-driven process selection in conjunction with the Orchestrator tags the subprocess with the goal. So for example, the subprocesses are Hit-home run, Hit-single, Hit-double, Hit-triple, Hit-Sacrifice Fly, and so on. They are also tagged with the circumstances they can be used. Hit-triple with bases loaded in Yankee Stadium or Hit-home run with baserunner on first and two outs.

The subprocess is also tagged with the circumstances that it can be used with—the entry condition. For example, Hit-home run with baserunner on first where left field fence is less than 355 feet.

By doing that, the process flow then can just call out the goal "Hit" and let the system determine which subprocess achieves the goal. It calls out "Hit" and gathers up all Hit-related subprocesses (single, double, triple, home run, and such) and then evaluates the entry condition. If the entry condition is "true" (there is a runner on first and the left field is less than 355 feet), then that ball is going, going, gone! In drier terms, Hit-home run. If none of the conditions are applicable, returning "false," he's outta there!

Using the Orchestrator and goal-driven process selection, you find a well organized and streamlined way of using BPM to accomplish your objectives, through the excellent Staffware Process Suite.

Company Culture

Staffware is strongly focused on the relationship between business processes and applications technology, however, they have one of the clearest perceptions of how CRM and BPM work together. They built their internal culture around the relationships that CRM demands.

Helen Donnelly, vice president of marketing at Staffware: "We believe that relationships are the key to business success, and with this mindset, we work to know our teams internally, as well as we do our partners and customers. Since inception, we have been a very customer-centric company. As such, our product development, sales, marketing, and support priorities reflect our customers' priorities."

But they don't stop with a good set of internal customer-focused processes. They spend money on things like research. In a 2003 study, Staffware was found to be the 14th highest investor in research and development among software and services companies. The average is 10.8 percent of the budget by the software companies. They were 21 percent higher than that! Not bad for a company that made $77 million.

Their optimism is unbounded for good reason. They accomplish their goals and do it well.

Their Strategy

Staffware is expanding their collaborative efforts as the core of their strategy for the next three years. They are aggressively pursuing an expansion of their partner networks, and increasing the number of vertical frameworks they provide. They already provide frameworks in financial services, telecommunications, insurance, pharmaceuticals, public sector, and utilities. They are going granular with some of their newer frameworks looking at such items as claims processing, mortgage processing, and customer service transactions. To do all of this, they are enlisting partners freely that can both act as service partners but also partners who can work with them to provide industrial expertise for target industries. Smart stuff.

CRM and BPM: Staffware's Take

Let's hear Helen Donnelly again: "Without knowledge of the customer, a business will fail to nurture and grow their base or provide best-of-breed, differentiated service. That's why CRM is crucial for storing and sharing the history of transactions and serves a critical role in the overall process flow across an organization. BPM, however, is the overarching arbiter of process. CRM is but one of many subcomponents working together to automate and streamline the processes that are the lifeblood of an organization."

My perspective is somewhat different. I see BPM as a subcomponent of a CRM strategy. If CRM were an application I would agree with her perspective, but as I hope I have established by now, CRM is an over-arching business strategy that has multiple components to develop and act on in order to guarantee success.

For example, a CRM system can tell you when a customer is due for an upgrade product or service. A BPM system, receiving such a notification from the CRM system, would initiate and monitor all the steps necessary to deliver the upgrade to the customer.

However, to her point, CRM-related business processes are not the only business processes that fall within a company's value chain. All the supply chain, financial, human resources (you won't find me calling it human capital management, the outlandish dehumanized phrase for the management of human activity at a company), and multiple industry specific practices are all part of the BPM universe. But CRM is the strategy that encompasses the value chain we now see in the customer ecosystem.

Staffware's BPM framework and engine fine-tune the way work is done at companies, and not just at the human level. They have defined processes that govern how people interact with paper documents, digitized images, and other systems and applications. I only hope that doesn't include things like taking Word files to lunch or breaking down the process of kissing pictures of your kids or cats. If not, then they are surely the BPM champs.

I go on and on about strategy and then tell you that I'm going to run five chapters on a more in-depth look at certain elements of strategy. Okay, you've now got the first element, BPM. The second element is arguably the most important of all: culture change and change management. Remember what I said before: if you're considering CRM, you're considering a change in the way you do business. If you're considering a change in the way you do business, you are going to have to change the way you think about doing business, which means an environment has to be created to support that change, which means that senior management has to change the way they think about doing business. We've covered the "considering a change in the way you do business" in this chapter, because BPM and VW is how you start developing those changes. The rest of that statement? Next chapter.

19

Culture Change, not Diaper Change: Managing a Dramatic Transformation

I magine this: you're going to an opera, because you promised you would, but you hate opera. Or this: you love the Yankees, but you live in Boston. Or finally, this: you're reading this book because you have to for a class or your boss, but you don't really have the slightest interest in CRM.

Take any one of those scenarios and tell me what kind of actual impact an opera or this book is going to have on you. Or what impact rooting for the Yankees all alone in Boston will have. When the opera is over, you'll breathe a sigh of relief and go back to your Outkast CDs. You'll always root for the Yankees (of course) but stay silent. And this book will sit under the drink you're nursing because you've flunked the test or were fired because you were never on board with the CRM initiative at your company.

But what if you did extensive reading on the history of the opera that you were seeing and it was really very moving? Or what if you convinced the entire city of Boston to abandon the Red Sox and root for the Yankees? What if you actually liked this book and were able to understand CRM a heck of a lot better as a result of it?

The results? You have a good time at the opera, the Yankees win the World Series to the delight of the city of Boston, and CRM is a subject you know so well, you ace the test or enthusiastically participate in the initiative at work, getting you a big year-end bonus.

That, attentive readers, is the difference between not planning, transforming, and managing the change in culture that CRM needs and doing so. You will need to change, and the environment around you will have to support the change, meaning it too must change. Transformation of your business culture is a vital step—perhaps the most vital step in making sure that a CRM initiative succeeds.

Why So Important?

CRM encourages resistance. It is a difficult system and outlook to implement, especially in business cultures that have been successful for years. At its best, when change is handled well, users enjoy the new business environment they are working in. It sweeps away the dusty behaviors and stodgy thinking that had begun to cripple the business. It allows for a foresighted approach to how the business needs to conduct itself over the ensuing years to the benefit of the customers, employees, suppliers, and partners. Not just the paying customers. In other words, the entire value chain is affected by the change in culture.

But there are a lot of obstacles in the way of successful culture change, because the elements are both substantial and minute. For example, in most companies, the users of a system are often not empowered in any way to create the system nor are they involved in the decisions to adopt it. They simply are told they are responsible to make it work. As we saw in Chapter 4 on sales and throughout many of the other chapters, this engenders resistance because there is no apparent benefit to a user from a system that is aimed at enriching the experience of someone else. The use of this kind of strategy and system also calls for cross-functional or cross-departmental cooperation and revealing data that was privately held. This is not how companies ordinarily work. Self-interest, often in the form of selfish interest, is the departmental chieftains' and their working minions' operational approach. Thus, users don't see the value to them, so why should they change how they behave?

But it isn't that simple.

Driving Miss(ed) Adoption

There are multiple reasons why users don't adopt a new strategy, outlook, or system. Some are obvious, some not; all are very human. Analysts have spent years looking at the cultural difficulties with CRM. Some recent studies are interesting.

In May 2003, Forrester Research asked executives where their CRM difficulties most appeared. Adoption was listed as the number one problem with 22.5 percent of the respondents citing it, over any other reason, including lack of strategy.

In an even newer Forrester Research study released in early 2004, even with nearly 75 percent of the respondents reporting that they were satisfied with their CRM effort, half of them still reported that resistance to process change was their most significant obstacle, which led to the most often cited difficulty of "driving adoption."

Equally as interesting in the same study were the 25 percent dissatisfied who claimed 25 percent of the time that they had usability problems; only 5 percent of the satisfied said that. Interesting correlation. More on usability later in the chapter.

The Model: General Behavioral/Social Psychological

Not so oddly, transforming a corporate culture to a customer-friendly culture, and from "whatever else it had been" culture (sales-driven, product-driven, no-organized-culture-to-speak-of-driven), is something that is framed by the general knowledge and principles of change and social psychology. The father of social psychology and change management, Kurt Lewin, identified a model for managed change in the 1940s that stands the test of time for any type of change:

- ▶ **Stage 1: Unfreezing** This is the most difficult stage. It often needs an organizational shock to occur. It is initially when at least the leadership knows that the old ways of doing whatever it is that you were doing are no longer appropriate. Failure isn't necessarily the motivation for this. It can come as a result of success and the need to improve upon that success. That is where the leadership comes in. They are able to think strategically to describe future opportunities if changes are made or difficulties if changes aren't implemented. If they can effectively get this across to their personnel, unfreezing could occur. What makes this so difficult is that there is a strong resistance to anything new and if it doesn't appeal to touch, taste, sight, or sound, then people have a hard time grasping it. It is all the more difficult to get the breakthrough understanding that comes with unfreezing.

- ▶ **Stage 2: Changing** People look for new ways of doing things and select an appropriate and promising approach.

- ▶ **Stage 3: Refreezing** The new approach is implemented and it becomes established as a supportive environment.

Crossing the boundaries of these stages are interactive elements that identify the dynamics of this change throughout the entire process:

- ▶ **Group productivity** What is going on in the departments or through the company that necessitates a CRM initiative? What is ineffective? What is effective?

▶ **Communications** How does influence work in the departments, among social cliques, at corporate headquarters, in the
field, or between these entities?

▶ **Social perception** How do the sales managers and their sales
teams perceive the stakeholders' idea that a CRM initiative is
necessary? What does that do to the sales group?

▶ **Intergroup relations** How do sales and marketing get along?
How does the board of directors get along with…well, they don't
get along with anyone, do they?

▶ **Group membership** As the changes are made, how do the sales
folks adjust? Poorly? Well? What is their response as a group?

▶ **Training leaders** Who are the leaders who need to get trained
in order to train the staff? A natural leader (see Chapter 17) who
is respected can be trained to train his group. These are trained
as change agents.

Finally, (at least for the purposes of this chapter) the forces of change
have to be accounted for. There are two basic forces—driving forces
and constraints. The drivers are those that move change forward such
as compensation plans that are aimed at customer satisfaction. A clear
mission and vision statement presented to the company for action is
another example of a driving force. Examples of constraints are fear of
job loss with the new accountability, or fear of job loss with the new
accountability, or fear of job loss with the new accountability, or…
The actions taken for change are increasing the driving forces while
reducing the constraints. The latter is the tough job. It's easy to provide
those things that are happiness-producing. It isn't so easy to alleviate
fears. Reality doesn't drive the fear's power, does it?

Change Dynamics

This change framework is dynamic and proactive. Lewin's entire pos-
tulate was that you can't understand an organization without trying to
change it. That means don't diagnose without intervention. Active
involvement in the change process will lead to the diagnosis, which
will change as progress is made.

The critical moments in this CRM change strategy are the transition
times. They are the delicate points that can make or break a change
management process. Edgardo Pappacena, BearingPoint's Global Leader

for Business Transformation, notes the need to manage the transition and the best practices that are available to do that:

> Although every CRM transformation effort is unique due to the specific business and organizational reality of each company, there are a handful of leading practices that all successful CRM initiatives use to mitigate the organizational and people risks associated with large-scale change transitions:
>
> - Early stakeholder segmentation to understand true "resistance to change" drivers
>
> - Audience-specific, two-way, continuous, staged communication strategy
>
> - Strong political "guiding coalition" and leadership alignment plan
>
> - Cascading approach to ensure local leadership involvement and adoption
>
> - Realignment of frontline employees' job profiles, roles, and responsibilities
>
> - Just-in-time reskilling strategy that addresses new technical, functional, and behavioral competencies
>
> - Focus on performance management to drive and reward new desired behaviors
>
> - Realignment of key HR practices (e.g., hiring, compensation, appraisal, and development) to transition to and sustain the new CRM environment

When you bring in the change management experts for your CRM initiative, spend a good deal of time understanding their approach and methodology. Dante identified a difference between the *vita activa*—the active life—and the *vita passiva*—the sedate life. It is the difference between changing a culture and merely diagnosing the need for the change. It is here that the difference between success and failure could well be lurking. *Vita activa* for everyone—on the house.

The Hidden Change Factor: Usability and Technology

Imagine that you've gotten buy-in from all your users. You think you've unfrozen, changed, and refrozen. All without a refrigerator! Your users go into the new system, smiling, glad to know that they are going to contribute to the happiness of their existing and potential customers. In fact, they are thrilled by the new compensation plan that is in place that rewards those interested in customer satisfaction. But when you log onto your new CRM vendor-bought system, what seemed great during the demos and the testing is now ugly, slow, and frustrating. Page load times are long; the analytics dashboards have to be read by PhDs in math; the new bouncy culture of the company isn't represented by the user interface. It's hard to find anything on the opening portal screens once you log in. It isn't long before your positive outlook erodes and you are back to using the wrong, but comfortable old system with Excel and Outlook. It was easier on the eyes, not as hard to figure out, and seemed to just go faster. It was familiar. The old system seemed a lot more *usable*.

Usability

Usability is one of the human factors most often overlooked when planning and dealing with corporate culture change. How your website looks and feels, and how your automated response system actually measures up in the response of a customer to it are all part of the thinking that has to go into the change in culture. Don't forget there is nothing more likely to limit or destroy strategic user adoption than a system that is hard to understand or use. The primary three reasons that someone repeats their visit to a site are content, speed, and ease of use. Usability and usefulness.

But usability is most often associated with technology. Technology is normally associated with performance-related numbers such as storage requirements, benchmark tests, and system "robustness." So the human factors involved in technology are ingloriously ignored to a bad end. At best, they are a rear-end test environment for users to see how well they respond to your completed new design.

The reality is that usability is perhaps the most important factor related to systems that you are going to install at your company. Usability needs to be considered a major design factor and is certainly a component of total cost of ownership. It is not just ease of use that determines usability, no matter how easy it is to qualify it that way. It also takes into account how quickly a system can be learned, how effective it is for regular users, whether users will remember how to use the system after a period of nonuse, and how errors in the system are managed by or, even better, prevented by the system.

Factors and Standards

In order to set a common standard for usability measurement, a number of companies, including Oracle, Microsoft, Boeing, and the National Institute for Standards and Technology (NIST), got together and created the Common Industry Format (CIF). The CIF is the standard for usability testing and reporting that began development in 1997. The idea was to construct a common set of tools, tasks, facility types, methods, and data types to allow an easy exchange of results between consumers and vendors. It worked. The CIF is the standard for reporting and analysis among the labs that do the work in this millennium. It is a specific list of procedures and detail needed to successfully complete the results of a usability survey or test. For example, this is a verbatim list from Section 5.4.4 on metrics:

Section 5.4.4. Usability Metrics

As defined in Section 4.1, usability is measured by three types of metrics: effectiveness, efficiency, and satisfaction.

The following information shall be provided:

Metrics for effectiveness.

Metrics for efficiency.

Metrics for satisfaction.

Effectiveness and efficiency results shall be reported, even when they are difficult to interpret within the specified context of use. In this case, the report shall specify why the supplier does not consider the metrics meaningful.

EXAMPLE

Suppose that the context of use for the product includes real time, open-ended interaction between close associates. In this case, Time-On-Task may not be meaningfully interpreted as a measure of efficiency, because for many users, time spent on this task is "time well spent."

If it is necessary to provide participants with assists, efficiency and effectiveness metrics shall be provided for both unassisted and assisted conditions, and the number and type of assists shall be included as part of the test results.

EFFECTIVENESS

Effectiveness relates the goals of using the product to the accuracy and completeness with which these goals can be achieved. Common measures of effectiveness include percent task completion, frequency of errors, frequency of assists to the participant from the testers, and frequency of accesses to help or documentation by the participants during the tasks. It does not take account of how the goals were achieved, only the extent to which they were achieved. Efficiency relates the level of effectiveness achieved to the quantity of resources expended.

This gives you an idea of the excruciating detail necessary to keep a CRM user happy about the new system that they are endorsing so chummily. It is serious enough for Oracle to invest in a usability laboratory—the Usability and Interface Design Department—under the able direction of Dr. Anna M. Wichansky, Senior Director for Advanced User Interfaces. The lab has 66 employees engaged full time in nothing but making sure that your attention doesn't wander and your beliefs in the system stay strong. Here's Dr. Wichansky on how they go about it:

> Usability testing is an evaluation process in which at least 8 and up to 30 users from the target market group are brought into a usability testing lab and run through a series of realistic, job-related tasks, using prerelease or released software. Usability engineers moderate the test session, and record users' performances and subjective reactions to the product. Software developers and UI designers observe test sessions live from a control room behind a one-way mirror, or remotely via streamed video over the Internet. We video tape record all sessions, and also log and time stamp each user behavior, to enable us to track time on task, errors, number of assists, task completions, and other objective usability metrics. We use standard usability surveys such as SUMI (Subjective Usability Measurement Inventory) (Kirakowski, 1996) after the user experience with the product is completed, to get an idea of users' subjective reactions to the product. Most important, we observe where users have trouble with the product and we formulate design recommendations to improve the issues we inevitably find *before* the product is released. The key points are:
>
> - Usability testing is an iterative process; redesigns are performed between tests which improve the product, and then it is tested again.

- We bring in users from outside who are similar in profile to our customers; we don't test ourselves.

- We have them do realistic, goal-oriented job tasks. They do not get written or verbal instructions in what controls to click, but have to formulate a product use strategy themselves at the time of the test.

- This testing is quantitative in nature, based on user performance with the product, as well as whether they say they like it or not.

So be wise. Even though we've redefined CRM over the past few years as a business strategy and not a technology, if your change management strategy doesn't include a well-designed technical system tested for its user-friendly capacity, then all the change agents in the world won't maintain the good will and support that was created by the strategy.

Results

Much of the published usability testing results are the work of Jakob Nielson, a guru who specializes in website design issues. In his article "Return on Investment in Usability" (Jakob Nielson's Alertbox, January 3, 2003), he mentioned the ROI derived from the redesign of an intranet: "Similarly, the estimated productivity gains from redesigning an intranet to improve usability are 8 times bigger than the costs for a company with 1,000 employees, 20 times bigger for a company with 10,000 employees, and 50 times bigger for a company with 100,000 employees." Whoa! That is a really substantial benefit. But that's a projected benefit. What about actual studies? Table 19-1 shows the results of a study of 842 companies done in 2002 by Nielson. The benefits are indisputable.

Table 19-1: Usability Redesign Success

Metric	Average Improvement Across Web Projects
Sales/conversion rate	100%
Traffic/visitor count	150%
User performance/productivity	161%
Use of specific (target) features	202%

How Do You Do It?

Change management is a methodologically nebulous field. There are as many approaches as there are toppings for California-style pizzas. The vast majority of approaches are based on the Lewinesque "unfreeze, change, refreeze" stages, but there are rebels opposed to even that time-honored set of dicta. The fundamentals remain the same— the social dynamics involved are pretty much what they always were. But each company has a different subset of those dynamics that has to be harnessed and saddled before it can be ridden.

There is one other thing that has to be considered when it comes to CRM-related change management. The environment that the external customer—be they supplier, partner, or paying client—comes to is the environment that changed so that they have to be considered in that change. It's not just a matter of what change you make, but what groups you impact, both internally and externally.

For example, you are a customer interaction center that has historically responded to customer queries in 48 hours and customer problems (trouble tickets) in 24 hours. You want to change the time to 24 hours for the queries and 6 hours for the customer trouble tickets. That is a major change in the way that the culture of your company works. Not only does it entail compensation plans for your CSRs meeting these new goals, and penalties for consistent failure, but it means that you might have to hire new CSRs, and improve the algorithms for optimization of the schedules of the CSRs and for queue management. Additionally, it means that the workflow and processes have to be altered so that trouble tickets are flagged differently (perhaps) and that there are values/weights attached to the queries and the customers making them. If they are a super premium gold, platinum, diamond-level SLA holder, they are handled differently than a brown sludge-level SLA holder. Finally, though, it means that the way the CSR handles the individual customer has to change. The buy-in from all levels for the change in program and culture has to be complete or nearly so.

So what methodology do you use that can effectively implement this level of culture change down to the singular CSR?

I'm not sure I've looked at all of the methodologies that are available, but I'm still supporting the one I supported in the last edition—the O2 methodology developed by RWD Technologies and used by such stalwarts as SAP. This has unique characteristics that can impact change more than a typical or traditional change management program, and yet best represents how change management programs work.

STEPPIN' OUT: O2: Change Management for the Masses

O2 is short for Opportunity Optimization. This is a change management process, from now on called OCM for organizational change management, owned by RWD Technologies, and licensed by such enterprise applications giants as SAP as their own. It is unique because of the level of mass and individually interactive involvement that the users have in the process. Unfortunately, often enough, the senior stakeholders are seen as the change agents because they are senior management. The users are left out, not only of the design process but of the change management workshops and facilitated sessions and are only involved after the fact. O2 actually provides a means to overcome that problem and still interact with the individual user as an agent of change. The underlying philosophy is "the more change agents, the better."

The framework for O2 is a series of three or four sessions that are initiated throughout the lifecycle of the change management project. They are supplemented by Web-based "pulse taking" surveys that use a validated survey instrument. These occur throughout the project life. The initial session is two days and involves between 50 and 150 key stakeholders at once, far wider a group than a typical change management meeting which involves about 5 to 25 key stakeholders. The change readiness survey is validated prior to the session. There are immediate results from the meeting and an action-planning workshop over the two-day period. O2 involves the right number and mix of stakeholders, which might include the power users, the management, the suppliers, and others who need to be there. The actual process should take about eight days, though the surveys are taken throughout the life of the project and could potentially go on longer than that.

Some of the questions that are asked in the course of the sessions include:

- ▶ How can we quickly and efficiently gauge the organizational readiness for our change initiative?

- ▶ We're (doing the mission). How can we assess what impact this will have on our organization?

- ▶ We've just gone live with our new system. How can we test how well the organization will commit to its utilization and ensure the outcomes we expected?

▶ How can we ensure the communications process throughout our implementation is really effective, understood, and accepted?

▶ Will the solution we're implementing require us to change our organization culture, and what would we have to do?

▶ Is there a way of benchmarking and measuring our progress in implementing the organizational change aspects of our program in order to make the needed course corrections along the way?

▶ We need to assess, anticipate, and mitigate the organizational risks associated with our solution implementation program and get the key people to take ownership. How do we best do that?

There is something of a resemblance to any planning process, but there are a few differences. For example, look at that last question. The fact that stakeholders and risk assessment are involved might seem to be enough to handle change. But what is interesting about good organizational change management is that it doesn't just identify the necessity of the task, but it specifies how to do it so that it can continuously assess organizational impact. The endgame is to align expectations with reality so that when reality does assert itself—and it always does—not only will the stakeholders not be shocked, they will actually be happy with the results. Additionally, it helps identify the support environment that will sustain the changes.

The Web-based surveys are short and are sent to the identified change agents or opinion leaders. They give the OCM team a chance to assess the state of the change cycle and to make corrections where necessary. The psychological value is the constant involvement of the change agents in the process, empowering and invigorating the larger enterprise and thus increasing adoption rates.

During the last two days—the summarization stage—detailed assessments are presented along with recommended actions from the change management consultants at the site. There are defined metrics and targeted action plans based on the reality curve identified by the change consultants for the particular company—nothing generic.

O2 is a step further along than the typical change management planning because of its involvement with both large groups of selected stakeholders and its high technology use of validated tools for surveys and interactions. Bravo.

There are other excellent OCM methodologies such as the intense three-day effort called Breakthrough Change (BTC) that was created by CRMGuru fellow guru panelist, Bill Brendler. This one is for a somewhat different audience than O2 and is an outstanding example of how to effect change in a short time frame.

Whatever methodology you use for organizational change management in your CRM planning, the one certainty is that you will need a change management program to monitor the success (or failure) of the cultural impact of your CRM strategy and to effect the transformation of your business to its new environment.

For the Record

For the record, I love opera *and* Outkast, love the Yankees, but live in Virginia where there are lots of Yankees fans, and I'm writing this book so I'm clearly interested in CRM.

20

Dancing to the Music: Implementing CRM

This chapter we're going to do something interesting. Because the drama in CRM is now at the level of a Law & Order episode (five times nightly on TNT), I'm going to let the companies that I think represent best and most glamorous of breed do the speaking here.

Implementations are projects. Where strategies have milestones and specific stops along the path, implementations have (theoretical) definitive ends and fully reinforced frameworks. That means they have a beginning, a cost to the project, and an end date that is agreed upon in a statement of work. They are tactical in execution, though strategic in thought. They are run by project managers from the company that is purchasing the application or suite of applications and the consulting services company doing the installation, configuration, customization, and maintenance. There is a wall that they reach.

You've probably gotten the idea that this is a phase of a CRM strategy that occurs after a vendor is selected. That raises some questions: How do you select the vendor? Why the vendor? Why not the software? Well, my fellow travelers in this journey, when you buy software, you buy an inanimate package. If there are problems with the software, they don't fix themselves. If there are questions with how to apply the software, the software won't ask you the questions. Or answer them. It is not (yet, anyway) self-healing, nor self-installing, nor self-customizing, though these things are becoming easier. It will take human intervention to make things happen.

When You Buy the Application, You Buy the Vendor

I have no doubt that when the first humans kindled fire, they were enchanted by the sparkling, crackly, bright orange and red flames—just before they stuck their hands into them. Unfortunately, you would think that if Jung were right the species memory would prevent that from happening again, but... When potential CRM customers have gotten to the point where they are selecting their vendor for the applications they want to use, they think "software" not "vendor." That is a big mistake, and, if that is the way you are considering your implementation, just like our ancestors and the flames, you're going to get burnt.

Software is not what you select when you prepare for an implementation. You select a purveyor of the software. The fact is that when you buy the application you buy the vendor. Repeatez après moi: When you buy the application, you buy the vendor. Most of the vendors will provide you with the functions and features you need in the software they created. However, the real issue here is not just what can they provide functionally, but what kind of company are they? Do they have a corporate culture you can live with? Are their salespeople giving you an honest picture of what you need, or what they need to get their commissions? Are they trustworthy? Stay tuned and I'll answer your questions, one at a time.

Vendor Genus

Selecting a vendor is no easy task. You are not just deciding what features and functions are useful to you if you select their applications, you're deciding how you want to do the implementation, and who should lead that implementation. For example, after software vendor selection, you have multiple possibilities on actually doing the implementation in the enterprise applications world. You don't have the same options yet, though you will, in the ASP world. I'm going to outline a few of the options. The "Best of" part at the end means that they provide what I see as the best quality of work in their class. However, that doesn't guarantee anything at all. They may not have the range or scope of services that you need. They may be a bad cultural fit for you. They may have services available but not be so good in the segment you want. The way it works is project by project, and company by company—whoever you are comfortable with, and do your due diligence on, will likely work.

Vendor's Consulting Services

Most of the larger CRM applications vendors have their own consulting services or extensive partner networks that do their implementations.

The benefit of using them is the extensive backup and expertise in the applications suite that you are installing. The downside is that they are expensive and utterly useless if you are using a best-of-breed implementation where you are installing and customizing multiple applications from several vendors. The last thing you want is the likely catfight if you get the competing vendor services in the same room. Additionally, often they are not as capable as a third party just in terms of sheer technical experience over a long time. They have people schooled in what they provide. Period. So use them with caution, but consider them if you have a single enterprise solution.

Best of: PeopleSoft Consulting; SAP Partner Network

Large Systems Integrator or Consulting Services Firm

The advantage here is that they have perhaps the best skilled people available and are technically vendor agnostic, though most of them are agnostic because of partnerships with multiple vendors, rather than none. The advantage of these large consulting firms or systems integrators is that they have vast experience that runs deep in not just applications, but methodology, processes, and industry-specific expertise. They can provide soup to nuts strategic services in addition to implementation assistance. But there is a real disadvantage. They cost a lot of money and often tend to do things in a big and very time consuming way, though many of them are trying to respond to the "do it faster and cheaper" model that's popping up all around the CRM world.

Best of: Unisys, Bearing Point in specific areas; IBM Global Services; EDS as an outsourcer for call center work

Boutique Firm

These are small specialty firms who are often the partners that are used by the larger vendors to do many implementations or have a vertical strength such as public sector, insurance, or perhaps sports. If they are good, they have the benefit of a highly skilled small company culture, which means that they are hungry. That means that they are willing to price themselves reasonably. That means they are willing to go the extra mile. What they don't offer is the added resources or usually the financial stability. But don't take me at the generic word. Investigate their finances. If stable, they can be the bargain of the century, getting big league skills at a Double A price.

Best of: ePartners

Internal Team

Don't even think about it. Let's put it this way. If you are a plumber, would you want one of your customers to come and try to fix your plumbing? I don't think so. Stick with your expertise and let the outside consulting firm or vendor consulting team use theirs. Implementing CRM cost effectively is fine. Implementing CRM on the cheap isn't. It will bite back if you try to do it that way.

Does that mean that an internal team can't do it? No, but it's as frequently successful as your sighting of a live dodo.

The Ropes

Vendor (or consulting services) selection is traditionally done in several ways. A request for proposal (RFP) is issued to multiple companies either as an open bid, inviting anyone in, or a selective one—meaning you invite specifically chosen appropriate companies to submit a response. Then based on traditional criteria that involve past performance, personnel experience, price, understanding of what is being proposed, and ability to perform, a company is graded and chosen if they have the highest weighted grade or subjectively chosen based on their response. There are often orals if it is a government bid and lots of meetings and solution demonstrations if it is private sector proposal. That's the way you do it, that's the way your father did it and his father before him. The lore of RFP response travels back to the days of the Anglo-Saxons, when Harold won the bid to invade England in 1066.

It also can be done without an RFP. Or done differently, even with an RFP. Let's take a quick look at some of the 21st century methodologies. One disclaimer. What I'm proposing is one of many ways to do your due diligence with vendors. Mine is somewhat unorthodox, but it works, though it will take time. Feel free to take any other route you care to. This one has no lock on the truth. It just allows you to get closer to those nuggets of truth that are often obfuscated by marketing "techniques," a.k.a. spin, a.k.a. hype.

Vendor Selection Can Be Fun

Each year CRMGuru, Dick Lee of Hi-Yield Methods, and David Mangen of Mangen Associates do a vendor satisfaction survey that I would highly recommend using as part of the selection process. The current version is called, "The State of Customer Relationship Management

Software, 2003–2004." Their results show that each year, even though there are slight improvements, the vendors don't look great. For example, in the recent survey, the highest rated three vendors are Best Software's SalesLogix at 73.51, then Microsoft at 72.31, and salesforce.com at 71.21. The highest rated enterprise vendor is PeopleSoft at 65.60, pretty close to the CRM industry average of 65.3. In statistical terms, according to the authors, the industry satisfaction rate in comparison to other industries is "very low."

The most meaningful factors that the more than 1,000 customers identified as most critical are the vendor's corporate stability and the vendor's customer focus, not functionality. So presuming that you are interested in learning the lessons that those who came before you learned and some of the lessons that I've evolved over time, here are some of the things that you can do to make vendor selection as painstaking and painless as possible—while protecting your back in the bargain.

Self-Interest Governs Business (and Life)

Lesson 1: Self-interest governs what you do and what the vendor does. No big surprise here, I would guess. Your interest is in getting the best price and best usable functionality to support your brilliant CRM strategy. Your interest is served if all of that meets your customers' needs and your ROI planning. The vendor's interest is served in providing you with the applications that you need or, depending on the vendor's salesperson, the applications you think you need at a price that earns their company a profit and the salesperson a commission. Both of you, one way or the other, are trying to serve customers.

Lesson 2: The application isn't the issue. Most CRM functionality is pretty much the same. The execution might be a bit different, some features and functions may vary, and the tools associated will work differently, but especially with the rise of web services, even the way that they speak to each other is similar. Additionally, the applications are inanimate. They are not breathing. Problems with them aren't solved by them. The problems are solved by people. That means that you have to have a relationship with the vendor that works in times of difficulty. That is a much more complex process than even the packaged software selection part. Naughty or nice is something you have to decide, not Santa—and before you pick the package.

Lesson 3: Your culture and the vendor's culture need to be compatible, not identical. No two companies are alike. However, having a culture that supports similar definitions of success, failure, or timeliness can be very important. Inchoate ideas of success or failure can lead to failure, that is, depending on how you define it.

Looking for Love in All the Right Spaces

So what do you look at and for in a vendor besides application price, functionality, usability, integration, and configurability? A few orthodox and somewhat unorthodox techniques first:

- ▶ **Experience** That comes with talking to references. By all means, speak to the references that have a similar profile to yours that the vendors give you, but recognize that they gave them to you for a reason. For the most part, they are going to say nice things, though some useful nuggets will emerge. Often, the vendor compensates the reference somehow to be a reference, perhaps with discounts on future upgrades. In this case it is worth going the extra mile to find out more from references that are, so to speak, "off the books." Go on the Web and through searches and user groups (look at stockholders discussion groups, if the companies are public) and cull company and individual customer names. Get names through word of mouth, printed media, whatever other sources you have. Call all the vendor customers you find. Some percentage of them will talk to you and you'll get the real scoop, good or bad. Ask them about the behavior of the sales, marketing, and support staff. Find companies that listened to their pitch and turned it down and find out why. Talk to the vendor's partners, especially those that partner with multiple vendors and ask for comparisons. Watch for the sales pitch with the partners, though. All this can be time consuming, but worth it to get the truth.

- ▶ **Finances** How much information about its financial condition will the vendor disclose? Are they candid with their employees and partners about their finances?

- ▶ **Gossip** This has more value than you could ever imagine. While all of us both love and are repulsed by gossip, there is one ironic fact. Gossip spreads because it seems credible somehow—via a personality pattern or a near-truth. The critical idea of gathering the industry scuttlebutt about your vendor choices is that there is likely a kernel of truth about their senior leadership's personalities which you might have to deal with: moves being made by that leadership (such as Oracle's attempted takeover of PeopleSoft), and what other companies say about the vendor, good or bad. If you strip the gossip of its venality, there is likely to be a nugget of truth that will be important in your selection process. Be careful, though, the gossip you hear could be an outright lie. Just don't discount gossip. Know what to do with it.

▶ **Play the margins** Find techniques to get some information at the edges if need be. For example, a Montana Supreme Court ruling in May 1998 found that the law requiring that the contents of requests for proposals not be revealed to competing offerors conflicted with the public's "right to know" provision in the Montana Constitution. In 1999, the Montana legislature amended Section 18-4-304, MCA to reflect the changes required by the Supreme Court. The outcome of this ruling is twofold. First, the contents of the submitted proposals are now open to public inspection, including competing offerors and the media, at the time set for the receipt of proposals. Second, all meetings involving the evaluations of RFPs are open to the public and subject to the open meeting laws. What this means is that if your vendor is bidding on a project with the state of Montana, you can go on the Internet and find out the vendor's pricing.

Matchmaker.com: Comparing Corporate Cultures

When examining the corporate culture of the vendor, you have to look pretty deeply. In fact, it is worth a trip to their corporate headquarters for a few days to meet with their senior leadership and speak with their employees too. Observe what goes on between the lines during the day-to-day business. Watch the corporate politics, learn how their salespeople are compensated for selling to you, see how the ordinary employee is involved day to day in the life of the company, find out how involved customers were in the creation of the applications you are considering. Pepper the leadership with questions and don't leave without a satisfactory answer. All of these affect whether or not they are a suitable match.

On the more formal side, find out if you can get a written statement of the core values that drive the company. Take an ISO9000 approach to the written values and see if the company actually adheres to them. This can be arduous, but it is an important piece of information for you to have to make your decision.

The information you want includes:

- **Financial statements** Don't just check for financial stability but for how they invest their dollars, such as in research and development, as a percentage of their total revenues and investments.

- **Employee turnover rates** Companies like SAS consistently prove that their employees love working for them, which says a lot about the culture you're dealing with.

- **Compensation** The metrics used for determining how sales, marketing, and support are compensated for customer satisfaction can tell you whether you are going to get hype when the salespeople are trying to sell you. There is a huge difference between compensation for the sale and compensation for satisfaction.

- **External analysts reports** I'd recommend CRMGuru and the Lee-Mangen work I mentioned above; Gartner, though they have a Siebel bias, but the work of Michael Maoz in particular is superb; META Group, especially Michael Doane's reports; and Forrester Group, especially the work of Erin Kiniken. On the smaller analyst company side, Denis Pombriant of the Beagle Research Group, Sheryl Kingstone of Yankee Group, Chris Selland, vice president Sell-Side, Aberdeen Group all provide top notch work.

Is this a complete guide to vendor selection? I presume that you know it isn't. I could write a book on that alone, and I'm having enough trouble staying to the page count I'm supposed to for this book in my quest to provide you with what you all need for CRM.

Remember two things:

- Take all the time you need to make your decision despite the pressures you feel.

- While you must include the statistical/functional, don't make the common mistake of forgetting the human factors.

When you buy the application, you buy the vendor.

How To: The Methodology

So what is it like to implement CRM applications or services? None of your business. These are deep secrets that vendors and integrators try to keep from you so that they, and only they, can reveal them—when you pay them to do that. However, as a public service, I am bringing these methods known only to vendors, integrators, and dark conspiracies into the daylight. But I'm taking a different route. Rather than do it myself, I'm bringing in two of the players. PeopleSoft, one of the best of the big enterprise CRM applications providers, and always the most cooperative and friendly, will represent the "how it's done" for the enterprise applications vendors and the bigger implementations. A team led by Sara Schrage, CRM services product line manager at PeopleSoft Consulting, put their piece together. On the ASP side, salesforce.com, represented by a team led by Bruce Culbert, executive vice president for global services, put their good work together.

Let's start with a couple of caveats. Don't try to compare the two methods. They are representing two different approaches for two different models. It is apples and kiwi fruit. Are there similarities? Sure. Are there differences? By the bucket. But when you are implementing CRM, you should have decided which of the models you are planning on using, so the comparison is not relevant. Learn the basics, but don't decide which approach is right for you based on only reading this chapter.

Also, be alert to the fact that since I've invited the two companies to do their own speaking, you are going to see two things. First, some self-promotion. There is nothing wrong with that. Who doesn't want to toot their own horn? What I've edited out is attempts by both to compare to each other. This isn't meant to be Crossfire. This is meant to be an education. Second, you might see some material I covered elsewhere. That is inevitable. I didn't write their materials and am trying to keep the editing to a minimum. But bear with it, take it with a grain of salt, and learn something. Both PeopleSoft and salesforce.com give very valuable insights into how the work goes in planning implementation, installation, configuration, and customization.

Hearing It from the Source: PeopleSoft on the Enterprise Deployment

Now, players, play on. We begin with PeopleSoft. Quotation marks are not used, but these are PeopleSoft's (edited) words.

Traditional implementations placed little emphasis on value. The main focus of a project team was the implementation itself, where decisions were made based on the benefit to the implementation. However, the decisions made and actions taken during the implementation process have a huge impact on the final value of the CRM solution. What was good for the project may not have been best for the company.

To illustrate the point, let's think of one of those home, car, and/or style improvement shows that consume the cable channels. The basic premise is always the same—a homeowner, junkyard warrior, or monster mechanic needs to solve a problem quickly and cheaply. The initial plan always looks great on paper. However, show after show, one of the team members gets preoccupied with their individual task, loses focus of the overall goal, and the entire project suffers.

For instance, during one recent home improvement show, two designers were trying to create a tiki-themed living room. The plan called for flaming torches, lush palms, and tropical print furniture. However, one designer got sidetracked on a small detail of the design— an artificial rain wall. The wall of water grew in size and scope until it dominated the remodel and the room felt like the backside of a waterfall—not a tropical isle. The living room had all the elements of the original plan—except the original goals and value.

Method to Maximizing Value

If the value of the CRM solution is impacted by actions during the implementation, how then do you guide those actions to create the greatest value? Value is no accident. The value you get from your system is a direct reflection of two elements—the importance value holds during your implementation planning and the methodology used to deliver that value.

Maximizing value is the guiding force in PeopleSoft implementations. To ensure the greatest possible business benefit, we developed a PeopleSoft-specific methodology that uses value as the performance benchmark and delivers the necessary combination of structure and flexibility to deliver on that promise.

These third-party satisfaction measures are directly linked to the ability of our methodology to pinpoint the value potential and build strategies to deliver and continually improve on that value. This is unlike a traditional implementation framework.

The Value of Structure and Flexibility in Planning the Implementation

The PeopleSoft methodology follows a three-part lifecycle—value assessment, value delivery, and performance measurement—overlaying the foundational strategy, planning, structure, construct, transition, and deploy implementation phases. (See Figure 20-1.) This framework provides the discipline and direction that drives implementation value.

It is an enterprise methodology, with specific activities, steps, and tasks to drive CRM implementation best practices. For example, end-user adoption is absolutely critical to CRM implementation success. Direct business benefit must be realized. It is for this reason that we built a specific Rapid Design and Build activity within our methodology that addresses the more iterative nature of CRM implementations. In this activity, refinements are made to the system by key end-users, resulting in a more tailored solution that solves business challenges.

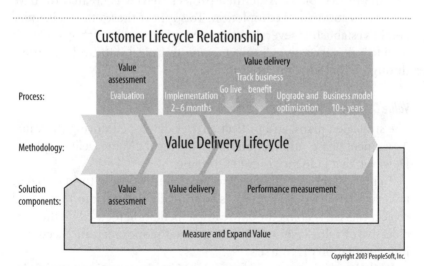

Figure 20-1: PeopleSoft's Value Delivery Lifecycle is the strategic part of implementation.

In addition to CRM-specific activities, steps, and tasks, PeopleSoft's enterprise methodology breaks a complete, end-to-end business solution into manageable phases, with each phase resulting in defined business value. Our methodology ultimately circles back in a continuous cycle of improvement, leveraging post–go live performance analysis to continually create greater value.

Value Assessment—Establishing the Blueprint

The first part of the PeopleSoft methodology lifecycle—Value Assessment—is where the implementation blueprint is established. At a high level, the work done here is like the first five minutes of the home improvement show we discussed above. In both cases, the "builder" and "owner" see what needs to be done and what challenges await. Plans are drawn and responsibilities are defined.

CRM value is determined by three elements—information, process effectiveness, and cost. For the implementation to create the greatest value, the Value Assessment phase must evaluate what information needs to be integrated, how processes can be rebuilt for greater effectiveness, and where overall costs can be reduced.

Our methodology addresses many of these challenges through built-in implementation best practices. Key objectives are identified and attached to quantifiable performance measures. Strategies become formal plans. A defined project charter is created to drive project execution and completion. To support these efforts, PeopleSoft has established several strategy and planning workshops that are used to guide executives, project teams, technical staff, and end-users through initial implementation phases.

Value Delivery—Where Plans Come to Reality

The strategies, plans, and project charter developed during the Value Assessment phase guide actions taken during the Value Delivery phase. However, that guidance is not automatic.

To prevent the overall objectives from getting lost in the day to day, tasks and project management is continually tied back to the overall project charter, keeping the entire implementation focused on the final objective of value creation. This eliminates scope creep and keeps the implementation on course.

With the iterative nature of most CRM implementations, the implementation course can seem a bit serpentine at times. One particular area where this balancing act is clear is customizations. Every customer believes they're unique. And they are. But does that uniqueness demand customization?

Customization adds to the total cost of the implementation and ownership. If cost is a major value for CRM, then, to maximize value, the implementation must hold customizations to a minimum. Our approach is to use configuration rather than customization, where possible, to accommodate unique processes. In essence, the process isn't changed; it's configured to match the end-user's needs. This balancing act requires substantial product and business process knowledge. This simple construct saves both time and money in implementation and production.

DIVIDING RESPONSIBILITIES

So who does what during the Value Delivery phase? Just like our home improvement team, a CRM implementation works best when everyone has clearly defined responsibilities. Unlike the TV show crews—which are crafted by the producers to create drama—the composition of the CRM implementation team is really a function of the existing enterprise resources, the overall objectives, and the options available through the enterprise vendor.

The need for flexibility is even more pronounced when deciding on how to build the right implementation team. The identified CRM value elements—information, effective processes, and cost should also determine team composition. The implementation requires a team that has the knowledge to cost-efficiently integrate information and deploy effective processes.

Because the resource mix, by definition, must be tailored to each CRM implementation, the most effective enterprise vendor is going to be the one that has a range of resource options available. At PeopleSoft, we support this need for flexibility through our Global Delivery Model. By providing access to more global resource options, we tailor our contribution to CRM implementations.

The PeopleSoft Global Delivery Model consists of six main resources—on-site consulting, Solution Centers, Off-shore Solutions Centers, hosting and application management, education, and partners. Each of these options has unique characteristics relative to the implementation.

On-site consulting is the most traditional resource. The more unique the CRM implementation, the more effective on-site consulting. Solution Centers are effective for structured implementations with predefined scope that provides more predictable, cost-focused, and accelerated solutions. The Off-shore Solution Center is best at handling very technical and structured tasks such as coding and interface development. Hosting and application management can be more cost-effective for organizations that don't have or want to support a large CRM infrastructure. Education helps train executives, IT staff, and end-users at all phases of the implementation. And partners can step in when the implementation requires expanded expertise or geographic reach.

PeopleSoft's Value Delivery Approach overlays the PeopleSoft methodology, a pure Internet methodology leveraged as the foundation for all PeopleSoft implementations, optimizations, and upgrades. The methodology breaks implementations into small, high-value components to drive scope, predictable results, and clear deliverables. The methodology comprises six phases—Strategy, Planning, Structure, Construct, Transition, and Deploy—each building on its predecessor. The early phases help identify, quantify, and build an effective PeopleSoft project plan. Later phases put that plan into action.

PHASE 1: STRATEGY

Strategy determines project course. In this phase, corporate objectives, business drivers, and project goals are accessed and mapped to their potential impacts and measurements. Critical business processes, current infrastructure, and application portfolios are also analyzed, resulting in the following two deliverables:

- An Executive Strategic Outline that includes a comprehensive list of an organization's major business drivers and business objectives.

- A high-level assessment of the major features to be included to achieve business objectives.

PHASE 2: PLANNING

Planning is all about building project mission, objectives, and performance measures based on strategic project objectives and business drivers. A format for developing a project plan is ultimately created that helps the customer team better understand project direction. Key deliverables at the end of this phase include:

- A framework for the project charter, explaining how the project will be conducted.

- A list of project objectives.

- An initial project plan with key milestones and defined deliverables.

PHASE 3: STRUCTURE

The Structure phase establishes a project framework. The information gathered in the Planning phase is used to identify, analyze, and prioritize any affected business processes and assess the software fit. The methodology helps define how the Internet will impact business processes, enabling better decision-making around gap solutions. At the conclusion of the Structure phase, customer will have:

- Documented business needs and identified and prioritized affected business processes.

- Assessed the fit of the software solution and identified gap solutions.

- Developed a comprehensive technical architecture strategy and scope.

- Defined the technical and functional specifications for the project.

- Developed a training plan for the project team.

- Finalized the project charter and scope.

PHASE 4: CONSTRUCT

The Construct phase represents the design, build, and configuration of the PeopleSoft system. As part of this work, initial system tests are conducted, critical plans are prepared, and documentation is written. Deliverables for this phase include:

- Constructed workflows and expected outputs.

- Complete test plans.

- A production support plan.

- A go-live contingency plan.

- A fully configured system into which historical and current data is loaded.

Phase 5: Transition

The Transition phase of the PeopleSoft methodology specifically represents go-live planning. Significant work activities include updating and finalizing system configuration and the setup of base tables; preparing the production environment; and conducting final user, system, performance, and parallel tests to verify that all data is converted, ultimately ensuring a smooth transition into production. An end-user training approach is also determined, which addresses defined training materials, a training environment, and how best to conduct train-the-trainer sessions. When finished, customers have:

- A fully tested, production-ready system.

- A complete end-user training approach ready for rollout.

- A tested cutover plan.

Phase 6: Deploy

The system is live! As a customer makes the transition, the Deployment phase focuses on end-user training execution, move to production, and post-production support. The PeopleSoft methodology also ensures a project review occurs and potential next steps are identified. At the end of this phase, customers will have:

- Closed the legacy system and turned on the new system.

- Moved all project support activities to the customer production support team.

- Trained end-users.

- Received go-live support from PeopleSoft Consulting

Performance Measurement—Where We Go from Here

When the CRM system finally goes live, the team is probably most interested in a few well-deserved beverages and a little rest. Who wouldn't blame them when, in all their excitement, the team overlooks the business benefits the system was supposed to deliver?

But real, quantifiable business benefits aren't just nice to have; they're the raison d'être for the implementation. At a minimum, the resulting benefits should justify the project. Ideally, the performance metrics aren't just a one-time snapshot; rather they become the foundation for continually generating greater value from the CRM solution.

With the PeopleSoft methodology, performance measurements to support this cyclical approach are built into the very fabric of the implementation. During Value Assessment, hard performance metrics are identified and applied to the objectives. During the Performance Measurement phase, predefined metrics are captured and the effectiveness of the solution is analyzed. Is the solution delivering as promised? If not, why? And, more importantly, are there areas where the solution, even if delivering as promised, can still be improved?

Using this post-go live analysis, one circles back through the entire Value Delivery Lifecycle. The process is essentially the same, just with a different starting point. Now instead of a wholesale system change, one is tweaking the solution for greater performance and deploying improvements for greater customer value.

PEOPLESOFT METHODOLOGY IN THE REAL WORLD

To illustrate this lifecycle, let's take a quick look at a real PeopleSoft CRM implementation.

A large telecommunications company was struggling to maintain customer service levels across 16 product and service lines when they came to PeopleSoft. Because the varied divisions of the company operated almost independently, the decentralization of information was damaging customer relationships. The fragmentation made sales forecasts unreliable and customer service levels inconsistent. No standard billing, order management, or provisioning processes existed.

> *This disarray became our common starting point for planning— our ground zero. Working with the company, we identified two key objectives that would result in greater value. For the customer, the CRM system needed to provide a complete and consistent 360° view of customer history, status, and installed products—regardless of where the record was accessed from within the enterprise. This consistency would ensure the same level of service throughout the organization and minimize customer frustrations. For the management team, the CRM system needed to provide an accurate assessment of vital customer statistics so the team could make more effective decisions.*

Both of these objectives required the consolidation of dozens of information silos spread throughout the enterprise. During the planning stage, we decided to use a phased implementation approach and started by replacing the multiple information silos with a single, centralized CRM system. This first step would provide a 360° view of the customer and act as the foundation for each additional phase of capabilities.

Our methodology provided the implementation framework as we worked through each phase of the project. With the flexibility to support a phased approach, the methodology maintained the structure and discipline essential to ensure the implementation delivered the value as defined by the objectives. This was accomplished by leveraging web-based self-service applications for the company's customers, partners, and suppliers. In the first phase, these applications fed back to a centralized repository within PeopleSoft CRM, consolidating customer information. Later phases added additional capabilities such as billing and executive-level decision-making support.

The final CRM solution not only met the implementation value objectives, it visibly exceeded the service level agreements. Billing, provisioning, and service order processing are more efficient. Customer service standards are consistently at a higher level throughout the enterprise. Lead generation and qualification are streamlined for better sales forecasting and cross-selling. And the system consolidation reduced maintenance costs and improved operationally efficiency, while the company expanded services into new regions and product lines.

By establishing metrics and by leveraging the PeopleSoft methodology, the telecommunications company is currently reviewing system performance and capabilities to identify areas for even greater value potential. PeopleSoft will work with the company to loop back to the Value Assessment phase, to craft objectives to exploit this new potential, and to develop plans to continually enhance the value of their PeopleSoft CRM solution.

For the Next Number: Salesforce.com

Implementations are not associated too easily with the net native solutions. However, they are necessary. They are done with a markedly different approach due to the markedly different model that is engaged. So take it away, salesforce.com!

SOFTWARE AS A SERVICE

Salesforce.com provides CRM solutions via the software as a service model. Customers of the service benefit both from the robust functionality included with the service and from the method by which it is developed, implemented, and maintained. Salesforce.com has recognized that the benefits of centralized, multitenant utilities such as power, water, and telecommunications can also be realized in the enterprise application software market. No company would invest the resources required to build its own power plant, transformer network, and power grid. Instead they subscribe to utilities, which spread the costs of this investment across a broad base of subscribers, providing full service at a fraction of the cost. These same economies of scale can apply to enterprise applications as well.

Like other utilities, salesforce.com developed a shared, multitenant infrastructure that delivers a valuable business service, specifically a robust enterprise solution for CRM. Whereas in a power utility that infrastructure consists of power plants, generators, transmission lines, and local power grids, in the salesforce.com model the infrastructure consists of data centers, server hardware, application and database servers, Internet connectivity, and application research and development.

Customers benefit from the utility model's economies of scale in multiple areas:

- ▶ *Continuous access to the latest in research and development*

- ▶ *Elimination of technical complexity from your business solutions*

- ▶ *Professional services focused on adoption and organizational enablement and customer success, not software development*

- ▶ *Industry-specific best practices driving the CRM business solutions*

- ▶ *Low initial cost and fast time-to-value*

CRM Success: The Salesforce.com Methodology for "CRM as a Service"

As an industry, we have learned that that the keys to CRM success are organizational commitment, speed, flexibility, user adoption, customer satisfaction, and superior ROI.

The "CRM as a Service" model emphasizes rapid user adoption, accelerated time-to-value, and maximum ROI. To achieve these results, our methodology is focused on customer success (see Figure 20-2). The following sections present an overview of the method.

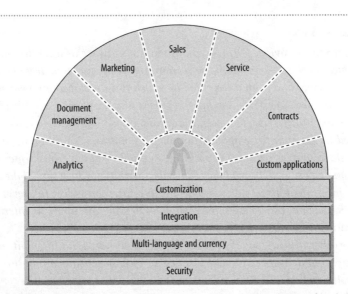

Figure 20-2: Salesforce.com provides "CRM as a Service." There is a broad range of on-demand solutions for small business and large enterprises.

Industry best practices, training, and end-user business support are priorities and are provided continuously throughout the lifetime of the customer's service agreement. Customers are immediately empowered through an iterative and highly visual and prescriptive design process that delivers results immediately while enabling continued value.

The Method

"CRM as a Service" provides an accelerated, iterative deployment methodology that emphasizes time-to-value and minimizes risk by leveraging the benefits of the model. Our method applies a solutions-focused approach to delivering the application, required process workflows, customizations, and integrations. The method spans people, process, and technology to ensure that the delivered solution maps directly to business requirements and that it delivers the appropriate ROI. In its simplest representation, it consists of four phases that mirror the evolution of a customer's organizational adoption of salesforce: Planning, Design, Deployment, and Support (see Figure 20-3).

Instant Provisioning: Eliminates Technical Complexity of Setup

The utility model enables us to provide instant provisioning of the application for our customers. In fact, customers typically sign up online at www.salesforce.com and activate their own application, a process which takes seconds.

Phase	Activities
Planning	Salesforce.com experts work with the customer to identify, refine, and document the objectives of the deployment, and to map out a detailed project plan that provides the roadmap to a successful implementation, integration, and adoption of the solution. Users begin to attend orientation training, to familiarize themselves with the basics of the service, and customers are introduced to their designated support team.
Design	We identify and document detailed configuration and integration requirements, configure the application as required to support the customer's processes, and develop any custom extensions and integrations as needed.
Deployment	We develop and deliver custom curriculum and training to end users and managers. Our experience in implementing over 10,000 customers in the "CRM as a Service" provider clearly illustrates the value of customized, focused end-user training to driving adoption and return on investment.
Support	We provide a broad support organization to ensure the ongoing success of the customer in using the deployed solution. This includes assigning a designated account manager to each account, providing tiered customer support offerings, and providing ongoing education services—all of which are included in the customer's subscription fees to the salesforce.com service.

Focus on Adoption Right from the Start

The "CRM as a Service" model requires high user adoption—if users don't adopt the solution and it's not constantly delivering the expected business value, they will not renew their subscriptions. Therefore, customers must receive real and sustainable value from the service. The utility model allows us to provide adoption-enhancing services early and often throughout the customer's subscription term.

Highly Visual, Iterative, Business-Driven Solution Design

Salesforce.com provides best practice–driven, industry-specific professional services. We apply a proven, prescriptive approach to accelerate time-to-value of the client's CRM solution, while at the same time working with the client to customize, enhance, and differentiate the solution to their specific needs. As a result, the application design and configuration is an interactive, iterative, and visual process. The customer can immediately see the impact of design decisions, and can tailor the functionality of the service to their specific business needs. This cost-effective, business-driven approach allows us to democratize the management consulting fees— so that even smaller customers are able to deploy a business-tailored solution that drives value into their business.

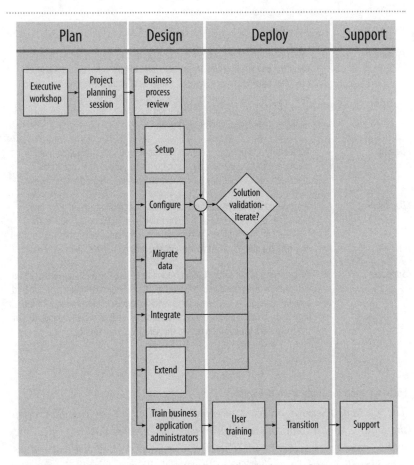

Figure 20-3: The salesforce.com method: Planning, Design, Deployment, Support

Emphasis on Training, Adoption, and Enablement

From day one, salesforce.com provides a catalog of dozens of specific training courses for its customers. These classes are offered online and include both self-paced courses and instructor-led webinars. Fees for these classes are included in the subscription fee, and users are encouraged to attend frequently. Customers will often begin attending these training sessions before the CRM project even begins, to learn about the application, its capabilities, and its fit within their organization. In addition, salesforce.com creates and delivers courses with customer-specific process and application training, developed during the course of an implementation and delivered to management and end users during the Deployment phase. After solution deployment and roll-out, our customers are offered a

constant opportunity to refresh and expand their knowledge of the service, indus-
try best practices, and service enhancements through our extensive continuous
education offerings delivered online and live in cities around the world.

End-User Support for Business Success

In addition to continuing education, we provide end-user support for every serv-
ice user worldwide. Consistent and expert end-user business and application sup-
port is provided to all of our customers. There is no dealing with third-party
integrators and VARS. Our customers get access to the experts in CRM when they
need it. Since our customers don't have to worry about technology support, our
end-user support is focused on customer adoption and success. This support also
begins at the outset of the relationship with our client and is shaped and tailored
to meet the specific needs of a particular customer or market segment. From day
one, every user and prospective user has access to expert services to help them
achieve their business goals.

Updates

One of the core tenets of "CRM as a Service" holds that upgrades should be fre-
quent, high-value, seamless, unobtrusive, and zero-cost (see Figure 20-4).

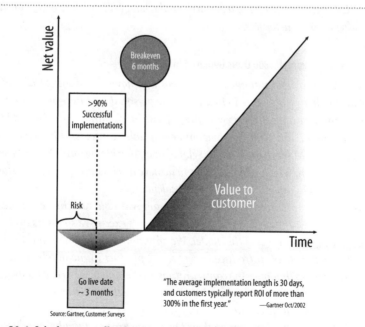

Figure 20-4: Salesforce.com offers frequent, incremental, low-cost, no-hassle updates

A subscription to the salesforce.com CRM service includes access to upgrades throughout the term of the subscription. Upgrades are applied centrally on our servers, by our data center staff. Customer data is automatically compatible with new releases. New releases are automatically deployed at no cost.

In our utility model, all salesforce.com customers are continually updated to remain current with the latest functionality and enhancements. New features are included in the subscription fees and generally require no marginal consulting fees. Packaged training services are available to train users on new functionality. Furthermore, because salesforce.com develops and operates the CRM service in a single, known hardware and software environment, we expend 100 percent of our R&D resources on adding new features for our clients. We upgrade the service on average three times a year, ensuring that our customers are always current with market leading functionality.

Results

The overwhelming business value driven by salesforce.com's "CRM as a Service" methodology are easily quantified, as evidenced by the rapid time-to-value. The business value of CRM is most commonly measured by the return on investment, or ROI. Many variables go into an ROI calculation, and among the most prominent is time-to-value, i.e., how long it takes to realize benefits from the solution.

Salesforce.com's "CRM as a Service" methodology allows us to accelerate time-to-value for our customers.

Time-to-Value Example: 800 Users Deployed in 45 Days

One recent implementation case study was a deployment of salesforce.com at a global supplier of integrated circuits for the personal and networked computer and communications markets with manufacturing facilities in the United States, Europe, Japan, and Asia. The customer was able to successfully deploy salesforce.com's CRM service to over 800 global sales, marketing, and channel users in a 45-day period, which allowed them to achieve a critical corporate milestone of deploying in alignment with their fiscal calendar.

Salesforce.com's Professional Services team was able to achieve this accomplishment by working closely with the customer's executive sponsors and leveraging the differentiators of the model. We provisioned the application well before the project stated. We introduced users to the product immediately for accelerated training, so that once the configuration was complete we needed only to provide process-specific supplemental training. We used the CRM service as a tool throughout design discussions, so that the business users could easily visualize the impact of design decisions on their forecasting process. Finally, we adopted an iterative approach whereby the company deployed sales functionality quickly—to meet its forecasting timeline—and followed the deployment by incrementally deploying additional functionality to drive further value.

Time-to-Value Example: 90 Days to Success

In another example, a global provider of document delivery solutions was able to deploy salesforce.com's CRM service to approximately 200 users in eight countries over a period of 90 days, during which the customer also integrated salesforce.com to its SAP back-end financials application. They offered this feedback: "Salesforce.com now manages our upgrades to the service automatically and with no charge... We have been amazed at the seamless, pain-free upgrade to the Winter '04 release... Salesforce.com is so easy to modify our sales managers change the screens themselves."

Furthermore, the web service model provided by the "CRM as a Service" integration layer simplified the process of integrating to SAP. It took 90 days.

Either/Or?

There is no either/or here. If you choose an ASP, then salesforce.com is the kind of methodology you are likely to use. If you go for an enterprise deployment, then what PeopleSoft is telling you is how they (and others like them) do their implementations. Both are valid. Both are thorny. Both are, when done well, successful. Learn from them, but don't choose because of them. Now let's trot over to the next chapter so you can see how to learn and then communicate what you learn to your colleagues.

21

Communications and Learning Management Does Not Equal Knowledge Dump

If you are a human being of any age, at some points in your life you've said, "Sorry, I misunderstood you." Or "Sorry, I didn't know what you meant." Each of these statements is preceded by the word "sorry" and that's exactly what you'll be if you don't see the importance of communicating knowledge throughout the life of a CRM initiative.

First and foremost, we are human beings. That means that the most important possible interaction in any CRM transaction is communication. We all understand the benefits of communications with our paying customers. But when you look at many CRM programs, you find that communications with employees, suppliers, and partners are either an afterthought or nonexistent.

We've already established that user adoption is one of the core issues of CRM initiatives. To restate it one last time, "If the users don't use, you're going to fail." No communications throughout the entire life of the program and they won't use it. You can make book on it.

The plans for communications and learning management are laced throughout the entire life of the program. They are always in place and ongoing. They are time-consuming, sometimes tedious. There is a lot of "manual" activity that can be involved in making them work, ranging from direct one-to-one conversations to inputting frequent updates. But they are completely, without qualification, necessary.

Communications Planning

There is a lot of confusion about this often overlooked piece of a CRM strategy. Because of CRM's intense customer focus, the communications plan is often thought of as how to improve communication with customers during the day-to-day operation of the business. In fact, products like NCR Teradata's CRM Communication Manager are designed especially for that purpose—aimed at the customer interaction center or call center and incoming/outgoing calls. While that is a valid part of CRM planning, it is not what I'm talking about here.

What I'm proposing are the channels and means to keep your stakeholders and general population apprised of the progress of the CRM initiative. There are multiple approaches and venues to work with, and because you are dealing with customer strategies, a significant number of internal and external constituencies to be concerned with.

Begin at the Beginning—and Honestly

Communications plans have to begin at the very beginning. In a sense, at that early stage, they are the most sophisticated part of the strategy being executed, because the concepts and mechanisms have to be a go from day one. Additionally, they have to be honest and set the expectations for delivery early on. This is not meant to be marketing. This is an honest day-to-day operational assessment of the progress of the initiative. Setbacks should be characterized as setbacks—but without politics, spin, or bitter opinion. The proposed solutions to the problems should be clearly defined. The mission and vision statements need to be communicated to everyone so that they get it.

Keep in mind that as, time rolls on, the iterative nature of this initiative is such that employees, customers, partners, or suppliers might be asked to take actions—perhaps participate in a focus group, take a survey, or just enter data somewhere. They have to be ready to do it, even though it is preparatory work for something that hasn't even begun yet.

Why not best face forward? Because it isn't ethical if it's untrue and it sets expectations to an unrealistic level. Optimism, sure. But keep it at ground level. Remember that this is meant to be an honest and frequent update to your members as a whole.

The announcement of the stakeholders and advisors is your first general communication with your targeted audience.

Who Is Doing the Communicating and How?

If I asked you this question, I'm most likely to hear, "Well, the stake holding team needs to be responsible and do this." The answer is yes and no. It is true that the stakeholders are responsible, but don't forget the value of the departmental or interest group leaders who can be brought into the fold to convey the right information and the right messages to their charges. These natural leaders or even the super-users are all perfect allies in the transmission. Bandwidth isn't only a radio wave. The amount of time and effort that must go into communications needs to be shared across the spectrum of leadership, management or not, stakeholders or not.

The Medium Is the Message

All the customer touch points need to be considered in the communications planning. Transmitting the message can be done obviously through e-mail, websites, direct mail, newsletters, phone calls, one-on-one conversations, group seminars, focus groups, departmental discussions, informal conversation in the hallway, office parties and going out for drinks and dinner. I prefer the latter as my favorite "touch point," but in substantial CRM plans, all or most of them are used.

What Communications?

The scope of this initiative demands several types of communications. They range from the legally mandatory to the tactical and operational to the emotional.

Mandatory Communications

These are top priorities when it comes to making sure that they are communicated. This can be a matter of law; it can be a company rule. But it must be communicated as needed by the CRM team via the more formal communications media being used. For example, if there is a company rule that is related to the form data has to take for financial entries (invoices, billings, or even compensation plans), then this shouldn't be communicated via word of mouth. If it involves mandatory employee meetings for the CRM initiative, the various media that reach the employees daily or weekly (with sufficient time) should be used. If there is a change in the law, which mandates a change in the disclosures to your customers, every channel has to be used to reach the appropriate targets that have to respond to the change. This, regardless of whether the recipient of the communication is local or remote It tends to be a proactive endeavor by the program office or those in charge of the CRM initiative.

Day-to-Day Communications

This is the most mundane, but potentially the most important question to be answered in the early stages of communications planning. What are the tools and media needed to provide easy access for the users and staff to the continuing daily messages that need to be transmitted?

The day-to-day can provide exciting communications of quick wins occurring in the earliest stages, especially publicizing things that can affect everyone's productivity or paycheck positively. More mundanely, the progress of the program can be updated regularly.

This is where perhaps a white paper on CRM or PowerPoint that explains the program, instructional materials, or even suggestions for improvements come in. They can reside on an intranet site that is devoted to the program and updated regularly by the team. Progress reports, specific instructions that need to be communicated, a library with supportive materials both from internal and external sources all need to be placed on the website and pushed to the population through e-mail.

What makes the site difficult is the amount of realistic time that can be put into its creation. While it seems that it would make sense to have a portal with customized messages for the varying target segments, that is a pretty costly proposition. A lot of companies will be reluctant to put forth the time, effort, and funding, given the demand of time pressure and keeping to some unknown budget. However, the closer to that ideal that you can come, the better.

Don't hesitate to use physical facilities too. A library where program reports can be read or other corroborating materials are stored is a valuable property in the CRM communications portfolio.

A Blog?

For those of you not "syncing up" with the world that lies in front of you, there is a true phenomenon known as a web log, or blog. The best way to define blogs is that they are instantly produced websites that operate as a diary or place where the freedom to express your untrammeled ideas is paramount. Most are run by teenagers whose acne-scarred opinions are quite clear and can make even someone who can handle almost anything thrown at them red-eared. But many blogs are run by adults and thoughtful teens presenting some of their thinking in a daily fashion and inviting response. Don't underestimate the value of a CRM blog that would do the same. It could be a good place for participants in the program to present their ideas or a member of the program management to run a daily diary. It can be treated as an educational service, with a running account of what is going on and the opinions of the writer or writers expressed freely. However, there are some dangers there. The limitations are the language and the level of content that is reproduced. What is off-limits has to be clear to anyone with access to the blog, and it would have to be moderated to some extent so that company trade secrets or really foul language aren't part of the writing.

The emotional value of this participation is undeniable. The direct interactive involvement of the internal and external users—or perhaps just the internal users—becomes an exhilarating force, as blogs have proven to be everywhere. Don't underestimate the value of the emotional and motivational in communications.

Emotional Communications

Informality and creativity rule this roost. This is how you engender interest, create excitement, and have fun. Conversations in the hallway can be your touch point, or if you prefer, your medium. Parties, barbecues to celebrate the kickoff, posters, flyers, and humor are all fair weapons in this part. But be clear. As much fun as you might want to have, you have remember that the fun is the motivator, but not the purpose. The goal is buy-in from the larger population involved in this program. If the emotions associated with your CRM initiative are "whoopee" or, at least, "cool," then the likelihood of success increases by leaps and bounds.

If it seems to play well at corporate headquarters, take your show on the road to your remote locations. Bring prizes, cheesecake, beverages, balloons—and your message—with you.

There is no harm in using the more traditional communications media for the emotional appeal. Websites, newsletters, even phone calls and e-mails can be of great value when trying to establish the spirit of your CRM program. The other stuff is more fun, though.

Who Are You Communicating With?

Your audience is not the same one you reached with ERP communications, which tended to be totally internal. Yes, it includes your stakeholders and advisors, but it also includes your employees, your business partners, and your suppliers. It includes selected customers, if appropriate. It also includes the "natural leaders" and power users who might not be stakeholders or on the advisory board. Each segment you identify as important to the program in different ways needs to have a personalized message that gets across what's in it for them.

While putting together the plan, identify the interest groups that have a stake in this, whether on the team or not. Identify the political alignments and the job roles of key users or leaders. For example, you might find that the sales team members are grouped tightly or that they are internally highly competitive. You might find that several of them align with someone who is a great supporter of the program or someone who isn't. You might identify key suppliers who are critical to your supply chain but have a significant group of relationships with other companies, or who are less critical but exclusive to you. Try to not only understand the positioning, but also the psychology of who you are dealing with, by segment for the most part, rather than by individual, though down to that level if necessary. Then develop the appropriate specific, honest message that you have to convey to each segment so that they stay apprised and onboard—or get onboard if they aren't. For example, if you are dealing with a department that isn't going to use the applications or be directly involved with the system or strategy, they still should be apprised of the general evolution of the program as it proceeds, because it will affect them and possibly their status in the company. Remember the simplest rule of social networking: everyone knows someone. That unknown someone could step out and hurt you. Network well and that unknown identity could help you.

An example: in 2002, I was at a Siebel user conference in Los Angeles, signing books in the Bearing Point booth as a featured author. While signing, I had a long conversation with a very intelligent guy who was trying to determine what direction he wanted to go in CRM. I gave him my card, and in early 2004, he contacted me again, having read the book and loved it. He then presented a business opportunity for me that was out of the blue. Our initial conversation at the conference had affected him (and me), and there was a resulting positive action from it, though two years later. That's why communications planning and targeted straightforward messages are important. You never know who you are going to affect.

Feedback

CRM success equals bidirectional communications. Get feedback through:

- ▶ Focus groups
- ▶ A place on the website that is available for gripes and suggestions
- ▶ Surveys
- ▶ E-mails with replies expected
- ▶ Good old-fashioned conversations between members of the team and "natural leaders"

In Sum: Communications Strategy

Clearly, this is a crucial and complex area and is of absolute necessity. Bruce Springsteen has a song called "Waitin' on a Sunny Day," that starts, "I'm waitin', waitin' on a sunny day, gonna chase the clouds away…" Well, the purpose of communications is not to wait. Create the constantly sunny day—bring information into the sunlight and bake it until it becomes knowledge. But it will take time, effort, and money to do so. Don't under-spend or under-expend. You'll be glad you didn't.

Learning Management Systems

Part of CRM's knowledge transmission belt is the learning systems that are in place. In many CRM initiatives, this is translated to "training." Implement the system, dump the knowledge on how the system runs, and wipe your hands of it. On to the next fiscally responsible thing.

Well, folks, that's not how it works.

Learning is not just training. Using only train-the-trainer to transmit classroom training is insufficient for something as vast as a CRM strategy. Now you have to think about classroom training, e-learning, blended learning, and learning management systems to aid your effort. Then you have to throw asynchronous learning, real-time learning, and content management into the pot. Then you stir as if your life depended on it and drink the brew—sweet or bitter, depending on your budget and your disposition.

First, some simple short definitions so that you can untangle this morass. These are from various sources identified in the parentheses following the definition.

Learning management system (LMS) "The infrastructure on which e-learning can be built and delivered. It is comprised of six main components: registration capabilities; management of curriculum and courses; skills and records management; student interfaces to courseware; administration; and external system application programming interfaces, including human resources and, optionally, enterprise resource planning systems." (Gartner)

E-learning "A wide set of applications and processes such as Web-based learning, computer-based learning, virtual classrooms, and digital collaboration. It includes the delivery of content via Internet, intranet/extranet (LAN/WAN), audio- and videotape, satellite broadcast, interactive TV, and CD-ROM." (American Society for Training and Development—ASTD)

Blended learning "Identifying how the learning audience can achieve mastery and improve business performance. It is a compromise between (1) business and performance objectives, (2) the way groups of learners learn best, (3) the various ways that the material can best be individualized, presented, and learned, (4) the available resources that support learning, training, business, and social activities, and (5) the ways to maximize capabilities for access, interaction, and social relationships." (Trainingplace.com)

Asynchronous learning "A type of communication that occurs with a time delay between steps in the dialog, allowing participants to respond at their own convenience. Asynchronous capabilities give learners access to course materials, including readings, embedded and streamed multimedia, and external websites. They also let learners participate in facilitated discussions, and complete assignments individually and collaboratively." (Robert Jackson at www.knowledgeability.biz)

Synchronous or real-time learning "A type of two-way communication that occurs with virtually no time delay, allowing participants to respond in real time. Also, a system in which regularly occurring events in timed intervals are kept in step using some form of electronic clocking mechanism." (Robert Jackson at www.knowledgeability.biz)

I'll leave the rest for you to find out. These are the various components of a possible educational strategy for the CRM initiative that could dovetail with your existing training and learning program or might be a new direction altogether.

Unfortunately, this can be an extremely expensive part of the CRM initiative, so often compromises have to be made between what business requirements demand and what you can afford. This is also not a small piece of the initiative. The level and variety of tools—and of course, vendors to provide them—is mind-boggling. You will have a strategic advantage if you already have a person in charge of your training and learning programs.

Aligning Learning with CRM Business Objectives

Learning programs for CRM need to be aligned with the strategy. What is put into place, using whatever means are necessary, is as ongoing a process as the CRM program itself. That means that the thinking toward how you are going to improve the education, communications, and participation of the workforce (and whatever external stakeholders and others you deem part of the effort) is going to be continually changing and improving. As you are looking for those small victories in the CRM program, you are looking for incremental improvements and additions to the learning program.

The level of agility that your users show in the adoption of the new processes will be dependent on how well they can assimilate the knowledge and new rules of the initiative. However, don't forget that as mission-critical as CRM is to the company, there are other things going on. Other initiatives perhaps. Certainly the day-to-day activity of the company. CRM learning has to be in line with the company's business activity and its overall learning strategy for that. But the need for the increased competency of customer-facing employees facing a sophisticated customer audience means that the use of the tools for learning will require an increase in quality of customer interactions as the result. The stakes are high and the results required, regardless of the intrusions on time by other company initiatives. So while the learning initiatives have to be in line with the business activity of the company, they have to stand out enough to get the users to use them day to day.

This doesn't happen overnight. Sales and customer service representatives have to continually be trained to do everything from learning the new system to figuring out new ways to recognize opportunity.

They have to constantly improve their people skills so they can inter-act with customers more appropriately and intelligently. We all know what happens when someone from level one technical support has little training. With training, they can be champs. Without it, you end up a chump.

This is being increasingly recognized by companies that are effect-ing an enterprise-level program. In 2002, IDC issued a report that recognized the trend: "By 2006, both ERP and CRM application ven-dors will integrate learning services directly into the business processes their technologies automate, resulting in ubiquitous, con-textual e-learning."

There are numerous questions that have to be answered to align learning with the CRM initiative (or any strategic venture, for that matter). I'll throw a few into the air and you catch the ones you want:

- ▶ What are the conditions for the training? Urgent, leisurely? Short term, long term, combination of both?

- ▶ What resources are available? What resources are needed?

- ▶ What budget is available to kick-start? What budget is needed?

- ▶ What is the content of the content? Is it mission-critical? Is it strictly educational? Are we dealing with procedural content? Behavioral?

- ▶ What kind of blend is the best for this company? Do we use CBT, classrooms, CD-ROMs, portals?

- ▶ How do we plan to keep this a successful investment as the busi-ness requirements change over time?

- ▶ What metrics can we establish that indicate successful CRM adoption related to the learning initiative? What kind of positive strategic gains can we capture?

- ▶ What feedback mechanisms do we have to capture satisfaction with the initiative?

Since this is tied to a CRM initiative, the training might have to include the partners or suppliers in the mix, especially when it comes to learn-ing the new CRM and/or partner relationship management or even supplier relationship management system subcomponents.

The Tools to Make You Cool

In the same study cited earlier, IDC stated: "Through 2005, e-learning services will increasingly be delivered as embedded components within enterprise portals, applications, and collaboration systems." There are dozens of media for delivering learning. Each of them has a different impact, both behaviorally and conceptually. For example, the purpose for using a CD-ROM for training might be to provide a permanent record of certain documentation or methods and to easily be able to courier that same information to a user at a remote location. The purpose of CBT or Web-based training could be to provide that remote user with an interactive, self-managed training that can be done at their leisure and at the same time capture the data needed to improve the results of that training for the training directors. Each has a conceptual reason.

Behaviorally, the media are different. For example, did you ever wonder why e-books remain a niche market and are by no means replacing actual books in print? From a behavioral, McLuhanesque sort of approach, one could say that e-books are part of a cold medium that has distractions galore, such as light sources. E-books engage a different part of your mind than the printed work does. They change the way you look at and retain knowledge or even the way you enjoy the wonderful use of language. Besides, who wants to fall asleep with a laptop on their chest?

This is merely to emphasize that the choice of media can affect behavior, retention, and other characteristics related to performance. The choice of delivery media has to be judicious, because not just what you deliver, but how you deliver can have a profound effect on learning behaviors.

Here are some possible media sources for both asynchronous and synchronous learning:

Asynchronous E-mail, message boards, chat rooms, forums, blogs, articles, books, FAQs, computer-based training, CD-ROMs, videos, streaming audio, tests, guides, context-sensitive help, knowledgebase

Synchronous Audio conference, Web seminars with Webex or similar tools, conference calls, videoconferencing, virtual classrooms, distance learning, classrooms with trainers, meetings, mentoring one to one conversations, focus groups, networking, parties

This is by no means complete, though it is highly representative of the available media. How you blend them is up to you and your CRM initiative. The one thing I hope you take away from this chapter is that you need to treat communications and learning as seriously as you treat your overall initiative. The days of knowledge dumps on nearly unsuspecting users are over.

Now on to a brief look at a few vendors and a Steppin' Out look at RWD Technologies.

The Few, the Proud, but Not the Many Vendors

The tricky part of looking at vendors is that some of them are CRM vendors with learning tools; others are learning vendors with CRM content. Will the thundering herds of vendors never cease? Anyway, let's take a brief look at a few types that exist and a few vendors that fit the types:

- ▶ CRM-specific tool vendors have emerged that support the creation and deployment of CRM business process–specific content. Some, like Brainshark and Presenter, provide hosted solutions via Webex or Microsoft's Placeware that cover the customer lifecycle and horizontal applications from sales to marketing to customer service. In fact, Presenter is owned by Webex. They handle the associated corporate training and communications. Others, like Knowledge Impact, are more application simulation tools that use Web-based training.

- ▶ Customer interaction center (CIC) vendors who integrate collaborative learning and skills improvement into their CIC systems are now a source of specifically focused learning tools. For example, Witness Systems uses its eQuality Suite to capture information from the various customer touch points and then analyzes the information. They provide both a learning framework and workflow design that can share the results and incorporate them into multimedia-based training initiatives. Other players in this field are Comverse and Knowlagent).

- ▶ The traditional CRM/ERP vendors (for example, Siebel, PeopleSoft, Oracle, E.piphany) have been adding enterprise training tools to their application suites to provide a highly integrated learning suite. For example, PeopleSoft provides what they call a User Productivity Kit. The kit includes a customization tool and prerecorded content that allow you to create

Web-based training, instructor-led training, performance support materials, and documentation. The upside is that if you've chosen a PeopleSoft or other enterprise vendor solution, the integration with the system is effective and the prerecorded content can save you lots of time and money. The downside is that they are nowhere near as robust as the Brainshark-level tools out there.

▶ Finally, learning management system platform vendors are offering CRM tools and courses that focus on basic CRM functionality. Companies like Docent and Click2learn, both of which rank in the Gartner leadership space in their LMS Magic Quadrant, offer these services. RWD Technologies offers a systemic learning framework that is easily customizable to CRM initiatives. They are the subject of Steppin' Out.

STEPPIN' OUT: RWD Technologies—If You Want to Know, They Already Do

I know these folks. They have been my client (past), some of them are my friends (present), and they have a really bright (future) when it comes to CRM and learning tools. They became my client because I saw they delivered e-learning, LMS, and blended learning more effectively and more progressively than any other of their competitors. I'm lucky enough to be in a position to work with only those companies I want to. Consider this my full disclosure and my unabashed admiration for the talent and tools RWD has.

RWD stands for Robert W. Deutsch, a former professor who founded this highly successful "who the heck are they?" company in 1988, devoted to lean manufacturing primarily for the automotive industry. However, in the early '90s, they started to provide training and documentation for Dow Chemical as they implemented SAP worldwide. They developed what they called an "adult learning model" for the enterprise systems, which led to a strong practice in providing these learning services to SAP implementations and later PeopleSoft and Oracle.

In the early part of the millennium, they created a new offering for their Enterprise Systems Division that involved a pharmaceutical product for CRM called OTIS, which married Siebel ePharma and Documentum, bringing their expertise to the majority of key pharmaceutical companies in a very short time. Since 2003, they have grown the CRM portions of their training business substantially, becoming a player despite a significant amount of under-the-radar marketing and little recognition from industry leaders. They are now 900 employees strong, with 16 offices worldwide, and close to $130 million in revenues. Not bad for word of mouth.

Shout Out to the Products: Awesome

RWD's product line is spectacular. I've seen it in action and seen countless feature demonstrations and I am always in awe of how well their "human performance management" products work. Three of them stand out in the world of learning.

Info Pak and Info Pak Simulator

Info Pak produces advanced and multichannel documentation. Procedural documentation for any system that you care to develop is created, converted to any format, and delivered to any medium, from print to Web libraries to directly within each transaction if that's how you choose to do it.

There are four tools that take care of this:

▶ **Publisher** This is a Microsoft Word–based template set that allows authors to record the actions that they perform and then create documentation for those actions step by step. This handles the recording flawlessly and the publishing is about as slick and interesting as you can get with the push of a few buttons and, if you need to, some editing. While nothing is ever that easy, this isn't too bad at making it easier.

▶ **Glossary** This is a custom glossary that allows the insertion of the glossary terms into the field description tables that Publisher creates to personalize the experience or to standardize it.

▶ **Web Architect** This tool allows the authors or Web designers to create website navigation pages that can link to the documentation or any media that exist for training (FAQs, videos, CBT, whatever). Drag and drop, hierarchical organization for the materials, and multiple views are possible using this adept tool.

▶ **Help Launchpad** The fundamental online performance support tools. This is context-sensitive in-screen support. Go to an Oracle screen, have some difficulty, follow links to instructional material and context-sensitive help.

Info Pak Simulator is a separate product. RWD calls it "reality-based training." I call it a flexible product that can provide the actual simulation of the transactions or interactions in a way that can instruct and make life a lot easier, though perhaps no grander. It works simply. As you use the application, the simulator records all interactions, ranging from your first mouse click to your last data entry. You then can edit the recorded functionality or add voice-overs or notes. When you're done, you export it to the Web as a Java applet or Dynamic HTML (DHTML) and voilà, you watch the simulation. It's record, replay. Editing is optional. What makes it even more interesting is that you can deliver multiple modes:

- ▶ Auto-playback, which is like watching a movie.

- ▶ Standard mode, which is step-by-step simulation.

- ▶ Self-testing mode, which offers no visible clues or instructions as in standard mode—you complete the task. If you fail, you get clues to guide you to the right way of doing it.

- ▶ Assessment mode, which is the self-testing mode plus data capture for grading, reporting, or data storage.

These applications come in a generic package or specialized versions for Oracle and mySAP.

University 360 LMS

University 360 is RWD's LMS crown jewel. This is their Java-based learning framework that provides student access and instructor or administrator access to all the blended learning resources your little heart desires. That means job aids, simulations, procedural documents, and synchronous and asynchronous tools for learning, ranging from CD-ROMs to virtual classrooms or even real classrooms. It can provide your remote users with their necessary CRM training materials and, for example, allow test-taking offline that will synchronize when the user gets back online.

Watch for these guys. They may be under Gartner's radar, but if you are implementing CRM for Oracle, SAP, PeopleSoft, or pretty much anything else, they may be appearing on a screen near you.

22

ROI and Metrics: Numbers Never Felt So Good

Return on investment (ROI), often calls for the most stringent metrics and benchmarks—because it entails highly specific results for your company. But, ironically, it is also arguably the most nebulous set of objectives any company contends with, because no two companies have the same plans or interests and no two companies want the precise same results.

ROI and Metrics—A Beautiful Combination

ROI has been all over this book. Rather than go through a lengthy discussion of how to plan ROI, I'm going to provide you with three case studies on successful CRM initiatives with great ROIs that followed the premises that I've been shoving down your intellects for the last 21 chapters. They will each represent a different result that will delight you or at least interest you in why CRM in the first place.

However, prior to that, I'm going to bring in another expert to discuss how you can define CRM metrics and look at scorecards. These same metrics will aid you in planning your ROI and your performance with those extraordinary customers that you would really, really, really like to keep. The gentleman is Dr. David Mangen, president of Mangen Associates. He is a distinguished statistician and also a fellow CRMGuru board member who understands customer metrics and how to create them better than anyone I've met in my considerable travels around the CRM globe.

Take my word for it. I'd rather be listening to him on metrics than me. Without further ado, Dr. David Mangen, statistician, raconteur, and a man with a great sense of humor—who, as you'll see here, also knows how to write about a difficult subject. There will be no test at the end of the lecture.

Dr. Mangen on Metrics

The metrics that can be used for assessing the total customer relationship fall into three broad classes—*customer-specific* metrics, which focus on the client's needs and specific issues that drive their desire to do business with your company, *diagnostic metrics*, which emphasize the customer's experience with doing business with your firm, and performance-based or *outcome metrics*, which emphasize the net outcome of the total relationship. Figure 22-1 presents the relationships among these metrics.

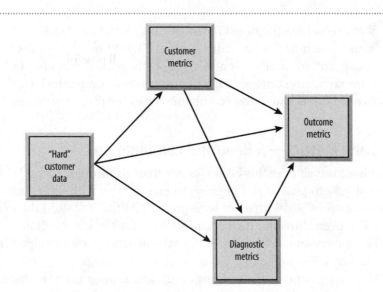

Figure 22-1: The relationship between customer, diagnostic, and outcome metrics

You will note that we've added another box to this diagram—"hard" customer data. We have added this because too often people consider factors such as the length of the client relationship, industry designation, number of employees, and so on as the most important characteristics of their customers—and indeed this information is very important. However, we want to differentiate that information from some of the "softer" customer measures that are ultimately far more important in specifying *who* elects to do business with you. Some examples of customer metrics might include:

- ▶ Customer desire for a partnering relationship with a supplier versus a transaction-based relationship

- ▶ Receptivity toward comprehensive solutions developed by a supplier versus the need to develop the solution in-house and maintain proprietary control of the final product

- ▶ A customer potential index, referenced by the number of products or services that the customer uses that a supplier is *able* to supply—regardless of whether or not the customer currently uses that supplier as the preferred current vendor

Note that the first two of these metrics clearly focus on psychological willingness to develop an intense, comprehensive relationship, while the third is a bit "harder" in that it addresses client potential.

By contrast, diagnostic metrics emphasize the nature of the customer's experience in doing business with a supplier. These can range from behavioral metrics to evaluative metrics. All possible touch points between customer and supplier are plausible areas for diagnostic metrics. For example:

- ▶ A behavioral metric might focus on the number of different sales channels that a customer uses when conducting business with a supplier. Note that depending on the type of business, use of a large number of channels could be a positive diagnostic (for example, the relationship is deep and the customer has flexibility in how they conduct business with you) or it could be negative (such as a relatively low value customer using a high cost, expensive sales channel).

- ▶ An evaluative metric might focus on the customer's satisfaction with error resolution, product satisfaction, or satisfaction with the sales channel.

Indeed, most of the measures included in typical customer satisfaction surveys emphasize diagnostic metrics, although some might argue that overall customer satisfaction, or stated customer loyalty, might reflect an outcome as opposed to diagnostic metric.

However, we shouldn't limit our consideration of diagnostic metrics to a mere focus on the customer alone. Recall that we have said that all of the different touch points that a company has with a customer can be considered as plausible areas where diagnostic metrics can be developed. What is one of the primary ways in which customers and companies interact and do business? Employees! Even in the increasingly virtual world that characterizes much of today's commerce, a great deal of business still requires the human touch. While we often will include some measures of that human interaction in our diagnostic measures of customer satisfaction (for example, evaluation of account executive effectiveness), this approach focuses on the *customer's* perspective of that relationship. Consider looking at the account executive's perspective, or all of your employees' perspectives. Staff members who are committed to their company, believe that they are doing valuable work, and feel both personally and financially rewarded for their efforts will do a far better job of communicating that message to your customers. In short, good employee loyalty fosters customer loyalty and ROI. Maybe our model needs to be a little more complex. So let's add something to Figure 22-2.

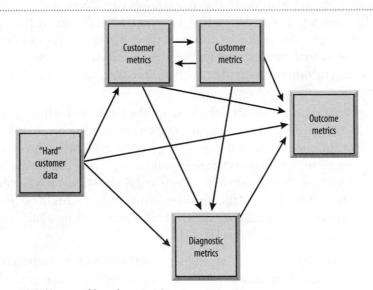

Figure 22-2: Now we add employee metrics

Developing Metrics

When trying to develop customer and diagnostic metrics, I often find it valuable to use a very structured, deductive logic–based model called the rational approach to measurement. If we're thinking about customer satisfaction, rather than sitting around and trying to cook up a bunch of questions that we can throw onto a questionnaire or a website, I start at the other extreme and ask three broad questions:

▶ *Who* are our customers?

- *What* do we do for our customers—in essence, what is our product or service?

- *How* do we interact with our customers?

From the answers to these, I build a small, multidimensional matrix. Consider one of the large financial institutions:

- The customer base includes consumers, small to large businesses, and other banks.

- Their product mix will obviously include traditional banking products such as checking, savings, and loans, but also business-oriented products such as night depository services and automated clearing house (ACH) services. They may also package and sell to other banks bundled mortgage and loan portfolios that may be used as investments by these banks.

- Customer interaction modes are quite disparate, but include branches, computer technology, phone systems, and personal relationships.

Clearly, the full multidimensional matrix is quite complex. Because we can only effectively visualize two dimensions on paper, let's focus on one customer type—consumers. The sub-matrix for customers might look something like Table 22-1.

Table 22-1: This is a multidimensional sub-matrix for consumers. Did you know you look like this?

	Branch	ATM System	Telephone Banking	Web Banking	Personal Banker
Checking					
Savings					
Secured Loans					
Unsecured Loans					
Mortgages					
Credit Cards					
Debit Cards					
Safe Deposit Boxes					
Investments					
Insurance					
Other					

Now, for each cell of this matrix, let's ask a few more questions:

▶ What do customers *expect* from this product service channel combination?

▶ What do customers *experience* from this product service channel combination?

▶ What do customers *like* about this product service channel combination?

▶ What do customers *dislike* about this product service channel combination?

Not surprisingly, the answer to each of these questions will be significantly different across each of the cells. Very few people expect to receive respect when using their debit card at an ATM, while almost all would have that expectation of a personal encounter with an assigned, personal banker who wants to invest your money. Some of the cells in the matrix may even be completely irrelevant and can be discarded.

The likes and dislikes for each cell will, in the end, probably be closely related to the gaps between expectations and experiences, and will define the evaluative component of the metrics. The different answers to the expectations questions will probably define many of the required customer metrics regarding wants and desires, and the experiences component will define many of the behavioral dimensions to the diagnostic metric portion of the assessment.

Now you're ready to start writing questions or developing indices for your metric program. By using this approach, you greatly increase the likelihood that you will capture all of the relevant data points you need, and identify any missing links in how you have evaluated your business processes.

If you've been reading this carefully and keeping track of everything that I've been suggesting, you may very well come to the conclusion that you'll suffer death from metrics, and that at the upper level of management you'll need a CMO—Chief Metrics Officer! To some degree, that is a valid point. I would certainly never recommend that senior management monitor every one of the metrics that could be developed from a comprehensive approach such as this. A select subset that cuts across the products and/or the channels should be selected from a statistical analysis of the data.

On one consulting engagement, my client proudly showed me the metrics that everyone within the company received on the fifth day of each fiscal quarter—this was their way of communicating the company's performance to their entire staff. The metric matrix focused on classic financial performance measures (almost entirely ignoring customers) and included 23 rows and 14 columns—322 different metrics. However, because all were drawn from financial performance measures, the correlations among these metrics were huge. The statistical analysis reduced the total number of metrics needed by financial management down to only two.

Outcome Metrics

Outcome metrics zero in on the end game of the relationship, with greater concern for some of the typical metrics used in an internal business evaluation. Sample outcome metrics include:

- ▶ Customer profitability
- ▶ Customer share of wallet
- ▶ Customer cross-sell ratios
- ▶ Repeat purchase rates

The end game is clearly the goal of any thriving, successful business, and we all work to achieve these successes. Maximizing the odds of success are, however, enhanced by learning to measure and outperform your competition on understanding your customer (customer metrics) and delivering a high-quality purchase experience (diagnostic metrics).

Using Metrics and Scorecards

Once you have developed a series of metrics that address the key components of your business, you will want to begin to systematically use these metrics throughout the organization. Many—if not all—of the metrics that we have discussed in this chapter can fit within the framework of the popular "scorecard" methods such as the Balanced Scorecard. Symbolically, the Balanced Scorecard is often represented as you can see in Figure 22-3.

We do not intend to endorse the Balanced Scorecard as *the* method to use for organizing your metrics or managing your business; rather, we use the approach of the Balanced Scorecard as a typical illustration of many popular approaches to organizing and reporting business metrics that address the interests of different key stakeholders within any organization.

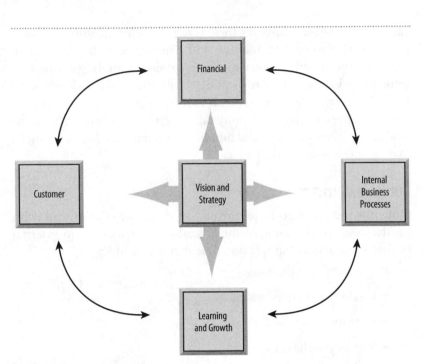

Figure 22-3: The Balanced Scorecard

Let's consider some of the different conceptual areas outlined in the Balanced Scorecard model, and compare those to the conceptual areas presented in our earlier model:

- ▶ *Outcome metrics* in our earlier model translate quite nicely into the financial metrics of the Balanced Scorecard.

- ▶ *Employee metrics* in our model largely correspond to the learning and growth metrics of the Balanced Scorecard, although our concern with employees extends beyond learning and growth to employees' perspective of the quality of service provided to customers.

- ▶ *Diagnostic metrics* in our model tends to focus on the interaction of the client and the company, while the internal business processes metrics of the Balanced Scorecard tend to emphasize the internal processes of the company to a greater degree.

- ▶ *"Hard" customer data* is largely ignored in the Balanced Scorecard, while we see it as the starting point of a model that looks at customer behavior. This is not terribly surprising, insofar as score-card models tend to focus on reporting outcomes, while these data elements tend to revolve around customer inputs into the system.

▶ Lastly, *customer metrics* in our model emphasize customer *requirements*, while in the Balanced Scorecard model the cus-tomer's perspective focuses more on their experiences—part of what we term diagnostic metrics in our model.

In short, there is considerable overlap between the content of the Balanced Scorecard model and the sort of business metrics that we recommend companies implement in their CRM systems. To be sure, there are some slight differences in emphasis, but the consistencies far outweigh the differences.

One final point regarding scorecard reporting: If metrics are devel-oped using the rational approach to measurement—as we have rec-ommended above—then scorecard reporting can largely replicate the differentiation of different concepts. Furthermore, reporting can also occur at the different organizational levels that are incorporated into the design of the measurement model.

The ROI

Now that we've established the metrics that can be valuable in deter-mining what we are going to do with our customers, let's look at com-panies that got actual results because they were smart enough to plan the strategy and define the metrics. But before we do that, a brief general look.

ROI Is What You Make It—So Make It Good

CRM ROI is so frequently debated, discussed, and wrestled with, I sus-pect that Vince McMahon is going to stage a pay per view event using some of his guys to address the issue. Unfortunately, the saying "ROI is what you make it" is true, but probably unsatisfactory when it comes to a real explanation. There are as many ROI "schools" and "opinions" as there are acronyms in CRM. Look at these comments from a few of my fellow panelists on the CRMGuru experts' panel. These are the most passionate and among the smartest devotees of CRM in the world. They are not at all alike.

▶ "CRM ROI should be about integrating the vendor's and customer's agendas and on an ongoing basis providing parameters
and frameworks for working out how to make the most money
for the vendor while producing the most satisfaction and
returns for the customer... Every industry and every company
in every industry will have a different answer, depending on
how they operate and what they are good at, and what their
existing set of customers have come to expect from them. The
only way to find out the most robust path to increased profitability is to compare the profitability outcomes of the most
likely scenarios that you can reasonably expect to be able to
implement." (Mei Lin Fung; see the Appendix for her treatment
on customer lifetime value)

▶ "The real measure of CRM success is change in customer behavior, which takes several years to measure. Because of the long time
frame (and because few companies benchmark customer behavior before implementing CRM), there's virtually no real statistical measurement done. Some companies (and consultants and
software companies) try to justify a CRM investment by cost efficiencies, but automating just to tighten up on operating expense
can and often does produce a negative change in customer behavior." (Dick Lee; see Chapter 18 for more on his work)

▶ "CRM's one of those tricky things, like getting married. On the
face of it, you know you're getting value, but you can't point to
any number that accurately, completely reflects that value. Of
course, if you're improving your measurable customer satisfaction, getting more share of your customers and lowering customer
churn, you're improving your company's business. If you're doing
it by using CRM, then your project's been a success; if you're doing
it by humming the theme song to Gilligan's Island on the way to
work, keep humming, mate." (David Sims, CRMGuru writer)

In other words, CRM ROI has both tangible and intangible features and
can't be easily determined. The results you want to get from CRM for
your company is your ROI. Increased revenue, increased customer satisfaction ratings, more products owned per customer, kisses and hugs
from 22 percent of your customer base, increased skybox sales, whatever. It's often hard to measure. However, the one factor that needs to

be constantly in the forefront of your mind, not your imagination, is that CRM's ROI is based on improvements to the customer experiences that result in something that is of value to you. Improvements in the customer experiences and increases in customer insight are what you want to see and use to get an ROI that makes you as happy as that now grinning customer who is proud to call you friend—even though he's never met you.

Yet planning ROI is important. While that might seem self-evident, the fact is that many companies try to develop a CRM initiative without planning any particular ROI. In 2003, Bearing Point did a study of 167 businesses with at least $1 billion in revenue. They found that 70 percent of the executives heading CRM initiatives don't develop an ROI. Only 6 percent set their ROI targets early in the implementation, with most of those that did plan an ROI jumping in later.

Those that do plan it don't necessarily plan it correctly. Gartner, in their report "Building Business Benefits from CRM: How to Design the Strategy, Processes and Architecture to Succeed," estimated in 2003 that 25 percent of the companies who are at least trying to plan it will plan it right—meaning defining the benefits, making the business case, and preparing the measurements of those benefits. The other 75 percent won't. Perhaps 35 percent will even additionally try to figure out the total cost of ownership. But 45 percent will only address the technology when it comes to planning the TCO or the ROI and 55 percent will ignore business processes that provide the ongoing measurement of benefits altogether. They see these problems going on through 2005 without too much alleviation. So what is self-evident evidently isn't.

There are three examples of vastly different ROIs below. The only thing they have in common is that they are CRM success stories. Enjoy them. If you're a smoker, light up a good cigar. If you're a drinker, sip a good Bordeaux. If none of that is appealing, just savor the company's victories. They taste extraordinary. But then, victory is always sweet. If it's a victory with finely wrought CRM, then it is sweet for customers and company alike.

Norwich City Canaries

Norwich City in England is the home of the Norwich City Canaries, a U.K. football club that has been spotty on the field for several years. It fluctuates between Division I football and a devoutly to be wished spot in the Premier Leagues alongside Manchester United, Arsenal, and lucrative TV contracts. The good news in 2004 is that the off the field success which filled the stands which inspired the team to first place which got them repromoted back to the Priemier League. Way to go!

However, on their business end, it has been anything but spotty. In fact, the success of this team is remarkable.

The Problem

The CRM program began in 1994 as a look at a team that was financially unstable and looking for a way to increase its ticket sales and merchandise purchases. The team understood from the beginning, unlike many of their American soccer league counterparts, that they were a business that had a team with devoted fans. They also understood that the systems and technology they would be implementing were dependent on the strategy they chose. They also knew that their success would depend on their effective ability to not just capture data, but to use interpreted data as the grounds for action. That meant providing the right kind of marketing messages and individualized offers that would bring the fans to the stadium and retain their commitment to the team. Their competition was the hard work that the community of farmers and blue collar workers was doing, often seven days a week.

Studies had been done in the U.K. that said that 83 percent of sports fans stayed loyal to the first team that they ever rooted for. How can you capture those fans and the potential revenue they drove when they don't seem to be able to find the time to come to the stadium?

The Plan

CIO Mario Zambas said their initial plan was to capture the data from the casual ticket-holders—those fans who would attend several games in a year. After five years of working on the strategy and spending time deciding on the right vendor, they launched their system in 2000. Within a year, they had captured highly granular data for 7,500 of those casual ticket-holders. As of 2004, that number was at 75,000. Among other things, this data included contact details, purchase history, likes, and dislikes. As the team successfully harvested and analyzed this data, it allowed them to segment and target tickets, promotions, and merchandise buys for the fans who had been nothing more than anonymous walk-ins before their CRM and business intelligence strategies were developed. The Canaries had some fascinating results. They found out that there were other customer segments that they hadn't even really considered when developing the plans, though they were aware of their existence. Among them were "facilities" customers—corporate and catering. Using CRM-related analytic and operational tools, they were able to distinguish the following really surprising segments:

Ticketing customers The fans who attend games.

Corporate customers Those companies who bought boxes at the stadium for business events of one sort or another.

Catering customers Those who were interested in using the sports facility for parties, weddings, large business meetings, trade shows, or other affairs that needed a place and food. These were accommodated by the 500 seat conference center and the on premise restaurant, "Delia's," named after the Canaries owner and famous British "telly" chef, Delia Smith.

Merchandise customers Those who purchased merchandise even without going to a game. Being a fan wasn't necessary for this segment. For example, a grandparent buying a jersey for their grandson's birthday, even though the grandparent never attended a Canaries game in their entire life.

The Applications/Services

The Canaries chose applications from a U.K-based IBM partner called Computer Software Group (CSG). This small, but highly effective company produced two types of applications that were appropriate to sports teams. Of particular interest, and the choice of the Canaries, is TALENT, a CRM application that is aimed specifically at sports. CSG has impressive credentials when it comes to the sports world. The applications are organized around an integrated database that is proprietary to the TALENT product line. They provide multiple modules, including TALENT Marketing, Loyalty, Ticketing, Membership, Corporate Sales, Merchandising, Accounts, Business Intelligence, and Web Sales. They also have a Smartcard interface if you need one. Their business intelligence wisely integrates with one of the market leading BI applications, Cognos. Better not to reinvent the football. CSG's success is an obvious sign of happy customers. Thirty-five percent of the premiership football clubs in the U.K. use them. I'm not sure what application TALENT has to U.S. teams, but watch CSG. They're going places—perhaps to a stadium near you.

The ROI

One year after their system went live in 2000, after five years of planning, the Norwich City Canaries sold out every home game and have continued this streak right through this year. They've capped their season's ticket sales at 18,750 and have a waiting list, despite Norwich City's highly dispersed population. They have a hugely successful catering business that competes with London's best hotels and restaurants for facilities usage. They hold events, concerts, and other entertainment. They provide individual offers based on the detailed customer profiles they've harvested, stored and analyzed. Their competition? The work ethic of the farmers who live in the area. They can't come to all games, but seem to be willing to attend at least several of the 24 home games that are offered during the season. That number wouldn't be possible if it weren't for their extraordinarily well done CRM initiative.

The Canaries' data is deep enough to be used to manage their problems too. For example, the Canaries lost one of their game sponsors at 10:00 A.M. one game day. Rather than despair over this lost source of revenue and potential social and political black eye, they ran a list of highly targeted sponsorship possibilities, using the data they had captured on their potential sponsors and matching data to the fans who would be interested in the sponsor's products. By noon they had 250 possibilities. By 1:00 P.M. they had a new sponsor.

Talk about scoring! CRM and BI team up and we get a great ROI tale. This is such a good story, I now root for the Canaries and I live in Virginia.

Sovereign Bancorp

Sovereign Bancorp, Inc., is a monstrous financial institution—a $40 billion Godzilla. It has 525 banking offices, about 1,000 ATMs, and 8,000 employees up and down the eastern and mid-Atlantic states. It sits in the top 25 of all banks in the U.S. While I get a headache just thinking about the size of this thing, pity the poor managers who have to manage it.

The Problem

Imagine something the size of Sovereign with no sales process. The closest thing to a process was to go from one deal to the next without any consideration of what happened to the existing clients and accounts. Their entire culture and compensation was based on "what have you done for me tomorrow?" While they had relationship managers (RMs), they had no relationships to speak of. In fact, they couldn't even handle prospect lists that were being generated from the marketing department. It was a random thing. "I'll check out this lead, and this one and this one and…" Unfortunately, "this one" might have already been checked out by another RM, so duplicate visits occurred with enough frequency to ring the alarm. Not only weren't they developing relationships with customers, but they couldn't even handle relationships among themselves. How could they acquire new customers when, as they were shaking hands on the deal, they were already effectively walking away? Customers could hardly feel very good about that approach, and word does spread.

The Plan

Sovereign realized that something had to be done. Not only did they have some areas of acute pain to solve, but they had to define a longer viewed actual customer value proposition. Even though there were points that had to be tactically addressed, Sovereign wisely understood that organization and automation alone were not the only answer. They knew they had to evolve new sales processes that understood the individual customer at the prospect stage. That meant when they were shaking hands with the prospect, they were thinking about how well they were going to treat the new customer, not how they were to move on to the next prospect. Thus, the prospect became the customer— before the deal was signed.

Kensington House, an outside consulting firm, spent three months working with Sovereign to create consistent, cohesive standards for its sales processes and to organize the kinds of cultural and operational changes to help Sovereign become a more customer-focused company. Sovereign also required a solution that could enhance its capacity to become a personal, trusted financial business adviser to its customers.

The Applications/Services

Salesnet was chosen as the solution of choice. The fact that they have an easy-to-use interface, are affordable as an ASP, and deploy quickly worked in their favor during the selection process. If you remember what I wrote in Chapter 4 on Salesnet, I mentioned that they spend time working to map customer sales processes to Salesnet solutions. This had a big impact on Sovereign as they established the standard processes they were going to use. Using Salesnet allowed Sovereign to automate and organize the sales processes effectively and allowed the relationship managers to increase their sales potential and not step on each others' feet. Salesnet uses its process focus and workflow to capture and distribute leads. It allows the RMs to take action on customer service requests.

The ROI
They had results. Oh, did they ever.

- ▸ Sovereign increased cross-selling and up-selling opportunities, resulting in an average customer moving from 2.5 products with the bank to more than 6. That is an extraordinary increase.

- ▸ Deployment was over five times faster than a previous Siebel implementation.

- ▸ Sovereign created a simplified and consistent system for the sales and forecasting process, enabling relationship managers to focus on selling.

- ▸ Equally as important, the strategy and use of Salesnet applied structure and visibility to the bank's sales and customer activities.

Brother International

Brother International Corporation (BIC) is one of the world's leading office and home office equipment suppliers. They provide everything from low-cost inkjet printers to high-speed networked laser printers to fax machines so sophisticated they can probably transmit edible food if pushed a little. BIC's revenue is a billion dollars plus and they've earned every penny with customers who seemed to be very satisfied with their products. Or were they?

The Problem
Unfortunately, despite Brother's financial successes, customers weren't satisfied nor was Brother. "Brother, can you spare another printer?" became an all too common refrain to the Brother National Service Division. Product configuration and troubleshooting was a frequent service issue and the high call volume was a nightmare. In 1996, they were getting calls from 1.8 million distinct callers and returning 46 percent of them. They used a very primitive database that couldn't even handle

the customer service history. It also was unable to place customer orders or provide any sort of inventory or delivery information—in other words, information about the supply chain. The result? You don't want to know. Over 12 percent return rate for products in the information and document sectors. That means printers, faxes, multifunction machines, and such coming back to a warehouse near them.

Between 1996 and 2000, the return call volume went up to 58 percent. But so did the calls per unit sold. In 1996, the calls per unit sold were 0.28. In 1998, it stabilized at 0.48 per product. That means almost half of the units had a customer calling in on it.

In other words, there were some serious problems.

The Plan

Brother International's effort was planned by a team led by CIO Dennis Upton. Dennis is one of the most articulate, intelligent, and good-natured CRM advocates in the customer world. He is often featured as a speaker at conferences because he presents what happened at Brother in a way that ordinary mortals like me not only understand but also can get excited about.

Brother foresightedly recognized that simply reducing returns by answering more calls was not the answer to their customer issues, though it was tactically crucial. They saw more fundamentally that they had to develop a CRM strategy that created core business processes aimed at customer satisfaction. The other issues, such as reducing returns and increasing callbacks were seen as serious, but as part of the strategy, not as isolated problems.

To start the program, Brother developed Total Customer Satisfaction (TCS)—a set of key performance indicators (KPIs) that would lead to the title result. They included the success factors and associated KPIs shown in Table 22-2.

Table 22-2: Brother International's Total Customer Satisfaction Metrics Matrix

Success Factor	Associated Performance Indicator	Associated Metric
Error-free order processing	On-time delivery, volume accuracy, return rate	Percent of orders delivered on time, percent of orders with correct volumes, percent of returns among sales order lines
Order processing speed	Sales order cycle time	Cycle time goods issuance, cycle time invoicing

The Applications

Even though Brother had been an SAP shop since 1994, using multiple back-office SAP products, when they first looked at SAP CRM in 1998, they passed on it. They were smart, because in 1998 SAP CRM was the product of SAP marketing's feverish imagination and was loudly decried by many. But by 2001, it was a functional product that, in combination with SAP's Business Warehouse (BW) to handle customer data and analytics, was too good to pass up. So Brother didn't. The benefits from just the implementation were superb. Nine databases were consolidated to one integrated database with more than a million customer records being added to at the pace of roughly 6,000 per day. They created a solutions database—a knowledgebase which covered all the products that were extant and being introduced so that their experienced CSRs could have the information they needed at their fingertips when they got an inevitable (though less inevitable) service call.

The cost of this was $1.7 million with about a $94,000 annual maintenance cost for 950 users. For enterprise CRM, this is downright reasonable. But were there real results? You betcha.

The ROI

Even conservatively, the ROI is estimated to be about 129 percent. Okay, but what's the real benefit? Brother is saving $1.6 million per year because the rate of returns has diminished from 12 percent to 5 percent. They are saving $1.80 per customer call processed. Where only 2 percent of the customers calling in had customer records in the system when the program started, within in six weeks, they had 20 percent of the customers calling with records in the system. Brother is saving $3.50 per work order processed due to a 20 percent reduction in work order cycle time. In other words, hard dollars are being saved. But most importantly, they are now on target to meet their goals for Total Customer Satisfaction.

Satisfied? I hope so. Now, go out and buy yourself a multifunction device—from Brother. Dennis Upton will be happy. So will you.

Finale

This chapter signifies the end of the strategy section that stretched your neurons and synapses from Chapter 17 through Chapter 22. Hopefully, you'll have something of an understanding of what it takes to create a CRM strategy. Not too easy, is it? But you can do it if you try. Really.

In the next set of chapters, we'll look at the culture and strategies and achievements of handpicked CRM vendors and integrators. You might as well know something about what they think as of 2004 and into 2007, and how they act with you and among themselves. This part is fun because there's no need to be nice. There's no need to be mean either, but there is a need to tell you the truth, so I will.

PART VI
The Ranks

23

Playing with the Big Boys: The Sandbox Survivors

I n 2002, when I wrote the second edition of the book, I had a chapter on these "sandbox playmates." Oh, what a difference a couple of years make, 17,520 little hours. The landscape showed itself to be a series of highly accelerated tectonic plates, changing the look of the CRM continent as companies rose and fell, devoured each other, were eliminated by cataclysm (bankruptcy), or just did what the old soldier did—faded away. CRM just doesn't look the same.

In 2004, on the vendor side, PeopleSoft, Oracle, SAP, and Siebel remain the behemoths, though behemoths that are attempting to reinvent themselves. On the integrator side, I had five in 2002: IBM Global Services, Bearing Point, Unisys, CSC, and Deloitte Consulting. Now, I have two: Unisys and IBM Global Services, with begrudging acknowledgement of significance to Accenture. Of the two who survived being voted off the second edition island—Unisys and IBM Global Services—the senior leadership is completely different. CSC's senior guy, Steve Olyha, is now Unisys's bossman. IBM Global Services is now being led by the former PwC CRM practice chief and well-known industry leader, Adam Klaber. Oh, that tangled web. CRM has changed so dramatically over the past two years that the criteria for my choices has changed as much as the landscape.

Criteria

I spent a lot of time eliminating a lot of companies to come up with the 2004 winners. Not on the vendor side—at least for this chapter. These vendors are a given. Companies like Amdocs, owners of Clarify, despite a noble effort to regain their lost market share just don't merit inclusion into this section of the book anymore, giant as they might have been. They don't have the success or influence on the market anymore that gets them recognized, by me at least. Consequently, PeopleSoft, SAP, Oracle, and Siebel are the automatic victors. However, I am judging all of the companies in Chapter 23–25 and basing my recommendations on dealing with them and my approach to help you understand them with three criteria in mind:

▶ **Achievements of the past two years** I allowed each of the vendor companies to choose the four achievements that they saw as most important. If they gave me more than that, I used author's discretion to cut it to four. If they gave me less, I didn't add any. The bold sentence is theirs. What follows is for the most part usually just a neutral commentary on each of the achievements, but not always. Use these choices to get a further insight into how each company thinks about itself. It is fascinating to see what and how these companies determine what's significant or what they want you to think is significant to them. If for some reason the company didn't respond in a timely fashion with the four choices, I chose my own for them and that is noted in the section. I cut out the most egregious marketing and comparative claims that were made in their submissions.

▶ **Current company culture** I'm a touchy-feely kind of guy. I think that the corporate cultures are not only unique to each company, but reflect the way that these companies will deal with their customers. In CRM, since we all make such a big deal about the relationships between yada and yado, it behooves these fine fellows and candidates to be what they eat. So I put a lot of weight behind the actual corporate culture and either like it, don't like it, or at least try to understand it. The results I pass on to you.

▶ **Strategy** The strategy for the coming year and for the next three to five years gives me a good idea of what these companies are planning to do. Do they have a zen-like harmonious relationship with and knowledge of the new customer universe? And how do they see themselves aligning with it? Is their strategy realistic or does it make little sense given the meta-forces that are governing business? I'm presenting it for you to judge, with whatever commentary I can make that seems to be useful. However, keep in mind, if they are recommended, it's because large clumps of their strategy make sense to me. Make your own decisions on my presentation and interpretation, *s'il vous plait.*

Why such a small number of criteria? Because there are eleven gazillion companies out there assessing the vendors' software features and technology or assigning them places in various squares and circles. There's probably even a company or two situating the integrators or software vendors in various sectors of Dante's Inferno, Purgatorio, or Paradiso. While I have no doubt of these things and sometimes don't even question their validity, what I'm trying to see is if CRM companies and practices actually practice CRM in their cultures and their strategies. Their achievements and their words tell me if they do. To a large extent, I have to trust them with the heart and soul of a skeptical optimist. You do too, when you are assessing them. I'm your eyes and ears, self-appointed with the conceits of an author. But at least I've done the legwork.

To get into any of these three chapters, I don't have to either have liked the company or admired them. I simply have to acknowledge them as a real force in the industry. Does that mean they practice CRM at their company? Not necessarily, but for me to have chosen them, it does mean they are at least making some honest effort. There is one company in this chapter, Accenture, whom I hesitate to recommend because of their culture and what seems to be little effort to change it. Thus, they won't get the level of coverage that the other companies will get. On the other hand, with the stepping down of Tom Siebel in May 2004 and what seems to be some actual effort to change, Siebel goes from sell to hold (metaphorically only—this isn't a stock pick) as a company to do business with in my opinion. Their efforts to change from what they were seem to be sincere and I want to acknowledge that.

I've always hoped to provide a substantial source of intelligence and opinion for you readers that I think is valid, based on my voluminous research, direct experiences, access to sources (partners, customers, employees, analysts, and so on) who have both solid information and compelling experiences too. I also take my big mouth into consideration.

Okay, enough already. Let's get it on!

Companies

The first four companies here are the biggest and most important CRM applications providers. These suppliers of Saville Row quality software are all characterized by one thing. They are very big. They are big in total revenue. They are big in employee numbers. They are big in geographical span .They are big in their strategic ambitions. And their egos are as big as Carl Sandburg's beefy Chicago. They are the pre-eminent players in the big enterprise CRM market. Each of them has a culture that is distinct to their company and that reflects how they will approach their future endeavors. The remaining two recommended companies are the large multiservice solutions companies that provide a complete range of CRM services and either have an impact directly in the market or are so absolutely creative or innovative that their inclusion into this section was unavoidable. They, too, are big. The companies returning to the list were put under the heaviest scrutiny, because, frankly, they have to maintain a cultural standard that I already know they are capable of. Wow. That's not so easy. But, for the most part, they have. I hope you noted, on the integrator side, there were some drop offs.

PeopleSoft

I have a soft spot for PeopleSoft. Lest you think me a mush head, my soft spot derives from my relationship to them for many years and their enduring success in the timeframe I've been dealing with them from ERP to CRM and through the more current enterprise applications. Their customers love them, their partners are happy to work with them, and their employees don't mind staying there. Keep in mind that these comments are based on over seven years of anecdotal and scientific evidence. I'm also not the only one saying things like this. During hundreds of implementations executed over several years, PeopleSoft has made customers happy, and the research shows it. In July 2003, the Data Warehousing Institute found that PeopleSoft had the highest percentage of customers who, given another chance, would still license their software. In September 2003, Forrester Research reported that PeopleSoft had the highest application ownership satisfaction.

Achievements 2002–2004

As I mentioned above, these are their choices, though my take on their choices is obvious here.

PeopleSoft acquires and merges with several companies—especially with J.D. Edwards. This is perhaps the most remarkable achievement of the last two years for PeopleSoft. Other strategic acquisitions included Vantive (before 2002, a core CRM leader at the time), Annuncio (EMA focused company), and Calico (interactive selling).

They've developed a best-in-class customer service solution. PeopleSoft CRM is a recognized leader in customer service and contact center solutions. This was Vantive's strength, and People-Soft has reinforced that strength.

They were the first to market with a pure-Internet CRM suite. In June 2001, PeopleSoft delivered on its promise to bring a complete, pure-Internet CRM solution to market by shipping People-Soft 8.0 CRM. Okay, I cut them a year's slack here. This was actually important beyond their own perception.

They have over 1,000 CRM customers, representing an impressive roster. Some of those customers include HP, Dell Computer, ABN Amro, Citigroup, Telecom Poland, and Orange UK.

Culture

PeopleSoft had to merge the culture of J.D. Edwards with their own culture, creating a link between Denver, Colorado (home of J.D. Edwards) and Pleasanton, California (home of PeopleSoft). Ironically, the more laid-back culture was J.D. Edwards, showing just how much PeopleSoft's culture had changed in the last three years of Craig Conway's stewardship. When PeopleSoft was founded and Dave Duffield ruled its roost, the culture was characterized by the most relaxed culture ever devised on the planet. When I was at the Pleasanton headquarters in 1998, I saw PeopleSoft employees working in shorts and tank tops and others working in that bicycle-specific spandex that you could see when cruising California bike paths. I heard of the "Raving Daves," the most prolific and not too bad rock band that any company had ever put together. I got a first line from Dave Duffield in the forword to a book I had written about PeopleSoft 7.5 that started "PeopleSoft was conceived on a beach in

Maui," one of the great opening lines for an IT book of all time. It was *loose*, man. But that was then, this is now.

I would have to say that the corporate culture of PeopleSoft is now more… corporate. It resembles many of its brethren that have been successful: big, beset by necessary policies and procedures, invested with corporate politics and egos. Yet, it still has a patina of what made it so much fun in the late 1990s. There are a few of the veterans around who carry the spirit and torch—highly competent senior management such as CIO David Thompson or CTO Rick Bergquist, who are both superb business people and good humans who were there "when."

While it ain't what it used to be, the culture is still something that needs to be reckoned with and affects what PeopleSoft does. There is a whole new ballgame at PeopleSoft, but the old ballgame is still remembered and revered.

What has remained consistent with its culture is their attention to customers. Despite the changes made from the Duffield-to-Conway eras, the one cultural consistency is that PeopleSoft not only knows how to listen to its customers, it knows how to engage them.

This is best represented not by the user groups (anyone has them), but by their customer advisory councils (CAC). These are close customers who play a major role in various aspects of PeopleSoft's internal culture and plans. For example, there is a CAC for product development that works iteratively and closely with PeopleSoft's development teams to decide what will be developed or incorporated into PeopleSoft's products based on the challenges that the customers face in their daily lives. This keeps PeopleSoft closely engaged with the customers, something that is often difficult to do in a company that's gone corporate. They meet formally twice a year and have a constant interaction informally throughout a given year so that the customer and PeopleSoft leaders and staff have a relationship.

Steve Roop, the vice president of CRM Product Marketing puts it happily, "The real strength of PeopleSoft is that not only do we offer best-in-class CRM solutions that are suited to our clients' needs, but we're known as the software vendor who is easy to do business with. Our customers know we're engaged for mutual success. Dave Duffield instilled that into our core values, and it's a legacy that lives on today. You might even say we're irrationally committed to their success. If a company is looking for a long-term, trusted partner, we're the clear choice."

The result is not only what you see with new products and solutions, but also it engenders the levels of satisfaction that I mentioned above and in the Dick Lee, David Mangen, CRMGuru study (see Chapter 20) that gave PeopleSoft the highest rated vendor satisfaction level among the big guys by the customers.

Strategy

If you remember earlier in the book, I mentioned that PeopleSoft had rather eloquently identified the change to a customer-driven corporate ecosystem from the product-driven version of the same through their articulation of Enterprise Resource Optimization (ERO). Customers drove the demand in the marketplace and now the companies had to respond to that demand in near real or real time equaled ERO. Well, they've done it again. They've understood the transition from the customer-driven corporate ecosystem to the customer ecosystem. To take that change on, they've introduced not a new form of ERO, but a new systemic concept and solution they call Customer Portfolio Management (CPM). Executing this is a significant part of their strategy and will be for some time to come.

CUSTOMER PORTFOLIO MANAGEMENT (CPM)

CPM starts from the premise that not all customers are the same and that the relationship with all customers is dynamic, not a static or even a falsely dynamic series of static snapshot slideshows. It is a program for identifying customer value to you and your value to the customer. It is a system for managing that value bidirectionally. It is a strategic look at customer strategies and the value derived from each customer based on that strategy. It essentially is a toolset that provides the means to determine whether the high value customer of today is the high, low, or medium value customer of tomorrow—or the day after, or whether they will be high, low and high value again.

For example, take AGF, a financial advisory firm in Canada. The traditional metrics they used to measure the success of their independent broker/dealers were based on the highest net assets under management. However, using CPM, they found something interesting. A 60-ycar-old broker who had a best value portfolio of high net assets had a customer base of mostly 50 to 70 year olds. Those customers were nearing retirement. When they retired, they would start redeeming their assets, so their long-term value was not as great as the traditional measurements suggested. All of a sudden, that 40-year-old broker with a medium-to-high value portfolio of 30 to 50 year old asset holders became more

582   CRM AT THE SPEED OF LIGHT: ESSENTIAL CUSTOMER STRATEGIES FOR THE 21ST CENTURY

valuable because of the continued investment opportunities represented by the younger group of asset holders. The older "elite" customers weren't necessarily the most valuable ones.

The insights that CPM provides goes beyond how to handle the customer data. The business advantage of PeopleSoft's CPM strategy is to provide the tools that give insight into present and future customer profitability, which means that there is a real business benefit that is being provided. What impresses me about it is that it is one of the key missing components in most of the systems that the vendors provide. It is a strategic solution that is not just a bunch of vertically specific processes but actually begins to look at the analysis of individual customer portfolios, which is not just treating customers individually, but understanding their business impact on your business as individuals. That means the identification of high value, high potential, and underperforming customers and also how to plan their treatment. Makes it almost like curing a medical condition, doesn't it?

SAP

SAP is well past the lumbering giant image they've had for so many years. While they still are **BIG** they are also on the move when it comes to CRM, becoming the most significant challenger to Siebel in market share of all of the enterprise vendors. They use their enormously flexible architectural platform, NetWeaver, in conjunction with the huge sums they spend on research and development to challenge the CRM market players at every turn. Will they become number one? They think so. I certainly wouldn't rule it out, so stay tuned. This could be a fascinating year or two.

Achievements 2002–2004

The first thing you see in these achievements is SAP's take on the top of the crop for them from 2002 until now. The text is my take on their take.

SAP's CRM has delivered a clear-cut ROI. As a result of SAP's vision and strategy (see below), that sees CRM as part of an overall organizational ecosystem and a massive investment in R&D, mySAP CRM has been able to provide an excellent ROI. Some examples of ROI case studies include customers such as Brother International (121 percent ROI), Waters Corporation (35 percent ROI) and Canada Post (26 percent ROI).

SAP CRM's market share has increased. According to UBS investment research for 2003, SAP captured 42 percent of the relative CRM market against the top five CRM vendors, eclipsing Siebel's 39 percent. While this is only one statistic against several others that keep Siebel at the top, the reality is that SAP is gaining ground. That much is unequivocal.

There has been a rapid increase in SAP's CRM customer base since MySAP CRM 4.0's June 2003 launch. More than 160 companies of all sizes, including many industry leaders with global brand names, are actively and successfully implementing the MySAP CRM 4.0, such as Colgate-Palmolive, Schwans Food Company, and Volkswagen Financial Services AG. All in all, they serve over 2,500 customers with their CRM solution worldwide.

NetWeaver is released in 2003. The delivery of NetWeaver is a singular moment in SAP history. It marks the transformation of the company from a closed loop products company to an open platform solutions delivery company. It is also the basis for SAP's move into the broader business ecosystem—the customer version. A truly important moment for this giant.

Culture

This is a surprise story. SAP has long had what I would characterize as cultural onus. They have been accused of being stiff, hard, difficult to get along with, and arrogant. They will be the first to admit this if you ask them—or rather, admit that they had once been that way. They aren't like that anymore, they would say. I would agree.

Oddly, but not out of character, their cultural change has been driven by a transformation in business mission and philosophy and technical architecture of all things.

In the mid to late 1990s, SAP's business model and technical architecture were driven on the idea that SAP was a homogeneous system that should be implemented that way. In other words, all things should be SAP. Implement SAP Sales and Distribution, Human Resources, Manufacturing, and such. Not competitors: SAP. That led to a culture that was driven by research and development to prove, both the superiority and the homogeneity. A culture that accepted partners who had that vision. All things SAP. I remember when I was working on developing an SAP practice and an alliance partnership, I told the SAP alliance guy that I was building a PeopleSoft partnership as well, in the interest of full disclosure. He told me that they wouldn't like that. I remember asking him if he would say that if I were Anderson Consulting (now Accenture). He was reasonable enough to say "good point" and drop the matter. But the fact that my desire to build other alliances was even in question was reflective of SAP's culture then.

But by the latter part of the 1990s into 2000, SAP realized that this was not the way to go in either business model or IT architecture. Open standards like Linux were in vogue. Customers were feeling empowered sufficiently to make SAP have to compete with other vendors for pieces of a modular strategy—and some won some and others won others. Growth and decision-making were becoming increasingly decentralized, as power was shifting to different parts of a company and often to lower levels than in the past.

What that implied was that customers were now looking at heterogeneous environments to drive their enterprise initiatives. SAP, when they realized this was the case, made the practical decision to recognize it and then to change what they did and how they did it. They developed an outlook that said that companies would be provided with a critical mass of core applications that had hooks into the heterogeneous systems and landscape that passed for company architecture and process.

"As a result, SAP had to open up more toward the outside," says Darc Dencker-Rasmussen, vice president of Global Initiatives at SAP. "We had to shed our more rigid structure of the past to deliver on this new technology and application set."

SAP launched a massive initiative with their customers to try to understand their requirements. "We had to come out of what we had thought was our perfect egg," said Dencker-Rasmussen.

This changed the relationships to the partner ecosystem too, while SAP built their own consulting services group. How is that? Well, SAP brings partners with them on all their engagements along with the consulting group and vice versa. Many of the solutions SAP delivers are partner-produced. This in an environment that has transformed from a product-out-the-door oriented galaxy to a solutions services universe.

The next step for the new partner ecosystem is to expand to distributions—downstream channels—to extend the value chain even further. SAP's relationship to American Express as their primary Business One distributor is a good case in point here.

Internally, the culture shifted quite dramatically. Bill McDermott, whom you heard from in Chapter 1, changed the incentives for the sales teams at SAP to compensate them for long-term relationships. One example of this is the change in the nature of the contracts that are signed for SAP solutions. Historically, the bigger the contract the bigger the compensation. Now the objective is longer-term phased contracts with customers implementing pieces of an SAP solution in phases. This is the new focus for sales in this new, more friendly, and yet utilitarian culture at SAP. It is still a research and development based culture but far more open than at any time in its past.

Darc Dencker-Rasmussen again: "When we look at the needs of business ecosystems, no other companies have the size and scale to build the depth and breadth of applications that can handle this ecosystem."

While I can't say that with their assurance, I wouldn't rule it out either. This is a formidable, very smart company capable of a lot.

Strategy

SAP's strategy for the next several years is something that I think is absolutely dead on. They are attempting to move beyond the enterprise into the business ecosystem by establishing a competitive value chain. That is not just the verbiage it sounds like. As our man Dencker-Rasmussen says, "We are committed to a dynamic environment to build a community and to build an ecosystem, not just to participate in one. That means we have to scale our ability to deliver and to increase the speed of delivery of new business processes." Whoa. That is one ambitious strategy. But they might very well pull it off. They are moving to this strategic epiphany by locking this idea into their NetWeaver strategy. CRM is NetWeaver as the ecosystem evolves.

NetWeaver

NetWeaver is their platform for SAP's strategy for thinking and acting beyond the enterprise. Each component of this significant platform for open architecture and integration is designed to work in those extended enterprise environments and in the larger business ecosystem. Each component has a clearly defined strategic purpose, not just a functional capacity.

> ▶ **The portal** This is one of the most CRM-critical components of the entire NetWeaver platform. Each role that the portal provides through its single sign-on and individual password gate

entry has personalized needs and views. As significant as the personalization is the underlying work going on. It links these personalized business functions to the appropriate data and applications across the entire value chain.

- ▶ **The distributor** NetWeaver provides a framework to distribute enterprise applications across any environment

- ▶ **The supplier** It can look at distribution and resale channel data and do demand forecasting for months ahead.

- ▶ **Business intelligence** It can do real-time analytics or static reporting and deliver it to a single portal user without exposure to other users.

- ▶ **Master data management** NetWeaver manages the appropriate customer views by role of the customer. It also can manage the appropriate changes to the master customer record.

- ▶ **Business process layer** NetWeaver can incorporate industry specific or general business processes through its business process layer. For example, order management can flow from the enterprise through the enterprise to the supply chain suppliers and back into the enterprise.

- ▶ **Field service/mobility** NetWeaver extends to pervasive devices such as your PDA—including the use of embedded analytics with real-time connectivity for those analytics—or will have that very soon. Right now, it can look at thin slices of specific customer or product data such as customer propensity to buy or product knowledgebase information or troubleshooting guides.

This is SAP's next few years, its platform for extension into that business ecosystem. Their idea is to build a community within this new ecosystem, not just to participate. That means in the long term, this R&D oriented company wants to take web services–based platforms like NetWeaver and allow companies to restructure their own business processes quickly and on their own, without writing code.

So far, not a bad start, don't you think?

Oracle

Over the past several years, Oracle has been an anomaly to me. They've done some things just so right and on the other hand…. But when it gets down to it, they are not only a market presence but a dominant one. Oracle is virtually built into the lingo of information technology (though the one at Delphi predates them when it comes to general language use). They have superb products, but had the reputation of being a little customer-challenged over the years. I always wondered about that and hadn't been that happy with them, but I have to say that they are certainly making significant strides forward, minus a few glitches here and there, when it comes to dealing with customers. I also have an explanation as to why they had so much cultural difficulty in their past. But they are working toward the change, especially as the customer ecosystem demands it. Keep it up, Oracle.

Achievements 2002–2004

Noticeably, this is a company that prides itself on technology, whether it be their culture, their coding, their features and functions. The achievements, according to Oracle, are very much functionally oriented, so pay close attention. They're listening.

Oracle changed the focus of SFA from administering a sales process to making it more effective. Management oversight, forecasting, opportunity management are table stakes. What makes SFA implementations successful today are projects that bring value to salespeople. Oracle is distinguished by solutions that drive sales effectiveness making deals bigger and making them happen faster not just administering the process and providing visibility.

They enabled service operations as an opportunity for profit, not just a cost of doing business. Customer satisfaction drives profitability. Oracle service solutions recognize that and allow customers to execute against it.

They now provide marketing that drives revenue, not just leads and contacts. Oracle's marketing solutions are built to deliver value to the sales process, not just drive higher levels of marketing activity through automation.

Culture

Oracle is another company making serious cultural strides, but it isn't quite there yet. I took a trip to their Redwood Shores campus and was very pleased with their facilities and even the perks of employee culture—within limits. The Redwood Shores campus (and that is what it truly is) is beautiful. Perhaps the most beautiful of all the work facilities I've seen since I've started seeing workplaces. Physically, there aren't too many facilities you can visit that have ponds and lakes with herons and cormorants diving into the clear waters. Nor can you often find five themed restaurants within the facilities for employees, or dry cleaning stations that will get your clothing back to your desk by the next business day. But that is no substitute for an overall climate that can best be explained by understanding what it is to live in a development environment.

The best way to understand the Oracle culture is to understand its roots. This is a culture steeped in technology, even more so than business. It is no coincidence and, in fact, is to their credit, that their concern is to get out the best applications possible. Their thinking is that if they develop great technologies, the customers will come to them. Much to their bemused bewilderment, that has been translated into arrogance on the order of "We don't need to go to the customers. They should come to us." Unfortunately, arrogant or not, this is a clear misstep in business strategy, for which they have paid many times over the past few years despite improvements in both the technical quality of their CRM and other applications and the recent improvements in their CRM functionality, always an Oracle weak point until now. (See Chapter 4.)

However, while ending up with a need to refocus their business model, this development-focused culture leads to true technology innovation. As stated earlier in the book, Oracle was one of the first companies to recognize the need to redirect CRM into a process focused model—the ubiquitous Oracle business "flows" as they called them. But even more impressive is the millions spent and the heavy personnel commitments to the Usability Lab at Oracle's Redwood Shores. You've seen the level that this takes in Chapter 19.

More importantly, in 2004, Charles Phillips, formerly Morgan Stanley's chief CRM analyst, and now one of Oracle's two presidents, has begun to work on transforming the culture. Oracle does recognize its past transgressions and is starting to spend time going to the customers and listening to them, rather than waiting for the customers to come begging at their doorstep. They have created a customer advocacy group to involve the customers in the planning of future Oracle solutions and products. All of this in a bid to make Oracle a more customer-friendly, but no less development-oriented culture. Go for it.

Strategy

Oracle's strategy for the oncoming years can be stated in one word: integration. Fundamentally, the principle is delivering CRM as an integrated part of a complete set of business applications. By orienting their functions and features around processes, they are able to deliver a solution that supports the customer transaction across the entire business: marketing, configuration, sales, fulfillment, billing, support, service, renewal, and so on. What makes it interesting is that they deliver this complete set of functionality in one implementation, on one single data model, and have built all of their applications on this same common basis. This allows for a nearly seamless experience, though nothing in the universe is seamless.

But the integration strategy based on a single model and a single instance permeates Oracle's strategic approach from here to five years hence, barring any new ecosystem interfering. The Oracle release of their customer data hub is a reflection of the first stages of this well thought-out approach. The customer data hub is part of Oracle's grid infrastructure. That is a mouthful of a sentence but is vital to the Oracle CRM strategy. Again, we're dealing with a development culture here, people, so let's explore it in plainer English.

SPEAKING SIMPLY ON THE GRID AND THE HUB

The Oracle enterprise grid allows you to manage your data and your resources as a single entity providing a thoroughly integrated, inter-meshed combination of processes and tools—all managed centrally—regardless of where the data or the resources come from. They are easily available to any user at any point from any vehicle (not car—communications medium) that the user has conveniently available, and all in real time. The customer data hub is a central repository for that customer record that has been through data cleansing and standardization so that it is recognizable and easily readable by those same disparate, singular users. It is "active" because the data is sent through the hub carwash and is cleansed and standardized before it ever sits in the repository's garage regardless of who the source (a.k.a. the manufacturer) of the data is. Any application has access to the data immediately upon parking, whether

Oracle or not, in near real time or even real time. All three hundred sixty degrees of it.

There it is in a nutshell. There is one thing that puzzles me, though. Oracle has arguably the best database in the world. It is that for my money. But I don't see Oracle actually taking advantage of that in their strategic thinking. Imagine this: you have the best database and a fully integrated stack of applications and processes built on a single instance of it. That's kind of a powerful message, but I don't see Oracle leveraging their database at all anywhere. Strange, very strange. But they still have a solid development-directed strategy in any case.

Imagine that. A development strategy governs this heavily technology-focused company. An innovative bunch, this. If they can only improve their relationships in the outside world, life could be good for them. Let's see how well Charles Phillips does.

Siebel

This is a company that has needed a sea change and finally launched the boat in 2003. Even though they had long been a favorite of the analysts, who tend to work on the left side of the brain, they had been under fire for everything ranging from poor financial performance (not unlike most companies in 2002–2003) to bad culture. But they still won award after award for their applications and frameworks; in fact, just about everything analysts had to offer from most of the CRM related Gartner Magic Quadrants on down. They continue to hold their own as the leader in an increasingly competitive marketplace. What is particularly heartening to me is that they are also beginning to make the transformations to their culture necessary to bring them to a world class level in all respects. By no means are they there yet when it comes to culture, but they are changing and for that, I tip my hat.

Achievements 2002–2004

It is always interesting to see the perceptions of one company against another's perceptions of themselves. Siebel's aim is squarely at market share and at areas that they have become newly good at, which makes sense given that they were already good at many areas in their application suite: PRM, call center, some of their vertical applications such as ePharma, and several others. They had been weaker in both analytics and integration, but have leapt to a solid position in the market both by 2004.

A decade of innovation and CRM leadership leads Siebel to its recognized number one position. There are some impressive numbers associated with Siebel's move to the top. They've invested over $1.4 billion in developing their CRM products. They have over 4,000 customers that total a phenomenal 2.37 million users of Siebel products. Those numbers are big enough to be almost frightening. Amazing.

Siebel CRM OnDemand provides comprehensive hosted sales, marketing, and service applications. Siebel and IBM form a powerful alliance that plays to the strengths of both companies so that a hosted service can be provided that is a genuinely useful entry into the marketplace. I wrote one of my TechTarget SearchCRM columns on the details of Siebel OnDemand and Siebel OnDemand: Upshot Edition (for smallest businesses) and found both of the offerings refreshingly useful and effectively targeted.

Universal Application Network (UAN) is introduced in 2002 and has dramatic results. The UAN is Siebel's integration platform, one that allows them to compete with enterprise application vendors, despite not having the back-end applications available. With the release of version 3.0 in 2004, they made major strides in both increasing their customer use and improving the capabilities of the platform. A 2004 Accenture study looked at integrating a CRM solution (Siebel) to two ERP systems (SAP and Oracle) across 20 integration touch points in the areas of customer lifecycle management, product lifecycle management, and order management. The study concluded that UAN accelerated time to market by 30 percent compared to the customer building a similar solution. And UAN required 45 percent fewer project staff compared to a custom solution.

Siebel Analytics leads market for customer analytic applications. When IDC Research issued their 2003 Worldwide Customer Relationship Management Analytic Applications Software Forecast and Analysis, they ranked Siebel as the market share leader in customer analytics and fastest growing analytic applications company. Siebel Systems captured 15.4 percent ($122.6 million) of the worldwide market for these applications in 2002, up from a 5.5 percent share in 2001, which is a substantial leap.

Culture

With the ascension of Jeff Pulver as senior vice president of marketing, and even more germane, with Tom Siebel, founder of the company and majordomo of the corporate culture stepping down in favor of IBM veteran Mike Lawrie, Siebel might well be on the road to recovery. The sales-at-all-cost culture that had dominated the company for so long could be on its way out the door. With 2004, a new era is possible at Siebel.

This isn't going to be easy, but then, cultural transformation never is. Mike Lawrie is used to an $80 billion revenue "bogie" (that's business development speak for "target") and he's used to IBM's rather different culture (see below). His current plan, according to the pundits and his own cautious initial statements, is to "stay the course" which might be fine in both strategy and culture, depending on what that actually means. Will he let the good guys continue to break the old habits that they are diligently working on? That remains to be seen. I'm betting he will, judging from what I've heard from those who have dealt with him.

What already has been a considerable improvement that I can directly attest to, as can many of my fellow CRM colleagues, is that Siebel has gone from a closed-mouthed hostility to "outsiders" to a dramatically more open company, not only willing to provide press, customers, partners, and even on occasion, rivals with considerably more information and support than in the past, but even to willingly admit their past transgressions and make attempts to redress them. It's like the section in the movie *Something's Gotta Give* where Jack Nicholson, as an older man who has been dating much younger women, has a catharsis and goes around seeing all his former girlfriends, attempting to both apologize and reach closure. Some slam the door in his face. Some let him have an earful about his transgressions. Ultimately, he and Diane Keaton get married and live happily because he and she have changed. Great movie. I hope Siebel senior management goes to see it.

Their new openness can be directly attributed to when Jeff Pulver became the vice president of marketing in 2003. It improved dramatically with Jeff's hiring and has continued unabated and unabashedly since that day. The winds whooshing through Siebel HQ are refreshing and even a bit warm.

Does that make me do a turnaround on Siebel? Not yet. I'm thrilled by the much needed changes in the culture that seems to be evolving.

I'm also glad to see that Siebel isn't claiming to be the gift of the gods to mankind any more and is willing to work more closely with its partners and allies—and even a few of its enemies every now and then. But the culture still needs to be repaired. It acquired the arrogance that I've blasted over the years a long time ago. But I have some real confidence that the effort will bear fruit. Since it's not up to me, I'm keeping my fingers crossed, though, of course, I have many ideas and suggestions. Hey, I'm a New Yorker.

The sales-oriented culture is changing, according to Kevin Nix, group vice president, Industry Applications, a nearly eight-year veteran and a really good person, even if he does root for the San Francisco Giants. "In boom times, there was no doubt, we weren't solutions oriented. We came across arrogantly sometimes. We didn't always ensure what the customer wanted. When the economy contracted, we had to change the ways we interacted with customers. Our sales folks started listening to the customers and make sure that the technology we were selling mapped to the actual needs of the customers."

One of the most significant cultural changes to make the customer friendliness more of a reality was the creation of a CRM strategy group, led by industry player Peter McCullough. This group provides strategic services to the customer for free. Another plus for Siebel on the side of good change. I'm not aware of any other major CRM company that does this.

But culture has to be responsive to all "customer" groups, including the employees, and that is the benchmark to which I always hold the companies that I review. Siebel claims that this has improved, though I have yet to see it in action. They have some employee perks—always have—like day care, a really good cafeteria, and a high quality fitness center in their San Mateo headquarters. Good things that help morale. People can work from home, have flex hours, and in some cases even have Siebel-funded home offices to work from. All strong employee benefits.

They have core values that have been their hallmarks: professionalism, customer satisfaction, courtesy, and a bias for action. The first three are really significant and are a matter for individual adherence, since each of them except professionalism has been something that Siebel has been questioned on over the years. I suppose I would say that the "bias for action" can be used for good or evil, since as a core value it's pretty much neutral.

While there are still some causes for concern, I'm cautiously optimistic about Siebel's chances to overcome their negative reputation and become a major force in CRM for the good, not just the sale. I say that because of the recent management shifts and the sincere desire to make the changes that I sense from Siebel. It doesn't hurt that they still have some of the best applications and solutions on the market. If the culture can shift to the side of the customer, welcome to their ecosystem, Siebel.

Strategy

Siebel's 2004 slogan reflects their desire to change, not just their culture, but their business model and strategy. It is "CRM for Everyone." It is probably best reflected by Siebel's acquisition of Upshot and OnDemand partnership with IBM over the past year—perhaps the most important move in Siebel's current history.

While their strategy is still focused on "what should we build," rather than "who should we partner with," there are some moves that will reduce the lone wolf emphasis. Most notably the partnership with IBM as their OnDemand hosting partner. "This was a no-brainer," according to Nix "It gave us a longer reach for our 'CRM for Everyone' approach. Large enterprise customers in a department, who had already standardized on Siebel, had a quick and easy ASP for other needs. This meant that products were running on the same technology—it was kind of like Burger King. You could have it your way. That way the concept of hosting versus on-premise isn't a religious issue. It is a business decision."

Since that particular battle often gets fought with the fervor of a medieval crusade, to reduce it to its proper proportions is a refreshing idea.

This aspect of their strategy was recently enhanced by their announcement of eight industry-specific OnDemand solutions that will be available in the summer and fall of 2004. The industries that will be available over the summer are insurance, high technology, automotive, and communications and media industries, while financial services, life sciences, manufacturing, and consumer goods industries will be available in the fall, making the OnDemand services a formidable competitor to the industry standards like salesforce.com, Salesnet, and NetSuite.

The other major face of Siebel's CRM strategy is built around the UAN. While Siebel continues to acquire companies to fill its technology and industry process holes (such as the recent acquisition of Eontec, a multichannel retail banking vertical solution), it strongly touts the UAN as a core part of its strategy. It comes from the recognition that in this multichannel integrated systems world we live in, not just one solution is likely to be used no matter how devoutly to be wished the idea is. Siebel is betting that the Unified Application Network, its integration framework, is the ticket to selling into existing PeopleSoft, SAP, or Oracle deployments and systems being held by other customers. Or at least that it will make them a stronger candidate on deals that will have extensive, open-ended integration in the future as part of the arrangement.

Siebel is also counting heavily on its release of Siebel 7.7, available to the public since April 2004. What makes this more than just a less buggy point release is the major improvements and additional functionality that Siebel is adding to the overall already strong application suite.

SIEBEL 7.7

This is one of Siebel's most significant upgrades, maybe a precursor to Siebel 8.0. If not, wow anyway. They have taken not only features and functionality into account, but TCO and usability, integration, and mobility, making this a massive improvement over an already good Siebel 7.5.3. Coupled with the upcoming Siebel/IBM OnDemand-hosted industry-specific services that will be available in fall of 2004, they are creating a powerful combination that actually meets their strategic objective of "CRM for Everyone."

What makes their features and functions improvements interesting is that they are very much oriented to the extended value, actually locating their ERM (Employee Relationship Management) applications appropriately as part of the value chain, rather than just some separate silo. While I have my already expressed concerns on their views of new sales functionality (see Chapter 4), I have no doubt whatever about their approach to marketing, which is fully integrated into the entire Siebel suite with strong best practices and processes. Apart from improved segmented and targeting tools, reflecting the interest in the marketplace on this matter, I'm particularly excited about the enhanced e-mail marketing capabilities, an area long under-recognized as mission-critical by most CRM vendors that provide the larger suites. Siebel redresses this for the whole industry with a comprehensive permission-based, personalized e-mail marketing campaign engine, rather than just focus on the campaign management that many vendors concentrate on. They have also made considerable improvements in their contact center and field service applications, both of which were already the best in class.

They have added substantial order management capabilities in this new release, ranging from asset-based ordering to quote and order validation and approval—all with a user interface that is almost easy to use. Imagine that.

Improvements to their ERM applications are noteworthy, though what excites me the most is the integration of ERM into the total system. That indicates to me that Siebel understands that employees are a customer group who are a link in a collaborative value chain. I'm almost as happy at that as I am about the improvements. The most important ERM improvement is probably the addition of a learning analytics engine and reports that can analyze training, helpdesk, and performance management for learning systems. This is something that has been sorely needed by CRM applications. Typically, it resided outside CRM systems in applications such as the learning management systems provided by RWD, which I discussed in Chapter 21.

The PRM improvements are incremental with perhaps the most important being the integration with their UAN 3.0 framework.

The industry specific solutions have been upgraded. There are now 23 separate industry solutions ranging from automotive to insurance to hospitality and travel to public sector to retail. Each of them has been dramatically enriched. For example, public sector added case and incident management, the latter valuable not just to local agencies, but also to federal agencies like the Federal Emergency Management Agency (FEMA) and law enforcement. In their hospitality and travel solution, they added Accrual Management to handle varying types of point-related programs such as frequent flier. All useful and valuable additions rife with best practices.

But they aren't just concentrating on the features and functions. What makes this even more interesting is that they have spent considerable time on usability—something they and their big ticket vendor rivals have been excoriated on time after time. Aside from the more typical improvements in navigation and screen layouts, they've added such useful improvements as a universal inbox that centralizes all "to dos" of any kind on a single screen, and iHelp, a context-sensitive embedded guide to using the applications.

Architecturally, integration is more enmeshed than ever, using service-oriented architecture to support increased application security, process, and data integration through the use of their newly minted Analytics Data Manager and External Business Components that link the configuration of Siebel's Business Components to external data sources.

This is one heck of an upgrade. Siebel-projected improvements to the TCO are extensive. For example, usability improvements between Siebel 7.5.3 and 7.7 reduce the related TCO by 53 percent; their integration improvements lower the TCO by 40 percent. These are excellent results, people. Look into it.

Unisys

In the second edition, Unisys was the surprise of the year. I had researched more than 40 companies and in the original round, Unisys didn't even appear on the radar screen. Like everyone else in the known universe at that time, except Unisys employees, I thought their business model was aimed at hardware and transactions like check services—they run over 50 percent of the world's check transactions on their hardware. They were generally impressive, but imagine my surprise when Mike Chuchmuch, then associate dean of the Unisys corporate university, now VP in charge of their change management practice, convinced me to take a first look. I did and never looked back. They made my top five in 2002. Now, it is no surprise despite the changes in my criteria, that in 2004, they remain among my final two integrators.

Achievements 2002–2004

What is glaringly obvious about Unisys's take on their achievements is that they are spotlighted on people and relationships. This is entirely consistent with their strategy and culture. Interesting, very interesting.

Their revenue, headcount and engagement numbers, and size grew substantially from 2002 to 2004. This was amazing, especially given that in 2002–2003 CRM wasn't exactly a growing concern. During this downturn, now thankfully over, Unisys grew in each of these areas in double digits. For example, their headcount grew 100 percent over the two years, 38 percent in 2003. The typical engagement size was twice what it was in 2001 by 2004.

They have been recognized as one the world leaders in CRM. They were named a "leader" in worldwide CRM practices by analyst firm

IDC and were one of only six companies included in Gartner's recent ranking of global CRM service providers.

They have a stable, growing global management team and staff. They have grown their staff and management team through hire and acquisition dramatically in the last couple of years. Yet they have had no management turnover at all and 1 percent voluntary turnover in staff.

They have developed strong relationships with their partners and increased their base of world class references across industries and geography. Most recently they have developed powerful, heavily invested relationships with Microsoft and PeopleSoft, on top of their other relationships with Siebel, SAP, Oracle, and E.piphany. They have exceptionally good references.

Culture

The culture of Unisys is likeability. Unisys SVP and general manager of the Global CRM practice Steve Olyha puts it very well, "Likeability and respect exist on our team. It is darn important to our culture. Our entire global operating model is designed to support likeability." How often do you hear these kinds of terms from a business, even as lip service?

I can substantiate that this is a lot more than lip service and is a sincere dedication, from my personal experience, which occurred subsequent to my interviews with key Unisys CRM leaders. Here's the story.

Those of you who read my dedication saw that my wonderful wife was diagnosed with a serious illness. I have a contract with Unisys to do a series of speaking engagements in the United States, Europe, and Australia that were scheduled to go during primarily June and July 2004. I made a decision—a no-brainer—that I had to be with my wife during the course of this trying time and the treatments necessary to beat it. I spoke with Unisys about this and told them that I understood the needs of business and certainly wouldn't be offended or hurt if they decided to break the contract and get a different speaker so they could stay on schedule. I had this conversation with their wonderful, warm, and very capable CRM marketing director Rose Lee and with, of course, Steve Olyha. There was no question for them. Without a moment's hesitation, they rescheduled all eight of the speaking engagements for the latter part of September 2004 and later, even though it meant delaying their own business plans to do so. "We know what's important." Likeability is perhaps too understated a word for a multi-billion dollar company with a global consulting arm with 38,000 staff that is still willing to treat human beings with dignity and respect and—likeability.

I'm not the only one with a good story to tell. I've spoken with multiple Unisys CRM clients in the course of preparing this book. I found that Unisys clients get treated as well as their partners, as well as their employees, and as well as their suppliers. Their cultural model, especially in the CRM practice, starts with "How do we make it easy for the customers to work with us?"

One of the answers to that is personal accountability around sales, delivery, and solutions. "Every time a person in our organization touches a customer, it's a brand impression," says Olyha, "which means that we have to ensure that the customer's experience is memorably positive. That way we can sell more and deliver excellence to a very satisfied customer."

They even evaluate their potential partners not just on the sales and delivery components that they can provide, but on the sales and delivery satisfaction that they provide to their customers and potential customers. They have an evaluation of partner customer satisfaction they call the customer value index (CVI). This is a client rating of the potential partner that means a lot.

As I've continually stated throughout the book, there has to be an element of self-interest satisfied to make these kinds of cultural paradigms work. If the employee is accountable for sales and delivery satisfaction, what do they get when they succeed? These are a few of their favorite things: promotion and money. There are personal and partner opportunities for successful satisfaction of this "likeability quotient" and, of course, penalties for either employees or partners failing, though I'm sure that Unisys doesn't believe in the death penalty.

ONE UNISYS

The cultural theme for Unisys in 2004 is "One Unisys." That means that they are moving to provide a stable management, a stable workforce that loves working there, and a worthy but small set of managed partner relationships that meet the likeability criteria mentioned above.

One of the most important pieces of a successful culture is providing that stable management team. A question and frustration that is constantly posed to me is, "Since it is ongoing, what happens to the CRM program when we have such a turnover in management? Even if we get buy-in and champions, they are usually gone within a year or two and we have to start over again." Without going into the answer, suffice it to say Unisys doesn't have that problem in their CRM practice. They have the same management this year that they had two years ago and will probably have the same management in two more years. Steve Olyha put it this way, "This is a stable bunch. Not only is management stable, but we have had only a 1 percent voluntary turnover, because we have such great people." I'll vouch for that.

Strategy

Laser focus characterizes Unisys strategy. Even prior to Steve Olyha's imprint on Unisys, they were always aimed at a targeted audience, but if you read the second edition of this book, when Steve Olyha was still at CSC, his approach was, to say the least, targeted. So the combination creates a strategic precision that led to some remarkable results over the past two years.

Before I describe the strategy precisely, I will preface it with one comment. Unisys is smart enough to walk away from solutions and opportunities that they haven't targeted. I have heard more than once from their competitors, "Why are you picking them? I don't see them competing against us ever." I hear this from two groups. One doesn't have the same targeted direction as Unisys and tends to be very opportunistic: "Find an opportunity and they will come." The other is companies that are jealous that they weren't among the companies chosen and Unisys was.

What is Unisys's strategic vision for the next several years? "We'd like to see the CRM practice go away and a value chain practice take its place," says Steve Olyha, with his usual foresight. They understand that the extended value chain is going to dominate the business landscape in the next few years as more and more businesses recognize that the customer needs to be at the core of their strategies and that the business ecosystem is already a customer hub, not a corporate hub.

But rather than just expanding their scope to cover all the facets—supply chain, demand chain, and support chain, a.k.a customer-facing solutions, back-office solutions, and channel solutions—they hone in on the areas and industries where they can have an impact.

Their primary strategic focus is on solutions that can supply and receive customer value and are tailored to their individual clients. One advantage that Unisys has is that it can provide the full spectrum of infrastructure and services, unlike the vast majority of its competitors. Consequently, when they are doing a CRM engagement, it becomes not just a software implementation, but an operating model and set of strategies for dealing with customers actively. They are vendor agnostic. So, for example, even though they have over 200 certified Siebel consultants, Unisys doesn't have a Siebel practice. They also have dozens to hundreds of trained consultants in PeopleSoft, Oracle, SAP, Microsoft CRM, and E.piphany in addition to Siebel, but no practices by that name. On the other hand, they are focused in certain industry-specific provinces such as pharmaceuticals, consumer packaged goods, retail banking, airlines, and the always popular federal, state, and local government sectors. They can develop a solution for any of the sectors using the most appropriate tools and methods to create the right mold.

With the targeted sectors and the appropriate tools, they can refine their strategy even more, always with the idea that customer strategies that span the extended value chain are the driving strategies of this era. This perception led them to spotlight business intelligence as a key strategic differentiator, using ExecuPoint, their mobile and real-time business intelligence solution as the wrapper for their offering. Business intelligence (see Chapter 9) is treated not as a gathering of insightful data, but as analytics that lead to actionable intelligence. The Unisys term is "differentiated customer treatment." Similar in concept to the customer portfolio management that PeopleSoft is providing the tools for, they have developed a set of strategies, methods, and tools to identify the high value and low value and in-between value customers of today and tomorrow. Additionally, they provide customer behavior analysis for their client companies so they can create the means and methods to treat these distinguishable customer clusters. Then they create a mobile and real-time environment for the customers to use this intelligence, using key performance indicators to see that the actionable intelligence is actually acted upon and the objectives set by the insight are met.

BLUEPRINTING

One other strategic specialty for Unisys is blueprinting. To put it simply (but by no means is it simple), blueprinting is a review of all levels of an enterprise so that the integration of processes and technology can be examined and effected and the cultural changes can be produced that will allow the integration to be as smooth as possible. The results according to Unisys are not a topline growth rate of 3 percent or a 10 percent cost cutting, but instead 30 to 50 percent across all sectors of the organization.

There are four stages to blueprinting: strategy, process, applications, and infrastructure. Even though the stages are distinct, there is no silo for any given process. Each instance of a process or component intersecting any other process or component is examined. I mean, this is thorough stuff. The idea is that this root-level examination can eliminate bad processes and identify best practices, making the customer considerably more effective.

Unisys is aimed at pushing these highly leveraged practices and segments through their next several years. They have had more success in the last two years than any other CRM practice that I have run across. It's hard to argue with that.

IBM Global Services

IBM Global Services in particular and IBM in general is unlike any other organization that ever populated the planet at any time. They are unique. They are astounding, organized, and even humane for an organization of their size. For example, Mike Lawrie, their former senior vice president and group executive for sales and distribution, left in May 2004 to head up Siebel. It was mentioned in the press that he was responsible for a target of $80 billion. That is one person with the overriding responsibility for $80 billion dollars. Eighty billion. Eight-oh-billion. What other company besides IBM can even mention that in a breath that is expelled over a century?

Yet, as big as they are and thus prone to "big" mistakes as they should be, I unequivocally recommend them because they have one of the largest and most effective CRM practices ever derived, and they make those mistakes less frequently than other companies that are in the same category. They can deliver pretty much anything. They strengthened that in 2003 with the acquisition of PricewaterhouseCoopers, particularly when they put Adam Klaber, PwC's former CRM chief at the helm of the practice. This is a guy with industry experience and thought-leadership street cred.

To give you some idea of the scope we are speaking of here, there are 11,000 CRM related employees that are split between 5,000 CRM consultants and 6,000 customer service representatives associated with CRM. And they are still hiring.

Achievements 2002–2004

IBM Global Services (IBMGS) achievements are results oriented, much like the culture and strategy of the company. There is no one "thing" that characterizes the four points—instead a substantial set of broad results that are simply the case.

Advancement of business process and industry expertise into IBMGS CRM's capabilities. This was accelerated due to their acquisition of PricewaterhouseCoopers's (PwC) consulting arm in 2002. While they had a strong industry-specific expertise, PwC provided increased strength and new capabilities in areas like public sector and financial services.

On-demand strategy and approach combined with CRM software partners. This is not only a good approach but a hallmark in the industry. Their alliances with CRM companies such as Siebel and Onyx in the on-demand market—in fact, with the OnDemand brand—is a landmark move that both attests to the staying power of hosted subscription services as well as the intelligence of IBM on adoption of a model like this.

Industry focus, breadth, and consistency of their CRM practices across the globe, evident in IBM thought-leadership and high analyst rankings. Everyone kind of claims this one, but IBM Global Services actually meets the requirements. Not only are they recognized as thought-leaders to some extent, better than most, but they are also consistently in the leader quadrants and the top positions of most analyst organizations. For example, they are classified as one of the few global integrator practices.

Development and leadership of business transformation services and global sourcing capabilities for CRM clients. The scope of the deals that they talk about are on the order of $1 billion—similar to the size of the outsourcing deal they signed with Swiss giant ABB in late 2002.

Culture

IBM Global Services and the integration with PwC created a new culture that at least spanned IBMGS, if not the entire company. Managing the growth spurt was not an easy task. IBM staff move from job to job in the company frequently, though they are 25- and 30-year veterans who don't leave the company. IBMGS treats them well. PwC, which came from the Big Five consulting/accounting arena, had a markedly different culture than IBM, and integrating the two perspectives has been difficult and not without its glitches, according to IBMGS sources. However, they seem to have gotten to the point where it's beginning to show some results.

The cultural metaphor they are attempting is to create a professional services environment or, as Adam Klaber, the partner in charge of CRM for IBMGS, says, "a business consulting environment." Interestingly, that is more in line with what PwC had, not IBMGS, but it's a wise decision since IBMGS is a consulting organization. The issue will be how to create that environment and still maintain the relationships that lead to highly loyal employees who remain at the company for 30 years or more. I have no doubt they will be able to do it.

Strategy

They can't do enough. Even with 5,000 consultants, a formidable fighting force, Adam Klaber has no illusions, "Alliance partners are the key to our go-to-market strategies. IBM provides the infrastructure and associated services. Our partners provide the applications." This partner-centric focus allows IBM to develop the framework for highly successful strategies such as their hosted OnDemand strategy that is best known for the IBM-Siebel alliance, but also is in league with several other CRM vendors such as Onyx. IBM is able to provide the hosted services, the vendors the applications. Just like the man said.

IBM bases its partner strategy on market share. They identify a market segment that they are interested in and find out who the corresponding leader is in that market. Klaber says, "We see this as CRM done right. We like to invest in where we see the market going and then work with the application leaders in that market to provide overall leadership."

But IBM isn't just all infrastructure and applications either. They are known to make strategic forays into thought leadership too. In May 2004, they issued a groundbreaking study on the factors that affect

CRM success and found that the softer side of CRM is the most influential. For example, their noteworthy study found that improvements from less than 15 percent to as much as 80 percent can be had if the human aspects of CRM, which "typically require conservative, incremental spending," are considered more seriously than they ordinarily are. Those are change management, learning management, and iterative involvement of the users in the redesign of the business processes around customer strategy and value. That is the kind of study that the industry needs and that IBM can provide.

One unambiguous fact is that the integration of IBM and PwC had a profound effect on IBM's CRM strategy and culture. IBM Global Services had always had the core technology expertise, but PwC was able to provide them with strategic management services such as process expertise and value creation skills that simply were not part of their equation in a meaningful way.

Because IBM is in a position to take on pretty much any facet of CRM they want to, they have a broad and deep approach. They have the assets—hardware, software, infrastructure, services, and outside relationships—to provide either on-premise or outsourced services for any size of institution. While they are focusing their attention on telecommunications, hospitality, public sector, and insurance, they can be opportunistic when it comes to possible other vertical domains or horizontal solutions. What makes this particularly valuable to their future clients is that IBM is one of the few companies that can provide not just the direct infrastructure with their services, but through their own resources and the resources of their partners (like Siebel, Onyx, and many others), the hosted services or the outsourcing that a company may need. To sweeten the pot, IBM is able to finance the deal for the companies that are signing the contracts. That is about as full service and complete as you can possibly get. Imagine: sign a deal with IBM, buy the hardware you need, buy all the CRM and related applications you need, decide whether you want it on-premise or OnDemand, go to IBM's financing services and get them to finance the arrangement for you, then have IBM Global Services come in and do the strategic and implementation services you need. Then have IBM introduce you to your future spouse through their dating service, secure tickets to a ballgame, and find your old college roommate for you. Okay, well, maybe not the dating or college roommate investigation services, but I bet they could get you the ballgame tickets. Their array is breathtaking.

Almost Done: The Case of Accenture

There is no denying Accenture. They are the CRM industry power-house when it comes to consulting firms. Few approach them for breadth, depth, and sheer scope of effort. Additionally, they are among the very few integrators or even vendors who understand the value of thought-leadership. I can't say that I've seen a lot that hasn't been self-aggrandizing, but I'll give them a B minus for their effort. The major-ity of their collegial competitors get a solid F for thought-leadership, so a B minus is something.

However, I'm too uncomfortable recommending them, even though they do some good work. My historic dealings with them have been ugly and while I'm not letting that influence what I think about them as much as I once did, they have a long way to go before I'm comfort-able in saying, "Yes, they've changed their culture." Even though, like any other company of their magnitude, it depends on whom you deal with, their culture hasn't changed sufficiently either in my experience or the experience of those I discussed it with for this book recently to merit my recommendation. But they can't be ignored either.

That said, I'll give you some useful information about them that is impressive. In 2002, they had 1,400 CRM clients who engaged them to do over 5,000 specific projects. There are 5,000 employees devoted to their CRM practice. Someone must like them. Their CRM revenue was a monumental $3.2 billion that same year. They have a strong value proposition for customer care and contact centers. They are also extremely good at marketing-related analytics utilizing a combination of CRM strategy, brand strategies, brand analytics, and customer insight analysis.

Clearly, they are a leviathan with a substantial presence and some-times really smart. I just don't like their culture. While the institution is big enough to have some islands of good practice and decent human instinct within it—which means you can trust certain individuals—as an institution, they have shown me that they are not terribly customer friendly despite their entreaties to the contrary, so I can't recommend them. However, because they do provide some real value-oriented thought-leadership in a truly practical way, I can't condemn them entirely either. My primary recommendation? *Caveat emptor*.

Well, that's it for the big guys. Enough with the giants who walk the earth. Now, let's head into the next chapter and deal with the smaller players—like Microsoft.

24

The Best of the Rest

O kay, they really aren't "the rest." That's kind of unjust, we still have the ASPs to go yet, but I couldn't think of what else to call them. Tough classification never stops me, a guy raised on the mean streets of East Meadow, New York. Well, actually, the kind of nice streets. In any case, I have two vendors aimed at the small and lower end of the midmarket, two aimed at the upper midmarket and lower Fortune 1000 (maybe 791 to 988?), and only one integrator. They all have unique personalities, excellent products, and have passed the bar when it comes to my criteria. That was tough in this category because there are dozens of pretenders and wannabes who just don't cut it. Some are good enough to make it, like Braun Consulting or Fujitsu Consulting, but don't have quite all the elements that I seek, though I wouldn't hesitate to suggest them to anyone.

As for the best of the rest, on with the show.

Companies

I've made some possibly eyebrow-raising selections here both by those I chose and those I didn't. Some of it was inadvertently easy. I was debating on whether to include ACCPAC in the best choices list here, and Best Software, owner of SalesLogix, bought them, to solve their entry into hosted solutions and to solve my dilemma. Ultimately, I chose Microsoft and Best Software as the companies that are best suited to serve the small business market, and E.piphany and Onyx as the companies best equipped to serve the larger end of the midmarket. All four of them can handle the lower end of the midmarket, and E.piphany and Onyx can even handle some of the large enterprise market.

Noticeable for its absence is Pivotal, acquired by Chinadotcom subsidiary CDC Software in December 2003 after some fascinating machinations, worthy of daytime soap opera. In October 2003, Pivotal announced that it had been acquired by Oak Investments, who also owns the solid CRM vendor Talisma. Just a few days after that, chapter choice Onyx announced a bid to acquire Pivotal which was rejected (too bad) by the Pivotal board of directors. Finally, after the theater curtains rolled down, in December, the CDC Software acquisition was announced—and had actually occurred too! Pivotal, who has a decent product, became part of CDC software. For my purposes, they have been too uncertain and have lost something in the market and in my eyes.

It was tougher on the integrator side. I looked at multiple companies, but I suppose I set a very high standard for integrators, since I know so many of them and have been involved with them as their partners or subcontractors or they as my clients over the last several years. I had to aim at those that served the smaller companies as well as not be averse to having high profile Fortune 1000 companies on their plate either.

While there were several excellent integrators out there, the only one that met my standard for this bunch was Hitachi Consulting. You'll see why when you read the section.

E.piphany

E.piphany is always creative. From the way they spell their name to their often cutting edge product offerings, to their current strategy, they take an innovative and pretty bold line of attack and usually make it succeed. Always make it succeed, no. They've had some periods where it just hasn't worked. But they are a continuing success story that has been classy and classic—going where no CRM company has gone before and making it revenue-producing. I'm not alone in this perspective. In March 2004, Gartner placed E.piphany in its "visionary" category for B2C CRM suites and for its marketing applications. No surprise—visionary. That they are.

Achievements 2002–2004

Since these achievements are delivered by the vendors, they tend to be not just interesting as individual milestones, but also are quite telling in the choices themselves. E.piphany's choices scream out that they are proud that they have turned a quality set of cutting edge applications into a revenue-producing venture that leaves satisfied customers in its wake. The nonbold commentary is mine.

E.piphany continued to focus the company directly on increasing profitability at the largest consumer-oriented companies through intelligent customer interactions. For more on this, see the E.piphany strategy section.

They delivered a modern and open enterprise CRM architecture based on J2EE and web services across entire suite of marketing, sales, and service. This is made particularly interesting by their strategy and their actual willingness to use their architecture to define their business model.

They grew revenues by 30 percent year over year in 2003 in a tough market. Since most of their competition were down in this number last year, that says something.

They continued to emphasize their marketing and analytics power and extended that real-time intelligence to sales and service offerings. This focus led to E.piphany growing its customer base, expanding existing relationships, winning competitive shoot-outs, and garnering press and analyst accolades—not a bad couple of years' work.

Culture

E.piphany understands that it is a 425-person company with roughly $100 million in revenue, which means that in the markets it competes in—upper end of the midmarket and the divisions and low end of the large enterprise—it has to rely on more than its resources, which are scarce by comparison to their competition. So they depend on a solid strategy and a strong culture. "We require strong prospect and customer satisfaction levels," says Steve Schultz, E.piphany's director of corporate marketing. "Our hunger to try harder comes because we are smaller. We can't afford to be arrogant."

In practical terms, this means that customer references are a critical part of the next deal, and they have to make sure that customer satisfaction is the centerpiece of their efforts. Whenever a vendor tells me that their customers are their culture (and they all do), I have to make sure that my skepticism is dissipated or I'll see it as just another marketing claim. When I asked E.piphany for proof, they provided it— AMR Research's Joanie Rufo and Lindsay Sodano, in their report

"CRM: Inflicting Pain or Profit": "In terms of overall satisfaction, no vendor was able to produce nearly as many satisfied customers as E.piphany. Besides being the most responsive, E.piphany's references cited more quantifiable benefits than any other vendor."

Strategy

E.piphany maintains its reputation as an innovator even in its strategy. Steve Schultz put it this way, "We want to be the CRM vendor of choice for the largest consumer-oriented companies that sell to end consumers." This simple statement actually flows into a coherent direction that E.piphany successfully capitalized on, as you can see by that 30 percent growth number above.

If you look at their pre-2002 strategy, it was focused around selling marketing analytics, their lead CRM product. An E.piphany product strength for many years, marketing analytics drove CRM into the sales channels that had high-volume customer interactions, which then opened the door for E.piphany's other products. Because the products provided a common view of the customer and the information for actionable intelligence, E.piphany focused on customer profitability as its key strategic message—because the better the information you had on the customer, the more significant the return from that customer. If that customer was in the consumer-oriented verticals such as telecommunications, retail, insurance, travel and leisure, or financial services, then E.piphany had the suite to provide the value.

But in 2003 and 2004, the strategy took another innovative turn. Not only was E.piphany going to concentrate on the consumer-oriented domains, but they were going to attack the marketplace in a way that none of their competitors were doing. They would plug in and augment. They understand that legacy systems meant investment—both financially and psychologically—for their customers. There were other systems the customer as concerned about. So plug and augment it was for their customers.

E.PIPHANY 2004: PLUG IN AND AUGMENT

E.piphany leverages its open architecture for its "plug in and augment" strategy. The architecture rests on a J2EE platform that is also 100 percent web services standards–compliant. It is not only capable of dealing with Java-based integration, but also .NET integration, making them one of the few CRM companies that can handle both platforms with equal facility.

Their architecture was created with the recognition that customers have heavily invested in legacy systems and third-party applications that they won't just dump. Consequently, E.piphany is able to go to the customer with an approach that says, "You don't have to implement all things at once. You can integrate a module of ours with your third-party application, or you can add some functionality to your legacy system—for now." By plugging in an E.piphany module—say, E.piphany's Interaction Advisor—you can increase your likelihood of success with real-time personalized offers and still have an Oracle Sales system in place. Plugging in a module without disrupting the existing applications but integrating with it through J2EE or web services compliance allows the customer to add new functionality with a deployment time usually under 90 days. This goes against the "rip and replace" approach that other vendors often take. Smart stuff.

Augmenting existing systems is the other aspect of E.piphany's go-forward strategy. Steve Schultz used the example of a telecommunications company in Switzerland that had been using a Vantive application for ten years. The Vantive application was mission-critical. What the Swiss client wanted from E.piphany was a single customer view for its call center agents and the functions that would allow the call center agents to cross-sell and up-sell to their customers. So that's what E.piphany did: implant functionality into a mission-critical legacy application.

Plug in and augment is both a smart, customer-friendly strategy and kind of diabolical. Given the quality of E.piphany products and the cost-effective approach they are taking, isn't it likely that the customer, if they have good sense, will eventually just go all E.piphany? E.piphany innovates once again with a kinder, gentler strategy that provides a business benefit typically in less than 12 months and gets E.piphany in the door with both feet. Innovative, smart… but who expects anything else?

Onyx

I admire Onyx. They are a company that kept a modest profile, letting their excellent portal products speak for themselves. Brent Frei, former CEO and founder, is an industry leader who is as modest as his company, a good person who doesn't feel the need to be out there more than necessary, refreshing in this industry that is rife with egotists and CRM divas. Even as a good fella, he is willing to make tough decisions when he has to. One of the toughest was to replace himself with a new CEO, Janice Anderson, when he felt it was time for a change. He wanted to get the company profile raised, so in 2004 he made the switch as this book came to press. This is not surprising, since Onyx is a company that could unflinchingly face change and deal with it—whether it was structural, political, product-related, or strategic. As a result, though there are many changes afoot yet, you now have the beginnings of a cultural shift and a reorganized, more efficient company that Janice Anderson can take the helm of. What has been consistent throughout has been the quality of their products, so with the changes and the products, their future looks really promising.

Achievements 2002–2004

As you can see if you read these achievements, Onyx faced changes starting in 2002 in all domains. Now, they're making money at it. Good show, eh?

Onyx migrated the application to an Internet-architected, multiplatform application that is 100 percent web services enabled. With the release of version 4.5 in 2003, their functionality surpassed anything that their client/server edition had to offer.

They launched their Embedded CRM strategy. This has enabled Onyx to partner with other solution providers who needed CRM, or pieces thereof, to complement and enhance their overall offering.

They transitioned the market focus of their business from almost exclusively midmarket to primarily midmarket with a growing percentage of business out of the large enterprise market. Approximately 20 percent of their 2003 business was large enterprise.

They strengthened their financial profile. Onyx took a number of financial measures, among them, aligning expenses with revenue and negotiating agreements to exit leases on excess facilities. This effective approach helped their operations generate $2.5M in EBITDA (earnings before interest, taxes, depreciation, and amortization) over the past four quarters ending with the first quarter of 2004. The cash flow from the business turned positive three quarters ago and has steadily increased.

Culture

If I were to characterize the Onyx culture in a phrase, it would be: an effective internally focused culture. They depend on themselves for their effort, which is not typical of the industry. For example, 70 percent of their implementations are done by their own professional services team—not partner teams—a reverse of the more typical VAR and partner channel arrangements that exist in the CRM world. According to Gordon Evans, the Onyx director of public relations, "We were characterized by an analyst about four or five years ago as a white hat in a black hat industry," which still seems appropriate today. They are a bit different from their competitors in several respects. They have only a small partner channel. Historically, they haven't been as aggressively sales and marketing–oriented as those same competitors. Even so, they have been successful. With this kind of culture, success falls on the quality of the products and the relationship of the company directly with its customers. This is a culture that does not depend on the middlemen, so to speak.

The accession of Janice Anderson as CEO means that what I write here today could change dramatically in the next twelve months as she gets her bearings. I expect we will see a new business model and market strategies as yet unknown. That, my friends, will stoke a cultural shift that is TBD, but could be dramatic. Let's see.

Strategy

Onyx strategy, in a nutshell, is "go deep." That means go deep into specialized processes and vertical markets. It means go deep as in Embedded CRM, as they call it.

They are particularly smart when it comes to using their strengths. There are no portals in the CRM world that are as good as Onyx's versions. They are using this benefit to sustain a highly successful vertical strategy. In 2003, 48 percent of their 2003 license revenues came from their vertical markets. Their strategy for the next several years is to expand their vertical presence and to improve their tools for customizing specialized processes—necessary for any vertical penetration.

They are one of the few vendors their size that seems to get the idea that the public sector is a vertical to die for in 2004 and beyond. They are working with local councils and boroughs in the United Kingdom to develop strong e-government functionality by 2005. They are active in a 311 initiative in New York City where they are providing preconfigured workflows and using their new business process tools for contact centers in the 311 market using a public sector product they call CitiServe and allying with Microsoft and Unisys to do so. I can't tell you how incredibly smart this entry into the public sector is. You saw that in Chapter 11.

Not ones to rest on their product laurels, they have added business process tools ranging from the Onyx 5.0 Process Scripting tool, which can provide dynamic branching and outbound marketing scripts, to process scripting with easy-to-use interfaces using the technology assets they purchased from VisualE. These visual mapping tools include graphic mapping and a forms builder that provides a user-friendly way of developing highly customized processes that can integrate well with the technologies in use at any given company.

The other important piece of their strategy is Embedded CRM, an intelligent OEM strategy that allows privately branded versions of Onyx to be embedded in systems provided by other vendors or customers. For example, Metavante sells a portal-based platform for regional banks that provides ASP-based services for bank tellers that is "powered by Onyx." Other companies embedding Onyx (either as "powered by Onyx" or where the Onyx name is invisible but the technology isn't), are Spain's Telefonica and Spherion among many others. This strategy is part of the recognition that customers have invested in systems they simply don't want to part with. By customizing specific processes and using the already award-winning portals, Onyx takes advantage—wisely.

Microsoft

There's a *Saturday Night Live* skit where the incredibly versatile and funny Christopher Walken plays a weird sort of gigolo at the Hotel Continental. His signature phrase when he sees a beautiful woman is "Wowie, wowie, wowie!" I think that I have to say that, in a nonsexist way of course, when it comes to the success of Microsoft in the CRM world.

Microsoft has amazed me for 15 years and yet, though I'm not surprised by Microsoft doing something well, they still surprised me with the MSCRM product—as you probably noticed earlier in the book. But what doesn't surprise me is that they had the foresight to understand the bigger picture, the willingness to invest the time and money to take the chances they had to, and the intelligence to use the partner business model they did to make this a successful product. Despite the continuous efforts to make them into some sort of "Evil Empire," let's face it, people, Microsoft is successful because we use and, gasp, *like* their products and not because they shove them down our throats. There are plenty of alternatives in the world of open source. We're not as stupid or devoid of will as the purveyors of "Microsoft is the epitome of evil" would make us to be. This goes for the 198 million users of Outlook and the installed base of MSCRM too. It's that Microsoft gets it, gets its partners, and, for the most part, gets us.

Achievements 2002–2004

Their choice of achievements is notable for its emphasis on customers and partners—more so than any other vendor in any other venue that I've selected as "The Ranks" choice.

They have developed and shipped the MSCRM product in 9 (and soon to be 14) languages and to 53 countries. They've done this all since February 2003, which is all the more remarkable for its speed—given MSCRM's more than adequate functionality.

Since the February 2003 release of MSCRM 1.0, they have developed a customer base of more than 2,500. This has been channel-driven from the beginning. These are not shelfware purchases—they have a very high usage rate.

Microsoft has created an extremely strong partner ecosystem. What makes this particularly interesting is that even though they have their own CRM solution, 775,000 partners, and tens of thousands of certified partners, they have not lost or damaged their partnerships with Siebel, Onyx, or Pivotal, among others. They have expanded their channel and kept it up at the same time. Not bad, creating a delicate balance between 775,000 different organizations.

With the release of MSCRM, they've been able to give their customers multiple choices for functions, technology, and environment. To highlight this, Holly Holt, the highly articulate CRM product marketing manager for Microsoft, tells me of a "redeployment tool that can take a pilot project or a hosted environment and move it to a new domain without disruption." Additionally, their APIs are open and available to their partners or anyone to develop useful tools and features for MSCRM. Slick and thoughtful.

Culture

This is a partner and customer-conscious culture where execution meets claims. Not only do they claim to be determined to make this culture work, but the way they work is operational proof of their claim.

They live on successful customer satisfaction. Every single employee, all 50,000 plus, is compensated for and accountable for meeting their Customer and Partner Experience (CPE) objectives—whether you are CRM or not, IT or not. This is not negotiable. The CPEs are the core of the way that Microsoft works and have a general manager, John Cahill, in charge of just that program.

Constant improvement is the other target when it comes to customer satisfaction. Three examples should suffice. First, each quarter there is a customer satisfaction survey. Each quarter, there is a partner satisfaction survey. The results are taken seriously and problems that are reflected in the results are fixed. Second, customer satisfaction issues are tracked every day. They don't have to be CRM-related—customer-related issues for Office System 2003 is fine too. The top ten issues are identified and dealt with as they are determined. They have an outsourced company that handles the tracking. Finally, they have a Customer Voice initiative that speaks with the customers all the time to see how much and how well they are using Microsoft applications. The questions are on the order of, are you using it? Is integration working and how? Are the commitments we made and messages told to you real?

Wowie, wowie, wowie.

Strategy

As much of a mega-institution as they are, Microsoft has perhaps the simplest strategy. It is partner-centric. They deliver all solutions through their partners. "We see a huge opportunity to deliver through them," says Holly Holt. "Our delivery pillars are productivity, usability, lower TCO, and integration. That's what our partners can deliver." To that end, much of Microsoft's strategy is embedded in the partner program I detailed in Chapter 6. In mid-2004, they developed a new program and certification for those partners who want to put the most effort into support of MSCRM and other Microsoft products. They call it their Certified Software Advisor (CSA). This is for the partners who are willing to make the investment into certified knowledge of the products, the customers, and the programs. This can earn those partners as much as 20 to 30 points higher compensation for business opportunities closed.

As long as MSCRM has been here, there has been speculation on Microsoft's ultimate plans with the product. No one, including me, thought that Microsoft would stop at the small business market nor would they limit themselves to CRM, per se, but would in fact go all the way to the Fortune 500 large enterprise market. Holly Holt again, "MSCRM will never be a fit for some of the Fortune 500. But we have sold into the divisions of some of the large enterprises. Selling into the semi-autonomous divisions or departments of these is a reasonable scenario." Does that slake your speculative thirst, reader? I thought not. At least admit that Microsoft thinks realistically about what it can do when. That's part of the reason for its success.

Microsoft, while strategizing in the here and now, also thinks ahead to the then. We've all read of the development of the next operating system code named "Longhorn" aimed at a 2005 release date. Well, on the CRM front, Microsoft is planning MSCRM version 3.0; yes, that's 3.0, not 2.0, even though 3.0 is probably three and a half years away and the number 2 comes before 3. Who knows what that will bring? We can only guess, which, when it comes to Microsoft, we customers all love to do. But Microsoft, to their credit, doesn't want to guess about what we customers need. They want to know what that is and to get their partners educated to do something about it.

Best CRM

There is no company that I know better, nor any company that I am just getting to know more. Confusing? Let me explain. Interact, the original SFA company, was founded by Pat Sullivan in the mid-1990s to serve a growing portion of the sales market that needed increasingly sophisticated sales functionality, but wasn't necessarily a Fortune 1000 company. Their product, SalesLogix, vaulted to the top of the pack easily for the midmarket and small business enterprise. Pat Sullivan also had extraordinary personal credentials, having been the cocreator of ACT!, the contact manager (see Chapter 4) known and loved by millions of salespeople. Multiple venues had voted him one of the great sales and marketing gurus of the 20th century.

In 2001, SalesLogix, by this time a real force in the SFA world, especially in that small and midmarket enterprise sector, was sold to the heavy-hitting $1.4 billion U.K.-based Sage Group, a company that had made its name with accounting products and placed under its also-acquired U.S. flagship company, Best Software. Boy, has this ever worked. Gartner, in early 2004, estimated that Best, with both ACT! and SalesLogix, has captured 25 percent of the SMB market worldwide, with sales that grew 13 percent in 2003 against a general growth rate of 5.5 percent for all vendors in this market—over twice the market pace.

Achievements 2002–2004

Acquisitions, products, and partners. They're saying "we've got muscle—intellectual and physical." They actually do, too.

Best Software got new ownership, a new management team, and a new philosophy. As you will see, Best Software changed its corporate leadership and with it refocused their outlook. They are now aggressively centered on customer satisfaction and retention as their core philosophy.

SalesLogix 6.2 release increased quality, usability, performance, customization capabilities, and added a new customer service application. I have no comment here except to say SalesLogix is always worth looking into.

They acquired ACCPAC CRM from Computer Associates. This one is really important. They added a hosted solution and thus a directly competitive dimension to their value proposition. They now offer both on-premise applications and hosted services. They are interchangeable.

They refocused on the partner channel. When I first met these guys in 1999, I was totally impressed with the fact that 86 percent of their revenue was from their partners. They went astray for a couple of years and it fell below 70 percent, but they are now more in harmony with their partners than ever. This was proven by their 2003 revenues, which were 100 percent through their channel.

Culture

This has been an enormously important facet of Best's success, but also a difficult thing to follow. Since the acquisition of SalesLogix, the culture has been changing from one of entrepreneurial innovation to a more conservative culture of "making it work well." This is partially driven by the fact that "Best is now getting used to being, not independent entrepreneurs, but a division of a much larger sized company," as Anthony Wooten, vice president of product management and product marketing for Best CRM, says. In 2003, Sage had roughly $1.4 billion in revenues, punctuating Anthony Wooten's statement with an exclamation point. Best Software was over 50 percent of those revenues and has 3,000-plus of Sage's 7,500 employees.

This is a culture of annuity streams from their customer base and to their employees—an unusual approach to corporate culture, to say the least.

Best Software culture is focused on more customer retention than the growth that small businesses crave. In fact, if you look at Sage's growth, a substantial portion has been by smart acquisitions ranging from the acquisition of DacEasy (I remember them!) in 1991 to ACC-PAC in 2004, both packages with accounting roots.

How does this affect them? Well, if you are customer acquisition competitive, your development efforts are aimed at announced due dates and product releases in a timely fashion. At Best, they are focused on nurturing their existing installed bases, so the products they release are released when Best Software thinks they are ready, no particular due date necessary, Jeeves. There is a sound fiscal reason for this less frantic approach since 60 percent of Best Software revenue is support and maintenance.

The annuity stream to the employees is intertwined with their organizational structure. Compensation isn't the "one big chunk for the closed deal," but instead is a steadily increasing income stream based on the relationships between the employee and the account that represents the customer. The better the overall long-term relationship, the more constant the increase in a regular income flow to the employee.

Strategy

Their strategy is a continuation of their culture, showing there is no disconnect between their policy and their practice. According to Anthony Wooten, Best strategy has three components.

SHORE UP THE EXISTING INSTALLED BASE

That means raise the level of customer satisfaction to protect the base or as Mr. Wooten calls it, "raising the state of play."

LEVERAGE THE EXISTING SAGE/BEST INSTALLED BASE

Sage and Best have a substantial non-CRM installed base with hundreds of thousands of customers and millions of users. Best sees this as fertile ground for growth, and as they acquire other companies to improve their enterprise applications offerings, the installed base comes with it. So there is a potentially endless fountain of customers for Best to drink from.

Their leveraging strategy dovetails with a study they completed in mid-2004 of 500 U.S. and 500 U.K. CRM users on the age-old question: single solution versus best of breed. The study subject wasn't surprising. The results were a little surprising only in the overwhelming size of the majority, not the choice of the majority. Single solution from a single vendor was the choice of 85 percent of the respondents with 10 percent not caring and only 5 percent calling for best of breed. That shows how far back the pendulum has swung in the last two years. While the results of a single study are not industry-definitive, they are important to the Best Software strategy because it means that the Sage/Best installed non-CRM applications base should be prone to wanting SalesLogix or the hosted ACCPAC solution.

To execute this strategy, they've created a Migration Center that works only with the installed base to cross-sell solutions and drive specific sales and marketing campaigns to the base, such as upgrading ACT! to SalesLogix. They are providing a new product called ACT! Premier, which is a version of ACT! using SQL Server, moving ACT! from just a flat-filed contact management product to a version with a relational database and increased functionality. The product features fall in between existing ACT! users and the needs of SalesLogix users. One of the most intriguing and user-friendly features is that the migration toolkit provided with ACT! Premier can pump data into SalesLogix and still use the ACT! interface, making the transition to SalesLogix a little less painful.

What makes this part of the strategy so appealing is that it recognizes the march of the customer ecosysem to the blue-collar needs of the users and doesn't ignore them for the money holders in management. Anthony Wooten again, "Sales optimization solutions should be totally separate from sales management functions. If users aren't using the solution, it's useless. It's optimization versus execution. Both are needed. Neither can be ignored. The car won't move if there is no one willing to drive it."

GROW THE SALESLOGIX BASE

Best realizes that to expand the base for SalesLogix, it has to appeal to the vertical marketplace. To do so means either acquiring the pieces that allow for the specialization or embedding SalesLogix into a vertical solution held by others. But there is a "horizontal" requirement too as the market moves to alignment with the customer ecosystem. There has to be the functionality of an extended value chain provided across all aspects of the enterprise. Anthony Wooten puts it rather colorfully, "We have to move the enterprise and then flip it from horizontal to vertical. Customers want a system to automate *their* business, and each horizontal piece needs to fit the vertical pieces. In the long run, vertical industries will dominate."

The verticals that Best is looking to are very specific. Not just accounting, but certified public accountants (CPAs), and they bought CPA Software to take care of that. They are aimed at real estate and construction. For that, they bought Timberline Software. They are very intelligently focused on the not-for-profit world and bought MIP Software for that.

While doing this, they (like the other recommended competitors) are cognizant of the need for a flexible integration platform. They are in the process of developing the Best Software Integration Framework (BSIF), which will enable vertically strong, horizontally integrated enterprise solutions across a common framework.

All in all, with this kind of clear strategy, and the deep pockets and strong commitments of their parent, Sage, Best is poised to go even beyond their Gartner-named 25 percent market share. With ACT! aimed at small businesses, Hosted ACCPAC aimed at midsized business, and SalesLogix aimed at the small enterprise, they are ready to rock. Not Amboy Dukes or Brewer and Shipley one-hit-wonder style rock, but Rolling Stones rock—permanent players on the scene.

Solutions Providers

This was a particularly difficult category, because it is populated with extraordinary organizations that are among the best and thousands of small fly-by-nighters and temporary inhabitants of the CRM universe whose position among the stars could supernova or just collapse in any moment of change at any time. To mix my metaphors, I had to look through the forest to actually find real trees. Only one company made my final list, but two others belong pretty close to it. They are Fujitsu Consulting and Braun Consulting, both of whom are excellent organizations with strong practices. As 2004 moves on, Fujitsu Consulting is cementing their market position by forming strong alliances with SAP and others. Braun Consulting, a Chicago-based group with a strong CRM strategic practice that emphasizes analytics and customer value, continues to do superb work with their clients. But Hitachi Consulting is my choice here.

Hitachi Consulting

Hitachi Consulting (HC) is the 2004 *CRM, Third Edition* surprise. When I began my research, they weren't even a thought. But someone I know decided to leave a good job and go to work for them, which piqued my curiosity, though it wasn't a book-related curiosity. I found out that HC has a serious CRM practice that, while it doesn't compete with the integrators like Unisys or the consulting firms like Accenture, has an interesting model, is growing, and has some substantial bucks behind it through parent company Hitachi.

That put them on my sonar and I began my usual vetting with calls, conversations, and research. They became book competitive. They met all the criteria that I had established for culture and strategy. But it wasn't a done deal at that point. The one thing that nagged was achievement *history*—this isn't meant to be a section on up-and-coming companies, but on established players. Hitachi Consulting had only been around for a few years. What sealed the deal for them is that they are the former Grant Thornton consulting arm, with chunks and soupçons of Arthur Andersen's consulting organization, and several others thrown in. My direct experience with Grant Thornton consulting and others who I know had that experience was always something that reeked of a classy organization, exceptional solutions provider, and fair and honest organization. So welcome, Hitachi Consulting.

Achievements 2002–2004

These are achievements chosen by a company that graduated recently from up and coming to a came up and still going status. The bold statements are theirs and the commentary is delivered without prejudice by me.

Hitachi Consulting was a great place to work through the downturn. During the economic downturn, Hitachi Consulting's

Customer Solutions practice continued to grow, while the market didn't. The parent Hitachi didn't waver for a minute and continued strong support while others were downsizing.

They integrated their CRM business and technology practices. In early 2002, they made the strategic decision to combine their CRM Business Consulting and CRM Applications/Technology practices. "The combination of these skills and experiences into a single integrated practice has significantly advanced our ability to deliver for our clients," says Brian Johnson, CRM practice leader.

They rebranded their consulting organization as Hitachi Consulting in 2003. Their heritage organizations included Grant Thornton LLP, Arthur Andersen, BDO Siedman, Experio Solutions, and others.

Culture

When it comes to culture, "inspiration" seems to be the word du jour for Hitachi Consulting. Here's three of their taglines or vision-related statements: "creating an inspired culture," "inspiring your next success," and "inspire the next."

However, inspiration is a lot easier to say than to, well, inspire. Their primary growth over the years 2000 to 2003 was fueled through acquisition, and inspiring is not a term you would typically attach to the cultural challenges that mergers and acquisitions create. But Hitachi was up to the task, forming the People and Cultural Advisory Team (PCAT) to handle the various corporate integrations. In a truly "CRMish" fashion they developed performance metrics that were used to measure employee satisfaction. The PCAT team then held the various departments and leaders accountable for meeting those key performance indicators.

For example, how to communicate was the basis for a culture clash. The Arthur Andersen veterans used voicemail far more than e-mail. Existing HC personnel primarily communicated through e-mail. So no one got back to each other. Distrust and arrogant behavior began to creep in and disrupt the venture. But rather than wait for it all to collapse, PCAT, using the 2003 rebranding effort as a jumping-off point, evolved a "best of the best" democratization process and solved the problem with the participation of all parties in the solution.

HC considers its culture to be socially focused rather than task focused. That means they aim their culture at customers, clients, markets, and prospects. "The difference is that task focused cultures are action oriented," says Johnson, "but socially focused cultures try to care about people as individuals."

They've managed to succeed as they continue to hire at a rapid pace through 2004. Each of the new recruits is trained and becomes part of this socially focused culture—a culture that does practice what it preaches—inspiration.

Strategy

Strategy fascinates me. The types and quality of strategies are often indicators of the maturity and social psychological state of organizations. For example, you can usually tell that a company is a longer-standing player when their strategy doesn't focus on geographies or size. The companies that tend to be more recent aim at size and location as a prime facet of their strategic effort. HC is more the latter than the former, but with a mature twist.

HC's immediately stated task is growth—move to critical mass in eight regional U.S. markets. They call it a 3-8-150 strategy: three industries, eight U.S. regions, 150 people in each region. The three industries that they are giving their attention to are the food and beverage/consumer goods market (one that I personally hold near and dear), the utilities industry including telecommunications, and the high tech and industrial manufacturing world. All of these are competitive markets that HC has been successful in. The idea is to focus heavily on those markets in the eight U.S. regions and not invest marketing dollars, intellectual capital, or develop alliances outside those industries. That way the $68 billion parent unit, Hitachi Ltd., can use its money judiciously.

They also are forming those alliances that can benefit them in these sectors with the expected players—Siebel, Oracle, PeopleSoft, SAP, Pivotal, and Microsoft.

HC is aggressively moving on the 3-8-150 strategy and will be close to achieving it as this book is published.

But they haven't forgotten the long term either. Not only are they looking to international growth over the next several years in both Asia and Europe, but they are planning on expanding their CRM offerings to business process optimization, providing offshore services and outsourcing, and expanding their industry footprint to most likely healthcare and financial services. How? Organic growth and the always pop-ular acquisition path. Between the growth tracks and partnerships, they can achieve the level of geographic and manpower expansion they want. Of this and Hitachi's deep pockets, I have no doubt.

But it gets more interesting and sophisticated in the second piece of their strategy, what they call intellectual capital. This is where the real strategic twist is—and their differentiator.

Their reasoning goes like this. Profitability and good rates are HC's primary business driver. Customers will be willing to look at high-value integrated delivery services models because they can provide consulting, best practices, customer value, technology, and thought leadership. These are all elements that when provided in a tailored package can drive business effectively for that customer. But the deci-sion on who should provide all of that and how it should be provided to the customer is not easy. Consequently, the better informed the potential buyer on what it all entails the more likely the buyer is to choose the company that gives them the right information. What that means is that HC (though, in truth, any company) has to have both a knowledgebase built up over years of successful services and project delivery, as well as a determinate point of view that can differentiate them from the pack. HC has designed a strategy that provides that kind of intellectual capital. For example, they can provide deep knowl-edge and content for sales force automation for the food service indus-try. This depth allows them to charge premium rates and provide a quality of effort and success that commands them.

As we've seen in this and prior editions of the book, this laser-focused strategy, coupled with a whole-brained CRM strategic frame-work, is the foundation for success. Hitachi Consulting, a maturing new kid on the block, is wise beyond its years.

CONTEST #2

This is the second contest. I'm disturbed about the lack of consulting services final-ists for this chapter. This contest is a simple one. Given my criteria (see Chapter 23 for them) and format, make a really solid case for why I should include another con-sulting services company of your choice in this mix. Make the case really com-pelling. It's okay if you represent the company either as an employee or contractor or public relations company, but pure marketing junk will diminish your case, believe me. So tread carefully if you are a representative and please disclose that fact in your e-mail. If you convince me, I'll make sure that the company you are argu-

ing for is covered in something I write that's in an appropriate venue, that the company goes on my permanent radar screen, and you'll win a $50 gift certificate to Amazon.com or a real Barnes and Noble store or Borders, whether you're independent or engaged with the company. There can be up to three winners in this contest. An added bonus: if you can tell me the one-hit-wonder songs of the Amboy Dukes and of Brewer and Shipley and provide the lyrics, I'll make your $50 gift certificate a $60 gift certificate. You have to win the actual contest to take advantage of this one-hit-wonder offer.

So we've covered the big boys and those that are focused in the smaller venues for the most part. That seems to be about it, doesn't it? Wrong. Now we move on to covering the companies that created that "disruptive innovation." The ASPs. The ranks continue to march ahead. (The Dave Matthews Band song "Ants Marching" starts to play as we exit page right.)

25

The ASP Is More than Cleopatra's Death Warrant

By any chance, have you noticed that the ASPs are all over this edition of the book? I'd say that after this chapter, it should be just about enough, wouldn't you? But they've had such an enormous impact—remember "disruptive innovation"—that their influence is unavoidable and even important. But, despite their continued entreaties, they still "ain't the biggest catfish in the deep blue sea," as an old 1930s song goes.

But, in this third edition, they've become contenders and will remain so. Not only can they stand toe to toe with the on-premise vendors, but there is a virtual parity with them, though they haven't actually reached that exalted level yet. If you paid any attention to the ASP marketing machines, you'd think they've seized the high ground from the dead enterprise vendors whose bodies are littering the valleys below, while the conquering ASP warriors stare satisfied and triumphant from the mountainous plateaus they now occupy. At least, that's what their marketing tells you. The only problem is that this isn't true nor does anyone even think it is. The fact is the ASPs are coming up on about a 10–12 percent market share. That's pretty good for a young upstart. They may not be dominant, but they are gaining strength. Don't let their size fool you; in this case, small *is* beautiful.

But I have a few beefs with these dudes. First, they never stop marketing. Never. Sadly, the marketing, while often entertaining, can get heavy handed. It has the sophistication of a hammer taken to a fresh egg. Here's the form it almost always takes when their press release hits my mailbox:

> "ASP #1 gets Customer #1 from ASP #2 (or On-Premise Vendor #2). This is followed by a quote from Customer #1 Vice President #213 about the superiority of ASP #1 over ASP #2."

You know what? I couldn't care less. Nor should you. For some reason, the ASPs think that this "customer theft" proves their superiority. It doesn't. For everyone who defects to you, I could probably find someone who defected from you, if I cared enough to do that. Maybe there should be ASP stats like they have in football and hockey—giveaways versus takeaways and you have an annual plus/minus ratio for the difference. The highest positive plus/minus wins. Wins what you ask? Just wins. Isn't that enough?

The ASPs spend more time than they should sniping at each other and the enterprise companies in a classic over-the-backyard-fence gossipy way. Sadly, not only does this detract from their message, but it can create some distrust. For example, in the course of interviewing eight ASPs for an article I was writing, two of them lied to me outright about their competitors. By the way, neither of the two made it to my selections for this chapter. I suppose they assumed that I wouldn't fact check. As a potential customer, I would be concerned about who I was dealing with. If you care to know who the scofflaws were, give me a call at the phone number listed in the introduction of the book.

Finally, I find little evidence that they are interested in thought leadership, only in marketing. That is a pity, because if they are truly the disruptive innovation they seem to be, then they have something of an obligation to provide the conceptual leadership that the market needs so it can understand the value of the disruption. Otherwise, they won't be able to sustain their momentum over a long period of time. One thing I've always found to be important is for the marketplace to have its intellectual leaders. Most human beings have good minds that need to be piqued and that need to have an understanding of what they are getting into. It's of the quality of "Oh, *that's* what you mean. That makes sense." While that doesn't necessarily promote the company, it does promote the idea.

An example: in late 2003, I was chatting with an Oracle CRM representative who had been at Siebel prior to Oracle. He told me that Siebel used the second edition of this book for their customers a fair amount. I said, "Why? I attack Siebel in the book." His response, "We knew that, but you validate the market." That blew me away because it was such an intelligent and subtle thing to do. Siebel, of all companies, was able to understand the value of thought leadership, and that shocked me. Actually, that was one of the first times that I began to understand Siebel beyond their historically arrogant behavior. To date, this level of subtlety has escaped the ASPs, though they try to make up what they lack in refinement with exuberance.

All that said, I really like the companies discussed in this chapter. All three of my choices are classy organizations run by smart, caring people. Their business models differ widely even though their value propositions are similar. One thing that characterizes all the choices is that they have very happy customers, which is certainly the result you want, especially if your business model depends on repeatable revenue. Repeatedly happy customers mean revenue streams that go on and on.

Why the Choices?

I considered four companies as finalists and chose three: salesforce.com, Salesnet, and NetSuite. The fourth one was RightNow. The reasons I didn't choose RightNow have nothing to do with their value proposition. They are a good company that specializes in hosted customer service. I see them as a value-added outsourcer, running call centers through the use of their hosted services or on-premise software. They seem to see themselves as one of the "net natives." I have a problem with their customer claims when they tell me that they have three million customers, which, I presume, means three million inbound callers to their hosted call centers. When I hear this, I am unclear on how they define customers. I define customers in the ASP market as users who are following the general business model (subscription services), not anyone who interacts with the service or product. It's their right to define their customer base any way they want to. It's my right to decide whether or not they merit the value that I need to provide my readers. Any uncertainty, however small or significant, means I won't warranty them.

This doesn't mean that I think they are not sound. RightNow's value proposition is pretty solid. They will provide you with their on-premise software or their hosted solution. They are the only one of the hosted brethren who has a selective upgrade policy, one of the missing and important features and functions that the others could benefit from. That means that rather than just uniformly automatically upgrading all the clients attached to the multitenant architecture, RightNow provides the opportunity for you to upgrade via e-mail with all features, some features, or not upgrade at all. Slick, indeed. Also, they are a great service to their locale, Bozeman, Montana. They are the biggest employer in town.

They did this all as a bootstrapped company—a company that used its own resources, not venture capital—to build itself into the successful 300-employee company they are today.

I'm also not covering Siebel in this chapter, though their CRM OnDemand services certainly merit ASP participation and status. However, these chapters are about companies and Siebel is covered with their OnDemand product in Chapter 23. Once is enough, though I doubt Siebel thinks that.

Now, on to the three recommendations. Remember, as I said in Chapters 23 and 24, under "Achievements 2002–2004," you'll see bullet points. These are the vendors' achievements through their own eyes. Even though I've chopped out the egregious marketing and put it in my voice, they selected their own. This allows you to get further insight into the company's thinking about itself, which is the purpose of these latest chapters.

Salesforce.com

Salesforce.com might be the number one CRM story of 2003–2004. At the time of this printing, about to go IPO, perhaps only eclipsed by Google's pending IPO auction, they have been a hot discussion topic for over a year and don't seem to be any less interesting. Marc Benioff, their CEO, marketer extraordinaire, and a good man with a truly charitable heart, has been featured in every business magazine known to our species. Salesforce.com is the reason that hosted solutions are seen as a disruptive innovation and they will continue to disrupt for a long while yet.

Achievements 2002–2004

As we've done in so many prior sections, here are a few bullets for you to peruse on the achievements of salesforce.com in the last two years:

- ▶ **Their vision of "no software" became a reality.** Many of the top names in computing technology such as IBM, Microsoft, Sun, and Oracle have adopted on-demand or software-as-a-service strategies. Purchasers discovered the advantages of the on-demand model which I outlined in Chapter 16.

- ▶ **They reached a 10,000 customer and 150,000 subscriber milestone in 2004.** After only five years of business, salesforce.com has nearly 80 percent of the market share, according to various analysts.

▶ **They successfully developed into a global company with operations in every region.** Salesforce.com now has operations across both the EMEA and Asia-Pacific regions. With on-the-fly translation in 11 languages and customers in more than 70 countries, across six continents and in every time zone, salesforce.com customers span the gamut, including global Fortune 500 companies.

▶ **The salesforce.com Foundation set an example for an integrated philanthropy model.** In the salesforce.com Foundation, Marc Benioff has created an inspiring new philanthropy model called the 1 percent model: 1 percent of employee time, company equity, and company profit are given back to the community. Since the foundation opened its doors with its first center in July 2000, it has grown just as quickly as the company. The foundation currently has more than 60 technology centers in 13 countries, employees have donated more than 10,000 hours, and approximately 50,000 adults and youth in the global community have been served. Awesome.

Strategy

Quick. What do eBay, Amazon, Google, and Yahoo have in common? Each of them is a ubiquitous service provider for marketplaces, retail, knowledge management, and news/content, in that order. You should have known that.

Salesforce.com wants to be a ubiquitous service provider for your applications in three to five years. I like that. They want to be *the* APS.

APS? Are you dyslexic, Greenberg? Is that a typo? Can't you spell?

No. No. Yes.

Salesforce.com wants to be *the* application provider service (A-P-S) the same way that Amazon is the retailer service or Google is the knowledge management service. They plan to be at this level in three to five years.

Two years ago, when I wrote the second edition, I criticized their strategy to provide enterprise applications services (back and front office) as too ambitious because they hadn't even gotten their sales force automation to work right. I wasn't wrong—then. To their credit, they fixed their SFA problems, created the sforce development platform and began to move in the direction of customized enterprise apps with sforce's release, especially with the spring '04 release of sforce 3.0 to realize that ambitious strategy.

Now their intention as an APS is to be the service provider for all applications that you might ever need, and to be the omnipresent provider at that. If you need to work on your sales opportunities or design your marketing campaign or handle your orders or just write a business letter from anywhere you happen to be, salesforce.com plans to be the one you use.

Tien Tzu, chief marketing officer at salesforce.com, has a colorful way of putting it: "The network is the computer. That's something that you've heard of for a long time. Software is something that needs to sit inside the network, not on individual desktops. We envision a scenario where everyone goes to work, fires up browsers, looks at Yahoo, does their personal stuff, fires up their applications, and it's all inside the network. We want to provide that service."

In their longer-term strategy and vision, the Internet is the public network and custom development is done to create your space within that public network. "You've probably heard this one before," says Tien Tzu, "but it's like the movie *The Matrix*. The whole world works within the public network, available to you anytime anywhere for anything."

The first step in this strategy is much more mundane than the vision suggests and fits within their one-year plan too. This is to build a substantial services component that specializes in using their sforce platform to develop customized solutions. Those solutions could be vertically specific processes or they could be embedding sales processes that you invented or they could be customizations of screens that are meaningful to you alone. But they all suggest providing customization as a service as the first step in salesforce.com omniscience as a global application utility.

To do this, they made a great move in December 2003, hiring Bruce Culbert, then the senior vice president of Bearing Point's Global CRM practice, as the executive vice president of their new services initiative, in charge of that critical first step toward APS status. Bruce is a long time industry leader who takes a visionary approach—but wait, you know that from Chapter 1, don't you? Okay. Just checking.

Additionally, they began to build alliance partners who are involved in developing code for their early rounds of customization. Over 10 percent of their traffic is through APIs, according to Tien Tzu. What that means for all of us lay folks is that customized applications and code drive 10 percent of their overall traffic, which means that partners are building their specialized applications. That is a community of self-interest growing up around their proposed future as the anointed APS. That is also in line with the cooperative business model that is needed to prepare to meet the needs of their customers.

Culture

Salesforce.com has a unique culture—unique not just to the ASPs but to the entirety of the CRM world. Of course, it is customer-centric, not particularly distinctive there, though their ways of going about it are. What distinguishes them is that their culture is philanthropic at its very core.

"Ah," you say, "but isn't that just good marketing that gains them some advantage in the competitive marketplace? They aren't really altruists, are they?" Yes, there is some marketing, but yes, they *are* corporate altruists.

Let's make the case for this fascinating culture. In early 2004, Marc Benioff, CEO of salesforce.com, coauthored a book with Karen Southwick entitled *Compassionate Capitalism* about this very subject. Here's the unfettered concept in a nutshell, taken from the book, "Whether it's Avon going door to door to raise money for breast cancer or Microsoft putting its software in libraries, companies (or people, for that matter) don't do anything out of unadulterated altruism. They do it because they figure it will help them in some way. However, the spirit of helping the community should permeate corporate philanthropy, even when it is predicated on business goals."

This isn't just verbiage to salesforce.com. They have a foundation, the salesforce.com Foundation, that has its headquarters and full-time employees in the salesforce.com San Francisco headquarters and is part of what Benioff calls an integrated business model, whose core value is service. That means that they see their needs as delivering market share and return and also returning something to the communities they serve.

Great words, but what about deeds and actions to back it up? Check out the following:

- ► Each new hire gets not only presentations on the foundation, but also does a half day of service work at one of 19 community centers or after-school programs that salesforce.com serves. Seniority level doesn't matter.

▶ To even get to the point of being a new hire, you are grilled during the interview process on your philanthropic outlook. If you don't have much of one, you aren't hired.

▶ Each time a local or regional office reaches a 30–40 employee threshold, they hire a full-time foundation employee to coordinate the foundation activities for that office in that region or locale.

▶ An employee steering committee is set up to help coordinate the philanthropic activities.

▶ Employees are encouraged to give 1 percent of their time and to contribute financially where and when they can to philanthropic activities and are supported in their efforts to do so.

They don't ignore customers either. Let's do something anecdotal. I'll tell you a story that is a tidbit, but shows how company cultures that actually ooze customer friendliness are quite different than those that merely claim it.

I spent some time as salesforce.com's guest at their corporate headquarters in downtown San Francisco early 2004, meeting with key leaders and employees of the company. As I was being escorted through the company to a number of prearranged meetings, we stopped at the desk of one of the salesforce.com vice presidents. He and I chatted and since this was in January 2004, I said something about their fiscal year closing on December 31, 2003. The VP told me that the salesforce.com fiscal year ended January 31, 2004. I thought that was a bit peculiar so I asked why. Boiled down to its essence, the answer was that most customers were closing their fiscal years on December 31 and if the salesforce.com sales people were trying to "get the deals in" before the year closed at the same time, this would be a great inconvenience to the customers, so they waited a month until the customers were done with their year. While I'm sure there is a case to be made for the business advantage of this approach to salesforce.com, this was an unguarded, unplanned-for remark on their part and reflects the thought that goes into their culture. I felt real good about these people when I heard that. Unguarded, customer-friendly, philanthropic. Yeah.

Salesnet

What can you say about a company that actually understands its mission and vision, and lives and breathes that every day? You can say, Salesnet.

Achievements 2002–2004

They transformed their product offering. Early in 2002, Salesnet realized that because of its comprehensive workflow modeling, customization capabilities, and exclusive focus on sales effectiveness, its core audience was primarily enterprise-class companies. These companies, like Staples, Tellabs, Software AG, Sovereign Bank, and American Express, already had business systems in place to handle core functions like financials, customer support, and marketing. What these companies, who were now increasingly adopting Salesnet's solution, needed was deeper integration capabilities, enhanced customization capabilities, increased team-selling functions, better mobility options (such as an offline version), and deeper workflow technology. So, by the middle of the year, Salesnet launched its enterprise edition—Salesnet Extended—and today, the award-winning application is supporting sales-focused CRM implementations ranging from 50 to 5,000 users per company. Note I said up to 5,000 users per company. Now do you see why I'm not a skeptic any longer about the scalability of the ASPs?

They expanded their distribution model. Salesnet was the first on-demand CRM company to launch a business partner program enabling its partners to sell, implement, and manage an online CRM services for their customers. The company announced the program in September 2003, but had been executing against the plan all year. The program marked the beginning of a dedicated effort for Salesnet to position itself as a "partner friendly" company. It's also a critical component to how the company plans to expand its bandwidth and substantially trail blaze into untapped vertical markets. From partnering with methodology vendors, like CustomerCentric Selling and Integrity Selling, to attracting traditional resellers who replaced or added to multiple other CRM vendors' solutions they carried, Salesnet has built a highly successful, repeatable method to get more feet on the street. In just six months, Salesnet had established profitable, revenue sharing reseller partnerships with more than 50 companies, which now account for more than 50 percent of Salesnet's new business.

They changed their direction with GPS. In 2004, Salesnet not only went back to its process roots, it totally expanded the as-a-service model. Salesnet's Guided Performance Selling (GPS) strategy leverages software-as-a-service, configuration-as-a-service, and integration-as-a-service.

With the software-as-a-service model and its configuration-as-service platform, Salesnet offered comprehensive, adaptable, and turnkey customization. For example, there is a CustomerCentric Selling (CCS) edition of Salesnet preconfigured with CCS templates, fields, layouts, and, of course, activity-based workflow technology. Customers who get trained in the CCS methodology can then go back and use Salesnet's CCS edition to fully reinforce the training. Good stuff, but it gets better. As part of its efforts to make life easier for its customers, Salesnet also offers admin-as-a-service. Adding new users, competing configuration or customization, helping to establish communication templates, and facilitating training can now all be done via Salesnet's team.

Integration-as-a-service provides more than 200 prebuilt system connections that enable integration cheaply and quickly. Salesnet also added 100 percent more APIs enabling even more flexibility for customers to push and pull data in and out of Salesnet remotely.

Strategy

Salesnet's strategy is nothing like their competitors, except in its purely generic sense. They want to dominate their market in their sector. They want to expand their functional offering, not natively, but through partnerships, and they want to be publicly traded. How? Even better technology, better process orientation, and better business execution than they have now.

Pretty straightforward, eh? Yes and no. The strategy is easy, the execution is complicated.

Technologically, they are not concerned. With the toolkits and availability of .NET APIs, the ability to integrate applications and processes are all that much easier and richer than they had been many years ago. That means that Salesnet can technologically execute highly specific "private label" versions that can be used by individual companies or individual industries such as high tech, financial services especially the often neglected subsector of regional banking, and life sciences verticals. Salesnet is acutely aware, more than any of their competitors, of the need to utilize a "leveragable ecosystem," as CEO Mike Doyle calls it, of partners and collaborators to develop their vertical or private label versions. The process expertise rests with those partners so that Salesnet can work with them to develop appropriate services and applications for the specific industry. For example, since mergers and acquisitions is such a significant part of the life of a regional bank, nimble, quick acting applications and services are a major part of the specific vertical treatment for regional banking.

To make this highly specialized set of services meet the standards that Salesnet is setting entails a lot of other aspects. As the number of global venues increases, so does the need to localize the services and globalize the efforts. Date formats and currency conversion become a part of Salesnet strategy, but so does an international distribution channel for the different services. Salesnet is developing a very significant channel of value-added resellers (VARs), distributors, and master resellers across the globe to handle the marketing of their new localized, verticalized, private label Salesnet suite. By year end 2004, Salesnet expects to have channels in the United Kingdom, Australia, multiple locations in Europe, and in China.

This channel is made powerful by an original equipment manufacturer (OEM) Salesnet version—a template-driven version of Salesnet that allows the partners and distributors to develop their own preconfigured solutions to their potential customers. For example, late in 2003, Salesnet announced its first public OEM distribution relationship with Encoda Systems, the leading global supplier of sales, traffic, programming, and financial systems for the broadcast and cable industry. Through this first OEM partnership of its kind, Salesnet's application has been integrated into Encoda's MediaExec CRM software system and is being marketed to 137,000 sales professionals in Encoda's existing worldwide customer base. And there's more to come: the company also signed a deal with Integrity Selling to distribute a branded version of Salesnet to 25,000 strategic partners throughout U.S., Canada, Australia, and New Zealand. So the channel is already spreading across the Channel and the international dateline successfully. Ride the wave, folks, it's a big one—maybe even a tsunami.

There is another side to Salesnet strategy that is linked to their extraordinary culture—an optimism tempered by good business sense. It is for that reason they have done something that no one else in their marketplace has done anywhere near the scale. They have deployed several customers with thousands of seats. Note I didn't say one thousand. I said thousands. They have convinced me almost singlehandedly that the net natives could scale to the level of an enterprise if need be. That was a big deal because I was by no means convinced that it could be. But they optimistically told me it could be done and then went and did it with several clients. Their strategy calls for expanding this sized deployment into the market that can handle the numbers: the large enterprises, Fortune 3500. If anyone could do it, I'm convinced Salesnet can.

Culture

Mike Doyle, CEO of Salesnet, is one of the industry's nicest CEOs. Dan Starr, chief marketing officer, is one of the industry's nicest CMOs. Donna Parent, communications and public relations manager, is one of the industry's nicest marcomm people. That is Salesnet in a nutshell. One of the nicest groups of people in CRM.

This level of goodness permeates the company and its core values. I have nothing but unabashed admiration for their values, their approach, and the way they live their corporate life.

"The company was originally composed of five developers who had spent three years developing a very advanced process engine," says CEO Mike Doyle. "I knew that if I was going to bring in sales and marketing people, I would have to change the technology-driven culture that was permeating the company at that time."

When his first team of senior executives met, they headed to an offsite resort near Bethel, Maine and discussed what they wanted to be and what they wanted to stand for. Once they figured that out, they went to a series of flea markets in the area to find ways to communicate what they wanted to be to their future customers.

Get this. Here is what they found and what they wanted to be. They bought:

- ▶ An antique fire engine, to show they were speedy and responsive.

- ▶ An antique telephone and gramophone, to show they can communicate and listen.

- ▶ A replica of the Mobil gas station symbol, the Greek mythological flying horse Pegasus, to provide inspiration and the desire to reach new, unheard-of heights.

- ▶ A two-handled saw, to reflect teamwork. It takes two people to work that saw. Can't be done alone.

- ▶ A ship's bell, for all good news, whether company or customer. Anyone in the office can ring the ship's bell, and all hands have to drop what they are doing and come listen to the happy tidings.

All these artifacts hanging from various nooks and crannies in the office are only the beginning of the indications of the relaxed and highly professional, fun-loving culture that is Salesnet. Each month, Mike Doyle holds fireside chats to keep all hands informed on what's up. Those who are direct reports to Mike also outline what's going on in their departments. Even more interesting is their "Hero of the Month" award. This award is from the direct nominations of the other staff. If the nominated member wins, the winner gets some money, the nominator gets some money, and the winner gets to wear a Spider-man cape—a "web-based action hero." Get it? Salesnet does.

NetSuite

If you look at the other two competitors, you find that NetSuite doesn't actually compete per se with them at all. They have an entirely different sort of product and a very different approach than their brethren. Their product is NetSuite 9.5. Their approach is outlined below.

Achievements 2002–2004

You'll note that NetSuite's take on their most significant achievements is based on their products and services. That dovetails very clearly with their strong business-focused culture and strategy.

- **They introduced NetSuite.** In 2002, a seminal moment for the company, they released their online integrated ERP, CRM, and e-commerce single database solution.

- **They introduced role-based dashboards.** New customized functionality and real-time data views based on user role became an integral part of their offering. This is important because you want to provide a UI and data that is different for a sales rep than a warehouse manager, for example.

- **They introduced "eXtreme" list editing.** Customers can edit a saved search without having to drill into each record.

- **They introduced partner relationship management.** A unique differentiator, this enables partners to sell with the same capabilities you give your own sales representatives and goes far beyond just lead distribution.

- **They introduced their customer center.** This enables companies to provide an Amazon.com-like customer experience. Customers can log in to your website to order items, see shipping status, do returns, and so on.

Strategy

Zach Nelson, NetSuite's CEO, wine connoisseur and thriving entrepreneur, says it clearly, "We organize our strategy around a simple proposition: what did the customer buy?" That straightforward statement drives NetSuite strategy in every facet of its business.

Remember, NetSuite is the only one of the three choices that is currently a fully realized, hosted enterprise application including PRM, a key differentiator as of now, with all the functionality of the typical enterprise application, though not as robust as the on-premise versions. But the functionality you will most likely need is there for you. What isn't there, won't be missed.

What makes their strategy interesting is that it is based around order management. "What did the customer order?" and "How are we going to handle it?" form the kernel of the application suite. The improvements in that are the strategies for the next year and the next three to five years. For example, an integrated data store with job-dependent views is one of the foci of the immediate period ahead. It's not just a matter of having a single customer record, but a specific view that is geared to the employee, the partner, the supplier, or the customer can be personalized as a view or a dashboard. "It would be having your view just as you do on Amazon.com," says CEO Nelson. "Customers will be able to see inventory levels for their orders, and even look at their data with some analytic slicing and dicing. The website thus would become the best salesperson."

By focusing on order management for strategic reasons, you begin to integrate all the features and functions that might have had some disparate capabilities. For example, if you are thinking about order management, you are thinking about how to get the order, how to handle the order once it has been placed, and how to ship the order and get it delivered to the customer. But that is a complex process. How to get the order not only implies opening up a new customer to an original order, but how to get further orders from the same customer. One of the new really cool pieces that NetSuite will be releasing to the application will be an automated bot (that's robot for those of you who are not geeky) that will identify upselling opportunities for the salesperson. It identifies nonintuitive relationships with customers that could lead to opportunities. It is a sophisticated correlation of customer behaviors with possible outcomes. By doing this, you are also able to manage upselling opportunities and even improve your forecast accuracy for those opportunities. This is still based on order management—you know what the historic customer bought and what your guy sold.

"This is a strategy that changes the way that CRM and ERP look. They have been internally focused, not about the customer. There are cultural implications to this strategy too. Most SFA doesn't take commissions into account due to the lack of order management. If you put the order as the hub, the processes take on a different flavor," says Nelson.

Culture

This is a business focused, but friendly customer-centered culture. Internally, they follow their own lead—they view NetSuite as a customer of NetSuite. It is a 400-person company that fits their target audience of 500-employee (or fewer) companies perfectly. The trite expression is that this is a culture and a company that "eats its own dog food." They use the applications, complain about them if there is something to complain about, and try to understand the minds of their customers as they would think about NetSuite. "If it doesn't work for us, it doesn't work for the customers" is the informal motto that drives the company's culture.

They are driven in other ways too. They are aiming at being the next great software application company and the one that provides the real-time view of business. "Companies really depend on us," says Nelson. "That's why we're willing to guarantee our 99.5 percent uptime in writing or our customer gets his money back."

Like all companies that have products, solutions, and processes for sale, they have strong development elements built directly into their corporate culture. They are proud that their code is compact and that what can often take 36 months to release for other companies takes 12 months instead because their programming is so efficient. Even the technology is based on this customer-centrism. They unearth problems that their customers have and they customize their applications to solve these technical or business problems.

All of this leads me to have no doubt that they will someday be as great as they say they will.

NetSuite 9.5

NetSuite 9.5 is a really fine product and is uniquely configured and structured to be a very different offering than any other ASP offering. It is a full enterprise application that happens to be hosted. It is no coincidence it sometimes resembles Oracle; Oracle owns a percentage of the company. But it can even exceed Oracle in a couple of ways. For example, NetSuite 9.5 is the only hosted product that offers a genuine partner relationship management (PRM) component. That means its functionality extends to the channel in all the facets that you know and love (see Chapter 6 for more on PRM):

- ▶ Joint pipeline and opportunity management
- ▶ Shared customer account management
- ▶ Promotional discounts and marketing campaigns
- ▶ Real-time inventory access
- ▶ Sales tools encyclopedia
- ▶ Back order status management
- ▶ Automatic quote generation
- ▶ Real-time credit card authorization
- ▶ Contract management tied to customer records
- ▶ Competitor tracking
- ▶ Sales analytics
- ▶ Referral and promotion code tracking

Those are only their PRM services and not even all of them. However, NetSuite 9.5 is a lot more than just PRM. It is a full-fledged enterprise application that covers all facets of CRM, ERP, and e-commerce. So not only do you get sales force automation and enterprise marketing automation, but you can get financial applications such as budgeting, supply chain management applications such as inventory, purchasing, and e-commerce functionality such as intranet publishing, web self-service, and even a web store that handles communications through XML.

This is all built on a J2EE, Oracle-centric (what else?) platform that is stable and communicates via web services. In fact, NetSuite 9.x won *eWeek* magazine's award for best CRM product of 2004. Best in show. Good show, NetSuite.

Well, folks, we're getting near the end. This is the final of the three chapters that I spend looking at "The Companies of CRM." Now we move on to the fun stuff. What the future of CRM is or isn't. After that, it's all up to you. While this is the third of a trilogy (third edition), it isn't either the Matrix trilogy (thank goodness) or the Lord of the Rings trilogy (too bad) and I'm certainly not Peter Jackson. But hopefully, you've gotten a lot from this book and even been excited at times. I have to assume you have because you've been willing to read this far, hundreds of pages and far, far away from the beginning of this major tome.

PART VII
Back to the Future

26

Peering at the Future Through Glasses: Bye-Bye CRM, Sort Of

If you've read the introduction, you know this is the last edition of *CRM at the Speed of Light*. Why? Because in five or so years, CRM as a separate discipline will go away or morph as customer strategies become a mainstream phenomenon and the entire value chain is coated with customer fairy dust. Darc Dencker-Rasmussen, VP of global initiatives at SAP, puts it eloquently, "CRM today is part of an extended value chain that will push itself into the broader business ecosystem."

This concept is at the very center of this edition of the book. CRM, which became a visible force about a decade ago, is now much more than it ever was anticipated to be. Not only is it currently a significant "on ramp" to the enterprise value chain, but it is becoming the basis for all corporate strategies and is "pushing itself into the broader business ecosystem." It started its life viewed as a technology, then became "a system, not a technology," then became "people, processes, and technology." It is now a philosophy and business strategy that is supported by those systems and technologies. It is a science and an art:

- It is the science of benchmarks and measurements for customer successes and corporate performance.

- It is the art of interpreting human behaviors and conditions to continuously gain more and more insight.

- It is the science of definition for increasing precision about how to effect a customer strategy using the appropriate tools and techniques.

- It is the art of knowing every single customer of your millions of customers without having necessarily known any of them.

▶ It is the science of planning, defining how you are going to craft a customer strategy within the realm of your own business ecology, working with your employees, partners, and suppliers—your extended value chain.

▶ It is the art of negotiation and managing cultures. How can you get the disparate elements that these different groups represent to collaborate without all the commensurate hurt feelings, political ramifications, and fundamental disagreements that always characterize this?

An all-encompassing, multifaceted and, when well crafted, beautiful piece of art, created using scientific principles.

There are practical implications of this vision of CRM's future. How is CRM going to look in the next year or two? Is it going to seize the strategic high ground and inaugurate the era of customer ubiquity or will it just be another $27 billion (2003 figures) big blip on the radar screen, because, mature or not, companies and customers just never got the idea?

As every good (or bad) consultant will tell you: that depends.

The Pundits

I'll preface my final remarks by telling you that everyone in the CRM world has a different opinion on this. Ultimately, you'll have to decide what you find to be a compelling vision—or develop your own (see Contest 3, this chapter).

I'm going to let a couple of friends of mine, skilled in the arts of punditry, weave their magic for a bit and present their own visions of CRM's future to you. While all three of ours vary somewhat, there are some common conclusions to be drawn which you'll find interesting, especially since you've gotten this far in the book. Without further ado, Paul Ward and Denis Pombriant.

Paul Ward

Paul K. Ward (www.pkward.com) is a CRM, branding, and customer value consultant based in the Washington, D.C., metro area. He regularly meets with top Washington-area executives to discuss business best practices, and has recently inaugurated an advisory group for the American Society of Association Executives to assist in creating ASAE member value. He writes for ASAE Global Link, ASAE Association

Management, and the Canadian Association. To me, he is one of CRM's more innovative thinkers, someone who puts the time into and understands the social psychological aspects that distinguish CRM from its more mechanical brethren like ERP. Read what he has to say on the future of CRM and social networking—a domain that should be of a great deal of interest to those of you involved in that collaborative value chain I speak of so much.

CRM and Social Networking: The Customer and the Phenomenon

One of Paul Greenberg's great insights is that the customer is now at the top of the market's food-chain. Businesses can't count on customer loyalty because no prospect or customer will be loyal to a company that clearly gives them less value. Businesses that have been relying on customer inertia are seeing their old-time customers leave because customer choice now has almost zero mass: it's the weight of a Google page as it streams in over the Internet.

So the challenge for business is to compete in real-time on value, which normally means hitting a quality mark for a given price point. Bradley Gale, in Managing Customer Value, *has a warning, though: "Historically, most companies have started... their quality improvement efforts with conformance quality... to achieve specifications before they even think about whether specifications are correct.... To win in the marketplace... business teams need a comprehensive understanding of total quality that is genuinely market-driven."*

The CRM market-driven revolution has been launched with the sound of a billion mouse clicks.

But the revolution doesn't end with companies finally delivering quality products at a great price. The Internet has ushered in two new phenomena you should pay attention to: the mesh and the lens.

The Mesh

While Paul's insight about the customer ecosystem is sinking in, companies need to be looking at the consequences of a well-meshed Internet. By 2000, Internet use was exploding. It's meshing could be measured in e-mail addresses, instant messaging accounts, the spread of online groupware, and the virtual company. But since 2000, the number of people connected to the Internet has more than doubled from even its 2000 results!

Our ability to find like-minded people is easier than ever. You and I aren't six degrees away from each other, but perhaps two or three.

This means that as world citizens, we can be influenced by good ideas really fast and really often.

The Lens

The consequence to business is that ideas about your product spread like wildfire. This was bad news for Nike when the word got out that they were employing laborers in sweatshop conditions. News like this, spread not just by news media but peer-to-peer using e-mail and web log, is often exaggerated or taken out of context and may well be wrong, but it plays a real role in shareholder value. Warren Buffet once said, "Our reputation is our only asset. Without it we are worthless."

You can bet if any company around the globe acts in a way that violates its brand equity, people will hear about it, because people will talk about it.

Thomas Friedman, in The Lexus and the Olive Tree, *says that one of the key drivers of globalization is the "democratization of information": "Thanks to satellite dishes, the Internet, and television, we can now see through, hear through, and look through almost every conceivable wall." But citizens of the world can do more than that—we can publish through every conceivable wall.*

We already see Web publishing by competing companies, nonprofits, NGOs, and our neighbor down the street, and if the message they send about a given wayward company or product gains resonance, soon the well-meshed Internet will get focused on the message to the point where it has a life of its own.

All this can happen without a plan, without predictability, and at almost any scale. Terrible work conditions of female workers in overseas Nike plants were reported in a private audit performed by Ernst & Young. The results were leaked to the Internet. Glen Morris of Advertising & Marketing Review *says, "In a pre-Internet world, Nike probably wouldn't be having this problem at all because of the communications barrier that existed then. It would have been difficult for anyone to find out about working conditions in foreign countries, and difficult for them to distribute that knowledge once they acquired it. Now, that kind of information travels to millions at the speed of light."*

The Social Network

Activists love to organize, too, so you'd not be surprised that groups like Global Boycott for Peace, Adbusters, and Consumers Against War rely on the Internet heavily to keep their constituents informed. But the real shift in the corporate landscape that will follow the customer ecosystem is something we might call the social network ecosystem.

People with some reason to interact with each other can create social networks. The reasons for interacting with each other may be compelling or casual (and that may vary over time), and the tools used to interact can also vary. The durability of a particular network, interestingly, doesn't depend on who the individuals are. They can come and go, and over time, the network may still exist without any of the founding players as part of the network! Just like the vast majority of the cells in our body aren't the same ones we were made of ten years ago, the whole persists despite the changing of the parts.

Because of the tighter and tighter meshing of the Internet, combined with self-publishing tools like blogs, e-mail, and other tools (see LinkedIn.com), social networks are increasingly spontaneously generated, as though they are an inevitable consequence of the great Internet conversation.

In fact, principles of complexity theory may well apply here. Groups of people, under the influence of a pervasive, compelling conversation, may be induced into a kind of phase-change. Just as water becomes ice at zero degrees Celsius, individual customers demanding value from your products may become a unified group demanding even more from your company at large.

The Dual Bottom Line

It has been said that the most successful companies of the future won't be the big ones; they'll be the fast ones. The power of the emergent social network will undoubtedly increase as global companies make their impact known, and you can bet that social networks will try to keep up with even the fastest corporation. The Internet will be the lens used by social networks to monitor bad corporate behavior, and the wallet will be the stick to whip corporations into shape.

The customer ecosystem and the social network ecosystem that overlays it will thus force companies around the world to look at more than how to create value from their products—they'll have to create value with their corporate behavior. Thus, value and values will be two measures consumers will use as they apply the Internet-focused lens to the market.

CRM and Social Networks

Ultimately, the linear, command-and-control nature of management systems such as CRM must accommodate the nonlinear way that information spreads to affect how a market views your business. It won't be easy to control those messages. You just won't have the resources to be on every chat room, every blog, and every listserv. You'll have two choices: keep your dirty laundry hidden and hope for the best, or become a part of the social network ecosystem by adapting your company to the best—and most ethical—practices you can.✸

Denis Pombriant

Denis Pombriant is the president of Beagle Research, Inc., and the former lead CRM analyst at the Aberdeen Group. He is an innovative thinker and the one who, as you've read in these pages, characterized the ASP market as a "disruptive innovation." He is one of the smarter analysts out there, willing to be an iconoclast who often is proven right.

On CRM's Future

CRM isn't going away, and it's not something you get over like the mumps or that weekend in Vegas. I expect CRM will expand and continue to diversify but only in relation to the larger changes that we will experience in business and society in general. For example, in their new book, The Support Economy, *Harvard Business School professor Shoshana Zouboff and co-author James Maxmin give us a tantalizing view of a business model of the new century that will ultimately shape what CRM becomes. Zouboff and Maxmin argue that the 20th century business model—which is the model on which CRM was created—was all about transactions in support of mass production and mass consumption. But increasingly our society is all about individuals, and if you are a vendor, making money is increasingly about supporting and catering to individual needs, desires, and aspirations. I believe that many of CRM's current shortcomings can be traced to a schism between a transaction-oriented business model that is being used to support an individualizing customer population. The schism will only grow.*

As our society becomes increasingly focused on catering to individual needs, the systems that run our interactions with customers will need to take on a greater share of the effort to interact with those customers as individuals. Trouble tickets? Forget about it. Tracking numbers? Anachronisms. The name of the game is solutions for everyone.

Some of the CRM systems of the future are already making an appearance if you know where to look. We have identified a new class of hosted CRM applications which we refer to as "Web Necessary" (WN) because they leverage the Internet to a far greater degree than "Web Friendly" applications that simply use the Net as a transport mechanism. WN CRM applications have at least three attributes in common:

▶ *They involve the Internet as an active part of the value proposition.*

▶ *They support innovative business processes that in most cases could not be easily supported any other way.*

▶ *They are collaborative, bringing together people from disparate roles, geographies, and organizations to participate in these business processes.*

The last point speaks most directly to the idea of individuation because by bring-ing together resources from literally anywhere, organizations will be able to sat-isfy individual requirements for products and services. Moreover, the ubiquity of the Internet, and that includes the wireless Internet, will make it possible for cus-tomers to access their preferred vendors (and vice versa) whenever necessary. Rather than the simple one-way transactions of the 20th century, the transactions of the future will be based on the bidirectional exchange of value, even if the value exchanged is in the form of information. For example, a service question about the life expectancy of the ice maker in a refrigerator may tell a manufacturer a great deal about customer need. Is the ice maker breaking down? What does that say about the age of the refrigerator itself and the need to replace it? Is there a need for a service call?

We should expect that CRM applications will increasingly mimic the way our social environment works in the years ahead. Given current trends toward indi-viduation, we can expect to find more applications that work through the Web to help us collaborate on solutions with our trusted advisors. ◼

CRM: Finally, Part of the Business Fabric

There are some clear lessons to be learned from both our visionaries (and me) in this chapter. CRM is becoming part of the fabric of a collaborative ecosystem that is bonded through trusted relationships. What makes CRM interesting in this context is not just its socio-political and human implications, but that it also provides the tools to measure and calibrate the success of the initiatives that are devel-oped to enhance and enforce the idea. It has an eminently emotional side but also the scientific means to improve relationships between people to the satisfaction of all concerned. However, we can't forget that it is a business initiative that is increasingly embedding itself into the social constitution. Its evolution is being defined by the customer ecosystem. Each individual customer is being provided a personalized set of services by a collaborative network that encompasses a set of enterprises brought to bear on the individual's needs and are trusted sources for that individual.

What exactly does this mean for you, the business person who is trying to earn a living and raise a family or live on the wild side or whatever it is you do that gets you going?

Start from the standpoint of your favorite consumer: you. When your needs are met, be they necessary or discretionary, base or intellectual, you feel happy. Businesses are all pretty much built on satisfying either these individual or organizational needs. Name one that isn't. The fact that businesses even have a value proposition proves the point. What's the value to you? If it fills organizational needs—say, capital equipment manufacturer—it is still based on producing equipment that is acceptable and useful to someone or a group of someones.

Imagine the possibility of being given:

▶ A strategy defined around producing value to fulfill *your* needs

▶ A collaborative value chain of all institutions and processes needed to fulfill your needs

▶ A set of measurements that reflect how successful (or unsuccessful) the collaborative value chain has been in fulfilling your needs and the ability to adjust the processes to improve the rate of success

▶ A system that provides insight into you so that improvements can be made

▶ Access to all the services you need for news, information, purchases, business, delivery, and on to infinity, from wherever you are in whatever circumstances you find yourself with whatever mechanics you need to access them

Remember this song from *The King and I?*

"Getting to know you
Getting to know all about you
Getting to like you
Getting to hope you like me…"

Right there are the fundamentals of CRM—of course without *actually* getting to know you.

We can argue the merits of the "not actually" part of this seemingly impersonal personalization all day, but reality is multidirectional here. We've spent considerable time talking about terabytes and millions of customer records held by companies. We all know that there is no way to go through those millions of records one at a time to make sure that customer service reps can personally involve themselves in the life of a particular customer. But, by the same token, do you really want to have to deal with a person every time you need to access some service, connected or disconnected? Or would you rather access the service with a click of a mouse or a flick of a wrist to open your cellphone? I think we can answer that one easily enough.

The idea is to form a discreet, but discrete partnership—a relationship based on getting value for giving value. CRM at its finest.

There is big, futuristic, visionary stuff to absorb here. But how realistic is it, really? How much can we already do? Technically, much of it. Culturally, we've only just begun.

What About Now?

Perhaps you've noticed that one of the perpetual themes of this edition has been the move toward customer services, not customer service. CRM, ERP, SCM product companies like SAP, Oracle, and PeopleSoft are morphing into enterprise solutions companies. Companies like Indus International are creating end-to-end service delivery models where they didn't play in that park before. Companies like Unisys and IBM are providing complete enterprise hardware, software, and solutions. Even the more traditional consulting firms are partnering with collaborators who can provide the missing pieces of their offerings—particularly services specialties. New collaborative models are linking the demand, supply, and support chains into a single enterprise value chain that is extended into the business ecology that used to be called, in Internet lingo, the "extraprise." Companies like ChannelWave on the one hand and salesforce.com on the other are providing solutions for this extended enterprise and its active value chain, though each is by no means the only answer. What is still missing is that while the customer ecosystem is a reality, most of the business world has not adopted the new business modes it calls for and is still operating on worn principles and old business models. Keep doing that and create the conditions for your own demise.

In sum, let's look at the differences between the still entrenched, outmoded business model that served us so well in the latter part of the 20th century and the new model that is critical for the 21st century. Table 26-1 is a high-level overview of some of those differences.

Table 26-1: 20th and 21st Century Business Models

20th Century Business Model	21st Century Business Model
Self-contained enterprise-wide efforts	Collaborative network
IT infrastructure that dealt with legacy systems and third-party applications within the company	IT infrastructure increasingly Web services infused to communicate with other companies' infrastructures and applications
Web-enabled architecture	Service-oriented architecture
CRM part of the corporate strategy	Corporate strategy is customer strategy
Customer-driven corporate ecosystem	Customer ecosystem
CRM a competitive differentiator	CRM is a mainstream strategic necessity
Integration of CRM, ERP, SCM; extends throughout the enterprise	Demand, supply, and support chain integration to a single value chain that extends beyond the enterprise
Web-enabled but primarily connected and desktop access	Connected or disconnected increasingly mobile access to all necessary services
Customer segmentation	Customer personalization
Near real time	Real time
Data driven	Process driven
Software-focused technology	Service delivery model

So this vision of the future isn't so far into the future, is it? Many of the 21st century model characteristics are exactly what I've been writing all these chapters about.

When I begin many of my speeches, I ask a series of questions about Amazon.com and barnesandnoble.com. The first question I ask is, "How many of you have ever had a direct experience with CRM that you consider good?" I'd say about 15 percent of the audience raises their hands. After some hands rose on shopping at Amazon.com versus shopping at barnesandnoble.com, what becomes apparent is that people are far more likely to shop (and have shopped) at Amazon because of the personalized experience and ease of use. Then I ask one final question, again, "How many of you have ever had a direct experience with CRM that you consider good?" About 90 percent of the audience raises its hands. I close that section with the statement, "The best CRM is when you don't know it is CRM." We're almost there.

CONTEST 3: FOR BEST VISION OF CRM'S FUTURE

Third and final contest, folks. Send me your vision of CRM's future and make the case for it. If you succeed to my liking, I'll give you a $150 gift certificate to Amazon.com. There will be up to two prizes awarded for this one, though I reserve the right to award none or three. It has to be a compelling vision—not necessarily mine, but compelling—and it has to be articulately proven. There is no limit on the length of the "essay," but the contest ends with the award of the second (or third) certificate or by the end of 2005, whichever comes first. Students reading this, maybe you could make it a class project. If you do and there is a winner in your class, I'll also work out something with the professor to come teach a session at your class, if you want me to. Don't worry, the winner still gets the gift certificate. E-mail me at paul-greenberg3@comcast.net with your entry.

So...Is CRM Ashley Judd?

Don't I wish? Sigh. Actually, if you can remember when you started Chapter 1 roughly thirty years ago, I asked that question and gave an example of the IHOP in my home town. Remember? If not, look back at Chapter 1's opening paragraphs. Now we're finally getting to the answer. As much we might wish it to be so, Ashley Judd really isn't CRM. It was a clever idea that led to some great customer service. If only it were part of IHOP's national customer strategy—if they had integrated this approach into their best practices because of the blatantly obvious customer value it provides. Or if they had aligned their enterprise to those customers like me who would love such an approach, or understood how to use this to make me a high value customer. Perhaps if they figured out how to segment our behavior and then came up with marketing plans to personalize the appeal to me (a Halle Berry endorsement, for example) with the means to measure the results. Maybe if they had developed an integrated system that could track the results and report back to them after analysis. If they had engaged partners and their entire company in this initiative and others like it to make this a pilot for a later national or international program, then I'd perhaps be able to say that Ashley Judd was part of an all-embracing customer strategy. And who wouldn't want to embrace Ashley Judd?

APPENDIX

Customer Lifetime Value Primer

Author's Note: Mei Lin Fung, the creator of this document is a colleague of mine at CRMGuru and a dear friend. If I were just a warm and fuzzy guy, I'd still include this appendix, becauase Mei Lin Fung is a dear friend of mine—a brilliant one at that. She's not only a whiz at CLV, but she's a person with a social conscience, who believes in doing good things in the world. In fact, she is currently working with a government or two establish on a concept of social value that could be revolutionary called constituent lifetime value. But, aside from a friend, you are reading the work of an industry veteran who has worked with Larry Ellison, Craig Conway, and Tom Siebel at Oracle and simply knows from whence she came and to where she goes.

Economic debate used to rage around the question: what is the ideal rate of savings? Economics Nobel Prize winner Franco Modigliani offered a key insight: it depends on the stage of the person's lifetime. A child's savings rate is negative, as is the case when the person retires. During the income earning years, the savings rate turns positive, increasing to a peak, and then declining. Customer lifetime value takes this notion and applies it to the customer relationship, as shown in Table A-1 (on next page).

Physical product costs are becoming a smaller part of the value of the overall purchase that a customer makes. The cost of providing services is becoming an increasingly larger part of the overall cost. The cost of services varies over the lifecycle of a customer. In an increasingly typical situation the cost of services will vary according to the lifecycle of the relationship. How are businesses going to accurately predict their cash flow or their profitability? How will decisions be made?

Table A-1: Customer Relationship Lifecycle

	Customer Relationship Lifecycle			
Stage	**Prospect**	**Newly Acquired Customer**	**Peak Customer Relationship**	**Declining Customer**
Revenue	None	Rising	Rise, peak and/or plateau, then start showing signs of decline	Declining
Customer Relationship Cost	Acquisition cost	Building relationship cost	Cost of retaining and creating satisfied customers plus cost of recruiting to the club of satisfied customers who give testimonials or referrals	Wind down relationship or retain as alumnus customer
Product and/ or Servicing Cost	No	Yes	Yes	Yes
Net Cash Flow	Negative	Increasing	Increase, peak/plateau, decline, plus indirect cash flow impact of recruiting customers (if satisfied) or discouraging prospects (if not satisfied)	Decreasing

Customer lifetime value (CLV) is a concept devised by Professor Paul Wang at Northwestern University and has been used extensively in direct marketing. It takes into account the changing dynamics of a customer relationship. It provides insight through objectively valuing the customer relationship based on net cash flow. To provide a comparable value in "today's dollars," net cash flow from future periods is discounted at the cost of capital to the business. CLV can be used to value the "portfolio of customer assets" of a business, very similarly to the way a stock portfolio is comprised of stock assets valued as the NPV of future income from each company whose stock is in the portfolio.

Activity-Based Cost Management

Service costing is going to have to become more accurate. Historically, average cost or standard cost has routinely been calculated for the components of products. Where activities now make up the bulk of the cost, it is necessary to determine standard costs for repeated activities.

The accounting profession developed activity-based costing/management (ABC/M) to address this need. ABC/M takes historical data from the standard accounting general ledger, and uses it to calculate the average cost of servicing activities. Using these average service costs, business managers can project in a systematic way the costs at different levels of service activity.

ABC/M is the critical component of the cost side of calculating customer lifetime value. In calculating CLV, the same techniques used on the cost side are applied to activities to generate revenue with one important difference: when looking at activity-based *revenue* projections, the revenue is not 100 percent guaranteed. We perform several steps to interest prospective customers in our product or service. We don't know whether or not the customer will actually make a purchase. CLV requires the introduction of "probable revenue." It requires making a guess. The guess needs to be tested and reviewed in order to improve the accuracy of the guess. Systematic learning about activities and their outcomes must occur to accelerate improvement.

Calculate Customer Lifetime Value

Can customer retention be converted to financial value?

- ▶ Net present value (NPV) = Valuing cash flow over time in today's dollars

- ▶ Expected value = Probability of event × outcome of event

Measuring the expected financial benefits from retention and referrals provides for sustained investment in customer care. It moves beyond good will and lip service. Quantifying the expected results provides metrics for measuring the impact of customer care programs and actions, turning data into knowledge that can be acted upon.

As an example, let's look at ACME, a fictional company that does business with the federal government, summarized in Table A-2.

Table A-2: An Example for CLV Calculations

ACME's Federal Government Business
The average sale is $2,000 per customer per year
The product margin is 50 percent of revenue (after selling costs)
Customer retention rate is 40 percent in the year after initial purchase

The next two examples will demonstrate the calculation of expected value and net present value for this segment of federal government customers. In the following section, we will look at how CLV can be used to create different activity paths for different segments of customers.

Example 1: Calculate Expected Revenue Over Two Years from a New Customer

Let's look at the two-year history of revenue from customers. In the second year, 40 percent of customers come back and make a purchase, while 60 percent of new customers never return. On average, how much revenue do you get from 1,000 new customers over two years?

	Year 1	Year 2
New customers	1,000	
Expected number of customers = 1,000 × retention rate of 40%		400
Average size of sale for each customer	$2,000	$2,000
Revenue	$2,000,000	$800,000
Expected revenue from 1,000 new customers		
Cumulative		$2,800,000
Average revenue from each of the 1,000 initial customers =		
Expected two-year revenue divided by 1,000 = $2.8M/1,000 or		$2,800

If retention rate was 60 percent, two-year revenue from each new customer would be $3,200.

Let's calculate the profitability to ACME of their customers, assuming that their product margin is 50 percent of revenue. Of 100 new customers in year 1, only 40 percent come back in year 2 to make a purchase.

Example 2: Measure the Profit from Increasing Customer Retention

The customer value model can be used to value customer retention. Customer lifetime value is the profit you earn from a customer over their lifetime. It is calculated as the net present value of the expected value of the profits you earn on sales to that customer in each of the years the customer remains a purchaser. Each customer provides ACME with $1,000 in profit each year that they are a customer. Net present value takes into account the cost of capital in order to discount future years' profits and restate them in today's dollars. In this example, the cost of capital is 25 percent.

	Year 1	Year 2
New customers	1,000	
Expected number of customers in year 2 = 1,000 × retention rate of 40%		400
Average profit for each customer	$1,000	$1,000
Total profit	$1,000,000	$400,000
Discount rate 25% factor	100%	80%
NPV profit	$1,000,000	$320,000
Expected profit from 1,000 new customers		
Cumulative		$1,320,000
Average profit over two years from each of the 1,000 initial customers =		
Expected profit by year 2 divided by 1,000 = $1.32M/1,000 or		$1,320

If retention rate were 60 percent, expected profit per new customer would be $1,480.

One of the great advantages of customer lifetime value is the ability to incorporate probability in the future years. Unlike cost analysis, which is determinate in that if you do an activity, you will incur a cost, revenue analysis is probabilistic. You can do an activity, but you cannot guarantee that the revenue will eventuate. You can increase the chances of a customer purchasing, but there are factors outside the control of the selling entity that can affect whether or not the purchase will occur. With CLV, you can take these into account.

Customer Lifetime Value Indices

The most valuable use of CLV is to differentiate customer segments with high CLV from those with low values. While calculating the absolute value of CLV may be a subject of debate, relative CLV for different customer segments may be calculated based on different costs of acquisition and retention. These relative measures are used to create the CLV index, which can range from 0 for the customer segments of lowest asset value to 1 for the customer segments with highest asset value. Today companies ranging from financial institutions like banks and insurance companies to retail and technology companies use CLV to distinguish between segments of customers, empowering front line sales to provide offers appropriate to customers of differing CLV—to make sure that their portfolio of customer assets are managed to maximize potential value.

Customer Segment Lifecycles

Let's look at a business targeting three very different types of customers, a gasoline service station in Sacramento, California, near Interstate 5, the main north/south highway on the U.S. west coast.

Segment 1: Neighborhood Customers—See Table A-3 for the Relationship Lifecycle

Characteristics: very regular repeat customers, usually start buying when they move into the neighborhood and stop buying when they move out.

Segment 2: Interstate Truck Drivers—See Table A-4 for the Relationship Lifecycle

Characteristics: repeat customers who make large purchases each time. Some have regular routes that take them past this gas station, others irregularly pass this station.

Segment 3: Leisure and Business Drivers Taking I-5—See Table A-5 for the Relationship Lifecycle

Characteristics: one-stop customers, looking for either the cheapest gas, a bathroom, or both.

Table A-3: Matrix for Segment 1, Neighborhood Customers

Segment 1: Neighborhood Customer Relationship Lifecycle				
Stage	Prospect	Newly Acquired Customer	Peak Customer Relationship	Declining Customer
Revenue	None	First fueling	Rises as second or third car from household starts fueling. Plateaus.	Moves away, revenue stops
Customer Relationship Cost	Gas station sign	Welcome Neighbor loyalty program	Track household purchases using loyalty card. Provide regular complimentary carwash, coffee coupons, or other loyalty reward for every x gallons.	Nothing
Product Cost	None	Cost of gas	Cost of gas	None
Net Cash Flow	Negative	Increasing	Increase, plateau	Decreasing

Table A-4: Matrix for Segment 2, Interstate Truck Drivers

Segment 2: Interstate Truck Drivers Customer Relationship Lifecycle				
Stage	Prospect	Newly Acquired Customer	Peak Customer Relationship	Declining Customer
Revenue	None	First fueling	Rises as driver returns. Plateaus, depending on route assigned.	Moves away, revenue stops
Customer Relationship Cost	Investment in superior food and rest stop	Friendly welcoming reception. Remember driver's name	Maintain high quality food, assure friendly food and gas service, clean restrooms, attractive separate rest area for smokers. Offer referral reward if other truck drivers come in based on referral, "Joe sent me."	Referral reward, "Joe sent me," not contingent on driver visit to gas station
Product Cost	None	Cost of gas and food	Cost of gas and food	None
Net Cash Flow	Negative	Increasing	Increase, plateau	Negative offset by profit from new customer

Table A-5: Matrix for Segment 3, Leisure and Business Drivers

Segment 3: Leisure and Business Drivers Customer Relationship Lifecycle				
Stage	Prospect	Newly Acquired Customer	Peak Customer Relationship	Declining Customer
Revenue	None	First and only fueling plus possible food purchase	None	None
Customer Relationship Cost	None	None	None	None
Product Cost	None	Cost of gas and food	None	None
Net Cash Flow	Negative		None	None

Customer lifetime value can be used to evaluate the value of the average customer in each of these segments. Tremendous insight into what it takes to pursue these segments of customer is already gained by creating the lifecycle tables to determine what would or could be done to attract and retain different types of customers with different needs and different priorities. For Segment 2, the interstate truck drivers, CLV can be used to evaluate what the break-even point is for numbers of trucks per day or per week, in order to be able to cover the investment cost of creating a superior food and rest stop. Depending on the location of other competitive gas stations and the services they offer, CLV might end up positive or negative. Negative customer lifetime value indicates that the operational lifecycle profits do not cover the investment cost.

A final note of caution: all calculation of customer lifetime value requires a working model or a hypothesis of what the customer relationship lifecycle looks like. This can be tested in a predictive model, with the goal of revising the model regularly to improve predictions over time. Be wary of CLV indices based on analysis done once some time ago, with relationship lifecycles not explicit. Circumstances change and relationship lifecycle activities and responses must change with them.

Afterword

When Paul asked me to write the afterword for the third edition of *CRM at the Speed of Light*, I couldn't pass it up. He promised me that he could lift the curse of The Bambino and that the Boston Red Sox would automatically win the 2004 World Series. So I accepted his offer on behalf of the people of Boston. If anyone can will such a promise, Paul can. He's just that type of a guy. And I've known this about him since we first spoke several years ago.

Paul had called my office to introduce himself and before I knew it, I had dropped everything and was engaged in a lengthy conversation and an instant friendship. We talked for over two hours. Granted, the two hours plus with Paul was information-packed, but I didn't know if I gave him what he needed to really understand our business. This was the first time this had happened to me. I joined Salesnet in March of 2000, and I was accustomed to fast-paced, whirlwind media interviews. After all, back then was the dot-com bubble. There was a lot of hype and plenty of press.

A few months later, I realized that the conversation went exactly how Paul needed it to go. He had been doing research for the second edition of *CRM at the Speed of Light*. He wasn't looking for just the facts or product features—he wanted to understand the flavor and culture of the company, not only at a business level, but also at a personal level. He realized that the people make the company and not the other way around. After reading the book and digesting Paul's candidness, I knew that our initial conversation had gone very well. He got it! He not only knew Salesnet, he felt what it was like to be a team member, a competitor, and most importantly, a customer of the company. The awareness he has continues to surface from his sincere interest in all aspects of the vendors he writes about.

CRM at the Speed of Light isn't textbook reading. It's real-world, offering a deep, truthful view of the companies profiled, which ultimately offers the greatest benefit to you. You're getting insight that has taken Paul years to acquire—beyond the business perspective and down to the personal level.

Take a deep breath. There's a lot to digest in *CRM at the Speed of Light*. Actually, there's a lot to digest about the CRM industry. Mergers, acquisitions, IPOs—everything is moving at lightning speed. And yet, Paul gets all of it. He's taken the time to thoroughly review who's who in CRM and cut through the hype. By taking a hands-on approach to evaluating offerings, interviewing end-users, and keeping a keen eye on industry trends, Paul has amassed an invaluable guide to make CRM work for today's results-driven businesses.

When I first spoke to Paul, I told him that what would make Salesnet win is its commitment to its customers. Clearly, where CRM is going today is into the hands of its customers. And it's the customers who are responding. According to Forrester Research, CRM market revenues will grow over 70 percent between 2002 and 2007. Keep in mind, though, that to sustain this uptake, CRM customers must "feel the love." They want to have control over the technology from implementation to integration. They want to have more adaptable and turnkey solutions. And they want results now, not two years from now. They won't tolerate a "not in my lifetime" mentality.

CRM has changed, and Paul's book empowers beginners to get in the know, while giving further insight to even the most advanced CRM gurus.

One more thought—back to one of my favorite interactions with Paul. In early 2003, he invited me to his house for a social visit. He shared his scotch, showed off his technical gadgets and gizmos (which, by the way, are truly impressive), and revealed that he was a closet Red Sox fan. Okay, maybe he didn't reveal that. As anyone who knows Paul knows he's a diehard Yankees' fan. But that's the level of rapport we had—and it happened in real time, or much like the title of his book indicates, "at the speed of light." This goes back to the promise that Paul made about lifting the curse of The Bambino—it may have been foolish for me to believe in his promise, but then again, at this point, I'm willing to take a leap of faith. After all, I know where Paul lives.

—Mike Doyle
Chairman and CEO, Salesnet
May 2004

P.S.: This is the year that the Boston Red Sox will lift the curse!

Author's Note: Yeah, right.

Index